LAKOTA AMERICA

THE LAMAR SERIES IN WESTERN HISTORY

The Lamar Series in Western History includes scholarly books of general public interest that enhance the understanding of human affairs in the American West and contribute to a wider understanding of the West's significance in the political, social, and cultural life of America. Comprising works of the highest quality, the series aims to increase the range and vitality of Western American history, focusing on frontier places and people, Indian and ethnic communities, the urban West and the environment, and the art and illustrated history of the American West.

EDITORIAL BOARD

RECENT TITLES

LAKOTA
AMERICA

A New History of Indigenous Power

Pekka Hämäläinen

Yale

UNIVERSITY

PRESS

New Haven & London

Published with assistance from the Annie Burr Lewis Fund.
Published with assistance from the Louis Stern Memorial Fund.
Published with assistance from the John R. Bockstoce Endowment Fund.

Yale University Press books may be purchased in quantity for educational,
business, or promotional use. For information, please e-mail sales.press@yale.edu
(U.S. office) or sales@yaleup.co.uk (U.K. office).

Set in Electra type by Tseng Information Systems, Inc., Durham, North Carolina.
Printed in the United States of America.

Library of Congress Control Number: 2018966994
ISBN 978-0-300-21595-3 (hardcover : alk. paper)
ISBN 978-0-300-25525-6 (paperback)

A catalogue record for this book is available from the British Library.

10 9 8 7 6 5 4 3 2 1

CONTENTS

Acknowledgments

I owe many institutions and individuals thanks for their help and support in writing this book. I have been extraordinarily fortunate to have Briony Truscott manage the Nomadic Empires project and wish to express my deep gratitude to her. Many friends and colleagues have read all or parts of the manuscript, spent time talking with me about my project, and offered their expertise. I would like to thank Rani Anderson, Sean Archer, Juliana Barr, Ned Blackhawk, LaDonna Brave Bull Allard, Kingsley Bray, Bruce Brown Wolf, Jay Buckley, Marcel Bull Bear, Jane Burbank, Richard Carwardine, Frederic Cooper, Julien Cooper, Brian Delay, Philip Deloria, Jane Dinwoodie, Willy Dobak, Tawa Ducheneaux, Marie Favereau, Alex Fire Thunder, Catharine Franklin, Gary Gerstle, Dakota Wind Goodhouse, Steven Hahn, Tiffany Hale, Ryan Hall, Richard Iron Cloud, Stella Iron Cloud, Mandy Izadi, Karl Jacoby, Goedarz Karimi, Ari Kelman, Tilda Long Soldier, Ben Madley, Bryan Miller, Kathryn Olivarius, Brian One Feather, Jeffrey Ostler, Sarah Pearsall, Laura Peers, Maya Petrovich, Marie Randall, Akim Reinhardt, Irina Shingiray, Mark St. Pierre, Alan Taylor, Tim Vasko, Michael Witgen, and John Wunder. I owe each of them a large debt of gratitude. I would also like to thank friends in the Oxford History Department and the Rothermere American Institute, especially Aileen Mooney and Jane Rawson, for all the help along the way.

I have presented parts of this book in seminars at the University of Cambridge, New York University, and the University of Oxford and wish to thank the participants for their comments and advice.

Elliott West and Richard White read the full manuscript for Yale University Press and gave exceptional feedback. I deeply appreciate their help. They and the other readers saved me from many mistakes. Those that remain are mine alone.

For their vital help I wish to thank the archivists and librarians at the Bodleian

Library; the Library of Congress; the National Archives; the Missouri Historical Society; the Missouri History Museum, Library and Research Center; the Nebraska State Historical Society; the Newbery Library; the Oglala Lakota College; and the State Archives of the South Dakota Historical Society. I also wish to extend grateful thanks to Mark Holman at the Sitting Bull College Library; Michael Moore of the Sitting Bull College faculty; Jennifer Martel at the Sitting Bull College Visitor Center; and Nicolas Texier at Service Historique de la Défense.

Lindsay Marshall offered efficient research assistance in Oklahoma, and I owe her a debt of gratitude. Morgane Muscat provided invaluable help with French colonial documents. Adina Berk at Yale University Press guided the manuscript into production with keen insight. I am very grateful to Eliza Childs for superb copyediting and for making the final stretch of the manuscript preparation so rewarding and enjoyable. It was a great pleasure to work with Bill Nelson again on the maps.

My dear friends Chris Rogers, Sam Truett, and David Wishart have helped me over the years in more ways than they know. And, as always, there is Veera Supinen who makes everything better.

The research leading to these results has received funding from the European Research Council under the European Union's Seventh Framework Programme (FP7/2007–2013) / ERC grant agreement no.615040.

A NOTE ON TERMINOLOGY

I use the word "Sioux" in this book as a cover term for seven related and allied people or *oyátes:* the Lakotas, Yanktons, Yanktonais, Mdewakantons, Sissetons, Wahpetons, and Wahpekutes, who together formed the Očhéthi Šakówiŋ, the Seven Council Fires. Sioux is a French corruption of Ojibwe word "Nadoues-sioux" which means "snake" and thus enemy. Here I use Sioux when describing events or action that involve more than one or all peoples or oyátes; the alternative would have been to list each group in every instance. Although problematic, "Sioux" remains the most common English term used by Lakotas and non-Natives alike, and many modern Lakota oyátes identify themselves as Sioux tribes. "Dakota" is a cover term for the four eastern people, the Mdewakantons, Sissetons, Wahpetons, and Wahpekutes.

The spelling of Lakota words follows *New Lakota Dictionary,* edited and compiled by Jan Ullrich (2008; 2nd ed., Lakota Language Consortium, 2011). I have used Lakota names for the seven Lakota tribes or oyátes unless a French or English name is dominant in the literature: Hunkpapas ("head of camp circle entrance"), Minneconjous ("plant by water"), Oglalas ("scatter one's own"), Sans Arcs ("without bows"), Sicangus ("burned thighs," hence the French term *Brulés*), Sihasapas ("Blackfeet"), and Two Kettles ("two boilings"). As for other Native nations, I have used their preferred spellings of their names: Odawas rather than Ottawas; Mesquakies rather than Foxes; Wyandots rather than Hurons; and Ho-Chunks rather than Winnebagos.

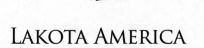

LAKOTA AMERICA

INTRODUCTION:
DARK MATTER OF HISTORY

In 1776 two nations were born in North America. One was conceived in Philadelphia, the other in the Black Hills of South Dakota, and they were separated by more than seventeen hundred miles. Exactly a century later those two nations would clash violently along the Little Bighorn River in what is today southern Montana. It was a collision between two radically different expanding powers that had conquered their way into the West, and its outcome was spectacular. Lakotas and their Cheyenne allies killed more than two hundred soldiers of the Seventh U.S. Cavalry, destroying five of its twelve companies. Remembered as Custer's Last Stand, the fight remains one of the most famous, intensely studied, and passionately debated battles in history.[1]

While the fight itself was not transformative—after all, the railroad was coming and the buffalo were almost gone—its ironies and symbolic resonances are unparalleled and, it seems, boundless: the worst defeat the United States suffered in the late nineteenth-century Indian wars and on the cusp of its centennial; a ferocious, flamboyant Indian fighter meeting his fate at the hands of Indians who disposed of him routinely and effectively; a single death that has refused to die as a metaphor, signifying, for different ages, heroism, ignorance, arrogance, and, perhaps most pointedly, savagery—first the Indians', later Custer's own. The Battle of the Little Bighorn was a moment when American history accelerated and turned violently. A perfect victory demanded a perfect retribution, and it sent the Indians into a spiraling decline and sealed the United States' continental hegemony. Within a year, Custer's Last Stand had spawned a reckoning that broke the power of the Lakotas and their allies in the northern plains.[2]

The Battle of the Little Bighorn fixed the Lakotas, embodied by Sitting Bull and Crazy Horse, in historical memory and made them an object of enduring fascination. A historical sequence that saw an Indigenous power deliver a humiliating blow to a rising industrial behemoth, only to soon suffer a devastating defeat by the U.S. military, continues to mesmerize because its meanings resonate so broadly—from America's imperial hubris to the moral complexities of the Vietnam War, from the present-day struggles between nation-states and non-state actors to the confounding unpredictability of history itself. Dee Brown's acclaimed work, *Bury My Heart at Wounded Knee*, remains the most read book on Native Americans in part because it captured those meanings so evocatively.[3]

The Battle of the Little Bighorn has both elevated and diminished the Lakotas in the American mind. Like the Battles of Yorktown and Gettysburg, it is a cultural touchstone around which American identity and self-understanding revolves. But unlike the American Revolution or the Civil War, the Lakota story lacks a comprehensive study. There are hundreds of superb works on different aspects of Lakota history from social organization to religious life to the shifting relations with the United States, but most of them take the Little Bighorn as a guiding coordinate, tracing the immediate events—essentially the military buildup—leading up to it. Through a quick rear-view look, Lakotas enter the scene fully formed as fierce horse-mounted hunter-warriors who give Lewis and Clark pause with their haughty confidence, a premonition of the carnage on the Little Bighorn three generations later. The Lakotas of our imagination are props that bookend America's westward expansion, present at its promise-filled inception and at its morally ambivalent finale.[4]

For Lakotas the clash with the United States, culminating in the horror of the Wounded Knee Massacre, was a shattering experience, but it did not define them as a people or their place in history. This book detaches their story from the mainstream historical coordinates, which have reduced them to a foil of the American condition. Here the Lakotas emerge not as quintessential villains or victims, but as central and enduring protagonists who contended with a range of colonial powers since the seventeenth century, variously diverting, foiling, and boosting their ambitions. They emerge as superbly flexible people who went through a series of geneses from pedestrian foragers to sedentary farmers to equestrian hunters to nomadic pastoralists, each a precarious attempt to carve out a safe place in a world where European newcomers had become a permanent presence. They come to life as fiercely proud people who easily embraced outsiders, turning their domain into a vibrant ethnic jumble. Perhaps most strikingly, they emerge as supreme warriors who routinely eschewed violence, relying on diplomacy, persuasion, and sheer charm to secure what they needed—only to revert to naked force if necessary. When the overconfident Custer rode into the Bighorn Valley on that June day, they had already faced a thousand imperial challenges. They knew exactly what to do with him.

Two centuries earlier, in the middle years of the seventeenth century, the Lakotas had been an obscure tribe of hunters and gatherers at the edge of a bustling new world of Native Americans and European colonists that had emerged in the Eastern Woodlands of North America. They had no guns and no metal weapons, and they carried little political clout, all of which spelled danger: the odds of survival were slim for people who lacked access to Europeans and their new technologies of killing. That crisis set off what may be the most improbable expansion in American history. Lakotas left their ancient homelands and re-invented themselves as horse people in the continental grasslands that stretched seemingly forever into the horizon. This was the genesis of what I call Lakota America, an expansive, constantly transmuting Indigenous regime that pulled numerous groups into its orbit, marginalized and dispossessed its rivals—both Native and colonial—and commanded the political, social, and economic life in the North American interior for generations. Just as there was Spanish, French, British, and the United States of America, there was Lakota America, the sovereign domain of the Lakota people and their kin and allies, a domain they would protect and, if necessary, expand. A century later, the Lakotas had shifted the center of their world three hundred miles west into the Missouri Valley, where they began to transform into a dominant power. Another century later they were the most powerful Indigenous nation in the Americas, controlling a massive domain stretching across the northern Great Plains into the Rocky Mountains and Canada.

It was an expansion that, in many ways, should not have been possible. Lakotas collided with numerous Native nations and maneuvered among four colonial empires, surviving endless crises. Yet they never numbered more than fifteen thousand people. They were not more warlike or necessarily better fighters than any of their Indian neighbors. They were creative and formidable diplomats, but so too were their Native and non-Native rivals. They had skillful leaders, but so did their adversaries. They believed that they had special access to otherworldly powers, but so did others. French, Spanish, British, and American colonists repeatedly underestimated their strategic proficiency, allowing them surprising openings, but in that the Lakota experience was more typical than exceptional. And yet it was Lakotas who humiliated the world's most powerful nation in battle again and again, hindering its westward expansion for decades. The Lakotas and their story, in short, are puzzling.

In this book I attempt to unravel that puzzle. All societies possess more or less the same human potential for innovation, change, self-preservation, and aggression. The key to Lakotas' success, at the most elemental level, is that they did something slightly different and unexpected with their potential. This book is, in its essence, about that something.

The central challenge in writing about the Lakotas is to make them unfamiliar again. Their mythical place in popular consciousness as the vanquishers of Custer and as the masters of the western plains has made their rise seem preordained. Even in the best histories, the Lakota expansion from the edge of the Great Lakes across America's heartland seems an inexorable march, driven by nearly limitless resources in the distance—buffalo, grass, space—and backed by an early access to guns and horses. Westward expansion was a foregone conclusion. Again, Custer's Last Stand as an attention-absorbing climax distorts, bending the Lakota history toward the there-and-then and tricking us to accept one moment of apparent invincibility as a template for an entire history. Teleology, a sense that things were destined to unfold a certain way, has rendered the story of the Lakota ascendancy too simple and easy. It has abstracted it from human experience, sanitized it of uncertainty, and drained it of meaning.[5]

This book steps outside of those teleological currents by resisting the urge to drive the story to its assumed culmination. Alive to the ever-present possibility that events could have turned out differently, it seeks to restore a sense of contingency to the story. The book's very composition is geared to that end. It replaces the traditional story arc of beginning, climax, and resolution with a more unpredictable narrative structure that is full of triumphs, twists, reversals, victories, lulls, and low points, big and small. If the book's Lakotas—haughty and imperial at one moment, fearful and vulnerable the next, prudent and accommodating the third—seem strange and unfamiliar, this portrayal has succeeded.

The Lakotas of this book may also seem unfamiliar in another, more elemental way. The Lakotas have become the embodiment of the horse-mounted Plains Indians, but here they spend most of their time in river valleys. Our understanding of the Lakotas has been distorted by what might be called the romance of the open plains. The continental grasslands, it suggests, exerted an irresistible pull on the newly equestrian Indians, who were drawn to their enormous bison herds, promise of unhindered movement, and potential for material and spiritual uplift. Such stories do capture an essential truth. The grasslands and their animal bounty did pull in Lakotas, whose foundation myths and values revolve around the bison and the hunt. But Lakotas' greatest political and military ambitions always focused on the few river valleys that cut across the seemingly boundless grasslands. Indeed, the most formative chapter in their history, lasting for three generations, took place not in the plains but on the banks of the great Missouri.

The mobile, horse-powered hunting way of life in the grasslands was a late development, a culmination of long history that has largely gone unnoticed.

This book recovers the untold story of the Lakotas from the sixteenth into the twenty-first century, and it also recovers the story of the North American interior, the immense swath of land stretching from the Great Lakes to the Rocky Mountains and from the Canadian Shield to the edges of the American South. The interior has long been a blind spot in American historical consciousness. In most histories of early America, the story centers on the continent's outer rim, where Europeans built colonial outposts and rooted themselves in the New World. That is where, supposedly, all the pivotal imperial rivalries over North America took place, France vying for supremacy with England on the eastern seaboard; Spaniards, Comanches, Mexicans, and Americans jostling for position in the Southwest; and Russians pushing down the Pacific Coast in search of pelts and challenging Spain's claims to California. The interior world was a sideshow, too marginal to stir potent imperial passions, too vast and vicious for proper colonies. It was Thomas Jefferson's imagined Louisiana whose settlement would take a thousand generations.

Jefferson's myopia will no longer do. The great interior, the setting of this book, was a dynamic, cosmopolitan, and intensely contested world. Dozens of Indian nations and four colonial powers sought to rule parts or all of it, producing a shifting constellation of expansions, conquests, retreats, and collapses. Here, for generations, Lakotas were key players within a larger coalition of seven Sioux nations, clashing or allying with nearly all the other contestants at one time or another. The Sioux confederation was formidable, but it was also dangerously isolated, separated by numerous Native rivals from the colonial frontiers where power-giving novelties—guns, powder, iron—flowed inland. Becoming central people, drawing Europeans and their goods to them, became an all-important quest for Lakotas and their allies. It was the most paradoxical of expansions, Indians cajoling European empires to come to them in a desperate effort to prevail over Native rivals. It took roughly a hundred years, but by the mid-eighteenth century the Sioux had succeeded. Their homelands between the Great Lakes and the Missouri Valley were a geopolitical hot spot where the most promising of the European imperial projects, New France, made its bid for continental hegemony with the Sioux nations on its side.[6]

It was then and there that Lakotas began to detach from the Sioux confederation, launching an expansion of their own that saw them becoming the dominant people in the great interior. It was a massive gamble. Drawn by bison and horses in the West, they were pulling *away* from the major continental trade corridors, entering a strange new world in the western plains that was on the verge of transforming from a backwater into an imperial crossroads. As Lakotas shifted westward, an array of competing empires rushed in, seeking to control the deep interior and its rivers, wealth of furs, and thousands of potential Native allies, only to realize that the interior was not theirs for the taking. The Spanish, French, British, and American Empires did not simply clash in the heart of the continent; they converged on the expanding Lakota realm. How Lakotas harnessed that imperial cauldron to serve their interests — how they learned to cut the newcomers to size — is one of the great untold stories in American history. By the time Lewis and Clark plunged — quite innocently so — into the cauldron in 1804, Lakotas were ascendant people who saw themselves as the rightful rulers of the North American interior. Like the French, British, and Spaniards before them, Americans had to readjust their imperial ambitions around Lakota ones.[7]

The great paradox of Lakota history is that by helping prevent the realization of other Wests — French, British, Spanish — Lakotas inadvertently paved the way for an *American* West and, eventually, their own downfall. Yet, as the pages that follow will show, for half a century after the Louisiana Purchase Lakota and U.S. interests converged rather than collided. The two nations pushed westward in tandem as military allies and trading partners. Lakotas transformed themselves into formidable equestrian people capable of shaping human fates on a vast scale, and Americans were their firm allies, one of the many peoples who had realized where power lay. How this happened, how two expansionist people managed to coexist in the same space, each feeling safe and certain of its supremacy, is a historical conundrum that needs an explanation.[8]

It also requires a new way of looking at Indian-white relations, empires, and space. North American historical writing has a long tradition in the study of cross-cultural relations and has spawned a number of models — the frontier, the borderland, the middle ground — that help explain how different societies and cultures have clashed and coexisted in the past. A set of assumptions, some clearly articulated, others more vaguely sensed, runs through this scholarship: that a collision of two expanding powers must result in either a retreat or a borderland where power and authority are perpetually contested; that empires are mutually repelling organisms that can overlap only at their far-flung edges; and that mutual weakness, inability to dictate terms to others, is the necessary ingredient for enduring coexistence between Indians and colonists.[9]

The history of the Lakota-U.S. relations challenges all those assumptions. Lakotas and Americans expanded simultaneously into the West, often claiming the same tracts of land and water. Their regimes overlapped and interpenetrated rather than brushed against one another, and yet they managed to coexist for two generations, well into the 1850s. How and why this happened was an outcome of many factors, but one was crucial: neither Lakotas nor Americans compromised their core convictions about themselves and the world. Convinced of the essential rightness of their respective beliefs and principles, they created a yawning mental crevasse where two expansionist powers could fit. They valued, desired, sought, and fought for different things and often talked past one another, which, ironically, made them compatible. It was only when nature itself failed to sustain both that coexistence became impossible.

The rise and might of the Lakotas, symbolized by the Lakota-U.S. wars of the 1860s and 1870s, was thus much more than some anomaly in a history that was rolling irresistibly toward U.S. hegemony. Expansion—territorial, commercial, and cultural—had transformed the Lakotas into an imperial power in the midst of another. Seen against this background, the Great Sioux Wars and the Battle of the Little Bighorn take on drastically new meanings. Lakotas were fighting for survival, to protect the bison and their sovereignty, but they were also fighting to keep alive a broader vision of America where coexistence through right thoughts and acts might be possible. By 1876 that vision had guided them for two centuries, pushing them into successful alliances with France, Britain, Spain, the United States, and numerous Native societies, keeping them powerful and safe. It was all but unthinkable to Lakotas that this America had run its course.

It is only in the last few decades that Native Americans have entered history as full-fledged protagonists. Earlier, for centuries, Native people lingered in the recesses of the American imagination as a kind of dark matter of history. Scholars tended to look right through them into peoples and things that seemed to matter more, that seemed to move history: conquistadors, monarchs, founding fathers; settler empires, nation-states, global capitalist markets. The Indians were a hazy frontier backdrop, the necessary "other" whose menacing presence heightened the colonial drama of forging a new people in a new world. While persisting in popular consciousness as America's foundation myth, those stories now seem hopelessly outdated, relics of another time and of different sensibilities. Today, Native Americans occupy the center stage as powerful historical actors who thwart colonial intrusions, reverse expected power dynamics, force newcomers to adapt to their way of doing things, and profoundly shape the creation of a distinctly American identity.[10]

The scholarly pendulum has swung abruptly—perhaps too abruptly. If Native Americans were for a long time stunted as historical agents, today it is the colonists and settlers who seem to be in danger of becoming caricatured, their motives and ambitions simplified, their complexity flattened. With the Indians commanding the center stage, the whites often appear as a monolithic mass hell-bent on conquest or as weak, hapless pawns in intricate Indigenous politics they could neither understand nor control. I have been guilty of such simplifying my-self, and I have aimed for a more balanced exposition in this book. I have tried to keep all the protagonists—Lakotas and their kin; the many Native peoples they had dealings with; and the French, Spanish, British, and American colonists who came to them—in the frame as rounded historical figures. This has meant taking the ideals, anxieties, and ambitions of the colonists seriously, tracing how they clashed and intertwined with Native ones, and how Lakotas and European new-comers created lasting shared worlds even when they misunderstood, hated, and killed one another.

Yet this book is decidedly a history of the Lakotas, written from sources that seek to convey their perspective, often in their own words. Its overarching ambi-tion is to understand how they saw the world and shaped American history. An extraordinary archive makes this possible to an unusual degree. Lakota commu-nities traced the passage of time by drawing on a buffalo hide a pictograph of one memorable event for each year. Lakotas call these calendars *waníyetu iyáwapi*. Waníyetu means "to be winter" and iyáwapi "to count." At once a record of the past and an act of remembering, of giving meaning to the past, winter counts are a unique source that allow us to capture the astounding variety and raw im-mediacy of Lakota experiences. Often emotionally charged, they show not only what happened but also how Lakotas felt about events and outcomes. They allow us to see Lakotas as dynamic and often contradictory people—formidable and full of bravado at one moment, in the grip of despair the next, then absorbed with internal politics and social drama. They draw attention to the mundane and reveal the sublime. Perhaps most important, as a body of historical record, winter counts capture what fascinated Lakotas and what mattered to them most. They uncover how Lakotas shaped their histories through selective narration and how their understanding of the past and themselves changed over time. They most emphatically do not adhere to Euro-American accounts of major historical events and developments. They open an alternative, counterhegemonic window into the American past, allowing us to observe Native motives and meanings di-rectly, without a foreign filter. *Lakota America* makes the fullest use yet of this Indigenous archive in writing Lakota history.[11]

The great pitfall of Native American history is a tendency to homogenize its protagonists, to portray Indians as staunch traditionalists averse to new things and ideas or as pragmatists resigned to the incongruities of the modern world. I do not want to essentialize the Lakotas, nor do I want to make them consis-tent. This book takes its cue from Iktómi, an ambiguous shapeshifting spider-

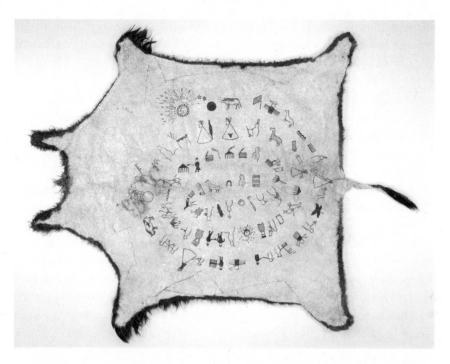

1. Lone Dog winter count. Winter counts were originally drawn on buffalo hides and later on cloth, muslin, and paper. Using ink and various pigments, the keepers of winter counts drew pictographs sequentially in spirals or rows, often covering more than a century in a single hide. Several times a year the keepers unrolled the calendars and retold the events, reinforcing the people's historical memory; the winter counts were essentially mnemonic devices for collective remembering. The pictographs of this winter count were drawn in a spiral on buffalo hide. Courtesy of National Museum of the American Indian, Smithsonian Institution (01/0617). Photo by NMAI Services.

trickster culture hero who embodies what is perhaps the defining characteristic of the Lakota people: their stunning ability and willingness to change. Like Iktómi, Lakotas were—and are—shapeshifters with a palpable capacity to adapt to changing conditions around them and yet remain Lakotas. Recurring metamorphosis, fragmenting and coalescing into smaller and larger units, enabled Lakotas to mobilize power on multiple registers and in various capacities: not only as bands and tribes but also as a nation and as leaders of large Indigenous alliances. By the time Lakotas came in close contact with the U.S. government in the early 1850s, they were in the midst of what was perhaps the most remarkable—and least known—of their self-reinventions. By 1876 that transfiguration was complete and reached its symbolic culmination in the Battle of the Little

Bighorn. Custer failed to see that change and led his men to certain death. He was not brought down by a mere alliance of Indians. He was brought down by the Lakota empire.[12]

When I started researching and writing this book, I knew to expect certain things about Lakotas and their history. Some of my assumptions turned out to be correct, more or less, but much of the writing was an exercise of recalibrating expectations. I knew Lakotas were highly adaptable people—all Indians had to be to survive settler colonialism—but their capacity to reimagine their place in the world over and over again took me by surprise. I knew they were powerful, but I could not foresee finding them shaping American history on almost a continental scale, expanding not only westward but also deep into the south and far to the north. I knew they were superior fighters but was astounded how often they forced things by restraining action. I knew that they were great orators, but I did not know just how searing—and historically significant—their use of irony could be when facing colonial agents. But the most elemental surprise was their sheer ubiquity. Lakotas and their kin were Native Americans who received eight-gun salutes in Quebec, inspired fear from the Mississippi Valley to the Continental Divide, ranged from the deserts of Utah to the Canadian plains, commanded the attention of the great global fur-trading conglomerates, and agreed to be feted in imperial centers in Montreal, St. Louis, New York, and Washington, D.C. That their most famous leader would tour the East to enormous crowds was less surprising than it was predictable.

The story begins not in the open plains of the West but in the Eastern Woodlands around the Great Lakes where the main protagonists are not the Lakotas but the Dakotas, their close kin. In the seventeenth century the Dakotas were the most powerful members of the Sioux confederation, and they held the center stage in Sioux politics for generations. But gradually, as the Lakotas transformed into an equestrian power and turned westward, they emerged from behind the Dakotas as the foremost Sioux division. A people reborn on horseback, they peeled off from other Sioux tribes, shedding old assumptions of the possible. But they also carried into the West a deep understanding of European newcomers, accumulated over a century of living on the fringes of French and British colonies in the East. Lakotas knew what Europeans were, what colonialism was, how empires operated, and how thin the line separating violence from conciliation would have to be. That knowledge was their greatest asset as they pushed into new worlds beyond the horizon.

1

A Place in the World

In the summer of 1695 two Indian emissaries embarked on a nearly one-thousand-mile journey from the western Great Lakes to Montreal. One was Zhingobiins, a Sauteur chief, and the other Tiyoskate, a war leader of the Mantanton band of the Mdewakanton Sioux. Five French traders guided their fleet of some dozen canoes. The two emissaries had a common purpose, for they were carrying an offer of peace and alliance to the French, but their journeys east could hardly have been more different. Zhingobiins was traveling through Sauteur lands and among allies, and many of the Indians and French traders and priests he met along the way were friends and kin. Tiyoskate, however, was entering a war zone. His people had been fighting the Great Lakes Indians for decades, and only the presence of Zhingobiins and the French now kept him alive. He may well have been the first Sioux to travel east neither to kill nor as a slave.[1]

When the convoy arrived in the island city in mid-July, Tiyoskate stepped into a new world. Along the shoreline sat massive vessels with towering poles draped in ropes and sheets, and the island itself was a jumble of sharp angles, soaring vertical walls, and the amplified sounds of confined spaces. A stench of excrement, animal entrails, and rot hung everywhere. The city was also teeming with Indians. At the behest of the governor of New France, Louis de Buade, comte de Frontenac, hundreds of Native envoys had gathered there, desperate to put an end to violence that was ruining their homelands. To maintain order in his crammed city, Frontenac had brought in much of the French colonial army, and an honor guard of seven hundred regulars, militia, and Natives received Tiyoskate and Zhingobiins in front of the council chamber where they were to meet the governor. The soldiers carried what Tiyoskate's people needed most: guns.[2]

When the council began, the person whose voice was heard most was Pierre-Charles Le Sueur, an explorer-trader and Frontenac's favorite. He was one of the Frenchmen who had escorted Zhingobiins and Tiyoskate to Montreal and, fluent in several Native languages, now served as a translator. Zhingobiins spoke first, asking the governor to sanction a war against the Mesquakie people who had killed many Sioux. Sioux now wanted to raise their dead by taking the war to Mesquakies with Sauteurs' help. Sioux "came to cry with us," he said. "Father, let us have revenge." Next to speak was Ginooczhe, an Odawa leader, who urged the governor to embrace the Sioux, "a bellicose Nation" that would make for a formidable ally. Odawas, he said, had already accepted Sioux as their allies and kin, ending years of deadly warfare. He urged the governor to do the same.[3]

It was Tiyoskate's turn. The young warrior spread two beaver robes at Frontenac's feet and began to weep. After crying bitterly, pleading the governor to have pity on him, he dried his eyes and spoke. "All the Nations have a Father who gives them his protection and has iron," he said, "but I am a bastard searching for a Father." He laid twenty-two arrows on the robes, naming "a Village of his Nation" with each, and asked the governor to send his traders to all of them. He begged the governor, "the master of iron," to accept him as one of his children and bring his guns and iron weapons to his people. "Take courage, great Captain," he said. "Reject me not, despise me not, though I appear miserable in his eyes," he pleaded. "All the nations that are present here know that I am rich and the little they offer you is taken on my lands." What he meant was a wealth of beaver pelts, the raison d'être of the French fur trade, two samples of which lay at the governor's feet. It was common knowledge that Sioux lands were the richest sources of thick winter pelts in the West.[4]

A veteran frontier administrator, Frontenac understood Tiyoskate's plea and its performative nature. Like so many before him, this Indian wanted his pity because pity evoked compassion and created obligations. Pity promoted, indeed demanded, a relationship. In begging the governor to be his father, the Indian was asking him to arm and thereby protect his people and, if necessary, to go to war for them. The young chief wanted Frontenac to be the father of the Sioux but on Sioux terms. He was asking him to be generous with his iron, but he also wanted him to be gentle and compassionate. Tiyoskate expected him to give guns and iron, not orders. Word of the governor's benevolence, he said, "compelled me to abandon my body to come request for his protection." For that the Indian expected the same from him: to abandon his body, to think and act like Sioux, and to transform himself into a kin of the Sioux. Frontenac was to give himself and become one with them.[5]

Like his predecessors, Frontenac was Onontio—Great Mountain—and a father to France's Indian allies, who were his children. Both a title and a social role, Onontio mediated quarrels among his children and cared for their needs.

In return he expected loyalty. True children of Onontio traded only with the French and went to war against the enemies of the French. When Frontenac embraced Tiyoskate and his people as his children, he did so "on condition that he would listen only to his father's voice." Once more Tiyoskate wept, now clasping the governor's legs, and said, "Take pity on me; I know well that I am incapable of speaking to you, being still but a child." But things would change, he continued. With the French on their side, Sioux would grow stronger, and Frontenac would soon see what they "could do when they had the protection of such a good father who will send them Frenchmen to bring them iron of which they are only starting to have knowledge." Sioux would grow from children into allies and they would learn to speak properly to their father. They would be equals.[6]

Tiyoskate did not live to see it through. Cross-cultural diplomacy in seventeenth-century North America was an intensely physical affair that involved handshakes, embraces, kisses, and tears. It may have been in one such encounter in Montreal that Tiyoskate contracted an alien pathogen. The pathogen developed into an illness that killed him after a month's struggle. No one carried his bones home; they remained in Montreal. His hope would have been that the French would dig them up once in a while, hold them, think of good thoughts, and then put them back, but it is unlikely that anyone asked about his last wishes.[7]

IRON FRONTIER

The threats and frustrations that brought Tiyoskate to Montreal in 1695 had eaten away at his people for half a century. The Sioux homeland, a fertile realm of forests, marshes, and lush grasslands around the upper Mississippi River watershed, had become a dangerous place. Sioux knew exactly the reason why: *wašíču*, people with other-than-human abilities, had appeared, wielding extraordinary powers. Long before Sioux would meet these people, they had learned about their power, which manifested itself in various forms: in fire-spitting sticks whose tiny projectiles killed from distances greater than a bowshot; in consciousness-altering liquid that eased spiritual transcendence; in diseases that consumed entire villages; in the softness of their fabrics, which gently hugged human bodies and dried remarkably fast; in the hardness of their iron that could slice through flesh and bone with astounding ease.[8]

The wašíču arriving with guns and iron were formidable, but they were also curiously generous with their wondrous novelties. A few well-worn beaver pelts could produce an iron knife, an ax, or a kettle: European traders preferred used pelts that had lost their coarse outer hair but retained the thick, soft underfur. The French colonists who pushed up the St. Lawrence Valley in the early seventeenth century had forged an alliance with the powerful Wyandot nation, granting them privileged access to their wares in exchange for beaver skins. Wyandots became middlemen who carried French goods from Montreal into the Great Lakes in the west—a region the French knew as pays d'en haut, or "upper country"—and brought back pelts procured from many Native groups. By the 1630s a sprawling trading network, anchored in Montreal and run by Wyandots, stretched deep into the interior, all the way to western Lake Superior.[9]

The quest for French iron drew the Sioux into war. Their main enemies were the Crees, powerful hunter-gatherers who ranged across a vast belt between Hudson Bay and the Great Lakes. Cree bands occupied the forests on the northern shores of Lake Superior, where they were within reach of the castor-rich Sioux country to the west and the burgeoning French-Wyandot fur trade to the east. When Crees made contact with Wyandot traders, Sioux immediately felt the repercussions. Cree war parties seeking beaver started to appear, fighting with iron axes and knives. The Sioux borderlands to the northwest became a war zone where bands gathered together for defense. "Their Villages are larger, and in a better state of defense," a French Jesuit reported in 1641, "owing to their continual wars" with Crees.[10]

Sioux were on the receiving end of violence because their border with Crees had become a technological frontier. Crees now had iron weapons; Sioux were isolated and ironless. Their age-old alliance with the Siouan-speaking Assiniboines with whom they shared an ancestral connection had unraveled—either over a woman or bison meat, according to oral traditions—and they had no ties to the French. When Jesuit missionaries met with a large Native assembly—probably Anishinaabemowin-speaking Sauteur Indians—at the rapids between Lakes Superior and Huron in 1641, they learned "of a certain Nation, the Nadouessis," who lived "eighteen days' journey further away" and "have never known Europeans and have never heard of GOD." Sauteurs, aspiring trapper-traders, seem to have depicted the Sioux as peripheral and uncouth to discourage French overtures to them. It worked. French colonists came to know them as Nadouessioux, a corruption of an Anishinaabe term *na·towe·ssiwak*, which means someone who speaks a foreign language. The Sioux had entered French consciousness as people beyond the pale.[11]

The Sioux were distanced from the French not only mentally. Nearly half a continent separated them from New France, and between them and the French traders lay dozens of Native nations, all of them inside the gun and iron frontier and all of them familiar with the European newcomers and their strange ideas and habits. All of these odds were stacked against the Sioux in ways they did not know. Each of those nations would have to be won over, pushed aside, or otherwise neutralized for the Sioux to find a secure place in the world. They were at once one of the most isolated and boxed-in people in North America.

OČHÉTHI ŠAKÓWIŋ

The Sioux may have been isolated, but they were not defenseless. Crees and Sauteurs fought with iron, but they were widely scattered and loosely organized. Sioux fought with stone, bone, and sinew, but they were numerous and united. Their numbers were estimated around thirty thousand at mid-seventeenth century, and their many villages possessed a strong sense of common identity as the *Očhéthi Šakówiŋ*, the Seven Council Fires.[12]

The Očhéthi Šakówiŋ was an alliance of seven *oyátes*, or "people," who understood themselves as relatives and were bound to one another and the universe by a pervasive life-giving essence, *wakȟáŋ*. The oyátes spoke different dialects and occupied distinct sections of their shared realm, having moved northwestward from their ancestral lands in the central Mississippi Valley over several centuries and in several stages. They were part of a larger movement of Siouan-speaking peoples who variously competed and cooperated with one another, gradually assuming distinct identities as they jostled for position. The great Siouan exodus was triggered by a warmer and wetter climate cycle that began in the ninth century, rendering the lands in the previously colder north and drier west more appealing. The collapse of the Mississippian mound-building cultures and their great center in Cahokia from the twelfth century onward gave a further impetus to the already itinerant Siouans. For centuries commercial gravity had pulled people toward Cahokia and the Mississippi Valley; as that pull faded, people scattered, seeking new attachments.[13]

The ancestral Sioux shifted slowly northwestward until they reached the pine-oak forests that were spreading to the west from the Great Lakes under the wet conditions. The Mdewakantons, Sissetons, Wahpekutes, and Wahpetons—collectively known as the Dakotas—laid down roots first, settling in the marshy woodlands between Leech Lake and the St. Croix River. Converging around Mde Wakan (Mille Lacs), their sacred lake, these four oyátes became the eastern face of the Očhéthi Šakówiŋ. The Yanktons and Yanktonais pushed farther, eventually clustering their villages around the upper Mississippi Valley. The Lakotas—or the Teton oyáte, a derivation from *thítȟuŋwaŋ*, "prairie village"—pushed farthest, settling on the lands toward the Minnesota Valley.

This was North America's ecological hinge, a transition zone where Eastern Woodlands and western grasslands met and overlapped, offering an unusual opulence of plant and animal life. Migratory animals—deer, elk, and especially bison—thrived there, shifting nimbly between habitats, inviting people to do the same. Lakotas did and became the most mobile of the Seven Council Fires. Their range extended ever deeper into the West during the cool and moist Little Ice Age when both grasses and bison proliferated. The herds were many and often numbered in the thousands, each animal yielding at least 650 pounds of

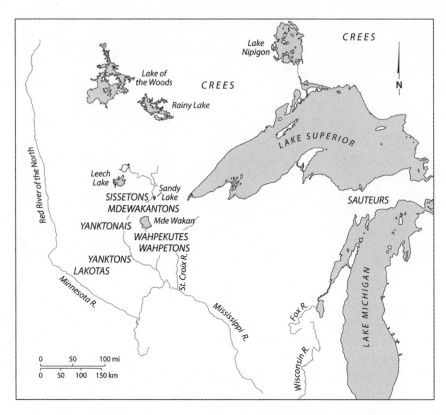

2. The Očhéthi Šakówiŋ in the mid-seventeenth century. Map by Bill Nelson.

food, pulling Lakotas in. Lakota traditions depict the West as both frightening and irresistible, a place where extraordinary people lived and where Iktómi wanted them to go. Their winter counts record great western gatherings from the fifteenth century onward. One of those spiritually charged meeting places was Pipestone Quarry more than two hundred miles west of the Mississippi Valley, where malleable reddish catlinite—ideal for making sacred pipes—was readily available. Great communal bison hunts, possibly in the West, appear in Lakota winter counts in the early sixteenth century.[14]

The Očhéthi Šakówiŋ was not a formal state or a confederacy. It had no over-arching governing structure or leaders who could speak for all members of the alliance. It was instead a manifestation of deep voluntary attachments that bound the seven fires together, the sacred number seven echoing the ancient unity of Sioux as a people. The Očhéthi Šakówiŋ was constructed from the bottom up, with language and kinship as its main cohesive. Its three major divisions—the Dakotas, Yankton-Yanktonais, and Lakotas—spoke different dialects, but all could understand one another, and the seven oyátes saw themselves as "real people" who were distinguished from strangers and *thókas*, enemies. Yet Sioux kinship was not exclusivist. For them belonging was a matter of behavior rather than blood: anybody capable of proper sentiments, words, and deeds could become a relative, *takúye*. From this mindset arose a confederation that was at once durable and exquisitely supple.[15]

Sioux's primary social setting was *thióšpaye*, a local band that stayed together year-round, forming a camp circle that could include more than twenty households, the round shape a manifestation of spiritual unity and cosmological order. The people with whom they shared a village were their first and best shield against the hostile world beyond, but they were also their main rivals for status and power. They were likely to marry someone in their village and village life defined their identity. Each oyáte consisted of several thióšpayes and each commanded a distinct territory, but the Očhéthi Šakówiŋ was not fixed in space. It was a human kaleidoscope where individuals, families, and bands moved around constantly, arranging themselves into different constellations as circumstances demanded; in the late seventeenth century their villages were known to range from a few families to hundreds of people. Instead of fragmenting the Očhéthi Šakówiŋ, the constant movement stitched it tighter together by creating a thick lattice of kinship ties that transcended local and regional identities. Sioux traced descent through both maternal and paternal lines, which maximized their potential to forge connections. Most Sioux had relatives spread across many thióšpayes and oyátes. They could travel anywhere within their realm and always be among kin.[16]

Ties of kinship, *wótakuye*, held the Sioux together, but so did the fear and aversion of outsiders who denounced Sioux mores and remained *thókas*. Sioux went to war for complex reasons—to protect their lands, to exact revenge, to secure hunting and trading privileges, to enhance their power and prestige by taking slaves, to preempt threats—and the threshold for a military campaign was low. Any Sioux could initiate one by visiting villages and inviting warriors to a feast and a dance, which turned war into a collective sacred endeavor. As they came together, warriors sang songs that anticipated the submission and metaphorical absorption of the enemy: "I am going to War, I will revenge the Death of such a Kinsman, I will slay, I will burn, I will bring away Slaves, I will eat Men." Sioux called the feast *šunkahlowanpi*, "ceremonial song of the dog." The fate of the slaves was also decided collectively by elders who listened to the warriors' accounts. Women who had lost fathers in battle received slaves and had the right to decide whether they lived or died. Men who had distinguished themselves in battle received captives to marry, to build up their households, and to bolster their masculine status.[17]

Certain of their fighting prowess and ability to "eat" strangers—to subjugate and neutralize them like they would domesticate dogs—the interconnected oyátes of the Očhéthi Šakówiŋ could mobilize massive numbers of warriors against their enemies. Known by their neighbors as "very strong," Sioux kept Crees and Sauteurs at bay. By the mid-seventeenth century the violence seems to have abated to an on-and-off-again borderland skirmish that sustained a neutral zone between the three powers. Although the competition for furs and iron had made their place in the world uncertain, Sioux remained powerful and relatively safe.[18]

What kept them safe, in the end, was the land itself. The seven fires commanded a vast domain stretching southeastward from Mde Wakan, "the center of the world," and tracing the Mississippi—Ȟaȟáwakpa, "River of the Falls"— near the Wisconsin River confluence where it curved northwestward, bulging out toward the northern latitudes where prairie meets forest. The Mississippi and Minnesota bracketed their core territory, a roughly sixty-thousand-square-mile mix of pine and broadleaf forests, marshes, parklands, and prairie. It was a superbly fertile domain that almost invariably impressed newcomers. In the fall countless lakeside stands of "marsh rye"—wild rice—seemed to yield abundant crops "without any Culture or Sowing," although women probably molded the soil to get larger harvests. Women dried the rice and later boiled it into a broth that sustained their villages through winters. In the spring and summer large schools of fish moved up the rivers, surrendering impressive catches, and Mde Wakan teemed with muskellunge, a large predatory fish. Spring was also the time to tap maple trees for juice, which Sioux boiled into syrup. In the summer there were wild oats, berries, plums, nuts, wild turnips, and *mdo*, a potato-like plant. Deer, elk, ducks, and geese flourished in the forests and around the lakes, and west of the Minnesota began the prairie of towering tall-grasses where massive herds of bison could be found in the summer and early fall.[19]

So bountiful was their domain that Sioux could feed a growing population essentially through wild foods and game alone. Sioux women did grow small crops of corn, but their lands were near the northern limit of corn cultivation and the harvests were unreliable. Farming was a supplementary resource that helped maintain a diet that many modern nutritionists would consider almost ideal: moderate or high in protein, moderate in complex carbohydrates, and low in saturated fat. They probably received enough iron and vitamin B-12, not too much cholesterol or sodium, and sufficient amounts of the essential omega-3 and omega-6 fatty acids.[20]

The Sioux are often thought of as quintessential people of the plains and the hunt, but that was a later development. In the seventeenth century they were consummate generalists who exploited multiple habitats, moving among wood-

3. *Guarding the Corn Fields*, engraving by James Smillie after Captain Seth Eastman, 1853. From planting to harvesting, horticulture was women's task. For centuries, Dakota and Lakota women protected their families and communities against the periodic shortages of carbohydrates, the major downside of a hunting way of life, by raising small crops and by gathering berries, fruit, and root vegetables. Courtesy of Getty Images. Photo by Science & Society Picture Library.

lands, parklands, grasslands, and marshlands in a carefully attuned annual cycle. Indeed, theirs was very much a watery world. Women harvested wild rice from birchbark canoes by pulling the stalks down over the side and gently beating the grain into their canoes with sticks. Men performed many of their duties—policing borders, visiting allies, moving trade goods—with light and fast canoes. Bands traveled to communal ceremonies, political gatherings, and war in fleets. One early observer portrayed them a "wandring nation" that commanded "a vaste countrey. In winter they live in ye land for the hunting sake, and in summer by the watter for fishing."[21]

By 1650 a modicum of stability had settled in the Sioux realm, which had been rocked by French markets, enemy trappers, and iron weapons. A new hybrid world of Indians, colonists, and commerce had expanded deep into the West, butting against Sioux borders and then faltering there. But, unbeknownst to Sioux, that distant new world in the East had already imploded, ripped apart by disease, death, and unprecedented violence. The ensuing chaos engulfed the Northeast and then washed over the Great Lakes. The turmoil reached the Sioux in the late 1650s and nearly broke them.

In the fall of 1638 a delegation of Jesuit missionaries met with Wyandots in the Great Lakes. Looking like "men who already feel the terrors of death," the Indians spoke in sighs, which only seemed "to incite them to vomit more bitterly upon us the venom which they concealed within." An old chief addressed the priests: "I am obliged to speak here, since all the other Captains are dead. Now before I follow them to the grave I must free my mind; and perhaps it will be for the good of the country, which is going to ruin. Every day it is worse than before; this cruel malady has now over-run all the cabins of our village, and has made such ravages in our own family that, lo, we are reduced to two persons, and I do not yet know whether we shall escape the fury of this Demon. I have seen maladies in the country before, but never have I seen anything like this."[22]

The malady was an extraordinarily virulent smallpox outbreak that had begun in Massachusetts in 1633. The death toll was staggering: more than 80 percent of New England Indians perished within a year. John Winthrop, a leading Massachusetts colonist, saw a divine intervention in that. "I am still as full of Companye and business as before," he wrote to a fellow Puritan in England, "but for the Natives in these parts, Gods hand hath so pursued them, as for 300 miles space, the greatest parte of them are swept awaye by the small poxe, which still continues among them: So as God hathe hereby cleered our title to this place." From New England, Native traders and warriors—the continent's most mobile people—transported the pox in all directions, carrying the multiplying virus in their seemingly sound bodies while it incubated—a window of ten to seventeen days, on average. Fast-moving parties could cover vast distances before expiring, and soon the zone of death extended from the Atlantic Coast to the Appalachians and from the Chesapeake Bay to the St. Lawrence Valley.[23]

The pandemic killed European settlers and their African slaves everywhere it went, but in relatively modest numbers: long exposure to smallpox and other viral diseases had fortified their ancestors' immune systems against crowd illnesses, which had gradually evolved into childhood diseases. For Native Americans, however, viral diseases were a lethal novelty. No one had acquired immunity against them, a vulnerability that was greatly magnified by the colonists who destroyed Indian crops and food caches to generate disastrous bouts of famine. Their immune systems were also more homogenous than those of Europeans, which rendered them more vulnerable to infections: once adapted to their relatively uniform immunological responses, pathogens could jump bodies with relative ease, spreading and killing much faster than in more heterogeneous populations.[24]

Entire villages could be inflicted within days and entire regions within weeks. The St. Lawrence–Great Lakes trade corridor became a disease corridor, channeling the pox far downriver in the east, to Lake Huron in the west, to Hudson Bay in the north, and to the Chesapeake Bay in the south. About half of the Natives in that vast expanse died. The death toll was equally devastating among the Haudenosaunee, the Five Nations of the Iroquois League, whose lands around Lake Ontario and along the upper Hudson River were surrounded by English, Dutch, and French outposts. About half of them, ten thousand people, had perished by the time the pox had run its course in 1641. Shattered worlds emerged everywhere in the pandemic's wake. Unburied bodies remained rotting on the ground, ghastly reminders of broken families and lineages. Starvation sapped villages that had lost too many hunters or farmers. Native converts turned against their missionaries, who seemed curiously invulnerable to the malady, killing them in rage. Despair and sorrow gripped entire communities, spawning apathy or, increasingly, violence to ease the pain.[25]

MOURNING WARS

Death demanded war, and nowhere as potently as among the Five Iroquois Nations. With the loss of half of their population, their world had suddenly become a deadly and menacing place. Iroquoia's central location in the midst of several Indigenous and colonial realms, once an advantage, turned into a liability: how could a confederacy that had lost half of its fighting power hold on to its extensive territory in a fiercely competitive milieu where multiple peoples jostled for power? Rather than turning inward, trying to cling to what they had, the Iroquois exploded outward. They had lost too many people and now needed new ones. They went to war to make Iroquois out of others.

The result was warfare more ferocious than anyone could remember. Iroquois war parties pushed north and west, raiding across a widening zone in months-long summer campaigns. A massive invasion broke the Wyandot world of villages, "the people of each scattering where they could." The Iroquois pursued the refugees to the interior, chasing them into the western Great Lakes. Once again people fled, and once again the Iroquois followed, now targeting virtually anyone they ran into. Several nations crumbled as political entities, and scores of Mascoutens, Kickapoos, Potawatomis, Odawas, and others abandoned their villages, retreating in the face of the most concentrated projection of power in seventeenth-century North America. A swelling diaspora carried fugitives deep

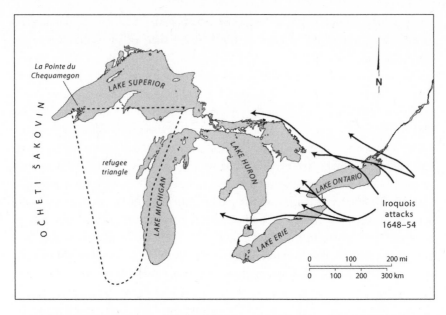

4. The Iroquois war zone and the middle ground in the 1650s. Map by Bill Nelson.

into the forests of the western Great Lakes, where distance gave them a measure of safety. In the mid-1650s the Iroquois dispersed the remaining Eries and then moved the war to the south against the Shawnees. An enormous swath of land between the Ohio Valley and the northern Great Lakes became virtually empty of people. It had become an Iroquois shatter zone.[26]

Iroquois war parties carried thousands of war prisoners into Iroquoia, where clan matrons slated them for slavery, adoption, or execution. Many, mostly women, became slaves who labored as farmers, household workers, and mothers. Many, almost invariably men, were "requickened" to cover dead kin. They were adopted into Iroquois clans and assumed the social role and name of the deceased, thereby repairing fractured lineages as newly born Iroquois. Some male captives were adopted and then killed to atone for slain relatives. Their bodies were cut up and boiled in a kettle. Whole villages joined in feasts where they consumed the corporal and spiritual power of their enemies, preserving it for new purposes.[27]

The Iroquois never invaded the lands of the Očhéthi Šakówiŋ, and if they ever captured or killed any Sioux, there is no record of it. Yet the Iroquois wars profoundly changed the history of the seven fires. The thousands of Indians who fled "the fury of the Iroquois" to the western Great Lakes were refugees, traumatized and desperate people in a foreign land that seemed "the very end of the world."

But soon they forged a new order out of the fragments of the old and made the strange lands their own. This entrenchment spelled trouble for the Sioux. An entire Indigenous world, alien and menacing, had materialized on their borders, alive with otherworldly powers. These newcomers not only had iron. They had guns.[28]

THE POLITICS OF PITY

The thousands of refugees who fled the Iroquois to the western Great Lakes had not entered empty lands. The lands belonged to Odawas, Ojibwes, Sauteurs, and others whose mobile villages dotted the area, clustering around strategic lakeshore locations at the Straits of Mackinac and Sault Ste. Marie. At first there was violence, but the unremitting Iroquois pressure drove people to seek safety in numbers. Resident Indians opened their villages to emigrants, who made their new homes points of resistance against the Iroquois. Intermarriage expanded and thickened long-standing kinship lineages, *nindoodemag*, which fostered co-operation across political and clan boundaries. Feasting, gifting, dancing, and sharing the sacred calumet pipe, they created a space of transcendence where they could connect with unearthly powers and reimagine the newcomers as allies. Carefully, through a thousand ceremonies, they ushered the foreigners into their homeland, Anishinaabewaki, which encompassed most of the lands around the Great Lakes.[29]

Most refugees pushed deeper into the interior, seeking sanctuary west of Lake Michigan. There they merged with the resident Indians who had no choice but to weather the emigrant surge. Local villages bulged into dynamic mixed villages, and new loyalties began to cohere. A measure of stability fell over this refugee world that stretched, in a triangular shape, from the upper Illinois River to both ends of Lake Superior. The greatest concentration of villages was in the middle, around Green Bay, where some ten thousand Indians resided, desperate for normalcy, belonging, and trade.[30]

The refugee triangle became a magnet for far-ranging independent French traders who lived in the West and, in the eyes of their countrymen along the St. Lawrence Valley, seemed to have gone native. The budding interior fur trade had ground to a near halt during the Iroquois wars, leaving New France without robes and revenue. A restart became possible in 1654, when the Iroquois agreed to a peace with the French. Craving guns and iron, Wyandots immediately guided more than one hundred Indians, mostly Odawas, to Trois-Rivières in the upper St. Lawrence Valley. Médard Chouart Des Groseilliers, a veteran trader who had lost his livelihood with the collapse of the fur trade, joined the Odawas on their journey back west. Two years later he returned to Trois-Rivières with fifty fur-laden canoes, which spoke of immense western riches: beaver populations had boomed during a trapping hiatus, and the interior rivers and lakes were teeming with castor. Although the Iroquois wars soon flared up again, the inland trade persisted. Odawas emerged as a key broker regime, running a burgeoning traffic that connected the American interior to Atlantic markets.[31]

Managing such a prodigious, multiethnic trade network was a daunting logistical undertaking, but it posed an even greater cultural challenge. Answers to that challenge spawned an extraordinary small new world in the heart of the continent. As the refugee villages morphed into trade centers, the French and the Indians had to find ways to coexist despite the yawning cultural gap that separated them. Neither possessed the power to dictate to the other, and so they were forced to accommodate one another. Through trial and error, they learned how to listen, how to pull back, and how to reconcile inevitable disputes over authority, trade protocols, crimes, punishments, and sex. They learned not to impose their own customs, but to rather appeal to what they thought were the meanings and practices of the other, practices that often seemed absurd and outright repellent. Often they misunderstood one another and frequently chose to misread one another, but out of those distortions emerged new meanings on which a fragile shared world, a middle ground, could be built.

The compromises took many forms. Hard bargaining over goods blended into gift giving in which fictive kin shared possessions. Much of the trade in skins and furs was conducted by Indian women whom the French simultaneously sought as sexual partners and sometimes married *à la façon du pays*, "according to the custom of the country." Murderers of French traders were condemned to death only to be pardoned and then "raised" with slaves or "covered" with presents. Indians appealed to their distant father in Montreal to look after their needs, and Onontio pretended to command his dutiful children through kindness and generosity. The Great Lakes middle ground was an artifice, a mutual fiction between people who hardly tolerated one another, but it survived because both sides needed it to survive. Word by word, concession by concession, the French and the Indians forged an alliance that stabilized the refugee triangle, allowing trade to flourish. Soon Jesuit missionaries followed. Suffused with utopian fantasies of "La Nouvelle Jérusalem" in the wilderness, they began building missions.[32]

The French-Indian alliance in the Great Lakes underwrote a dramatic expansion of the fur trade, which then thrust a gunpowder revolution into the Sioux world. Fleets of French traders and Odawa middlemen carried guns into the rich castor lands in the western Great Lakes, where greatest profits awaited. Sauteurs, Wyandots, Odawas, and other Lakes people acquired enough guns to contain Iroquois war parties from the east. But they also carried their guns against the Očhéthi Šakówiŋ in the west. They needed more pelts to fuel the fur trade and more game to feed their crowded villages, and the largest concentrations of both could be found in the lands of the Sioux. Wyandots, a French trader noted, "so rash as to imagine that the Scioux were incapable of resisting them without iron weapons and firearms," joined forces with Odawas to drive out to "secure a greater territory in which to seek their living." The refugee triangle began to bulge westward, turning the Očhéthi Šakówiŋ's eastern border into a battlefront.[33]

It was the kind of warfare Sioux had never seen. Trapped on the wrong side of the technological frontier, they had been cut off from a revolution that had multiplied their enemies' killing power. Sioux still relied on the energy of their own bodies to wage war. Stone points and bows had long ago amplified their capacity to inflict damage, but Sioux warriors were still constrained by the limits of human strength: the force of an ax stroke or the reach of an arrow ultimately depended on their own ability to generate power. Their enemies, however, now commanded unimaginable power that had been harnessed from the natural world and condensed into an explosive substance. Packed behind a bullet, gunpowder's sulfur, charcoal, and saltpeter produced a chemical reaction that sent a piece of hot lead at speed faster than an eye could see. Gunpowder provided more than an amplification of human power; it opened a way to tap into the immense energy stored in the earth's mineral wealth. The muzzle-loading smoothbore flintlocks the enemies of the Sioux carried into battle were more than weapons; they channeled wašíčuŋ, mysterious and incomprehensible sacred power.

The eastern border of the Sioux became a terrifying place where they fought from a position of daunting material and psychological disadvantage, facing steel with flesh. They confronted enemies that could kill from distances far greater than their own weapons could reach and suffered wounds their healers could not mend. Sauteurs became a "terror unto them," waging "a cruell warre" with instruments they "never have seene." Sioux tried desperately to secure guns. They captured a party of Odawas, whom they called spirits because they had iron. They returned these spirits home and sent emissaries to Odawa villages. They wept over everyone they met, beseeching them to "have pity on them, and to share with them that iron, which they regarded as a divinity." But the Odawas became contemptuous, dismissing them as "people far inferior to themselves, and as incapable even of waging war." They fired their guns, which "so terrified the Scioux that they imagined it was the thunder or the lightning, of which the Outaoüas had made themselves masters in order to exterminate whomsoever they would."[34]

The performance affirmed the inequity between the Odawas and the Sioux and announced on which side power lay. Odawas and their allies wielded extraordinary powers and had no intention of surrendering their advantage. Sioux "loaded them with endearing terms, and showed the utmost submissiveness," but this "humiliating attitude" only deepened Odawas' revulsion. Perhaps the struggles over hunting rights cut too deep or perhaps the Sioux did not quite know the proper rituals of war and diplomacy of the Lakes world. Unlike their neighbors, Sioux did not burn their captives, considering it indecent "for men to be so cruell," and their custom of ceremonial weeping was not common in the Lakes. Or perhaps there were simply too many of them. Whatever the reason, Sioux remained outsiders. Odawas, Wyandots, and others would shun alliances with them and keep driving into their hunting lands.[35]

The expanding refugee triangle was just one of many hostile fronts converging around the Očhéthi Šakówiŋ. Looking east from their core region around Mde Wakan, Sioux faced enemies across an arc extending from the Leech Lake all the way south to the Des Moines Valley—a massive war zone where they fought some dozen nations, vying for hunting rights, trade, and predominance. Then, disastrously, Crees and Sauteurs joined forces against them. The new allies, a terse French report noted, sent "companys of souldiers to warre against that great nation" to capture its deep reserves of prime castor. Neither Crees nor Sauteurs had kinship ties with Sioux, and both considered them an alien people who could be killed and whose possessions could be taken. The enmity with Sauteurs was particularly damaging. Ranging across the length of Lake Superior's southern shore, Sauteurs could exert strong control over the western flow of guns and other trade goods—and stop it from reaching the Sioux.[36]

Gunless and ironless, Sioux had to retreat. To avoid clashes with their many enemies, they increasingly hunted on the western side of the Mississippi, but this drew them in conflict with the Iowas, Siouan-speaking hunters and farmers who lived to the south of the seven fires and hunted bison in the grasslands west of them. On all sides the Sioux domain began to cave in. Cree warriors pushed into Mde Wakan, threatening Sioux fisheries and rice fields. Sauteur war parties invaded Sioux hunting grounds through the western tip of Lake Superior, a natural gateway into the contested beaver-trapping grounds. A group of Odawas settled on Prairie Island on the Mississippi and began to raise corn on Sioux lands. The power dynamics had become horribly stacked against the Očhéthi Šakówiŋ.[37]

Yet the seven fires possessed a singular advantage: they were more numerous than any of their enemies, boasting a population that, by some estimates, was thirty times larger than that of the geopolitically privileged Sauteurs. Their isolation rendered them vulnerable, but it also protected them from contagious crowd diseases: there is no record of epidemic outbreaks in the Sioux country

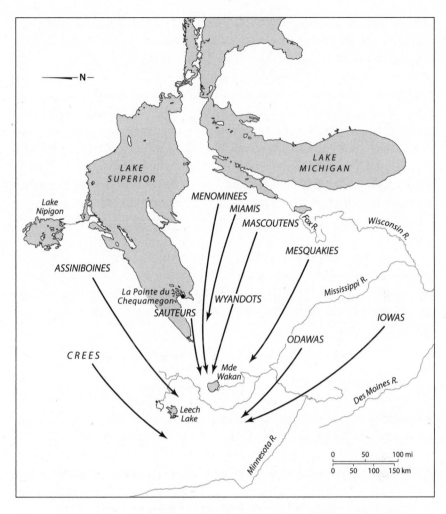

5. The Sioux war zone in the mid-seventeenth century. Map by Bill Nelson.

in the seventeenth century. Sheer numbers allowed Sioux to hold on. Their enemies could kill them, infringe on their lands, and steal their peltry, but they could not conquer or undo them. Sioux could bring thousands of warriors on a battlefield to keep out enemy war parties whose numbers rarely exceeded a few hundred.[38]

Numbers also made them impossible to ignore. The French traders who followed the refugee Indians west spoke of Onontio's love for his children, pledged to take care of their needs, and armed them against Sioux. But all the while French officers kept gazing past them at the seven fires, which had taken an un-

yielding hold of their imagination. La Nouvelle France was a small colony surrounded by much larger British ones and the formidable Iroquois, but how great
might New France be with thirty thousand Sioux on its side?

The French seemed to have found in Sioux the key that could unlock the continent and its immense wealth for them. Yet they struggled to implement consis-
tent policies to win the Sioux over. Having originated as an eclectic religious and
commercial venture, New France did not seem to be able to decide the shape
and character it should assume. Even after the king took the colony under his
direct control in the 1660s, the French did not seem to be able to decide whether
to center the Indian trade in Montreal through Native middlemen, to concentrate it in fixed posts in the interior, or to allow *coureurs de bois* (runners of the
woods), wide-ranging independent traders, to carry goods into distant Indian villages.[39]

The result was a constantly shifting and chronically unstable commercial and
geopolitical landscape that remained Sioux's greatest challenge for nearly a century. They met it with a policy that was resolute in terms of ends—securing guns,
iron, Onontio's love, and safety—and extraordinarily supple in terms of means.
But first they needed to find openings.

DEAD OR ALIVE YOU HAVE THE POWER OVER US

In the spring of 1660 a band of Mdewakanton Sioux walked for several days to
visit Sauteurs, carrying the bones of their ancestors. They had been summoned
five months earlier to a village by Ottawa Lake south of Lake Superior where a
great gathering would take place. As they now made their way east, these Sioux
entered a world of strangers and enemies who for years had tried to destroy them.
But if the bones of their dead would join the bones of departed Sauteurs, the past
could be buried and the violence would end. The bones could remake the world
in a ceremony the Indians knew as the Feast of the Dead.[40]

The peace process had been set in motion a year earlier by hunger and bloodshed. Pierre-Esprit Radisson, a French adventurer-trader who was wintering
among Sauteurs, wrote how his hosts, caught between the Iroquois to the east
and the Sioux to the west, had become the "very Image of death." He also wrote
about a massive battle between Sioux and allied Sauteurs and Crees. Many had
died on both sides and a Sauteur chief had lost an "eye by an arrow." But with his
remaining eye the chief had seen what had to be done. "His courage being abject," he had announced that "he himselfe should be ambassador & conclud the
peace." He had traveled to Mille Lacs to reach out to Sioux. But the "wound was
yett fresh," and Sioux had recoiled. Sauteurs returned home, but within a year
they made a new effort by calling the Sioux and Crees to a feast.[41]

Now the moment was at hand. When the Sioux ambassadors reached the Sauteur village, they met Radisson who was once again visiting Sauteurs, now with his brother-in-law, Médard Chouart Des Groseilliers, who had been instrumental in opening the Great Lakes trade. The ambassadors seized the opportunity to forge ties with the French. Their wives—each had two—offered the Frenchmen gifts of wild rice and Indian corn. They then greased the Frenchmen's feet, undressed them, and clothed them with buffalo robes and white beaver skins. "After this they weeped uppon our heads untill we weare wetted by their tears," Radisson marveled. The ceremony culminated in the smoking of the calumet, which put an end to hostilities and created bonds of affinity and obligation. The ambassadors perfumed the clothes and armor of the Frenchmen, who in turn threw "tobbacco" into a fire, causing a violent explosion—the Sioux's first experience of gunpowder. Almost all of this took place in silence. The ceremony resumed the next day, now in words and through an interpreter. The Indians sat down, but Radisson and Des Groseilliers made a "more elevated" place for themselves to "appear in more state." The Frenchmen accepted the calumet and told the envoys that they had taken them in their protection.[42]

French protection was precisely what the Sioux wanted if it translated into trade, guns, and iron. They had made themselves small and pitiful to invoke generosity. They stripped and dressed the strangers so that they could be born again as allies. This initial meeting between the Sioux and the Frenchmen was followed by eight days of feasting, which then transformed into a grand council. Thirty young Sioux men, armed with nothing but bows and arrows, their faces painted with many colors and their ears pierced in five places, entered the council house. They were warriors and they spoke of war, explaining how they had brought their wives with them "to take their advice, ffor they had a minde to goe against ye Christinos (Crees), who were ready for them."[43]

The fact that wives made themselves visible announced Sioux's commitment to end the violence that was consuming their world: women's presence in public meetings conveyed peaceful intentions and helped create a common ground. The next day, with great gravity and modesty, Sioux elders entered the council lodge, carrying calumets and dressed in long buffalo robes that reached the ground. While the ambassadors handed out gifts of beaver and buffalo skins, their spokesman made "a speech of thanksgiving," declaring that they had come to make a sacrifice to the French. He implored the French to visit them and bring their merchandise to keep them alive. An old man placed a calumet at the Frenchmen's feet, covered them with his robe, and spoke: "Yee are masters over us; dead or alive you have the power over us, and may dispose of us as your pleasur."[44]

Radisson and Des Groseilliers imagined themselves as life-givers who alone had the capacity to unite the fractured Indigenous world with their goods and love. "We weare come from the other side of ye' great salted lake," they told the assembled Indians, "not to kill them but to make ym live; acknowledging you for our brethren and children, whom we will love henceforth as our owne." Because the fur trade required stability, they exhorted the Indians to commit to "an universall peace all over the earth" and urged the Sioux to embrace the Crees, whom the Frenchmen had already adopted. Sioux should "lead them to ye dance of Union, wch was to be celebrated at y death's feast and banquett of kindred." If Sioux continued their war with Crees, Radisson and Des Groseilliers warned, they would not see them in their villages. The Sioux ambassadors, apparently, said nothing. Radisson then traveled three days to a Cree encampment and brought back a delegation.[45]

The Cree emissaries melted into a large audience of Sauteurs, Sioux, Odawas, and others who had gathered to witness the culmination of the peace council in the Feast of the Dead. Women danced to music, young men competed at climbing up a greased pole, and everyone took part in a feast. Gift exchanges of "most exquisite things, to shew what his country affords," ensued; the Frenchmen received three hundred beaver robes. Informal marriages were concluded "according to their countrey coustoms," turning strangers into relatives. Finally the time came for the main participants to unite the bones. Sauteurs unearthed ancestral remains and bestowed them on Sioux who reciprocated. Enemies held the bones of their enemies and reburied them in a common grave, thus resurrecting as relatives. More than a thousand people watched as "two redoubted nations" did "what they never before had": they became one.[46]

All this Radisson and Des Groseilliers observed with growing delight. "This feast ended," Radisson wrote, and all headed home "well satisfied." The two adventurers thought they had pacified the interior and refitted it to the needs of the fur trade, but in truth they had played a role far smaller and more ambiguous. For all their humility and submissiveness, the Sioux ambassadors had arranged ceremonies and exchanges to forge a new reality where the Sauteurs could become allies, the French could become protectors, and trade could flow freely into their villages. What the Sioux needed was a thorough geopolitical realignment of the American interior. They needed the essential elements of power—the wašíčuŋ of New France, the gun frontier, even the Sauteurs—to shift west.[47]

THE IROQUOIS OF THIS COUNTRY

The Sioux vision for the West complemented French designs for the interior. Where Sioux wanted merchandise and peace to flow west, the French wanted furs and loyalty to flow east. Sioux, superior hunters whom Radisson called the

"Nation of the beefe," were the key to French designs. The animal-rich Sioux country promised to become what Mexico and Peru had been for Spain—a source of easily extractable wealth—but the French knew that it was too big and too distant to be claimed with missions and forts, the basic tools of French imperialism. Instead of bringing the French Empire among the seven fires, the agents had to bring the seven fires into the French Empire. And so, as the Feast of the Dead ended, Radisson and Des Groseilliers headed west with a party of Sauteurs to deliver the Sioux into the fold.[48]

During the council with Sauteurs, Sioux emissaries had boasted to Radisson and Des Groseilliers about the many attractions of their country. Working hard to enhance their reputation, they promised the Frenchmen would find smooth roads and bridges across rivers "for not to wett our feete." More pointedly, they assured that the lodges of their wives and daughters would always be open to them—a promise of intermarriages that would cement an alliance by turning the French into kin. When the pair arrived after "seaven small Journeys," they were not disappointed. They were taken to the Mde Wakan area, the spiritual and political center of the Sioux world, where they found themselves in a town of skin "cabbans." They were told that "there weare 7,000 men. This we believed." They also seemed to believe that there were mines of copper, pewter, and lead, as well as mountains covered with "a kind of Stone that is transparent and tender, and like to that of Venice." Radisson learned how the Sioux "retire in winter towards the woods of the North, where they kill a quantity of Castors." He believed their pelts were the best "in the whole world." Cree lands, he concluded, were richer in castor, but Sioux castor was "far better." Radisson and Des Groseilliers stayed for six weeks and left "loaden wth booty."[49]

Things changed rapidly after this. The refugee triangle had long been the primary destination of French traders, but now commercial gravity shifted north and west around a Sauteur-Sioux axis. A small, resource-rich peninsula at the southwestern corner of Lake Superior the French knew as La Pointe du Chequamegon became the focal point of the interior trade. Chequamegon belonged to Sauteurs and their villages became a cosmopolitan neutral zone, a "Babylon" of "libertinism," where guns, food, and captives exchanged hands, where customs and ceremonies blended, and where new kin were made. Jesuits built a mission, Saint-Esprit, for the swelling Native population. "More than fifty Villages can be counted," the priests rejoiced, "which comprise divers peoples, either nomadic or stationary, who depend in some sort on this Mission."[50]

Sioux, too, benefited from the rise of the Sauteurs. With the bones of their ancestors now resting near Chequamegon, they were welcome at the region's thriving fairs where they found ready markets for their coveted castor. At long last guns and iron became available. And just as they had explained to Radisson and

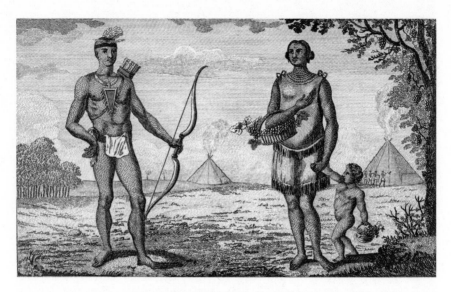

6. *A Man & Woman of the Naudowessie.* From Jonathan Carver,
Travels through the Interior Parts of North America, in the Years 1766, 1767, and 1768.
Courtesy of the John Carter Brown Library at Brown University.

Des Groseilliers, trade brought peace. To their southeast the formidable Illinois raided slaves across a widening zone while simultaneously fighting a two-front war against the Sioux and Iroquois. Desperate to carry their slaves through Sioux territory to the Lake Superior gun markets, Illinois approached the seven fires and made peace with them "in order to facilitate their coming to La Pointe."[51]

Sioux had won a tenuous access to an enormously complex world, and they had to quickly learn how to navigate it. Careful not to alarm their new allies, they visited the Chequamegon fairs "only in small numbers, and as if on an Embassy." Like the Iroquois, they had to tread cautiously on the margins of the shared Indian and French world that was coalescing in the western Great Lakes. Jesuits dubbed them as "the Iroquois of this country, beyond la Pointe"; the Feast of the Dead may have joined them to Sauteurs, but they remained foreigners to most Lakes Indians. "They speak a language that is utterly foreign, the Savages here not understanding it at all," the Jesuits observed, and their "manners and customs are quite extraordinary." To the Jesuits whose sensibilities had been molded in decades of proselytizing among more sedentary Indians, the Sioux seemed unworldly and vulgar. Their calumet-centered ceremonies seemed pathetically simple and their hospitality verged on the insulting: "when any stranger arrives," complained Father Jacques Marquette, "they feed him with a wooden fork, as one would a child."[52]

Their acts of generosity and kindness misinterpreted and their pleas for pity ignored, Sioux remained outsiders. They had made a concerted effort to be accepted and included, and it had failed. The carefully fashioned realm of good thoughts fractured and violence flowed into the cracks. By the late 1660s Sioux were once again at war with most of their neighbors who held them "in extreme fear." The access point to the eastern markets through Chequamegon closed up, and they turned inward. "They have the wild oats," Marquette wrote, and "keep their world inviolate." Sensing a growing detachment, Marquette sent them gifts and a "message that they must show due recognition to the Frenchman wherever they met him, and must not kill him or the Savages accompanying him." Their response gave him a pause. Sioux refused to visit Chequamegon and rejected the gifts. "I could wish that all the Nations had as much love for God as these people have fear of the French," the dejected priest complained. "Christianity would soon be flourishing." Another missionary wrote of a "King of the great nation of the Nadouessiouek," who "reigns over a vast country beyond the Vermilion Sea." There was no such king, of course. As the Sioux became increasingly aloof, imagination started to replace facts.[53]

French assertions of Sioux detachment may have been exaggerated — there was so much in the interior world the French could not see or know — but it did not matter. Perceptions bled into policies and the seven fires were once more deemed strangers. When they were paired with the Iroquois, who were tearing down New France, they had already lost their quest for centrality. Occasional traders would visit them, but iron and guns would concentrate elsewhere, consigning them to the receiving end of the Native arms race. Odawas entrenched themselves on the Straits of Mackinac between Lakes Huron and Michigan — a key gateway to the west — where they were ideally positioned to dominate the reviving fur trade. Five hundred miles and thousands of merchandise-hungry Indians separated the Sioux from the straits, leaving them isolated and vulnerable.[54]

THEY HAVE EATEN ME TO THE BONE

In around 1670 Sioux captured a Wyandot hunting party from Chequamegon that had entered their lands. One Sioux chief was so incensed by this that he nearly attacked the young men who had seized the Wyandots. The chief had recently "sung the calumet" to Sinagos, a brutal slaver and war chief of Odawas who were close allies of Wyandots, and he was desperate to protect this lifeline for his village. He decided to personally deliver the Wyandot captives home and set out with three warriors and a woman. When approaching Chequamegon, however, the Wyandots fled. At the village they said they had escaped certain death in Sioux hands. The Sioux ambassadors continued to Chequamegon regardless and were cordially received by Sinagos. But the Wyandots convinced Sinagos to hand the Sioux over to them. They boiled and ate them.[55]

Things fell apart after this. Sioux retaliated by killing Wyandots and Odawas, who responded by killing Sioux. The Sioux-Sauteur alliance dissolved into chaos, and the lands between Lake Superior and Mde Wakan became a battle-ground. The French tried to mediate, but the bloodshed escalated through kin-ship networks as grieving men sought to revenge slain relatives. Enmities con-gealed into hatreds and violence swept over the length of the Očhéthi Šakówiŋ's eastern border where "a general League" had formed "against a common foe." Mesquakies, whose lands west of Green Bay butted against the Sioux domain, were "fully resolved not to treat" the Sioux "more humanely than they are treated by them."[56]

Yet the border held. Enemy war parties raided along the Mississippi, turning it into a battlefront, but few risked pushing into the Sioux country beyond the river. Some thirty large Dakota, Yankton, Yanktonai, and Lakota villages dotted the vast realm, each protected by boggy marshes and each ready to pull together and "give prompt aid wherever it is needed." They "made themselves feared by all their neighbors," using the bow and arrow "with such skill and readiness as to fill the air with shafts in an instant." Now "exceedingly numerous," Sioux seized the initiative and carried the war to their enemies, striking deep into the Great Lakes. The result was a massive diaspora. If in the 1650s the Iroquois had been a hammer that pounded westward fleeing refugees against an anvil that were the Sioux, in the 1670s the positions were reversed: Sioux now delivered the blows while Iroquois remained passive. The western Great Lakes began to empty as people either fled or wasted away. The peninsula linking Lakes Superior, Michigan, and Huron became a new refugee center for people who had been twice dispossessed in a single generation. The Jesuits abandoned Chequamegon and moved east to Sault Ste. Marie. There they rejoiced how the fear of the Sioux pushed the refugees "almost in one spot," making it easier for the priests to find them and "show Them The Road to heaven." More concerned with survival in this world, the refugees embraced the Jesuits and their god as life-givers who could help them destroy the Sioux. A Sauteur chief, his body coated with scars from years of fighting the Iroquois and Sioux, thanked the Jesuits for "praying for us to JESUS, The God of war."[57]

In 1672 the Lakes Indians mobilized French resources against the Sioux. Odawas visited Montreal and brought back only muskets and powder, "intending to march against the Scioux, build a fort in their country, and wage war against them during the entire winter." When Sinagos moved Odawas toward the Sioux country across the refugee zone, handing out gifts, his party kindled kinship obligations in village after village, becoming a mobile rallying point for shared vengeance, "a body of over a thousand men, all having guns or other powerful weapons of defense." Sinagos's army managed to surprise small villages, but Sioux quickly regrouped and "slew them in great numbers, for their terror was so overwhelming that in their flight they had thrown away their weapons." Nearly all of them perished "by fighting, by hunger, or by the rigor of the climate." Demoralized, the coalition collapsed into infighting: "the disorder among them was so great that they ate one another."[58]

Sioux captured Sinagos and decided to make a statement. "Unwilling to burn" the prominent chief, "they made him go to a repast, and, cutting pieces of flesh from his thighs and all other parts of his body, broiled these and gave them to him to eat—informing Sinagos that, as he had eaten so much human flesh and shown himself so greedy for it, he might now satiate himself upon it by eating his own." Then they sent one of Sinagos's slaves back home so that "he might faithfully report what he had seen and the justice that had been administered."[59]

If this was an attempt to intimidate Odawas or to communicate restraint, it did not work: Lakes Indians remained resolute to destroy and consume the Sioux. In the midst of the bloodshed, Mascoutens and Illinois invited Father Claude-Jean Allouez to what "seemed to be a feast for fighting." "You have heard of the peoples called Nadouessi," the master of the feast told the Jesuits. "They have eaten me to the bone, and have not left me a single member of my family alive. I must taste of their flesh, as they have tasted of that of my kinsfolk. I am ready to set out against them in war, but I despair of success therein unless you, who are the masters of life and of death, are favorable toward me in this undertaking." Allouez heard the pleas but flinched at mass violence. The Jesuits, he explained to his distraught audience, were "but the weak servants of the great God of Armies." It took a threat from another European empire to prompt the French into action.[60]

TEN THOUSAND ONONTIOS

In 1670 dreadful news reached New France: King Charles II of England had chartered a new fur-trading enterprise and granted it a monopoly over all lands whose rivers drain into Hudson Bay, an area fifteen times the size of England. Making matters worse, Radisson and Des Groseilliers, the pioneer trader-explorers, had grown disillusioned with the prospects of the French fur trade and deserted, taking their deep savoir faire of Indigenous diplomacy to the service of London merchants, who seemed to possess not only the money but an unfettered commercial focus to fulfill the pair's dream of an inland fur empire. Hudson Bay lay hundreds of miles to the north and west of the St. Lawrence Valley, the spine of New France, but it anchored a vast fan-shaped river system that opened multiple entryways to the interior. Suddenly, the English seemed poised to reach nearly every Native nation in the interior, threatening to cut off New France from its hinterland.[61]

The news came at a particularly unfortunate time for the French: the Sioux wars had effectively closed the West beyond Lake Huron to trade. This presented a mortal threat for New France, whose empire did not exist outside of its Indian alliance system. The eastward retreat of the Lakes Indians also meant an eastward retreat of the French Empire. The pays d'en haut, the sphere where French traders, missionaries, and soldiers could safely operate, had shrunk dangerously. This alone would have been damaging, but the contraction occurred just as a new imperial rival entered the scene in the form of the Hudson's Bay Company.

The French did what they habitually did when facing imperial crises: they reached out to Indians. In the summer of 1671 a seasoned inland trader, Nicolas Perrot, brought Simon-François Daumont de Saint-Lusson to Sault Ste. Marie where, in front of Jesuit priests and two thousand Natives, the commissary claimed for Louis XIV all the "territories lying between the East and the West, from Montreal as far as the South sea, covering the utmost extent and range possible." The pageant was meant to preempt English claims to the interior, but it was delivered to the people who mattered most: the Indians whose allegiance made and unmade European empires in seventeenth-century North America.

The pageant was also a response to the Indians' pleas for French aid. Saint-Lusson had come to offer the king's iron and protection to his suffering children and to renew their alliance. In return, he expected obedience. "You know about Onnontio, that famous Captain of Quebec," Father Allouez exhorted the Indians through a translator. "Beyond the sea there are ten thousand Onnontios like him, who are only the Soldiers of that Great Captain, our Great King." Not only did this king decide "all the affairs of the world," Allouez explained, warming up to his topic, but he had "enough hatchets to cut down all your forests" and "kettles to cook all your moose." (The priest who recorded the speech may have considered it somewhat grandiose. Regardless of the historical weight of the occasion, he cut his account short, simply noting, "The Father added much more of this sort.") When the ceremony ended, Saint-Lusson set out west in search of the Northwest Passage, a fabled water route across the continent to the South Sea — the Pacific Ocean. With the Lakes Indians back in the fold, the French gazed to the west, dreaming of unforeseen riches.[62]

But others dreamt, too, and not of commerce or cities of gold. The multiethnic Native community that had sprung up in Sault Ste. Marie under the shadow of Sioux war had become something of a Jesuit success story: "This Place, to which The abundance of whitefish Caught there gives considerable importance, daily becomes more beautiful and more comfortable, — especially since the savages apply themselves to planting Indian corn there." In the deep interior Sioux aggression was pushing the French and the Indians to tighten their bonds. As long as there were horror-struck people who "blackened themselves and fasted in order to dream of the Nadouessi," the French and their god and guns would be needed. Without knowing it, Sioux held the future of France's North American empire in their hands. The English challenge to French dominion had made the Očhéthi Šakówiŋ a pivot around which the continent's imperial fortunes turned. War between France and Sioux could deliver the interior to England, whereas peace between the two could secure it for France.[63]

Though largely unaware of their geopolitical weight, Sioux could nonetheless capitalize on it. They seem to have already begun a conciliation with Sauteurs when, in the winter of 1678–79, the Sauteur leader Oumamens met Marie Daniel Greysolon Dulhut, a fiercely ambitious French trader, at Sault Ste. Marie. Oumamens saw in Dulhut a useful mediator who, as Onontio's representative, could extend the French alliance among the Sioux and Sauteurs. Oumamens took the eager Frenchman on and in the spring escorted him to the western end of Lake Superior, where they came to a mixed Sioux-Sauteur village. Sioux and Sauteurs had already begun to forge peace; Dulhut, it seems, was brought in to open access to French goods that would make the Sioux-Sauteur alliance powerful and enduring.

Sioux and Sauteurs made peace on the very ground over which they had clashed. When the conference ended, they sojourned among one another on the marshy borderlands between their domains, turning them into a common ground. A year later Dulhut invited Crees and Assiniboines to a rendezvous near the western tip of Lake Superior to "make peace with the Nadouesioux, their common enemy." The Indians spent the winter hunting together in the forests somewhere about Dulhut's camp, burying grievances and becoming relatives. Abruptly and decisively, the interior geopolitics had swung around a prodigious Sioux-Sauteur-Cree-Assiniboine alliance.

If not earlier, it was now obvious that, rather than the world-changer he imagined himself to be, Dulhut was but a useful instrument in Native diplomacy that followed its own goals and course. His hero fantasy collapsing, Dulhut retreated to it. Reporting to Quebec and Paris, he cast himself as a latter-day conquistador-merchant who had engineered a crucial Indigenous alliance, which could be expanded to wrench the entire Indian trading system from the English orbit back toward New France. In true New World adventurer tradition, Dulhut believed he could achieve this almost single-handedly. He worked tirelessly to realize his ambition, at times seriously hurting English ventures and winning favor with the governor of New France, but his efforts would not bring a single Sioux to Montreal.[64]

TO SUCKLE THE NADOUESSIOUX WITH HIS BREAST

Sioux did not want to go east, neither as diplomats nor as traders. They wanted people to come to them. They wanted the French to bring iron to their villages and they wanted their allies to live with them. To be powerful in late seventeenth-century North America meant having allies and kin. Distances were enormous and people lived far apart, which meant that access to resources— goods, humans, markets—was critical. So was a capacity not to move. Travel was dangerous and arduous—it took French traders three to four weeks to paddle downriver from western Lake Superior to Montreal and twice the time to paddle back—which meant that immobility connoted power: the weaker traveled to the more powerful, and markets were not so much opened as brought in.[65]

The French did just that. In 1681 Jean-Baptiste Colbert, Louis XIV's minister of finance, announced a new form and purpose for France's North American empire. Instead of a fixed enterprise centered on the St. Lawrence, Colbert now envisioned an expanding commercial sphere extending deep into the interior. The impromptu arrangement of independent traders and Native middlemen was replaced by a *congé* system of trade licenses and permanent posts. The coureurs de bois were legalized. Colbert's edict opened inland trade just as the Sioux-Sauteur peace made the interior safe for French traders. The result was a flood of traders to the west.[66]

The fur trade and trapping had declined during the relentless wars, and the Sioux country became known as "a nursery of beavers," a luring pool of wealth just beyond reach. With Colbert's reversal, the pent-up demand for Sioux castor carried the gun and iron frontier into the Sioux country in a single lunge: the number of guns reaching the West in the 1680s may have doubled from the previous decade. Coureurs de bois pushed among Sioux from the western tip of Lake Superior, and Dulhut sent traders through Green Bay and the Fox and Wisconsin Rivers, where canoeists had to negotiate but a short portage and a few rapids. It was a natural route to the Sioux country and soon became the main pathway into the West. Enjoying a generous commission from the governor, Dulhut built a post in the headwaters of the Croix River, within easy access from the core of the Sioux country around Mde Wakan. At long last Sioux had broken Lakes people's grip on the fur trade and opened access to guns and iron.[67]

This was a terrifying development for the Great Lakes Indians. All of a sudden French traders began to push through their lands to arm their archenemies. Emboldened, Sioux and Sauteurs sent, in 1681, a force of eight hundred warriors against Mesquakies, whose villages near the Wisconsin-Fox route threatened their lifeline to the French. They killed fifty-six. Mesquakies, along with others, accused the French of betrayal and started attacking Sioux, trying to divert the flow of goods into their own villages. French agents worked hard to appease all, mediating quarrels, handing out gifts, and arranging murder trials. No one worked harder than Perrot, France's most proficient Indian trader and envoy, who now became a linchpin of French ambitions in the West. Practiced in Indigenous diplomacy, he presented himself as the embodiment of the French-Indian alliance. Facing an angry Mesquakie village in 1683, he addressed them with arresting bravado: "I have learned that you are very desirous to eat the flesh of Frenchmen. I have come, with these young men whom you see, to satisfy you; put us into your kettles, and gorge yourselves with the meat that you have been wanting." Mesquakies recoiled, refusing to eat—to kill—their "father," and the emboldened Perrot demanded submission: "Vomit up your prey; give me back my body . . . if you cook it, [it] will stir up vapors that will form stormy clouds which will extend over your village—which will be in a moment consumed by the flames and lightnings that will issue from them." "Nothing more was necessary to secure the return of the captives," he concluded.[68]

Two years later Perrot, the self-designated savior of France's western empire, made a bid to consolidate the Sioux alliance. Launching from Green Bay with Abenaki refugees from New England, he intended to build a post on Sioux land. But the plan, word of which soon spread across the region, alarmed Mascoutens and Kickapoos. For decades the flow of French goods had stopped at their villages, whereas Perrot's endeavor would make the Sioux the terminus, reducing Mascouten and Kickapoo lands to a mere thoroughfare—just as the fur trade was starting to boom. Mascoutens and Kickapoos pleaded with Perrot not to abandon them and asked him to show the place in the West where "they should light their fires." They sought, in effect, to expand their realm westward with the fur trade by piggybacking on Perrot's venture.

Suspended between old allies and new, between the eastern past and the western future of the French Empire, Perrot made a tortured compromise. He presented Mascoutens and Kickapoos the calumet and promised to always offer his breast for them to suckle. They would follow him to west. Yet, at present, he was going to "give suck" to the Sioux. Onontio's milk of iron and guns would reawaken them as allies.[69]

YOU WISH TO MURDER ME AND THEN TO WAR AGAINST THE NADOUESSIOUX

Perrot and his men, the Abenakis, the Mascoutens, and the Kickapoos—the French-Indian alliance in miniature—simply walked in. Mascoutens and Kickapoos proceeded to hunt bison on the grasslands in the west, while the French sought out their patrons and "found on the ice twenty-four canoes of the

Nadoüaissioux, delighted" to see them. The Sioux, most likely Dakotas—took them to their village, where the Frenchmen divulged that they had brought Abenakis, Mascoutens, and Kickapoos with them in the Sioux country. There is no record that the Sioux objected. Virtually overnight, the Očhéthi Šakówiŋ shifted shape, opening its borders to former enemies and strangers.[70]

Like most Native peoples in the interior, Sioux did not understand territory as an exclusive bounded domain of one people. A border was not a line on the ground that kept out strangers. It was a space, sometimes a specific place, perhaps a river or a wasteland, where one kinship sphere ended and another began. Borders were more emotional than physical; they were felt rather than seen. They were also dynamic. Sioux saw in every person a potential kin, which meant that their society had no predetermined boundaries. A tightly policed boundary that kept enemies out could vanish, almost instantly, with peace and good thoughts.[71]

That mindset had already allowed Sauteurs, Crees, and Assiniboines to enter the Sioux country, resurge as allies, and gradually blend into takúkičhiyapi, the Sioux circle of kinship. Perrot was attempting a similar merger. He built his trading house, a log fort he named Saint-Antoine, at the foot of Lake Pepin on the borderland between the seven fires and the Lakes people. The post thrived. Before long at least a dozen traders were working there, carrying goods up the Mississippi into Sioux villages and arming many of them for the first time. Yanktonais visited the post from the west—Perrot may well have been "the very first white man they had ever seen"—and a Mdewakanton band relocated from the lower Minnesota River near the fort, which became known as the post of the Nadouessioux. Soon Perrot built another fort, Bonsecours, just below Lake Pepin.[72]

But the French also traded with several Lakes peoples, who had begun to edge toward the Sioux domain, the emerging hub of the western fur trade. The post of the Nadouessioux became a gravitational center where many Lakes tribes traded and mingled with Sioux, Sauteurs, and French, trying to find the proper sentiments, acts, and rituals to make this nascent accommodation work. The Sioux, Onontio's youngest children, could learn from Onontio's older children how to share their homelands with a multitude of strangers, how to welcome them without relinquishing authority, how to diffuse quarrels with the right words and gifts, and how to cope with the notion that French goods and love were no one's prerogative.[73]

A tighter and entirely aboriginal common ground took root around the Mde Wakan, where Sioux had welcomed their Sauteur allies, who now traded with them and went to battle with them. The natural bounties and the relative safety of the Sioux country drew in scores of Sauteurs who gradually left "their native

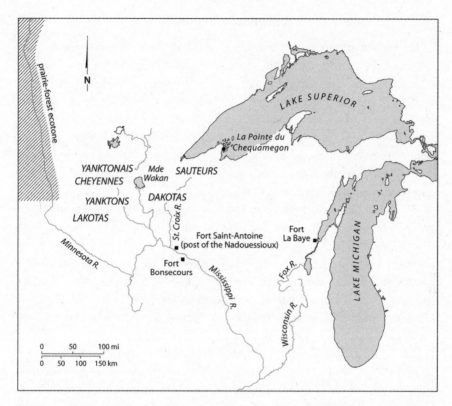

7. The Očhéthi Šakówiŋ domain in the late seventeenth century. Map by Bill Nelson.

land." The common ground expanded farther west when Sioux and Sauteurs opened their domain to the Cheyennes, a relatively small Algonquian nation. There, on a transitional zone between the Eastern Woodlands and the western grasslands, Sioux, Sauteurs, and Cheyennes lived in mixed villages, collecting wild rice on lakeshores and hunting buffaloes, elk, and deer. Sioux women married across ethnic lines, maximizing potential identities and serving as a glue that kept the alliance together. In doing so they nurtured peace and fostered war.[74]

Unfolding deep in the great interior, this Indigenous appeasement was one of pivotal turning points in early American history. The interior world had begun to curve around the Očhéthi Šakówiŋ. Dangerously isolated just a few years earlier, the Sioux country emerged in the 1680s as a central place where commercial and diplomatic circles converged. The Sioux now had allies, iron, and guns — and the eye of the French. There would still be tests and trials, but the power dynamics had shifted decisively in their favor.

A GOOD SUPPLY OF GUNS

The French attention only intensified when, in the early 1680s, the Iroquois launched yet another major offensive—their third since the 1640s—this time targeting the southern Great Lakes in an effort to seize captives and furs. Backed by English guns and markets—the Five Nations and the English colonies had forged a series of treaties known collectively as the Covenant Chain—Iroquois war parties swept into the lands south and west of Lake Michigan, attacking Miami, Illinois, Otoe, and Mesquakie villages and killing and capturing hundreds. Once more the Indians fled, seeking safety anywhere they could. The Iroquois had created yet another shatter zone.[75]

This was a disquieting development for the French who saw English ambition behind every Iroquois act. French explorers had learned in the early 1670s that the Mississippi flowed not to the Pacific but to the south, and in 1679 René-Robert Cavelier de La Salle sailed down the river all the way to the Gulf of Mexico and claimed it for France. The sea route promised more pelts and power, and the key to it was a swath of land between Lake Michigan and the lower Ohio and middle Mississippi Valleys. The French named the area the Illinois Country and planned to attach it with forts to their empire.

But the Iroquois onslaught revealed the Illinois Country to be the soft underbelly of the French Empire. In 1680 an army of eight hundred Iroquois and their allies devastated the Grand Village of the Kaskaskia, a stronghold of the Illinois Confederacy and a critical cog in French imperial designs, and carried hundreds of Illinois into captivity. The onslaught created a momentary power vacuum in the region, exposing the pays d'en haut to Iroquois attacks from the south. Not a single fort stood between the Iroquois and the western Great Lakes, the heart of France's inland empire.[76]

New France was soon tottering. With its Indian allies being destroyed "on all sides," the French governor warned in 1686 that if the Iroquois attacks were not stopped, "the Colony must be put down as lost." This made the relationship with the Sioux a priority. Only an alliance that linked the Sioux, the interior's foremost military power, with the Lakes people and the French could contain the Iroquois. Every fight in the Sioux country was a fight that could have been waged against the Iroquois. But to win the Sioux over the French would have to privilege them with guns, iron, and love, which risked alienating the Lakes Indians, New France's ancient shield against the Iroquois. This was one of the many painful compromises the French had to make to save their empire in a world where they had to balance multiple Native interests. French agents, embodying Onontio, asked their children to breathe fire on the Iroquois, while simultaneously rechanneling the gun flow among the Sioux. Feeling betrayed, Onontio's oldest children lashed out in fury. The French simply did not have enough goods, the essential cohesive of the alliance, to go around.[77]

French agents mediated desperately, but tensions mounted around the post of the Nadouessioux. Mesquakies and Mascoutens remained "implacable" against Sioux, "whatever the peace which they had made together." In 1689, with his grip of developments slipping, Perrot took possession of "all the places where he has heretofore been and where he will go." He acknowledged the Sioux as the "proprietors" of their lands and yet claimed them for his king all the same, trying to salvage French authority in the West by attaching it to his personal presence *and* the territorial power of the Sioux. There is no record of Native reaction, which exposes the impotence of the act. Not long after Mesquakies and Mascoutens set out "with all their families" against the Sioux and destroyed a village of eighty lodges near Perrot's fort. They "cut to pieces all who offered resistance" and "practiced unheard-of cruelties on their captives," which numbered in the hundreds. Having lost fifteen warriors in the battle, Mascoutens reportedly burned two hundred women and children in revenge and killed many more on their way home. Still, they had hundreds of Sioux captives left.[78]

Violence had become routine in the Sioux country long ago, but carnage on this scale was unprecedented. Shock effects reverberated across the West. Miamis, fearing Sioux retaliation, asked Perrot to mediate and sent a calumet to the Sioux through him. Perrot visited the ruined Sioux village and covered the dead with gifts and placed them in shallow graves so that Onontio could learn about their loss. "God allows you to weep," he told the mourners, "but he declares against you and will not aid you if you set out on the war-path." Sioux burned their flesh in grief, and Perrot promised to redeem their kin "whom I will draw out from the mouths of your enemies." Ten captured Sioux women eventually returned home, having been freed by Mesquakies who dreaded Sioux reprisal and denounced Mascouten actions. Miamis sent a delegation among Sioux, brought back two redeemed captives, covered their dead with kettles, and "swore the entire destruction of the Maskoutechs." Onontio's family was growing and splintering, hurting and struggling to heal all at once.[79]

Sioux understood the regenerative power that was built into violence. Just as losing kin to death or captivity fractured lineages, redemption could mend them and create new bonds. They saw how redemption brought them closer to the French, Miamis and Mesquakies, making them more powerful and allowing them to sing "funeral calumets" against the Mascoutens. They could handle the bloodshed. Perrot could not. He worked hard to free the Sioux captives, whose presence in Mascouten villages fueled violence, but there were too many of them. Captives remained unredeemed, and the western Indians kept fighting one another rather than moving against the Iroquois, whose raids were ruining the pays d'en haut. By 1695 Perrot's dream of an anti-Iroquois alliance was dead. Mascoutens, who "no longer placed bounds to their conduct with any one whatever," feared that the French, Miamis, and Sioux might unite to destroy them, while Mesquakies planned to attack Miamis and then relocate, with their remaining Sioux captives, among Iroquois. In the spring Perrot and his associates embarked on a customary supply voyage to Montreal. Their last act was to send some Sioux, whom they had redeemed, back to their own country. Perrot never returned to his post. Financially ruined, he settled on his land grant along the St. Lawrence Valley.[80]

Perrot's departure turned out to be a boon for the seven fires. Without French mediation, Onontio's older children were defenseless against the vengeance of the Sioux who outnumbered them many times over. They retreated east en masse, exposing themselves to Iroquois attacks to escape Sioux ones. And Sioux did not remain without trade for long: they were simply too powerful and too rich in castor to be ignored. Governor Frontenac installed the audacious coureur de bois Le Sueur in Perrot's place and commissioned him to open trade routes west from Lake Superior, search for lead and copper mines in the upper Mississippi country, and bring peace to the West—all of which would help the French subdue the Iroquois. Le Sueur built a post on Peleé Island on the Mississippi to serve as a new center for Sioux trade. Backed by Frontenac, he intended to build a private trading empire in the Sioux country under official screen. One of his first acts was to escort Tiyoskate to Montreal.[81]

DEAD SCIOU TIES MY ARMS

Sioux were ready. They were now powerful enough for Tiyoskate to face Onontio in the presence of his older children. He knew he could appear small in front of him, give his body away, and still make demands. He wanted a more complete relationship with the French, and he wanted Onontio to share his wašíčuŋ with the Sioux. If Onontio would do that, Sioux would fight for him. They would be allies and equals, and no one could eat them again.

Had he lived to see it, Tiyoskate would have been both troubled and pleased with the outcomes. In 1695 there was only one trading post—Le Sueur's—in the Sioux country. This was less than what Tiyoskate had hoped, but the post soared in relative importance when, only a year after his visit, the French crown made yet another turnabout and closed all inland posts save Frontenac, Michilimackinac, Saint-Joseph, and Le Sueur's. Traders were banned from Montreal, and the Indians were expected to carry their furs there themselves. The booming fur trade in the West had created a glut of beaver in Montreal, severely cutting into profits, while the Jesuits, increasingly vocal, condemned the fur trade as a corrupting influence that hindered proselytization.[82]

Le Sueur's post, one of the four that survived, brought the Sioux tremendous power. They were said to be selling thousands of beaver skins at a time when most tribes thirsted for trade. In the summer of 1697 a Mesquakie chief traveled to Quebec to visit Frontenac. A dearth of goods and gifts had thrown the pays d'en haut into chaos, and Mesquakies had clashed with Sioux. Just two years earlier Mesquakies could have demanded Frontenac to punish the Sioux, but the world had changed. Tiyoskate had won Onontio's love, the fur trade had contracted dramatically, and yet the Sioux had prevailed. The dead "Sciou ties my arms," the Mesquakie bewailed. "I killed him because he began; Father, be not angry with me for so doing."[83]

The Sioux post prevailed against all odds, reflecting the Očhéthi Šakówiŋ's growing commercial and geopolitical weight. In 1699 a group of French colonists led by Pierre Lemoyne d'Iberville founded the province of Louisiana on the Gulf Coast. The new outpost galvanized an old French dream of linking the St. Lawrence basin, the pay d'en haut, and the Mississippi Valley into a great crescent-shaped empire stretching from sea to sea. Such an empire would confine the Spaniards into the Southwest and lock up the English on the Atlantic Coast, eliminating foreign threats once and for all. As the dominant power in the upper Mississippi, the Sioux were critical for French ambitions. D'Iberville asked Le Sueur—who was married to his cousin—to buttress French presence among them. His former sponsor Frontenac now dead, Le Sueur seized the opportunity. After d'Iberville secured him a license to explore the Mississippi for ore, Le Sueur formed a Compagnie des Sioux and led some twenty men up the Mississippi in merchandise-laden canoes into the Sioux country.[84]

Their ascent was a crash course into the messy realities that lay bare the absurdity of French imperial dreams: naked, bleeding coureurs de bois assaulted by a massive war party of Mesquakies, Sauks, and Potawatomis heading downriver to kill Sioux; rumors of caves filled with saltpeter and rattlesnakes; an Indian envoy seeking to confess a murder of a Frenchman somewhere in the woods; Canadian voyageurs carrying letters from Jesuits reporting rampant carnage upriver; a Sioux war party canoeing far downriver to avenge dead kin. Finally the expedition reached the Sioux country near the junction of the Minnesota and Blue Earth Rivers where, on a high bluff, Le Sueur promptly built Fort L'Huillier—named after a Parisian patron—to launch into illegal beaver trade. The fort was in the western Sioux country, and a delegation of eastern Sioux demanded Le Sueur to move the post eastward. Le Sueur ignored their protests, perhaps because he learned that the western Sioux—the Lakotas, Yanktons, and Yanktonais—had more than a thousand lodges, lived only by the chase, and ventured deep into the animal-rich prairies. This was the kind of fur industry he wanted.

Fort L'Huillier became a magnet for Lakotas, Yanktons, Yanktonais, and Dakotas who now looked to the south for guns and iron. The Iowas and Otoes followed them there, eager for trade and protection, and in Montreal Governor Louis-Hector de Callière maneuvered from a distance to prevent the Lakes Indians from raiding the Sioux, desperate to appease his older children who felt betrayed by the French who now seemed to favor the Sioux. D'Iberville thought that there were some sixty coureurs de bois active among the Sioux, and Le Sueur believed the Sioux had become masters of other Native nations because they now had "a good supply of guns." Sioux finally had the kind of relationship with the French that Tiyoskate and others before him had sought. Meeting at the ruins of the Sioux village Mascoutens had destroyed five years earlier, Oucantapai, a Mdewakanton Sioux chief, gave Le Sueur a slave and a sack of wild rice. His people, he told him, were now Onontio's loving children and "thou must therefore no longer consider us Scioux, but as Frenchmen."[85]

TINY ISLANDS

Seventeenth-century North America was a vast Indigenous ocean speckled with tiny European islands. The Spanish, English, and French newcomers claimed vast chunks of the continent through the doctrines of discovery and *terra nullius* (no one's land), but such claims mattered little on the ground where the Indians controlled the balance of power. Through shrewd diplomacy, warfare, and sheer force of numbers, the Indians held the line. In 1700 French settlement remained tethered to the St. Lawrence and a small foothold on the mouth of the Mississippi, and the Spanish possessions amounted to two isolated clusters of missions in New Mexico and in Florida. English settlers were more numerous and assertive, but they too huddled on the margins, expanding up and down the coastal lowlands rather than inland. Conquistador fantasies stayed alive, but they were becoming increasingly detached from reality.

Yet, wherever they planted themselves, the colonists were a force to be reckoned with. Their fringe outposts were pockets of dense military-technological power that could shape developments far beyond their borders. The Europeans fought, dispossessed, and enslaved nearby Indians, whose ability to resist was severely compromised by disease epidemics. The more distant Indians in the interior required more subtle measures, for the colonists could not simply rely on pathogens to obliterate them. Numerous and fiercely independent, the interior Indians could be neither killed nor commanded; they needed to be cajoled and co-opted. The key instrument for achieving this was a frontier post. Europeans thought of trading posts and missions — military forts would come later — as means to claim and control faraway lands. Indeed, an inland post brought the frontier into existence and demarcated it by announcing that the lands around and behind it belonged to the people who had built it. Posts made empires.[86]

Such ideas were laughable to the Indians, who thought that land belonged to those who lived on it and whose ancestors lay in it. They almost invariably welcomed trading posts and missions on their lands because they were concrete expressions of the newcomers' largesse — both material and spiritual — and of their willingness to share their power. A trading post was particularly desired because it signaled a commitment to a particular people and its needs. This is why the Indians competed so fiercely to secure them. A single post could dramatically change their fortunes by opening access to the new technologies that had irrevocably changed the parameters of the possible. Reliable access to guns, powder, and iron was a promise of safety, prosperity, and otherworldly power, while lacking them spelled hurt, retreat, and shame.[87]

At the turn of the century Sioux knew both sides of the equation. Since the 1650s they had seen how French trading posts proliferated in the western Great Lakes among their enemies, rendering them horribly vulnerable. An alliance with Sauteurs in the late 1670s punctured the imagined wall that cast them as outsiders. They had their own post from 1685 onward and, at last, a secure access to firearms. Guns gave military teeth to their overwhelming demographic strength, making them the epicenter of interior politics. French officials saw them as the last best hope to contain the Iroquois and save New France, and they worked hard to integrate them into their alliance system. For decades Sioux had grappled on the margins of the bustling Indian-European world of trade and alliance that had emerged in the east; now that world began to converge around them, bestowing them with substance and power. They now had options and, it seemed, time to weigh them.[88]

HOMMES DE PRAIRIE

The long struggle for allies, trade, and relevance had been spearheaded by the four Dakota fires, the Mdewakantons, Sissetons, Wahpetons, and Wahpekutes. They had played a key role in the birth of the all-important Sauteur alliance and in nurturing the relationship with the French, and their lands around Mde Wakan were the place where most foreigners sought access to the Sioux. To the outsiders they seemed "the masters of other Scioux." But the long struggle involved all seven fires. No oyáte or thióšpaye was immune to the seemingly endless blows or denied the rewards when they finally came.[89]

Distance shielded the Lakotas, the westernmost Sioux division, against the hardest blows—the massacres, the repeated border conflicts, the exasperating indifference of French traders. They remained a shadowy, enigmatic people to the French, who caught only glimpses of them. They were "Nations *Tintonha*," "*The Inhabitants of the Meadows*," who lived in the West "certain Seasons of the Year." Eventually, to facilitate deepening western excursions, growing numbers of Lakotas moved permanently west of the Mississippi. By the late 1690s the French knew the lands around the upper Minnesota Valley as the Lakota domain—"Pays et Nations des Tintons"—and few years later Le Sueur was struck by the geographical and cultural distance that separated Lakotas from their eastern kin: they did not gather wild rice or use canoes, and they kept to "the prairies between the Upper Mississippi and the river of the Missouris" where they had no fixed villages.[90]

What to the French seemed a Lakota detachment from the eastern Sioux was actually a part of a larger strategy of fueling the growing fur trade. When the trade took off, Sioux needed large quantities of castor: one gun cost approximately ten skins of winter beaver, and the thousands of Sioux warriors needed thousands of guns. The greatest castor reserves lay to the west, in lands still beyond the fur trade's long tentacles but within Lakotas' reach. Each fall Lakota bands left for the western prairies beyond the forest line, spending months in scouring the rivers and streams for thickly furred beavers and living in light deerskin lodges. While there, they lived off the bison, which seemed to grow more abundant with distance, and clashed with the resident hunter-farming peoples who saw them as invaders. Already in the late 1680s the the Arikara Indians on the Missouri River—more than two hundred miles west of the Lakota domain— seem to have been engaged in grueling wars with the westering Lakotas.[91]

By the turn of the century the Lakotas were a growing and often violent presence on the tall-grass prairies west of the Minnesota River. But they were sojourners, not conquerors. They were in the West, but the West was not theirs. Each spring they returned east to the precious prairie-forest ecotone where they could enjoy one of the best diets on the continent. There, they reconnected with their kin, traded skins for iron, shared the calumet, and reaffirmed their place in the world as one of the Seven Council Fires. Sicangu Lakotas came together with their kin every seven years to make offerings to Wakȟáŋ Tȟáŋka, Great Spirit, and reaffirm their interconnectedness.[92]

Lakotas were suspended between western promises and eastern realities. Their firsthand experience of the new world of Indians and Europeans was limited, but they knew its challenges and opportunities intimately through their eastern relatives whose sufferings and successes were theirs. They knew what not having allies or guns meant, and they had learned that people were capable of aston-

ishing violence to secure them. They knew that the world had changed irrevocably and that no one could ignore the European newcomers and their wašíčuŋ.
And they knew that this new world was an unforgiving place where people often
were expiring if they were not expanding.

When Lakotas finally pushed into the West in the early eighteenth century,
drawn by its tremendous possibilities, they carried with them a specific set of
convictions about the world. They would have to adapt to new western realities,
but so too would the West have to adjust to theirs.

2

FACING WEST

'In early August 1680 knotted cords of maguey fiber began to appear among the Pueblo Indians in the Spanish kingdom of New Mexico. Specialist runners — "the swiftest youth" — carried the cords from village to village, delivering in each a message from Po'pay, a Tewa religious leader from the Pueblo of San Juan: count days by loosening the knots and the morning of the last knot start killing the Spaniards. The colonists learned the secret of the knots from captured messengers two days before the set date, but by then it was too late. On August 10 New Mexico erupted into a rebellion.[1]

Within three days all Spanish settlements save Santa Fe in the upper Rio Grande Valley had been destroyed. Twenty-one Franciscans and more than four hundred settlers were dead. When the surviving colonists trapped in Santa Fe fled south to El Paso, the Indians set out to cleanse their world from Spanish contamination that had persisted for three generations. They razed churches and shattered their bells. They replaced Christian names with Native ones. Not a single Spanish word was to violate the newly Indigenous soundscape. Even horses began to disappear from the Rio Grande Valley. Troubled by their tendency to trample corn fields and their tremendous power that symbolized Spanish might, Pueblos sold the animals to the bordering nomads. It was to be as if Spanish colonialism had never happened.[2]

But it had, of course, and it would happen again. Native reign in the Rio Grande lasted for twelve difficult years. The Pueblos revived community rituals and forged new ties, but they also quarreled over Po'pay's extreme vision and struggled with droughts and Apache raids. Civic leaders, medicine men, and warriors competed for authority within communities that descended into civil wars. In 1692, shocked by La Salle's expeditions along the Gulf Coast, a Spanish army reconquered the divided Pueblo realm with a brutal campaign. The Spaniards ruled again along the Rio Grande, but the world around them was not the same. The surrounding hunter-nomads now had enough horses to shift to mounted warfare. Before long, they were raiding New Mexico for more. One of those groups, the Comanches, built a powerful raiding economy on New Mexico's borderlands, reducing the Spanish colony to a subjugated hinterland they could mine for horses, captives, and corn with seasonal invasions.[3]

A new technological frontier centered on the horse had been launched into the North American interior. Nomadic raiders kept most of the stolen horses for themselves, but they did trade some to their allies. Indigenous trade fairs that had been for food and luxury exchanges became horse markets, and new ones emerged to channel the swelling equine flow. The main current was northward along ancient trading routes that traced the Rocky Mountains to the Pacific Northwest and fanned out across the continental grasslands toward the Missouri Valley.[4]

The quickest proliferation occurred in the Great Plains, the birthplace of the modern horse, the single-hoofed *Equus ferus caballus*. The arrival of Spanish horses in these grassy steppes was in fact a homecoming, a closing of nearly a million-year exodus that had taken the *Equus* westward across the Bering land bridge into Asia, Africa, and Europe—and then back into the Americas with Columbus and other conquistadors, now fully domesticated and disciplined to carry a human rider. The Great Plains, along with the rest of the hemisphere, had been horseless for over ten millennia, for all large mammals had died off during the great Pleistocene extinctions that also eradicated mammoths, giant sloths, and other megafauna. Back in their original niche, the *Equus* flourished, opening new worlds of possibility for those who could secure them.[5]

Comanches called the horse a "magic dog," which captures the magnitude of the change. The dog, the only Native American domesticate north of Mexico, could carry a load of about fifty pounds on its back and haul seventy-five pounds on a travois; the horse could move four times as much weight while traveling twice the distance in a day. This spelled more wealth—household utensils, tools, weapons, clothing, foodstuffs, religious items—and larger homes in which to store that wealth in. It meant a new kind of nomadism, one that transcended human and canine power to carry things and did not require giving up all but the bare minimum of possessions. And unlike the dog, the horse was at once a hunting tool and a weapon, allowing its owner to both chase game and kill enemies more efficiently. Horses elevated and empowered human beings and made the world smaller and its bounties more accessible.[6]

Roughly at the same time as the Pueblo Revolt unleashed the horse frontier northward, the consolidation of English commerce in Hudson Bay and New

8. Sioux Indians with a travois. The image shows two Lakota women as well as a
child seated on a travois in around 1890 at the Rosebud Reservation. The Lakota
travois technology dates back to the early eighteenth century. Courtesy of John A.
Anderson Collection, Nebraska State Historical Society, RG2969-PH-2–225.

France's liberal trade policy thrust the gun frontier westward. Separated by more
than a thousand miles, the two technological frontiers began inching slowly
toward each another, propelled by Native traders. Where the two frontiers would
converge and overlap would be the continent's strategic sweet spot, a place of
vast advantage. Whoever happened to be in that spot would wield enormous
power.[7]

BASTARD CHILDREN

In the late seventeenth century, the French knew all too well the hard certainties on which their New World empire rested: that they were numerically
weak; that their empire could not survive without its Indian allies; that those
allies had to be placated with cut-rate goods; that the alliance system might unravel without an external threat that bound the Indians and the French together;
and that the Iroquois were that threat.

And then it was not like that anymore. The Iroquois invasion into the Illinois
Country in the mid-1680s turned out to be the last of their great onslaughts. It
was a military overstretch—too many warriors ranging too far—and it left the

Five Nations exhausted and vulnerable. The Iroquois were also divided. The absorption of thousands of captives had spawned pro-French, pro-English, and neutral factions, fueling internecine violence that loosened the Iroquois League at its seams. The eruption of the Nine Years' War between France and England in 1689 turned the Iroquois lands between New France and the English colonies into a battleground. When the war ended in a wary stalemate in 1697, the Iroquois were near collapse and eager for peace. Against English objections, they opened negotiations with the French, trying to preserve their sovereignty.[8]

This set in motion a massive peace process. Sensing an opportunity to forge a peace among New France, the Iroquois, and the Great Lakes Indians, the French sent envoys among the tribes to invite them to Montreal. The Lakes Indians embraced the opportunity to end the Iroquois wars that had made life uncertain for them for half a century. In August 1701 more than one thousand Indian envoys gathered in Montreal to negotiate a settlement with the Five Iroquois Nations and Governor Louis-Hector de Callière. It was the largest known peace conference in the continent's history. The Sioux were not invited.

It was not long before word of what unfolded in Montreal reached the Očhéthi Šakówiŋ. The news was shocking. Onontio had embraced the Iroquois as his children and brokered a peace between the League and some three dozen Native nations, dramatically expanding his family. With a single move, the geopolitics of the interior had been recentered, spawning a new geography of inclusion and exclusion. An alliance of that magnitude would change everything for those who were not part of it. By not asking the Sioux to witness his adoption of the Iroquois, Onontio had turned his back on them.[9]

After the Great Peace of 1701 the French made a concerted effort to extend the rewards of the alliance—Onontio's merchandise and love—among the Iroquois. Through careful play-off politics, the Iroquois managed to preserve their peace with the French without alienating the English, accepting traders and gifts from both to shore up their new policy of neutrality. Backed by both empires and restrained by neither, the Iroquois extended their hunting range deep into the West. English traders followed, hoping to expand their markets into the interior in the Iroquois's wake, and the French built Fort Pontchartrain du Détroit by the strait joining Lake Huron and Lake Erie to stop them. And then, in 1702, another war broke out between France and Britain—the War of the Spanish Succession in Europe, Queen Anne's War in the English colonies—fixing French attention firmly in the East. The West, including the Sioux country, became a sideshow.[10]

At the turn of the century, Sioux had felt confident of French benevolence. Le Sueur's Fort L'Huillier supplied them with guns and iron, keeping them safe.

A pocket of mutual accommodation had emerged around the fort, allowing the French and Sioux to trade and coexist despite the cultural differences that separated them. Both had learned specific metaphors and rituals that smoothed out disputes and both knew how to appeal to the conventions of the other, however strange they may have seemed. Sioux had embraced Le Sueur as a powerful relative who took care of their needs: "It is for thee to see," chief Sacred Born told the trader, "whether thou wishest them to live or die; they will live if thou givest them powder and ball."[11]

In the spring of 1701, just before the great peace council in Montreal, Le Sueur traveled down the Mississippi to Mobile with a cargo of furs and minerals. French authorities promptly accused him of illegalities: his patron d'Iberville was suspected of working to monopolize the Mississippi River trade at the expense of New France. Le Sueur never returned to his post. Thirteen traders had stayed behind among Sioux to man the post, but a Mesquakie-Mascouten attack sent them into a panicked flight to the Gulf Coast. A new trader was dispatched from Montreal with a substantial load of merchandise, but all his wares were stolen by Mesquakies. No one was sent in his stead. Alone and exposed, Sioux were once again bastard children without a father.[12]

Scarcity descended on the West. There was not a single trading post left. Soon the Indians had masses of beaver pelts, sewn into robes of nine, but no one to buy them. They could obtain guns and iron only through Louisiana-based coureurs de bois, who were driven by profits, not politics, and would not mediate disputes among Native nations. Deprived of Onontio's care and goods, the Great Lakes middle ground began to crumble. Like Sioux, France's Indian allies in the pays d'en haut felt betrayed by Onontio, who had taken his merchandize among the Iroquois. Many felt that the previous governor, Callière, had loved them better than the new one, Philippe de Rigaud de Vaudreuil.[13]

Scarcity brewed resentment and violence. Lakes Indians sent delegations to Montreal, demanding for themselves the guns and iron that were still trickling among Sioux. They wanted Vaudreuil to cut the Sioux off. Fearing that English agents could persuade his disgruntled children to attack New France—Queen Anne's War was heating up—Vaudreuil abandoned the Sioux. He granted the Lakes Indians "the freedom to make war" on them and prevent them "from making war on the Iroquois that I consider as the only nation that is important for me to keep." With the interior slipping away from them, the French made a calculated choice to sacrifice the Sioux to save their Indian alliance and, by extension, their North American empire. The Sioux replaced the Iroquois as the necessary menace that pushed the French and the Indians to preserve their alliance. The seven fires were forced away from the world that only a few years earlier had embraced them. Rather than lash out, they turned inward and westward, seeking something new and definite. This was the beginning of the Lakotas' long expansion into the West.[14]

In the winter of 1703 Sicangu Lakotas walked above the bison, a thousand beasts under their feet. Beneath them they could see the broad faces and glimpse the massive bodies halted in mid-motion. There were rows and piles of them, a vast, jumbled pool of preserved meat. A lake's ice coat had collapsed under a buffalo herd and then hardened again to seal the drowned animals in, leaving Sicangus a huge natural refrigerator of meat. Whenever they needed food, they could simply cut through the ice and bring up a carcass. The meat lasted an entire year. A Sicangu winter count remembered it as "Camped cutting the ice through winter."

The next year was equally bounteous. Sicangus killed a great many buffalo in a single hunt, dried the meat, and stored it in pits. The meat sustained them the whole winter. Then, in 1708, they brought home horses from Omahas who lived west of them. Catapulted by the Pueblo Revolt, the horse frontier had leapt from New Mexico to the Missouri Valley by the late 1680s and then into prairies where it kept inching eastward just as Lakotas began pushing west. Sicangus were in awe of the creature, of its tremendous power and its keenness to obey subtle commands. They called it *šúŋka wakȟáŋ*, sacred dog.[15]

These events probably took place deep in the western prairies where they coincided with a wet climate cycle that created a superabundance of grass and game. They capture Sicangus' sense of the West as a world of wondrous things. They also capture a striking and growing contrast between the East and the West in Lakota consciousness. The East was becoming a dangerous and uninviting world that seemed to have no place for the seven fires. The West was not free of dangers, but it was full of promise and pulsing with wašíčuŋ: sacred dogs that could do the work of many canines, grasslands teeming with buffalo, lakes filled with meat. The West was pulling Sicangus in.[16]

There were acute push factors as well. Shut out of French gun markets, the seven fires were exposed to attacks from Crees and Assiniboines, who had a reliable access to firearms through Hudson Bay British traders and the highly mobile coureurs de bois. Trade "gangs" led by trading captains forged far-flung networks that channeled muskets across the northern woodlands to the tune of four hundred guns a year. Now, more aggressively than ever before, the northern Indians raided into the Sioux territory to lay claim over the prime beaver lands. Mde Wakan, long the political nerve center of the Očhéthi Šakówiŋ, became a front line in bitter beaver wars.[17]

Pushed by northern aggression and pulled by western promises, Sioux began to shift westward—first band by band, then tribe by tribe. The four Dakota fires made the upper Mississippi and the Minnesota their strongholds. Yanktons and Yanktonais continued farther, leaving the forests and marches for the open western prairies, while gradually separating from one another. But it was Lakotas who led the way. Expanding an ancient practice, they pushed deep into the West. Sicangus, together with their close relatives Oglalas, followed a southern route, with Yanktons in tow. Two other Lakota fires—the Saones and Minneconjous— edged westward farther north, trailed by Yanktonais.[18]

Slowly the traditional western sojourns transformed into niche conquests. The four Lakota fires began to carve out small enclaves deep in the tall-grass prairies. But they faced resistance nearly everywhere they went. They were new-comers who did not have much to offer to Omahas, Otoes, and other prairie people. They did not have enough guns to sell, which prevented a potential trade in horses, and what they could have shared—essentially meat and hides—the prairie people did not want, for they were skillful hunters in their own right.[19]

The conflicts centered on river valleys, the cradles of human existence in the prairies. River valleys offered reliable low-saline water, high-calorie riparian grasses, fertile soil, firewood, and shelter against the elements during colder sea-sons. All farming, all trapping, and much of the hunting and gathering took place on their wooded banks. Villages could not survive anywhere else. For Lakotas, river valleys were both havens and obstacles. They needed them to survive in the West, but most of them were already taken. All the magnificent things—the bison, the horses, the vitality of the prairie—would be denied to them until they had access to the streams. This was the paradox of the grasslands: they were an immense reservoir of space and wealth that pinned people down. They promised material liberation through seemingly unlimited natural bounty, while requiring uncompromised control over small ribbons of water and fertile earth. One of the earliest winter counts of the Yanktonais relates how they "chased the Arikara into the water."[20]

It did not have to be this way. Prairie Indians, Missouri villagers, and Sioux all honored the calumet ceremony, sharing a common cultural base that could have spawned peace on the ground. And had there been peace, individual Lakota bands could have sought inclusion into the riverine villages, offering their numbers for common causes. Yet neither peace nor cooperation came to pass. Whether it was because the increasingly nomadic Lakotas had no interest in vil-lage life because their demoralizing experiences with the French had made them wary of strangers, or because the villagers rejected them as aggressive intruders, for now, and for the next half a century, well into the mid-eighteenth century, war would drive Lakota policy in the West. Unable to access the river valleys and their people, Lakotas set out to conquer them.[21]

EIGHT VALLEYS

The conflict became both pitiless and protracted. In 1700, as they pushed westward, Lakotas knew what lay ahead, for they had learned the basic geography of the prairies during their age-old western excursions. Stacked ahead of them, like the rungs of a ladder, lay eight major rivers that sliced through the boundless swath of prairie from north to south. These rivers—which Europeans would name Des Moines, Little Sioux, Floyd, Big Sioux, Red River of the North, Sheyenne, James, and Missouri—virtually invited Lakotas in, providing a feasible frame for expansion. Instead of an extended war of attrition, it could be a sequence of smaller conquests. Lakotas could carve out a western domain for themselves one valley at a time.

The river valleys were essential also in another, less obvious way. As Lakotas and their allies spread out into the western prairies, the Očhéthi Šakówiŋ began to loosen at its seams. Thióšpayes and oyátes grew detached from each another as they shifted westward and seized more territory. Conquest had a shattering effect. The Očhéthi Šakówiŋ had always been a headless polity—there were no institutions for overall governance—and expansion threatened to push decentralization to a point where key elements of effective foreign policy—sharing of information, face-to-face deliberation, coordination of diplomatic and military action—became unfeasible. In the end, it was the river valleys that kept Lakotas and their allies unified. To simply survive in the West, all thióšpayes and oyátes had to remain bound to the bottomlands, a shared biological imperative that brought them into close proximity, sometimes in small units and fleetingly, sometimes for weeks and months and in massive numbers. Though intermittent, such gatherings doubled as political meetings where vital matters were debated and exposed to public scrutiny and sanction. They sustained a spirit of unity, synchronized local policies, and made expansion possible. This would be a great constant in Lakota and Sioux history.

The expansion accelerated when Sicangus and Oglalas clashed with Otoe farmer-hunters on the Des Moines, forcing them to retreat to the Little Sioux and finally to the Missouri. Not long after, Sicangus and Oglalas reached the lower Big Sioux, where they fought Omahas, Poncas, and Iowas whose fortified earth-lodge village presided over the valley. Loosing perhaps as many as a thousand warriors, the villagers sought shelter along the Missouri, which became a refugee zone. At the same time to the north Saones and Minneconjous also pushed westward. This northern prong of Lakota expansion was closely entwined with the migrations of Cheyennes, who were retreating west under Cree and Assiniboine attacks. Cheyennes moved to the Sheyenne River where they built a large palisaded village and began raising corn. Saones and Minneconjous

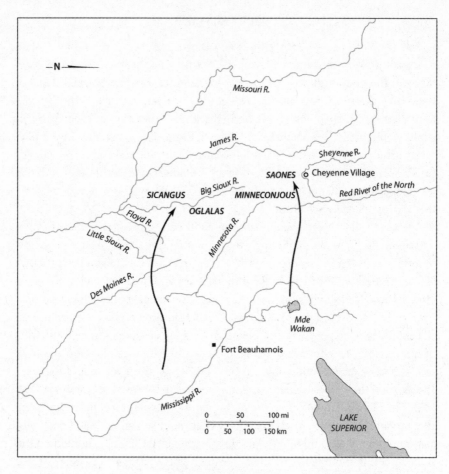

9. Pathways to the West: the eight valleys, early eighteenth century.
Map by Bill Nelson.

trailed their Cheyenne allies to the west trading and at times living with them. The Sheyenne River village became a crucial asset for them, serving as a food depot as they kept inching away from the rice stands in the east.[22]

By the early eighteenth century the Očhéthi Šakówiŋ had bulged around two hundred miles into the West: the Big Sioux rather than the Minnesota now marked its western border. The expansion was spearheaded by Lakotas, who were now within striking distance of the Mníšoše ("muddy water"), the Missouri, the largest and the lushest of the eight prairie valleys. Dozens of villages, many of them squeezed there by Lakota pressure, dotted the middle stretch of the valley like unevenly strung pearls. It was the greatest concentration of humans and wealth in the heart of the continent: as many as fifty thousand people may have lived in grand riverside villages that abounded with horses, corn, squash, bison robes, human energy, and power. Lakotas' westward thrust had created a villager bulwark that now threatened to foil it.[23]

Despite their strength, the villages and their possessions, especially horses, exerted an irresistible pull on the newcomers. Early eighteenth-century Sicangu winter counts are a litany of raids and clashes with the Missouri villagers as well as the Pawnees, who occupied a large domain in the central Great Plains north of the Republican Valley. Braided with triumph and terror, the counts capture how Sicangus kept pushing toward the villages despite daunting odds. The terror centered on horses. In 1715 Sicangus were struck by a mounted raid, possibly for the first time: an unidentified people attacked them "on horseback but killed nothing." A year later Sicangus were less fortunate: "Came and attacked on horseback and stabbed a boy near the lodge," reads the count. The pictograph shows an enemy warrior on a rising horse, dangling a speared child in midair. The attacks, apparently, were too swift and shocking for Sicangus to identity the enemy.[24]

Lakotas could have given up the fight, abandoned their quest of a western domain, and returned east, to the familiar and safe. They had not yet crossed any threshold—economic, cultural, or mental—that would have moored them in the West. But there seem to have been just enough successes to balance the setbacks and horrors. There were good hunts, especially in heavy snow when hunters with snowshoes could pluck snowbound bison, and there were victorious defensive battles and successful raids to avenge slain kin and restore spiritual balance: a Pawnee war party "annihilated"; an Arikara man hunting eagles killed; two Arikaras left dead "among the lodges"; Pawnees who "camped alone with their wives" killed. And then, finally, there were successful horse raids. Pushing west from the Big Sioux on foot, Sicangus infiltrated Missouri villages, hurrying back with mobile loot. It was probably women who pioneered the equestrian way of life by using horses to carry and haul possessions. It would be a long time until men dared to ride horses to war.[25]

Lakotas found themselves in a technological and military limbo. They could not yet fight on horseback, and their access to firearms remained precarious. The contraction of French trade after 1700 shrunk the flow of manufactured goods, leaving the seven fires without a dependable weapons source. Moreover, flintlocks were delicate devices and tricky to repair, and metal could become so brittle in subzero temperatures that barrels simply exploded. Lacking spare parts and blacksmiths, Lakotas could do little to stop the depletion of their reserves. In 1707 a Sicangu man named Corn killed his wife and fled. He returned a year

10/10a. Battiste Good winter count, 1704–5 and 1715–16 (details).
These two Sicangu winter counts capture the resistance and
violence the Lakotas faced when they started moving westward in
increasing numbers in the early eighteenth century. The captions
for the counts read, respectively, "Killed fifteen Pawnees who came
to fight winter" and "Came and attacked on horseback and stabbed
a boy near the lodge winter." Courtesy of National Anthropological
Archives, Smithsonian Institution (NAA INV 08476807 and NAA
INV 084746806, details).

later with three guns he had acquired from the British, possibly Hudson's Bay
Company traders. The guns were said to be the first known to his people.[26]

While Lakotas floundered in an extended liminal phase, their enemies were
rapidly harnessing firepower. Queen Anne's War had set off a vicious rivalry between the French and British over trading privileges in the lands between Hudson
Bay and the Great Lakes. Both armed the Indians liberally, trying to win them
over, and the Indians shifted their trade between different posts, paying little
attention to the flags they flew. Several Cree and Assiniboine bands became specialized trapper-traders and increasingly ambitious. Spurred on by muskets and

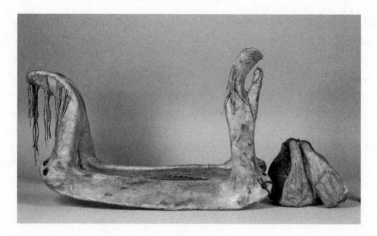

11. Lakota woman's saddle. In charge of transportation of household goods and other possessions, women played a key role in developing the Lakota horse culture. The hard saddle had wooden side pieces and high front and back pieces to help women carry packs of household goods and children on horseback. Courtesy of Department of Anthropology, Smithsonian Institution (E361490–0).

blacksmiths, they soon dominated trapping and trading across a vast semicircle around Hudson Bay. In the south the sphere dipped into the prairies, exposing Lakotas, Yanktons, and Yanktonais to technologically overpowering enemies.[27]

In the early eighteenth century Sicangus may have been the only Native group in the continental grasslands to simultaneously possess guns and horses. But it mattered little. They were only starting to experiment with equestrianism and their gun supply was unreliable. Their position on the nascent gun-horse borderland signaled potential, not power, and they were in a fundamental disadvantage when facing well-armed Crees and Assiniboines who could kill from the safety of distance with far superior firepower. The Crees and Assiniboines *were* the gun frontier in the Indigenous interior, whereas Lakotas were scrambling to acquire both muskets and mounts. They were feverishly trying to turn themselves into a true horse and gun power, but until they did, they would be dangerously exposed.[28]

HOT AND BLIND SPOTS

In 1712 the lower Great Lakes erupted into violence. The French strategy of packing its Indian allies around Detroit to block British expansion had turned the region into a seething hodgepodge of incompatible ambitions and intrigue.

French agents tried to mediate between their new allies, the Five Iroquois Nations, and their old ones who resented Iroquois presence and hunting in the region. Miamis demanded that French boil Le Pesant, an Odawa leader whose followers killed Miamis, sought to dominate French markets, and yet seemed ready to abandon the French if the Iroquois and the British would buy their pelts. The Iroquois, the center of rumors and fears, maneuvered to deflect the interior trade from Montreal to Albany, a radical reorientation of continental geopolitics that would make them the dominant middlemen. Reeling under pressure, French agents scrambled to find common causes to defuse the anguish. When Odawas wanted to make war on Sioux, a French agent not only authorized the attack but offered to join them with Wyandots, Miamis, and Iroquois.[29]

French attempts to calm the mounting tensions were already failing when more than a thousand Mesquakies moved to Detroit with their own allies. Their arrival threw all the rivalries over trapping and trading rights into a fever pitch. Mesquakies claimed to be rightful owners of Detroit and thus infuriated a number of rivals who began killing them in a concerted effort to eliminate them from the area. Mesquakies lay siege to Fort Detroit, and the French, confused and unnerved, could do little more than watch their alliance system collapse into bloodshed.[30]

The Mesquakie wars deepened the Očhéthi Šakówiŋ's already decadelong isolation. Suffering heavy losses, Mesquakies retreated to Green Bay, from where they raided across the pays d'en haut in search of vengeance, nearly paralyzing the fur trade. Sioux saw an opportunity in the carnage. Sioux and Mesquakies had feared and killed one another for decades, but now they were both Onontio's outcasts and hurting as a consequence. Caught between two aggressive fronts, Mesquakies were eager for respite and sought refuge in Sioux country. Sioux took them in.[31]

The 1713 Treaty of Utrecht, which ended the War of the Spanish Succession, further intensified the enmities. The British accepted a French prince as the king of Spain, and France recognized British claims to the lands around Hudson Bay and a British "dominion" over the Iroquois. The treaty made the lower Great Lakes and the Ohio Country a free trade zone and stipulated that the Indians could trade freely with either nation. The British had secured an inviolate control over the Northeast and Hudson Bay, whereas the interior, the core of the French Empire, became a site for a free-for-all rivalry for Indian allegiances.[32]

As North America's imperial map was being redrawn in European palaces, European rats were gnawing their way into another kind of contribution to geopolitical struggles. In 1714 the fur merchants in France made an astounding discovery: the huge surplus of pelts stored in their warehouses had been devoured by vermin. The demand for pelts skyrocketed, launching a swift revival of the French fur trade in North America. Traders pushed once again into the West, reopening old posts and building new ones. The fur trade became a big business run by a small group of wealthy bourgeois who employed wage-earning voyageurs, and the crown made certain that commerce continued to serve political ends. Soon the interior was speckled with posts, many of them fortified. Michilimackinac and Detroit, roughly equidistant from Montreal, anchored French trade in the West, while British traders pushed in through the Ohio Valley. The Ohio Country now became the hot spot in the British-French rivalry for dominion in North America.[33]

The hot spot created a blind spot. A reinforced Fort Michilimackinac looked to the north to contain the Hudson's Bay Company to its frozen sea, and Detroit looked to the east to block British traders from Pennsylvania. Fort Chartres in the Illinois Country faced west to extend France's commercial reach into Spanish territories and to the south toward Louisiana and its growing export markets (thus creating a rival to the Montreal-bound network). Coureurs de bois forged a trade route, *chemin de voyageurs*, that took them from the Mississippi-Wisconsin confluence directly west to the Missouri and its beaver-rich western tributaries. Sioux and Wyandots were reduced to seeking micro-openings into a bustling French trading empire that seemed to have turned its back — or its many backs — to them. Neither could do little more than wait for crumbs that might fall from the great table of commerce Onontio had set for his favorite children: an errant coureur de bois, an occasional Sauteur trapping party willing to trade.[34]

BRING UPON THEMSELVES A WAR WITH ALL THE NATIONS

Sioux and Mesquakies were both outcasts, but Mesquakies were also something else: after the damage and pain they inflicted across the pays d'en haut, they were widely and fiercely feared. Desiring a stronger French presence in the West, Governor Vaudreuil claimed that Mesquakies were agents of Iroquois, who in turn were agents of British, who wanted chaos in the Ohio Country to loosen France's imperial grip. Their close association with the denigrated Mesquakies would become a growing problem for Sioux.[35]

By 1720 the Mesquakie wars had made the French Empire dangerously brittle at its center where a bridge area linked the Great Lakes to the Mississippi Valley. Viewed from Quebec, the region was in a political limbo: France claimed it, but it was entirely beyond its control. Jesuit priest Pierre François Xavier de Charlevoix, who had been commissioned to search for a water passage through the continent to the imagined Sea of the West, a Mediterranean-like inland extension of the Pacific that would offer a new sea route to China, was appalled to learn that

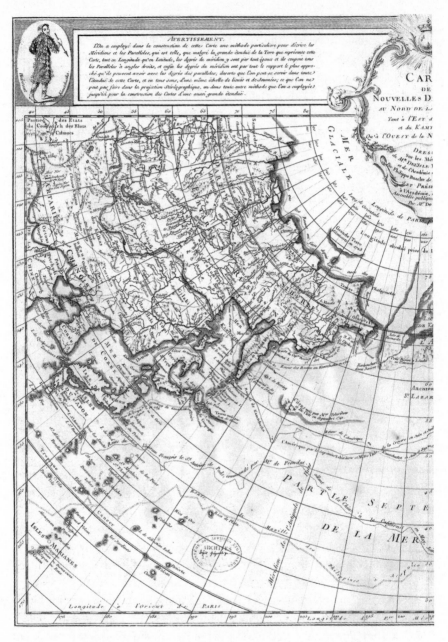

12. The Sea of the West as depicted by Philippe Buache and Joseph-Nicolas de L'Isle, *Carte des nouvelles découvertes au nord de la mer du sud tant à l'est de la Sibérie et du Kamtchatka qu'à l'ouest de la Nouvelle France*, 1750. French explorers and traders believed that there was a Sea of the West not too far to the west of the Mississippi Valley. Eager to gain access to China and its markets through North America, the French spent considerable time and effort to find

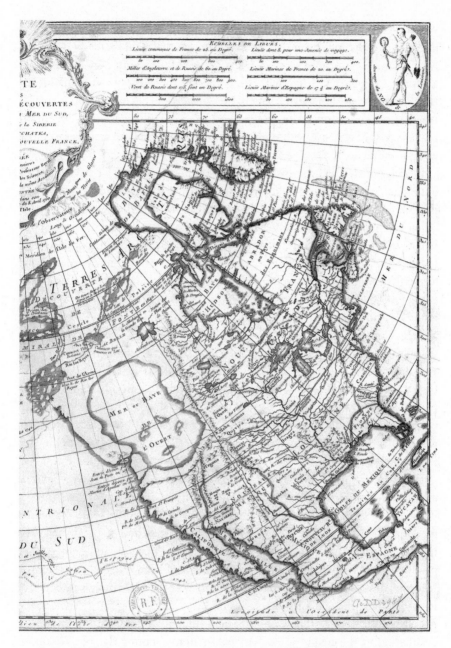

an all-water route to that sea. This map by two prominent French cartographers shows an enormous "Sea or Bay of the West" (Mer ou Baye de l'Ouest) covering much of the western interior. Such imagined geographies profoundly shaped French imperial ambitions in North America. Courtesy of Bibliothèque nationale de France.

warfare had all but closed the upper Mississippi and Illinois Rivers for French navigation, inflicting "great damage upon the mutual Commerce between the two Colonies." Not only was Louisiana being severed from New France, but a door was opening for the Spaniards to ascend the Missouri and look for the Northwest Passage, Charlevoix feared. Mesquakies had become an anathema for New France and a burden for Sioux. The Mesquakie alliance was pulling Sioux into an abyss of violence with multiple Native peoples and on a collision course with New France.[36]

French policies had driven Sioux into the thorny alliance with Mesquakies, but French policies also opened a way out. Fearing that Lakes Indians would seek protection from Mesquakies among the British in the Ohio Country, French officials began to lean toward the extermination of the Mesquakies, hoping that it would keep Lakes Indians in their orbit. Agents in charge of interior posts were ordered not "to hold back the ones who want to make war" on Mesquakies and to incite the Indians to unite forces to "destroy them entirely." But Mesquakies could not be destroyed as long as they were allied to the formidable Sioux and found asylum among Lakotas deep in the prairies. The French and Sioux began a careful reconciliation. Sioux asked for missionaries, a request that almost invariably prompted the French into action, and the French offered to build them a trading post on the shores of Lake Pepin on the Mississippi to "succor them in their needs." Sioux grasped the opening and were promptly awarded: La Compagnie des Sioux had Fort Beauharnois running by late 1727, furnishing goods for political ends. Trade, the French hoped, would frustrate Mesquakie efforts "to win the heart of the Sioux, who will always reject their offers as long as they see the French on their territory."[37]

Fort Beauharnois was a troubled success. As Mesquakies were sidelined, Sioux emerged from their shadow, hungry for merchandise. Ninety-five Dakota lodges immediately settled at Lake Pepin, and during the first winter some three hundred Lakotas camped near the fort. Mesquakies, isolated and desperate, harassed the fort, forcing Sioux to choose sides. They chose iron, guns, and France. They gave up their Mesquakie "hearts," which prompted French agents to anticipate "the total destruction of That Wretched Nation." Fort Beauharnois was reopened in 1731 to Sioux's "great satisfaction," its business split among fifteen traders who managed six canoes. In that winter a French-Iroquois-Wyandot army "caused the destruction of the majority" of Mesquakies, thus securing the Fox-Wisconsin artery for French traffic. Trade boomed, and the following year Fort Beauharnois sent tens of thousands of "very good skins" east, establishing itself as one of the most profitable French trading posts in North America and a major source of firearms. It was now, at long last, that the seven fires became a true gun power.[38]

This could have been the culmination of Sioux's nearly century-long search for a proper relationship with the French, the moment when Sioux and French interests finally aligned. Yet Sioux treaded carefully. They "appeared well intentioned towards the French," the traders reported, "and had no other fear than that of being abandoned by them." They showed little interest in the faith of the Jesuits who had settled among them and they refused to feed the priests. Dependent on French goods but cynical of French intentions, Sioux wanted loyalty and compliance. They did not want the French to extend the artful but fragile accommodation of the middle ground among them; they wanted the French to enter a Native ground and conform to Sioux customs. They expected the French to behave like, essentially to be, Sioux. This was less a matter of policy than of what the French called *mentalité*, a way of seeing the world and being in it. To win the Sioux over, the French would have to shift from their still new imperial mode into a much older Indigenous one and embrace its logic and lessons.[39]

A LITTLE DOOR TO CHINA

On the night of June 6, 1736, a party of twenty-one Frenchmen set out in three canoes to cross Lake of the Woods to the east. They were part of a larger exploring expedition that had run out of food, and they had been sent to fetch supplies from Fort Kaministiquia on the northern shore of Lake Superior, more than three hundred miles away. They paddled vigorously for several hours and then set a camp on a little sandy island to have breakfast. At the same time another party was approaching the island from the opposite side. They too landed and started to move through the underbrush toward the French.

When the hundred Lakota and Dakota warriors descended on the resting Frenchmen, the surprise was complete. They killed them all. Sixteen days later a French search party arrived at the site. They found their compatriots arranged into a statement. Their bodies rested in a circle, their severed heads wrapped in beaver skins. Most of the heads did not have scalps. The leader, Jean-Baptiste Gaultier de La Vérendrye, lay on his stomach, headless, his back sliced with knife cuts and a stake sticking out of its side. His body was "decked out with garters and bracelets of porcupine quill."[40]

Jean-Baptiste de La Vérendrye and his associates had been brought into the West by an audacious plan. During the long slump of French fur trade in the early eighteenth century, British merchants had filled the vacuum, carving out a vast trading hinterland that reached deep into the interior from Hudson Bay. They worked through Crees and Assiniboines, who used British muskets to establish themselves the foremost long-distance traders in the continent's northern half. Soon they dominated trapping across an enormous semicircle extending outward from Hudson Bay. The Indigenous interior was turning rapidly toward the British, threatening to cut off the French Empire from the West. This was a grave danger. The symbolic and potential value of western North America for France had soared after the Treaty of Utrecht, which, in the spirit of a new balance of power doctrine among European empires, banned both British and French ships from the Spanish Pacific. This left a water route across North America as France's best chance to access Mexico and its silver as well as to reach the throbbing markets of the Orient.[41]

The French finally acted in 1731 when Governor Charles de Beauharnois de La Boische assigned Pierre Gaultier de Varennes de La Vérendrye—Jean-Baptiste's father—to build a string of French trading posts into the interior and, while at it, find the elusive water route to the Pacific. If successful, the plan could deliver not only much of North America but also a healthy slice of Asian markets for France. A continent-wide French belt could isolate the British in Hudson Bay, open access to Mexican silver, and force the Indians to privilege French traders over all others. On a broader scale, a water route through the continent might bring France closer to China and its riches and turn the comparatively modest colonies of New France and Louisiana into pivots of a globe-spanning French Empire.[42]

But in between the French and China stood the Sioux who now seemed entirely immune to French ambitions and demands. Beauharnois and La Vérendrye's lofty design thus hinged on the loyalty of Crees whose trapping and war parties dominated access to the interior regions where the route to the Pacific might be found. The most promising prospect for the passage seemed to be the "River of the West"—the Missouri—where semi-urban white-skinned "Mantanne" Indians were rumored to dwell. The French became obsessed with the Mantannes, and to reach them they had to win Crees on their side. Crees responded eagerly to French overtures—La Vérendrye was well-versed in Native diplomacy and generous with his goods—but a Cree connection threatened to draw the French into a war with the redoubtable Sioux, whose enmity could swiftly undo all French designs for the West.[43]

La Vérendrye worked hard to forge a truce between Crees and Sioux, but he had stepped into a deep-rooted Native conflict he could neither understand nor diffuse. When Crees insisted on raiding Sioux, the exasperated Frenchman directed them to attack Lakotas, apparently not realizing that this would draw the French into a conflict with the most numerous of the Sioux divisions. And while La Vérendrye presented himself as Onontio's surrogate promising peace and protection, he and his men openly engaged in Indian slave trading—which had been legal in New France since 1709—alienating the very people they were trying to win over.[44]

The contradictions came to head in 1734 when La Vérendrye, crumbling under pressure, armed a war party of over six hundred Crees and their allies whose hearts were "bitter against the Sioux." He sent Jean-Baptiste, his eldest son and "dearest possession," with them "as another myself" and cautioned them not to attack Sioux. "Who could tell whether my son would ever return," he asked his diary. The massive force promptly attacked Lakotas. They took several captives and sold some of them to La Vérendrye. Jean-Baptiste survived, for now. Two years later René Bourassa dit La Ronde, a prominent slave trader and La Vérendrye's business associate, left with a female Sioux slave for Michilimackinac, but they were stopped by a large Sioux party seeking to avenge the French-sponsored Cree attack. The woman directed the warriors to Lake of the Woods, disclosing that they would find Jean-Baptiste there.[45]

The massacre at Lake of the Woods was targeted at killing the young La Vérendrye who was a living symbol of French betrayal. In a world where empires were still loose and decentralized, individual agents often came to embody policies and their failures. The massacre was also a response to Onontio's gun trade with Crees and a declaration of war on the nascent French-Cree alliance. French had not wanted this war because killing disrupted trade and exploration, but Crees had. They had methodically co-opted the French into their decades-long conflict with the Sioux, and now they had succeeded. The prairie-forest borderlands between Lake Superior and the Missouri Valley became a sprawling war zone where Crees and their Assiniboine allies vied for supremacy with the seven fires. French agents tried to stop the killing, but the war only escalated, driven by rivalries over hunting grounds and the need to avenge slain kin. Crees, who now received guns from the French while still trading with the British at Hudson Bay, emerged as major contenders for dominance in the continental interior, commanding a bulging sphere with sheer firepower.[46]

The Sioux-Cree conflict put Sauteurs in an impossible position. They were caught between two expanding powers, and their homelands threatened to become a battleground. They had to choose sides. Crees were an immediate presence, pushing south into the Sioux country through Sauteur lands, and their growing commercial prominence promised the Sauteurs a lucrative role as middlemen. Sioux, by contrast, were becoming increasingly elusive. Sauteurs' alliance with them had been primarily with the eastern fires, but the sprawling Cree war boosted Lakotas' political weight. The Očhéthi Šakówiŋ was turning west and pulling away from its old allies. And so Sauteurs chose Crees, ending their generations-old alliance with the Seven Council Fires, and began killing Sioux. Sioux fought back, killing Crees, Assiniboines, Sauteurs, and French.[47]

French dreams of finding a route to the Sea of the West dissipated into violence and fear. When Pierre Gaultier de Varennes et de La Vérendrye finally made it among the Mantannes—the Mandan Indians who lived along the Missouri Valley—in late 1738 with some six hundred Assiniboines, the visit was fraught: Lakotas were rumored to be prowling around, spreading fear. The French stayed for just ten days, too sickly and too anxious to seek the Sea of the West. Another Vérendrye expedition four years later was a timid and desultory affair. The Vérendryes hoped to glimpse the Sea of the West from a mountaintop, but a threat of Indian attack pushed them to turn back. The French never built a western fort that could have turned the river into a jumping-off point to the Pacific.[48]

The French push for a continental empire had stalled. It had been a bold but not an unfeasible plan. In the early eighteenth century New France had enjoyed a range of advantages that made it the most likely contender for dominance in North America: a hard-won peace with the Iroquois, a firm grip on interior fur trade, a powerful mother country committed to overseas expansion, and unmatched experience in Indian diplomacy. The door to the Pacific and China lay wide open, for Spain had not yet extended its reach to California, and the western Indians would have eagerly welcomed French traders and goods. But Lakotas closed the door. France's North American empire would never span the continent.

WITH REFLECTION AND DESIGN

In early May 1736, a month before the massacre at Lake of the Woods, a party of fifty-four western and eastern Sioux warriors passed by Fort Beauharnois on their way southeast to redeem a Ho-Chunk captive. The post commander, Jacques Legardeur de Saint-Pierre, protested that it was not necessary for so many of them to deliver a single woman. Sioux said they were also going to hunt turkeys for arrow fletchings. After some time the party returned to the fort and, with the traders watching, danced with two fresh French scalps for four days.[49]

Four months later ten Sioux emissaries presented Saint-Pierre a gift of fifty-seven pounds of castor, nine deerskins, and two female slaves, denouncing the Lake of the Woods killings. The next day another Sioux party arrived in the post. Its leader wore a French silver coin as a pendant. Saint-Pierre recognized the coin and demanded to know its origin, but the Sioux laughed and said nothing. Saint-Pierre "ripped the seal off with the ear." A retaliation came three months later when Sioux burned down a French fort intended for Ho-Chunk trade. Confused and alarmed by the sudden turmoil, Saint-Pierre confronted Sacred Born, the prominent Mdewakanton chief, demanding to know why his people were harassing and insulting the French. The response gave him a pause: Sioux were doing so "with reflection and design."[50]

That design was part of a much larger strategy to mold the interior world to meet the needs of the Očhéthi Šakówiŋ. The French had envisioned Fort Beauharnois as an extension of their alliance network to the west of the pays d'en haut where they could challenge the Hudson's Bay Company in the imperial rivalry over furs, Indian allies, and territorial claims. Although the fort was one of the most profitable fur-trading depots, the French thought that the Sioux were not exploiting their rich trapping grounds to their full potential and urged Ho-Chunk and Sauteur trappers to move into the upper Mississippi Valley. With friction intensifying around the fort, the French burned it in the winter of 1737 and left.[51]

The massacre at Lake of the Woods and the violence around Fort Beauharnois were connected: they were manifestations of a new uncompromising Sioux policy toward the French and other European powers. Like its previous reiterations, French Indian policy in the 1720s and 1730s had been a bitter disappointment to Sioux: it had armed them and made them stronger, but in the end it had made their enemies even stronger and better armed. Sioux were determined to ensure this would never happen again.

That demanded coordinated political action. It required that war became a collective Sioux effort and that the many oyátes and bands talked with one voice. In the late 1730s, in the wake of La Vérendrye's explorations, the French built a string of trading posts in the woodlands and parklands just to the north of the Sioux territory, hoping to block the northern flow of furs and allies to Hudson Bay. Violence followed the trade to the west. Crees, Assiniboines, and Sauteurs gravitated toward the new posts and began to winter in the parklands on outer edges of the woodlands, within a striking distance of Sioux territory. Come spring, they pushed to the south, seeking furs that were still thick. For several months each year Sioux were reduced to looking to the north for raids by superbly armed enemies who could push in nearly anywhere across a five-hundred-mile borderland that extended from Lake Superior to the upper Missouri Valley. So relentless was the violence that Governor Beauharnois anticipated imminent collapse of the Sioux barrier. The Sioux "nearly died of hunger because they were afraid to hunt," he wrote approvingly. "It would be a great boon if we could destroy them because they occupy the finest Hunting grounds."[52]

Such was the extent of the battle zone that the wide-ranging Sioux seemed to be waging a single war—which, in effect, they were. They could have pulled back to protect a core territory farther south in the prairies, but instead they did the opposite: they lashed out. Their war parties started policing an extended borderland, tracking and attacking invaders, and they took the war deep into the homes of their enemies, seeking captives and blood to cover their dead. The borderlands turned into perilous no-man's-lands. Much of the violence on both

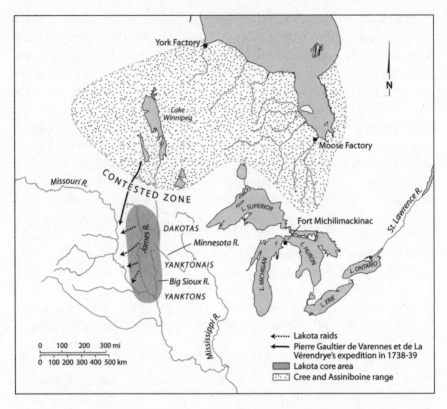

13. The contested interior in the middle decades of the eighteenth century.
Map by Bill Nelson.

sides was indiscriminate: culpability mattered little in a war in which kin avenged kin. Dakotas formed the front line of defense around Mde Wakan and on the upper Mississippi, absorbing most of the damage, but they held the line. They also strove to keep diplomatic channels open. In 1739 Wabasha and Sintez, two young Mdewakanton chiefs, visited Beauharnois, asking him to mediate the violence in the interior.[53]

RIVIÈRES DE SIOUX

The Sioux, in fact, were expanding. While fending off Cree and Assiniboine attacks from the north and east, they fought other wars in the south and west. Warriors from all seven fires gathered together in the heart of their domain to form large war parties that canoed down the latitudinal prairie rivers to raid Iowas, Omahas, and Otoes along the lower Missouri Valley for captives, corn, and horses. Such was the frequency of the attacks that two of the key arteries became known as *rivières de Sioux*. But the main direction of expansion was toward the west. Soon Lakota war parties pushed beyond the Big Sioux River, raiding Arikaras and Hidatsas along the upper Missouri Valley.[54]

The thriving gun trade at Fort Beauharnois in the east had translated into growing military prowess in the west. None of the Missouri River villagers fought with firearms, which gave Sioux a psychological and tactical advantage, encouraging plundering. Many of the villagers were refugees, driven from the prairies by Lakotas and struggling to carve out a place for themselves in the crowded Missouri Valley. Yet the villagers were not easy targets. Trade with Crows and other plains nomads to the west supplied them with horses, allowing many of them to shift to mounted warfare in the 1740s. This made raiding them a risky proposition. Facing mounted warriors on foot, Lakotas, even though carrying guns, seem to have absorbed damage as often as they inflicted it.

The Sicangu winter count for 1742 shows an unidentified enemy on a fearsome horse, carrying a long spear and looming over a prairie turnip and a digging stick: Sicangu women were ambushed while gathering food. The next winter a war party of some one hundred mounted warriors surrounded a Sicangu camp without warriors, who were out hunting. A woman pointed the enemy party toward the hunting ground, and the horsemen descended on the Sicangu men. It was a memorable event because the horseless Sicangus beat the odds, repulsing the mounted aggressors with mere spears. The pictograph is filled with hoof prints, engulfing both the village and reaching toward the hunters.[55]

Lakotas feared these horse warriors, but they would not stop attacking them. The enemy horses of their winter counts were menacing beasts, but they were also irresistible creatures, precisely because they imparted such awe-inspiring power. Lakotas wanted and needed that power, and the Missouri villages were the only place where it was available. The Mníšoše would remain a battlefront.[56]

WE CAME TO COMPLAIN OF IT TO YOU

While Lakotas spearheaded the Očhéthi Šakówiŋ's war effort in the West, the eastern oyátes led its diplomacy. In 1741 a Cree and Assiniboine war party of over two hundred had descended on a prairie Sioux camp. The battle lasted for four days, and the well-armed northerners killed 160 Sioux warriors and uncounted women and children. They took so many captives that their procession stretched for half a mile. They sold many of them to French traders who took the captives to thriving slave markets in Montreal: the prolonged western wars were a boon for French merchants eager to traffic in Indian slaves. A year later La Colle, a Cree chief, announced in the presence of French traders that a large coalition of northern Indians would soon fall on Sioux, determined to "create all the carnage they can." Sioux, he said, "were only good to eat," and he wanted "to kill enough of them to feed his village." The chief sought to fill his people with sacred reckoning, but his passion had a material element as well: men like the Vérendryes were buying all the Sioux slaves they could and paid good prices for them. For Assiniboines and Crees, Sioux were at once commercial rivals, fearsome enemies whose very presence strengthened their communities through martial kinship, and prized commodities in colonial slave markets.[57]

Diplomacy in such a milieu was literally a matter of life and death. Sioux wanted very specific things from the French—guns, iron, mediation, and a relationship that yielded them—but to have them they had to consider what the French could and could not do. Onontio could not embrace them if they killed too many of his children, but he could welcome them if they appeared weak and pliant. Sioux held back, refraining from vengeance, an extraordinarily difficult thing for their chiefs to do, as the people who had lost kin needed retaliation to restore spiritual and emotional balance and doubted leaders who failed to provide it. It is possible that the chiefs rechanneled the need to replace dead relatives with captives by attacking an Illinois village along the Illinois River. Sioux restraint gave the French room to maneuver, and in 1742 Governor Beauharnois called all western nations to a council in Montreal. This time Sioux were among the invited.[58]

Paul Marin de La Malgue, a leading French trader who had worked at Fort Beauharnois, escorted two prominent Mdewakanton chiefs, Sacred Born and Leaf Shooter, to the imperial city. There, in the presence of emissaries from several enemy nations, the two chiefs addressed Beauharnois, making a series of claims on the governor. They stressed the Očhéthi Šakówiŋ's difficult position in the fringes of French and Indian middle ground—on "the other side of the half of the earth"—and asked Beauharnois to accept the calumet and extend his benevolence over their nation. They recounted their people's tortured history with the French, reminding the governor of their repeated efforts to reach out to them. They emphasized their bond with Marin, which could anticipate a new relationship with Beauharnois, and they publicized their restraint in the face of the hurt Assiniboines, Crees, and others had inflicted on them, imposing a moral responsibility on the governor to protect them as his children. Rather than meeting violence with violence, the chiefs said, "We came to complain of it to you."[59]

Six days later, Sacred Born and Leaf Shooter addressed the governor again. The chiefs had had a busy social schedule in the city, and something had happened. Montreal, along with the rest of New France, had entered a golden age. It was a nexus of a thriving fur trade and boasted a growing bourgeoisie class. Its businesses and households were run by a substantial population of Indian slaves, who worked as dock loaders, millers, weavers, shopworkers, and housekeepers. The city's elite had hosted Sacred Born and Leaf Shooter in their homes, and on one of those occasions the chiefs had been served by very young, newly baptized Sioux slaves. The emissaries demanded a new audience with Beauharnois and, suppressing their disgust, told him how the children had "started to cry when they saw us." They asked the governor to free them and, exerting pressure, intimated how slave traffic fueled unrest among their people, making it necessary for the French to placate them: "Though I am a Chief, the young men do not always do my will," one of the emissaries said, "that is why I beg you to have pity on me." Pity, as always, commanded obligation. "My Father," the chief continued, "this is the reason that leads me to ask you to grant us an officer"—a trader in charge of a post—"in our villages, to give us Reason." It was a thinly veiled threat: if Onontio refused them his munificence, the violence in the West would continue, senselessly.[60]

Beauharnois replied four days later. It was an awkward speech, the governor's discomfort and vacillation palpable. The new Sioux demands after the slave debacle had placed him in a precarious position where, suddenly, he had to grant Sioux more concessions than to others. Although suffused with patriarchal authority, his message progressed to accept the Sioux demands one by one, culminating in a plea. He first accepted the calumet "to make you know how much I wish peace and tranquility to reign among the Nations of My Children." But if refused, he would breathe fire: "If you do some bad action again ... I will unleash all my French people and the nations who do not wish for anything better than to charge at your villages to get revenge for all you have done in the past." He recounted past grievances only to put them behind, promising to "reconcile all things." He returned the two slave children, having probably bought them from their owner. Sidestepping the question of a post—"I have to first see how you behave"—he gave Sioux what they wanted most: his generosity. "My Children, as I see you naked, I give you what you need to cover yourselves." He handed out gifts and a drink of his "milk"—brandy—and implored them to sit and drink and smoke quietly in their villages, "listening to my word." Marin would follow them into the West and look after them.[61]

THE OCHETI ŠAKÓWIŊ AND THE FRENCH DOMINOES

Unlike Tiyoskate's pioneering intervention in 1695, the 1742 council produced profound and lasting results. Sacred Born and Leaf Shooter had faced the French and their Indian allies with poise and force, securing Onontio's love and protection. But unlike half a century earlier, the momentum of historical change was now on the side of the Sioux.

In 1744, after thirty years of peace, a new war, King George's, broke out, creating disorder that worked to Sioux's advantage. British warships blockaded the St. Lawrence, nearly stifling France's imperial trade. Beauharnois handed out licenses for free, but the interior trade languished, alienating the Indians from the French. Soon a virulent Indigenous rebellion washed over the pays d'en haut, throwing French officials into a panic over the emboldened British "who have no other Object than to Make Themselves masters of all the upper country through the Sole medium of the Savages whose minds they have won." But Sioux remained peaceful, trading with the wide-ranging coureurs de bois. When their young men killed three coureurs, four "chiefs of the Lakes and Prairies" delivered the culprits, "bound and tied," to French officials, and then traveled to Montreal to ask for pardon for the transgression.[62]

The accommodating stance paid off richly. When the hot war ended in 1748 the French and British became entangled in a cold war over the Ohio Valley, a contest in which the allegiance of Indians was the key to victory. When the armies withdrew, traders from Pennsylvania and Virginia took over the fur business in the Ohio Valley, their primacy underwritten by cheap goods, a steady supply of liquor, and a string of posts. Ejecting British traders from Indian villages and erasing British military presence from Ohio became an urgent priority for the French. It was a daunting challenge for the materially puny New France—its population just exceeded fifty-five thousand—and any chance of success demanded that peace prevailed elsewhere on its far-flung borderlands. The last thing the French needed was a war with the numerous Sioux who could bring a massive army in battle.[63]

And so, in 1749, the new governor, Jacques-Pierre de Taffanel de La Jonquière, formed a partnership with Paul Marin and authorized him to open trade with the Sioux. With such backing and mission, Marin became more than a regular frontier official: he was to transform the Sioux from a barrier into a bridge and extend the French Empire deep into the West. Marin promptly arbitrated a truce between the Sioux and the various Green Bay peoples, thereby safeguarding the Fox-Wisconsin route into the Sioux country. He then proceeded among the Sioux, who were eager to expand the peace: they handed over a captive, a son of a Cree headman, so that Marin could take him home. "The young man did not wish to leave that nation"—a rare glimpse into how captivity shaded into belonging and kinship in the Sioux world—but Marin was confident that peace could be established in the West. He brought his son Joseph and a cadre of traders into the Mississippi Valley where they built three posts to serve the Sioux: Fort Vaudreuil below the mouth of the Wisconsin, Fort Duquesne somewhere on the upper reaches, and Fort La Jonquière on the western shore of Lake Pepin.

Trade could now flow where needed, and soon regular trade parties frequented nearly all Sioux villages between the Mississippi and Minnesota Rivers.[64]

Here, the Sioux desire for guns, iron, and protection met the French desire for profits and power to create an odd hybrid world where two peoples could simultaneously pursue their expansionist ambitions and yet coexist, cooperate, and feel secure. For French officials the peace with the Sioux was part and parcel of their enduring quest to dominate the West. The dream of finding a water route to the Sea of the West resurfaced once more, and Joseph Marin was assigned to replace his father as commander and find the elusive passage. The French envisioned the Sioux country both as a beaver reservoir that siphoned prime castor eastward and as an imperial crucible where westbound French merchants and explorers would consolidate a mighty empire spanning from ocean to ocean. A century earlier the Iroquois had been the most powerful Native nation on the colonial frontiers. Now the Sioux were. French agents saw in them a most useful proxy: the more powerful and loyal they became, the stronger the French position would be. A dominant Sioux nation, attached to the French, could finally secure the continental interior for France.[65]

Marin fils implemented the French policy, and he did that with care and deep insight. At thirty-one he was already one of France's most experienced frontier officers. He had explored the pays d'en haute since the age of thirteen, had fought the Indians in the South, and managed the relationships with the Sioux at Green Bay. He understood the protocols and politics of the fur trade, was fluent in Dakota, and knew enough of the culture and mindset of the Sioux to win their trust. He was New France's best ambassador for an empire in the West.[66]

Marin's tenure in the West was a culmination of a long Sioux quest to harness the fur trade and the French Empire itself to serve their needs. In Marin Sioux had a guardian who understood the importance of right words, gestures, and rituals and could find the proper emotional register to be effective. The first meeting at the Wisconsin-Mississippi confluence in the fall of 1753 set the tone. Marin had sent invitations to a peace council along with three boatloads of gifts, and Sioux welcomed him with the calumet. Marin promised to send traders to mediate disputes over hunting privileges and sent more gifts through Dakotas to "Prairie Sioux"—Lakotas, Yanktons, and Yanktonais—whose overwhelming military power could derail any peace process. Then, throughout the winter, he hosted various Sioux bands at Fort Vaudreuil, attending to their needs with gifts given in Onontio's name. He demanded nothing in return but asked the Sioux to hunt "well all winter long so they could get what they needed from the traders," camouflaging a forthright credit system with the metaphors of love and compassion. Knowing that he had stepped into an active war zone where Sioux had killed and had been killed by Assiniboines, Crees, Sauteurs, and Lakes Indians for years, Marin also acted as an arbitrator, covering the dead with gifts, exhorting the bereaved to mourn peacefully, and handing out soothing brandy.[67]

Fort Vaudreuil became a focal point of a vast new fur trade domain that yielded the French a remarkable annual profit of 150,000 francs. It was first and foremost a Sioux post. A large Dakota village camped next to it throughout the winter, reflecting a larger retreat from the violence that continued to rage on the northern borderlands, and Marin sent repeated invitations to the more elusive Lakotas in the West. And while Marin worked hard to bring the Sioux in, his traders spread out to live among Sioux bands. They almost certainly married Sioux women à la façon du pays, converting fictive kinship ties with biological ones.[68]

Inevitably, and perhaps purposely, such preferential treatment alarmed the enemies of the Sioux, prompting them to seek inclusion through appeasement. Fort Vaudreuil became a pivot around which Indians forged an alliance. "The Sioux played lacrosse against the Sakis and the Wisconsin Foxes [Mesquakies]," Marin noted in his diary in December 1753, pleased with the tranquility, but failing to underline the momentous rapprochement between Sioux and Mesquakies, whose alliance had unraveled into ruinous violence twenty years earlier. From that lacrosse field the peace process widened, pulling in group after group until Mesquakies, Sauks, Winnebagos, Illinois, Menominees, Dakotas, Lakotas, Yanktons, and Yanktonais were all on board. It was a peace "of the greatest consequence," Marin later reported. Without it, violence would have cut off the Illinois Country from Canada and its *habitants* "would have been forced to abandon their settlements."[69]

Marin behaved and, it seemed, thought like a Sioux, which nearly erased the boundary between them. He remained, ardently so, an officer of the French Empire in his reports, but his actions on the ground made it difficult to say where French interests ended and Sioux interests began. That convergence culminated in the most unexpected of arenas: territory. Land, along with trade and alliance, was the root cause of all conflicts between colonial powers and Native nations, but Marin became a passionate advocate of the Očhéthi Šakówiŋ's territorial integrity. In the winter of 1753–54, he recorded a speech by Dakota chiefs, who asked him to have pity on them for they were "completely changed, defeated, and naked." They had no robes to cover Marin because they had not been able to hunt, fearing attacks from Sauteurs who "want to take our territory."[70]

Blood and bones, the chiefs insisted, both underwrote and demarcated the Sioux domain: "Here is a map of the Mississippi. No one could be unaware that from the mouth of the Wisconsin to Sangsue Lake [Leech Lake], these territories belong to us. At all parts and on the little rivers we have had villages. One can still see the marks of our bones which are marks of the Cristinaux and the Sauteux having killed us. But they never run us off that way. These are territories that we hold from no one except the Master of Life who gave them to us."[71]

This became Marin's doctrine. His advocacy of Sioux rights may have been rooted in a business dispute—Louis-Joseph Gaultier de La Vérendrye, the commandant at La Pointe and the youngest son of Pierre Gaultier de Varennes, had sent Sauteurs to hunt for him in the upper Mississippi Valley, which Marin considered his jurisdiction—but the end result was a genuine alignment of interests. "The Mississippi belongs to the Sioux and doesn't belong to the Sauteux at all," Marin wrote to a friend, and he promised to Dakota chiefs to take their case to Onontio in Montreal. Guided by Sioux, Marin had married commerce and culture, embedding the profit-driven fur trade into the familial language and logic of alliance. Sioux supplied New France with castor, fueling its pursuit of a western empire, and French traders furnished Sioux with guns and iron, meeting their needs by sharing their seemingly limitless wealth.[72]

The French saw the Sioux as a critical piece in their contest for the interior with the British. In the late 1740s, as Indian rebellion kept the pays d'en haut in a state of unrest, the Ohio Country seemed to be sliding irrevocably to the British. And once it fell, the French feared, the pays d'en haut, the Illinois Country, and Louisiana would all topple like dominoes. The Sioux alliance was essential for French efforts to reverse the momentum. It kept alive the idea of the French as benevolent fathers at a time when many inland Indians saw them as power-hungry tyrants. More pointedly, peace with the Sioux in the West allowed the French to focus resources against Britain in the Ohio Country. The link was concrete enough to become domestic: as Marin fils mediated Indigenous disputes in the West, his father led an army into the Ohio Valley to build forts, reign in Indian rebels, and arm Native allies.[73]

Two flashes of violence accelerated the French-Indian rapprochement. In the summer of 1752 a war party of more than two hundred Odawas, Ojibwes, Potawatomis, and Frenchmen attacked Pickawillany, a Miami village near the Ohio Valley, where chief Memeskia—known as La Demoiselle by the French—sheltered British traders. They captured Memeskia and three traders and dragged them outside. They killed one of the traders, cut his heart out, and ate it, and they boiled and ate Memeskia in front of his relatives. The attack was a sensation, and it sent British traders fleeing from the Ohio Country in panic, leaving behind a firmer French-Indian alliance.[74]

Two years later an ambitious but inexperienced British officer led a regiment of colonial troops into the region to attack Fort Duquesne, a new French stronghold at the forks of the Ohio. His under-planned assault was a failure, leading to a humiliating surrender. Like the horror of Pickawillany, George Washington's capitulation at Fort Necessity triggered a mass flight of British subjects from the Ohio Country. Together, the two battles buttressed the French-Indian coalition, emboldened French imperial officers to defy British posturing, and pulled France and Britain toward a cataclysmic conflict. When the contest over the Ohio Valley spiraled into the French and Indian War and then into the global conflict of the Seven Years' War, the interior was once again securely in the French orbit.[75]

CASTOR AND CARBOHYDRATES

The French were not the only big winners in the 1750s. If the Sioux peace helped the French secure the Ohio Country and contain the British, the French trade helped Sioux to prevail over their rivals and continue their expansion into the West. The tempo and scale of the Sioux warfare increased, reflecting a growing assertiveness of Lakotas, who now emerged as the dominant power among the seven fires.

The booming trade in the Mississippi Valley drove Lakotas deeper into the prairies in search of castor. Impatient with rival hunters from the Missouri River villages, they fought more intensely and widely: almost every midcentury Sicangu winter count records a clash with some enemy group or another. Sicangus now had guns, enough to seize the prairies and their beaver streams all the way to the turbulent, meandering Mníšoše. It was sometime during this westward thrust that they launched their first mounted raid. "Went on the warpath on horseback to camp of enemy," the caption for the 1757–58 count reads, "but killed nothing." In spite of the underwhelming outcome, it was a transcending event. Sicangus had accumulated enough know-how to wield a lance on a beast galloping at twenty to thirty miles per hour, enough animals to put an entire war party on horseback, and enough confidence to launch an attack. Sicangus edged westward in a close partnership with Oglalas, who probably began experimenting with mounted warfare around the same time.[76]

Sicangus and Oglalas pushed to the James River and beyond, entering the Coteau du Missouri, a poorly drained plateau that flanks the eastern side of the Missouri River. The Coteau was an inferior trapping and hunting country, and Sicangus and Oglalas moved rapidly across it, facing little resistance. They touched the Mníšoše amid several Arikara villages that housed thousands of people. For Arikaras the Missouri was *tswaarúxti*, Holy Water, along which all of their history had happened. They lived in some thirty villages on its banks and were determined to keep the newcomers out. Sicangus and Oglalas found a rela-

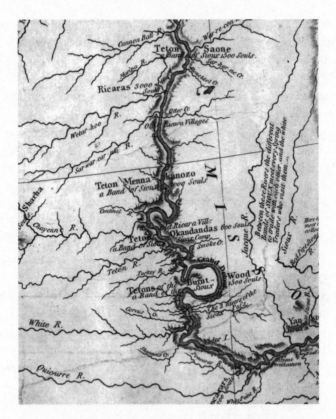

14. The Big Bend of the Missouri. Detail of William Clark,
*A Map of Lewis and Clark's Track, across the Western
Portion of North America from the Mississippi to the Pacific
Ocean*, Samuel Lewis, copyist; Samuel Harrison, engraver.
Philadelphia: Bradford and Inskeep, 1814. Courtesy of
Library of Congress, Geography and Map Division.

tively safe niche in an eastward protruding meander that would be later known
as the Big Bend of the Missouri. Stretching out for thirty miles in near full circle,
the bend enveloped a fertile, grass-covered island that teemed with bison, elk,
and other game—a superb base from where Sicangus and Oglalas could raid Arikaras for food, horses, and captives and dominate the prairies to the east.[77]

Around the same time another Lakota wave—the Saones and Minneconjous—
reached the Mníšoše some seventy-five miles northward, next to another Arikara
village cluster. Saones' and Minneconjous' westward thrust was spearheaded by
their Cheyenne allies, who had fled to the Missouri after Sauteurs burned their
great village on the Sheyenne. Band by band, Cheyennes touched the Missouri

just above the Grand River junction. There, on both banks of the channel, they built several villages, entrenching themselves in the Missouri world. Like Arikaras to the south of them, they constructed earth houses and planted corn and squash. Mandans to their north embraced them as trading partners. The Cheyenne villages were prosperous and safe—only one of them was fortified—and they pulled Saones and Minneconjous in.[78]

These were precarious footholds of enormous significance. The two Mníšoše bases were like hooks that kept the stretched-out Sioux domain anchored in the West. They formed a front line of defense deep in the interior, shielding the Sioux villages and campsites along the James, Big Sioux, and other prairie rivers from enemy incursions. They were also crucial supply depots that allowed Lakotas to operate across the length of the prairies, combing the far western streams for beaver and then carrying the pelts hundreds of miles to the east where they procured guns and iron. Before the Missouri footholds, this was a dangerous enterprise for a very specific reason: carbohydrates were scarce.

Lakotas did not sow, and while they did gather berries and edible roots, their prairie diet was low on carbohydrates and alarmingly high on protein. In the dead of winter when the body fat of bison plummeted, protein poisoning became an acute threat. When calorie intake from protein neared or exceeded 50 percent, Lakotas became exposed to nausea, fatigue, and dangerously low blood pressure and heart rate. If the situation persisted, diarrhea, loss of appetite, and elevated metabolism would set in even if they were getting enough calories. If there was no remedy, the body's ability to utilize proteins themselves could become compromised and death would follow. Before winning bases along the Mníšoše, Lakotas had to be careful not to venture too far from the Mississippi Valley where wild rice and corn were available. Afterwards, they had ecological safety nets at both ends of their domain. It was then, and only then, that the prairies truly belonged to them.[79]

SHAPESHIFTERS

Iktómi, the son of Inyan, the Rock, was once Ksa, or wisdom, the inventor of language and stories and names and games. But he was troublesome and cunning and lost his title, becoming Iktómi, a spider-trickster spirit and an imp of mischief who can speak with every living thing, fool gods with potions, manipulate humans through the strings of his web, and protect them from menace. His features are that of a spider, but he can assume any form he wishes and make himself invisible. When a human, he paints his face with red and yellow, encircles his eyes with black, and wears a deerskin coat with bright beads: a true Sioux warrior. His temperament, like his form, is supple and ambiguous. It is neither good nor evil.[80]

Iktómi is the mythological hero of the Sioux, a symbolic embodiment of their essential qualities and ideals as a people and, when they act recklessly, a warning of how not to behave. Shapeshifting involves potent spiritual power and it can be at once rewarding and dangerous, unpredictable and uplifting. Mirroring the shapeshifting trickster, Sioux were a pragmatic and adaptable people who considered extreme fluidity, even separation, both natural and necessary. That malleability sprang from the alchemy of kinship. Sioux understanding of the universe and belonging was based on clear categories: the larger Sioux community consisted of *ikčé wičháša*, "ordinary people," who formed one kindred community, takúkičhiyapi, beyond which all was danger. But these categories were also dynamic and contained the potential of inclusion. Although people outside the circle of kinship were strangers and enemies, kinship could be extended to them through *wólakȟota*, bonds of peace. The Sioux *were* allies, which was not a static condition but an active spiritual mandate to embrace others. That embrace can include anyone capable of proper behavior and thoughts. It is theoretically limitless.[81]

By the mid-eighteenth century the Sioux had shifted shape many times over. They had opened their lands and villages for real and potential allies—Sauteurs, Cheyennes, Mesquakies, Frenchmen, and many others—while contending with numerous rivals as they struggled to find a place in the rapidly changing world. They had reached out to Onontio far in the East—Sioux visits to Montreal had become almost commonplace—while expanding aggressively in the West. The boundary of the four Dakota oyátes shifted gradually west and south from Mde Wakan as bands sought safety from violence and trade along the Mississippi and Minnesota Rivers; Lakotas expanded their domain all the way to the Mníšoše in search of beaver, bison, horses, and captives. Along the way they pushed aside the Iowas, Otoes, Omahas, and Poncas, turning the prairies into a shatter belt of displacement and destruction—a western version of the mid-seventeenth-century Iroquois shatter zone in the Great Lakes. As Lakotas gradually took over the vacated lands, they turned the Očhéthi Šakówiŋ into a territorial giant that commanded nearly one hundred thousand square miles of land—the second largest Indigenous domain in North America after the rising Comanche empire in the southern Great Plains.[82]

The conquest fostered a distinct political and cultural identity. Band by band, Lakotas detached from the main Sioux body, whose interests remained fixed to the east, and made the western grasslands their home. They became the nomads and bison hunters of the prairie; they were re-creating themselves in the West. In Lakota mythology, Iktómi is a helper spirit who can convince people to scatter or come together. Knowing how and when to do that was the basic requirement of successful nomadic hunting: Iktómi was guiding the Lakotas through a precarious metamorphosis, shifting shape with them in the vast new world in the West.

The new life came with a cost. As Lakotas inched westward and became full-fledged nomads, their priorities changed, diverging from those of their eastern kin. Around midcentury that divergence threatened to deteriorate into a civil strife. The four eastern Dakota fires were desperate to have peace with Crees, whose raids were sapping their strength, but "Sioux of the Prairies"—most likely Lakotas—attacked Crees with whom they clashed over hunting rights. "Sioux of the Rivers and the Lakes were very much disturbed," a French official noted, "and did not cease to fear that the Cristinaux would take vengeance upon them for the attack." To escape retaliation, Dakotas put survival over kinship. They "desired to have an interview" with Crees, the official reported, "with whom they were resolved to ally themselves to go and make war upon the Sioux of the Prairies, who continually were attacking them, and even carrying away their women as prisoners."[83]

Splintering was a real possibility; it happened time and again in the Americas when colonial expansion forced Native peoples to disband and relocate. With their two thousand warriors, Lakotas could hold off the Crees, but Cree aggression posed an existential threat to Dakotas, who lacked the military muscle. Westward expansion was distancing Lakotas geographically and psychologically from their eastern kin.

Yet the Sioux endured as one people. Two centuries of colonialism had ushered in a new world of unforeseen perils and possibilities that extended deep into the heart of the continent. Lakotas, Dakotas, Yanktons, and Yanktonais thrusted themselves into that world, trying to make it fit their needs and ambitions. To succeed in that they, too, had to change. By the mid-eighteenth century, the Očhéthi Šakówiŋ was expanding, contracting, and loosening at its seams all at once, coming on the verge of disintegration, only to find cohesion in its collective traditions, shared history, and age-old commitment to the idea of a single kindred community. It survived because of, not in spite of, its startling malleability and ability to shift shape.

Another, equally profound, metamorphosis sustained that shapeshifting. In the early eighteenth century Lakotas experienced two technological revolutions—one brought about by horses, the other by gunpowder—when North America's two great technological frontiers converged on them. They had expanded westward toward the horse frontier carrying the gun frontier with them, and they became the first Indigenous nation on the continent to fight on horseback with substantial firepower. They now occupied a place of vast advantage. The world seemed wide open.

3

THE IMPERIAL CAULDRON

In the middle of the eighteenth century, as North America's two most powerful empires descended into protracted wars that neither would survive, the Očhéthi Šakówiŋ had become a colossal force in the deep interior. It dominated the tall-grass prairies in the heart of the continent, controlling a vast territory stretching from the upper Mississippi to the Missouri Valley. A century earlier the Sioux had been powerful but isolated people at the margins of the new Indigenous and colonial worlds that took shape on the continent's fringes; now they were a central people who commanded attention and refused to be ignored. For generations old and new worlds of North America had tended to skirt the Očhéthi Šakówiŋ. Now those worlds butted against it, denting and twisting in the process.

To the south Sioux faced a refugee world of their own making. Omahas, Poncas, Otoes, and Iowas, all previously prairie people, had fled to the middle Missouri Valley under pressure from the westering Lakota oyátes. The retreat had brought the villagers a measure of protection, but it also distanced them from colonial markets. The villagers looked south for help and forged ties with French coureurs de bois who were eager to exploit the niches that arose in the blind spots of the formal, fort-based imperial trade. By the 1720s Étienne de Bourgmont, a deserter, lived with a cadre of illegal traders among Indians in the lower Missouri Valley. This was a volatile world—most coureurs de bois were after quick profits, not time-consuming mediation—but a shared desire for trade kept it alive.

It was also a highly contested and surprisingly cosmopolitan world that challenges the notion of the American interior as an insulated periphery. The French were reported to have built two large towns among Pawnees on the Loup River west of the Missouri, which prompted the Spaniards in New Mexico to send an expedition of more than a hundred soldiers and Pueblo Indian auxiliaries to stop French advances. Pawnees and Otoes surprised the party and killed one-third of it, delivering a debilitating blow to Spanish ambitions in the heart of the continent. French trade along the lower Missouri burgeoned, emboldening Bourgmont. He was elevated to lower nobility and named the commandant of the Missouri River. To seal his achievements, he escorted in 1725 a delegation of Osage, Otoe, Missouria, and Illinois headmen and a Missouria woman to France where they saw Versailles, the Opéra, Hôtel des Invalides, and the fifteen-year-old King Louis XV. Such impulsive and grandiose ventures fueled intensive rivalries among the many Missouri River nations that sought a favored place in French schemes. Entire villages moved along the river to better position themselves toward the French, turning the Missouri Valley into an elongated geopolitical chessboard. At midcentury the jockeying for position showed no signs of abating.[1]

The new Missourian refugee world blended into the much older Missourian village world along the river's upper section. Arikaras, Mandans, and Hidatsas, too, had become exposed to Lakota attacks. They had all but yielded their old hunting grounds east of the Missouri to Lakotas who then extended their raiding operations into the great valley itself. By midcentury the village world had shrunk dramatically. Blocked from their hunting grounds east of the Missouri, Arikaras, Mandans, and Hidatsas curled inward, seeking sustenance close by. With bison hunts in the open prairies increasingly dangerous, they relied more on fish, fowl, and fruit. The villager hegemony along the great river began to crumble.[2]

To the east there was the hybrid world of Native powers, French traders, and French imperial agents. This was a world born of weakness, which, ironically, made it so resilient. Unable to dominate one another, the Indians and French had to accommodate one another in ways that were mutually beneficial. Most of the Indians on this middle ground were Algonquian speakers who had repeatedly sabotaged French attempts to reach out to Sioux, who very much wanted the French Empire to embrace them because they needed its goods and technology. By the 1750s they had succeeded, and the Sioux country became the most viable part of what survived of the battered French-Indian middle ground. The Očhéthi Šakówiŋ tied the French Empire to the West, keeping alive the dream of continental Franco hegemony. When the French and Indian War entered its third year in 1757, that dream seemed more attainable than ever. A series of brilliant, unexpected victories against the British promised a future belonging to the French and their Native allies.[3]

This configuration—the expanding Očhéthi Šakówiŋ at the center, forcing others to fit to its form—seemed entrenched at midcentury. The horse-mounted, gun-using Lakotas were poised to become a domineering military power in the deep interior, and they had their Dakota relatives and French markets behind them. Indeed, just as Lakotas encroached upon the village world along the Missouri, the French and their Native allies were chasing the British out from the Ohio Country. Nearly a thousand miles separated the two war zones, intimating the new coordinates of power in North America. The future seemed to belong to the French Empire that was fastened far in the West by the ascendant Lakotas.

THE GREAT MYSTERY WAS CRAZY

North American imperial history was in many ways typical. Across the globe, colonial empires built posts and forts, hoarded trading privileges, dispossessed and co-opted Natives, and fought one other, often through aboriginal proxies. But North America's imperial dynamics were particularly volatile. In the morning of September 6, 1760, in the final hours of the French and Indian War, General Jeffrey Amherst, commander in chief of the British forces in North America, received Louis-Antoine de Bougainville, a French emissary, in his headquarters on the heights around the Island of Montreal. Amid rumors that a peace to end the global war between sprawling British- and French-led alliances was at hand in Europe, Bougainville proposed an armistice. The French position in North America had become hopeless. Three years of stunning victories had turned into three years of demoralizing losses, and now three British armies besieged Montreal, where four thousand French troops, more than half of them sick, waited helplessly. Sitting low in the river, the city was defenseless against British shelling. The North American conflict was effectively over—with the fall of Montreal, the French would be cut off from their Indian allies in the interior, their true power base—and the question was merely how many more French soldiers would have to die. Amherst responded, contemptuously, that he had come for Canada and would not "take anything less." Governor Pierre de Rigaud de Vaudreuil accepted his terms. The next day the French dominion in North America was officially terminated.[4]

Around the same time two Oglala bands approached one of the Arikara villages in the upper Missouri Valley, pleading to be pitied. They begged for corn and asked to be taken in. Arikaras made peace with them and allowed them to settle near their earth-lodge village on the river's eastern bank. Oglalas married into Arikara families and under their tutelage started to plant crops.[5]

The two events were related. The French and Sioux had expanded into the West in tandem, and the disintegration of the French Empire left the Sioux reeling. The troubles had begun with the outbreak of the French and Indian War. Joseph Marin left the Sioux country during the first year of the war, and the rest of the French traders followed soon after. By 1759 the Royal Navy had banished the French fleet from the North Atlantic, crippling France's ability to supply its Indian allies, and when Vaudreuil surrendered in Montreal, most Sioux had already been several years without reliable access to powder, ammunition, and guns. It may have thus been out of desperation that some Oglala bands sought entry among Arikaras. Lacking munitions, they could not impose their will on the villagers, but they desperately needed their produce to close the nomads' chronic carbohydrate gap. They embraced a radical transformation to survive in the West.[6]

There was nothing unusual about Lakotas forming close ties and moving to live with former enemies: the Očhéthi Šakówiŋ transmuted constantly to include and exclude foreign peoples. The Oglala-Arikara bond, however, was different. Arikaras had been enemies for generations and injuries had hardened into hatreds. A number of Oglalas may have seen the submission to Arikara patronage as shameful and a betrayal. When fighting later broke out between Arikaras and Oglalas, some Oglalas fought their relatives who had stayed with Arikaras. Oglala winter counts record how a civil strife erupted in 1763 and lasted for two years. These were winters when "They who talk alike fought each other." A camp circle dominates the top of each pictograph and below them stands a man with an arrow sticking out from his back.[7]

Oglalas reunited soon, but they had become manifestly weakened. They abandoned the village experiment, which closed off an entry point into the Missouri world and its resources. Appeasement gave way to violence. Oglalas and other Lakotas staged raids into the Arikara villages, but they absorbed more damage than they inflicted. Arikaras had fortified their villages with trenches and palisades, and they fought with guns, killing from relative safety. Suddenly Lakotas were stuck, their expansionist momentum expended, the sheltering Mníšoše just beyond their grasp. They could not enter the valley, but they could not retreat either. Larger bison herds had drawn them to the west, and pulling back would have meant moving toward scarcity. Retreat to the east would have also meant moving into a commercial void, for the French and Indian War had left the interior trade in shambles.[8]

In 1763 a British expedition assigned to take possession of the French forts in the western Great Lakes received a Dakota delegation at Fort de la Baye des Puants—soon to be renamed Fort Edward Augustus—at Green Bay. Several Indian delegations had already visited the fort, eager to secure the munificence of the new father, King George, but Dakotas left the deepest impression. They were, Lieutenant James Gorrell wrote, "certainly the greatest nation of Indians ever yet found." "They can shoot the wildest and largest beasts in the woods, at seventy or one hundred yards distance," and even their dances were extraordinary, a model to other nations. They supposedly had thirty thousand warriors and, the lieutenant mused, kept "regular guards in their chief town or metropolis, relieving once in twenty-four hours, and are always alert": a seat of a wilderness empire. It was a fabrication to conceal a profound weakness. Desperate for British goods, Dakotas portrayed themselves as a disciplined military behemoth capable of guaranteeing the safety of British traders in the west. If their enemies "wished to obstruct the passage of traders coming up," they boasted, the British should "send them a belt, and they would come and cut them off from the face of the earth, as all Indians were their slaves or dogs."[9]

Dakotas had awed the impressionable lieutenant, but it was to no avail. At the time Dakotas were cajoling the British at Green Bay, the interior had already descended into yet another war. The Treaty of Paris in February 1763 had outraged the Great Lakes Indians by handing their lands over to Britain without any consultation. France had lost all its North American possessions and Spain, having joined the war late as France's ally, ceded Florida to Britain, but its loss was more than compensated by secret treaty a year earlier which gave it Louisiana and New Orleans. A few strokes of a pen had divided the continent into British and Spanish halves separated by the Mississippi, leaving the eastern Indians to negotiate their rights and needs with an empire that cared little about either. Insulted and exposed, Odawa war chief Pontiac and other Native leaders led thousands of warriors into a rebellion that swept across the interior from the Susquehanna to the Mississippi. Indian trade ground to a near halt, and Fort Edward Augustus was abandoned.[10]

Far in the West Lakotas grappled with the fallout. They could no longer expect guns from their Dakota relatives who had no traders among them and struggled to fend off Sauteurs who seemed determined to "swallow them all up." Cheyennes along the Missouri were their only source of trade, and it was not enough. Cheyennes traded some corn and horses but had no guns to sell, and they were struggling to maintain a viable farming economy in their Missouri niche amid the escalating violence. Packed against an Arikara-Mandan wall, Lakotas were unable to either advance or retreat and were absorbing mounting losses.[11]

The West was turning into a dead end for Lakotas. The late 1760s emerge as a dark period in their winter counts: mounted, gun-wielding enemies storming their camps; women joining men in fighting enemies; Lakota warriors defecating next to their lodges, bows in their hands, too afraid of venturing out for fear of enemy attacks. It was a low point. "The great mystery was crazy," declares an Oglala winter count for 1770–71.[12]

THEY BURNT THE MANDANS OUT

In 1771 Oglalas and Yanktonais attacked a Mandan village near Apple Creek, some two hundred miles north of the regular Oglala camping grounds. "They burnt the Mandans out," notes the pithy Oglala account. "A Big Battle took place," echoes the Yankton one. An Oglala contingent had circumvented the Arikara barrier, connecting with their Yanktonai kin in the north to strike the unsuspecting Mandans. There was little glory in it. Betraying their weakness and apprehension, the Oglala-Yanktonai party burned down the village rather than seeking military honors by facing Mandans on a battlefield. It was a momentous victory nonetheless, and Oglalas and Yanktonais made the most of it. They captured many women and children and forced Mandans to retreat upriver. Yanktonais settled in the area, built semi-subterranean earth lodges, and began growing crops.[13]

The sacking of that Mandan village was a turning point that marked the beginning of a long Lakota ascendancy along the river. The upper Missouri villages began to fall with shocking rapidity. While their Yanktonai allies carved out a riverine foothold in the north, Sicangus and Oglalas raided Arikaras, Pawnees, Otoes, and Poncas in the south. Some Sicangu and Oglala oyátes crossed the Missouri near the White River, opening a base for attacks from the villagers' rear. Not even the most heavily fortified villages were safe. An Arikara village sitting on a high terrace on the east bank of the Missouri became a scene of carnage. Arikaras fought Lakotas to their lodge doors, choosing to die in their homes. The attackers left seventy-one corpses, some of them scalped, some decapitated, and some mutilated, in plain sight. Hundreds more died and disintegrated as burning earth lodges collapsed into graves.[14]

The renewed Lakota onslaught was partly driven by hunger. In the early 1770s a severe drought gripped the North American interior. Bison herds withered along with the grass, forcing Lakotas to subsist on drowned buffalo carcasses floating down the Missouri. Under such conditions, Missouri villagers' caches of dried corn, squash, and seeds became irresistible targets, encouraging war parties to test their defenses. When the dry spell passed, the raids continued, now fueled by sheer capacity, for the Lakotas were on the verge of emerging as a formidable horse and gun power, capable of mobilizing large numbers of mounted warriors with muskets.[15]

The accumulation of horses happened gradually through persistent raiding, breeding, and careful winter care. Winters could take a heavy toll on horses, and Lakotas had to devote considerable time and energy in pasturing, sheltering, and treating their mounts. Horses appear in several Lakota winter counts in the 1770s, indicating intensifying equestrianism. Families began to compete for the largest and best herds. One Oglala band with strong horses experienced this bluntly when some of their kin became envious and killed several of its horses. Lakotas may have not yet been able to put all their people on horseback, the critical threshold of mounted nomadism, but they were mastering the art of cavalry. They already possessed the necessary numbers to shape the world to their needs; now they accrued the necessary technology to capitalize on their demographic might.[16]

What made the equestrian takeoff so consequential was that it coincided with the revival of the gun traffic. The long slump of the interior trade passed in the late 1760s when British officials, alarmed by the virulence of Pontiac's War, adopted the French system of diplomacy and gifts. By 1767 free trade was restored in the West. British traders may have lacked French traders' diplomatic acumen, but they lacked none of their entrepreneurial flair. Independent traders from Montreal, New England, and elsewhere pushed in growing numbers to the Great Lakes and the Mississippi Valley, and by the early 1770s the fur trade had largely recovered.[17]

When Peter Pond, an independent trader from Connecticut, carried goods into the Minnesota Valley in 1773, he found the Dakota trade in full, exhilarating swing. He conducted brisk trade in beaver, otter, raccoon, wolf, and deer skins as well as in "Drid & Grean Meet," but another trader nearby had traded with Dakotas for several years and was well liked among them. "I perseaved," Pond noted in his idiosyncratic phonetic style, "that he Seamd to have a Prefrans & Got more trade than myself." The rival explained that Pond "had not Hit on ye Rite Eidea": a successful trader left needles and other small items "on the Counter" for the Indians to steal—his version of gift giving. Pond tried it and "found it to Prove well."

When he traveled east in the summer to restock at Fort Michilimackinac, he learned of recent hostilities between Dakotas and Sauteurs. British agents assigned him to deliver three wampum belts to Dakotas and escort them to a peace council at Michilimackinac, while other traders would do the same with Sauteurs. Dakota and Sauteur delegations united and proceeded together to the east, a startling procession that "excited the Cureosatay of Everay Nation South of the Lake of the Woods." They all wanted peace, Pond realized, so that trade could flow freely. At Michilimackinac the Dakota and Sauteur envoys made peace and ended a century-long on-and-off-again war. They agreed to the Mississippi as a boundary line.[18]

Dakotas received traders from the south as well. In early 1764 a group of French colonists established a settlement near the Mississippi-Missouri junction and named it after Saint Louis, the patron saint of Louis XV, who had just handed over the site, along with the rest of the French North America, to Spain. News traveled slowly across the oceans, and the French did not learn until months later just how outmoded the name was. They kept it nonetheless and went on with their business, which was the fur trade. Dominated by French merchant families,

St. Louis quickly emerged as the focal point of the interior trade, its commercial tentacles reaching up the Mississippi and Missouri Valleys. Downriver, French bourgeois also dominated New Orleans. The first Spanish governor did not arrive until 1766 and was ousted by the city's merchant elite after two years. All the while and throughout the Spanish era, French traders continued to ascend the Mississippi from St. Louis, competing for trading privileges with Dakotas and other prominent trappers. Boats with thirty-six pairs of oars brought in manufactures, wine, cheese, and ham for trade fairs.[19]

What belonged to Dakotas belonged to Lakotas. Goods did not flow automatically from east to west, but familial ideals of sharing obliged Sioux people to take care of each other's needs. What Lakotas needed was munitions. The great pan-Sioux trade fairs, now held along the Minnesota rather than the Mississippi, became a vehicle for moving guns to the west, where Lakotas carried them into a war over the Missouri Valley. In exchange, Lakotas supplied their eastern kin with mounts. By the mid-1770s Yanktons had a "Grate Number of Horses," which allowed them to become skillful mounted hunters who could "Kill as Much Meat as thay Please."[20]

1776

The Lakota resurgence was so forceful that it propelled several bands into unfamiliar lands far beyond the Mníšoše. These Lakotas were Indigenous explorers who pushed toward the elusive horizon, drawn by legends of mythical places and momentous events in distant lands. But the lands they entered were not empty, and they clashed with the formidable Pawnees in the Platte River country and with the Crows, powerful horse people, near the Rocky Mountain foothills, triggering enmities that would last for generations.

At some point during these long-range ventures Lakotas came to an elevation that emerged from the green flat like an anomaly, black and glowing. The singular mountain uplift was covered with ponderosa pine whose needles sparkled black from a distance. It was crowned with a series of rugged granite towers that rose high above the sea of grass below. At the foot of the rocky mass deep subterranean caverns seemed to reach down to the very core of the earth. There was nothing ordinary about the place, and Lakotas considered it a world of transcendence, a being in its own right. It was the center of the world, the first place created on earth and the place where the bison emerged from a cave, small as ants, sucking the breath of life and inflating with each gasp. It was there that Iktómi invited the first humans from an underground village onto the earth's surface and saw them grow into the Seven Council Fires. And it was there, along the Racetrack, a shallow depression of reddish sandstone and shale that circles the Black

Hills, where two-leggeds raced against four-leggeds and won, thus securing for themselves everlasting prosperity.[21]

In 1879 American Horse, an Oglala elder, recited his people's winter count to a U.S. Army officer, William Corbusier. The count pinpointed the Lakota discovery—or rediscovery—of Pahá Sápa, the Black Hills, "the heart of everything that is," in 1776. This was the first entry of the winter count, marking the beginning of history for American Horse's people and, symbolically, for all Lakota people.

This version of Lakota history placed Lakotas and the United States on similar historical trajectories: in 1776, according to American Horse, not one but two nations had been born in North America, both destined for greatness, discoveries of new lands, and, perhaps, respectful coexistence. In 1879 the history of the Lakota-U.S. relations seemed anything but respectful. American Horse had lived through the U.S. invasion of the Lakota lands, the loss of the Black Hills, and the killing of Crazy Horse, but perhaps parallel origins could prefigure parallel futures.[22]

Historical similarities were palpable from the outset. The American Revolutionary War was transformative for both Americans and Sioux. The sprawling war disrupted Atlantic trade, leaving both to scramble for resources. Americans alleviated their supply problems in 1778 when France recognized the United States as a sovereign nation, declared war on Britain, and offered loans and soldiers. Sioux, meanwhile, were being cajoled by British agents who were eager to recruit the interior's dominant power to their side and keep them from allying with the Spaniards who supported the Patriots. The thriving Sioux-British trade in the prewar years transformed almost seamlessly into military cooperation.

Wabasha, the Mdewakanton chief who had visited the governor of New France in Montreal almost three decades earlier, became a key mediator. In his youth he had confronted the French in Montreal; now the British welcomed the senior statesman, "a prince of an Indian" with "uncommon abilities" who seemed to preside over some kind of Indigenous empire. In the spring of 1776 Wabasha traveled east with a hundreds-strong multinational Native force to join the British in the liberation of Montreal from Patriot troops. They arrived too late—the Continental Army had already retreated, wrecked by smallpox—but Wabasha proceeded to Quebec, where Governor Guy Carleton received him. Wabasha offered the governor the calumet and the services of fifteen thousand warriors from "the most distant of your children," and Carleton hosted the chief at a state dinner, probably in the imposing Château Saint Louis. Before leaving Quebec, Wabasha was taken aboard HMS *Isis*, a fifty-gun man-of-war, where he received an eight-gun salute.[23]

British agents saw in the Sioux an ally who could deliver interior Indians behind Britain, and Sioux saw in the British an ally who could deliver guns for a fight against common enemies. Wabasha received a general's commission from his hosts and in 1780 brought two hundred Sioux warriors to join a thousand-strong British-Indian force on an attack on the Spanish garrison at St. Louis. The campaign failed, delivering a serious blow to the British war effort in the West, but the alliance yielded Sioux what they needed most: guns, lead, and powder continued to flow in, sustaining their power in the interior.

Wabasha worked tirelessly to preserve that flow. He brought warriors to protect a British supply depot at Prairie du Chien near the Wisconsin-Mississippi confluence and conspired with British agents. "One cannot imagine the expenses which the English are incurring and the exorbitant amounts of merchandise which are continually consumed among the Indian tribes, in order to attract them to their side," one Spanish official agonized. "Le Feuille" — Wabasha — "the great chief of the Sioux, has boasted of taking St. Louis," fretted another. "This party will come, I believe, by the Mississippi." Wabasha's expansive diplomacy kept the Spaniards agitated, and his reward for that was a privileged position in British trade, which recovered quickly as the Revolutionary War began to abate. Traders flocked into Sioux lands, and many Sioux families married their daughters to British husbands, thus helping their communities secure firm trading privileges through kinship ties. Some British traders pushed up the Des Moines River deep into the Sioux country, possibly connecting with Lakotas.[24]

WARS, PATHOGENS, AND WORLDS REMADE

Even as the British were shifting on Sioux orbit through marriages and wóla-khota, a quieter but far more powerful agent had entered the scene, blindly altering power dynamics across the continent. The smallpox epidemic began in late 1775 in Quebec and spread down the eastern seaboard with the peripatetic British and Patriot armies. The epidemic's most significant intrusion into the war came in 1781, when it caught up with the loyalist African Americans who had joined the British Army in a march across the South. In September General Charles Cornwallis was besieged in Yorktown, his black allies dying in masses and his soldiers succumbing to malaria. When Cornwallis surrendered, his army had nearly melted away under the double pathogenic assault. The first British Empire had come to an end.[25]

While smallpox was thriving in the war-ravaged East, it found another opening some fifteen hundred miles to the west. This epidemic originated in Mexico City in August 1779 and moved from there to New Orleans, San Antonio, and Santa Fe by December 1780. There trade became the principal vehicle for transmis-

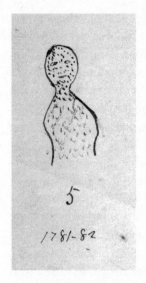

15. Cloud Shield winter count, 1781–82 (detail). "Many people died of smallpox," reads the caption for this Oglala winter count. The dots mark smallpox pustules that clustered in parts of the body where they caused most pain: face, neck, palms, soles of the feet, and back. Courtesy of National Anthropological Archives, Smithsonian Institution (NAA INV 08746902, detail).

sion. Comanches, who dominated the lands amid those colonial capitals, were infected and seem to have passed on the pestilence to their trading partners, some of whom transmitted it into the Missouri Valley. Carried by equestrian Indians, the malady could travel far during its long incubation period, and a trading expedition may have reached the Missouri with the virus before succumbing to it.[26]

Dying began in 1781—just as the British Army was wasting away at Yorktown—among Arikaras and Mandans. Lakotas contracted the disease around the same time, possibly while raiding. Oglala and Sicangu winter counts record two successive years of smallpox. They depict human figures in agony, their faces and torsos covered with red spots, documenting the infection's aggressive spread from small blood vessels in the mouth and throat across the body until sharply raised, pus-filled blisters covered the skin; they capture the ineffectiveness of traditional healings methods in the face of an alien organism. There is no way of knowing how many died. Lakotas' migratory way of life and dispersal into small hunting bands gave them a measure of protection against the pestilence, but cold and erratic weather around the outbreak must have compromised their ability to fight off the virus.[27]

While the epidemic ravaged Lakotas, it nearly ruined the villagers. The virus found in the crowded villages an auspicious setting to spread. Arikaras may have lost more than three-fourths of their people, and they abandoned all but seven of their thirty-two villages. Mandan losses were similarly catastrophic. Their eight villages were reduced to two, and their thirteen clans became seven. The Hidatsa population was cut by half. An ancient political geography collapsed in a matter of months as the combined villager population of tens of thousands was reduced to roughly eight thousand. Thick clusters of Arikara, Mandan, and Hidatsa villages melted into thinly sprinkled nodes; permanent settlements no longer governed the riverscape. Cheyennes, too, were afflicted. Most of them abandoned their Missouri villages, making an abrupt and uncertain leap to a nomadic existence in the open plains to the west. Only one band, the Masikotas, stayed along the Missouri, attaching themselves to Lakotas.[28]

Though also weakened by the pox, Lakotas were able to capitalize on the wreckage, pushing into the vacated lands. Some forty years later a Mandan elder would remember how Lakotas "were not very dangerous" before the pox, capturing the enormity of the onslaught that followed it. Pressed by Lakotas, the remaining Arikara villages huddled into a marginal section of the river basin where "dryness and barrenness does not supply animals with their regular pasturage." North of Arikaras, Mandans abandoned their remaining villages in their ancestral lands near the Heart River and moved upriver to a place that became known as the Painted Woods. Later explorers would find a shatter zone haunted by the remains of what had been a bustling village world: one "Old Indian Village" after another, all destroyed by "the Soux and Small Pox." Trying to find safety in numbers, Mandans approached Arikaras with whom they had had a tortuous and often violent relationship, and the two groups mounted a joint attack against Oglalas. It ended badly. Oglalas drove them back, killed twenty-five, and captured a boy who had joined the war party, possibly as a guard.[29]

Lakotas, by virtue of simply having lost fewer people than their rivals, were now ascendant. A long stretch of the Mníšoše north of the Big Bend belonged to them. They had become "the dominating nation" on the east bank of the Missouri, marking the culmination of a sustained westward thrust. But the entrenchment in the Mníšoše also fixed Lakota imaginations on what lay beyond. The Missouri watershed was a transition zone where the pervasive flatness of the East gave way to a distinctly varied landscape of the West. Mandans preferred the West so much that they believed that the east bank was some kind of failure in conception. Ohmahank-Numakshi, the lord of life, had shared the work of sculpting the landscape with the first man, who was given the responsibility of the east side. The result was underwhelming: "All is level, so that it will be impossible to surprise buffaloes or deer, and approach them unperceived. Men will not be able to live there. They will see each other in the plain at too great a distance, and will be unable to avoid each other, consequently they will destroy each other," the lord of life complained. "See here," he said of the west side, "I have made springs and streams in sufficient abundance, and hills and valleys, and added all kinds of animals and fine wood; here men will be able to live by the chase, and feed on the flesh of those animals."[30]

It was not before long that Lakota women pitched tipis on the west bank, carving out first footholds in what would soon become known as the American West.[31]

THEY KILLED ALL

The Mníšoše was home, but it was also a base for further expansion. The decade following the smallpox outbreak saw Lakotas waging a multifront raiding war along the valley. They struck Arikaras, Mandans, and Hidatsas to the north and Omahas and Pawnees to the south, seeking horses, corn, captives, and vengeance. The depleted villagers fought back desperately, sometimes relying on shock tactics. Pawnees captured the frozen body of a Sicangu warrior named Skinned Penis and carried it to their village where they played haka stick game with it. The event was recorded in several Lakota winter counts, capturing the virulent anger that demanded retribution. One by one, Lakotas forced their rivals to pull back. Having lost huge numbers to smallpox, Assiniboines and Crees all but gave up their efforts to seize Lakota hunting grounds and retreated north to recover. Sicangus remember 1781–82 as "Came and attacked on horseback the last time winter." It may refer to any number of people: Arikaras, Mandans, Hidatsas, Assiniboines, or Crees.[32]

Lakotas also clashed with their old Cheyenne allies who had given them shelter on the Sheyenne River and later on the Missouri. Missouri villagers remembered the collapse of the alliance as a major event that marked the ascendancy of nomads on both sides of the valley. Lakotas had turned against Masikota Cheyennes, perhaps rejecting them as rivals over commerce and limited riverine resources. One observer noted how Lakotas, "always wandering, left little for capture to the enemy, who often knew not where to find them, and the Chayennes, settled there, were every day exposed, in spite of their superior courage, to some particular catastrophe." Forced to choose between village life and survival, the Masikotas "abandoned agriculture and their hearths and became a nomadic people." But even the withdrawal from the Missouri did not bring respite; chased by Lakotas, the Masikotas retreated toward the Black Hills. As Lakotas chased Cheyennes to the west, they also collided with Crows whose homelands encompassed the northeastern Rocky Mountains and the grasslands west of the Black Hills.[33]

Lakotas were venturing deeper into the western short-grass plains, but it was the Mníšoše that absorbed their ambitions. Arikaras and Mandans tried to put distance between themselves and Lakotas, but Sicangus and Oglalas closed in, extending their domain northward one camping and pasturing ground at a time. This was territorial warfare stemming from the elemental need to secure foraging grounds for sustenance. In 1787–88, returning from a failed horse raid in the west, Oglalas joined with Yanktonais to attack a Mandan village near the Painted Woods and reportedly killed all. The attack took place during an intense cold spell and famine that had reduced Lakotas to eating roots. Several counts noted that the winters were so harsh that crows died in droves. They "froze in the air and dropped dead near the lodges."[34]

By around 1790, pressured by Sicangus and Oglalas, Arikaras had retreated into two consolidated villages near the Cheyenne River. It was a painful diaspora. Arikaras had to cram a large and decentralized political organization into a tiny pocket, and they struggled. "This nation, formerly so numerous," one trader observed, "is reduced to about five hundred fighting men" and was afflicted by "the lack of agreement" among their leaders. As existing kinship networks and lines of authority unraveled, chiefs began fighting over followers, deepening the crisis. Dispossessed and destabilized, Missouri villagers no longer posed an immediate threat to Lakotas who recalibrated their foreign policy accordingly.[35]

A COMMONWEALTH OF COTTONWOOD

The man walked into the silty brown water and swam toward the approaching head in the distance. He met him in midstream, stopped, and shook his hand. There, in the middle of the Missouri, Lakotas and Mandans watching the ceremony from opposite banks, the two men made peace.

Around that same time, the early 1790s, Oglalas made peace also with Omahas, and the following winter saw some Lakota bands moving their tipis into an Arikara village to winter there. These were strange years in other ways as well. Oglalas carried a U.S. flag among all the neighboring tribes and saw a white woman, clearly a curiosity: a party of American traders traveling with a woman had made its way among Lakotas and invited them to a trade fair on the Minnesota. Just as their Dakota relatives had quickly grasped commercial openings in the East, so too were Lakotas now seizing commercial opportunities in the West. If they brought peace to the upper Missouri Valley, trade might flourish, bringing prosperity and safety.[36]

The nascent conciliation was an extraordinary opportunity for the long-suffering Missouri villagers. Sometime soon after the midstream encounter, Mandans at the Painted Woods sent a calumet pipe among all the Indians of the northern Great Plains, allies and enemies alike, inviting them to "a great peace council" in their village. It was an audacious bid to reclaim their long-standing primacy in a rapidly changing world and it seemed to work. About eighty years later Mandan chief Running Face told the trapper Joseph Henry Taylor of a great gathering of peoples: "From the far north came the frost eared Assinaboines and their tandem trains of dogs; from the west came the black leg Anahaways, well dressed, haughty and silent. From the northwest came the plumed and painted Gros Ventres, and with them as guests rode the gaily dressed Crows, with suspicious hearts and prying eyes. And from the south came up the Yanktoney with their cold stare and silent tongue, riding bands of stolen horses."[37]

Even the Sissetons from the distant east had sent a delegation. Mandans opened their village to the mixed assembly. They had had a good harvest and they had a lot to offer: "pumpkins, squashes, melons and corn were bountiful—the season of the tinted leaves had brought them clear balmy days, so that this grand comingling of these northern nations was but a continuous spread of gormandizing feasts"—a banquet for nomads.[38]

Yet grievances and suspicions ran deep. The fragile accommodation collapsed when a young Yanktonai man approached the daughter of a Mandan chief. "She was winsome and beautiful," Taylor wrote, he "a stranger and an enemy,—one who had, perhaps, embued his hands in the blood of their murdered relatives." Mandan men failed to separate the couple, and their exasperated chief ordered the Yanktonai killed. Enraged Yanktonais shot the chief's daughter and fled. But they were not gone. "With the light of morning came war—the sack of camps and villages ... the burning of forests of timber and the wide ranges of dry grass upon the plains." There is a winter account of Lakotas attacking a village of fifty-eight lodges and killing everyone in it.[39]

The carnage disheartened the Mandans. They fled upriver, pushing north until they reached the three large Hidatsa villages at the mouth of the Knife River. Hidatsas took pity on them and allowed them to build villages nearby. A few years later, fearing a Lakota attack, Arikaras abandoned their two Cheyenne River villages. One group sought refuge in the west and the other fled to the north into the Mandan country, which emerged as the new center of a shriveled upper Missouri village world.[40]

Nearly a two-hundred-mile expanse of the Mníšoše now lay vacant ahead of Lakotas. They pushed in, seizing an enormous reservoir of water, grass, game, timber, and shelter. Their greatest prize were the groves of grand and sturdy cottonwoods lining the valley and its western tributaries in lush clusters, offering a host of blessings: protection against frigid winds and storms, fuel for cooking and warmth, and nourishing bark to carry horses through the nutritional crunches when grass lay frozen or dead dry. Soon Lakota villages stretched out along the Mníšoše and its western feeders—a sprawling, expanding commonwealth of cottonwood. It was the single most important expansion in the history of the Očhéthi Šakówiŋ. This was the moment when the long struggle to amass horses, guns, and military power translated into an unqualified and reassuring success. Lakota history had entered a new phase, a decades-long era when the Mníšoše was the center of their world.

Lakotas had carved out a safe and bountiful domain along a life-giving river in a long and often brutal war, but they were not some blind conquering machine bent on subjugation and annihilation. They were capable of shifting from violence and war to diplomacy and peace fluidly and swiftly. The Arikara-Mandan alliance in the north unraveled soon, and Arikaras approached Lakotas, who accepted the overture. The two united against common rivals—Mandans, Hidatsas, Assiniboines, and Crees—who variously joined forces against them. There were stories of a two-thousand-strong Lakota-Arikara army that suffered a devastating loss against Mandans and Hidatsas who fought on horseback, felling pedestrian Lakota and Arikara warriors with arrows and bullets and taking many captives. After the battle Arikaras moved back downstream and built three fortified villages near the confluence of the Grand River. Soon two to three thousand Arikaras lived there, surrounded by extensive fields of corn, beans, and squash.[41]

Those villages were a key to Arikaras' reentry downriver. Their crops of corn, beans, and squash—the celebrated three sisters—provided Lakotas with a reliable source of carbohydrates and essential vitamins and amino acids. The Arikara villages became crucial supply depots for Lakotas who often camped near them, especially during late summer and early fall when green corn, a sweet and scarce delicacy, and ripe corn, the bulk produce, were available. A day's canoe trip downriver, on what was now Lakota territory, stood the ruins of old Arikara villages, a silent reminder of the Lakota ascendancy over the river world. And two days' horse ride upriver on the east bank stood the new tipi villages of Saones, the vanguard of that ascendancy.[42]

Lakotas loomed over Arikaras. The two were said to have the "same character and attitudes," but it was not a relationship of equals. Lakotas, one observer noted, "visit them and make great promises to live in harmony and friendship with them in order to smoke their tobacco, eat their corn, freely hunt buffalo and beaver on their lands in the autumn and winter, and in the spring they withdraw to the other bank of the river from where they usually return to kill them or to steal their horses." It was a revealing but also a superficial assessment of a relationship that stretched both people to their limits. Arikaras would not reduce their villages to mere resource depots for Lakotas who in turn would not include Arikaras into their circle of kinship through wólakȟota. The two nations were neither allies nor exactly enemies.[43]

Lakotas knew how to exploit such ambiguities. The prosperous Saone domain

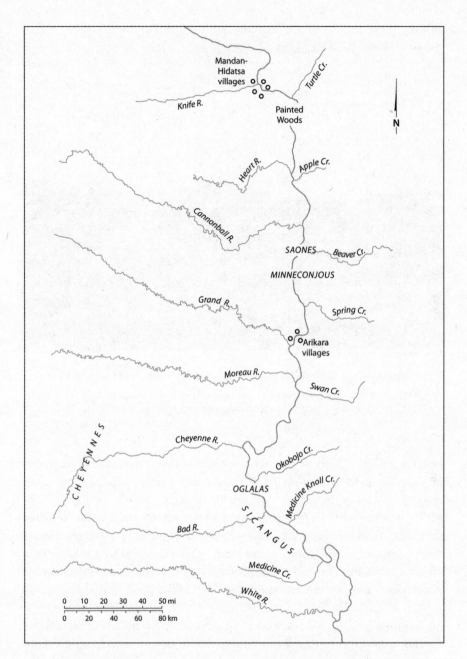

16. The Missouri Valley, c. 1802. At this time many Lakota bands probably camped on both banks of the Missouri and along its many tributaries. Map by Bill Nelson.

17. *Arikara Village of Earth-Covered Lodges, 1600 Miles above St Louis*, by George Catlin, 1832. The Arikara villages occupied the Missouri-Grand junction for three decades. Courtesy of Smithsonian American Art Museum, © Photo Scala, Florence.

near the Arikara villages drew other Lakotas who were attracted to its proximity to a carbohydrate cornucopia. Most Lakota oyátes were in the process of becoming specialized hunter-trappers, and they needed dependable supplies of garden produce to do so. No other source in the interior was more secure than the politically reduced and yet economically still robust Arikara villages. Saones' old Minneconjou allies came, as did many others, people who would become known as Sans Arc, Two Kettle, and Sihasapa Lakotas, settling along the Mníšoše under Saone auspices and within easy reach of Arikaras.[44]

On the banks of the Mníšoše Lakotas were coalescing as a nation, increasingly prosperous, confident, and capable of coordinated collective action. It is therefore not a coincidence that it was there and then that an outsider first learned about a remarkable ceremony. "As soon as this heavenly body appears on the horizon, the dance begins," he wrote. "The young men and women, separated on either side of the dance ground, holding the ceremonial calumets in their hands, dance to the sound of the drum and rattles. . . . They dance with their hands raised toward the sun, and they follow it in the same way as this heavenly body rises above the horizon." They danced from sunrise to sunset, stopping only briefly to eat and smoke, always offering "the first morsels of their food and the first pipefuls of tobacco" to the sun. "At the conclusion of these dances, the goods brought as offerings to the sun are distributed to the people they know to have the greatest need of them." A ceremony of gratitude, humility, and solidarity, this was *Wiwáŋyaŋg Wačhípi*, the Sun Dance.[45]

UPRIVER TRADE

While Lakotas were entrenching themselves in the upper Missouri Valley, almost a thousand miles downriver another power center was also gearing up for expansion. For decades St. Louis had functioned essentially as a frontier trading outpost, blocking British and then American encroachments into the Trans-Mississippi West, which, by the 1763 Treaty of Paris, belonged to Spain. French in language, customs, and mood, the city was a thriving relic of the co-operative French-Indian policy that survived in the *moeurs* and sensibilities of the Frenchmen and Frenchwomen who had stayed put as Spanish subjects. St. Louis merchants had developed a brisk trade with the nearby Indians who lived along the Missouri's east-west running lower section. Much of that commerce focused on—and stopped at—the villages of the formidable Osages who reaped great profits by channeling manufactured goods among the more distant groups in the western plains. Some St. Louis traders pushed past the Osage bastion among Kansas, Omahas, Pawnees, and Otoes, but few managed to venture farther. No one had ascended the Missouri beyond the mouth of the Big Sioux, reported the governor of Louisiana in 1785.[46]

By 1790 the lower Missouri Valley had become saturated with St. Louis traders who began looking upriver for untapped markets and fur domains. The middling traders also felt stymied by the growing power of the Chouteaus, the leading St. Louis dynasty that dominated the lucrative Osage trade. These commercial impulses converged with the geopolitical ambitions of Spanish officials who agonized over imperial challenges from the north. British traders from Canada—"much more enterprising than those of the Illinois and of Louisiana"— had established themselves among Mandans, deflecting the upper Missouri fur trade north from its customary southbound flow. St. Louis merchants' profit margins dropped from up to 300 percent in the 1770s to 25. Desperate to secure the lucrative trade and block the British challenges to Spanish sovereignty, St. Louis officials began granting licenses to trade in the far reaches of the Missouri. There, they calculated, the British would be contained. And there, they imagined, would be a water route to the Pacific Coast, the key to an everlasting Spanish Empire in the heart of North America.[47]

It was not to be. The Franco-Spanish traders who secured licenses were about to crash into a Lakota barrier they did not know existed. Spanish exploration of the interior had lapsed during the sprawling colonial wars of the 1770s and 1780s, and Lakotas had rearranged the geopolitics of the upper Missouri country without the colonists learning much about it. In 1793 an enterprising trader, Jacques d'Eglise, embarked upriver to visit Mandans, only to be stopped three hundred miles from his destination by Lakotas and Arikaras, who confiscated most of his goods and "kept him from making profit." D'Eglise's interception was more than thievery; it was policy. St. Louis traders were determined to push far upriver to maximize their client base and drive out British rivals, and their main target was the Hidatsa and Mandan villages, which thus far marked the outer edge of British activities. Lakotas, however, were determined to prevent the traders from moving past them. They wanted to cut off their rivals and reserve the bulk of the critical goods—guns, powder, lead—for themselves.[48]

These conflicting ambitions permeated the Missouri River trade with chronic tension: the Indians were constantly maneuvering into position in the elongated trade chain, trying to hoard and block the flow of goods, whereas the St. Louis traders were bent on pushing as far upriver as possible. In this rivalry over position and access, Lakotas held a distinctive advantage: they were nomads. Mandans and their Hidatsa allies had to wait in their villages for the traders to come, whereas Lakotas could move up and down the valley at will, camping wherever needed to encounter trade convoys. Spanish officials and St. Louis merchants envisioned the Missouri as an ordered commercial corridor where the sites, rates, and practices of exchange were predictable and where all-water transportation guaranteed free movement of people and goods deep into the interior. Before long, the governor of Louisiana envisioned, "a line of forts will be established on the Missouri which will be extended to the South Sea"—the Pacific. Lakotas' vision was more focused and more attainable. They sought to puncture the Missouri trade corridor at strategic points and divert the movement of people and goods into their camps.[49]

It was a momentous and risky initiative for them. For generations, they had looked to the west and north for territories that yielded crucial resources. Now they turned south to embrace a commercial windfall they could sense was coming. But like their Dakota kin a century earlier, they would have to maneuver both gently and ruthlessly to make themselves central.

LIKE A PACK OF FAMISHED WOLVES

In 1794 the schoolmaster Jean-Baptiste Truteau tested the Missouri's commercial waters. He was backed by the Missouri Fur Company, a new partnership headed by a pitiless and chameleonic adventurer-financier Jacques Clamorgan, and his directive was to open trade with "all the nations ... above the Ponca nation," build a fort in the Mandan country, and look for a waterway to the Pacific. He was specifically instructed to "fix a very high price on everything." Leaving St. Louis in early June with eight men and a pirogue, the expedition rushed upriver, hoping to pass the Kansas, Otoes, Pawnees, and Poncas while the villagers were out on the plains hunting bison. The traders wanted to save the bulk of their goods for the magnificent autumn fairs of the Mandans.[50]

After nearly three months of hard rowing up the muddy, meandering river, however, game became scarce, and the traders grew hungry. Smoke in the horizon revealed the reason: a Lakota hunting party was marching ahead of them, clearing the river flats of deer and bison. Truteau tried to keep his distance from the slowly moving hunters, but the stalling caused him "extreme anxiety": other French traders had recently clashed with Lakotas near the Arikara villages, and he feared retaliation. He sent two men upriver among Arikaras "as much to bring back provisions as to invite them to come to meet me to protect me from the abuse of the Sioux."[51]

About to embark upriver again, the French were stopped by a cry from the opposite bank. Truteau saw "several Indians who were descending the hills opposite us" and "called out to us in Sioux asking who we were, where we came from, and where we were going." "On this occasion," he admitted, "I had no little distress." Hungry, outnumbered, and scared, the French were trapped. Truteau, who had learned to speak Dakota passably during an earlier sojourn among Yanktons, demanded the Indians to declare their intentions. One of them declared to be "of the Yankton Sioux nation" and named "all the Frenchmen, of past and recent times, who had most often visited his village." Truteau was one of the listed. The spokesman also shouted that their women and children would be arriving soon, a confirmation that theirs was not a war party. Relieved that he had encountered not Lakotas but Yanktons, "fairly civilized Indians," Truteau asked the Yankton to send in two of his men. Three swam to him.[52]

Truteau took the men into his merchandize-laden pirogue and set upriver, the rest of the Yanktons following the vessel "like a pack of famished wolves." The pirogue got stuck in a shallow, and the Yanktons dragged it into their camp. The camp was not what Truteau expected. It contained only three Yankton lodges; most of its residents were Lakotas, "fierce, uncivilized people." Without realizing it, the traders had entered the Lakota country. Lakotas lit a fire at the edge of the woods and assembled around it. Most of them refused the tobacco Truteau offered, and when they learned that the traders were heading among Arikaras, they raised "loud murmurs." Truteau tried to defuse the tension by speaking good thoughts of "Great Spanish Chief, their father," who, "knowing their distress due to the lack of powder, balls, knives, and other merchandise so necessary to life, had taken pity on them," but he also insisted on continuing upriver. He urged Lakotas to accompany him in the Arikara villages where they would "find all their necessities provided." Only fixed settlements mattered in imperial commercial logistics, which for centuries had revolved around colonial headquarters, permanent inland posts, and port cities.[53]

Through their eastern kin, Lakotas had heard of this sort of maneuvering before and were not convinced. They denounced the Franco-Spanish trading policy in its entirety. The French who traded with Arikaras were "bad men, always talking evil against them and urging that nation to kill them," and the powder the French traders carried upstream "would only be used to kill the Sioux." The traders would not move beyond them. A Yankton man, acting as an intermediary, urged Truteau to "open up the bad roads by means of large presents of merchandise" and "called all the men, young and old, the women, and children of all ages and of both sexes." This too failed. Lakotas and Yanktons swarmed around Truteau and took what they wanted. "This was genuine plunder," the trader protested, only to promptly arrange another round of gift distributions—cloth, tobacco, knives, axes, blankets, vermillion, flints, gun worms, a barrel of powder, and "a proportionate number of balls."[54]

The pillage may have been spontaneous, but it delivered a clear political message. It asserted Lakota jurisdiction over the burgeoning upriver commerce and cut the French down to size. "My distress and my anguish were without equal," Truteau lamented. Soon after, Lakota spokesmen challenged Truteau directly on the question of upriver trade. They had sent messengers upriver, they warned, and the Missouri would be bordered on both sides by Lakotas who, "once alerted, would be on the lookout for me everywhere, would pillage me, and perhaps kill me and my men." It was better for Truteau to "remain with them and build a wintering lodge," because all Lakotas "would come to trade many peltries." Lakotas portrayed Arikaras as weak nothings who, "having been attacked by the Indians of the north," had "abandoned their lodges without taking the time to harvest the corn."[55]

Trade—its flow upriver and its impact on Indigenous politics—was the crux of the clash, but the underlying problem was social. The French and their patron the Spanish king did not have a proper relationship with Lakotas who "had no Spanish father." They had received no gifts from the king who seemed to have embraced many downriver Indians as his children. The king was a stranger, which meant that Truteau and his men were strangers, too. They were interlopers and ignorant of Native realities. Lakotas demanded that the French recognize their sovereignty over the upper Missouri and act accordingly. They should bring gifts from their king, share their wealth with Lakotas, and secure their commerce in the Lakota country with a fort. They should respect the territorial boundaries of the Lakota domain—which stretched across the Missouri channel and encompassed the Arikara villages—and acknowledge the Lakota right to decide who would be granted access. Once the French accepted this, great things would happen, but first they had to find the right thoughts and words and become kin through wólakȟota. Truteau had not, and he found himself puzzled and battered.[56]

If Truteau's sojourn among Lakotas was suffused with ambiguities, so was his departure. During the prolonged wrangling, some Yanktons, who seemed to be afraid of Lakotas, had surreptitiously signaled to Truteau to reject the Lakota demands. And when Truteau and his men slipped out of the camp at sunset, they were assisted by Yankton women. The French descended downriver, their half-empty pirogue now much more navigable, and set up a winter camp. In the spring they made another effort to reach Arikaras. They were now held back by Poncas and Omahas who tried to dissuade them from pushing forward, but they did finally make it to the Arikara villages in the summer of 1795. Along the way they heard reports of other expeditions: the upper Missouri trade was starting to boom.[57]

Lakotas and Yanktons had baffled Truteau, which may well have been their intention. Truteau believed the events had been masterminded by a "diabolical old man" residing somewhere outside the camp. Maybe it had. The whole affair had a distinct air of performance: Yanktons luring Truteau's pirogue into the Lakota camp and then furtively signaling to him not to yield to Lakota demands; Yanktons trying to temper Lakota greediness, only to partake in the appropriation of Truteau's goods; Lakotas denouncing the French and Yanktons extolling them as life-givers who "gladdened all the nations who received them well." The dissonances may have been a negotiation tactic necessitated by the particular spatial dynamics of the Missouri commerce: upriver groups had to find ways to prevent the St. Louis traders from supplying their enemies, but they could not alienate them too much lest they stopped coming altogether. Lakotas could extort the traders and still count on them to come—such was the pull of the upriver commerce—but the coercion had to be carefully administered. Yanktons' role may have been to soften the twinge of Lakota assertiveness. Truteau himself concluded, not with little admiration, "all the Indians of this river . . . are sly and tricky. They have more knowledge than many people believe."[58]

But the division may have also reflected a genuine tension between Lakotas and their Yankton relatives. The Yanktons residing among Lakotas were visitors who lived in the upper Des Moines Valley from where they had easy access to the Missouri trade channel—hundreds of miles ahead of the Lakotas. Yanktons, in fact, had been one of those downriver groups that had for decades enjoyed a privileged position in the St. Louis–based commerce. They had strong ties with Franco-Spanish traders and had been "well received by the Great Spanish Chief," most likely in New Orleans. But the expanding upriver trade now threatened to sideline them, perhaps prompting them to intervene. They may have been cajoling Truteau, in plain sight, to turn away from Lakotas.[59]

In the heart of the continent, Lakotas were rearranging the world around them to meet their needs, and no one was unaffected, not enemies, nor newcomers, nor kin. Lakotas insisted on an unhindered connection between St. Louis and themselves, which in many ways was an unnatural thing. The continent's most coveted commodity—guns—would somehow have to move upriver past thousands of Indians who were desperate to stop the traffic right where they were.

IMMENSE WEALTH

By the mid-1790s Lakota dominance in the upper Missouri was an accepted fact. The Mandan villages had to remain central to the St. Louis commerce for political reasons—British trade in the Mandan country showed no signs of abating—but what preoccupied the merchants most was how to move upriver without alienating Lakotas. They resigned to pay tolls for access. A major, thirty-two-man Missouri Company expedition with an outsized agenda—drive out the British, find a water route to the Pacific, and look for a colony of Welsh Indians, the purported progeny of a twelfth-century Welsh prince who was said to have sailed to America—allocated an entire boatload of goods to "flatter" Lakotas and secure a right-of-way through their country. The expedition nearly sputtered out on the lower Missouri where Omahas demanded guns to fight Lakotas who ranged up and down the valley and reportedly received "silk flags" from the British in the north. Another corporation, Clamorgan, Loisel and Company, earmarked substantial funds for Lakotas "with reservation that they will not trouble the privileged commerce of the Company." Lakotas had turned one of North America's great commercial arteries into a tribute-yielding machine: they could reap massive profits by simply allowing people and goods to pass by.[60]

In 1796 the much-battered Truteau wrote a report of the upper Missouri trade. He noted the Lakota stranglehold on the commerce and proposed a way to avert it: travel north in spring when Lakotas were out on the plains hunting. But he also noted something unexpected: Lakotas had become the region's "greatest beaver hunters" and "could furnish more beavers than all the nations besides" without compromising quality: "Their beaver is worth the double of the Canadian for the fineness of it's fur and parchment." The explanation to the prodigious beaver production was alarming. Lakotas had begun to trade pelts eastward to their Dakota kin who in turn channeled pelts to the British in the north. Spanish Louisiana was now bleeding furs into Canada through the formidable Lakotas and their allies. The leakage was serious, for Lakotas could "roam all the rivers and streams" across the upper Missouri watershed "without fear of anyone."[61]

Lakotas were thus plugged into two enormous trade systems, one anchored in St. Louis and New Orleans, the other in Hudson Bay and Montreal. Both systems were run by private merchants backed by imperial might, and both were alive with continental ambitions. In the late 1770s prominent Scottish merchants had formed the North West Company in Montreal to compete with the London-owned Hudson's Bay Company, which had dominated the Canadian fur trade for decades. The Montreal-based traders pushed into the Great Lakes and the prime fur regions in the upper Mississippi Valley, forcing the Hudson's Bay Company to do the same. Soon both companies had agents among Dakotas, competing fiercely for clients. Traders sought Sioux wives to secure trading privileges and supplied their new Native relatives with guns, powder, and ammunition. Dakotas then carried those guns against Crees, holding their enemies at bay. Soon the North West Company ran three ships on Lake Superior, carrying Dakota pelts east and keeping the upper Mississippi trade firmly in Canadian hands. "The goods that they bring are superior to those brought us from the Capital," Zenon Trudeau, the governor of Upper Louisiana complained, "and they give them at better bargains."[62]

Trudeau's frustration was more than routine imperial wrangling over jurisdiction: the Dakota trade policy was denying Louisiana a fortune. That this could happen had been evident for some time. In 1794 François Luis Héctor Carondelet, the governor of Louisiana and West Florida, estimated that the "commerce and trade of the Missouri would produce—without imposing any burden on the royal treasury and without extraordinary effort—immense wealth for Louisiana." However, most of that wealth now seeped north through British networks. The Mandan villages had been a known leaky valve for years, but now furs were pouring into Canada also through Lakotas. Carondelet planned to stop that flow with two new military forts, one on the Des Moines River and the other on the Minnesota, the heart of the Dakota country. Not only would such forts force the fur flow to its natural destination in New Orleans; they would save Spanish Louisiana itself. "Many settlers would flock to their vicinities, both from our settlements and from Canada, and from the banks of the Ohio. Within a few years they would have several posts in those districts more populous than that of St. Louis at present, and could serve to protect the part of Louisiana higher up on the Missouri from the usurpation of the English and Americans."[63]

Carondelet did not get his forts, but he kept fighting. Three years later he asked the Royal Treasury for a ten-thousand-peso subsidy for the Missouri Company "to conserve the dominion of Missouri" against Canadian incursions. The battle line had shifted decisively from the distant Mandans to Lakotas. "English companies of Hudson Bay and Canada," the governor explained, were inciting them "against our Company." Time was running out, because behind the British there was an even graver threat. "His Majesty's settlements in Ylinoa [Illinois]," Governor Trudeau warned, "have opposite them, on the east bank of the Misisipi, settlements to the same number, belonging to the United States of America. Their population is at the present time slightly greater or less than ours, but the United States have powerful means for their increase, namely, the eye of a good Government on whatever can bring its population from such to such a point."[64]

PERPETUAL FRIENDSHIP AND CLEAR ROADS

Lakotas had become a force field that twisted and bent human endeavors around them. Their enemies avoided them, their allies gravitated toward them, and those still outside their sphere cajoled them. Louisiana's Spanish merchants wanted to trade with them, while high-level Spanish officials wanted to eliminate them. No one could ignore them.

A crossroad in continental flows of commerce and technology, Lakotas' Missouri domain had become a major center of geopolitical power. Power radiated outward from their territory for "they were feared and dreaded by all of these others [Indians] on account of the fire arms with which they are always well provided." Those firearms were remarkable. Gun technology had leapt forward during the revolutionary wars of the 1770s and 1780s, settling on a new standard: the simple, light, and durable North West gun, which featured an oversized trigger bow that could accommodate a mittened finger and a thin, smooth-bored barrel that could launch either buckshot or round ball. It was the most lethal and coveted weapon on the continent.[65]

Lakotas also enjoyed an advantage in equestrian technology. They were still building up their horse herds, but they already had a decisive edge over their rivals. None of the villagers around them possessed large herds, and many of them were not even trying, reserving the precious riverine habitats for farming rather than pasturing. Lakotas could now hunt on the Mníšoše's western bank without disturbance, ranging out into the plains toward the massive bison herds that only seemed to grow thicker toward the west. At home along the Mníšoše they had Arikaras living in their midst, growing corn, squash, and beans for barter under pressure. Sustained by a steady inflow of protein, fat, and carbohydrates, Lakotas were growing rapidly in numbers. Pierre Chouteau, a member of the wealthy St. Louis fur-trading family, estimated their population at fifteenth thousand in 1804, expecting it to be "beaucoup plus considerable" in the future. The estimate was inflated by nearly half, but it captures how large Lakotas loomed in the American interior.[66]

Native neighbors sensed it, too. Cheyennes, who had been rivals since the early 1780s, returned to the fold. They embarked on vigorous beaver and otter trapping in a boggy zone north of the Platte River and bartered the processed pelts with Lakotas for merchandize. Once again, the Cheyenne connection became a crucial lifeline for Lakotas. Cheyennes were still raising corn and their horse herds were now growing explosively along the fertile Cheyenne River, and they supplied Lakotas with both. Soon the two people were camping together again, rebuilding their alliance through wólakȟota.[67]

Lakotas were extending their reach also far to the south along the Mníšoše. In 1797 Missouri Fur Company manager James Mackay invited Lakotas to a parley at an Omaha village "so that they might hear the Parole of their Great Father the Spaniard." A month later four "principal" chiefs came to accept Mackay's presents. The trader found the conference "tiresome" in detail, missing the elemental point: the Lakota headmen were reaffirming with their sheer presence their privileged relationship with Spain in the very home of their rivals some two hundred miles downriver from the core Lakota territory. Under their great chief Blackbird, a savvy and ruthless politician who used arsenic to eliminate rivals, Omahas had inserted themselves as major contenders in the lower Missouri River trade, but now they were mere spectators in a Lakota-Spanish parley. There is no record of what Omahas thought when they listened to Mackay urging Lakotas "to Traffic & live in perpetual friendship with the white children of their Great Spanish Father ... who from pity & regard for his red children wished to have the roads Clear." Clear roads spelled wealth for Lakotas and marginalization for Omahas.[68]

Rather than trying to resist, Omahas cast their lot with Lakotas. While wintering on the Missouri in 1796–97, a Franco-Spanish trader learned of a group of four hundred Indians visiting Omahas with a gift of 150 rifles and six kegs of brandy. The visitors, the trader reported, expected Omahas to share the liquor with Octotactas, a splinter group of the Iowas, "in order to go and make war upon the Kance [Kansas], the brandy being intended to give courage to the warriors in battle." These visitors—probably Sicangus who lived closest to Omahas—shared their wealth with hope of turning rivals into allies and to co-opting them to fight *their* enemies. The lavish gift bespoke less of compliance with a Spanish-sponsored peace than of confidence. With their control of the Missouri trade secure, naked force was no longer necessary. Flush with newfound wealth and power, Lakotas could shift from coercion to persuasion.[69]

Yet the threat of violence never disappeared. During their long struggle to carve out a place for themselves in the upper Missouri Valley, Lakotas adopted a demeanor that enabled them to survive and thrive in the fiercely contested interior world. It meant an existence on the knife-edge of violence, switching from accommodation to aggression whenever necessary and doing the exact opposite the minute the circumstances shifted again. They had embraced the world for what it was—erratic, nurturing, menacing, and uplifting at turns—by accepting unpredictability as normal.

SHE RAN AWAY

The Lakota country at the turn of the century was a busy commercial thoroughfare. Lakotas still had to occasionally police the Missouri to enforce compliance, but mostly they waited in their camps for traders to come. Lakota winter counts for the period are filled with references to men with brimmed hats and short hair, bringing in guns and iron. These were people Lakotas had come to know as wašíčus, persons with white skin and special possessions suffused with extraordinary qualities, wašíčuŋ.

Most prominent among these wašíčus was The-Good-White-Man who brought several trading parties into Oglala villages. In the first encounter Oglalas had allowed him to advance past them after he promised to return with weapons that allowed them to kill game with little labor. Making good on his pledge, the trader brought several expeditions into the Lakota country. Oglalas remembered him as "the first white man to trade and live" with them. An Oglala count depicts him with a flintlock musket in the middle of a large Oglala circle, and a Sicangu count shows his hands in a kind of benediction, emulating the Lakota gesture for "good." The escalating commerce permeated the Lakota country, reaching bands that had not yet received traders. "A trader brought them their first guns," reports one Oglala count. "The first white men ever seen and who used iron," reads an early entry in the winter count of the Hunkpapas, an emerging oyáte.[70]

The thriving trade demanded a robust set of rituals and institutions to structure it. As always, ceremonial smoking, gift exchanges, and carefully chosen words preceded exchanges, but the steady trade encouraged Lakotas to embrace a new practice: intermarriage. Marriages between European traders and Lakota women had occurred before, but became common only when men like The-Good-White-Man acquainted themselves with Lakota traditions. Marriages à la façon du pays provided traders with a slice of domestic normalcy—food, companionship, sex—during their long trips and promised advantages over competitors. For Lakota women and men, marriages were a means to embed trade in a deeper social bedrock. Trade marriages created kinship ties that bound individuals, families, and ultimately societies together through the social alchemy of intimacy and caring. Marriages not only sustained markets; in a way they were the market. Kinship bonds demanded sharing, which is why Lakotas considered trade marriages vital for their commercial ambitions. Something of their importance and of their instrumental and coercive nature is captured in an Oglala count from 1799–1800 which depicts a woman "who had been given to a white man" and "was killed because she ran away from him."[71]

That woman had been essential, but neither her name nor any other details made it into the historical record. She was but one of many. During the first century of Lakota expansion, men—warriors, chiefs, envoys—had been the public face of Lakotas, fighting, hunting, trading, and negotiating a path into the West and into ascendancy. They were the first line of the Lakota expansion. But beside them were the women—mothers, daughters, laborers, healers, elders—who tended to children, prepared food, processed pelts (and perhaps traded them), mended wounds, integrated strangers, and preserved knowledge, building a cultural and domestic foundation that held everything together.

THE GREAT SIOUX RENDEZVOUS

Trade was the single most important political concern for Lakotas in the late eighteenth century, but it was not the only one. The last decade of the century was dominated by warfare, reflecting their rising military might. They ranged far to the north, raiding Mandans and Hidatsas for corn, and kept Arikaras confined in their villages, enforcing the all-important food trade. Eventually, an entire band settled among Arikaras, who took them in "to avoid making too great a multitude of enemies among the Sioux nation, who could certainly overpower them." Arikaras accommodated the Lakota colony "out of fear" and "to obtain guns, clothes, hats, kettles, ... which are given them in exchange for their horses." The Lakota-Arikara bond was at once coercive and accommodating. The 1797–98 winter count of the Two Kettles—another emerging oyáte—depicts an Arikara woman who was captured "while gathering 'pomme blanche,' a root used for food." Raids like this were routine, but they could have unforeseen outcomes. This woman was "the God Woman" and "holy." When captured, she said, "'I am a Wakan Tanka,' meaning that she belonged to God." She was clearly familiar with Lakota beliefs—not at all surprising given Arikaras' location in the midst of Lakota oyátes—and may have assumed the role to awe her captors. But she may have also been a religious leader capable of appealing to many other-than-human forces. Lakotas released her.[72]

Lakotas were also expanding their sphere of operations far beyond the Mníšoše, following a distinct seasonal cycle. They chased the bison in late spring and early summer and again in late fall, gathering together for large communal hunts.

Since bison herds had declined east of the Missouri, Lakotas now hunted almost entirely in the western high plains, where they clashed with Crows over hunting rights. In early spring they traveled east to trade with Yanktons, Yanktonais, and Dakotas. Reflecting Lakotas' growing weight within the Očhéthi Šakówiŋ, the great Sioux rendezvous now took place on the James River, some 150 miles west of its previous site on the Minnesota. These were enormous gatherings as one Missouri trader reported: "This concourse is sometimes composed of a thousand to twelve hundred lodges, about three thousand men bearing arms. Much trading is done there. Each man brings different articles, according to the places over which he has wandered. Those who have frequented the St. Peter's River [Minnesota] and that of the Mohens [Des Moines] furnish guns, kettles, red pipes, and bows of walnut. The Titons [Lakotas] give in exchange horses, lodges of leather, buffalo robes, shirts and leggings of antelope-skin."[73]

The great rendezvous was also a medium of collective renewal which drew the Očhéthi Šakówiŋ together. Distance and different interests inevitably created tensions among the seven fires, and the rendezvous was an opportunity to defuse them: "Although very often this general meeting produces disturbances among tribes already unfriendly," the trader noted, "it serves more commonly for their reconciliation." With their generations-long experience in dealing with European empires, Dakotas had "become mediators among our fierce hordes and make them see the necessity of unity among them." Dakotas urged Lakotas to "treat the French kindly," but, inadvertently, they also delivered "a terrible blow at the peace of the traders of the Missouri by informing the Titons of the value of the merchandise upon the St. Peter's River." Fierce competition among Canadian fur companies and economies of scale had brought the price of manufactured goods down in the east, whereas the Missouri trade was still a robust frontier business of high risks, high costs, and spur-of-the-moment deals.[74]

Dakotas were educating Lakotas, but they were also furnishing their relatives with the most precious commodity of all in late eighteenth-century North America: information. Pooling knowledge, the seven fires accumulated an exceptionally broad understanding of North America's imperial and Indigenous landscapes. Together, they had dealings with the Spaniards, British, Scots, Louisiana French, Canadian French, Americans, and dozens of Native nations. Occupying the center, they had a 360-degree panorama of the continent and its peoples.

THE CRADLE OF EMPIRES

The late eighteenth-century North America was a world of many possibilities. On treaty documents and official maps things looked clear-cut and neat: a contiguous block of land for each of the three empires. The territories west of the Mississippi belonged to Spain by the 1763 Treaty of Paris, and the 1783 Paris treaty gave Spain Florida and thus an unbroken shoreline around the Caribbean. The 1783 treaty also gave the Ohio Valley, the crucible of imperial rivalries, to the United States, confining the British to the north of an imaginary line running through the Great Lakes. The division was not perfect—there were quarrels over the exact borders and Britain maintained illegal forts in the Great Lakes—but the overall framework granted each empire a distinct power base. The Gulf of Mexico had become a "Spanish lake," shielding Mexico against foreign intrusions, while British Canada boasted an immense fur hinterland, which was rapidly developing into a transcontinental trade system. The United States claimed vast tracts of Indian land, which settlers were filling with such fervor that Washington believed nothing "short of a Chinese wall" could restrain them. The design was meant to diffuse the chronic imperial rivalries that had kept North America in a state of turmoil for over a century.[75]

The geographical certainty of maps belied the messy realities on the ground. The 1783 treaty gave Britain and the United States unhindered access to the Mississippi and placed the United States' western border in the middle of the river, but in practice Spain controlled Mississippi navigation because it held New Orleans. The larger problem was that the Mississippi was a poor natural boundary. Much more than just a river, it was a trunk line of an enormous system of naturally navigable tributaries that connected 1.5 million square miles of the interior to the Gulf of Mexico and Atlantic circuits. The Mississippi watershed was the master key to the continent, feeding everything—people, ambitions, commerce, violence, power—toward the center. In the late eighteenth century imperial rivalries focused to an astonishing degree on the big river and its great tributary, the Missouri.[76]

On paper the Mississippi and Missouri belonged to Spain, its claims buttressed by the vast hinterlands of Louisiana and the vital port city of New Orleans. On the ground, however, Spain was an absentee landlord at best. Violations of territorial boundaries were constant and blatant, fueling rampant intrigue. British traders pushed from Canada into Spanish Louisiana via the Mississippi, Red River of the North, and Missouri, which practically invited them in by offering waterborne transportation deep into Spanish territory. When Great Britain and Spain clashed over trading privileges in Nootka Sound in 1790, the British seriously considered pushing down the Mississippi River and ousting Spain from Louisiana and Florida, only to be thwarted by Jefferson's offer to Spain to annex New Orleans and Florida: the last thing the British wanted was a strong U.S. presence on the Caribbean rim. Jefferson's bid was soon forgotten, but American settlers pushed in nonetheless, gravitating toward the Mississippi's incomparable gift: superior farmland next to sea access. "Thus they are becoming our neighbors," wrote the Spanish governor of Louisiana in 1793, "clamoring threateningly for the free navigation of the Misisipi. If they obtain their purpose, their ambition will not be limited to this part of the Misisipi." Left unchecked, he warned, Americans were poised to capture "the rich fur-trade of the Misuri" and "the rich mines of the interior provinces of the very kingdom of Mexico."[77]

And then there were the French who had not left North America as much as moved to steer its futures from a distance. France supported the colonials during the Revolutionary War to weaken the British Empire and snatch away its Atlantic trade. After the war, the French shifted their attentions to Louisiana, which, if recaptured, could serve as a buffer to the Caribbean sugar colony Saint-Dominique, perhaps the world's most valuable piece of land. When Spain refused to negotiate over Louisiana, French agents set out to take the province by force. In 1792 Edmond Charles Genet, the French minister to the United States; George Rogers Clark, a former general of the Continental Army; and an assortment of revolutionaries and discontents hatched a plan to drive Spain out of the Mississippi Valley, capture New Orleans and Florida, and, as imaginations soared, liberate Canada from the British yoke. An army of Kentuckian frontiersmen under the French flag was already in place when President Washington ordered the expedition stopped on pain of military strike. Had the plan succeeded, it was not at all clear to whom—France or the United States—the backcountry army would have offered Louisiana.[78]

In the eighteenth century, then, it seemed that there could be four Wests—British, French, American, and Spanish—of which the last appeared the most unlikely. Yet the Spanish officials clung to the Louisiana buffer zone, which in their minds shielded the Mexican silver mines against covetous empires, and sought ways to hold on to it. Their solution was creative, bold, and desperate all at once. Chronically short of people and funds, they aimed to co-opt and neutralize their rivals. Instead of trying to block the westward flow of Americans, they embraced it. They opened Louisiana and West Florida to American settlers and granted American merchants trade licenses in New Orleans. Land grants and profits, they gambled, would turn American emigrants into loyal subjects who would defend Spanish Louisiana against other Americans—not an unreasonable scenario at a time when the United States was gripped by backcountry separatism and appeared to be splintering in its expansive trans-Appalachian setting. The settlers might even carve independent pro-Spanish colonies out of the young republic. The Appalachian hydrological divide split the United States into eastern and western halves, the former tethered to the Atlantic seaboard, the latter pulling toward the Mississippi and New Orleans through the Ohio, Tennessee, and other westward flowing streams. The United States was not yet a consolidated nation, and a lasting multicultural, Mississippi-based Spanish Empire with American satellite colonies seemed a real possibility.[79]

What American emigrants were to Spanish Louisiana in the east, Lakotas were in the north: a vital borderland buffer that helped keep Spain's North American empire intact. The outbreak of the Anglo-Spanish War in 1796—a spillover of the French Revolutionary Wars—heightened Louisiana's and Lakotas' strategic weight. Fearing a Spanish invasion from Louisiana, British agents in Canada sought protection in Lakotas—"a nation unquestionably composing the best Indian Warriors in America," an army of thousands, "all mounted"—and planned to send them "down the Mississippi and to engage any Enemy they might meet." Such an invasion could have crippled the militarily feeble Spanish Louisiana, opening the continent's midsection for Britain.

It never happened. Spanish officials had gotten an essential thing right: having grasped Lakotas' geopolitical centrality, they had granted them a privileged status in the Missouri trade, calculating that gifts and goods would turn them into trusty allies who would reject British overtures and blunt British ambitions. Like the American immigration scheme, the rapprochement with Lakotas was a gamble, for it could and did alienate a host of other Native nations in the interior. Yet both gambles paid off. Lakotas remained neutral and welcomed Spanish traders, while thousands of Americans settled in Louisiana, drawn by its cosmopolitan milieu. In 1800 failed Kentuckian land speculator Daniel Boone resided in the Femme Osage District in Upper Louisiana, holding court under the "Judgment Tree" and serving as both judge and jury. Not far from him lived Moses Austin, an up-and-coming lead-mining magnate. Like many others, they were forging new lives, businesses, and local governments under the auspices of the Spanish king who had the Lakotas on his side.[80]

Lakotas needed the Spanish Empire to last. More than a century of negotiating the chronically unstable imperial landscapes of North America had taught them that empires were most useful to them when they were at once prosperous and seriously threatened—fit to operate but too frail to dictate. The Očhéthi Šakówiŋ had forged a truly functioning relationship with New France only around the mid-eighteenth century, when the French dominated the interior fur trade but faced an existential threat from British settlers and soldiers in the Ohio Valley. The late eighteenth-century Spanish Empire was weaker and more distracted than the French Empire had ever been, but if it survived, it could serve Lakotas well.

4

THE LAKOTA MERIDIAN

Napoleon Bonaparte was a decisive emperor and a fickle colonist. The man who revolutionized military organization, built a European empire with determined battles of annihilation, and reformed Western Europe's legal landscape with the radical Code Napoléon was also a colony-builder who did not seem able to decide what to do with France's sprawling overseas possessions.[1]

In 1799 the newly appointed First Consul inherited a troubling situation in the Americas. The Jay Treaty four years earlier had been a disaster and an insult to France. By initiating a rapprochement between the United States and Great Britain, the treaty threatened to undercut French interests in the Caribbean, where France held several small but highly lucrative colonies. No longer, it seemed, could the Caribbean-bound French ships find safe harbor, provisions, and repairs in American ports. The United States had turned its back on its steadfast revolutionary ally just as France was moving toward a massive conflict with Britain over global dominance.[2]

But there could be a quick remedy: buy Louisiana back from Spain. If retroceded, the vast province would yield a variety of commodities for Atlantic commerce and it could be harnessed to produce food for France's fabulously rich sugar colony of Saint Domingue. Louisiana's strategic center, New Orleans, would serve not only as a crucial port but also as a lure to pull in independent-minded backcountry Americans; by dangling it, France could sever the trans-Appalachian states from the rest of the United States and deliver them to the French fold.

France's eagerness to buy coincided with Spain's eagerness to sell. In the late 1790s Spanish policymakers came to realize that they could never, not with the number of settlers available to them, turn the money-draining province into an effective buffer for the Mexican silver mines. A French Louisiana, backed by

French military might, could achieve what a Spanish Louisiana could not: contain the growing, sprawling United States.[3]

Napoleon seized the opportunity. In a secret treaty of San Ildelfonso in 1800 Spain swapped nearly 9 percent of North America for the Grand Duchy of Tuscany, which Napoleon promised to conquer for Spain, and in October 1802 the Spanish authorities handed Louisiana over to France. The transfer, Thomas Jefferson feared, posed an existential threat to the United States by blocking it from the Mississippi Valley and New Orleans. "There is on the globe one single spot, the possessor of which is our natural and habitual enemy. It is New Orleans, through which the produce of three eighths of our territory must pass to market," he warned. With formidable France now that natural enemy, nothing in the interior seemed certain.[4]

As colossal as it was, Louisiana was merely a part of a larger imperial package. What the French wanted most was to reestablish their rule in Saint Domingue, where an infectious slave rebellion had carried an ex-slave, Toussaint Louverture, into power. Napoleon secured a pledge of support from Jefferson—the sage of Monticello was terrified that the Caribbean slave rebellion might spread into the American South—and dispatched an armada of fifty thousand men, the largest naval invasion force ever to cross the Atlantic, to overthrow Louverture. A new and mightier New France beckoned. Anchored in Saint Domingue, it would encompass the Mississippi watershed and embrace Francophone Canada, confining the United States to the East and securing the West for French settlement. In the summer of 1802 another French fleet of twelve ships was being prepared near Rotterdam. Its destination was Louisiana and, along with soldiers, it was to carry two hundred medals to the Indians.[5]

But the French invasion crumbled against Louverture's army and yellow fever within a year. As French soldiers lay incapacitated by the black vomit, Jefferson withdrew American support, and Napoleon abandoned the campaign and his dream of a new French Empire in America. By then Jefferson had already dispatched James Monroe to Paris to purchase New Orleans and as much of the Floridas as possible. When Monroe arrived in Paris in early April 1803, he learned that Napoleon had made a new offer: not just New Orleans but all of Louisiana for $15 million, 530 million acres at three cents per acre. It was an emergency measure. Fearing that Louisiana might be grabbed by the British, who already had entered it via the Mississippi and Missouri Valleys, Napoleon handed over the province to the United States for virtually nothing. A deal was struck, and Napoleon shifted his sights to Europe, North Africa, and Asia.[6]

There was nothing unusual about this kind a diplomacy in which enormous chunks of territory were reduced to pawns in a global geopolitical game, but the outcome of this particular round was unusual. While European empires routinely swapped lands they meant to exploit from a distance through colonial outposts and joint-stock companies, this time the transfer was colossal and the beneficiary was a nascent settler state poised for continental expansion but uncertain of its legal right to expand its territory. "You have made a noble bargain for yourselves," said the French Foreign Minister Charles Maurice de Talleyrand, "and I suppose you will make the most of it."[7]

Talleyrand referred to the unspecified boundaries of Louisiana, oblivious of the fact that making the most of the bargain would inevitably require coming to terms with the Native powers on the ground. The people who lived on the land that was transferred from France to the United States were neither consulted nor informed because they were thought to be too few and too uncivilized to matter. In actual fact, "Louisiana" as marketable real estate was an imperial fiction, for Indians controlled almost all of it, the largest portion belonging to the Sioux. When the Indians of this Louisiana eventually learned about the final transfer to the United States, they considered it ludicrous. But it did not take them long to realize that the newcomers with their outlandish claims could not be ignored.

SMALLPOX USED THEM UP AGAIN

There were no signs of Louisiana's dizzying changes of status in the upper Missouri Valley. Traders still came every year and most of them still spoke French. And even if Lakotas had come to know about the imperial machinations, it would have mattered little because so many of them were dying. Winter counts for 1801 and 1802 depict figures with blotted faces and torsos: another smallpox epidemic. The pestilence struck Sicangus, Oglalas, Minneconjous, Two Kettles, and Yanktonais in the wake of an intensely cold winter that had sapped their strength, leaving many pregnant women dead. For Oglalas it was "Smallpox used them up again winter."[8]

The outbreak was an upshot of the growing Missouri River trade, an inherently cramped activity that turned the densely inhabited valley into a disease corridor. Impervious to the imperial transfers, the Franco-Spanish Clamorgan, Loisel and Company dispatched several trade convoys upriver. St. Louis merchant Régis Loisel built Fort Aux Cèdres, a large structure walled with a thirteen-and-a-half-foot-high picket fence, on Cedar Island near the Big Bend to serve Sicangus— the first fixed trading post in the Lakota country. Loisel's partner, Hugh Heney, managed to ascend the Missouri all the way to the Cheyenne confluence where he traded with Oglalas. There were other signs of growing traffic as well. Several winter counts around that time mention shod horses, a novelty for Lakotas. Lakotas were also becoming more particular in their preferences, demanding not only guns, powder, balls, metal utensils, woolens, and blankets but also blue glass beads, brass wire, and iron for arrows and spears.[9]

Pathogens piggybacked on commerce. Like the previous major smallpox epidemic two decades earlier, this one realigned geopolitics along the Missouri. Lakotas suddenly lost a large portion of their most important resource—people—and they maneuvered ferociously to hold on to what they had. Operating as autonomous bands and oyátes but responding to similar challenges in broadly similar ways, they tightened their grip on the trade. In the fall of 1803, just as the news of the Louisiana Purchase began to trickle in, Loisel planned to send a party upriver from Fort Aux Cèdres to trade with Oglalas, Saones, and Cheyennes. Sicangus stopped him in his tracks. Four chiefs—Black Buffalo, the Partisan, Medicine Bull, and Manzomani—seemed inclined to allow Loisel to proceed, but an "old soldier," Mato-kokipabi, "without taking the trouble to refute them or to explain his own reasons," laconically declared that the goods would not move upriver. The four chiefs accepted this without a word. Pierre-Antoine Tabeau, one of Loisel's employees, believed the chiefs to be secretly delighted by this "as they hoped themselves to trade the peltries of the strangers by an intermediary commerce to which they are accustomed and to sell to us then with profit—what actually took place."[10]

The staged, performative tone of the affair echoed Jean-Baptiste Truteau's experiences among Lakotas eight years earlier. Truteau believed that his upriver push had been thwarted by an "infernal old man" who may well have been the "old soldier" who now blocked Loisel's advance. Mato-kokipabi embodied a hard-line Sicangu policy in a highly competitive and unpredictable milieu where a growing traffic promised unforeseen profits, fueled rivalries, and spread deadly pathogens. Led by Mato-kokipabi, Sicangus strove to establish themselves as the principal gateway for upriver trade, a position that would yield them considerable power and profits.[11]

There were deeper layers beneath such cold commercial calculations. As elsewhere in the interior, politics were intensely personal. Tabeau understood the old warrior's hard stance on upriver trade to be "founded upon a particular revenge against the Saones, who had lately stolen some of his horses." Such acts were not uncommon in the rapidly changing Lakota society where status was becoming increasingly linked to horse wealth and where young men sought to make their mark by challenging and shaming established senior men. But the roots of the old warrior's frustration cut deeper still. He had presented his daughter to Loisel in marriage, but "reason, prudence, and economy" had compelled the trader to decline. By rejecting the marriage, Loisel had rejected an offer to share resources between relatives. He was left with hard bargaining between strangers.[12]

KIND OF SERF

In the fall of 1803 Tabeau, Loisel's right-hand man, led seven traders among Arikaras, slipping through the Sicangu bottleneck. There, more than a hundred miles upriver, he came to understand the true extent of Lakota power along the Missouri. He spent two years with the Arikaras, observing firsthand how Lakotas molded the valley's human geography to serve their needs, locking the Arikaras into a relationship that was intimate and unforgiving, mutualistic and exploitative all at once.

Covering events from around 1800 onward, Tabeau's account began with a murder. Kakawita, a prominent Arikara "known as the bravest of the Ricaras and as the foremost poisoner," had killed the brother of Black Buffalo, a renowned Sicangu chief who had visited Arikaras "upon the faith of a recent treaty." "Vengeance was not delayed," and the killing "cost the life of five or six Ricaras and the peace of all the others, who dared not leave their lodges." Violence, along with smallpox, raged for some time among Arikaras. But then, to Tabeau's bafflement, Sicangus made peace. Confused by the sudden turn of events, he attributed it to the "interest of the one" and "the weakness and stupidity of the other." In fact, what he was witnessing was an intricate Indigenous system of collaboration and manipulation working exactly as intended.[13]

Corn, it turned out, was ripe. It was the time of the fall harvest, which for Lakotas meant trade. "In this season," Tabeau observed, they "come from all parts loaded with dried meat, with fat, with dressed leather, and some merchandise." Sicangus, Oglalas, and Saones came to Arikaras as traders, but not as equals: a long history of violence had rendered the exchange markedly asymmetrical. They camped on the plains near the Arikara village, "which they openly pillage without anyone opposing them except by complaints and feeble reproaches." This was more than simple looting. Alive with masculine prowess, Lakotas were announcing their dominance by challenging Arikara men's capacity to protect their property and kin. "They steal the horses and they beat the women and offer with impunity all kinds of insults."[14]

To further boost their bargaining power, Lakotas used naked force to create artificial demand for their own exports. They pitched numerous tents around an Arikara village, "forming a barrier which prevents the buffalo from coming near." Unable to access the bison, Arikaras had to get their meat from Lakotas, who had time on their side: they had rendered "assured objects of subsistence"—game—"precarious" and could "fix, as they wish, the price of that which belongs to them and obtain, in exchange, a quantity of corn, tobacco, beans, and pumpkins that they demand." It was "a ruinous commerce" that forced Arikaras to buy even bows and arrows from Lakotas, although they were "surrounded by woods suitable for supplying them."[15]

Lakotas had blended raiding and extortion with diplomacy and exchange into a flexible economy of violence that left the Arikaras weak and needy. Tabeau thought they saw in them "a certain kind of serf, who cultivates for them and who, as they say, takes, for them, the place of women." The gendered language was carefully considered. Two generations earlier Oglalas had lived as farmers under Arikara tutelage, but now they were people of the hunt and ascending. While diminishing the Arikaras, they treaded carefully not to alienate them to a point of rebellion. Tabeau realized this and yet failed to avoid becoming a foil for Lakota stratagems. He complained bitterly how Lakotas, having returned from a trade fair on the Minnesota, "announce that merchandise is abundant and wonderful there, give in detail the price of each article and make the Ricaras understand that I treat them as slaves." Lakotas were manipulating markets and perceptions to their advantage. While forcing Arikaras to pay inflated prices for their exports, they still managed to paint the St. Louis traders as the real exploiters and villains.[16]

Outplayed by Lakotas, Tabeau struggled with the fallout. Hoping that Arikaras' "customary mildness, long known, would induce the government and the traders to provide them constantly in the future," he earmarked a good portion of his powder for them. It was too late. Arikaras denounced Tabeau as an outsider who had "seen them without breech-clout, without powder, and without knives" and yet had refused to share his wares. He faced constant insults and demands for largesse and, in the end, declared his bid to win over the Arikaras a failure. They were, he reported, "not a fit subject for a special trade expedition."[17]

That declaration began a long marginalization and vilification of the Arikaras, once one of the most renowned traders in the American interior. The vilification took time to take root, but once it did, it fixed the Arikaras in the American imagination as an irredeemable menace. It committed the United States to destroying them, inadvertently paving the way for a Lakota hegemony in the upper Missouri Valley.[18]

CHAINS

Three thousand Arikaras had become virtual vassals of Lakotas, their economies and very lives remolded to accommodate the new masters of the Missouri. Tabeau wrote off the entire valley from the White to the Heart River—a 250-mile stretch of prime fur country—and shifted his sight to the Mandans farther north. "A post among the Mandanes," he mused, "would be a gathering-place for more than twenty nations and would be the means in determining the Ricaras to take up a station nearby." He envisioned a vast trade emporium extending upriver from the Mandans to embrace the Cheyennes, Crows, Shoshones, and many other people. The plan was as ambitious as it was improbable, for Lakotas would not allow it.[19]

Lakota winter counts for the early years of the nineteenth century bespeak of a sudden surge of ambition. Lakotas seemed to be everywhere in the upper Missouri country, trading, parleying, raiding, dancing. Ranging across an expanding radius, they stole curly haired or "woolly" horses from Arikaras, Crows, Pawnees, and Assiniboines, and fought Omahas and Poncas in the south, carrying countless men, women, and children into captivity. Hundreds of miles to the north, they made peace with the Mandans, preempting once more Tabeau's designs for upriver commerce. They welcomed Little Beaver, a white trader who did business with them for years. And every year they danced with the calumet, tightening their binds, forging new alliances, and preparing for wars that bent the great interior onto their orbit.[20]

Unable to contain Lakotas, smaller groups sought protection under their auspices. It was not easy because Lakotas were not a centralized polity bound by fixed policies. Each headman was free to follow his own agenda, which either attracted followers or not: the size of any leader's band was the measure of his competence. In the fall of 1803 Omahas and Poncas extended a peace offer to Sicangus, hoping to secure better access to trade. Black Buffalo, recently "elevated to the first rank," found himself being "urgently entreated" by them. But Black Buffalo's ascendancy alarmed the Partisan who was "envious of the honor and the presents which his rival would receive." A "fidgetty" man "who is seen in the selfsame day faint-hearted and bold, audacious and fearful, proud and servile, conciliator and firebrand," the Partisan sent six of his warriors to attack the Poncas and abort the peace. Poncas retaliated but struck the wrong band— Black Buffalo's, not the Partisan's. Black Buffalo lost all his seven horses.[21]

He had also lost face, "reduced all the winter to serve as a beast of burden," and was obliged to retaliate. The politics of vengeance took over. His Sicangus killed more than half of the inhabitants in a Ponca village and seventy-five people in an Omaha one and carried dozens into captivity. Poncas and Omahas nearly collapsed as polities. They abandoned their villages and tried nomadism, but life on the plains was alien to them and they kept dying. Tabeau found the "formerly very numerous" and "fierce horde" of Poncas "very mild" since the carnage, and Omahas negotiated a truce with Oglalas to redeem their kin from captivity. Concentrated in a single village far to the south, Omahas and Poncas no longer posed any challenge to Lakota interests: the first village downriver from the Sicangu domain was a Yankton one.[22]

Tabeau, who witnessed most of these developments, recognized the raw force of Lakotas but disparaged their lack of vision and political organization. "If this nation had more insight and policy, it could form a chain that would render it yet more formidable to all of its neighbors than it is. But their separation and mutual remoteness, necessitated by their form of hunting which does not permit of their living together in too great numbers," caused the Missouri-based Lakotas and the Mississippi-based Dakotas to "regard each other as strangers."[23]

But Lakotas and their eastern kin did in fact form the kind of chain Tabeau thought they should in order to fully capitalize on their overwhelming numbers. The difference was that theirs was a seasonal, on-off alliance and therefore not so easy to see. The Očhéthi Šakówiŋ had become an imposing alliance of seven divisions extending from the Ȟaȟáwakpa to the Mníšoše and beyond. For much of the year that alliance lay loose as individual bands sought pasture, game, and goods in different corners of their massive domain. But every spring they came together in trade rendezvous that doubled as political meetings where the decisions and disputes of the year were exposed to public scrutiny. During those crucial days and weeks, oyátes shared resources, pooled information, identified threats and opportunities, and smoked the calumet, reaffirming their shared identity as the Seven Council Fires.

Cut from the same cultural cloth, Lakotas mirrored the exquisitely malleable Očhéthi Šakówiŋ in character and composition. In the late eighteenth and early nineteenth centuries, as their presence along the Mníšoše grew, Lakotas shifted shape once again, now bending to the contours of the river that bestowed them with unprecedented power. The multi-oyáte Saone coalition loosened as Minneconjous peeled off, carving out a distinct niche downriver. Seeking better trading opportunities, many Minneconjou bands migrated all the way south near Sicangus who operated as gatekeepers into the upper Missouri trade. Sans Arcs, Two Kettles, Sihasapas, and Hunkpapas may have also begun to separate from the Saones around this time and move downstream.[24]

It was an unusually rapid transfiguration and it did not unfold without difficulty. "Time people were on prairie. No water," notes a Hunkpapa winter count. "Time people had no horses," reads another. But it was also restorative and exhilarating for this may have been the moment when Lakotas assumed their sacred form as seven oyátes and became "allies against all others of mankind." Oral histories relate how, in a time before time, Lakotas "expanded and grew to have seven bands." Articulating a distinctive intermesh of the sublime and the practical in the Lakota way of being, Slow Buffalo, a prominent chief, announced: "We are seven bands and from now on we will scatter over the world, so we will appoint one chief for each band." "The Mysterious One"—Wakȟáŋ Tȟáŋka—

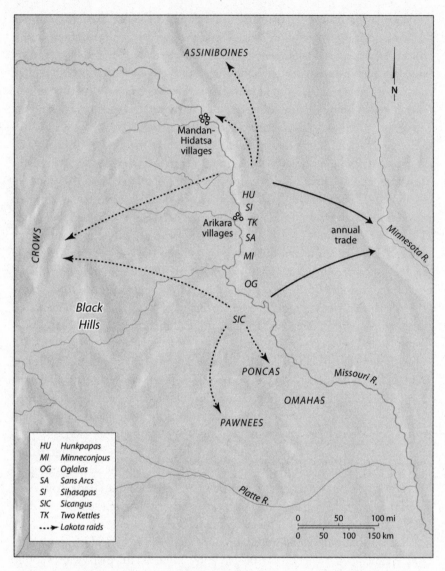

18. The seven Lakota oyátes in the early nineteenth century. Map by Bill Nelson.

"has given us this place, and now it is up to us to try to expand ourselves. We will name every person and everything." He sent chiefs to the east, west, and north, but not to the south, for "other people would come from that direction."[25]

Splitting and linking up, oyátes spread out along the upper the Mníšoše, narrowing the spaces among them. What gaps remained they stitched together through mobility. Thióšpayes moved constantly up and down the channel, seeking trade, tribute, horses, game, pasture, and firewood. In doing so, they brushed against one another, connecting and partially shading into one another. Each grouping and regrouping, whether large or small, was a socially charged occasion where not only individuals but extensive kinship networks came together and interlocked. In 1801 Hunkpapas adopted horse tails as a symbol of leadership, suggesting how mobility and power were becoming intertwined, and three years later Oglalas and Yanktonais performed the *huŋká* adoption cere- mony by singing "in praise of one another using horse tails." It was the first time a holy man officiated the ritual by wielding "a wand with pendant horse hair," and it marked a deepening synthesis among horses, humans, and belonging. The upper Mníšoše became a nomad's space where mobile Lakota bands coalesced around the liquid spine of their world.[26]

ON THAT NATION WE WISH MOST PARTICULARLY
TO MAKE A FRIENDLY IMPRESSION

In the fall of 1804 the Lewis and Clark expedition crashed all but blindly into the expanding Lakota domain. It was not because of lack of preparation. It was rather a failure to see, learn, and adapt.

Thomas Jefferson, a sentimental rationalist, a supremely eloquent advocate of individual freedom, and a lifelong slaveholder, saw the world through ideal forms and stark dichotomies. That is also how he saw America. On his imaginary map the continent was a symmetrical whole of two matching halves with the Missis- sippi as a unifying axis—the West the mirror image of the East. Each half had a pyramidal spine—the Rocky Mountains the western equivalent of the Appala- chians—and a crucial artery: the Missouri was for the West what the Ohio was for the East, the great channel of movement and commerce that attached a vast interior hinterland to the Mississippi, the pivot where the two Americas con- verged and could become one. For Jefferson this was reassuring and sublime and he saw destiny in it: just as the American settlers were already moving down the Ohio toward the Mississippi, they would soon be pushing up the Missouri, ex- tending the American republic from sea to sea. It was carved in stone.[27]

Anxious to secure the West with American presence on the ground, Jefferson had in 1801 begun to educate his private secretary Meriwether Lewis about its natural history and geopolitics, molding the physically imposing scholarly man into a hybrid of a frontiersman and a polymath who could execute the critical first plunge into the unknown as the leader of the Corps of Discovery, a new unit of the United States Army. Lewis recruited a retired army officer, William Clark, as his co-commander, and the pair spent nearly a year preparing for a projected two-year journey to the Pacific. When the Louisiana Purchase was finalized in the summer of 1803, Lewis and Clark started preparations and in December established Camp Dubois near St. Louis, where they awaited the official transfer in early March. The commanders made the most of the wait, interviewing fur traders, pouring over their maps and journals, and recruiting and training interpreters, guides, and boatmen. As the scraps of information cohered, they grew anxious. Their greatest challenge might not be logistical—somehow navigating largely unknown rivers for thousands of miles—but political. The continent, and the Missouri in particular, was full of Indians. One crew member braced himself "to pass through a country possessed by numerous, powerful and warlike nations of savages, of gigantic stature, fierce, treacherous and cruel; and particularly hostile to white men."[28]

Jefferson had handed the captains a monumental task. They were to inspect the flora and fauna, pioneer an all-water passage to the Pacific, end British dominance of the inland trade, harness the Missouri for U.S. commerce, and project U.S. sovereignty into the West—a mission that gathered urgency when, in the fall of 1803, Jefferson began seriously contemplating the removal of all Indians into the West and envisioning an expansive trading empire built on an Indigenous substratum. Jefferson's vision, then, hinged on forging friendly relations with American Indians, which in itself did not seem an insurmountable challenge. The fur trader maps from the late 1790s suggested an ordered, village-dotted Missouri corridor where the explorers could find food, shelter, and tractable Natives. The maps were essentially address books that would guide Lewis and Clark all the way up to the Mandan country where the charts went blank.[29]

Jefferson sent Lewis extracts of Jean-Baptiste Truteau's journal, which detailed Lakotas' aggressive trade policies along the Missouri. Jefferson's selections were both hyperbolic and disquieting. Lewis learned about a Lakota nation that possessed "from 30. to 60.000[?] men, and abound in fire-arms," a gross exaggeration that captures how ubiquitous Lakotas had become in the deep interior. "Although you will pass through no settlements of Sioux," Jefferson advised, "you will probably meet with parties of them. On that nation we wish most particularly to make a friendly impression, because of their immense power."[30]

Beyond that, however, Lewis and Clark possessed little concrete knowledge about the upper Missouri or Lakotas. A few days before their departure, Clark made a note of "a Mr. *Teboux* [Tabeau] who is at present... up the Missouri [and] can give us much information in relation to that country." The captains anticipated Lakotas to be critical to their success, but could not predict much more beyond a hazy "probability of an opposition from roving parties of Bad Indians." They prepared special bundles of gifts for the village-dwelling Otoes, Poncas,

Omahas, Arikaras, Mandans, and the unknown "foreign Nations" beyond the Mandans, but the Lakotas did not merit one. It was as if they did not belong on the explorers' imagined map of sedentary Indians.[31]

What the explorers lacked in knowledge, they tried to make up in merchandise, matériel, and military discipline. Jefferson had initially envisioned a compact expedition of "ten or twelve chosen men," but the co-captains expanded their crew to forty-odd men and stockpiled Indian presents which included, among other things, 4,600 sewing needles, 2,800 fishhooks, 130 rolls of tobacco, and a large assortment of beads, each item listed and catalogued with such determined precision that certainty itself seemed to arise from it. Clark equipped the bow of their fifty-five-foot keelboat with a bronze swivel cannon that could fire a one-pound lead ball or sixteen musket balls with enough velocity to cut through a man. He also mounted two swiveled blunderbusses, heavy shotguns that used musket balls and scrap iron on the stern. Each of their two pirogues was also armed with a swivel gun, and Lewis carried an air rifle that used compressed air to launch projectiles to impress the Natives.[32]

Lewis and Clark felt ready, but things were changing so rapidly in the upper Missouri country that much of their information was already dated when they embarked in early May. The documents they had consulted painted Lakotas as an aggressive but ephemeral presence along the upper Missouri, detached from the more structured villager world. Like nearly all portrayals of the era, they depicted nomads as capricious opportunists who ruled by terror and possessed but a vague understanding of territoriality. If the picture was menacing, it was also reassuring: whatever power such brutes wielded was surely but an anomaly arising from the absence of a firmer, more civilized rule, the kind the captains were determined to deliver upriver.

A SPOONFUL OF YOUR MILK

Yet a speck of doubt had taken root. Lewis and Clark had set their sights on the Pacific, but they knew that the first leg would be the most critical part of their endeavor. A gateway into the far West, the Missouri was the crucible where Jefferson's imperial vision would either congeal or crumble. Jefferson himself wrote a month after the expedition's departure that the crew "must stand well" with the Osages and the Sioux "because in their quarter we are miserably weak."[33]

The Corps of Discovery was to establish peace among the river's many Native groups and make them understand that their lands now belonged to the United States. They were to be pinned down and arranged into a neat row extending eastward toward the seat of a new father in Washington who would protect and provide for them. Thus reconstructed, the Missouri Valley would become an orderly commercial highway where each Native nation would enjoy equal access to American benevolence. Lewis and Clark were harbingers of empire, but they were also harbingers of Enlightenment. Jefferson—and, by extension, Lewis and Clark—envisioned the West as an inhabited wilderness on which a new rational order could be inscribed through a new science of remaking people and worlds. It was a brash and profoundly ironic vision. Jefferson, a republican purist who loathed the idea of a robust federal government, had launched a massive projection of state power into the North American West to mold its people into his model of an enlightened man—such was the hold of the Louisiana Territory on his imagination.[34]

The Jeffersonian vision had its first serious test in early August when the Corps met with Otoes and Missourias above the Platte confluence. The captains stuck to the script, parading for the Indians, instructing them with speeches, and "making" chiefs with medals. They shot the air gun and thought that the Indians were "happy to find that they had fathers which might be depended on." But when the expedition reconnected with Otoes two weeks later, the mood had changed. "I came here naked and must return home naked," Big Horse complained in the coded language of kinship. He expected gifts to keep his young warriors from going to war; "a Spoon ful of your milk will qui[e]t all." He asked the Americans to act like kin and provide goods that sustained social relationships, but the captains had little patience for such quotidian concerns. Driven by the Jeffersonian vision of a moldable Missouri Valley, they pushed on, imagining their expedition essentially as a single multi-stop diplomatic intervention geared for maximum efficiency.[35]

Not long after, far upriver, a more pointed intervention took place. Tabeau was there to witness yet another demonstration of growing Lakota power over the Arikara villages. The Arikara coalition, "wearied by its losses," accepted a peace overture from Mandans and Hidatsas and prepared to send a peace pipe to them. Arikara envoys traveled upriver among the Mandans who received them "with open arms loaded with presents." Custom demanded that Mandans send a delegation to Arikaras to confirm peace, but they never made it. Lakotas forced them to turn back, aborting the conciliation. They now commanded the upper Missouri with an iron grip.[36]

THOSE NATIONS ABOVE WILL NOT OPEN THEIR EARS

After two and a half months of travel—navigating sandbars, snags, collapsing cutbanks, and the five-mile-per-hour current, drinking the silty water, and battling dysentery—the Corps of Discovery reached the James River junction. The Americans had entered Yankton lands and set the dry prairie on fire to announce themselves. On August 29 the expedition came across a large party of Indians who quickly understood that this was no ordinary trading party; the bulky keel-boat and the heavily armed crew proclaimed a different kind of purpose. Lewis and Clark had tobacco, corn, and iron kettles packed into a canoe and sent it across the river. The next morning, as Yanktons crossed the river in full regalia, the captains, also in dress uniforms, put up a flag and ordered a gun salute. Lewis delivered his stock speech about peace and trade, after which the captains distributed gifts, believing that they were creating chiefs by simply recognizing some individuals as such with medals.[37]

Yankton chiefs responded the following day—a common Native custom—speaking through Pierre Dorion, the Corps' accomplished interpreter who had lived for many years with Yanktons and was fluent in their dialect. Lewis had proposed a new relationship by invoking a different kind of future. Yanktons demanded that the Americans conform to established practices by appealing to the past. "Listen to what I say," demanded Shake Hand. "I had an English medal when I went to See them, I went to the Spanoriards they gave me meadel and Some goods, I wish you would do the Same for my people." Medals and gifts symbolized generosity and commitment, Shake Hand insisted, not power and submission. Unimpressed with the abstractions of the Great Father's authority, Yanktons focused on the most tangible thing in front of them: the two merchandise-laded pirogues on the riverbank. Aware of the expedition's upriver ambitions, Yanktons made a bid. The Sioux, not the Arikaras or any other villagers, should be the focal point, Half Man insisted: "We open our ears, and I think our old Frend Mr. Durion can open the ears of the other bands of Soux." "But I fear those nations above will not open their ears, and you cannot I fear open them."[38]

Lewis and Clark duly recorded Half Man's words and continued upriver. They left Dorion behind with instructions to arbitrate a peace between the Yanktons and their neighbors. The stopover had been hasty, bordering on dismissive, stripping off the expedition's authoritative veneer to reveal what it really was: an undersized reconnaissance venture that needed to move fast before the wide-ranging British might stop them.

KILL TWENTY SUCH NATIONS IN ONE DAY

The Americans entered the drier short-grass plains in September, finding themselves moving through a faunal bounty of prairie dogs, coyotes, deer, elk, pronghorns, goats, jackrabbits, and bison herds that covered the grasslands into the horizon. They knew they were approaching the Sicangu domain when they saw "a great Smoke" on the west bank. If Lewis and Clark had largely managed to follow their own script among Yanktons, they now entered a Lakota one.[39]

Sicangus had probably observed the Corps for some time from the riverbanks, tracing its arduous progression upriver. Finally, on September 23, they decided to enforce border control by sending three young to swimmers to the keelboat. The boys communicated through sign language that there were two camps close by. The captains gave them tobacco, sent them off with an invitation to a council at the mouth of the next river, and began to prepare "all things for action in Case of necessity." Next day, as the boats approached the site, the expedition's hunter, having camped alone on an island, shouted that his horse—the expedition's last—had been stolen. Five Sicangu warriors came to the riverbank, asking to get on board. Americans demanded the horse back, claiming that it was intended as a gift to their chief and shouting that they "were not afraid of any Indians." The warriors pulled away. The Americans made camp at the mouth of the Bad River and anchored the boat seventy feet offshore where they had a broad firing range over the site. They put most of their men on board, close to the guns and ready to flee.[40]

The council took place on a large sandbar in the Bad, which Lakotas knew as the Tranquil Water. Lewis and Clark found themselves incapacitated even before the talks began. Having left their principal translator with Yanktons, they now discovered to their shock that their second interpreter, Peter Cruzatte, hardly spoke Lakota; Lakotas seem to have spoken Omaha, which Cruzatte translated into English. Lewis gave a cursory speech, which the captains augmented by staging a military parade and handing out gifts. They recognized Black Buffalo as "the grand Chief" and invited him and two other headmen, the Partisan and Medicine Bull, on board the keelboat to show them "Such Curiossities as was Strange to them." Those included whiskey, "¼ a glass" each. The chiefs were "verry fond" of it and "Sucked the bottle after it was out."[41]

This was the Corps' standard spectacle of imperial theatrics and it was ill-fitted for the ascending Sicangus. Without fully realizing it, Lewis and Clark had stepped into a dynamic Indigenous world where power rested on rivalry. Sicangu leaders competed, often fiercely, for trade, prestige, and followers. Individuals and families gravitated toward competent leaders who could look after their needs and eschewed those who could not. It was an ethos that fueled chronic friction, but it also bestowed the Lakota society with tremendous flexibility and staying power. Whenever and wherever Lakotas faced challenges or spotted opportunities, they could cluster around leaders best equipped to see them through. At times of crisis the entire Lakota society could realign around new political coordinates.[42]

In the fall of 1804 Lakotas were in the midst of such a realignment. Diseases, new commercial prospects, and growing military power had opened up the continental interior for them in unprecedented ways, fueling aspirations and inciting rivalries. Recognizing Black Buffalo as the first chief of the Sicangus was a mistake, for it alienated the Partisan, a war leader who had for years vied with Black Buffalo for preeminence. A lavish distribution of trade goods could have diffused the situation, but Lewis and Clark were not traders. The Partisan moved to derail the American-Sicangu accommodation that threatened to marginalize him.

Clark realized that things were spinning out of control when the Partisan began feigning drunkenness "as a Cloake for his rascally intentions." Clark and seven men forced the chiefs into a pirogue and ferried them back ashore. Clark disembarked, but Sicangus refused to leave the vessel. Three young Sicangus seized its bow cable, and the chiefs said that they "were poor and wished to keep the períogue with them"—that much was clear from the hurried, mangled translations. Clark insisted on getting back on board, but Sicangus refused him, saying that "they had soldiers as well as he had." The Partisan declared that the Americans could not advance because he had not received enough presents. He would hold the pirogue as a toll.[43]

Clark, who had been born into a culture of politeness that hinged on gestures and words that gave no offence, felt that the insults were becoming "So personal." He drew his sword, triggering a rapid escalation. Lewis, on board, ordered the blunderbusses and the swivel gun to be loaded. Black Buffalo sent off the three young men and grasped the cable himself while the Partisan "walked off to the Party at about 20 yards back, all of which had their bows Strung & guns Cocked." Clark, getting "warm," told "in verry positive terms to them all" that "his soldiers were good, and that he had more medicine on board his boat than would kill twenty such nations in one day." The expedition, he said, "must and would go on." Black Buffalo said that "he had warriers too and if we were to go on they would follow us and kill and take the whole of us by degrees." Clark responded that a simple letter to "their great father the president" would "have them all distroyed as it were in a moment." Black Buffalo released the cable, and Clark offered his hand to him. The chief walked past him to his warriors. With Sicangus "pointing their arrows blank," Clark could but watch as the two chiefs calmly walked into position, arranging their men into a face-off.[44]

THE WHITE VILLAGE

Had someone lost nerve and fired, the Lewis and Clark expedition could have become a footnote in history. Sicangus would have in all likelihood prevailed against the outnumbered Americans, and even if they had not, news of Sicangu deaths would have traveled upstream faster than the wašíču procession, prompting other Lakota oyátes to retaliate and abort the expedition. And had that happened, American expansion into the interior may have been delayed by years, perhaps long enough for the British to entrench themselves in the upper Missouri valley and the Pacific Northwest strongly enough to contain U.S. expansion to lower latitudes.

But no one flinched at the Bad River. Black Buffalo defused the situation by appealing to the most obvious thing that separated them from the Corps: families. He "requested that their women and children See the Boat as they never Saw Such an one." Black Buffalo acknowledged that the Americans were not merchants, nor "loaded with Goods, but he was Sorry to have us leave them So Soon—they wished to come on board." Clark took Black Buffalo, Medicine Bull, and two "Brave men" in. They proceeded about a mile upriver and "anchored out off a willow Island." "I call this Island bad humered Island," Clark wrote in his journal that night, "as we were in a bad humer."[45]

Next day, with Black Buffalo guiding the convoy, the boats sailed four miles upriver. The Americans had entered the heart of the Sicangu country and felt diminished. Sicangu warriors lined up on the riverbank, observing them: hundreds of staring faces showing "great anxiety" and appearing "generally ill looking." Black Buffalo indicated a landing site near a village, and the Americans anchored one hundred yards from shore.[46]

The Corps had been brought into one of the foremost centers of power in the American interior. Clark went ashore and then he was swept into midair, twenty hands holding him on a white buffalo robe. From this elevated and enfeebling position—he was not "permitted to touch the ground," he later protested to his journal—the explorer was offered a sumptuous display of Sicangu power and grandeur. Mostly he saw white. He was carried into a ring-shaped village of some one hundred tipis, all of them made of tanned white buffalo robes, precious luxury items. He also counted many Omaha captives, taken in a recent raid, before he was "put down in the grand Councl house on a White dressed robes." Before long he was joined by Lewis, also carried in. The two captains were placed next to a six-foot sacred circle reserved for medicine bundles, calumet pipes, and pipe stands. The smell of roasting dog and bison meat filled the lodge. They faced two chiefs, and around them sat seventy warriors in a circle. They saw one American and two Spanish flags. As the captains processed the coded messages—Sicangus' access to otherworldly powers, their international reach, their commitment to peace—an elder spoke softly, asking the newcomers to have pity on his people.[47]

The graphic messages were vital because the Americans, lacking a skilled interpreter, could not understand much of what was said. The council became a spectacle of hard negotiation through dimly understood signs and gestures. A "great Chief . . . rose in great State" to address the congress, but a flustered Clark only discerned that the speech was "to the Same purpos" as that of the elder. The chief then offered the calumet and made a "Sacrifise to the flag," evoking a relationship of peace and sharing with the Americans, a proposition that may have been sanctioned beforehand by the seventy Sicangu men present. Then a procession of women arrived, delivering a different kind of message. They "Came forward highly decerated with the Scalps & Trofies of war of their fathes Husbands & relations, and Danced the war Dance, which they done with great chearfulness untill 12 oClock." The exhausted captains asked to be excused, at which point Black Buffalo offered them women—an attempt to turn the obstinate newcomers into kin, to fit them in. The captains promptly refused the offer, and Black Buffalo, the Partisan, and two other chiefs accompanied them to the keelboat. They "Staid all night," preventing a nocturnal escape.[48]

The next day saw the diplomacy shifting from an assertion of collective Sicangu power to its flipside: the decentralized nature of Sicangu politics. Clark was taken into individual meetings with the Partisan, an unnamed elder, and Black Buffalo, and then back into the great lodge where another scalp dance was performed, some eighty women holdings Omaha scalps on sticks. The round of meetings laid bare the Lakota political system, its inherent egalitarianism and emphasis on personal relationships. Sicangu leaders were forging all-important bonds between their bands and the Americans that would be the sinews of any relationship they might have in the future. Sicangus could embrace the distant Great Father if he took pity on them and sent them gifts, but here, on the ground, these Americans would have to be fitted in as kin or not at all. Sicangus again offered Clark a woman for the night, asking him to "take her & not Dispise them," and again he refused. Withdrawing, he stepped into a pirogue, which slammed against the keelboat's anchor cable and broke it. Both vessels began to rock violently, and Clark shouted an alarm. Reactions on both sides revealed the anxiety that had built up during the outwardly polite talks. Within minutes two hundred armed Sicangu warriors lined the shoreline. The Americans took that as an attempt "to Stop our proceeding on our journey and if Possible rob us." Clark could not sleep that night.[49]

In the morning the Americans were determined to move on, but the familiar scene played out once again. There was a gathering of warriors by the boats, a now-expected demand that the expedition must stay put, and a seizure of the keelboat's bowline. The Partisan demanded a flag and tobacco as a recognition of his chiefly status, and Clark, losing his calm, threw a carrot of tobacco on the ground, shouting, "You have told us you are a great man—have influence—take this tob[acc]o & shew us your influence by taking the rope from your men & letting go without coming to hostilities."

But it was Black Buffalo who asserted his authority. Overriding the Partisan, he asked the Americans to give tobacco to the warriors holding the cable. Lewis warned that they "did not mean to be trifled with," to which Black Buffalo responded that "he was mad too, to See us Stand So much for 1 carrit of tobacco," a put-down that seemed to hit its mark. Lewis, his poise crumbling, threw the warriors some more tobacco, and Black Buffalo released the cable. The Corps rushed upriver.[50]

AS TO THE CHILD

Lewis and Clark were always more circumspect about their failures than their triumphs. The Sicangu episode was, at best, a disaster averted. Instead of recognizing chiefs who could visit the president in Washington, the captains had been reduced to pawns of fiercely competitive Sicangu politics. Clark fell silent in his journal about the humiliation. "I am verry unwell I think for the want of Sleep" was all he was willing to divulge.[51]

It did not have to be that way. In 1804 the Sicangus, along with several other Lakota oyátes, were firmly integrated in the St. Louis commercial system as major traders. Had the Americans recognized that and acted accordingly by extending them preferential treatment, things may have unfolded differently. Black Buffalo and other Sicangu leaders were not trying as much to prevent the Americans from continuing upriver as to integrate them into *their* trade emporium as suppliers. Sicangus played a critical role in regulating the Missouri commerce and knew that a total block of upriver traffic risked killing the trade for good. But instead of savvy traders, Lewis and Clark saw rowdy and uncouth nomads and dismissed them as predators to be avoided.[52]

By the time the Corps pushed ahead, Lakotas had already taken measures to thwart their efforts to draw the upriver villagers into their fold: Lakota agents may have already reached the Arikaras. There were inklings of new troubles, and the Americans "prepared for action." Along the way they saw tangible signs of Lakota power: the riverbanks were dotted with abandoned Arikara villages, a silent testimony of smallpox and the explosive expansion of Lakotas in the valley in previous years.

When the Corps arrived in the cluster of three Arikara villages at the confluence of the Grand River on October 8, they witnessed, without realizing it, yet another upshot of Lakota expansion. The walled villages were built to capacity, lodges crammed in "close together." The area teemed with so many dialects that "the Different Villages do not understade all the words of the others." People had simply melted away underneath their leaders, who were now "captains without companies," competing for supporters in a milieu of deepening "insubordination and discord." The Corps had entered a refugee center, a "tower of Babel" full of different people "compelled to Come together for protection" against Lakotas.[53]

Lewis and Clark set to work. They met with resident French traders, including Pierre-Antoine Tabeau, and Clark delivered the standard speech to the gathered Arikaras. They lavished gifts and "made" three chiefs—Kahawissassa, Pocasse, and Piaheto—"one for each Village," and "Shot the Air gun, which astonished them." This, at long last, was the kind of reaction the explorer-diplomats expected, but then came a rude awakening: Clark spotted two "Sioux in the Council." Lakotas, it turned out, were manipulating Arikara politics from within. The two Lakota emissaries had come "to interceed with the Ricaras to Stop us."[54]

The available information Lewis and Clark gathered before their departure had depicted the Lakotas as a commercial barrier, fixed around the Big Bend, and a kind of hovering menace around the upper Missouri. But things had changed dramatically in a few years, and the captains now began to understand how thoroughly the Lakotas dominated the upper river through their mobile power politics.

An alliance between Americans and Arikaras—which could have been extended to include Hidatsas and Mandans when the expedition pushed farther upriver—posed a serious threat to Lakota interests, and they counted on Arikaras to reject the Americans. The two Lakotas shadowed Lewis and Clark for two days, forcing them to confer with Arikaras under surveillance. Lakotas, Clark noted pithily, held "great influence over the Rickeres, poisen their minds and keep them in perpetial dread." He later composed an account of the close and coercive relationship: "Though they are the oldest inhabitants," Arikaras "may properly be considered the farmers or *tenants at will* of that lawless, savage and rapacious race the Sioux *Teton*, who rob them of their horses, plunder their gardens and fields, and sometimes murder them, without opposition.... They maintain a partial trade with their oppressors the Tetons, to whom they barter horses, mules, corn, beans, and a species of tobacco which they cultivate; and receive in return guns, ammunition, kettles, axes, and other articles.[55]

But some Arikaras had recognized an opportunity to unfasten the Lakota grip and they seized it. Aware of the confrontation with the Sicangus downriver, Kahawissassa promised the Americans free passage upriver: "Can you think any one Dare put their hands on your rope of your boat. No! not one dar." He then accepted Lewis and Clark's offer to mediate among the upper Missouri villagers: "When you Get to the mandans we wish you to Speak good words with that Nation for us. we wish to be at peace with them." It was a risky maneuver, and Arikaras needed American protection to see it through. Chief Pocasse pledged to visit "his great father" in Washington, while raising "a Doubt as to the Safty on passing the nations below particularly the Souex." The message was clear: if Americans wanted peace and trade to flourish along the Missouri, they would have to first contain the Lakotas.[56]

The talks stirred both "terror and confidence" among Arikaras, Tabeau learned. By "leaguing themselves" with Mandans against Lakotas, they could, at long last, escape "the slavery of the Sioux." When the Americans left the Arikaras in mid-October, an Arikara leader, Too Né, was with them. The expedition passed a Lakota camp. Lakotas knew the Americans were heading upriver to forge an anti-Lakota alliance between Arikaras and Mandans. The time for talk was over: "Those people only viewed us & did not Speak one word." They were waiting for the Americans to leave so they could undo the damage they had done.[57]

The Corps arrived in Mandan and Hidatsa lands in late October and, with sixteen hundred miles of the Missouri behind them, set up a winter camp. Mandan chiefs sat down with the captains and agreed to host them. The Americans built a stockade and barracks they would call Fort Mandan slightly downriver from the two Mandan villages. The Corps had won entry into the greatest trading citadel of the northern Great Plains. Horses, blankets, guns, metal utensils, beaver pelts, buffalo robes, leather clothing, meat, corn, *Dentalium* shells, pipestone, and other necessities and luxuries exchanged hands in the great Mandan trade fairs, which attracted nomads from the western buffalo plains, St. Louis merchants from the south, and Canadian and Native trappers from the cold north. Lewis and Clark wanted the Mandan trade for the United States, and to have it they needed Mandans, Hidatsas, and Arikaras to form an alliance—and denounce the Lakotas.[58]

AN EYE OF SORROW

Back in the Arikara villages, Tabeau observed how Lakotas were already working to foil such an alliance, which "would become formidable for them." Lakotas meant to keep the three people separated through divide and rule politics. Only nine days after the Corps' departure, an Oglala band camped below the southernmost Arikara village. "By this maneuver, the three [Arikara] villages lie between the Sioux and their enemy," the Mandans. The maneuver also "closed the entrance to the buffalo" and brought Oglalas nearer to Arikara "horses which they carried off every day." As days passed Oglalas tightened the circle and stepped up horse raiding, the helpless Arikaras looking at them with "an eye of sorrow and regret." Regret-induced reevaluation was exactly what Oglalas were after. If Arikaras embraced Mandans and Americans as allies, they would have to survive without horses, bison, and the mercy of Lakotas.[59]

The Corps of Discovery's tenacious effort to create a unified villager front in the upper Missouri had prompted Lakotas to tighten their grip on the valley: they consolidated their power literally in the expedition's wake. As the Corps pushed upriver, Lewis and Clark fantasized about leaving behind a new imperial order of satellite Native villages bound to distant American centers in St. Louis and Washington. But underneath the veneer of authority they had instilled with medals and flags and promises, a stronger Lakota America emerged. Wašíču presumption had provoked an imperial Indigenous response.[60]

THE PIRATES OF THE MISSOURI

Lakotas were Lewis and Clark's greatest challenge. So ubiquitous were the Sioux in their thoughts and journals that Clark managed to spell the name twenty-seven different ways in his inspired orthography. And yet the captains never fully grasped how thoroughly Lakotas had eclipsed their enterprise, not even when Lakota tentacles reached them in the relative safety of Fort Mandan more than two hundred miles upriver from the Big Bend where their expedition had begun to falter.

Upon their arrival in the Mandan the country, Lewis and Clark immediately learned of a recent Lakota raid on the nearby Hidatsas, and Big White, the headman of the lower Mandan village, gave them a brief history of his people: "the Smallpox destroyed the greater part of the nation" after which "the Sioux and other Indians waged war, and killed a great maney, and they moved up the Missourie." In late November "an army of *Sioux*" attacked Mandans, and in February 1805 Americans themselves became targets. Twenty miles downriver from Fort Mandan, a party of 105 "Souix Savages" stopped members of the Corps and stole two horses. Not long after messengers brought a letter from Tabeau in the Arikara villages, warning that Lakotas were planning to come and "kill everry white man they See." But the messengers also said Arikaras were eager to move near Mandans and "join them against their common Enimey the *Souis*."[61]

The Arikara overture sent the imagination of the usually commonsensical Clark running. When an Arikara delegation was reported approaching in early April, Clark expected "the arrival of the whole *ricarra* nation" in the Mandan and Hidatsa country, a concentration of Native power that, at long last, could check the indomitable Lakotas. Four Arikaras showed up. The captains promised the pitiful contingent the Great Father's protection and sent Too Né downriver with six "well armed" soldiers and Joseph Gravelines, a veteran French trader-interpreter who was fluent in Arikara. They urged them not to yield when being "fired on by the Siouxs."[62]

Lewis and Clark fell silent on their personal feelings, but Clark's hurt seeps through the compiled observations on the Missouri Indians he put together at

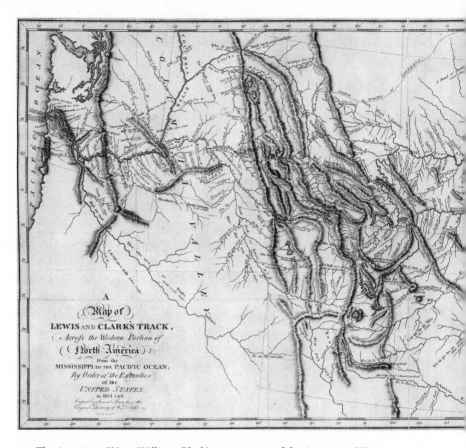

19. The American West. William Clark's master map of the American West
was at once a scientific triumph and an act of cartographic dispossession.
Although highly accurate in its description of the physical landscape, it left out
several Native nations, thereby making the Missouri Valley and western North
America appear sparsely inhabited and thus free for the taking. William Clark,

Fort Mandan. The Indians had acted nothing like the captains had hoped. They
had welcomed America's merchandize but not its paternal embrace; they had accepted the Americans as traders and potential allies, but not as their sovereigns.
They had, in other words, refused to be "discovered" by the Corps and brought
into the American fold as the children of a new great father.[63]

No Indian nation had done more to undermine the Jeffersonian vision than
Lakotas. Clark denounced them as "the vilest miscreants of the savage race, and
must ever remain the pirates of the Missouri." Like many explorer-colonists before them, Lewis and Clark were greedy learners who knew that their success

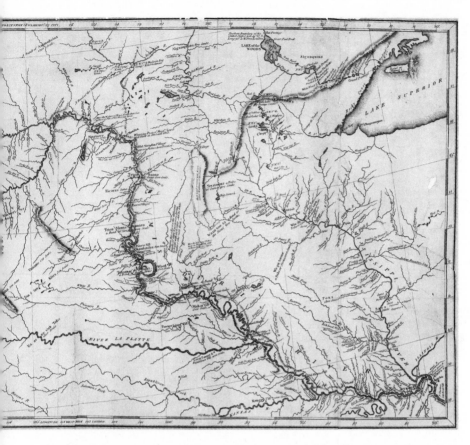

A *Map of Lewis and Clark's Track, across the Western Portion of North America from the Mississippi to the Pacific Ocean,* Samuel Lewis, copyist; Samuel Harrison, engraver. Philadelphia: Bradford and Inskeep, 1814. Courtesy of Library of Congress, Geography and Map Division.

or failure was largely determined by how well they understood the worlds they meant to appropriate. But the captains had learned much more about the flora and fauna than about Lakotas who remained a specter-like menace to them. Clark's was a planter's view of the world, and he saw in the nomadic Lakotas an organizationally shallow robber regime that preyed on weaker, less mobile, and less capricious people who lacked their propensity for swift violence. He counted the Corps as one of their victims. Lakotas, he told in 1810 to Nicholas Biddle, who wrote the first narrative of the expedition, were "a cunning vicious set," a condemnation echoed by Patrick Gass, a sergeant of the Corps, whose

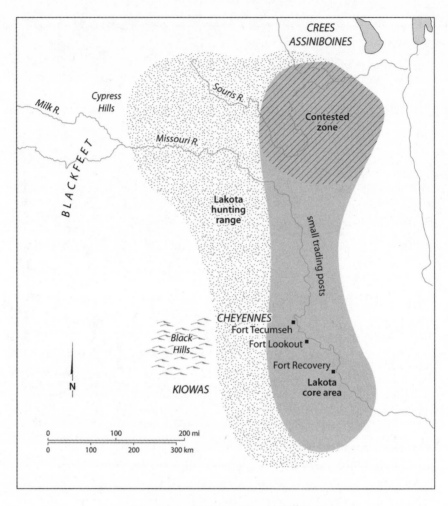

20. The Lakota Meridian. Map by Bill Nelson.

published journals were reprinted six times between 1808 and 1814 in London, Paris, Weimar, and Philadelphia. "It appears that these people," he instructed his audiences, "are an unsettled, ferocious, blood-thirsty race."[64]

Clark's influential denigration obscured more than it revealed. Rather than landless pirates who preyed on tillers and travelers, Lakotas were protectors of a newly established Indigenous hegemony. Lewis and Clark had sought a radical realignment of power in the American interior on an east-west axis, and they had crashed hard into the Lakota Meridian, a long, integrated south-north oriented corridor of power in the heart of the continent. Lakotas had transformed the Missouri's longitudinal section into an imperial valley through diplomacy, persuasion, and raw military force. Almost all the people Lewis and Clark tried to win over were already in Lakota orbit as allies or dependents. Instead of delivering Native peoples into the U.S. fold, Lewis and Clark muddled through the Lakota Meridian as also-rans.[65]

A LONG CIRCUIT WESTWARD

When the Corps left Fort Mandan in the spring of 1805, Lakotas once more asserted themselves in its wake. A year later two Canadian traders, Charles McKenzie and Alexander Henry, joined Le Borgne, a powerful Hidatsa chief, on a diplomatic mission to an Arapaho-Cheyenne-Lakota camp on the Knife River. Le Borgne was desperate to make peace with the nomads who cast a threatening shadow over his village, and he carried a large American flag as a demonstration of his political clout. But it was the nomads who dominated the encounter. The Canadians witnessed Lakotas' equestrian prowess in its raw, exuberant infancy. "The neighing, snorting, and prancing of such a large company of strange horses, meeting each other suddenly and being restrained by their riders, had really a very spectacular effect." The nomads adopted Hidatsas as allies in an expeditious ceremony. A Cheyenne leader, "posted in their center, mounted on a handsome black stallion," embraced Le Borgne's flag.[66]

> As soon as this great man had performed the ceremony of embracing the flag, his whole party came on full speed amongst us; at the same moment orders were given for us to proceed, and every one of them selected one of our party, whom he adopted as his comrade, which is done by riding up to and embracing him.... The bustle and noise of so many horses galloping and prancing through the ranks, while the war chiefs of all parties, now being intermixed, passed from right to left at full speed, each making his own arrangements in his own language, had quite a martial appearance. The substance of those speeches was to welcome each other, give mutual thanks for the present happy and auspicious occasion, and express their wishes that they might henceforth live like brothers, and bury in oblivion all former animosities.[67]

Yet Hidatsas remained wary, anticipating violence. Just a week after, back in his village, Le Borgne urged Henry to be on guard "as the time was nearly arrived when the Sioux frequented those parts, as they could subsist on berries" and "corn would soon to be fit to steal during the night." He advised Henry to "make a long circuit westward" when retuning to Canada.[68]

The longer route was necessary because the Sioux were in the way. The Sioux—Lakotas, Yanktonais, and Dakotas—had already extended their reach far to the north of the Mandan-Hidatsa country, clashing with Assiniboines and

Crees along the Souris River. Near that distant northern river, on a high hill, there was a base known as the Dog Lodge, "a remarkable place which the Sioux warriors often frequent in their hostile excursions." Soon Lakotas and their allies were patrolling the region "in hopes of falling in with Assiniboines and Crees who frequently hunt along this river": they were staking their claim to disputed hunting grounds. Canadian traders soon dubbed them as "the natural enemies of all the tribes in these parts."[69]

A few years later Lakotas met with the powerful Blackfoot Confederacy in the Cypress Hills some three hundred miles west of the Souris Valley. They formed a pact and agreed to divide hunting territories with the hills as the western boundary of the Lakota domain. Having solidified their control over the upper Missouri Valley, the increasingly nomadic and mobile Lakotas began shifting their ambitions on the vast animal-rich plains around them. Expansion fueled expansion. The conquest of the Missouri had created a slingshot effect that carried Lakotas far beyond the valley.[70]

THEY WOULD CERTAINLY KILL HIM

Lewis and Clark had traversed the Missouri Valley one imperial expansion too late and found it hard to accept. When they returned from their arduous and exhilarating journey to the Pacific sixteen months later, they once again plunged into the Lakota Meridian, which had only grown stronger during their absence. Mandans and Hidatsas were reeling. Whooping cough had ravaged their villages, and Lakotas had intensified their raiding. Lewis and Clark made one more bid to check the Lakota ascendancy. They invited Mandan leaders to visit Washington. The president, they promised, would listen to their troubles, send traders among them, and protect them.[71]

The offer was as unrealistic as it was alluring. Black Cat of the Mandans wanted to see "his Great Father" but said that Lakotas would "certainly kill him if he attempted to go down." Lakota hold of the upper Missouri seemed now nearly absolute, confining the villagers to the north. Clark asked René Jusseaume, a Canadian trader who had lived among Mandans and Hidatsas for fifteen years, to coax the villagers. He did find one headman, Sheheke, willing to go. What resulted was hardly the kind of embassy Lewis and Clark had in mind: one chief, a few women and children, and Jusseaume, a Canadian, braving Lakotas' river hegemony. When the Corps set out downriver on August 17, all Mandan headmen saw them off, crying. As Clark was about to embark, the chiefs asked him to sit "one minit longer with them." They wanted to talk about Lakotas. It was more a lamentation than anything else. After the Americans left, they said, Lakotas would come and "kill them." Clark told them to fight.[72]

By late August the expedition neared Sicangu territory, and the explorers grew anxious. They spotted some eighty armed warriors on the northeast bank and hoped they were Yanktons, Poncas, or Omahas. Clark walked toward them on a sandbar, and three Indians swam to him. They were Black Buffalo's Sicangus. Painful memories flushing over him, Clark had an interpreter tell them they were "bad people." American traders were arriving soon, he warned, and were "sufficiently Strong to whip any vilenous party who dare to oppose them." Sicangus told him to cross so they could kill them all.

Clark and his men resolved to stare at the Sicangus, thinking that it "put them some Agitation as to our intentions." Then, quietly, they continued downriver. Twenty-four days later they arrived in St. Louis, finding the city bubbling with expectation, ambition, and opportunism.[73]

NON-STATE ACTORS

Whatever the idiosyncrasies brewing within him, the chameleonic General James Wilkinson was a product of his time. The late eighteenth and early nineteenth centuries were the Age of Revolutions when, suddenly, almost everything seemed possible. If thirteen quarrelsome colonies could oust the world's most powerful empire, if a provincial corporal could become an emperor and the conqueror of Europe, and if a former slave could rise to liberate a fabulously wealthy Caribbean sugar colony, what prospects then could be found in the North American interior where an overstretched and apparently tottering Spanish Empire seemed to be the dominant power?

The convoluted career of Wilkinson provided one answer. After a checkered service in the Continental Army, Wilkinson became a land speculator in Kentucky and then reached out to Esteban Miró, the governor of Spanish Louisiana, offering to deliver the Kentuckians into the Spanish fold in exchange for trading rights on the Mississippi. Charming, enterprising, and witty, Wilkinson became Agent 13, feeding the Spanish information about American designs in coded messages while rising in the ranks of the U.S. Army he had rejoined. December 1803 found him in New Orleans to officially take possession of Louisiana as its first U.S. military commissioner, a position that did not prevent him from informing the Spaniards, in exchange for a pension, on how to best check U.S. westward expansion. He tipped off the Spaniards about the goals of the Lewis and Clark expedition and then lobbied himself, grandiosely, into the post of the first governor of the Louisiana Territory, in which role he began conspiring with Aaron Burr, who in turn maneuvered to carve out a piece of the continent for himself. Whether that piece was to be New Orleans, the western states of the Union, or a new empire that hugged much of the Gulf Coast remained unclear. But then the general dropped the mercurial Burr, latched onto the man whose trust underwrote his survival, and began to plan expeditions to quench Jefferson's insatiable hunger for western facts. If Lewis and Clark embodied Lakotas' first exposure to America's geopolitical ambitions, Wilkinson embodied it for Dakotas.[74]

As the governor of the Louisiana Territory, Wilkinson operated in a world that was suspended between imperial ambiguities and national certainties and where little seemed fixed or self-evident—boundaries, identities, loyalties, futures. Not unlike the Sioux, Wilkinson operated at the margins of weak European empires, and the first meeting between the two proceeded admirably. In May 1805 Wilkinson received in St. Louis a large Dakota embassy. The envoys, "handsome, able bodied men," said that they had denounced their "old father," the governor of Canada, and were seeking a new one. They said they had recently killed a drunken French trader and now asked Wilkinson to pardon them, but there was a larger underlying agenda: they were making a bid to reclaim their old trapping grounds along the upper Mississippi for which they needed American support. Wilkinson pardoned the Dakotas and considered their request.[75]

It was an intriguing prospect for Wilkinson who did not seem to be able to resist a scheme when one presented itself. Was there a private fur trade fiefdom to be won through the Sioux? Lewis and Clark were still far in the West, their "perilous and expensive" enterprise uncertain under British infiltrations from Canada, and the upper Mississippi was still largely beyond American reach. There was a window for an enterprise. Wilkinson assigned, without authorization, Lieutenant William Zebulon Pike to reconnoiter the upper Mississippi and invite prominent chiefs to visit him. Somewhat defensively, with "small private means, not with any view to Self interest," he also dispatched John McClallan up the Missouri where the agent met the returning Lewis and Clark. When British traders moved to apply for American citizenship—the 1795 Jay Treaty allowed them to apply for naturalization on the basis of residence—Wilkinson promptly denied them, later admitting that his actions may have been "somewhat extrajudicial."[76]

Wilkinson's hard stance threatened to dismantle the entire economic and social world of Dakotas. It threatened to sever their life-giving commercial linkages to Canada and break up the many Dakota-British families that had become rooted in the very fabric of the Dakota society. By the time of their meeting with Wilkinson, Dakotas may have also learned from their Lakota kin at the spring rendezvous about the Lewis and Clark expedition and its imperial ambitions. From Sioux perspective, American aggression and arrogance were palpable in 1805. It demanded a response.[77]

One response came when British officers at Fort Amherstburg at the mouth of the Detroit River received a delegation of Sauks, Mesquakies, Odawas, and Potawatomis. They carried two pipes—of war and of peace—and a message from the Sioux. The Sioux had asked all of them to share a common dish and spoon, hold their territories in common, and "confront the new white nation now encroaching on Our Lands." The peace pipe was for the British. The Sioux invited them to join a confederacy of ten nations against "the White Devil with his mouth wide open ready to take possession of our lands." These devils were the Americans, and the war pipe was traveling to bring the British and Indians into a united front against them.[78]

The American countermove was already in motion with Pike readying to lead twenty soldiers up the Mississippi to locate its source, clear British traders from the area, and negotiate land sales with Indians. The enterprise was inspired by and modeled after the Lewis and Clark expedition, except that Wilkinson operated privately. Pike's hastily organized expedition left St. Louis in early August 1805; just two weeks later Wilkinson issued a proclamation barring foreign traders from the Missouri and Mississippi Valleys. Pike pushed all the way to Leech Lake, which he mistakenly identified as the source of the great river. But the expedition did make contact with several Dakota bands in the great confluence area where the Minnesota, Chippewa, and St. Croix Rivers merge into the Mississippi.[79]

He found Dakotas engaged in intensive hunting for British markets. He also found them widely dispersed, striving to harvest the declining animal populations for enough pelts, and fighting the Chippewas over trapping rights. He organized a summit and arranged as public a display of American power as he could in the heart of the Dakota domain. He had his men improvise a tent out of sails and invited Canadian and Scottish traders to witness a meeting with six Mdewakanton leaders. He announced that the United States had bought Louisiana from France and proposed to buy a piece of it again, now from the Mdewakantons for a military fort. The Mdewakantons agreed, because Pike promised that a trading post would supplement the fort. Americans were "many and strong," he said, and would come in "large boats." Two chiefs, Little Crow and Penichon, signed a treaty.[80]

Pike returned to St. Louis with a conspicuously terse document—barely 250 words—and confident that it had extended U.S. sovereignty among the Dakotas. The treaty was never proclaimed, and Wilkinson dispatched Pike on another unauthorized expedition, this time to survey the Arkansas and Red Rivers in Spanish territory. Meanwhile in the upper Mississippi Valley, Dakotas had no reason to believe that they had not been heard or that Americans would not care for their needs.[81]

THE IMPERIAL VALLEY

While Pike's arrival in St. Louis in April 1806 went largely unnoticed, the return of the Corps of Discovery five months later was a sensation. Lewis and

Clark brought back stories of spectacular natural phenomena, dozens of exotic Native peoples, and a dizzyingly expansive setting for the new American empire to realize its potential. And what resonated powerfully in the business-possessed St. Louis, they also reported of handsome profits that could be made. Clark's published letter to Jefferson in a Kentucky paper spoke of a land "richer in beaver and Otter than any country on earth" in the headwaters of the Missouri and Yellowstone, but most of the dissemination was word of mouth. If Clark's conclusion in his journal is any indication of what he relayed verbally, then even the Lakotas had become a prospect: "their trade might be made valuable if they were reduced to order."[82]

News of Lewis and Clark's discoveries had been relayed back to St. Louis, and when the Corps approached the city in the fall they encountered several trading outfits pushing upriver. Like traders, American policymakers expected an imminent consolidation of American commercial and territorial hegemony in Louisiana. At a dinner in St. Louis honoring the expedition, toasts were given to Jefferson, "The friend of science, the polar star of discovery, the philosopher and the patriot," to "the memory of Christopher Columbus," and to the Missouri itself, now poised to become "a vehicle of wealth to all the nations of the world." The Missouri did quickly become a commercial thoroughfare, but the immediate windfall would not be for the Americans.[83]

The first inklings that something was amiss surfaced in late 1806 and early 1807 when three expeditions embarked upriver. The first was led by Joseph Gravelines, whom Jefferson had dispatched to inform the Arikaras that their chief Too Né had died in Washington. Gravelines arrived with gifts and delivered the president's speech, which stated that the Americans were "all gun-men" and "numerous as the stars in the heavens." It also offered agricultural advice. The supreme corn farmers fell silent on Jefferson's lessons. What they did say stopped Gravelines in his tracks. "There was no other liar but their Father," they began, and announced that they had "resolved to do the same as the Sioux in stopping and Plundering all and every boats that would ascend as far as their villages." They seized Gravelines's boat. The affair bore a conspicuous Lakota imprint. In fact, as the subsequent events suggest, it may well have been orchestrated by Lakotas living among Arikaras.[84]

While Arikaras harangued Gravelines, two other expeditions were already ascending the river. The first belonged to Manuel Lisa, an energetic and opportunistic New Orleanian who would come to incite the disgust of Meriwether Lewis, the hatred of the Chouteaus, and the fear of James Wilkinson who had blocked him from developing trade routes with Spanish Santa Fe—an extra-legal endeavor the governor reserved for himself. Having devoured Lewis and

Clark's information, Lisa had quickly put together an expedition of over fifty men to tap into the rich fur lands in the Missouri's upper reaches. In Lisa's wake came a large government expedition led by Ensign Nathaniel Pryor, another member of the Lewis and Clark expedition, who had been assigned a compli-' cated agenda: escort a large Lakota delegation back to their village from a visit to St. Louis, deliver the Mandan chief Sheheke back to his village from an extended visit to Washington, and carry goods into both Lakota and Mandan villages. He had been given twenty-two traders, fourteen soldiers, and two boats to make it happen. The traders were under the command of Auguste Pierre Chouteau, a member of the powerful merchant family.[85]

Lisa's party passed the Sicangu chokepoint at the Big Bend without trouble, but it was stopped at the southernmost Arikara village where Lakotas and Arikaras levied a heavy toll in guns, powder, and ammunition — "about half of his goods," an astonishing boon. The Pryor expedition that followed left the Lakota delegation at Sicangu villages near the White River, where Pierre Dorion, Jr., the son of Lewis and Clark's interpreter, sponsored a trade fair for more than three hundred Lakota tipis. An Oglala winter count depicted the peaceful event as "Many people camped together and many flags flying."[86]

But when the flotilla continued upriver, it too was stopped at the first Arikara village — by Lakotas. Lakotas had maintained for years an internal colony among the Arikaras who had to endure "almost all the year a large crowd." More than six hundred warriors lined the riverbank, all of them brandishing guns, most of them probably just taken from Lisa. Lakotas shouted that Arikaras and Mandans were at war, thus breaking the news that Lewis and Clark's peace effort had indeed failed. With warriors "chewing their bullets," the Americans prepared to fire. Lisa, they learned, had diverted "the storm which threatened *his own boat*" by telling the Lakotas and Arikaras that the next expedition was coming specifically to trade with them. Chouteau offered to trade half of the goods earmarked for Mandans, but Lakotas prohibited him from moving on. Fighting broke out. Lakotas killed four of Pryor's men and chased his expedition downriver, Sheheke still on board. The humiliated Pryor reported that "even One Thousand men might fail in the attempt" of delivering Sheheke home.[87]

Lisa and his men, meanwhile, proceeded to the Yellowstone-Bighorn confluence where they built Fort Raymond, opened trade with Crows, and harnessed an impressive load of furs — a nucleus for a vast Rocky Mountain fur trade empire Lisa envisioned. Lisa returned to St. Louis buoyant and partnered with William Clark and the Chouteaus to form the Missouri Fur Company. In the spring of 1809 he launched another major expedition, now with 160 men, heading toward Fort Raymond. The brashly ambitious Lisa had grasped the logic of the Missouri trade and moved more carefully now. When pushing upriver, his crew built a new post for Sicangus on Cedar Island. The post was managed by a French trader Lakotas called Little Beaver. He was well liked and his post flourished. When he died in an accidental powder explosion, seven different winter counts reported his demise. The Missouri Fur Company lost in the blast a fur cache worth between twelve and fifteen thousand dollars.[88]

While fur traders like Lisa quickly adapted to the Missouri's geopolitical realities and conformed to Lakota expectations, government officials sought to avenge the attack on Pryor. In the summer of 1809 Meriwether Lewis, Wilkinson's successor as governor of Louisiana Territory, assigned Pierre Chouteau to deliver retribution "for the reputation of our Government, as for the security which it would Give to the future navigators of the river Missoury." He was also to escort chief Sheheke back home; the Mandan's protracted presence in St. Louis had been an acute embarrassment for Lewis, underscoring U.S. impotence in the face of the Lakota barrier. Yet Chouteau's target was not the Lakotas who had orchestrated the attack on Pryor, but the Arikaras: "exterpate that abandoned nation if necessary," read the order. Lewis had based his decision solely on geography, focusing on location rather than culpability. Three years after his epic expedition, Lewis still could not comprehend the Indigenous politics along the Missouri.[89]

Lewis had instructed Chouteau to recruit American traders and Indian auxiliaries along the way and "form a body of five hundred and Fifty." The governor's instructions were painstakingly thorough, detailing how the various auxiliaries should sequence their movements when approaching the Arikaras to ensure peaceful passage. When Chouteau encountered a Lakota party, he tried to recruit three hundred warriors. He was flatly refused and warned that any attempt to incite the Missouri tribes against one another would be severely punished. Six Lakota headmen joined Chouteau upriver and, once among the Arikaras, demanded he pardon the villagers. "I shall Ground my arms," Chouteau announced to Arikara chiefs, "untill new orders can be received from your Great Father who alone can pardon or destroy," a futile attempt to assert American authority that had already been repudiated. Arikaras were not for Chouteau to punish. They belonged to Lakotas. Chouteau was allowed to continue upriver, and he managed to deliver Sheheke back to his people. The chief died three years later, killed, according to a Mandan tradition, by the Sioux.[90]

REDUCED TO ORDER

By the early nineteenth century the Lakota river policy, founded on mobility, visibility, and ubiquity, was an accepted fact. Placating the "Pirates of the Missouri" had become the new normal, a necessary evil that had to be factored in as a built-in cost for the American fur trade to reach its full potential. Almost all American expeditions, small and large, had to abide by it. The New York–based fur trade mogul Jacob Astor's 1811 four-boat expedition to the Pacific Northwest—it was to connect with another Astorian expedition that had taken the *Tonquin* around Cape Horn to the mouth of the Columbia River—had to stop to furnish Lakotas with sacks of tobacco and corn near the Big Bend. The same year the near-ubiquitous Manuel Lisa was allowed to pass beyond the White River only after he promised to rebuild the burned Cedar Island post. Nicholas Boilvin, an Indian agent at Prairie du Chien, wrote that the Sioux "command the balance of power . . . and influence all the other indians on the Missouri and Mississippi in whatever political steps they may take." He believed that placating the Sioux "is alone sufficient to defend this frontier against" British inroads from the north. Out of fear and necessity, the Americans had to make the Lakotas integral for their burgeoning commercial and political ambitions in the West.[91]

A new narrative of the Lakotas began to emerge. By monitoring south-to-north traffic along the Missouri, Lakotas held the United States' imperial expansion hostage, forcing its traders and agents to pay to access the lands and resources in the far West. But from that edgy dynamic genuine accommodation emerged. From Lakota perspective, the Americans had merely conformed to the practices that had prevailed along the Missouri for a generation. Like the Spanish and French traders before them, the Americans had learned to share.

This changed the tone and methods of Lakota foreign policy. Lakotas no longer had to rely on naked force to be noticed. Instead of actual violence, they could rely on threats of violence to secure their needs. Rhetoric and calculated bravado began to replace raiding and war as principal foreign political tools. Lakotas were a haunting presence along the Missouri, one of the hot spots in early nineteenth-century North America, regulating commerce, managing allegiances, and enforcing behaviors. Rather than being "reduced to order" by American might as Clark had anticipated, the opposite had happened. Lakotas were reshaping the interior in their own image.

It was hard work. Lakotas and their Yankton and Yanktonai allies now policed a four-hundred-mile stretch of the Missouri, which required diplomacy that was measured, swift, and portable. A constant theme that emerges from the reports of American traders along the Missouri is a sense of being shadowed by Lakotas moving along the banks, ready to interfere with any transgressions. When Lisa built a trading post near the Mandan-Hidatsa villages, Lakotas attacked and killed some two dozen.[92]

It also required new kinds of leaders, at once assertive and adaptable, men who could be accommodating as well as intimidating, could speak eloquently at one moment and mete out brutal violence the next, and possessed the sang-froid to face down the agents of a burgeoning empire that boasted millions of people and awesome technologies—in short, charismatic individuals capable of imperial posturing. Lakotas already had such leaders in Black Buffalo and others; they would need more.

ALL THE RIVERS ARE TO BE SHUT

Leadership was essential because a sprawling transatlantic war was about to arrive at the Lakota country. The War of 1812 was a contest over the futures and survival of British Canada, Native America, and the United States, and it pitted, on the whole, the British and Indians against the expansionist but shaky American republic. For many Indians the conflict became their last war of independence, a desperate effort to secure a sufficient land base with British help before it was too late. The most powerful among them were the Dakota Sioux. But some Indians allied with the Americans. The most powerful among them were the Lakota Sioux.[93]

This did not mean that the Sioux were divided or in conflict. The United States and British Canada were abstractions that meant little to the Sioux, who saw societies not as monoliths but as aggregates of individuals and groups that could pursue distinct policies. Commerce was the essential issue. Dakotas had traded for decades with British merchants who lived among them, married into their families, and supplied them with crucial goods. They were kin. But this did not prevent Dakotas from embracing Americans as potential allies. Behavior transcended nationality, and Americans would be welcome if they said and did the right things.[94]

But they did not. Americans were stingy traders, shunned kin ties, and gravitated toward the Missouri rather than the Mississippi. In 1810, with rumors of an imminent war between the United States and Great Britain circulating in the upper Mississippi Valley and with the word of Shawnee leader Tecumseh's anti-American coalition spreading across the interior, U.S. officials realized that the Indians were turning away from them. An alarmed trader reported that the Indians declared all rivers "shut against" the Americans and that "their Old English father" promised to take "his beloved red children" under his protection again. Roughly a week before official declaration of war by the United States, the Dakota chief Red Wing warned a U.S. agent that his people will "abandon forever any connection with the Liars who have uniformly deceived us."[95]

The war triggered a rapid realignment of loyalties in the interior. Some Dakotas, along with many Menominees, Sauks, Odawas, Ho-Chunks, Wyandots, and Chippewas, joined the British, who siphoned provisions and guns to the western Great Lakes, hoping to pull interior tribes to their side. By the summer of 1813 British agents had mobilized some three thousand western Indians for operations in the lower Lakes. The warriors came with their families, bringing their numbers to around ten thousand. Nearly a hundred Dakotas were part of the large British-Indian coalition that filled the Americans with dread.[96]

This was a decisive moment. Had the British mobilized their Native allies into a concentrated attack on St. Louis, the U.S. nerve center in the West, the War of 1812 might have become as much a western war as it was an eastern one: Dakota Sioux already wanted to carry the war to the Sauks and Mesquakies to the west to secure their own position along the Mississippi. But the British Army focused its efforts on the East to secure Upper Canada's exposed heartland, and the moment passed. Thereafter the war did not proceed in line with Dakota interests. Robert Dickson, a red-haired Canadian trader who had married a Dakota named Blue Eyes Woman, worked tirelessly to keep them in the fold, but his pleas lost traction with hunger; Dakotas would remember the War of 1812 as "Pahinsha-shawacikiya," "when the Redhead begged for Our help." In September the U.S. Navy defeated the Royal Navy on Lake Erie, and in October Tecumseh died in the Battle of the Thames, leaving the pan-Indian confederacy reeling. Fighting a foreign and losing war on foreign soil, Dakotas had had enough. They would protect their own borderlands, but they would not enter the larger war.[97]

Nor would Lakotas. British traders and agents pushed south among Mandans and Hidatsas where they incited the villagers against the Americans. That William Clark, Louisiana's newly appointed governor, could tolerate, but any further advances down the Missouri would have brought British agents in touch with Lakotas. That Clark could not accept. Pro-British Lakotas could have opened the upper Missouri Valley to Britain—a southbound protrusion that could have foiled the U.S. war effort in the West. Clark recruited the ruthless Manuel Lisa as a subagent for Indian Affairs. Lisa worked hard to keep the Lakotas neutral, trading with them even when he had no real market for pelts and supplying posts with horses, meat, vegetables, and blacksmiths. The war became a nonissue for Lakotas. They did not fear the British and they had the Americans right where they wanted them: in St. Louis and along the Missouri, committed to supplying them with goods and services.[98]

THEY LIVED IN LARGE WOODEN HOUSES

Lakotas stayed out of the War of 1812, but the war years were a dynamic time for them. There were exhilarating advances in equestrian technology: several winter counts record how Lakotas captured their first wild horses with lariats somewhere in the western plains. The practice signaled a larger expansion of the horse culture across the grasslands. Herds of wild mustangs had multiplied in the southern plains to the point where animals began spreading into colder northern latitudes, and Lakotas may have adopted the use of the lariat from their more experienced Cheyenne allies.

There were also far-reaching political developments. Lakotas fought with Crows in the west, clashing over horses and hunting rights, while also engaging in active diplomacy with Pawnees and Kiowas to the south. The talks were often tentative, rendered so by the very dynamism of the rising horse nations of the plains. Comanches, Kiowas, Crows, and other plains nomads were now rapidly accumulating horses, their ambitions growing along with their herds. They were jockeying for position in the western steppes, competing for the richest hunting grounds, the best riverine pasturelands, and key trade corridors.[99]

Though still bound in the Mníšoše, Lakotas were not exempt from these rivalries. Most of their oyátes had begun regular bison hunts in the West where, at the edge of the Black Hills, they sometimes wintered with Cheyennes. The western excursions drew them into conflict with Kiowas, who were in a habit of traveling to the Black Hills from their southern homelands around the Arkansas, where they lived in an alliance with the powerful Comanches. Lakotas could ill afford a war with Kiowas, who had become prominent middlemen, carrying Comanche horses to the North Platte where they traded with Cheyennes. In 1815 a Lakota delegation traveled there to hold a peace council with Kiowas. It went badly. A Kiowa tried to steal Lakota horses, and a Sicangu warrior buried a hatchet in his head. Lakotas drove the Kiowas all the way into the Rockies. It was a major event, recorded in numerous winter counts, for it anticipated Lakota expansion into the West.[100]

Lakotas were not plains nomads yet. They ventured into the grasslands to hunt and trade and raid, but they did not feel safe out in the open. They were still building up their horse herds, and the Black Hills were dominated by Crows and Cheyennes who commanded the western grasslands from the rocky bastion. In around 1815 Sans Arcs astonished other Lakotas by building dirt lodges at Peoria Bottom above the Bad River. They then did something even more unexpected: they built large wooden houses, which they occupied for at least two years. The pictographs of the boxy structures appear at once cozy and utterly alien on the buffalo hides.[101]

FROM THIS DAY YOU MUST DATE YOUR CHANGE

In the city of Ghent in the Netherlands, meanwhile, the United States and Great Britain signed a treaty that ended the War of 1812 and restored status quo ante bellum. The British had pushed vigorously for an Indigenous buffer state in the Great Lakes to curb the United States' territorial ambitions, but they lacked the necessary leverage. They had lost their supply lines, had withdrawn from the Upper Midwest, and had failed to bring the militarily overpowering Očhéthi Šakówiŋ onto their side and open a sizable war theater in the deep interior, failures that rendered the buffer state unattainable. Given the lopsided distribution of Americans on the eastern and western sides of the Mississippi, the military victories forcing the United States to yield would have had to be won in the West and imposed in the East, but Sioux neutrality crippled Britain's western designs. The Treaty of Ghent secured the United States' hold on its 1783 borders and consolidated its hegemony east of the Mississippi. Britain would never again seriously interfere with American ambitions of continental expansion.[102]

In the summer of 1815, seven months after the Treaty of Ghent, U.S. officials invited the western Indians to a council at Portage des Sioux just north of St. Louis. Two thousand Indians showed up, and Americans made treaties with Lakotas, Mdewakantons, Wahpekutes, Sissetons, Wahpetons, and Yanktons. The pithy compacts pardoned past aggressions and brought the Sioux under the protection of the United States. The Americans understood the last article as a corroboration of U.S. jurisdiction over the Sioux, but the seventy-two Sioux delegates who touched a pen probably understood it as a confirmation of the prewar status quo whereby Americans traded with them without dictating to them. When U.S. soldiers began building an unauthorized fort at Prairie du Chien a year later, Mdewakanton chiefs approached British agents in the upper Great Lakes, pleading for help in preventing their "final extinction." It was only when the agents refused them that the chiefs realized that they would have to face the United States without British counterweight. Their fall from power was shockingly fast.[103]

Left alone to face the Americans, Dakotas were soon reeling. In 1818 Benjamin O'Fallon, a newly appointed U.S. agent for the Sioux and William Clark's nephew, led two heavily armed keelboats up the Mississippi and Minnesota to stop Canadian incursions and establish American authority in the region—an enterprise that echoed his uncle's famous expedition fourteen years earlier. O'Fallon found the Sioux divided and quarrelling over trade. At a Mdewakanton village, chief Shakopee, "ferocious and savage," complained that his warriors lacked guns and could not contain their Chippewa enemies. O'Fallon urged them to "be always last in war" and place their faith in "the Great Spirit." "I cannot restrain them," he admitted. "If they come upon you, make them drink your balls." O'Fallon recorded Shakopee's response with satisfaction, missing its bitter irony: "Yes, we will scratch them with our tow [sic] and finger nails and we will knaw them with our teeth."

Pleased with his efforts, O'Fallon turned back, assessed the Minnesota for

military forts, and brought his boats to another Mdewakanton village near the
Mississippi junction. Announcing his arrival with swivel guns, he delivered a
speech to a headman named Grand Partizan: "Sioux, I have come to tell you
we have done submitting. . . . From this day you must date your change, or this
river's surface will be covered with our boats, & the land with troops who will
chase you, as you do the deer of your plains." Cut off from the British trade and
political support, the Mdewakantons accepted O'Fallon's gifts—a little whiskey
and some goods—and demands. Within a year the U.S. Army started planning a
military fort at the Mississippi-Minnesota junction on lands Pike had purchased
fourteen years earlier.[104]

O'Fallon had succeeded where Lewis and Clark had failed. While the Corps
of Discovery had inadvertently prompted Lakotas to strengthen their hold of the
Missouri and its peoples, O'Fallon had extorted from Dakotas a tacit acceptance
of a military fort on their lands. Fort Snelling was in operation by 1820 and was
soon accompanied by St. Peter's Indian agency. The complex marked the beginning of a growing American presence in Dakota lives. It became a hub for the
growing fur trade, which soon cut into the region's animal populations, creating
food shortages and entangling Dakotas into chronic wars over hunting privileges
with Chippewas and Ho-Chunks. Indian agents tried to mediate, but they lacked
the know-how to be effective. Things came to head in 1827 when Mdewakantons
and Wahpetons killed two Chippewas in a council at Fort Snelling under a U.S.
flag. The fort commander, Josiah Snelling, imprisoned several Dakota warriors
and demanded the culprits be turned over to him in return for their release. He
was given a few men whom he handed over to Chippewas. Chippewas let them
run before shooting them down. Then they scalped them in front of the shocked
American officials.[105]

A century earlier, less than fifty miles downriver from Fort Snelling, the French
had built Fort Beauharnois to serve Dakotas. That trading fort had been the focal
point of a deep Dakota-French accommodation that stabilized the upper Mississippi Valley, fueled the expansion of the fur trade west of the Great Lakes,
and made the Dakotas the dominant power in the interior. Now the region's
dominant fort was a military establishment that heralded U.S. sovereignty over
the Mississippi Valley, monitored the Dakotas, and staged U.S.-sponsored public
executions of Dakota people.

FORTS, RAIDS, AND RATS

The aftermath of the War of 1812 was a great divide in the history of the
Očhéthi Šakówiŋ. While Dakotas suffered a precipitous decline in the disori-
enting postwar milieu, Lakota fortunes soared. Lakotas had every reason to think

of their 1815 treaty with the United States as a commitment to continued equilateral collaboration. They would have neither understood nor accepted the notion of a distant government claiming jurisdiction over them, and they embraced the Americans as allies who had been integrated into their expansive network of kinship and sharing. The Americans did not disappoint. The years after 1815 saw the greatest concentrated expansion of Lakota prosperity and power yet.

When New Orleans reopened for traffic with peace, the pent-up thirst for pelts triggered an explosive resurgence of the Missouri trade. Americans set out to eliminate the British threat from the north once and for all. President James Monroe authorized the Upper Missouri Agency to manage the Indians, and the War Department sent in two expeditions with an unequivocal assignment: eradicate British trade on U.S. soil and use military forts to close the river to Canadians. The panic of 1819—a product of lax credit and real estate speculation—gave a further boost to the fur trade, which required small initial capital investments. While banks failed and people lost their farms and jobs in the East, the fur trade continued to boom in the West.[106]

No other place boomed like the upper Missouri Valley, and no one benefited more than Lakotas. Drawn by land policies that privileged U.S. citizens over Spanish residents, settlers from Kentucky and Tennessee poured into the lower Missouri Valley, unseating the formidable Osage traders. The focal point of commerce shifted decisively upriver, delivering a bonanza for Lakotas. Winter counts record, with palpable anticipation, the commercial surge that turned the Lakota Meridian into a bustling center of the fur trade: by 1823 there were seven new trading posts. Winter counts also speak of unusually bountiful bison herds at that time, which buttressed the commercial takeoff during its critical early stages, and Americans now praised Lakotas for placing the traders "under their guardianship." A German traveler was struck by the mental shift. In St. Louis he had heard the Sioux being denounced as "the treacherous enemies of all white," but a journey upriver revealed a different image: "the more loyal of the aborigines under the care of the American government."[107]

Experience had taught Lakotas that even one well-supplied trading post could bring about a dramatic change in fortunes; now, suddenly, they had many. Three major companies competed for their trade, maintaining large and well-stocked posts within their reach. There was the Columbia Fur Company's Fort Tecumseh just above the mouth of the Bad River; the St. Louis-based French Fur Company's Fort Lookout near the White confluence; and the Missouri Fur Company's Fort Recovery below the White. Then a new player, John Astor's colossal yet nimble American Fur Company, extended its reach into St. Louis and launched a systematic takeover of the Missouri commerce. By 1827 it had

21. *Sioux Indians at Camp,* by George Catlin, early 1830s. Catlin captured the key
elements of Lakota prosperity and power in the early nineteenth century: reliable
access to sheltering river valleys, maturing equestrianism, booming robe trade, and
increasingly ambitious western hunts. The painting also highlights the centrality of
women's labor behind the Lakotas' commercial prowess. Courtesy of Getty Images.
Photo by Herbert Orth/The LIFE Images Collection.

either eliminated or absorbed its major competitors, enjoying a virtual monopoly
on the upper Missouri. Its crown jewel was Fort Tecumseh, which served as a
nerve center for a network of local posts. The fort sat in the heart of the Sicangu
and Oglala country, confirming Lakotas' privileged position.[108]

The ruthless competition among the companies benefited Lakotas because
they were now by far the most powerful Native nation in the region. Unlike
the French and British traders, the American companies, preoccupied as they
were with each other, could not actively manage relations among the Indians.
Spurred by growing markets and restrained by none, Lakotas tightened their
grip on the Missouri artery and the lands around it. They were growing rapidly
in numbers, and their neighbors consumed resources they needed. They raided
Pawnees, Poncas, and other villagers for horses, captives, and corn in the south,
and contended with Assiniboines and Crees over bison ranges in the north. They
attacked Hidatsa boats on the Missouri and clashed with Crows far in the west,
stealing horses and inching into the contested bison ranges toward the Black

Hills, inadvertently pushing their rivals into a tightening partnership with the United States.[109]

Thanks to their tributary relationship, Arikaras enjoyed a measure of protection against Lakota raids, but then they miscalculated. Eclipsed by Lakotas and snubbed by Americans who considered them disruptive and unworthy of a major post, Arikaras struggled to retain their position as traders. In March 1823 they stormed a Missouri Fur Company's Lakota post near the White and in June attacked a hundred-strong trapper party, killing fourteen and wounding eleven. Some of the terrified mountain men scrambled to safety—among them Hugh Glass, soon to run into a bear and frontier mythology—while others rushed downstream to bring reinforcements. An entire army came. An unprecedented punitive campaign led by Colonel Henry Leavenworth accrued allies as it ascended the river and brought 230 soldiers, seven hundred Lakota and Yankton allies, and a company of mountain men before two Arikara villages on the Grand in early August.[110]

The motley expedition prepared for bloodshed, and "whole pieces of cotton were torn up into bandages for those expected to be wounded." Lakota cavalry charged, repulsed a mounted Arikara counterattack, and then shifted back, urging Leavenworth to move in with infantry. He did not. The next day the colonel ordered artillery shelling, but the soldiers overshot the village. Leavenworth tried an infantry attack and, damagingly, asked the Lakota horse warriors to stand back. After several hours of desultory fighting he disengaged. Leavenworth sat down and smoked with Arikara elders who pleaded for peace. Lakotas stole some American horses in protest. Leavenworth, fearing that the disgruntled Lakotas might join the enemy, spent the third day coaxing the Arikaras to sign a treaty, ignoring his officers who demanded a charge. Again none came. But the common Lakota-American front had terrified the Arikaras. On the morning of the fourth day, the soldiers found the village empty, except for an old woman, the mother of a fallen chief. The Arikaras had slipped away at night, seeking refuge among Mandans. The mountain men burned the villages. For the disgusted Oglalas, the "abundance of corn" they carried home was the only thing worth recording of the desultory campaign. The vast quantities of wasted cotton bandages entered into Lakota lore as a symbol of the United States' military timidity.[111]

Lakotas were appalled by Leavenworth's tentativeness—twenty years later they would still be ridiculing his expedition—and condemned the U.S. soldiers for not subduing the Arikaras, who returned to their ruined villages a year later. A large expedition of eight wheel boats two years later up the Missouri did little to repair the Americans' damaged reputation. The wašíčus brought gifts, and Lakotas signed a treaty. They would handle the Arikaras on their own.[112]

Generously supplied by fur companies, Lakotas no longer needed the Arikara trade. The villagers had turned from a magnet into an obstacle, and Lakotas wanted them gone. The removal of the upper Missouri villagers became policy — even if it meant losing access to precious corn. In the winter of 1828–29 Lakotas killed two hundred Hidatsas in one of the bloodiest recorded Indian-Indian fights, and their raids filled Arikaras with such terror that they starved even when bison teemed around them. Lakotas burned them out for good in 1832. Arikaras fled south to the Loup, a tributary of the Platte, where they survived in "poverty and desolate state" with their distant Skiri Pawnee kin. Several thousand Lakotas and Yanktonais moved to occupy the abandoned village sites at the juncture of the Missouri and Grand, which pleased the region's Indian agent who was eager to see the Arikaras banished. Even germs seemed to side with Lakotas. In the winter of 1831–32 a highly virulent smallpox virus killed half of the Pawnees, leaving them exposed. In the fall a well-armed Lakota party attacked the six thousand survivors who had seven guns between them. Their Indian agent immediately applied for a leave.[113]

The Grand River domain became a staging area for northbound raids into Mandan and Hidatsa villages which, like the Arikara ones, had become impediments. In 1833 Oglalas "killed many" in an attack on a Hidatsa village, and the following spring an unidentified Sioux party reduced two Hidatsa villages to ashes. Mandans and Hidatsas could not stop the onslaught because they were struggling with another invasion as well. Norway rats, big, voracious rodents had migrated up the Missouri with the growing fur trade, reaching them in the mid-1820s. Multiplying with shocking speed—females averaged fifty offspring a year—these invaders quickly gnawed their way into Mandans and Hidatsas' underground granaries and began feasting on their provisions. They devoured the villagers' power from within—at a rate of hundreds of pounds of corn a day. Soon the villages were engulfed with burial scaffolds.[114]

The United States did almost nothing to stop the attacks. On the contrary, in 1832, the very year Lakotas banished the Arikaras from the upper Missouri, the Americans came to them with a remarkable novelty: vaccines. The smallpox outbreak that had devastated the Pawnees, along with many other tribes, had prompted Congress to pass a vaccination act to save the Indians from "the destructive ravages of that disease." Beyond humanitarian impulses, government officials also saw a vaccination program as a singular tool to win the goodwill of the Missouri Indians and detach them from British traders and agents. Physicians were dispatched up the Missouri where they vaccinated most Yanktonais and Yanktons and nine hundred Lakotas against smallpox. They made it among the Sioux on the Bad and vaccinated several hundred people. They did not even try to reach the Mandans and Hidatsas.[115]

22. *Distant View of the Mandan Village*, by George Catlin, 1832.
The Mandan village Mih-tutta-hang-kusch, located three miles above the
Knife River, was one of the many Missouri villages that the Lakotas considered
variously as competitors, allies, sources of tribute, and obstacles. Courtesy of
Smithsonian American Art Museum, © Photo Scala, Florence.

Lakotas and their Dakota, Yankton, and Yanktonai allies had taken a persisting
hold of the American mind as the mighty Sioux. A kind of Sioux exceptionalism
began to emerge. Inquisitive visitors marveled at their proficiency with firearms
and their "fine" looks and "very prominent cheekbones" and thought that they
were "more attentive to their dress" than other Native people. An 1824 U.S. Army
report, based on an exploration of the headwaters of the Minnesota, estimated
the total Sioux population around sixty thousand. It was a gross exaggeration,
perhaps three times too high, and as such revealing: the Sioux loomed ever larger
in the American interior and imagination, eclipsing all others.[116]

LIKE A LITTLE VILLAGE

By the early 1830s the Lakota Meridian encompassed all of the Missouri Valley
from its northern turn to its western one. Only the Americans had a meaningful
presence there, and they were staunch allies, posing no threat. The Americans

23. *Fort Pierre on the Missouri*, by Karl Bodmer. From *Voyage dans l'intérieur de l'Amérique du Nord, execute pendant les années, 1833 et 1834*, by Prince Maximilian von Wied and Karl Bodmer, Paris, 1840. Courtesy of Library of Congress, Rare Book and Special Collections Division.

had boats and guns and cannons, but they did not seem to be capable of using them effectively. They were great traders but poor soldiers. The most impressive thing about them were their life-giving vaccines and their trading posts filled with goods.

In 1831, after massive flooding, the Missouri channel shifted around Fort Tecumseh. The American Fur Company dismantled it and built a new post, Fort Pierre, on the west bank for Lakotas. Fort Pierre epitomized the improbable trajectory of Lakota-American relations, the close alliance the two people had forged out of troubled beginnings. In 1804 Lewis and Clark had nearly clashed with Sicangus at the mouth of the Bad, but now Fort Pierre stood three miles above the Bad confluence, a linchpin of a common ground that brought Lakotas and Americans together in a formidable alliance in the heart of the continent. Lakotas had already brought "an immense and almost incredible number of buffalo robes" to Fort Pierre in the spring of 1832 when they heard of a giant "*medicine-canoe*" moving upstream toward them: John Astor's 120-foot-long side-wheeler, the *Yellow Stone*, was steaming up the Missouri from St. Louis. Six to seven hundred Lakota and Yankton lodges gathered near the fort to welcome the Americans and their wealth-bearing machine.[117]

Fort Pierre symbolized the dramatic rise of the Lakotas. The quadrangular post was an imposing structure surrounded by three-hundred-foot walls and boasting two two-story blockhouses with embrasures, a fifteen-acre enclosed garden, and comfortable living quarters for over a hundred employees, some sixty of whom specialized in Sioux trade. "From the roof of the block-houses, which is surrounded with a gallery, there is a fine prospect over the prairie," reported the German prince Alexander Philipp Maximilian zu Wied-Neuwied, "and there is a flag-staff on the roof, on which the colours are hoisted." Maximilian estimated the value of stores at eighty thousand dollars—a supermarket of the steppe.

Yet it was Lakotas who made the greatest impression. "Indians, on foot and on horseback, were scattered all over the plain, and their singular stages [scaffolds] for the dead were in great numbers near the Fort; immediately behind which, the leather tents of the Sioux Indians, of the branches of the Tetons and the Yanktons, stood, like a little village." It *was* a village, one of the many mobile Lakota camps that dotted the Lakota Meridian in an ever-changing constellation. Fort Pierre was an American outpost within seasonal Lakota settlement. In one of the tipis lived an "old interpreter, Dorion, a half Sioux" with "his Indian family." He was the son of Pierre Dorion, Lewis and Clark's talented interpreter who had talked the Corps of Discovery through the Lakota gauntlet. From the poles of his tipi "scalps fluttered in the wind."[118]

5

THE CALL OF THE WHITE
BUFFALO CALF WOMAN

First there was but a speck. From out of the immense flat a figure emerged slowly, as if floating, gleaming white in hot air. The two men on the hill saw that it was a woman and that she was wakȟáŋ, holy, so they waited. As the woman grew larger, they saw that she was carrying a bundle and that her hair covered her body like a robe. One of the men lowered his eyes, but the other kept staring at her. She saw that he desired her and asked him to come near. A cloud concealed them. When it dissolved, the woman stood alone, a pile of bones and snakes at her feet. She turned to the other man and told him to go back to his village and have his people prepare a lodge for her.

When she arrived four days later, the village was ready. She entered a large medicine tipi, singing,

With visible breath I am walking.
A voice I am sending as I walk.
In a sacred manner I am walking.
With visible tracks I am walking.
In a sacred manner I am walking.

She circled the lodge sunwise and instructed the people to build an altar of red earth with a buffalo skull in the center. She opened her bundle and took out a pipe, holding its bowl with her left hand and the stem with her right. She walked around the lodge four times, evoking the great sun and "the circle without end, the sacred hoop, the road of life." She lit the pipe. Its red stone bowl, she explained, signified the earth and the buffalo whose four legs stood for the four directions of the universe and the four ages of man. The smoke rising from the bowl was the living breath of Wakȟáŋ Tȟáŋka, the Great Spirit, and the wooden stem stood for all plants growing on the earth. An attached fan of twelve feathers stood for the eagle and all the birds of the air.

Ptesáŋwiŋ, the White Buffalo Calf Woman, had brought the gift of the sacred Buffalo Calf Pipe, *Ptehíŋčala Čhaŋnúŋpa*, by which Lakotas would live from thereon. With the pipe they would "walk like a living prayer," their feet resting on the ground and the pipestem reaching to the sky and their bodies "a living bridge between the Sacred Beneath and the Sacred Above." The pipe, the woman said, was a gift from Wakȟáŋ Tȟáŋka who smiled upon them because they had become one with the universe: "earth, sky, all living things, the two-legged, the four-legged, the winged ones, the trees, the grasses. Together with the people, they are all related, one family. The pipe holds them all together."

It would also hold Lakotas together. The surface of the bowl, the White Buffalo Calf Woman revealed, was marked with seven incised circles, standing for seven ceremonies that would guide Lakotas to live well. She taught them the first, the Sacred Pipe Ceremony, and promised to reveal the others in time. Although she would soon leave, she would return. She would look upon them always.[1]

The White Buffalo Calf Woman had come to Lakotas at a time of famine and confusion. The two Lakota men who first met her were hunters, sent out by their chief to find bison for his starving village. Lakotas were starving because their lives had no structure or meaning. "There was nothing sacred before the pipe came," Left Heron, an Oglala elder, recounted later. "There was no social organization and the people ran around the prairie like so many wild animals." The pipe changed all that. "With this pipe you will be bound to all your relatives," the holy woman announced. "By this pipe the tribe shall live." Instead of as strangers, Lakotas would embrace one another as kin, which would give their lives order. The pipe also established a pact between humans and buffaloes. "I represent the Buffalo tribe," the woman said. "When you are in need of buffalo meat, smoke this pipe and ask for what you need and it shall be granted you." When, after several days, it became time for the White Buffalo Calf Woman to leave, she turned herself into a white buffalo calf. She bowed to the four sacred directions and vanished, leaving behind a promise of order and plenty.[2]

The story of the White Buffalo Calf Woman is ancient, reaching back to a time when Lakotas first emerged as a distinct, self-aware people. The story acquired new urgency in the early nineteenth century, when Lakotas made their second concerted push into the West, this time from the Missouri Valley, their home for more than half a century. It marked the beginning of a new phase in their history, a phase that saw their expansion becoming increasingly intertwined with the American expansion. It was a phase that centered to a remarkable degree on the Black Hills.

WAYS TO THE WEST

Lakotas had frequented the Black Hills from their Mníšoše homelands since the late eighteenth century, drawn by the region's spiritual primacy, unique climate, and reliable bison herds. The White Buffalo Calf Woman appeared to them in Pahá Sápa, the Black Hills, when the buffalo were scarce and people were suffering. But Pahá Sápa became known as North America's paramount bison hunting range, the place where hunters could find game even when herds were failing everywhere else. This was the gift of the White Buffalo Calf Woman—and of the area's higher elevation that caught greater rainfall and, consequently, offered more pasture and bison.

Lakotas responded to Pahá Sápa's seductive pull. Every year they hunted in the western grasslands, following the protective passageways of water and trees toward the Pahá Sápa two hundred miles away. On these western excursions they may have joined forces with Cheyennes who had already made the western plains home and regularly hunted in the Black Hills. Pahá Sápa loomed ever larger for Lakotas as a source of prosperity and rebirth, but they were beyond their control.

The Black Hills had been inhabited since time immemorial, the thousand-year-old rock art on its sandstone boulders a testimony of a deep human connection to the place. People had prayed, hunted, and farmed on the hills, which stood out like a lush island in a dry sea of grass. But in the late eighteenth century, as the horse frontier inched northward across the western plains, the Black Hills became nomads' domain. Several newly equestrian people vied for control of the region. Slowly, in the early years of the nineteenth century, Cheyennes emerged as the dominant group. They formed an alliance with the Arapahos and made the Black Hills theirs.[3]

Lakotas had access to Pahá Sápa through their tightening alliance with Cheyennes, and the hills and the buffalo plains around the Black Hills beckoned them to the West. Getting there was, in the end, an intensely mundane matter of acquiring the necessary technology: procuring horses, tending them, and building up substantial herds. This happened, gradually, in the course of the 1820s and 1830s, when Lakotas amassed enough mounts for large-scale equestrian warfare. Prince Maximilian, the German explorer-traveler, observed the equestrian takeoff in its early stages when successful individuals "frequently possess from thirty to forty horses" and could put all their relatives on horseback.[4]

Horses translated into mobility and power, fueling western expansion. For decades the Mníšoše had been the home of Lakotas and seat of their power; now it became staging ground for increasingly ambitious western expeditions. Geog-

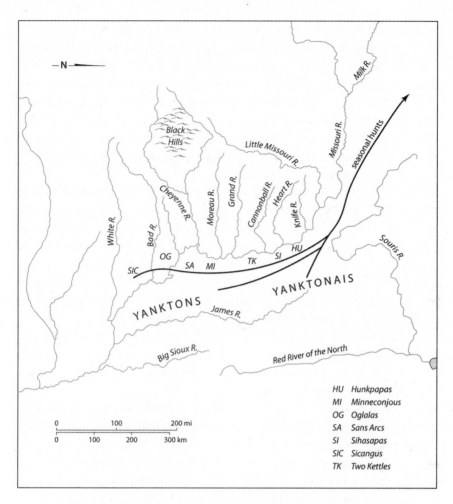

24. Ways to the West. The western tributaries of the Missouri River served as avenues to the West and toward the Black Hills. Map by Bill Nelson.

raphy itself seemed to invite Lakotas in. From the Mníšoše's west bank a string of rivers pointed like fingers toward unprecedented animal wealth and spiritual fulfillment beyond the horizon, pulling them in. Eight great tributaries—the White, Bad, Cheyenne, Moreau, Grand, Cannonball, Heart, and Knife—all flush with riparian forests, veined the western plains, providing all the means necessary for a grand leap toward the life-affirming Pahá Sápa.

The eight roads were not activated all at once. Oglalas and Sicangus were the first to turn west, ascending the White and Bad which offered reliable water and wood, serving as superb passageways. As they inched upriver, they clashed with

Kiowas and Crows, pushing the former to the south and the latter to the west. Sicangus joined forces with Cheyennes against the Kiowas, while Oglalas spearheaded campaigns against Crows under the leadership of Bull Bear whose boldness and resolve seemed to have given their operations particular sharpness. By the late 1820s Crows had retreated from the Black Hills into the Powder River country a hundred miles to the west, and Oglalas and Sicangus established themselves on Pahá Sápa's eastern side. By that time Sans Arcs, Minneconjous, Two Kettles, Sihasapas, and Hunkpapas had also begun to shift west, establishing the Cheyenne and Grand as entryways.[5]

Lakotas had turned west, decisively, but they remained people of river valleys first and people of the plains second. They ventured into the western grasslands and Pahá Sápa from multiple points along timbered river valleys and moved back regularly along those same valleys to the Mníšoše, which remained vital to their cosmology and economy. Essentially protrusions of the Missourian riparian woodlands, the White, Bad, Cheyenne, and other tributaries provided Lakotas with safe and familiar pathways into the West. When they began pulling away from the Missouri, they were not so much casting themselves loose on the open plains but extending their old riverland world into the West.[6]

This tripartite pattern—a trunk line in the east, an elevated, magnet-like anchor in the west, and a row of arterials in between—formed the core of the Lakota world from the 1830s onward. It was in those three places where Lakotas spent most of their time—cooking, eating, sleeping, socializing, smoking, praying, raising children, tending horses, preparing hides, making clothes, tools, and weapons—and where most of them entered and left this world. This was the homeland Lakotas would defend against invaders and, when needed, expand.

The western tributaries were keys to land and wealth and power, but they were also conduits into a perilous new world, for they carried Lakotas toward greater aridity. The western Great Plains lie in a long rain shadow cast by the Rocky Mountains. Pacific winds pump moist maritime air eastward, but the air sheds much of its moisture while climbing up the Rockies. The shadow effect is strongest in the west, the 98th meridian marking a default line where evaporation exceeds precipitation and the soil starts to go dry. The grass cover reflects this, becoming shorter toward the west. Around the 105th meridian densely tufted blue grama and buffalo grasses become dominant and the plant canopy shrinks down to a few inches. The bison had adapted over the millennia to these semi-arid conditions, thriving on the stunted short-grasses that retained protein in their dry stalks, making them ideal winter forage. Tens of millions of them lived in the plains, their huge bodies a hunter's delight.[7]

That was when the Black Hills began to loom large in a material sense. When severe droughts struck the grasslands, the bison tended to seek relief in the high-altitude microclimate around the Black Hills where summers were cooler, rainfall higher, and pasture more lavish. Lakotas did the same. This introduced a new dimension to Pahá Sápa's allure: it became a sanctuary and a meat pack. Lakotas gathered there to sit out droughts and subsist on buffaloes that seemed to give themselves up—just like the White Buffalo Calf Woman had promised. The control of Pahá Sápa became a spiritual and material imperative without which nothing in the world was secure—not its unearthly bounties, not the hunt, not the survival of Lakotas as a people. Hand paintings on Pahá Sápa's rocky planes—red spots marking slain enemies—bespeak of the violent struggle that turned the mountain range into an exclusive domain of Lakotas and their Cheyenne and Arapaho allies. By the late 1820s Lakotas were wintering in Pahá Sápa. The Black Hills belonged to them.[8]

THE NEW HYBRID

Control over the Black Hills and the Missouri tributaries was Lakotas' principal ambition, an end in itself. But the new western lands were also staging areas for broader ventures. Most immediately, they served as bases from which Lakotas could access the astounding animal bounty that now surrounded them.

To the south of Pahá Sápa Lakotas found herds of wild horses that seemed to grow ever larger the farther they pushed. Plains winters grew progressively colder from south to north and thus more taxing for horses. The quantity and quality of natural forage dropped sharply, depleting the herds: too many foals perished in the vicious cold. Millions of feral horses—descendants of sixteenth-century Spanish strays—roamed the southern and central plains, but the North Platte was a fault line beyond which hardly any wild horses could be found. Arrival in Pahá Sápa brought Lakotas very close to that fault line, and now they crossed it with relish. Edwin Thompson Denig, a fur trader who spent more than twenty years in the West, described the boon: "the wild animals were pursued from one to the other until so fatigued as to be lassoed, after which they were thrown down, bridled and either packed or ridden by the fearless cavaliers. Frequently 40 to 60 head of horses were brought home as the fruits of a single expedition."[9]

These were astounding hauls that allowed Lakotas to compensate for severe winter losses and complete their drawn-out equestrian takeoff in a matter of years. The consequences were nothing short of revolutionary. Just as steam power was fueling an accelerating industrial revolution in the United States, equine power ushered Lakotas into a new technological age. The horse was more than a tool or a bigger and more muscular dog; it was a means to access the immense pool of energy that spread out boundlessly—and seemingly uselessly—right under

Lakotas' feet: grass. Horses were magnificent, empowering creatures of spectacular strength, but what really made them so useful for Lakotas lay in their stomachs. The dogs could tap grass energy only indirectly, by consuming the flesh of the herbivores their masters procured for them, whereas horses harbored symbiotic bacteria in their large intestines that enabled them to digest enormous quantities of cellulose-rich grass. Horses, in a purely mechanical sense, served their masters as finely tuned organisms that converted inaccessible plant energy into tangible and instantly exploitable muscle power. It was an extraordinary shortcut that redefined the limits of the possible: the plant biomass of the Great Plains may have been a thousand times greater than that of animals.[10]

With supercharged equestrian mobility Lakotas could harness the seemingly infinite pool of plant energy and reimagine their place in the world. The moment when they could put all their members on horseback was a moment of transcendence that saw humans and horses blend into one another to form a new kind of society. Lakotas reinvented themselves, with stunning speed, as equestrian hunters and herders who relied on horses to move, feed, clothe, protect, enrich, and perfect themselves. In the 1830s the mounted chase became the preferred and then the only method of procuring bison, and the Sun Dance became an annual event, securing a more bountiful and safer future for the people.[11]

But there was a catch. The rapidly growing horse herds also introduced new burdens and uncertainties. There were two major problems. The first was ecological. The expanded Lakota realm was a mélange of sturdy grasses where large mammals thrived, but the abundance hid a structural vulnerability. Horses and bison, the paired foundation of the new Lakota economy, were competing species. They ate the same grasses—up to an 80 percent dietary overlap—and their survival strategies were conspicuously similar. Just like Lakotas and their rivals, horses and bison competed for riverine habitats and their gifts. Both needed the perennial streams, protective bluffs, and cottonwood bark to survive the frequent dry spells and harsh northern winters—and this was just the ordinary years. When the rains failed for extended periods of time, things turned brutal. Superbly adaptable organisms, grasses survived droughts by storing vital nutrients in their sprawling root systems. They literally withdrew underground, sometimes leaving grass-eaters with as little as 10 percent of the normal forage supply. When that happened Lakotas faced the off-putting challenge of balancing the needs of their horses with those of their prey. Nature pitted the two halves of their economy against each other.

The second problem was more straightforward: horses needed a of lot care. They had to be broken, trained, protected, treated, fouled, gelded, pastured, and watered. Each horse needed roughly twenty pounds of grass and up to ten gallons of fresh water a day and regular intakes of salt. The search for sustenance became constant. A Lakota thióšpaye with five hundred horses was likely to exhaust an area of three to four acres of grass in a day, which meant that villages had to be moved frequently, always an arduous task that involved dismantling and pitching tipis, packing belongings on travois and horses and unpacking them again, and scouting and keeping guard while on the move. For all the work horses did for Lakotas, they demanded their share of labor input, too.[12]

At some point in time Lakotas had to make a choice. There came a moment when they faced an invisible threshold where a foraging way of life would have to transform into a new hybrid of bison hunting and horse pastoralism. They crossed it. Rather than favoring one facet over the other, they embraced both. It was a daunting experiment that demanded discarding familiar practices, recalibrating traditional values, and imagining novel ways of being in the world.

Like most hunter-nomads, Lakotas lived by a carefully orchestrated annual cycle of activities; now that cycle had to become much more intricate and flexible. Winter was the most critical phase. Nature yielded little, and people and animals had to get by with less. The names of the winter months—the Moons of Shedding Horns, Hard Times, and Popping Trees—evoke the harshness of the northern winters that assumed distinctive physical manifestations: trees splitting in frigid cold, epidemics of snow blindness paralyzing villages, the necessary transition into heated tipis. Suddenly, the open plains became all but unlivable, and Lakotas moved into riverine lowlands where they could find timber, water, grass, and shelter against the elements. Broad and level bottomlands lined with steep bluffs and cottonwood groves were favorites. What made this tricky was that the bison, too, gravitated toward the same spaces, seeking similar things. The bottomlands were in danger of becoming overcrowded.

Lakotas had to find ways to allocate finite resources for themselves, their horses, and their prey. Their solution was both drastic and simple: they slowed down and dispersed. For several months each winter they did as little as possible, conserving their and their horses' energy. Steered by women, thióšpayes scattered along river bottoms, isolating themselves from one another to conserve the limited supplies of the still-nutritious short-grass stalks. So entrenched was this strategy that when a Sicangu band once wintered on a hill, it earned a mention in a winter count. They dwelled near enough to the bison to launch quick family hunts but kept enough distance to avoid grazing competition between horses and bison. They moved only when all grass was consumed or when the accumulated camp refuse became intolerable. Women rounded out diets with dried meat, preserved vegetables, and pemmican, a high-calorie mixture of dried bison meat, fat, and berries; men made bows, arrows, and other tools; and children col-

25. The South Fork of the Cheyenne River. With its thick cottonwood groves
and nearby protective bluffs, the South Fork of the Cheyenne River was one of
those essential river valleys that provided shelter and nourishment for the
Lakotas and their animals. Photograph by the author.

lected cottonwood bark for horses. Winter was sedentary time, allowing elders to
educate children about past events, traditions, and ceremonies. This was the time
when winter counts were drawn.

March—the Moon of Snow Blindness—marked the shift into spring, a time
of transition. April was the Moon of Fattening, and Lakotas stepped up bison
hunting. Carbohydrate reserves were low, and women tapped boxelder trees for
sap, dug wild turnips and potatoes, and picked fruit and berries; May was the
Moon of Planting. Then equine matters became a priority. Men broke in year-
lings and two-year-olds, castrated unfit stallions, and selected studs for breeding.
Since the average gestation period is close to a year, spring was also the time of
foaling. When grasses started sprouting on the plains, bands filtered out of the
river valleys into the open to fatten their thinned mounts, moving frequently to
maximize fresh pasture. Women and men danced and dreamt of medicine ceremonies to revive depleted horses, make their mounts swift, and ensure fine colts.
Rejuvenation was the all-important matter.

Quickening action marked early summer. With their diets rounded up and with their horses restored to form, Lakotas began raiding again. Raiding was becoming a routine, an effective industry that secured a steady inflow of horses, and the villages transformed into veritable staging grounds for outgoing and incoming war parties. This was the time when Lakotas exploded out of their core domain in all directions. They carried horses into their villages to replenish diminished herds and brought in captives to ease labor burdens. In June the bison congregated for the rut, signaling for Lakotas to launch collective hunts, and mobile villages containing hundreds of tipis set out to the open plains. Throughout all this women kept amassing crucial carbohydrates: the high summer months were the Moons of Good Berries, Cherries Blackening, and Harvest.[13]

The Sun Dance was the religious and political pinnacle of the Lakota annual cycle, the moment when the Lakota way of belonging reached its most poignant manifestation. Preparations for the ceremony began in early summer under the guidance of *wičháša wakȟáŋs*, holy men to whom sprits had entrusted sacred words, and culminated in July at the height of the growing season when great gatherings could be held. Moving into a predetermined site, Lakotas arranged their tipis into a circle, into rows, or into elongated lines along river valleys, the clusters symbolizing the rekindled collective ethos. The great camps were essentially overlapping and interlocking circles of kinship that crisscrossed the entire campground, connecting each person, each family, every band, and every oyáte together, enveloping everyone and everything into one great web of belonging. Entering a Sun Dance camp was a socially charged act of embedding oneself into a single kindred, takúkičhiyapi. The moment Lakotas entered the ceremonial camp and took their places in the sacred circle, both cosmic and human order could be restored. Societies came together to perform their ceremonies, dramatizing and reaffirming the essential Lakota values: bravery, generosity, fortitude, and wisdom. The great summer gatherings were the only time in a year when Lakotas could come together as a collective, and they always doubled as political councils where headmen from multiple oyátes discussed trade, diplomacy, cooperation, and war. For a few intensive weeks Lakotas lived, prayed, and conferred together, binding their expanding nation together and reaffirming their spiritual attachment to the land. That sense of togetherness and belonging was not fleeting; renewed annually, it has persisted into the present.

The summer gathering dissolved into fall hunts, the nutritional pivot of the yearly cycle. Elders performed buffalo-calling ceremonies and sent out scouts to locate herds. Almost invariably they found them, for the westward protruding Lakota domain was like "one continuous range for the buffalo." Once the scouts returned to the camp, they lit their pipes and revealed the coordinates. Women mobilized the entire village, "overhauling wardrobes, tipis, travois and harness, and putting all in good repair," and the camp moved toward the herd, guarded by its police force, *akíčhita*. Now the mounted chase, the sharp edge of the new horse-powered Lakota economy, revealed its exhilarating efficiency.

If the herd was small enough, mounted hunters surrounded it and shot down the beasts they needed, sometimes killing the encircled animals on foot. If the herd was larger, hunters rode straight into it, launching arrows and bullets into the sides of the panicked animals. A successful communal hunt, directed by experienced hunters and policed by akíčhitas, lasted but an hour or so but yielded vast quantities of meat, fat, and hides, enough to last for weeks. Those who could not take part in the hunt could claim the meat of a beast by tying its tail, a custom that ensured that no one went hungry. After each hunter had claimed the animals he had killed, women moved in. They disassembled the carcasses into hides, meat, bones, bladders, and brains; packed the parts on horse-drawn travois; and took the bounty back to the camp. There they carried out a second round of processing, turning the bloody miscellany into bow strings, powder containers, dressing tools, clothing, tipi hides, and fine robes for the market. Almost everything that did not become a tool, clothing, or shelter became food. Women prepared huge amounts of pemmican, enough to last much of the winter, and stored dried meat in deep pits for spring when food would be scarce. Lakotas had entered a new era of abundance and safety.[14]

A GEOGRAPHY OF VIOLENCE

Galvanized by suddenly magnified power, Lakotas expanded their hunting and pasture ranges out into the bison-rich plains around Pahá Sápa. It provoked an immediate backlash: almost all resident Indians saw the Lakotas as aggressors and mobilized to drive them back. The result was an ever-shifting geography of violence. Conditioned by both macro and micro factors, bison migrations were highly unpredictable, which meant Lakota hunters had to be ready to venture in any given direction from the Black Hills—and fight any number of people they might encounter on their way. This was the primary cause behind the sprawling Indian-Indian wars in the high plains: a hunting-pastoral way of life demanded an unusually high people-to-land ratio.

In the 1830s and 1840s a broad pattern took shape. In the north and west Lakotas clashed frequently with Crows and Shoshones, who ventured to hunt on the plains east of the Powder River. In the south, along the Platte and Niobrara, they collided with Pawnees, Omahas, Poncas, and Otoes who left their villages twice a year for extended bison hunts in the West. Here the competition over hunting rights became particularly vicious because the herds had begun to thin out. The villagers hunted disproportionate numbers of buffalo cows, whose supple hides were favored by American traders, compromising the herds' reproductive capacity. As the increasingly self-assured southbound Lakotas clashed with the increasingly desperate westbound villagers, the central plains erupted into carnage. Omahas, an Indian agent at Council Bluffs reported, begged him for guns and ammunition to hold back the Lakotas who seemed "resolved on exterminating this little band of Indians."[15]

The curious thing about the violence was that it made the contested hunting ranges even more enticing. Rivals tended to avoid places where they were bound to run into enemies, and some of those places became buffer zones, no-man's-lands people entered with caution if at all. That made them veritable animal preserves. Soon several game-rich buffer zones emerged on the borderlands of the expanding Lakota realm. The largest lay in the south between the forks of the Platte where Lakotas and their Cheyenne allies clashed with Comanches and Kiowas who ventured northward from the Arkansas Valley and with Pawnees and other eastern villagers. Another major buffer zone sprawled to the west and north where Lakotas, Crows, Shoshones, Utes, Arapahos, and Cheyennes "settle their difficulties." Both zones were rich in game, intensely coveted, and hotly disputed.[16]

A paradoxical dynamic took shape. The Indians knew that violence created buffer zones, but they also believed that more violence could unlock those zones and open access to animal bounty. While that ambition remained an elusive possibility, in the short term it provoked self-perpetuating cycles of killings and retributions. Lakotas and their rivals never denied one another's humanity, but they came to see one another as irredeemable enemies who could be exploited, conquered, or dispossessed.

GRAVITATION

Lakotas had three distinctive advantages in the intensifying wars: numbers, trade, and an ability to incorporate others. Their population surpassed ten thousand and kept growing, buoyed by improved hunting prospects, American vaccines, and an expanding territory, which allowed their bands to disperse, put distance between one another, and thwart the spread of infectious diseases. Lakota winter counts record no epidemics between 1820 and 1837, suggesting a level of epidemiological safety few American Indians enjoyed.[17]

Prosperous and safe, the Lakota realm became a gravitational center for people around it. The three-thousand-strong Cheyennes tightened their alliance with Lakotas, bringing their combined fighting force to near three thousand warriors. Yanktons and Yanktonais, too, were drawn in. Unlike their Lakota kin, they struggled to plug themselves in the Missouri River trade, operating in the shadow of the weakened but still active Mandans and Hidatsas. "Keen traders," the villagers took advantage of Yanktonais' "suffering condition," bargaining hard and reducing them to "a state of poverty." In 1835 Mandans and

Hidatsas attacked a Yanktonai camp on the Knife River, killing and capturing nearly two hundred people. Thousands of Yanktonais and their Yankton relatives sought safety among Lakotas, trading their deteriorating hunting grounds for the buffalo-teeming western plains where they joined Lakotas in hunting, trading, and raiding along the great river.[18]

Old preexisting kinship ties eased the inclusion of Cheyennes, Yanktons, and Yanktonais into the Lakota orbit. A more striking sign of Lakotas' increasing pull was the case of the Poncas, always a small tribe. Many Ponca families severed their age-old ties with Pawnees and Omahas and attached themselves to Lakotas, who gained a number of warriors willing to fight their former allies. Living so close to Lakotas, one of their headmen explained, "they would be necessarily obliged to war against the Pawnees, as long as the Sioux did." The Lakota-Ponca merger was a disaster for Omahas who became refugees reduced to "prowl over the country like so many hungry wolves." Their farming economy collapsed, leaving them "exceedingly poor and destitute."[19]

Poncas survived as a people by shedding much of what had made them Poncas. Like the Cheyennes before them, they sided with power, abandoned their earth-lodge villages, and became nomads. They hunted and camped with Lakotas in the open plains, settling down only briefly near the Missouri to plant small patches of corn. They blended into Sicangu bands and largely disappeared from the historical record. A single mixed Sicangu-Ponca band, the Wazhazhas, reminded outsiders of their absorption; the Wazhazhas were widely known as a Sicangu band. How the Ponca/Wazhazhas coped with the abandonment of the ancient ceremonies and traditions embedded in village life, and how they felt about joining Lakotas in attacking people who once had been kin, they did not reveal.[20]

While Lakotas grew in numbers and influence, their enemies were either stagnating or losing ground. A smallpox epidemic in 1832 killed about four thousand Pawnees, about half of their population. Variously mixed war parties of Oglalas, Sicangus, Cheyennes, and Poncas descended on the debilitated Pawnee villages, stealing horses, raiding food caches, taking captives, and burning fields and villages and killing women to deter resistance. When Pawnees moved out west to hunt, they faced the superbly mobile Lakotas and their allies who were resolved to keep them out. Crows kept testing the sinew of the nomad barrier that cut them off from the plains buffalo, but their forays were becoming increasingly costly.[21]

Lakotas were ascendant, and their burgeoning presence in the interior translated into a potent commercial pull. As they shifted their operations toward the Black Hills and the Platte Valley, they grew reluctant to carry their hides and pelts to Fort Pierre on the Missouri and demanded that traders come to them. The American Fur Company relented and established small moveable posts along the White, Cheyenne, and the South Fork of the Cheyenne, their locations determined by Lakota and Cheyenne hunters. Several winter counts recorded the modest structures, usually simple dirt houses, for they meant unprecedented access to guns and goods. An Oglala count for 1831 marked a major event: Red Lake, a white trader, brought goods into their camp in a wagon, the first they ever saw. In that year the American Fur Company was reported to have extracted fifty thousand buffalo robes from the Lakota country.[22]

It was a galvanizing haul, dwarfing anything that had been reaped from the plains, and it whetted the traders' appetite. In the summer of 1834 wašíču runners began arriving in Lakota villages: a new trading post was being built for them on the North Platte, about a hundred miles south of the Black Hills. Sensing a shift in commercial geography, veteran traders Robert Campbell and William Sublette had decided to open a new post in the lee of the Laramie Range. It was an audacious move. The American fur trade had expanded through the curving Missouri deep into the Rocky Mountains where numerous brigades of mountain men scoured the streams and valleys for beaver, but there were no fixed posts in the grasslands in the middle. Sublette and Campbell's post, popularly known as Fort Laramie, hurled the fur trade into that gap with a single thrust. Their western leap echoed that of Lakotas and was in fact prompted by it. After decades of intensive hunting, beaver and bison populations had visibly declined along the Missouri, whereas the western plains teemed with buffalo. Lakotas were following bison and Americans were following Lakotas into the West.[23]

Fort Laramie solidified Lakotas' ascendancy. It was built for them and it remained the only post in the western plains for years, giving them a decisive advantage over other Native groups. Although relatively modest in size—an eighty-by-one-hundred-foot rectangle with a fifteen-foot cottonwood palisade—the fort abounded with goods: guns, lead, copper kettles, steel knives, hatchets, awls, blankets, tobacco, beads, vermillion, and alcohol. Steamboat transportation had been instituted on the upper Missouri in 1832 when the *Yellow Stone* pushed all the way up to Fort Union near the Missouri-Yellowstone junction, covering eighteen hundred miles in less than three months. Steam power had suddenly shrunk the Missouri artery to a manageable length.

In 1836 Astor's American Fur Company bought Fort Laramie and began supplying it with annual ox-wagon caravans from Council Bluffs and Fort Pierre, both steamboat stops. The fur giant established branch posts in Lakota camping grounds in the West and soon received more than half of its robes—tens of thousands of them—from the Lakota domain. Then the rival-imitators came. A cluster of posts mushroomed on the eastern bank of the South Platte, and Fort Platte challenged Fort Laramie's regional monopoly on the North Platte,

26. *Sioux Dog Feast*, by George Catlin, 1832–37. Although the Lakotas shifted
their trading operations farther west, Fort Pierre continued to serve as an important
diplomatic venue where Lakota headmen received and negotiated with foreign agents.
This image, likely from 1832, shows the feast Lakota headmen arranged for U.S.
dignitaries traveling on the *Yellow Stone* side-wheeler. Two Oglala chiefs, Ha-wan-je-
tah (One Horn) and Tchán-dee (Tobacco), had their lodges arranged into a semicircle,
allowing 150 warriors and leading men to observe the proceedings: the erection of the
flagstaff, the smoking of the calumet pipe, and the meal served from seven kettles.
Courtesy of Smithsonian American Art Museum, © Photo Scala, Florence.

drawing in hundreds of Lakota and Cheyenne families at a time. For Lakotas the
competition meant enhanced bargaining power and such novelties as Belgian
guns, Spanish blankets, Italian beads, and Chinese paint. All their bands were
"said to be friendly to the whites," and hundreds of Lakota tipis often enveloped
Fort Laramie, proclaiming Lakota primacy at that vital spot.[24]

THE DIVERGENCE

The westward shift of the fur trade accelerated a long process of economic-
military divergence that saw the northern Great Plains parting on two con-

27. *Fort Laramie*, by Alfred Jacob Miller, 1848.
Courtesy of the Walters Art Museum, Baltimore.

trasting trajectories along the nomad-villager divide. While Lakotas experienced
a sustained commercial boom, the villagers found themselves increasingly marginalized. Beaver populations in their homelands had nearly collapsed and
bison herds were shrinking at an alarming rate. Pawnees, Omahas, Otoes, Iowas,
Kansas, and others saw their trade sink to almost nothing. Their meager fur
output secured them a few cheap guns, which hardly seemed worth the trouble:
often they simply bartered their pelts and horses for whiskey, deepening their
poverty and decline.[25]

Mobility was the key to Lakota success. Just as steamboats compressed time
and distance along the Missouri channel, mounted hunting and transportation
compressed the vast steppe expanses, making their animal wealth more accessible, exploitable, and moveable. The interior between the Missouri and the
Rocky Mountains became a single economic system fused by steam- and horse-
powered transportation. The system was not without its challenges and hard-
ships—the Missouri iced over for several months each year, and long winters
drained horses and their owners—but no other region in the interior could compete with the northern plains in terms of transportation efficiency and sheer economic output. By 1840 some ninety thousand bison robes were shipped each

year from the region to eastern markets, yielding the fur companies more than half a million dollars. The robe trade was becoming big business, and its main axis extended from St. Louis to the Lakota country.[26]

Among the many interior Indians Lakotas eclipsed were their Dakota kin to the east. The booming Missouri traffic demoted the Mississippi-Minnesota trade to a sideshow. One company after another abandoned the region, allowing a single corporation to achieve virtual monopoly. Prices for pelts plummeted, and competition for outlets became vicious, pitting Dakotas against Sauks, Mesquakies, and Chippewas. Everyone suffered, and Dakotas collapsed into poverty; Mdewakanton-Wahpekute pelt output for 1834 was 118. In 1837 the U.S. government brought Dakota leaders to the capital where they signed off Sioux lands east of the Mississippi to make room for a growing flow of settlers. In exchange, they received annuities—yearly payments of food, guns, tools, and cash—which allowed them to halt their steep population decline. They had traded land, their most precious possession, for survival, and it set a dangerous precedent. Soon much of their treaty funds was going directly to private traders as a payment for necessities.[27]

WEALTH OF WOMEN

George Catlin, a self-taught American painter-ethnographer, witnessed in the late 1830s how the fur trade had turned the Lakota country into a bazaar: "In the heart of their country is one of the most extensive assortments of goods, of whiskey, and other saleable commodities, as well as a party of the most indefatigable men"—fur traders—"who are constantly calling for every robe that can be stripped from these animals' backs." Catlin captured the rapid commercialization of the Lakota world, but he also captured a more essential truth: the rise of Lakotas was a product of hard, grinding work. Behind the wars, raids, trade fairs, and diplomatic missions were thousands of everyday chores that made Lakotas what they were but rarely received notice. Catlin did notice. Having witnessed the violent dispossession of Native Americans in the East, he believed that all Indians were doomed, "melting away at the approach of civilization," and he wanted to record their "domestic habits" and ceremonies for posterity. "Amongst those tribes who trade with the Fur Companies," he wrote, "the women are kept for the greater part of the year, dressing buffalo robes and other skins for the market."[28]

"Our home life began in the tipi," remembered Oglala chief Luther Standing Bear, and the tipi in the Lakota world was the woman's domain. Women owned the tipis—their poles, covers, and much of the wealth in them—and they owned the horses that hauled the household from place to place. The wife was the center of the tipi—the smoke flaps were "women's arms"—and she decided how its interior space was arranged and decorated. Women raised and taught children in tipis, cared for elders in them, and told stories in them, and for all that they were deeply respected. A woman could expel an unruly husband from the lodge and divorce him.

Men were the public face of the Lakota nation, but by custom and practice they consulted wives and mothers before taking major decisions. Women knew intimately the material, psychological, and spiritual needs of their families and relatives, and they counseled and challenged their husbands and sons who voiced the family consensus. Sitting Bull's closest councillor was his widowed mother, Her-Holy-Door, who lived with him and offered him affection and advice into his early fifties. Women actively shaped Lakota foreign policy by pushing men into war, by pressing for peace, and by raising children committed to Lakota values and institutions.

Women possessed both personal and collective autonomy, had their own societies, and often enjoyed more extensive kinship networks than the men did. Like men, they could seek sacred power through the Sun Dance and the vision quest and become *heyókȟas*, thunder dreamers, who communicated with Thunder Beings, received special duties from them, and instructed others, both women and men, of their mysteries. They did not belong to their fathers or husbands. But the commercial boom that washed over Lakotas in the 1830s and 1840s brought dramatic changes to women's lives and relations with men. Women's sphere began to narrow around the indispensable buffalo robe.[29]

The making of a robe began with the slaughter and skinning of a beast, but someone had to transform the bloody, gristly hide into a supple, water-resistant robe that could warm a gentlewoman's back, soften a baby's bed, or keep a workingman's feet dry and warm somewhere in the East. That task belonged to the women. Women scraped all the flesh and fat off the skin with a sharpened bone, rubbed boiled buffalo brains on it to soften and tan it, and soaked and stretched it several times over. Women also raised and dismantled tipis, hauled water and fuel, collected wild plants and salt, dug food caches, cooked and cleaned, manufactured household utensils and garments, and tended the young and old, providing the all-important labor that made Lakotas dynamic and powerful. When the fur trade began to boom, women's work increased exponentially. By a long tradition, Lakota men were hunters and warriors and could not be employed in fur dressing, which meant that women would have to process the tens of thousands of robes Lakotas brought to market each season. A skilled tanner could finish twenty-five to thirty-five robes in a year—which fetched three to six guns—whereas a skilled hunter could bring down ten bison in a single chase. This made women's labor the most critical resource of the robe trade, which, in effect, was a mechanism for connecting western female labor and expertise to eastern demand for furs.[30]

Women's labor was the bottleneck in Lakotas' quest for goods and wealth, and like many other Indigenous societies enmeshed in colonial markets, they widened that bottleneck through polygamy. The practice was ancient among the Lakotas, but it grew dramatically with the robe trade. Prominent hunters, warriors, and providers with the means to offer the generous gifts that validated a marriage were in a position to acquire multiple wives whose collective labor made their households rich. When a man acquired a wife by "purchase" — paying a bride price — he gained the right to marry her sisters as well, and a highly successful man could have several sister wives sharing his lodge as well as a number of other wives living in separate tipis outside the camp circle. When Maximilian noted that "wealthy people sometimes have eight or nine wives," the emphasis on wealth was well taken: as women's value as robe processors increased, so too did the bride price, for fathers demanded to be liberally compensated for the loss of their daughters' labor. Red Cloud, an eminently gifted man of a middling lineage, paid twelve superb horses for the right to marry his first wife, Pretty Owl, and married his sixth wife when he was twenty-four. Some prominent men also married *wíŋktes*, two-spirit persons who embraced a woman's social role and dress and lived in polygamous marriages.[31]

"The brave or chief, who has the greatest number of wives," observed Catlin, "is considered the most affluent and envied man in the tribe," for his lodge was "the most abundantly furnished with the luxuries of civilized manufacture." The number of wives became a key measure of male success. Wives elevated men by making them wealthy through their labor and by embodying their husbands' martial and commercial prowess. Women did share their households' successes, but not equally. First and sister wives who shared a lodge with their husbands were in a position to enjoy the privileges of wealth: a large tipi in the camp circle; coffee, sugar, fabrics, dyes, and other imported luxuries; the joy and status of being able to help the less fortunate; the opportunities to council influential husbands on political matters; the time to join women's societies, stage ceremonies, become visionaries, and specialize in competitive craftwork that brought comparable status to military coups. There, in a sphere of relative privilege, the ancient ideal of equivalent and complementary gender roles persisted. But a growing number of women found themselves marginalized in the new commercial milieu. Many were harnessed in the arduous task of processing robes, but the products of their labor no longer belonged to them. At some point in the early nineteenth century buffalo robes became men's possession, a commercial product they could trade as they saw fit. The proceeds, excitement, and prestige of trading was men's alone.[32]

Like trade itself, polygamy was a mixed blessing for Lakota women. Becoming one of the several wives of a wealthy man could bring status and security to a widow or a young woman whose family could not afford the customary gift exchanges of horses and other valuables between parents-in-law. Wives in plural marriages could also rely on one another in raising children, sharing household work, and receiving personal care during pregnancies, and there was both status and security in belonging to a large household with many children. There was no cultural stigma attached to women in polygamous marriages.

Yet plural marriages seem to have loosened the emotional ties between husbands and wives, fostering heightened male bravado in which women were reduced to objects of male rivalry. In the eighteenth century, when trade was still a small part of the Lakota economy, men and women had shared the burdens and fruits of the hunt relatively equally. That collective ethos began to crumble in the early nineteenth century, challenged by a detached, even cavalier attitude toward women and marriage. That attitude was visible when a man, at a dance of his society, threw a stick in the air and declared that it was his wife and any man who caught it could have her. The attitude was there, too, when two men who were *kȟolás*, friends who had pledged to look after each other in war and life, chose to exchange wives. It was there when young unmarried men seduced young women only to publicly humiliate them for having yielded to them or when adult men "stole" each other's wives to flaunt their masculine prowess. It was there when men mutilated wives who had been deemed lazy or unfaithful, and it assumed a pointed physical manifestation in two-tiered villages where the perimeter was dotted with humble, sometimes dilapidated tipis housing adopted captive women who formed a growing portion of the Lakota labor force.[33]

Polygyny was becoming an investment that helped some men accumulate extraordinary wealth through female labor and climb the social ladder. Prosperous married men came to dominate the marriage market—the majority of "purchased" marriages were for second or third wives—and soon the demand surpassed the supply: there were not enough women for all. The more successful some men became, the larger the pool of men who struggled to marry at all. It was a dangerous social pathology that threatened to divide the Lakota men into fully franchised and marginalized individuals. When polygyny became essential for social ascent, it drove Lakota men to see one another as rivals rather than comrades.[34]

MEN OF SUBSTANCE

In the early nineteenth century Lakota men were born into an increasingly competitive world with an uneven playing field. Boys were raised to be brave and ambitious in war, hunting, horsemanship, and courtship, and aspiring young men had to participate in several raiding expeditions to accumulate enough horses for a dowry. Many accomplished this in their late twenties after which they could settle down to family life, gradually give up raiding, and assume the role of an elder. As their families grew, they could marry off their daughters to other prominent men, receive handsome bride prices, and embed their families into expansive kinship networks that brought prestige, prosperity, and security. The most successful men — those who had become *wiča*, complete men — could sponsor extravagant feasts and giveaways in their sons' name, paving their way within the fiercely competitive male sphere. Many celebrated Lakota leaders were born into this kind of privilege and were in turn able to bestow their sons with similar benefits. If competent, their sons could succeed them as hereditary chiefs and assume their names. They Fear Even His Horses the Younger and American Horse the Younger belonged to old and highly esteemed lineages, their names both a privilege and an obligation.[35]

If not quite aristocracy, such men nonetheless possessed decisive advantages over others. Sitting Bull was born into a long line of chiefs and raised by two powerful uncles — Four Horns, a prominent band leader, and Looks-For-Him-in-A-Tent, a renowned war leader — whose eminence reflected on him, propelling his rise among aspiring Hunkpapa men. Camp heralds publicized his exploits as a hunter and a warrior — he earned his first military honors at fourteen, chasing a fleeing Crow on horseback and bringing him down with a hatchet-blow to the head — a position of advantage that blended with his innate spiritual prowess, physical courage, and quiet charisma to elevate him above rivals. He had a powerful dream in a vision quest at a young age and became the leader of the prestigious Strong Hearts warrior society in his mid-twenties.

Curly Hair was the son of Crazy Horse, who was the headman of the leading Hunkpatila band of the Oglalas, which traced a proud lineage of elders and holy men. At the time of Curly Hair's birth in 1840, his father's band included over ten tipis of blood relatives and in-laws, all of whom looked to Crazy Horse for spiritual and political leadership. Curly Hair was a child of privilege who grew up having his first steps and words celebrated with public feasts and gifts to the poor. Through his Minneconjou mother Curly Hair found another set of supportive kin relations and a further source of esteem: his family was the key proponent of an Oglala-Minneconjou alliance that shaped Lakota politics for a generation. His family promoted solidarity in both oyátes through giveaways, accruing admiration and followers; High Backbone, an ambitious Minneconjou headman, adopted Curly Hair as his protégé, engaging him in two-way character-hardening play fights and equestrian feats. When Curly Hair became a man and assumed his father's name, he was primed for success. Young women wanted him for a husband, fathers wanted their daughters to marry him, young men wanted to be his kȟolá, and warriors were willing to follow him into war.

Men like the young Crazy Horse inevitably overshadowed less privileged men who lacked their kin connections, family wealth, and fame. For them the path for social recognition was paved with toil, anxiety, and violence—relentless raiding that gradually, often after several years, yielded enough clout to court women and enough horses and robes to pay bride prices. Lakotas raided and fought several neighboring groups in the mid-nineteenth century, but they did not do so as a monolith. Elite men raided horses to augment their possessions, but, backed with wealthy relatives, they could also afford to focus on collecting coups—war honors earned through audacious exploits like touching the enemy with a hand or a coupstick in the midst of hot battle—which further solidified their credentials as leaders. For other men raiding was an economic necessity that could consume their lives into early middle age. Some of them succeeded in turning themselves into warrior-traders with several wives, but many died trying. Their raw, anguished ambition to become men of substance was a latent impetus behind the expansion that made Lakotas the masters of the northern plains. Red Cloud, who lacked the pedigree of some of his rivals, spent nearly twenty years raiding before he dared to make a formal bid for chieftainship.[36]

THE LORDS OF THE PLAINS

In 1834–35 Pawnees and their Arikara allies attacked a Sicangu camp on the Niobrara and stole dozens of horses. It proved to be the last large-scale villager attempt to stop the Lakota expansion. Lakota warriors pursued and defeated the attackers within a short distance of their village, killing twenty-two and recovering the stolen horses. Manning a temporary Lakota post near the Cheyenne River, Denig recorded the aftermath and its heated masculine self-aggrandizement: "The successful warriors returned bringing the head, hands, feet, and other parts of the enemies' bodies into camp. The hands and feet were stuck on sticks and paraded through the village by old women."[37]

From there the violence escalated rapidly. Winter counts record how Lakotas "went to buy corn and the Rees [Arikaras] killed six of them as they did not want them around," and how mounted Lakotas fought with Pawnee footmen "on the ice on the North Platte River," killing seven. Pawnees retreated from their western village around Cedar Bluff, a hilly island near the forks of the Platte that

28. American Horse winter count, 1836–37 (detail). This Oglala winter count depicts a battle between Oglalas and Pawnees on ice. Both sides had guns and bows, and the pictograph shows blood stains on the ice. Plains Indian warfare is often portrayed as a quintessential summer affair, but in reality raids and battles took place in all seasons. Courtesy of National Anthropological Archives, Smithsonian Institution (NAA INV 08746929, detail).

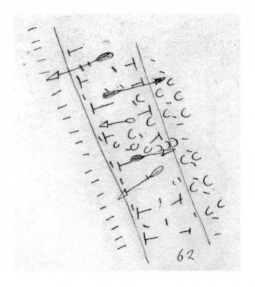

was sacred to them. They still launched large-scale hunts into short-grass plains, but fighting shifted east into Pawnee homelands. Pawnees owned some six thousand horses and produced up to fifteen thousand bushels of corn each year—magnets for Lakota raiding parties and their Ponca auxiliaries. Red Cloud cut his teeth as a warrior in these campaigns. The first raid he participated in brought home fifty mounts.[38]

Pawnees were still formidable, carrying a reputation as skillful warriors whose "position in the midst of jealous and ever active enemies" was "an unimpeachable evidence of their martial eminence." But in 1837 the smallpox returned to the Missouri Valley, now on board the *St. Peter's*, an American Fur Company steamer. The company decided not to quarantine the diseased vessel, and a succession of epidemics erupted as the steamer completed its rounds, leaving behind "one great *grave yard*." More than twenty thousand Plains Indians may have perished, most of them village dwellers; Pawnees lost twenty-five hundred people, mostly children. Lakotas, too, were struck, but several hundred of their members had been vaccinated five years earlier, compromising the virus's ability to spread. Lakotas became beneficiaries of the catastrophe: suddenly, they faced a dramatically weakened village world.[39]

The debilitated villagers struggled to hold on to their lands under the Lakota onslaught, and fighting became desperate. "They think it necessary to contend for every inch of ground," John Dougherty, the U.S. agent for the Pawnees, wrote in 1838. "Otherwise their natural enemies will soon get possession of the whole buffalo country." As if to prove him right, the next winter a multi-oyáte Lakota party operating far from their homelands killed as many as one hundred Pawnees. "The day is not far off when the Sioux will possess the whole buffalo region," Dougherty warned, "unless they are checked." For a while there was hope. In 1841 the new Pawnee agent, Presbyterian minister John Dunbar, established a mission for his charges on the Loup River north of the Platte. Two years later some three thousand Pawnees lived on the site, a foundation for what Dunbar envisioned as a peaceful community of Christian Native farmers. Instead, it was a death trap.

At dawn of a late June day about five hundred mounted Oglalas and Sicangus descended on Pawnee lodges around the mission in a coordinated attack. Horse soldiers closed in on the panicked villagers from three sides. Pawnees withdrew and then gathered together and climbed on the roofs of their lodges. Lakotas feigned a retreat, trying to draw Pawnees out in the open, but failed. They "returned to the combat with renewed fury," charging through the streets and dodging Pawnee arrows and bullets raining from above. They drove off Pawnee horses—fear of enemy raids forced Pawnees to keep their horses inside their villages at night—and then started to burn lodges, tearing down their earth cover to set the thatching underneath on fire. As the flames ate their way toward them, Pawnee warriors kept fighting, trying to shield their fleeing women and children. When the fighting ended around noon, Pawnees had lost seventy people, two hundred horses, and more than half of their lodges. How many Lakotas were lost was unclear, for they threw their dead and fatally wounded into the burning lodges so that Pawnees could not torture the living and mutilate the dead. Dunbar, along with several Skiri Pawnees, watched the battle from a distance, unable to do a thing to help his protégées. The survivors withdrew south of the Platte, and Lakotas began patrolling the area, making sure they would not return. Missouri traders reported that Lakotas "declared themselves to be the lords of the plains, and are resolved on exterminating the Pawnees and Omahas, if not all the border tribes."[40]

The destruction of the grand Pawnee village had effectively secured for Lakotas the plains and its bison south to the Platte Valley, but Oglalas and Sicangus remembered the battle for a different reason. "In the fight with the Pawnees," reads an Oglala count, "they captured the medicine arrow which the enemies had stolen from the Cheyennes." Four sacred arrows were Cheyennes' most hallowed possessions, a gift from their prophet Sweet Medicine who had bestowed the arrows to them in a time before time so that they could organize themselves properly, kill buffaloes, and defeat their enemies. A Pawnee hunting party had captured two or three arrows in a chance encounter, and Cheyennes had managed to negotiate the return of all but one arrow. It was that arrow Oglalas and Sicangus retrieved on the Loup. They took it to Cheyennes who redeemed it with one hundred horses.⁴¹

Unlike Poncas, Pawnees never abandoned their villages to become nomads, not even when it was clear that sedentarism threatened their survival. They could not imagine life without villages and corn, and their ceremonies, social order, and sacred knowledge were all tied to specific tracts of land. The Pawnees stayed put, subsisting at times on roots and begging food from American traders and travelers, and Lakotas kept raiding them for resources. Pawnees had figured prominently in Lakota winter counts for decades, and although Lakota attacks on Pawnee villages increased in the 1840s, the counts do not mention them: raids had become routine.⁴²

Pawnees were under siege. When Lakotas burned their village near Dunbar's mission in 1846, the minister and his partners fled instantly. No one was sent in their stead, and the raids continued. A year later Indian agents sent in farmers to teach the starving Pawnees how to extract more from the soil, but Lakotas would not allow it. Seven to eight hundred warriors attacked the one remaining Pawnee village on the Loup, destroying "everything about the village that could be readily destroyed." Pawnees survived on roots, only to be struck by cholera in the spring of 1849. They built a new village on the lower Platte, as far from the Lakotas as possible.⁴³

The smaller village groups—Omahas and Otoes—posed less of a threat, but that did not shield them from attacks. The seemingly blind Lakota wrath against these tiny groups puzzled the government agents who were trying to Christianize them and settle them into reservations. The key explanation was drought. The period from the mid-1820s to the mid-1840s was extraordinarily wet, supporting large bison populations and booming trade. In 1845–46 there were "immense quantities of buffalo meat," drying racks straining under strips of fresh meat, and "much feasting." It was a zenith: a severe drought struck the western high plains, ending the boom. Ponds and creeks dried up and grasses saved themselves by withdrawing underground, sprouting only minimal surface growth to conserve their root systems. The bison herds mirrored the grasses. By producing fewer off-spring, the bison survived the dry spell as a species.⁴⁴

When Lakotas attacked Omahas at their Big Village on Elkhorn Creek near the Missouri in 1845, it was the second time they banished the villagers from the site. Omahas retreated south to the Platte-Missouri confluence, but Lakotas now chased them relentlessly. In the winter of 1846–47, together with Poncas, they killed seventy-three in a single attack, more than 6 percent of the Omaha popu-lation. Another burst of raids prompted an agent to warn that, without a U.S.

intervention, the Pawnees, Omahas, and Otoes "will soon be extinct." Omahas begged the United States to buy their lands so that they could receive annuities—farming tools to fend off starvation and guns to fend off the Lakotas.[45]

Otoes reacted differently. Abject poverty and starvation kept eating into their numbers, fueling internal schisms, alcoholism, and spite. A vicious spiral set in. They traded their paltry yield of robes and pelts for whiskey and soon had only a few horses and guns left. Embittered, they lashed out, attacking missionaries and traders, alienating the Indian agents who controlled their annuities and thus accelerating their decline. Their world collapsing, they split into small villages on the lower Platte, hoping to elude Lakota war parties. It failed. In 1847 more than three hundred Lakotas descended upon them. There were nine hundred Otoes left and their numbers were dwindling.[46]

Horrified and humiliated by the seemingly unstoppable violence and human suffering unfolding before them, U.S. agents denigrated Lakotas as irredeemable savages "determined to exterminate" their neighboring tribes. They killed villagers because that was what savages did. The agents failed to see the underlying causes of the violence. Lakotas did go to war to fulfill the warrior ideal, but they conquered and dispossessed entire groups because those groups were rivals and threats. Each farming village absorbed crucial resources—grass, water, timber—Lakotas needed for their horses and burgeoning bands; each village occupied a precious segment of a river valley that could have accommodated a Lakota village or a bison herd. In 1847—when effects of the drought were already evident—some 110,000 bison robes and 25,000 bison tongues were shipped down the Missouri, and Lakotas were the main contributor to that profusion. The season that preceded the record harvest was the first when they could hunt without opposition from the Cannonball in the north to the Platte in the south.[47]

THIS MUST BE AN END

The fate of the Pawnees and other plains villagers had been sealed by the 1837 smallpox epidemic, which plunged their numbers onto a lower plateau from which they never recovered. Within a decade Lakotas had cleared tens of thousands of square miles of western grasslands and prime bison country of rivals— the foundation of an expansive plains dominion.

A similar dynamic of death and conquest unfolded in the upper Missouri Valley, where villager losses were even more horrifying than among the plains villagers. When the *St. Peter's* made a stop at an American Fur Company post near the Knife River, the virus found a fertile ground for spreading. Mandans had not been struck by smallpox for fifty-six years, which meant that only the elderly were immune. Almost everyone got smallpox, and almost everyone who caught it died. Of sixteen hundred perhaps only three hundred survived. The survivors lacked the strength to dig graves and had to cut holes in the ice and throw the bodies in the river. A U.S. Indian agent was certain that they "will cease to exist as a nation." The nearby Hidatsas lost at least half of their people. Arikaras, having fled Lakota aggression south among the Pawnees five years earlier, had returned north just before the outbreak. One-third of them died, and the survivors occupied one of the two remaining Mandan villages near the Knife. Lakotas came the following winter. Francis Chardon, the region's only remaining fur trader, wrote down what he saw: "I beheld the Mandan Village all in flames . . . this Must be an end to What was once called the Mandan Village, upwards of one hundred years it has been standing, the Small Pox last year, very near annihilated the Whole tribe, and the Sioux has finished the Work of destruction by burning the Village."[48]

On the margins of his entry Chardon wrote "20 Skins," the day's acquisition. The next day he reported having secured forty robes and twenty-six pounds of beaver from Lakotas. The jarring conjoining of annihilation and petty trade in Chardon's journal offers a clue to Lakota motives. After decades of intensive hunting and trapping, animal populations had begun to fail along the Missouri, fueling competition and animosity. The decimated Missouri villagers could hardly feed themselves, not to mention produce surplus for nomads. They were now simply competitors for dwindling resources. Mandans and Hidatsas retreated into a consolidated village dozens of miles north of their old village sites, desperate to put distance between themselves and Lakotas. The village, Like-a-Fishhook, was to be the last earth-lodge settlement in the northern Great Plains.[49]

The villagers' ruin marked at once Lakotas' final conquest of and withdrawal from the Missouri Valley. By neutralizing the villagers as rivals, they had also obliterated a vital resource that had sustained them on the Missouri for generations. Like-a-Fishhook was an impoverished refugee center, and the heady days of tribute extraction were gone. Lakotas would occasionally come and raid the village, but the greater attraction was trade at the nearby Fort Berthold, built by the American Fur Company in 1845.[50]

By the late 1840s almost all Lakotas had made the western plains their home, visiting the Mníšoše only periodically to bring their robes to steamboat stops for downriver shipment. Only Two Kettles, a small oyáte of some five hundred people, remained attached to the river. They made quick forays into the West, but did not engage in large-scale raiding, and were known as superior hunters and tactful traders who were "extremely fond of getting well paid for their skins." Their semi-permanent villages near Fort Pierre were the last substantial Lakota bridgehead on the Missouri, which had lost its centrality in the Lakota universe.

Like the Americans in St. Louis, Lakotas began to see the river as a means to an end, a trade artery that linked them to the larger world, generating wealth and power.[51]

For a long time the Black Hills were a sanctuary and supply depot that anchored Lakotas in the West. They were the terminus for extended, often dangerous westbound sojourns through immense grasslands Lakotas did not yet fully know or control. But in the late 1830s Joseph N. Nicollet, a French scientist leading U.S.-sponsored expeditions into the West, reported that hundreds of Lakota lodges dotted the Black Hills: the Lakota world as a whole had shifted westward. Its spatial logic was inverted. Pahá Sápa became the center of the Lakota world, and the Mníšoše became a destination for eastbound sojourns through the grasslands that had become Lakota territory.[52]

Pahá Sápa was "the heart of everything that is." It was a place where life itself began, where Lakotas entered the present world, and where ancient petroglyphs revealed the future. Now Pahá Sápa was also the economic and political core of a new western dominion whose gifts must have seemed providential. When Lakotas took the crucial step into the West in the 1830s, they unleashed themselves from the Mníšoše's vital but declining carbohydrate reserves, plunging into a perilous nutritional limbo. They found a new haven in Pahá Sápa, a crossroads where mountain and steppe habitats and boreal and deciduous forests meet. In that extraordinary spot elevation created a singular microclimate that sustained rich and diverse plant communities — hundreds of native species that yielded edible seeds, tubers, pods, and petals.[53]

Those wild plants were more than food; they were a key to the West. By helping close the chronic carbohydrate gap, they allowed Lakotas to live in the western grasslands year-round and gain access to their immense animal wealth. The Great Plains may have supported close to thirty million bison in the early nineteenth century, and one of the largest concentrations was found around the Black Hills where abundant grass growth, relatively mild winters, and protective river bottoms and gullies provided nurturing niches for the bulky bovines. Observing their new world from high up, Lakotas could see the animals blackening the plains toward the horizon in the summer and revealing themselves with clouds of steam, their "visible breath," in the dead of winter. That winter vapor must have seemed like destiny, evoking the way the White Buffalo Woman had first come to Lakotas, promising a new age of prosperity.[54]

Pahá Sápa concentrated the Lakota political life as never before. The Missouri had pulled all the Lakota oyátes into its sheltering fold, but the river also encouraged dispersion along its long channel. Pahá Sápa, by contrast, was a single gravitational point where all the oyátes gathered, sharing the sacred space and its material bounties. Pahá Sápa became one of the main arenas for the Sun Dance, which took on new significance now that Lakotas had arrived in their mythical place of origin. Thióšpayes came together as oyátes by forming a tribal circle that replicated the sacred hoop and contained a circular arbor where a sacred cottonwood tree stood. There, for a few intensive midsummer days, people danced in prayer, reconnecting with flesh-and-blood relatives and otherworldly ones. Everyone was renewed and everyone became one with the universe. They all thought alike, forming a single kindred, just as White Buffalo Calf Woman had promised.[55]

When the ceremony ended, bands sometimes stayed together for weeks. People hunted together, visited relatives in different oyátes, married across band and tribal lines, and deliberated political matters. The gatherings were a reaffirmation of spiritual unity, but the large multi-oyáte congregations now also functioned as temporary headquarters where Lakotas formulated and debated policies that would preserve their nation that was once again shifting shape.[56]

THESE DRESS ELEGANTLY AND EXPENSIVELY

In the winter of 1830 Lakotas killed some twenty Crows at Mathó Pahá (Bear Butte) about twenty miles north of the fabled Racetrack. Crows had attempted to surprise a Lakota camp in an unusually snowy winter, but Lakota herders had detected them. Numerous winter counts recorded the battle, underscoring its importance: it marked the beginning of a war that would last, with short respites, for nearly half a century between Lakotas and Crows—the longest known war in the history of North America.[57]

That the battle took place at Bear Butte was significant. Lakotas had banished Crows from the Black Hills in the 1820s, but the violence persisted, turning a vast arc stretching from the hills toward the North Platte, the Big Horn Mountains, and the Yellowstone into a battleground. At stake were spiritually significant places like Mathó Pahá and Mathó Thípila Pahá (Devil's Tower) where Crows, Lakotas, and Cheyennes gathered to hold ceremonies and seek visions. At stake were also robes, protein, carbohydrates, and timber. The contested terrain, an alluring mosaic of steppes and mountains punctuated by a series of lush and well-forested river valleys, was rich in bison and wild plants and made for some of the best horse pastures in the Great Plains. The fighting became unyielding, bringing violence to the doorstep of the Lakota villages. An 1837 Oglala winter count reported one such incident: "Black-face, who painted half his face black from the nose down, camped away from the circle and was killed by the Crow, he and his whole family."[58]

The Crow war presented a singular challenge for Lakotas: it was their first full-blown conflict with other horse nomads. Crows were formidable warriors who had acquired horses long before Lakotas, possessed more animals per capita, and were generally known as superior equestrian fighters. They were also well integrated in the fur trade. They visited Fort Union near the Missouri-Yellowstone confluence every year and also rendezvoused with Rocky Mountain trapper-traders who considered the quality of Crow beaver pelts second to none. From both outlets guns, powder, and lead flowed into the Crow country. The experienced fur trader Denig considered the Crows "cunning, active, and very intelligent in everything appertaining to the chase, war, or their own individual bargaining." Powerful and confident, they looked the part to Denig's nineteenth-century sensibility. "The warrior class is perhaps the handsomest body of Indians in North America. They are all tall, straight, well formed, with bold, fierce eyes, and as usual good teeth. These also dress elegantly and expensively."[59]

The Crow-Lakota conflict was an uncompromising tug-of-war over the control of the borderlands that separated the Black Hills from the Crow country to the west. This meant that Crows were fighting in terrain they knew intimately and that Lakotas were entering foreign lands to face an enemy that matched or surpassed their firepower and horsemanship. But Lakotas had a number of advantages that compensated for their weaknesses. Their population dwarfed the five-thousand-strong Crows, and their clustering in Pahá Sápa allowed them to coordinate military action at an unprecedented scale. At the moment the Black Hills became home, they also became a front line.

SO INVETERATE IS THEIR MUTUAL ANIMOSITY

In 1835 Lame Deer, a Minneconjou chief, shot a Crow warrior twice with the same arrow. He seems to have shot the man from a distance, ridden to him, and pulled out the arrow to shoot him again. Was it a coup de grâce to a wounded enemy, bravado, or just hatred? Whatever the motive, the Crow war was clearly testing Lakotas to their limits. The exact context for the killing cannot be retrieved, but it can be imagined: two supremely mobile war parties engaged in a deadly hide-and-seek, each trying to elude and awe the other, both desperate to prevail.[60]

Denig observed how bloodshed became routine. The war unfolded in a seemingly endless cycle of raids and counterraids, "the Crows generally killing most and the Sioux getting the most horses." Denig attributed the deadly cycle to an ingrained "exterminating custom," flattening a complicated war to an ethnic feud. In truth, Lakotas and Crows hated one another because they vied for a limited supply of resources. Both needed horses to thrive as nomads, and both needed secure access to bison to succeed as hunters. Both also needed imported technology—guns, powder, bullets, metal—to protect themselves, which made them competitors over American markets. The proliferation of trading posts in the western plains, on the very borderlands that separated Crows and Lakotas, drew both in, raising tensions to a fever pitch. Lakotas and Crows killed one another not because they were different but because they were so alike.[61]

The thriving robe trade also spawned new wars. Determined to protect their privileged position in the fur trade, Lakotas pushed farther west and north to hunt. Before long they were fighting Arapahos, Utes, Shoshones, Flatheads, and Rocky Mountain trappers who had sided with their enemies. Winter counts capture the magnitude of the suddenly inflated war zone. In the winter of 1838–39 at least two Lakota warriors "carried the pipe around" to organize war expeditions, and the next year Lakotas "killed an entire village of Snake or Shoshoni Indians" and one hundred Pawnees. There were carefully planned, stunningly successful raids — "Sitting-Bear, American Horse's father, and others, stole two hundred horses from the Flatheads" — as well as opportunistic ones: an Oglala party, perhaps returning from a failed expedition, "killed a Crow and his wife who were found on a trail." Victorious war leaders rose to prominence, drawing followers. The Hard, a Minneconjou, led an attack that "killed" seven to twenty lodges of Arapahos, a coup that was recorded in several winter counts, and Feather-in-the-Ear, also a Minneconjou, seemed to be waging a personal raiding-revenge war. He stole "30 spotted ponies" from Crows, a feat that merited mention in five counts, and sponsored "a feast, to which he invited all the young ... braves, wanting them to go to war with him" against Shoshones, perhaps to avenge a dead relative. Feather-in-the-Ear was not the only one hurting. Oglala winter counts for 1842–43 note that "Lone Feather said his prayers, and took the warpath to avenge" dead kin. Other counts seem to record the mixed outcome: Oglalas "killed four lodges of Shoshone and brought home many horses," but Feather-Ear-Rings was slain, blood stains around Shoshone lodges marking his demise. Lakota raiding parties ranged from the lower Platte to the foothills of the Rockies, covering a five-hundred-mile span, the largest active war zone in mid-nineteenth-century North America, bringing in Crow horses and Crow captives and military coups.[62]

It was both rousing and draining, bringing Lakotas near a breaking point. Raiding could yield lavish booty, but organizing a raiding expedition was a taxing affair. Feather-in-the-Ear's recruiting feast — princely enough to merit a winter count — captures something about the length men were ready to go to establish themselves as warriors. Anyone had the right to assemble a raiding party, which infused the male sphere with chronic rivalries, jealousies, and spites. When prominent men managed to collect large numbers of warriors around them, raiding — and its corollary, trading — could split entire oyátes.[63]

Alcohol inflamed an already charged situation. With the booming robe trade came whiskey, the fur trader's primary instrument to win over Native customers and raise profit margins. Like most Lakotas, Oglalas seem to have drunk moderately, but cutthroat competition drove the traders to push the liquor traffic to new levels. Things came to a head in 1841. Over the preceding years Oglalas had begun to gravitate behind two competing headmen, Bull Bear, the leader of the Kiyuksas (Breaks One's Own), and Smoke, the long-reigning chief of the Itéšičas (Bad Faces). Bull Bear's Kiyuksas resided near Fort Laramie and hunted in the upper reaches of the North Platte where they clashed with Crows and Shoshones. Their success enticed entire Sicangu camps to join them. The ambitious Bull Bear resented the ascendancy of the more accommodating Smoke among the traders. To assert himself, he publicly killed Smoke's favorite horse. Sometime later an Itéšiča man stole a Kiyuksa woman, provoking Bull Bear to storm into Smoke's camp. The confrontation, fueled by drinking, led into a brawl that left seven dead. Among the dead was Bull Bear, reputedly shot by Smoke's twenty-year-old nephew Red Cloud. The Oglala oyáte split into two factions. The Kiyuksas established themselves south of the Platte under their new chief Whirlwind, while the Itéšičas began to shift north, ranging from the upper North Platte toward the upper Grand and Powder River Valleys.[64]

The Kiyuksa-Itéšiča split was an internecine crisis, the kind Oglalas had known before: eighty years earlier an Oglala band had briefly sided with Arikaras to fight other Oglalas. Bands were constantly vying for position in the changing military and economic circumstances, forming coalitions and going their separate ways in a ceaseless cycle of shapeshifting that was considered both necessary and normal. The division into Kiyuksa and Itéšiča blocs endured—it was still evident in the 1870s—but not because of some irresoluble animosity. It endured because it served specific strategic purposes. In the 1840s Lakota ambitions shifted decisively west. With the bison herds receding under the double assault of market hunting and drought, Lakotas turned to the sprawling short-grass steppes stretching out from Pahá Sápa toward the North Platte, the Rocky Mountains, and the Yellowstone Valley. Ranging far and wide, disconnecting and uniting again, Oglalas became a frontier oyáte that drew in aspiring warriors from other oyátes, growing rapidly in numbers.[65]

THEY CANNOT EXIST LONG AS A NATION

Contemporary observers often portrayed the Lakotas as ruthless conquerors, but the reality was more complicated. In the winter of 1844 Crows and Shoshones killed some thirty Oglalas who had been led into a snowstorm and an ambush by their celebrated war leader Male Crow. More than one hundred Lakota warriors fled the site in shame. Among them was Male Crow's brother Crazy Horse, the father of Curly Hair who would later receive his name. Crazy Horse put together a war party, "said his prayers," and set out to avenge Male Crow and the other slain warriors. The expedition dissipated in a liquor-fueled gathering at an Oglala village at the forks of the Laramie where grieving relatives denounced Crazy Horse for the cowardice of surviving.[66]

A year later Francis Parkman, the soon-to-be-famous traveler-historian, witnessed the painful aftermath of unavenged deaths, finding "the whole nation" in mourning near Fort Laramie. An Oglala chief, Whirlwind, he learned, had sent messengers among all Lakota bands "within three hundred miles, proposing a grand combination to chastise the Snakes [Shoshones], and naming a place and time of rendezvous." Parkman believed that "five or six thousand souls" were "slowly creeping over the prairies" toward the meeting place. Traveling with a group of American and Canadian trapper-traders, Parkman connected with Whirlwind's camp and became a witness to a confusing pageant. "Horsemen suddenly appeared into view on the summit of the neighboring ridge. They descended, and behind them followed a wild procession, hurrying in haste and disorder down the hill and over the plain below: horses, mules, and dogs, heavily burdened *travaux* [travois], mounted warriors, squaws walking amid the throng, and a host of children. For a full half-hour they continued to pour down" until, "as if by magic," "a miniature city" sprang up on the steppe.

The bustling village began shifting across the Laramie plains, eventually joining forces with the village of White Shield, a renowned Oglala headman. The joint camp arrived at the rendezvous and proceeded into Shoshone lands, "farther westward than we have ever been before." Yet no attack materialized. White Shield said he could not fight. He had given his war arrows away, he explained, and one of his men had had bad dreams. Parkman struggled to understand why the formidable Lakotas would shy away from battle, although he recorded the very reasons into his journal: men launching hunts that yielded "immense quantities of meat and hides"; women processing the fresh hides and treating visitors with "rich, juicy hump-ribs of a fat cow"; scouts staying constantly on the watch for enemies. Lakotas had reassessed the situation and converted the revenge party into a hunting and scouting one. They were staking out new, game-rich lands in the contested western borderlands with their American visitors serving as witnesses of a quiet invasion that promised to deliver a flood of robes for American markets. At night, as if to announce themselves to their enemies, women dropped pieces of buffalo fat into their tipi fires, turning lodge after lodge into a "gigantic lantern." Soon the village was a sea of sparkling light.[67]

Parkman expected Lakotas—whose "superb, naked figures" left a deep impression—to match his image of noble savages who fought for national honor and personal glory, and their failure to do so left him appalled. He failed to understand that the Lakotas, a quintessential warrior society, were disciplined opportunists who shifted nimbly from war to trade to diplomacy and back again. They fought protracted wars only if they served their collective interests and helped them survive as a people. Their willingness to endure decades-long wars was dictated not by some ingrained military imperative but by the fundamentals of warfare—manpower, matériel, geopolitics, and momentum. As of now the fundamentals were on their side.[68]

Spearheaded by Oglalas, Lakotas pushed deep into the Rockies to raid the mobile Ute, Shoshone, and Flathead villages that speckled the foothills, plateaus, and river valleys in an ever-changing constellation. Small long-range operations, repeated over and over during warm seasons, produced a steady flow of horses and captives into Lakota camps. By carrying the war far into the West, moreover, Lakotas contained the violence in enemy lands and kept it far from their own. There are very few records of Ute, Shoshone, or Flathead attacks on Lakota camps in the plains.

Crows were closer by, but Lakotas kept gaining ground on them. By the late 1840s attrition began to wear the numerically disadvantaged Crows down. Crows were also caught between two aggressive fronts. While fending off Lakotas in the east, they waged a grinding defensive war against the powerful Blackfeet who pushed in from the north to poach the superior Crow horses. "Situated as they now are," Denig warned, "they cannot exist long as a nation." Parkman captured their desperation and trepidation while traveling with Oglalas. Several Crow war parties had been on the prowl for Lakota hunters, but instead of attacking, they settled for engraving signs on a tree "to signify that they had invaded the territories of their enemies." One of the parties had come across a Lakota burial site. Crows tore down the bodies from their elevated scaffolds and "blew them to atoms."[69]

A POINT ONE HUNDRED MILES WEST

In 1847, after a long absence, Assiniboines reentered Lakota winter counts when they killed two Minneconjous. The two nations had clashed decades earlier, but the conflict had abated when the Assiniboines withdrew westward to become middlemen between the Blackfeet and Canadian traders. Supplied with horses by the Blackfeet, Assiniboines adopted the equestrian way of life and began shifting south toward the bison and the American Fur Company's Fort Union near the Missouri-Yellowstone confluence. Denig, who was married to an Assiniboine woman, observed how some five thousand Assiniboines settled on the Missouri by 1837—just as *St. Peter's* carried smallpox up the river. Nearly two-thirds of them died.[70]

Yet Assiniboines persevered in their new homelands. Denig deemed his wife's kin to be superior traders. They hunted bison around the Yellowstone confluence, raided Crows for horses, and conducted brisk trade at Fort Union. In 1844, as their wars with Lakotas began to go against them, Crows offered Assiniboines a truce. "In a few years these two nations became good friends," Denig noted, "Crows giving the others a good many horses" and "furnishing them with hides and meat." In return, Crows gained a much-needed ally. With Crows on their side, Assiniboines seem to have felt strong enough to face the northern Lakotas—Hunkpapas, Sihasapas, Sans Arcs, Two Kettles, and Minneconjous—who were inching westward along the Knife, Heart, Cannonball, Grand, and Moreau Rivers.[71]

Lakotas sought allies, too. Minneconjous made peace with Arikaras and relocated their village next to an Arikara village in the upper Little Missouri Valley, "a point one hundred miles farther west than their former range." This joint-use accord was extended to the Sans Arcs, Sihasapas, and Hunkpapas, who also began camping in the valley. It was a superb base. "Here they find game," reported Denig, "continue the war on the Crows, visit the mouth of the Yellowstone occasionally, murder straggling white men"—trappers who entered their lands without approval—"and help themselves to whatever horses the forts in that neighborhood can furnish."[72]

It was into this world that Sitting Bull, Gall, Spotted Eagle, Touch the Clouds, John Grass, and other warrior-leaders were born. Northern Lakotas were more loosely integrated into the world of the wašíčus than Oglalas, Sicangus, and Two Kettles, who had become deeply enmeshed in the fur trade. Suspicious of the wašíčus' intentions and loyalties, they learned to keep them at arm's length, "seldom visiting the forts either on the Platte or Missouri, and never seeing whites except a few fur traders during the winter season." Suffused with a warrior ethos, theirs was a more isolated world where raiding defined hunting grounds and boundaries, generated wealth and status, and kept bands and oyátes safe and prosperous. Jumping Badger—or "Slow"—killed his first enemy, a Crow, when he was fourteen, and received from his father both a shield and his name, Sitting Bull. This Sitting Bull, it was said, eventually owned more than a hundred horses, a pool of redistributable wealth that brought him respect, followers, and power. The Hunkpapa war chief Gall would earn more than twenty coups in his life. Both made their mark as warriors first and political leaders second.[73]

MORE LIKE THE GREAT SPIRITS THAN ANY OTHER

The Lakota takeover of the upper Missouri Valley in the early nineteenth century had been a major turning point in the history of the American interior, signaling the rise of the nomads. The Lakota expansion into the short-grass plains west of the Missouri marked another seismic shift of power in the great interior.

Until then the northwestern Great Plains had been used by many but were home to few. They had largely been a meat-and-robe reserve for people who lived else-where—nomads in the Rockies and villagers along the Missouri. Now the vast region, one of the world's best hunting grounds, belonged to Lakotas. There were about thirteen thousand of them, and their largest oyátes, the Oglalas and Sicangus, were among the most connected Native people on the continent, with several thriving trading posts within reach. With the rapid disintegration of the Comanche empire in the southern plains under a punishing drought and mounting pressure from a booming state of Texas, Lakotas emerged as the most powerful Indigenous nation in North America.[74]

The Lakota ascendancy was not simply a matter of harnessing raw military force for expansion. In 1898 Short Feather, an Oglala elder, told James R. Walker, a physician-anthropologist, that his people "are more like the Great Spirits than any other of mankind. . . . The spirits are jealous of the Sioux but they are more friendly to the Sioux than to any other of mankind." The securing of Pahá Sápa had brought a sense of expanded power and transcendence, which shaped Lakotas' understanding of themselves and their place in the world.[75]

In the course of the 1830s and 1840s Lakotas fought and defeated scores of people and absorbed uncounted numbers as captives. Seen from the vantage of their rivals, they often appeared ferocious conquerors bent on annihilation. But while they dispossessed entire societies, they also embraced former enemies. Their vision for the West was supple and capacious. They saw in most people, even in their rivals, potential allies who could be brought in their fold as kin through ritual adoption. Their quest to control game, pasture, water, and trade in the West coexisted with a spiritual mandate to balance the world by extending wólakȟota to those capable of proper behavior and thoughts.[76]

That cultural imperative had fed the larger Sioux expansion across the prairies in the previous century, and now it fed Lakota expansion across the northern plains. Strategic pluralists, Lakotas fused trading, raiding, coercion, and diplomacy into a protean economy of violence that allowed them to simultaneously exploit and embrace others. Sustained expansion was turning them into an imperial power that commanded extensive hinterlands of extraction, managed an intricate system of dependencies, and manipulated human relations on a vast scale. Numerous Indigenous groups found their fates intractably linked to the Lakotas, some of them becoming victims or vassals, others blending into the Lakota fabric as allies. The Americans who sold guns and merchandise to Lakotas realized only too slowly that they were subsidizing an Indigenous regime that was becoming too big for them to reign it in.

Lakotas were reshaping the world around them to meet their needs, and to do that they, too, had to change. The winning of the West was immensely rewarding, but it was also fraught with danger. The seemingly boundless plains were at once a liberation and a predicament. In the mid-nineteenth century there may have been two hundred Lakota thióšpayes, covering the northern Great Plains from corner to corner. The Lakota nation seemed to be imploding in its suddenly magnified setting.

The White Buffalo Calf Woman had said she would visit Lakotas from time to time to see that they remained true and whole. It was in her message and in the rituals she had bestowed upon them that Lakotas learned how they would survive as a nation. There they found the way to balance the intense localism of plains life with a collective ethos that could hold an expanding nation together. When a Lakota elder said that there was no social organization until they received the sacred pipe from the White Buffalo Calf Woman, he could have been describing the dispersal and disorder that followed from expansion. When the White Buffalo Calf Woman said that the pipe would bind Lakotas to all their relatives, she was offering a way out of the chaos. The way was kinship.

The pipe laid the foundation of the Lakota nation by reaffirming the centrality of kinship as the essence of social order. Smoking it was an act of humility and submission, an acceptance of the pervasive relatedness of all living things, but out of that submission remarkable rewards would arise. The White Buffalo Calf Woman herself was the smoke, a conduit between humans and Wakȟáŋ Tȟáŋka, and the first smoking of the pipe established kinship and prayer. When Lakotas smoked and prayed, they created a compact with Wakȟáŋ Tȟáŋka, who would look after their needs by sending buffalo. The pipe created a compact also between the different tribes of humankind for it turned enemies into allies and strangers into kin. "The spirit in the smoke will soothe the spirits of all who thus smoke together," a Lakota elder explained in 1896, "and all will be as friends and all think alike."[77]

The ideal Lakota society was that universal system of kinship in microcosm. Kinship ties emanated outward in concentric circles from nuclear families to extended families, to thióšpayes, to oyátes, to the Očhéthi Šakówiŋ, and, through wólakȟota, to non-Lakotas willing to embrace the Lakota ethos and way of being. This was a voluntary and intensely intimate social order whose primary unit was a thióšpaye, a tight-knit kin group of roughly ten to twenty extended families occupying a distinct section of the Lakota domain. Each thióšpaye had a leader, *itȟáŋčhaŋ*, who spoke for his people, and a council of distinguished men who made final decisions about formal camp movements, communal hunts, foreign relations, and war. All decisions were made by consensus, and the itȟáŋčhaŋ announced resolutions through a crier, although an itȟáŋčhaŋ with several brothers and cousins in a council could greatly influence outcomes. The council appointed a select few among the accomplished warrior-hunters as *wakíčuŋzAs*, deciders, who were responsible for organizing hunts, distributing the yield, and arbitrating disputes, while the itháŋčhaŋ appointed akíčhita marshals who enforced the council's decisions, with brutal force if necessary. The strict organization coexisted with open competitiveness and plasticity: anyone could challenge the itháŋčhaŋ for headship and anyone could leave a thióšpaye at any time. An itháŋčhaŋ who failed to keep his followers prosperous and safe soon found himself without any.[78]

REINVENTION OF TRADITION

This was traditional. The tribal circle and the sacred hoop date back to the long prairie era and the ensuing Missouri epoch. But the move into the plains triggered a shift in political power from band to tribal councils. Around the time Lakotas established themselves in the Black Hills, a new term, *načá*, entered their political vocabulary. Apparently a loan word from the Arapaho term for "chief," it designated a member of the tribal council, its very appearance suggesting the institution's growing importance for the oyátes. Načás had to be powerful men in their respective thióšpayes, but their authority rested on their prominence in oyáte-wide politics. As a new type of chief, the načás embodied a growing centralization of Lakota political life.[79]

Another new centralizing institution was the huŋká ceremony by which prominent older women and men symbolically adopted members of other families, becoming their guardians. The ceremony arose from a crisis. It was introduced in the 1830s by Bull Bear who needed to secure followers after his clash with Smoke split the Oglalas into rival factions. The huŋká created a kinship bond and an obligation to share wealth not only between two individuals but between two families, allowing Bull Bear to retain his position as a headman. His innovation flourished and spread, giving rise to a cadre of leading men whose kinship networks webbed together multiple thióšpayes and oyátes. Like načás, these were leaders whose political vision cut across traditional band and tribal lines. They made their reputations as warriors but consolidated their power through their ability to bind people together. Many of them sat in tribal councils.[80]

The traditional tribal councils became the core of a new and more integrated Lakota political order that took shape around midcentury. The most tangible expression of the councils' increasing political weight was a revolutionary institution of shirt wearers, *wičháša yatáŋpikAs*, a select group of "praiseworthy men," who came to form a kind of administrative committee that executed the decisions passed down by councils. Shirt wearers were men in their thirties and for-

29. *Sioux Indian Council, Chiefs in Profound Deliberation*, by George Catlin,
1832–37. These headmen may have been načás, members of one of the Lakota tribal
councils. Courtesy of Smithsonian American Art Museum, © Photo Scala, Florence.

ties who had displayed uncommon bravery in facing enemies and exceptional
generosity among their own. As a badge of office, they wore sheepskin shirts
decorated with quill-worked bands and locks of hair taken from enemies. The
shirts were "owned by the tribe," and the shirt wearers were in turn "owners of the
tribe." Embodiments of peoplehood, their duty was to bind their oyátes behind
council decisions through moral authority, lead attacks on enemies, and serve as
peacemakers with outsiders. Being a shirt wearer was a position of great privilege.
Minneconjous were said to have only six or seven praiseworthy men, Oglalas and
Sicangus but four.[81]

New shirt wearers were appointed in sumptuous ceremonies at the tribal
council lodge during the Sun Dance. With the entire oyáte watching, akíčhita
marshals rolled up the covers of the massive tipi and a herald called the council
members and band ithánčhaŋs to take their places behind the honor shirts
hanging on racks. Akíčhitas escorted the candidates into the exposed tipi where
they were stripped to their breechclouts and led to sit on buffalo robes. A pipe
was passed around the circle of councillors and ithánčhaŋs and then among the
candidates. As the elders dressed each candidate with a shirt, an orator explained
how their lives now belonged to the tribe. Living embodiments of an ideal

Lakota, they would have to live exemplary lives and never show fear, anger, jealousy, or avarice. Most shirt wearers came from wealthy families with the means to sponsor the elaborate initiation ceremonies, but their new role as carers of the people compelled them to share their possessions with orphans, widows, the poor, and the aged. The ceremony ended with a feast that celebrated the shirt wearers' merger with the tribe.[82]

Senior men in tribal councils were amassing unprecedented power, and it did not happen without resistance. An already existing generational fissure widened dangerously. Tribal councillors, usually men in their fifties, sixties, and seventies, represented experience and restraint, and they were responsible for determining how to best balance diplomacy, trade, and war to secure their oyáte's future. Their growing power fueled bitterness among younger men who needed combat to prove themselves as warriors and providers. Both positions were considered and deeply felt: a poorly targeted or timed raid could tangle an oyáte into a destructive war, exactly the kind of misfortune the councillors were assigned to prevent, but long periods of peace could jam the war-driven social engine that turned boys into warriors, husbands, and leaders. Things were geared to escalate, for tribal councils employed shirt wearers, always active men, to restrain other active men, pitting members of the same oyáte against one another. Shirt wearers were deeply admired, but underneath that veneer of respect simmered a pool of resentment. Crazy Horse's fall from grace in the aftermath of his relationship with the already married Black Buffalo Woman was so precipitous in part because his position as a shirt wearer had turned him into a focal point of the virulent friction between Oglala councilmen and Oglala warriors. Left unattended, generational discord could have led to social splintering as ambitious young men distanced themselves from the councils and their policies.[83]

The great genius of the Lakota political system was its prodigious capacity to absorb and dilute built-in tensions. If tribal councils solidified the power of senior men, younger men found a countervailing instrument in traditional men's societies. The societies were voluntary fraternal organizations that sponsored dances and feasts, planned war parties, served as akíčhitas, and fostered cooperation through specific codes of conduct, infusing the larger society with hard military discipline that underwrote Lakota power. Societies competed openly for members and prominence, comparing war records, staging horse races and other games, and stealing the wives and horses of rival society members. Within their bounds young men found a legitimate outlet for their competitive impulses. The "gallant and dashing" son of the Oglala chief Bull Bear had already stolen several wives in his early twenties, noted Parkman, and young men "would always follow him to war."

Although most men's societies traced their origins to a vision or a spirit encounter, they served specific political purposes. They provided a platform for various interest groups—aspiring young men, active hunter-warriors, families with young children—exerting pressure on tribal councils. Some societies were explicitly organized to oppose tribal councils and sometimes a society erected its own lodge within the tribal circle next to the council lodge, underscoring the dualism of Lakota politics. According to tradition, Red Cloud formed the White Owners society to constrain the Oglala tribal council. Consummate shape-shifters, Lakotas understood power as a pliable substance that could be carved up, shared, and transferred fluidly among different institutions and bodies of people, and it was this expansive concept of power that allowed them to keep their bustling and polarized nation on a common orbit. Lakotas shaped power into a reflection of themselves: they rendered it mobile and supple.[84]

Just as Lakotas moved through their annual cycle, scattering and gathering together again, so too did they shift power from people to people and situation to situation. As long as a thióšpaye stayed put, a band council was in charge, arbitrating disputes, managing relations with other thióšpayes, and authorizing war parties. Once approved, a war party fell under the authority of a *blotáhuŋka* who led the campaign with several deputies and akíčhitas. Successful parties returned home with blackened faces, and the people rushed to seize their weapons and booty, symbolically stripping the leader of his power. It was understood that its concentration in his hands had been but a temporary necessity.

When a council chose to move the entire camp for a hunt, trade, or cere-mony, authority shifted automatically to wakíčuŋzAs and akíčhitas. Camp moves were highly charged events—a poorly executed one could mean a clash with an enemy or famine—and wakíčuŋzAs and akíčhitas commanded them with unquestioned authority. WakíčuŋzAs determined the route of the daily travel, and akíčhitas, their faces striped black to signal authority, maintained order, punishing any offenders swiftly, whipping them or destroying their pos-sessions. Harsh punishments were considered normal, "the soldier's right," and not even headmen were immune. If a traveling thióšpaye encountered enemies, wakíčuŋzAs and akíčhitas transferred leadership to a blotáhuŋka who assumed full authority: akíčhitas washed off their stripes to defer to him and repainted them after the danger subsided. When the camp settled down again, wakíčuŋzAs oversaw the distribution of meat and hides and reassumed their role as overseers of camp affairs. At the moment the tipis formed a circle, their doors facing in-ward, the council regained its primacy, infusing the inner space of the circle with its quiet authority.[85]

Akíčhitas and wakíčuŋzAs were also in charge when, in late spring, thióšpayes gathered together, preparing for collective summer hunts and ceremonies.

When thióšpayes reached a meeting ground, each took its designated place in the great camp circle, melting into the sacred hoop. Each sent its head itháŋčhaŋ to the council lodge at the hoop's center and, as though through osmosis, authority shifted to a tribal council. The council deliberated matters involving all thióšpayes, and since decisions required consensus, they were binding. These were the occasions that saw a multitude of local cells coalescing into formidable tribes and, if necessary, multi-oyáte and international coalitions poised to inflict debilitating damage on enemies and invaders. When Lakotas mobilized for large-scale war, tribal councils could bestow a few wakíčuŋzAs, drawn from warrior societies, with temporary coercive power.[86]

POWER IN MOTION

All seven Lakota oyátes lived by this ethos, keeping people and power movable and channeling both wherever they were needed. This made Lakotas appear far more formidable than they actually were, allowing them to dominate an oversized portion of the continent: their population density was less than one person per ten square miles. Their ascendancy rested not on inviolate territorial control but on a horse-powered capacity to connect and exploit key strategic nodes—river valleys, prime hunting grounds, corn-yielding Native villages, trading posts, Pahá Sápa—which allowed them to control resources without controlling people. Ranging widely but ruling lightly, they moved constantly through space, seeking trade, tribute, plunder, pastures, and game, and it was that mobile action that demarcated their territory and supremacy. Theirs was a malleable, forever transmuting regime—call it a kinetic empire—built on mobile power politics.[87]

A deep historical irony pervaded this nascent empire. Lakotas did not rise to power by forcing others under direct control or by making things predictable. They ruled by doing almost the exact opposite, keeping things—violence, attachments, borders, power, themselves—fluid and in motion. The Lakota world was a dynamic human mosaic where families, bands, and allies shifted around constantly, arranging themselves into various constellations as circumstances demanded. For Lakotas mobility did what capitals, bureaucracies, and standing armies did for sedentary empires: it kept them safe and united, empowering them to maintain enduring relationships of hierarchy and difference.

By the mid-nineteenth century Lakotas commanded human life around them. To their east and south there was a shrinking belt of villagers whom they had either absorbed into their body politic or reduced to tributary producers of food and animals. In the opposite direction they raided numerous nomadic tribes for horses and captives across an expanding sphere that stretched deep into the Rocky Mountains in the west and into the Canadian plains in the north. A

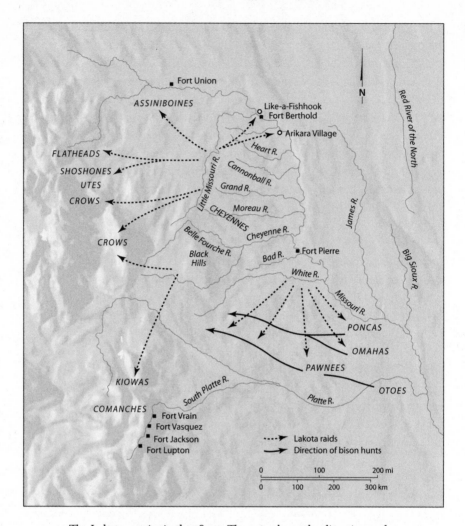

30. The Lakota empire in the 1840s. The map shows the direction and scope
of Lakota raiding and hunting expeditions. Map by Bill Nelson.

bird's-eye-view would have revealed a world of nearly constant movement and
action, a human kaleidoscope of ever-changing shapes and patterns.

It was in that fast-twitch changeability where the strength of the Lakota political system lay. It made possible stunningly rapid military mobilizations, massive concentrations of warriors in any part of the colossal realm, and annual
nationwide migrations to the heart of their world. It also contained a startling
capacity for absorbing internal strife, allowing dissidents to go out on their own,
establish distinct political identities, and yet remain full-fledged members of the

Lakota nation. It may seem fitful and arbitrary and, to a degree, it was. The splitting of the Oglala oyáte into rival factions in the 1840s may or may not have happened without Red Cloud's heated decision to pull the trigger, but the spur-of-the-moment killing was the precipitating event. Entire oyátes could split up with startling ease, almost as if by accident. The striking thing about the Oglala rift was not its sharpness but its normalcy: all oyátes had survived similar ruptures, and some of them may have had their origins in turmoil.

The White Buffalo Calf Woman had helped Lakotas remain a single unified kindred in their sprawling plains dominion, offering them the essential rituals and ideas that held their expanding and fracturing nation together. However, while embracing her vision, Lakotas also remained true people of Iktómi, ready to assume a new mood, a new form, or a different point of view when the world failed to conform to their expectations. The White Buffalo Calf Woman taught Lakotas how to access the world—the Wakĥáŋ Tĥáŋka, the buffalo, and the gift of kinship—and how to unlock its infinite possibilities for human betterment. Her message was fundamentally uplifting and laced with a sense of arrival and fulfillment. Iktómi taught Lakotas to accept the world as it was and adapt themselves to its ever-changing contours. His message was one of pragmatism and humility.

Between the two visions there was a vast imaginative space for Lakotas to envision nearly endless possibilities in the world and for themselves in it. As the nineteenth century approached its midpoint, Lakotas had thought and willed their world into yet another shape, into an Indigenous empire.

6

EMPIRES

On March 11, 1824, without authorization from Congress, Secretary of War John C. Calhoun created a new division within his department. He called it the Bureau of Indian Affairs and appointed his friend Thomas L. McKenney, a former superintendent of Indian trade, to head it. McKenney was assigned two clerks and a messenger to assist him, and with that the United States had its own colonial office. As McKenney and his clerks set to work, managing the United States' relations with the hundreds of sovereign Native nations living within its claimed borders, their small agency, which soon became known as the Indian Office, became a nerve center of a formal U.S. empire.[1]

There was much to do. In 1793 a New England inventor had applied for a patent for a simple machine with a rotating wooden cylinder covered with tight rows of wire hooks. The cylinder could be spun with a belt-and-pulley mechanism, and when balls of cotton were fed into it, the comb-like grid separated seeds from fibers, producing pure lint. Eli Whitney's cotton gin was a sensation that unlocked the immense economic potential of the Deep South, stirring its people to imagine their world anew as the Cotton Kingdom. Cotton mills popped up across the inland South, turning it into the earth's largest source of the essential fiber and the launchpad of the industrial revolution.

The American South and American slavery were at the heart of that revolution. The Jeffersonian vision of a yeoman republic gave way to a new South of slave capitalists, investors, bankers, and steamboats. Slave plantations and farms burgeoned in number and size, fed by a forced diaspora that moved nearly four hundred thousand black slaves from the old slave states to new ones by 1830. The South now produced roughly half of the world's raw cotton, a staggering output that spawned a new finance-insurance-shipping nexus that welded southern slavery and northern capital together and embedded both in an emerging global economy. Cotton and slavery had become normalized as the key to America's prosperity, and growing numbers of national leaders committed themselves to their continued expansion by gearing up to eliminate its main obstacle: the tens of thousands of Indians living in lands that had suddenly become the most desirable real estate in North America. For the Cotton Kingdom to thrive, the Indigenous southerners would have to give way to a white-owned black multitude.[2]

The idea and practice of mass-scale Indian removal was as old as the United States itself. Between 1778 and 1815 the new republic negotiated sixty-five treaties with Indian nations, negotiating ever-larger land transfers in exchange for annuities. The cotton boom shifted the practice into overdrive and stripped it of lingering constitutional scruples. As a general in the U.S. Army, Andrew Jackson fought relentless wars against southern Indians, forcing them to sign away tens of millions of acres and paving the way for a continental empire. As president, he signed Indian Removal into law in 1830 and allowed Georgia and other southern states to extend their laws over Indian nations within their borders to appropriate their lands. Fearing that such a unilateral extension of state authority could corrode the rule of law and federal authority, Chief Justice John Marshall issued two landmark decisions that plunged Native peoples into a legal limbo. As "domestic dependent nations," Marshall maintained, the Indians were exempt from state laws but could not enter into treaties with foreign countries or cede their lands to them. They were neither fully domestic nor fully foreign, not quite sovereign yet not mere wards of the United States either. Semi-autonomous polities within a much larger one, their sovereignty was precariously conditional, at once inherent and bestowed upon them by a dominant power that had assumed a unilateral right to manage them. They were subjects of a rising imperial power that was already seizing Indian lands faster than it could sell them to its denizens.[3]

The Indian Office was an instrument of that empire and an embodiment of its pointed ambiguities. When Jackson chose to ignore Marshall's rulings, allowing all eastern states to proceed with removal, the Office became the front line of imperial expansion, now driven by a logic of elimination. All of its agents were not Indian haters—many liked and cared for their wards and objected to removal— but they served an administration that had no patience for Indigenous peoples in the East, whether poor farmer-hunters, nations with long-standing treaty relations with the United States, highly educated slave-owning Cherokee planters, or Indigenous intellectuals. Jackson harnessed the Office to implement a wholesale removal of Natives from the East and, by extension, the expansion of slave capitalism across the South.[4]

The Indian Removal was a brutal, sustained campaign of ethnic cleansing executed by often corrupt and inept patronage government employees—and America's crash course into empire building. Although removal failed to deport all Native Americans east of the Mississippi, its successes—roughly one hundred thousand Indians cleared out, a hundred million acres of fecund black soil opened for cotton, the future of slave capitalism secured—conditioned the Americans to see themselves and the world in a new light. They had always thought big, but now their ambitions reached a new scale altogether. They believed that they had secured perfect settler sovereignty over a massive block of North America with what appeared a single, concentrated push, and they began to look at the rest of the continent in the same way: blocks of land, blocks of wealth, blocks of people, all attainable and transferable, all theirs to control if they so willed. They had little reason to think that the feat could not be repeated in the West. The southern Indians had possessed what white southerners deemed as impressive qualities—some of them could read and rule over others, and some had lived in city-like villages with large, well-tended farms—but what was there beyond the western horizon? Scattered nomads, a feeble Mexico, an Indian Territory full of subjugated people, an empty vastness.[5]

In the mid-1840s Mexican Texas had fallen to enterprising American emigrants and was on the verge of becoming an independent state and the vanguard of a new Anglo-centric hemispheric order. It was a pregnant moment, a crossroads where the United States could pull back to avert a potentially destructive overreach or embrace an uncertain expansionist future with all its rewards and dangers. Expansion had many opponents. Northern expansionists had not wanted Texas, southern expansionists did not want the original Oregon country, and antislave northerners and slave-owning southerners wanted only those parts of Mexico that held modest numbers of Mexicans. John Louis O'Sullivan, an obscure New York journalist, wanted Americans to meet their future boldly and accept their God-given right, indeed an obligation, to take over the world from lesser powers and people and make it better. He was building on a long tradition of providential thinking in the United States that revolved around a notion that God had a special plan for Americans. O'Sullivan called his version of the plan a "manifest destiny."[6]

REPLENISH THE EARTH

In practice, on the ground, the expansion of the United States was anything but manifest. Expansion was hard and often hideous work, a result of design rather than of destiny. It was also wrought with discord. There was little agreement among the Americans about the size, shape, and character of their nation—whether empire would be the best way to secure their place in the world or whether a small and more compact republic would be safer after all. The question, in its essence, was who could be included and who could not.[7]

Three years after O'Sullivan's appeal, on a February day in the White House, with large maps spread out in front of them, President James K. Polk and his cabinet sat down to discuss an urgent matter: how much of Mexico should they take? The Mexican-American War had ended, at least temporarily, in an overwhelming U.S. victory, a rout that owed much to the activities of the Comanches, Kiowas, and Apaches who had raided northern Mexico for years, weakening its defenses and thus inadvertently paving the way for the U.S. invasion. General Winfield Scott now occupied Mexico City, and there was a truce but no treaty. The pressing question was territory and borders. The war had begun over a disputed strip between the Rio Grande and Nueces, and it was clear to both sides that the border would have to move. But for Polk and his cabinet the real issue was of a different magnitude altogether.

Viewed from Washington, Mexico seemed a natural addition to a nation that was exploding toward the Pacific by way of Louisiana and Texas; the question was the exact size of the appendix. There was a broad consensus that the Nueces strip and San Francisco Bay should be included, and 37° N was quickly established as a new northern boundary. But opinions differed widely on the southern one. Most in the room insisted on a direct line from the mouth of the Rio Grande to the Pacific along 26° N—a thousand-mile-wide chunk of land that would have turned ten Mexican states into U.S. soil. Some argued that they should simply take the whole of Mexico. In the end cooler heads prevailed, and the United States annexed only New Mexico and Alta California. The Treaty of Guadalupe Hidalgo transferred half of Mexico to the United States.[8]

There was a direct mental strand between the Indian Removal Act and the Treaty of Guadalupe Hidalgo, between the debates over the Indian Removal and the debates over the Mexican annexation. Key U.S. policymakers had developed an imperial mindset, a collection of attitudes, convictions, and habits that allowed them to see humans, nations, and entire societies as pawns on an immense geopolitical chessboard. Jackson, Polk, and their officials poured over maps and drew new lines on them, rearranging the world into a new shape. Indian Territory in the West was now the home of removed southern Indians and El Paso was now a U.S. town because they had drawn the lines so. It was in many ways but a reiteration of the centuries-old European imperial ethos which had pushed Spain, Portugal, France, and Britain to carve up the world into empires, but it was new to Americans, and many of them reveled in it. Washington's dream of an expanding empire of liberty, Jefferson's utopian schemes for Louisiana, and Monroe's famous doctrine had been early versions of the imperial mindset, but it was only in the 1840s that Americans possessed the means—sufficient administrative capacity and an ability to borrow money on a vast scale—to start turning imperial abstractions into reality through state-sanctioned violence.[9]

The continental grasslands figured only marginally in these designs. Policymakers in Washington looked straight through the plains nomads into New Mexico and California where the imperial stakes were highest. Seemingly devoid of extractable wealth (except for furs) and securely embedded within U.S. borders, the Great Plains became a kind of halfway house where the Natives could learn the arts of civilization in splendid isolation under the tutelage of a select group of missionaries and government agents. A line of forts running down from Fort Snelling to west-central Louisiana marked a "permanent Indian frontier," demarcating a sizable reserve in the heart of the continent where the Indians could safely modernize themselves.[10]

It was yet another imperial scheme, as ambitious as it was improbable, created by default: Americans did not need the plains yet. The reserve contained Indian Territory along with some thirty nomadic and semi-nomadic societies, tens of thousands of people who had little in common beyond the imposed label "Indians." Violence between resident and newly displaced groups broke out immediately, but the Indian Office persisted with its mission of molding the western Indians into Christian farmers capable of entering national life. Such were the odds that some believed it would take a century. Others lacked that kind of patience. In 1846 Missouri senator Thomas Hart Benton laid out a more immediate future for the nation. Delivered in a hemispherically pregnant moment when the Mexican-American War had just opened and the Oregon boundary dispute with Britain was still undecided, he wanted Americans to embrace harder realities. "The white race alone received the divine command, to subdue and replenish the earth. . . . Civilization, always the preference of the whites, has been pressed as an object, while extinction has followed as a consequence of its resistance." The window for adaptation and survival, he warned, was closing rapidly for Indians with the Unites States' imminent continental dominance. "I cannot murmur at what seems to be the effect of divine law."[11]

Given Americans' palpable disinterest in the continent's grasslands at midcentury, it seemed that the Plains Indians were looking at a century of relative freedom. Several Indian Office agencies along the Missouri and in the central plains monitored the domineering Lakotas from a distance, but Lakotas received no government annuities and visited the posts only intermittently, leaving the agents to often report mostly on what they learned from traders and other tribes. The news was always mixed—robust trade laced with violence—but there was very little the agents could do. For Lakotas the agencies were little more than sites for occasional social visits. Many agents thought highly of them, praising them as good Indians.[12]

While Americans were preoccupied with Mexico and Oregon, Lakotas were preoccupied with Crows, horses, buffalo, and snow. All that was routine, and the winter counts for the period focus on everyday peculiarities. Snow fell so thickly that some camped in pine woods to find shelter. Hunters broke their legs when thrown off their horses in deep snow. The father of American Horse captured and killed a Crow woman, who turned out to be a hermaphrodite. Crows stole two hundred horses from Minneconjous and then tried to enter the Black Hills. Lakotas killed seven wildcats, "man eaters." A Lakota was shot in the cheek. One winter reported a sudden dearth of bison, but the rituals the White Buffalo Calf Woman had given them restored abundance: 1845–46 was one of the most plentiful winters in memory. The world was as unpredictable as ever, but Lakotas knew how to restore the balance and keep themselves virtuous and safe.[13]

But then, just nine days after the signing of the Treaty of Guadalupe Hidalgo, gold was discovered at Sutter's Fort and everything changed.

SEEING THE ELEPHANT

They were welcome at first. One could hear them from safe distance, chock-full wagon-dwellings creaking and groaning, their wooden wheels squeaking under the burden, iron rims juddering over rocks, men yelling at their beasts, whip snaps cutting through the air. They often traveled with children and were friendly, and only some of them were powerful men with many wives. They welcomed visits, shared their food, and readily traded mules for horses. They explained that they were only passing through, heading to a great lake or the great ocean far beyond. Unlike the French trader-explorers a century earlier, they seemed to know exactly how to get there. Lakotas worried that the travelers disturbed the bison, and in 1846 They Fear Even His Horses, a rising Oglala leader, brought to Fort Laramie a petition that the *tȟuŋkášila*, the Great Father, compensate Lakotas for the damage. They wanted the president to preserve peace through gifts of goodwill.[14]

Then came the flood. The news of Sutter's motherlode reached the East, triggering a rush. In 1848 fewer than two thousand California- and Oregon-bound overlanders had crossed the plains along the Platte, but the next year brought some twenty-seven thousand hopefuls. In that summer a party of the Army Corps of Engineers heading to the Salt Lake came upon five tipis by the North Platte. They approached them carefully, waving a shirt like a flag, but received no answer. In the smallest tipi they found a teenage Sioux girl "richly dressed in leggings of fine scarlet cloth," her decomposing body "wrapped in two superb buffalo-robes." Like the four other tipis, it was a tomb, holding a corpse of a person who had prepared or been prepared for death. Soon after a Minneconjou hunter, "having killed a buffalo cow, found an old woman inside her." An abandoned woman may have sought shelter against the elements inside of a carcass, but some Lakotas saw in this as the return of a monster that appeared from time to time to swallow human beings.[15]

A deadly bacterium had been carried west by the overlanders, turning the Platte Valley into a "boundless city of the dead," of human-swallowing monsters, of hastily dug graves that left hands, legs, and heads sticking out from the earth. "Many died of the cramps," reads a Lakota winter count, depicting a kneeling, twisting man dying of diarrhea dehydration: cholera's signature symptom. A global pandemic had begun in the Ganges River delta and spread across Asia to Europe and the Americas, jumping human hosts through digested fecal matter and killing them swiftly, sometimes in a matter of hours. The crowded Platte Valley was a nearly ideal conduit for the bacterium to spread. Reluctant to move far from the protective valley, infected overlanders defecated on its banks, contaminating the current with deadly bacteria. The life-giving water turned into poison.

Having left the "melancholy scene," the engineers pushed ahead and the next day encountered a Lakota band that had contracted the disease on the South Fork of the Platte and "fled to the emigrant-road, in the hope of obtaining medical aid from the whites." What wašíčus had wrecked, they seemed to believe, wašíčus could mend. They asked for "a little coffee, sugar, or biscuit" and spoke of a large village nearby with many people "very sick." The engineers entered the village and visited the lodges, their physician administering medicine to the inflicted who swallowed it "with great avidity" and "absolute faith in its efficacy." Yet the devastation was enormous. The Lakotas the engineers had tried to save were probably Sicangus who often camped along the Platte and its forks. In 1849 they would lose every seventh of their people. "Whole villages were swept away," Josephine Waggoner, a Hunkpapa, related, and the "odor from the dead bodies could be scented for miles."[16]

It was a biological invasion, the kind that had played out a thousand times across the Americas since 1492: fortune-seeking newcomers from distant lands arrive; Natives welcome them and their wares and more newcomers come; pathogens jump bodies, people die, and attitudes harden. Lakotas had been able to regulate the entry of outsiders into their lands for nearly two centuries, but this gold-triggered deluge was uncontainable: more than fifty thousand emigrants came in 1850. That year Lakotas were hit hard by the smallpox, while the stream of overlanders with its thousands of wagons and tens of thousands of oxen, cattle, horses, and mules filled up good campsites and exhausted forage along the Platte and its tributaries. It was now that the most acute threat to peace emerged: the bison might disappear, precipitating violence among the Indians and against the whites. A year earlier, sensing an impending explosion, an Indian Office agent on the Upper Platte had asked: "What then will be the consequences, should twenty thousand well armed, well mounted, and the most warlike and expert in war of any Indians on the continent, turn out in hostile array against all American travellers through their country?"[17]

Fear and anxiety began to dull the hope and high excitement among the prospective overlanders, and there was much talk about seeing the elephant, which evoked the rich imagined rewards at the trail's end and the all-too-real dangers along the way. Many emigrants saw the journey across the plains as a plunge into a wilderness world devoid of law and order. They started to form companies and draft constitutions, trying to become itinerant mini-governments capable of managing and protecting their members. Yet scores of overlanders perished each year, struck down by disease, accidents, and Indians. Lakotas grew wary of touching anything American—abandoned wagons, discarded goods along the trail, food offered—while growing more vocal about killing whites.[18]

The United States' umbilical cord to its new West Coast territories was becoming dangerously frail. If the powerful Lakotas were to go to war, there would have been nothing to stop them: two military posts, Fort Laramie on the site of the now-abandoned trading post and a modest Fort Kearny on the middle Platte, were supposed to guard the entire central plains. Just as the Očhéthi Šakówiŋ had once stood between the French and Asian markets, thousands of well-armed Lakotas now seemed to be slipping between Americans and California, the richest place on earth. Suddenly, the Great Plains and its Native inhabitants became a national priority.[19]

THE BIG ISSUE WINTER

The runners arrived in the spring of 1851, delivering the same message at each thióšpaye and oyáte: a great gathering would take place in early fall at Fort Laramie to resolve the mounting tensions along the Platte. They invited all Lakotas, Yanktons, and Yanktonais to come and join several other plains nations for great council and a giveaway. Agent Thomas Fitzpatrick, a former trader-trapper-guide whom the Indians knew as "Broken Hand," would be there, and Colonel David Mitchell, the superintendent of Indian affairs in St. Louis, would address the Indians. This was unprecedented to most plains nations, but not to Lakotas, Yanktons, and Yanktonais. As members of the Očhéthi Šakówiŋ, they remembered countless summits over the centuries where imperial agents and governors had welcomed, listened, and cajoled them. If anything, such an invitation was long overdue: sixteen Oglala and Sicangu headmen had already asked for a council five years earlier.[20]

Lakotas knew how to prepare and stage a spectacle. Aware that the wašíču envoys would have to balance competing tribal interests, they had plotted to secure their preeminence well before the talks began. Oglala and Sicangu councils appointed four "honored men" to lead the talks with Fitzpatrick, and a Lakota delegation held preliminary meetings with the agent at Fort Laramie. To ensure mass Lakota representation at the summit, They Fear Even His Horses, the head of one of the most renowned Oglala lineages, toured camps across the Lakota domain, coaxing them to attend. So formidable was the Lakota presence along the Platte that Pawnees decided not to come. And so it was that the "grand old Sioux Nation" was the first to arrive, riding in slowly, chiefs carrying an old American flag their nation had received from William Clark in St. Louis in 1807. They led rows of warriors and a multitude of women and children who steered a large herd of packhorses pulling travois and lodge poles. The Arapahos and the "dignified, the wiry, agile, intelligent and brave Cheyennes" soon followed.[21]

If staged to announce power and primacy, the entrance had the desired impact. It was clear from the start that it was the nomad alliance of Lakotas, Cheyennes, and Arapahos the agents would need to placate to have any meaningful settlement. Ruling the central and northern plains "at their own sweet will," noted First Sergeant Percival G. Lowe, "they did not want peace with other tribes. Why should they?" "They were rich in everything that people of nomadic habits needed, and as to peace, why, what would life be to them without war? Nature supplied all their needs." When the Shoshones arrived, they did so by "moving very slowly and cautiously." Around them Sioux women "howled in anguish for lost friends who had died in battle with these same cautiously moving warriors." A lieutenant "had 'boots and saddles' sounded so as to be ready whatever happened." A mounted Lakota chief charged toward the Shoshones, and a Shoshone chief "raised his gun ready to fire." A French interpreter rushed to intervene, and the Lakota chief allowed himself to be led back to his camp. The next day a massive assembly of Indians, agents, and interpreters moved thirty-five miles east to the North Platte–Horse Creek confluence in Lakota territory where Sioux tipis and horses filled out much of the assigned camping grounds on both sides of the North Platte. Sioux and Cheyennes arranged several tipis into a large, amphitheater-like council lodge.[22]

If Lakotas knew how to awe, so did the Americans. The Indian Office had planned the summit for two years. Superintendent Mitchell wanted "to impress the Indians of the Prairies with some just idea of our greatness and power," and the Office assigned one hundred thousand dollars for the task. Where Lakotas relied on thinly veiled military threat, Americans relied on tested imperial strategies of cajoling and co-opting the Natives. Some ten thousand Indians had gathered around Horse Creek, and the agents set out to classify them all by identifying chiefs and counting their followers. Headmen were given uniforms and warriors received medals and certificates connoting different ranks from major general to lieutenants. But the busiest among the wašíčus was Father Jean-Pierre De Smet, a renowned Belgian Jesuit, who would baptize hundreds of happily indulging Lakotas.

With the processing completed after several days, Fitzpatrick invited all the recognized headmen to a grand council in a great arbor with a cannon shot. He assigned each a place in a circle around a flagpole. He then introduced Superintendent Mitchell who stated his government's agenda in staccato style. He acknowledged that overlanders were disturbing pasturelands and bison and offered as compensation fifty thousand dollars worth of "provisions, merchandise, domestic animals, and agricultural implements" per year for half a century. In return, the United States expected the Indians to allow free travel along the Platte and to military forts on its banks. He also insisted that all hostilities among the tribes had to cease and counseled each tribe to elect a head chief to command all the bands and all the warriors.[23]

The uniforms, medals, elections, and baptisms were part of a larger process of social engineering aimed at domesticating and modernizing the Indians. The Indian Office sought to convert the decentralized plains tribes into coherent nations under supreme leaders who would be closely attached to the U.S. government. Once reformed, each nation would be assigned a reservation, a "colony" of its own, where its members could learn to farm, worship, and live properly under the tutelage of agents and missionaries. The new chiefs were a federal creation whose main function was to sign treaties and authorize land cessions that would undo the very nations they were entrusted to lead.

Mitchell would not reveal it to his audience, but the Horse Creek council was but a piece in an ambitious—and ad hoc—federal plan of rearranging the midcontinent. The reservations served a double purpose: they were meant to be safe havens for Indians, while also freeing land for overland trails, forts, and settlers. The U.S. government planned to carve out the Great Plains—the heart of what was supposed to be a permanent Indian Territory—into three blocks. Lakotas, Crows, Assiniboines, Mandans, northern Cheyennes, and northern Arapahos would occupy a northern reservation; Comanches, Kiowas, and Plains Apaches would live in a southern one; and southern Cheyennes and southern Arapahos would occupy one in the middle. Two overland avenues, the Oregon

Trail along the Platte and its southern counterpart, the Santa Fe Trail along the Arkansas, would separate the three reservations from one another. Eventually, as the nomads shed their "wild energies," "an ample outlet of about six geographical degrees" would open for settlement. It was a radical spatial solution to what was essentially a racial problem. The Indians would be isolated and contained, and the United States would have its safe passage across the continent.[24]

It was a vision as ambitious as it was myopic. Gazing toward the Pacific past the Indians, the federal agents failed to identify the most immediate obstacle to their grand design. The Lakotas whom they tried to pacify with made-up titles also thought in terms of large-scale geopolitics and, like Americans, they had grown to command the world around them like an imperial power. They discussed Mitchell's proposition in a private council, forged a broad consensus, and then announced their position.[25]

"We have decided differently from you, Father, about this Chief for the nation," proclaimed Clear Blue Earth, the main Sicangu spokesman. "We want a Chief for each band, and if you will make one or two Chiefs for each band, it will be much better for you and the whites. Then we will make soldiers of our young men, and we will make them good men to the whites and other Indians. But Father, we can't make one Chief." A supple and diffuse political system, Blue Earth explained to the agents, was essential for Lakotas who split up and coalesced in an endless nomad's cycle. What he left unsaid was that shared leadership also served as a buffer against the not-so-hidden attempt to manipulate Native polities by grooming a powerful head chief with close ties to the U.S. government. Considering the question closed—and quite likely offensive—Blue Earth ended with an impatient demand: "We are poor people, and want very much to see the presents you told us were coming."[26]

The government agents shifted the talks on tribal boundaries and presented a map of reservations. Black Hawk, the main Oglala spokesman, responded: "If there is anything I do know, it is this country, for I was raised in it. . . . You have split the country, and I don't like it. What we live upon, we hunt for, and we hunt from the Platte to the Arkansas." Lakotas would follow the bison, Black Hawk warned, and would not heed some lines on a map. The agents had proposed the Platte as the southern border of the Lakota domain, but Lakotas demanded the central plains all the way south to the Arkansas—much of it still a Pawnee territory—as well as more territory in the West. They did so by the right of conquest. "These lands once belonged to the Kiowas and the Crows," Black Hawk explained, "but we whipped these nations out of them, and in this we did what the white men do when they want the lands of the Indians."[27]

There were no Pawnee delegates to protest, and so the commissioners agreed to Lakota hunting rights south of the Platte. Those rights denoted to Lakotas what Americans understood as title, for they delineated territory in terms of access and resources rather than boundaries. The agents also accepted a stipulation that tribes could hunt outside of their reservations, a tacit acknowledgment that raw military power, not maps drawn in faraway Washington, would determine de facto tribal borders. It was abundantly clear to the U.S. delegates who would benefit from that open-ended arrangement because Clear Blue Earth told them to their face how it was going to be. "We are a large band," he said, "and we claim half of all the country; but, we don't care for that, for we can hunt anywhere."[28]

Lakotas had been the United States' staunch allies for decades, and Mitchell yielded to their demands. He acknowledged the Lakota right to range freely as long as peace among the tribes prevailed. Now Lakotas were willing to make a concession, too: they would elect a head chief. The widely respected They Fear Even His Horses, the obvious choice, wisely declined, and Mato Oyuhi, a young Sicangu leader, reluctantly assumed the role. He had neither sought nor wanted the honor but accepted it as a symbolic gesture. Mitchell handed him a bundle of goods. Mato Oyuhi immediately gave it all away, keeping nothing for himself or his kin.[29]

The delivery of the treaty goods had been delayed in St. Louis, and the massive herds of horses had nearly exhausted the grass on the banks of Horse Creek and the North Platte. The vast Indigenous congregation had been in place for over two weeks, and the stench of accumulated human waste was so thick that the army troops moved their camp two miles away. Finally word arrived that the gift convoy would reach Horse Creek in a day, and Fitzpatrick rushed to secure signatures for a treaty. Clear Blue Earth, Mato Oyuhi, and three other Sicangu headmen as well as a Two Kettle chief came forward and touched the pen to acknowledge a document they considered subordinate to the words that had been exchanged between the two people. The next day twenty-seven wagons pulled in. Lakotas, Yanktons, and Yanktonais formed a great circle and had the goods— tobacco, coffee, sugar, kettles, knives, beads, brass sheets, cloth, coats, trousers, and blankets—arranged in the middle for their inspection. When U.S. agents tried to count the Lakotas to determine the amount of goods they would need, Oglalas moved children from one tipi to another to hide their cholera-depleted numbers. Eighteen fifty-one became "the Big Issue Winter."[30]

Once the distribution, made in the name of the Great Father, was finished, the Indians dispersed, rushing to start fall hunts that had been postponed by the drawn-out talks. Lone Horn, a Minneconjou headman, was a part of an Indian delegation that was taken to Washington where he was shown naval yards and arsenals. He was received at the Indian Office and the White House, and President

Millard Fillmore presented him a medal and an American flag that made him "one of us" and "part of the same people." Government agents believed he was properly impressed and would advocate peace among his followers. Others were more sceptical. "The news from Fort Laramie fails utterly to justify expectations," a Swiss-born American Fur Company clerk grumbled. "Uncle Sam made no display of military power to impress the Indians."[31]

THEY MADE PEACE WITH THE CROWS

The treaty document the agents sent to Washington was as ambiguous as the talks that had preceded it. As the 1851 Horse Creek Treaty read, Lakotas would allow the construction of roads and posts along the Platte and receive in return an annuity of ten thousand dollars for fifty years—their share of the total of fifty thousand dollars—which both sides understood as a compensation for the damages emigrants would inflict on riverine resources. The treaty recognized Lakota title to nearly one hundred thousand square miles north of the North Platte, by far the largest Native domain ratified, and obliged Lakotas to live in peace thenceforward. The agents included in the stipulation of head chiefs, but it was plain to all that it was a dead letter.[32]

Yet the U.S. agents believed—or needed to believe—that the plains nomads had been pinned down and boxed in, securing U.S. access to the far West by the force of law. The government, the chief commissioner reported, was now poised "to throw open a wide extent of country for the spread of our population westward." Lakota chiefs, however, had insisted that their domain would be defined by the needs of the hunt and by action on the ground; they had made it clear that, whenever necessary, their expansion would continue. They did not remember the treaty for its territorial stipulations, which they probably considered irrelevant. Instead, they memorized it for the "Great distribution," a largesse that had spawned a tighter bond with the Americans. They also remembered the talks for the wašíču obsession with the Platte River. They thought the river had special meaning and started to call it the "Holy Road."[33]

In his report Superintendent Mitchell exulted how easy it had been to manage the unlikely multitribal gathering: "The different tribes, although hereditary enemies, interchanged daily visits, both in their national and individual capacities." Mitchell read this as obedience. His proudest achievement was a map that divided up "the country into geographical or rather national domains." The map, he wrote, was "fully approved and sanctioned by all." In truth, the Indian-Indian feasts had constituted a full-fledged shadow council that eclipsed the talks with the U.S. agents. Several winter counts for 1851 ignored the talks and the treaty with the United States altogether, instead highlighting a peace with Crows, nego-

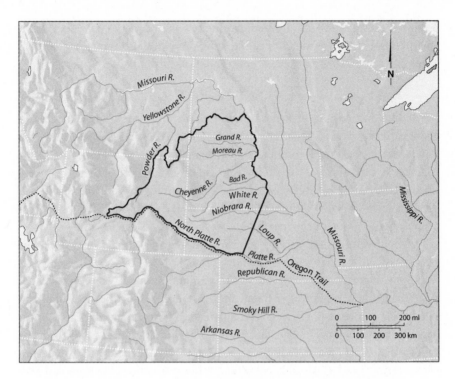

31. Lakota territory as determined in the Horse Creek Treaty of 1851.
Map by Bill Nelson.

tiated in private and without wašíču mediation. The geopolitical context that mattered to Lakotas most was Indigenous.[34]

Such dissonances were useful. The meeting between Lakotas and Americans was a meeting between two fundamentally different powers. The exhilarating capture of the northern plains had imbued Lakotas with a sense of arrival as a chosen people, while many Americans believed that they had a divine mission to expand their territory and institutions across the continent. Lakotas and Americans seemed fated to clash, but their different understandings of power, property, territory, and rule delayed the collision. Americans were content with a cartographic proof of U.S. sovereignty. They thought that reservations and annuities would discipline and hem in the nomads. Lakotas, old hands at managing imperial agents, believed that their words had forced the wašíčus to recognize their right to harness whatever resources they needed to survive, a right that reduced any territorial arrangements to a paper abstraction. Lakotas sought the land's resources, whereas Americans coveted the land itself. Shot through with such misunderstandings, the Horse Creek Treaty allowed both to claim they now possessed the right to rule the midcontinent as sovereign powers. Each could envision itself as the sole master of the same place because each imagined the world differently. The two regimes coexisted on separate mental planes.

HE WAS NOT KILLED

Wanting and valuing different things, Lakotas and Americans were able to begin a careful accommodation. Lakotas allowed the U.S. Army to refit Fort Laramie into a military fort, but next to it stood the Upper Platte Indian agency which served Lakotas and their allies. And a few miles downriver there was a new trading post run by James Bordeaux, a veteran merchant who had married two Sicangu sisters. Lakotas considered Bordeaux kin, calling him "The Bear," and his post became one of the focal points of Sicangu and Oglala yearly cycles—especially after his ex-partner Joseph Bissonette opened a competing post nearby. Bissonette, too, would have two Lakota wives and a total of twenty-one children with them. Over time these Lakota-wašíču families spawned a new Oglala band, Wágluȟe. Although often denigrated as "Laramie Loafers," they served a vital role in Lakota foreign policy by sustaining trade with Americans through periods of conflict when official trade halted. By marrying wašíču traders, Lakota women kept alive the long Lakota tradition of deep cross-cultural coexistence that dated back a century and a half to Nicolas Perrot, Pierre-Charles Le Sueur, and Fort L'Huillier in the Eastern Woodlands. Northern Lakotas sometimes wintered close to Fort Laramie, and Oglala headman Smoke settled near the fort and his family began planting gardens there. The Oglala council approved this as it bolstered Lakota territorial claims against wašíču presence.[35]

Crows posed a tougher challenge. They may have made peace with Lakotas, but tensions remained high. A kind of perfect storm had formed in the central plains. The drought that had gripped the region since the mid-1840s lingered, leaving the bison to subsist on a perilously stunted grass cover, and yet the robe trade continued to eat into the herds at the annual pace of roughly one hundred thousand. The clinching component was the Horse Creek Treaty itself, which opened the floodgates for overland traffic: in 1852 alone seventy thousand emigrants crossed the plains, turning the Arkansas and Platte Valleys, once havens for the bison, into mile-wide dust highways. Herds had all but disappeared from the Missouri Valley, and now they were thinning out in the grasslands. Plainswide buffalo wars seemed imminent.[36]

In the fall of 1853 Alfred Vaughan, the Indian agent for the Upper Missouri, learned that Yanktonais had clashed with a Crow party of some three dozen and "exterminated the whole of them." Violence exploded across the plains as people summoned kin and allies to avenge their dead. The distribution of annuities at Fort Laramie was a disaster. A young Minneconjou tried to seize an over-lander ferry, and the soldiers tried to arrest him. Shots were fired, and five Minneconjous died.[37]

Lakotas intervened. The people to whom war, according to Francis Parkman, was "the breath of their nostrils," became peacemakers. Having solidified their position as the dominant power in the interior, they sought to preserve the status quo. Lone Horn, back from Washington, set out to conciliate the Crows whom his people had fought, feared, and hated for years. In the winter of 1852–53 a Crow party of fourteen got lost in a snowstorm and stumbled upon Lone Horn's Minneconjou village. Unfazed, a Crow chief named Flat Head took a calumet and entered Lone Horn's lodge where a medicine feast was being held. He pressured Lone Horn to accept the pipe and, to an apparent surprise to all, "was not killed."[38]

Lone Horn's mercy initiated a conciliation—a shapeshifting—that saw several Lakota and Crow headmen seeking new ways to relate to one another. The bison had been the cause of war and now it became the means to ending it. The long-contested Lakota-Crow borderlands between the Black Hills and the Powder River Valley were one of the great neutral zones in the interior, teeming with game but utilized by few. Lone Horn and Crow chief Big Robber reenvisioned the neutral zone as a joint-use one. In exchange for hunting privileges in the West, Minneconjous and other Lakotas allowed Crows to come and trade with Americans on the North Platte and extort supplies from overlanders.[39]

Spurred by a conspicuous capacity to recalibrate attitudes toward strangers willing to show restraint and compassion, the joint-use zone quickly transformed into an Indigenous common ground under the spiritual mandate of wólakȟota. The new allies visited each other, exchanged gifts, staged communal ceremonies, joined forces against Pawnees, and shared trading rights at American posts: Minneconjou and Two Kettle counts for 1853–54 depict striped "Spanish blankets," a luxury item imported from Mexico by an enterprising American merchant who traded with both Lakotas and Crows at Pumpkin Butte in the heart of the joint-use zone. So firm seemed the Lakota-Crow bond that the Upper Platte agent proposed a joint agency and trading post for Minneconjous, Crows, and Eastern Shoshones 120 miles west of Fort Laramie—an idea that would have been all but unthinkable just a few years earlier.[40]

MAKE THE GROUND BLOODY

In the spring of 1854 agent Vaughan hosted more than a hundred Hunkpapa and Sihasapa lodges at Fort Clark on the upper Missouri. A "full council assembled *peremptorily*" and Lakotas, "with every manifestation of hostility," refused the Great Father's gifts: they preferred "scalps and stealing horses to any thing he could give them." Not long after, downriver, Vaughan met a band of one hundred Yanktonai lodges. He gave them "good and proper advice" and handed out annuities, only to face chief Red Leaf who "drew from his scabbard a huge knife and cut each one of the sacks and scattered the contents furiously in every direction." He threw a keg of gunpowder in the river and some fifty warriors fired their guns on it. After just three years, the Horse Creek Treaty seemed dead.[41]

Tensions between Lakotas and Americans had mounted steadily since 1851. At first the exotic overlanders—"rich English lords who were traveling for adventure," "rich French gentlemen" seeking "the thrill of hunting"—could be entertaining, but as the bison herds continued to diminish, Lakotas grew resentful. The overlanders killed too many animals, consumed too much timber and grass, carried death on their bodies, and, it was said, did not smell right. Many Lakotas thought that the smell of coffee and bacon frightened the bison and that herds avoided places where they had scented whites. The unthinkable—that one day the bison might simply die off—suddenly seemed a possibility. Lakotas relied on traditional buffalo-calling ceremonies to protect the herds, but they also blamed the wašíčus.[42]

And then the wašíčus betrayed them. In 1852 Indian agents told them that payment of the annuities, the compensation for lost game, had been reduced from fifty years to ten. The Great Father somehow had changed his mind, and suddenly his largesse seemed anything but genuine. Wašíčus seemed to expect the bison and Lakotas to promptly vanish from the plains; indeed, the superintendent of Indian affairs at St. Louis thought the modification of the treaty "very proper, as the condition of these wandering hordes will be entirely changed during the next *fifteen* years." Furious, Lakotas planned to destroy Fort Laramie, which had turned from a symbol of wašíču amity to a symbol wašíču hostility. "The soldiers of the great father," Lakotas warned the fort's Indian agent, "are the first to make the ground bloody."[43]

Fear, loathing, and confidence blended into an explosive mix at Fort Laramie. A twenty-four-year-old lieutenant named John Grattan wanted to "crack it to the Sioux," boasting that "with thirty men, he could whip the combined force of all the Indians of the prairie." Lakotas announced that they could "easily overcome any party or number that may be sent against them." Grattan was not unique with his vitriol: "Every outpost soldier wanted the trophy of taking an Indian scalp back home with him," Josephine Waggoner learned. Lakota-U.S. relations were balanced on a knife-edge of violence, and it took but a single cow to tip things over. In mid-August 1854 High Forehead, a Minneconjou, shot a lame cow near the overland road. The animal had belonged to a Mormon emigrant heading to the Great Salt Lake Valley, but it was unclear whether the animal had strayed or was bought by Lakotas. Mato Oyuhi, camping with his Sicangus eight miles downriver, went to Fort Laramie and offered the Mormon any horse in his personal herd. Pressured by belligerent officers, Lieutenant Hugh Fleming demanded Mato Oyuhi to hand over High Forehead.[44]

That Mato Oyuhi could not do, not without High Forehead's consent. High Forehead was his guest and under his protection. Mato Oyuhi returned to his village, and Fleming authorized Grattan to arrest High Forehead, sending him off with two cannons. Grattan recruited twenty-nine volunteers and brought along an interpreter, Lucien Auguste, who got thoroughly drunk during the march. Grattan pressed on. When the party reached a small bluff, the Lakota village came into view. Sprawling along the Platte, it seemed to have no end. There were some six hundred Sicangu, Oglala, and Minneconjou tipis, nearly five thousand people and more than a thousand warriors. Alarmed officers wanted to abort the mission, but Grattan ignored them and marched straight into the village. He faced Mato Oyuhi at the edge of Minneconjou tipis. High Forehead sent a word that "he would die first" than surrender, and Mato Oyuhi said it was "their custom to make a demand four times." With Auguste slurring insults and Grattan doing nothing to restrain him, the talks turned vicious. Grattan, mounted, deployed his men in a single rank and trained the cannons at Minneconjou lodges. Lakota warriors were already filing around the soldiers, and women and children were evacuating the village. Grattan returned to his men and ordered them into a firing position. A shot rang out and a Lakota collapsed. Mato Oyuhi turned away and began walking toward his tipi. Grattan unleashed a volley, and Minneconjous fired back. Mato Oyuhi collapsed, three holes in him; Grattan dismounted and launched a hurried cannon round that overshot the tipis. There was no time to reload, and Lakotas killed Grattan and five soldiers where they stood. The rest retreated toward a rocky elevation across open prairie but were cut down by two converging masses of mounted warriors. Only one managed to reach Fort Laramie but he soon died of his wounds.

The next day Lakota men, women, and children visited the corpses. They crushed their heads, cut off their limbs, and filled them with arrows. Men exposed their genitals to them, shaming them forever. Then they left the site, broke into an American Fur Company house, took all annuity goods stored there, and dispersed for the hunt. Mato Oyuhi died somewhere along the way. When soldiers later retrieved Grattan's body, they had to remove twenty-four arrows from it. They were able to identify him only by his pocket watch.[45]

The mutilations were a response to Grattan's arrogance and the unnecessary violence he had unleashed, but there were deeper reasons to Lakotas' wrath. The unilateral decision to cut the annuity payments had taught them that the U.S. government saw them not as allies but as wards, a quasi-nation under its patriarchal control. It was an insult and a rejection. For half a century, from Lewis and Clark's thwarted imperial posturing through Colonel Leavenworth's pathetic leadership to the booming fur trade and the Horse Creek council, Lakotas had been in charge of the situation, allowing the wašíčus to operate in the West under their auspices. They had seen Americans as friends who entered the interior with their approval, because Americans—traders, soldiers, government agents—told them so. After Lewis and Clark, the Americans who came to them spoke almost invariably of cooperation and respect, promising favorable terms and treating them with the humility expected of newcomers. The treaty amendment and Grattan's savagery were so shocking because they were so unexpected. At least ten winter counts recorded Mato Oyuhi's demise, capturing a collective disbelief and growing disgust.[46]

That disgust became visible to Americans in the fall when Minneconjous and Sicangus launched a flurry of raids along and around the Platte. Large and small war parties attacked military forts, mail stations, trading houses, and emigrant wagon trains, taking horses, mules, and lives. Spotted Tail, Red Leaf, and Long Chin engineered an ambush of a U.S. mail party that yielded a strongbox containing ten thousand dollars in gold coin: it was the "Plenty of Money Winter." Others announced that "next spring they will keep parties constantly on the emigrant road, and kill all they find." They Fear Even His Horses and other moderate Oglala leaders tried to restrain the warriors and sometimes returned stolen stock, but the raids continued, as promised, through the winter into the spring and then summer, spreading fear along the Oregon Trail. At a time when many Native nations were treading carefully, hoping not to antagonize the formidable United States and trying to keep it at arm's length, Lakotas did the exact opposite: they made themselves as visible as possible, defying the aggressive wašíčus and flaunting their power. It seemed to work. There were frantic reports of thirty thousand Lakotas along the overland road, and, conspicuously, no American response.[47]

AFTER YOU HAVE WHIPPED ME WILL YOU MAKE MY HEART GLAD

A genuine anti-Indian racist, Lieutenant Grattan was an embodiment of the United States' hard metamorphosis into an empire. The annexations of Texas and Oregon and the Mexican Cession had increased the territory of the United States by 66 percent and brought tens of thousands of new people into its fold. These people were different. Their skin, in general, was darker, and they spoke foreign tongues: the acquisitions of 1845–48 may have doubled the number of languages spoken in the United States. With conquest, the nation's ethnic and racial composition became infinitely more complex, its suddenly expanded borders containing masses of Hispanics, Mexicans, Chinese, and new Indian tribes. This was the human face of manifest destiny realized, and many recoiled at it. Secretary of War Charles Conrad proposed that the entire population of New Mexico be uprooted and moved somewhere else, and California's first legislature asked for federal help to remove all Natives from the state. An unsettling patchwork of different races, creeds, customs, and loyalties, the American West was a massive racial crisis in the making.[48]

And then Lakotas killed Grattan and launched a frightening raiding spree along the Platte, the heart of a virtually defenseless Nebraska Territory: excluding Texas and New Mexico, the U.S. Army had fewer than two thousand men between the Mississippi and the Rockies. Lakotas had made life dangerous in the central Great Plains, where a seething dispute over the expansion of slavery—soon to erupt into "Bleeding Kansas"—had rendered the survival of the Union itself uncertain. The last thing the nation needed was an Indian war in the midst of it. The Lakotas had to be reined in. The new secretary of war, Jefferson Davis, insisted that Grattan's demise was the result of "a deliberately formed plan, prompted by a knowledge of the weakness of the garrison at Fort Laramie." It was an open rebellion against federal authority and it had to be crushed. "A prompt and decisive blow on the Sioux," recommended the retired Pawnee agent John Dougherty, "would be worth to us, for years to come, millions of dollars and many strong armies."[49]

The time for reckless lieutenants and half measures was over. The U.S. Army bought Fort Pierre from the American Fur Company for a base of operations, turning a post that had sustained a generation of Lakotas into a threat. It caused "great dissatisfaction" among Two Kettles, who had lived around the post. Next the War Department summoned General William S. Harney from a vacation in Paris to subdue the Lakotas. Ambitious, innovative, stubborn, and blunt, Harney was one of the army's most experienced generals, who had tracked pirates in Louisiana, fought in the Black Hawk War in Illinois, designed riverine tactics that vanquished the Seminoles in Florida, and led General Winfield Scott's dragoons into Mexico. He had witnessed the rise of the American empire at firsthand from the battlefield. Now he brought all that accumulated knowledge to the plains where he was to "whip" the Lakotas.[50]

Fort Laramie's new Indian agent, Thomas Twiss, sent a message to Lakotas in mid-August. Finding the "whole Indian country in a state of feverish excitement and alarm," he felt he had to "act promptly or not at all." He declared the North Platte as a boundary between "hostile and friendly Sioux" and directed all friendly bands to move south at once. He met with They Fear Even His Horses of Oglalas and Big Partisan of Sicangus and ordered them to "drive away from amongst them all hostile Indians, on pain of being declared enemies." By early September he had "about 4,000 souls" in a single village on the Laramie River, thirty-five miles north of the fort. The rest of the Lakotas, about ten thousand people, were labeled as hostiles. Harney now had a target and a plan. A mere technical military victory would not do. He insisted that the Indians "must be *crushed* before they can be completely conquered." He would have to "destroy more of them than they do of us." He was making real the maxim that state power is often most potent at its margins.[51]

Headquartered first at Fort Leavenworth in Kansas and then at Fort Kearny, Harney put together an expedition of some six hundred dragoons, infantry, and artillerymen. Ten percent of the regular army now under his command, he marched up the Platte in late August. Expecting to face seven thousand Lakota warriors, he declared, "By God, I'm for battle—no peace." On September 2, 1855, he reached the gorge of Ash Hollow on the lower North Platte where he located a village of Sicangus, Oglalas, Minneconjous, and Cheyennes spread out along Blue Water Creek, almost within sight of the emigrant road. Sicangus, led by Spotted Tail and Little Thunder, sent the general a message, warning "that if he wanted peace he could have it, or if he wanted war that he could have that." Spotted Tail offered to come and see Harney.[52]

Sicangus learned Harney's decision next morning at first light when wašíču soldiers came rushing up the Blue Water. Lakotas started to move upstream, but Harney sent in word that he wished to talk. Little Thunder rode to him, "holding an umbrella over his head as a flag or insignia of truce." The talk lasted nearly an hour, Harney reproaching the chief for Grattan and "depredations" along the emigrant road. Little Thunder, who had had nothing to do with the Grattan fight, explained that "he himself was friendly and finally that he did not want to fight." He asked for an hour to remove women and children from the camp and offered his hand to Harney, who refused it, saying that "he could not take the hand of a man whom he expected to fight in a few minutes, unless they came to some definite conclusion." Harney told Little Thunder to go and join his men and tell them that "a battle had to settle their differences."

The perfunctory talks had served a strategic purpose. While Harney faced the chief, his dragoons were circling around the village to attack its rear. When Little Thunder left, Harney ordered the infantry to advance. The Lakotas and Cheyennes fled, and Harney directed the infantry to fire—a signal for the dragoons to close in. Trapped, the Indians rushed into a small ravine, and the soldiers "poured a plunging fire upon them with our long range rifles, knocking them out of their saddles, right and left." The cavalry followed the Indians into the open plains, "and for five miles the fight continued, a perfect melee." The Americans lost five men, but struggled to determine the number of Native casualties "as the field of battle extended over so great a space." One soldier reported eighty-six dead. Harney also took seventy captives, all of them women and children. The soldiers found pieces of clothing that belonged to Grattan's men and stolen papers from the destroyed mail coach and accepted them as evidence that they had killed hostiles. It was the worst military defeat the Očhéthi Šakówiŋ had suffered in more than a century.[53]

Harney sent some of the captives to Fort Kearny and took the rest to Fort Laramie, where he met with the leaders of the more than two-thousand-strong peace contingent. Their chiefs "begged for their lives—only asked to be allowed to live," he reported, mistaking regret over bloodshed for submission. There was no peace yet, he warned, and ordered the Lakotas to stay south of the Platte while he would march through the Lakota country to Fort Pierre, asserting his "prestige." He demanded the surrender of the mail party raiders and said that if his conditions were not met, he would hand his Lakota captives over to their "worst enemies." The army would chase the Lakotas down, "their buffalo would all be driven away," and the Lakotas "would be no more." In late October Spotted Tail, Red Leaf, Long Chin, Red Plume, and Spotted Elk rode into Fort Laramie, dressed in buckskin suits and singing their death songs. They were shackled and placed in army wagons with their wives and children and taken to Fort Leavenworth in Kansas where they were kept for a year as prisoners of war. By giving up themselves and their families, these chiefs underwrote peace, opening the door for future accommodation.[54]

Harney announced a council at Fort Pierre in March 1856, and all Lakota oyátes sent delegations. They were taken into a makeshift council house made of two big hospital tents where Harney, sitting on a dais, laid down his demands. They ranged from the expected—the surrender of anyone who had killed whites, the return of stolen property, safe passage for emigrants—to the absurd. Lakotas, the general insisted, should start "cultivating the soil," replace bands with a military-style chain of command, and stop all internal horse trade, which he saw as an engine of intertribal warfare. "Any band that refuses," he warned, "I will make war with them." Their relatives still held hostage, Lakotas accepted Harney's treaty, which effectively reaffirmed the territorial status quo. Each oyáte elected a head chief who was supposed to restrain his warriors, and Harney restored annuities. A winter count grasped Harney's extortion: "Putinska captured women and children and made peace." Putinska means "white beard," but Lakotas also called Harney "The Butcher" and "Woman Killer." Recognizing the

32. Chief Spotted Tail, 1872.
Courtesy of National Anthropological Archives,
Smithsonian Institution (NAA GN 03118B).

hardness of the man, the Hunkpapa chief Bear Ribs, Mato Oyuhi's successor as the nominal leader of the Lakotas, articulated a moral challenge that would echo for decades as Lakotas and Americans struggled to define their relationship. "To fight me you are able," he said. "After you have whipped me you will make my heart glad."

That winter President Franklin Pierce pardoned the Fort Leavenworth prisoners, and in the fall the notoriously aloof Hunkpapas and Sihasapas arrived in Fort Pierre to collect their first annuities; repelled by Harney's tactics, the militant and moderate Lakota factions began to converge. The Americans, meanwhile, became dangerously fractured. In 1849 the Indian Office had been transferred from the War Department to the newly established Department of the Interior, which fueled bitter rivalries between Indian agents and army officers. In designing and dictating the Fort Pierre treaty, Harney encroached on the Indian Office's jurisdiction, further alienating agent Twiss who condemned Harney's hard-edged methods. Twiss complained to commissioner of Indian affairs, who convinced key members of Congress that Harney's treaty was too expensive to be put into operation. The clash exposed a fault line within the federal government between the military officers and Indian agents that would complicate U.S. Indian policy in the plains for decades.[55]

By then Harney was already fighting the Seminoles in Florida, convinced that he had left behind reduced Lakotas and pacified plains. Indian agents tended to agree. "It is truly gratifying for me to state," agent Vaughan wrote, "that there is universal peace and quiet prevailing among the various tribes under my charge." Lakotas were peaceful and Yanktons, living around the now all but barren Missouri, had begun "to see the necessity of permanently locating themselves, and of cultivating the soil." For Vaughan the reason was clear: "the affair on the Little Bluewater on the 3d September has opened their eyes."[56]

AN EMPIRE IN DENIAL

The Harney massacre had opened Lakota eyes but not in the way Vaughan assumed. Federal agents and soldiers believed that the Lakotas had been vanquished and could be soon handed over to missionaries, schoolteachers, and farmers who would process them for civilization. The nomadic barrier in the plains seemed to be melting away, opening the heart of the continent for railroads, family farms, cities, and agrarian states. They were not entirely wrong. Lakotas *were* making themselves scarce, but not because they had been defeated or domesticated. They were deliberately withdrawing from the world of the wašíčus, distancing themselves from Americans and their institutions. They shifted shape once again, swiftly and decisively: the wašíčus all but disappeared for years from their winter counts.[57]

Lakotas continued to collect annuities at Forts Laramie, Pierre, and Clark with akíčhitas ensuring orderly distribution, and they rarely harassed overlanders along the Oregon Trail. For Americans this was reassuring, a confirmation that the Lakotas had been tamed and diminished. With the formidable Lakotas finally where they wanted them, their unspoken imperial design for the West seemed nearly complete. The vast Indian Territory was teeming with tribes, each under close supervision and cultural programming by a distant imperial governor, the superintendent of the Indian Office in St. Louis, and his field officers. Dozens of strategically placed military garrisons buttressed that bureaucratic assault, punishing offenders, supressing rebellions, and staging symbolic shows of force. Harney's march through the Lakota domain after the Blue Water massacre was a calculated act of imperial posturing aimed at turning an Indigenous territory into a dominion of an empire that refused to see itself as one.[58]

But however much Americans denied the imperial character of their nation, the signs of empire were all over the map. Holding a multitude of culturally distinct peoples within their extended borders, the United States erected an unusually severe imperial regime that subjugated one bloc of unlike people after another, absorbing them into its fold on its own terms. While the U.S. Army pushed into the far recesses of Florida to remove the remnant Seminoles to Indian Territory, American emigrants were flooding California, dispossessing the region's Indigenous societies with genocidal bent. And while twenty-five hundred troops dispatched by President James Buchanan were imposing U.S. sovereignty and laws upon a defiant Mormon theocracy in Utah, the U.S. Cavalry invaded the heart of the Comanche realm, delivering a crippling blow to a century-old Indigenous empire.[59]

That swell of American imperial ambition reached the Očhéthi Šakówiŋ in 1857 when U.S. agents began pressuring Yanktons to cede their lands between the Missouri and Big Sioux Rivers. The Big Sioux Valley "is of unusual fertility," noted the superintendent of Indian affairs and recommended negotiations to buy it. By then squatters were already moving into the valley, and a delegation of Yankton leaders traveled to Washington where they signed a treaty that gave them annuities for fifty years and transferred about 96 percent of their lands to the United States—"their entire country," as their disillusioned agent noted. Hundreds of miles west in the Upper Platte Agency, Twiss saw similar prospects in that area's "exceedingly fertile" land. He pressed the federal government to carry "into effect, with all means and force at its command, the colonization of these wild tribes on military reservations." He meant the Lakotas, Cheyennes, and Arapahos, whom he wanted to shield against an imminent settler wave from east.[60]

Reports like Twiss's formed a documentary trail that officials and historians would later trace back to explain the economic and political collapse of the imposing Lakotas. A distinctive and enduring narrative took shape: though Lakotas would humiliate the U.S. Army on the Bozeman Trail and at the Little Bighorn, the rot had already set in the 1850s, plunging the Lakotas on a downward spiral. Against this background, the Little Bighorn was an aberration and a fluke, an embarrassment that gave the United States the resolve to bring down a Lakota regime that had long outlasted its time.[61]

Twiss and other officials failed to see that, at midcentury, Lakotas were in the midst of a dramatic new expansion that would last for a generation, all the way to the Little Bighorn. Rather than teetering on the brink of collapse in the face of the American empire, Lakotas were expanding an empire of their own.

THESE BLACK HILLS MUST BE LEFT WHOLLY TO THEMSELVES

The renewed Lakota expansion began with what may have been the most significant political summit in Lakota history. In the spring of 1856, in the aftermath of the Harney talks, Hunkpapas and Minneconjous sent a pipe across the Lakota domain, summoning all seven oyátes to a council near Mathó Pahá in the northern edge of the Black Hills in a year's time. In August 1857 most Lakota chiefs arrived. It was the time of the communal summer hunt, so the headmen traveled with all their people. The oyátes arranged themselves along the Belle Fourche River just north of the butte, their lodges forming a village that meandered for miles along the valley as a tangible manifestation of their collective power.[62]

A huge council lodge dominated the council ground as a symbol of Lakota unity, and Four Horns, a renowned Hunkpapa shirt wearer, sponsored a calumet dance, rekindling bonds with warriors of other oyátes. Any tangible policies, however, had to be forged leader by leader, thióšpaye by thióšpaye, oyáte by oyáte, and clique by clique, and there was not much time: horses would soon exhaust the grass along the valley, forcing the gathering to break up. This was a daunting challenge because Lakotas were a collection of competing interest groups and factions. Dominated by young men who were born into a world where the wašíčus would start a war over a cow, warrior societies wanted battle, whereas tribal councillors advocated trade and accommodation. A broader division threatened to pit the Oglalas, Sicangus, and Two Kettles, the oyátes with closest ties to Indian agents and traders, against the Hunkpapas, Minneconjous, Sans Arcs, and Sihasapas who were deeply cynical about the wašíčus and their intentions. An influential Hunkpapa headman, Little Bear, driven by his "hatred for the white man," had recently avowed to see to the "destruction of all traders in the country." Twenty-six-year-old Sitting Bull, already a war chief among the increasingly isolationist Hunkpapas, emerged as a leading hard-liner with his uncle Four Horns, High Backbone of the Minneconjous, Red Crow Feather of the Sans Arcs, and Red Cloud of the Oglalas.[63]

As was the custom, the grand assembly broke up into countless little councils. Headmen and warriors met with their counterparts in other oyátes, each encounter a politically charged chance to build consensus. When people came together again for public talks, a broad unanimity had been reached. At its core was an artful—and tremendously risky—compromise balancing band autonomy with national unity. Lakotas would fight to protect their lands and way of life, but individual bands could continue to collect treaty annuities if they so wished. Lakotas would not sever their ties with wašíčus, but they would keep them at a distance. A particular substance, gold, galvanized that principle. The assembled

Lakotas decided that "any Indian who should show the gold fields in the Black Hills to white men, should die, and the whites thus made aware of the presence of gold there should also die, for fear that the country would be taken from them."[64]

A U.S. Army expedition surveying a military route from the mouth of the Big Sioux to Fort Laramie and the South Pass encountered large numbers of Minneconjous, Hunkpapas, and Sihasapas near the Black Hills in early September, almost immediately after the council had ended. Lakotas forced the expedition to stop, preventing it from entering Pahá Sápa. The soldiers stayed put for three days, and their leader, Lieutenant G. K. Warren, received a firsthand summation of the decisions of the great Lakota council.[65]

What he saw was a blueprint for an empire that was reinventing itself and its relationship with the United States. Lakotas and Americans could still be bound by wólakȟota, but Americans would have to accept that there were places where they could and could not go. Lakotas would uphold the wašíčus' "privilege of traveling on the Platte" and "up and down the Missouri in boats," but the interior to the north and west of that perimeter would be closed to them. Only traders would be allowed, and they would have to limit their operations to Forts Pierre and Laramie. "No white people should travel elsewhere in their country," they said, "and thus frighten away the buffalo by their careless manner of hunting them." The core of the Lakota world would be inviolate: "These Black Hills must be left wholly to themselves." Any intruders would be shot. So vital was this principle of territorial sanctity that Lakotas were willing to give up annuities to block wašíču access. "If the presents sent were to purchase such a right," Bear Ribs had Warren inform the president, "they did not want them. All they asked of the white people was, to be left to themselves."[66]

Beyond words, Lakotas provided a graphic demonstration of the centrality of the Black Hills. "Encamped near large herds of buffalo, whose hair not being sufficiently grown to make robes," Warren wrote, "the Indians were, it may be said, actually herding the animals. No one was permitted to kill any in the large bands for fear of stampeding the others, and only such were killed as straggled away from the main herds. Thus the whole range of the buffalo was stopped so that they could not proceed south. . . . The intention of the Indians was to retain the buffalo in their neighbourhood till their skins would answer for robes, then to kill the animals by surrounding one band at a time and completely destroying each member of it." Lakotas had learned to control the highly unpredictable bison migrations and assemble the beasts for commercial purposes in the protected isolation of Pahá Sápa. Warren grasped the message: "Their feelings toward us, under the circumstances, were not unlike what we should feel toward a person who should insist upon setting fire to our barns." Any infringement of the Black Hills would be considered a declaration of war.[67]

Yet Lakotas asserted their own right to expand. Indian-Indian relations in the interior, they insisted, were not for the wašíčus to manage. If annuities were a way "to induce them not to go to war with the Crows and their other enemies," Bear Ribs said, "they did not wish them. War with them was not only a necessity but a pastime," he explained, trying to convey to the lieutenant how young men needed war and raiding to establish themselves as warriors and providers and live full and meaningful lives. He condemned the wašíču interference not only as unwarranted but hypocritical. "General Harney had told them not to go to war," he said, "and yet he was all the time going to war himself." Bear Ribs "knew that when General Harney left the Sioux country," noted the nonplussed Warren, "he had gone to the war in Florida, and was at the time in command of the army sent against the Mormons." Bear Ribs was employing the most basic imperial re-source—knowledge of the wider world—to stump the U.S. officer.[68]

Bear Ribs spoke for all seven Lakota oyátes, outlining a hard-edged national policy toward the Americans and rival Native groups, and his assurance unsettled Warren, who had served under Harney at Blue Water Creek. "They are still nu-merous, independent, warlike, and powerful" and had the Mandans, Hidatsas, and Arikaras producing corn for them under "sufferance," the lieutenant re-ported to Washington. They "contain within themselves means of prolonged and able resistance to further encroachments of the western settlers," he warned, and predicted more violence. "Under the present policy of Government, which there is no reason to believe will ever be changed, these encroachments will continue and new wars will result."[69]

Warren saw a solution in the geopolitical dynamics of the Indigenous interior and the expanding settlement frontier. The Indians, he wrote, could not simply retreat, "for the region to the west of one tribe is generally occupied by another with whom deadly animosity exists." This, he thought, constituted an engine of spontaneous dispossession. The Indians would grind against one another and crumble away, "disease, poverty, and vicious indulgence" accelerating the pro-cess. "The present policy of the Government seems, therefore, the best calcu-lated that could be devised for exterminating the Indian."[70]

Warren had captured the corollary of manifest destiny, the myth of the van-ishing race which taught Americans that Native peoples were destined to melt away in the face of white civilization. Believing that the extinction of the en-tire race was imminent, the War Department did exactly what the young lieu-tenant, facing the formidable and indignant Lakotas in the heart of their world, thought it should: it waited. The federal government left the Lakotas in the hands of Indian agents who were soon terribly overstretched: one of them traveled forty-eight hundred miles in nine months, moving from one agency to another. But the news they delivered was stirring to the army: everywhere, from the Missouri to the Upper Platte, the bison were still gripped by the drought and dying, leaving the Lakotas reeling. In 1856 only twenty-two thousand bison robes were shipped down the Missouri, less than one-fourth of the annual average of the 1840s, and the thirteen thousand Lakotas were eating away their commissary to the tune of some eighty thousand animals a year. Only in the Crow country did the herds seem to hold. "Their country abounds with everything Indian life requires," reported Lieutenant Warren. That was where Lakotas needed to go.[71]

THEIR TRACKS CAME CLOSE TO THE TIPIS

Joint-use accords had given Lakotas access to Crow lands since 1851, but the arrangement was fragile, interlaced with raids and counterraids. In the summer of 1856 a hundred-strong Hunkpapa hunting-raiding party detected a Crow camp near the Powder-Yellowstone junction. Hunkpapas waited for the dark to launch a raid, seizing a huge herd of horses, but Crows chased them down and forced a battle. Sitting Bull charged toward a Crow chief, blocked a shot with his shield that sent the bullet through the length of his foot, and shot down the Crow holding his instantly useless single-shot flintlock. Loud Bear chased another Crow and snatched off half of his war bonnet. Hunkpapas returned home with the horses and the story of the year when "half a war bonnet was torn off a Crow Indian who was determined to go to war with Sioux."[72]

The adversaries met later that summer and restored peace, but the next year Crows launched a series of raids on Lakotas. Things became brutal. An unsuspecting Crow party traveling with women visited Lakotas, and a young warrior shot four arrows into one of the women. The following decade was a decade of war, punctured with brief truces, and Lakota winter counts are a litany of fights, victories, and defeats. In 1857 the largely Lakotanized Twiss relocated the Upper Platte Agency more than a hundred miles upriver in comfortable houses of an abandoned Mormon way station at Deer Creek, where he lived with his Oglala wife Wanikiyewin and their pet bear. By doing so, Twiss inadvertently created a launchpad for Lakotas to push into Crow territory. Lakota war parties could stock up on munitions at the agency and then take the Crow trail toward the prime buffalo range in the Powder River Valley. A young Oglala boy Amos Bad Heart Bull witnessed the stream of raiding expeditions and would later draw dozens of pictographs of the warriors and their deeds. By the end of the decade Lakotas dominated the Powder River country and began raiding into the Bighorn Valley one hundred and fifty miles to the west, often joining forces with their Cheyenne and Arapaho allies.[73]

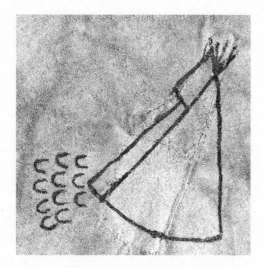

33. Lone Dog winter count, 1861–62 (detail).
Although the bison herds were visibly declining
from the mid-nineteenth century onward, their
size fluctuated wildly from year to year with
weather conditions. Several winter counts for
1861–62 record large herds. "Buffalo were so
plentiful that their tracks came close to the
tipis," records this Yanktonai winter count entry.
Courtesy of National Museum of the
American Indian, Smithsonian Institution
(01/0617, detail). Photo by NMAI Services.

A Lakota winter count for 1861–62 exulted over "an unusual abundance of buffalo," while a Yanktonai count reported that "buffalo were so plentiful that their tracks came close to the tipis." The bison seemed to be coming to Lakotas because Lakotas were expanding toward them. The concerted push into the West meant for Lakotas a reaffirmation of their bison-centered way of life. The lands east of the Black Hills could no longer sustain them. Overland traffic and decades of intensive market hunting had crippled the bison ecology, fueling despair and resentment, whereas the lands to the west teemed with game. The plains to the east had also become a place where the U.S. government "sends diseases to cut them off," whereas the West seemed to have few or no wašíču s. There Lakotas could still find life's necessities and fulfill their traditional social roles. There Crazy Horse and an entire generation of Lakota men sought visions and made their marks as warriors and providers, amassing military honors and excess meat that brought them respect, distinction, and songs.[74]

The Lakota-Crow borderlands became a westward bulging war zone. This placed the Crows into a tightening circle for they were already locked in a grinding border war with the powerful Blackfeet who coveted horses, which were scarce in the cold north. Crows were also becoming desperately isolated. The Yellowstone, a key artery into their country, became "infested by hordes" of Blackfeet and Lakotas who choked down the Crow trade raid after raid. Struggling to secure guns, Crows deposed chiefs who had advocated alliances with Americans and Lakotas. U.S. agents denounced them as "insolent, audacious, and lawless" and wrote pithily about them in their annual reports. Lakotas, meanwhile, collected regular annuities at their agencies and sometimes received goods earmarked for Crows.[75]

The wars would continue into the 1870s, but a kind of culmination came in 1863. By then Lakotas were driving the Crows up the Bighorn Mountains, and in the summer a Lakota-Cheyenne-Arapaho war party found a large Crow village on Pryor Creek, some fifty miles west of the Bighorn. Warfare was by now a routine, and both sides quickly organized themselves for battle. Crow women moved their tipis into a tight circle behind a line of warriors while the allies formed a line half a mile wide. A lone Cheyenne rode toward the Crow cordon and was at once filled with arrows. The allies charged across the creek to envelop the Crows who quickly moved warriors to close the flank. Waves of attacks and counterattacks swept back and forth, and horses fell in droves, breaking clear battle lines into a jumble of man-to-man fights. Crazy Horse chased a Crow into the village and scalped and killed him there. He Dog, another rising warrior, snatched a saber from a Crow and struck him with it, scoring a coup. When the allies detected signs of Crow reinforcements, they packed their dead and wounded on horses and fled.[76]

The battle may have been inconclusive, but the fact that it took place deep in the West was significant: much of the Crow realm had become a militarized zone where life was reduced to mere survival. The next year their agent reported that Crows "dare not go into their own country on the Yellow Stone." That summer found most of them on the Musselshell River, and some fifty lodges of refugees huddled on the Milk River 250 miles north of the Yellowstone, "waiting in the hope of receiving their goods there, as they had been driven from their country by the Sioux." "But in this they had to be disappointed," for the goods never arrived. Lakotas had attacked a mackinaw boat carrying Crow annuities, forcing it to turn back. It was an acute embarrassment for the agents, but they found a silver lining: some Crows now declared a desire to join Americans against Lakotas. Several Lakota winter counts for 1864–65 note how Crows pushed into a Minneconjou village and tried to steal horses. Four of them were caught and tortured to death. Mentions of Crow raids declined precipitously in winter counts.[77]

The well-organized and well-mounted Crows had reigned over a sizable do-main that disguised their relatively small population of about five thousand. The upshot was that Crows had placed relatively little pressure on the bison, which remained so numerous that they considered hunting a routine that required neither great numbers nor elaborate planning. Much of that animal bounty now belonged to Lakotas whose expansion had secured them five fertile river valleys—the Tongue, Rosebud, Little Bighorn, Bighorn, and Yellowstone—each filled with bison and enveloped by lush grass. When women and children joined men in the West, bringing in tipis, belongings, and horses, these valleys became home. It was there that Pretty Owl, Red Cloud, Snow-on-Her, Red Woman, Sit-ting Bull, and many others raised their families, securing their world for genera-tions to come.[78]

THE UNSEEN EMPIRE

The Lakota expansion into the Crow country violated the Horse Creek Treaty, but the government did next to nothing to quell it. Lakotas, after all, were pushing the Crows high up the northern Rockies where that "insolent" tribe posed no threat to America's overland arteries and hegemonic pretensions. The same ap-plied to the Eastern Shoshones, Assiniboines, and even Mormons whom Lakotas began raiding as the Crows retreated. Soon Lakotas were ranging west of the Big-horns and north of the Yellowstone.[79]

But elsewhere Lakota policies were a direct affront to the United States. In 1853 Cheyennes carried "the pipe around to invite other tribes to war against the Pawnees," and many Lakotas responded to the call. They killed more than one hundred. Lakotas also raided plains villages along the Missouri and south of the Platte, taking horses and captives and corn and trying to monopolize access to the bison. As if to assert their prerogative to deal with their Native neighbors as they saw best, in the spring and summer of 1860 Lakotas and their allies attacked the Pawnee reservation on the Loup eight times, each strike a blatant violation of the treaty that granted them annuities on the condition of keeping peace. The United States allowed Lakotas to stage raids, wage wars, and expand their empire in its midst without taking effective action to stop them. This passivity is one of the great puzzles in the history of U.S.-Indian relations.[80]

Gold, once again, was at the heart of things. In 1858 rich veins had been dis-covered in the Rocky Mountain foothills in western Kansas Territory. A hundred thousand "fifty-niners" rushed in along the Solomon, Smoky Hill, and Arkansas Rivers, heading toward Pikes Peak where their shared dreams converged. About half of them returned home the same year, crossing the plains back east. The two-way mass migration left behind wrecked river valleys with pulverized banks almost devoid of game, grass, and timber. Those valleys belonged to Cheyennes and Arapahos, their sanctity guarded by the proudly militant Cheyenne Dog Soldiers. As tensions mounted along the trails, the army sent in soldiers to keep order. The continuing flow of gold through the central plains became a priority for the federal government, and Lakotas slipped into a liberating blind spot. The already limited military oversight shrunk to almost nothing.[81]

The blind spot only grew when the United States descended into civil war. In 1860, pressured by federal agents, moderate Cheyennes and Arapahos accepted a reservation on the Arkansas River, signing away most of their lands. The Dog Soldiers declared the treaty unlawful and began killing anyone—Indians, ranchers, Union freighters—who competed for diminishing resources. Terrified that the Confederates in New Mexico might join with the Dog Soldiers to invade the Colorado goldfields, the Union built a frontier army out of volunteer regiments and assigned it to punish militants across the central plains. Chasing the ultra-mobile nomad warriors absorbed the bulk of the resources the Union could make available in the West. Every raid, fight, and flight the Dog Soldiers staged worked directly to Lakotas' benefit by keeping the Union preoccupied. Lakotas had a virtual free rein to arrange the world as they saw fit. It was not a coincidence that they were raiding all over the place and enjoying best hunts for a long time during the early years of the Civil War.[82]

The United States was not only stretched thin; its failure to counter Lakota expansion was also a failure of imagination. While Americans were otherwise preoccupied, Lakotas extended their range of operations to the U.S.-Canadian border in the north, the central plains in the south, the Missouri Valley in the east, and the Continental Divide in the west—an expansive outer rim of extraction and dominance. They were consolidating an empire, of a kind Americans could neither see nor understand. Built around a shifting tribal alliance rather than a state, it was a distinctly fluid organism that reflected Lakotas' vision of the world and their place in it. They desired power, prosperity, and respect, but they did not seek direct control over foreign people or territories to secure them. Their dominance rested on a capacity, underwritten by military power and mobility, to do certain things—raid, extort, intimidate, and kill—over and over again and across vast distances. Spectacular foreign political action, punctuated with ominous lulls, allowed them to achieve what traditional empires achieved through institutional control: harness resources, create dependencies, enforce boundaries, and inspire awe. Lakotas were a presence even when absent.

Unable to recognize the nature of the Lakota regime, U.S. officials became cogs in it. Lakota foreign policy revolved around a distinctive annual cycle, shifting from long-distance war expeditions to opportunistic small-scale raids to trade excursions to diplomatic missions to political gatherings at Pahá Sápa.

Visits to government agencies were embedded into that cycle. In the fall, after summer hunts and raids, Lakotas visited one of the four forts available to them—Laramie, Pierre, Union, and Clark—to collect annuities, which they considered an entitlement. Federal agents typically vacationed in the summer—the busiest raiding season—so they tended to be unaware of treaty violations when they met with Lakotas in the fall. In September 1859 agent Twiss, just back from Washington, the Great Father's "council-lodge," praised Lakotas for not having harassed the fifty-niners during his absence and handed out "a large present of annuity goods." He said nothing of Lakota raids in the Crow country and elsewhere because he probably knew nothing of them. The agents worked hard to collect information during the ten or eleven months they spent in the Lakota country, but they could gather only scraps: raids in distant places mostly by unidentified leaders and bands, rumors of rendezvous with illegal traders, extortions along overland trails, stories of summer excursions.[83]

The U.S. empire was built on institutional prowess and visibility, whereas the Lakota empire was an action-based regime, which gave it a fickle, on-and-off-again character. It could be all over the map one moment and nowhere to be seen the next. Long-distance war trails and sprawling raiding spheres became activated for a few months each year, only to become inert again, a seasonal cycle that repeated itself year after year and decade after decade. It was a regime of dominance and hierarchy, but it was not static, which made it difficult to see. The agents never did.

Nor did the agents ever grasp the magnitude of wealth, resources, and people that kept pouring into the Lakota domain: hardy, agile pinto horses with their blotched coats that served as natural camouflage siphoned out of the Crow country; heavier and darker American mounts poached from military and trading posts along with cattle and mules; captives taken from Pawnees, Omahas, Shoshones, Assiniboines, Crows, and wašíču overlanders; guns, powder, ammunition, and swords secured from independent traders and government agencies; luxurious Navajo blankets imported from the Southwest; corn, squash, berries, sugar, and other foods gathered, pilfered, and extorted wherever possible. Even annuities intended for other groups sometimes flowed in: Arapahos accused Twiss of diverting their goods to Lakotas. That influx solidified the material base of the Lakota empire, boosting its military strength, its mobile power politics, its labor force, and its prestige and allure.[84]

BIG FRIENDS

The inflow of wealth also set the Lakotas apart: theirs was now the largest, richest, and safest Indigenous domain in North America. Their prominence

34. *Sioux Village near Fort Laramie*, by Albert Bierstadt, 1859.
Although romanticized, the painting captures the prosperity and power of the
Lakotas at midcentury: the spacious tipis, the vast hunting grounds around their
villages, and secure access to river valleys and American markets. Blanton Museum
of Art, The University of Texas at Austin. Bequest of C. R. Smith, 1991.

pulled numerous Native groups into their fold as allies and dependents. Viewed
from the central and eastern plains where American expansion was rapidly
eroding Indigenous sovereignty, the Lakota realm emerged as a safe haven exuding prestige and power. More fundamentally, it embodied hope. Militants, discontents, and asylum seekers from other tribes who refused to accept the United
States' imperial claims began to gravitate toward it, hoping to secure a lease on
survival. If they found the right thoughts and words, Lakotas took them in.

Cheyennes and Arapahos had been close allies of Lakotas for generations,
trading with them, joining them in fighting common enemies, and camping
with them in the Black Hills. But the alliance reached another scale altogether
at midcentury. Entire bands shifted into the Lakota orbit, pushed by the horrific
conditions in the central plains and pulled by the promise of a better life among
the Lakotas. Their absorption was as fast as it was thorough. As earlier, Cheyennes and Arapahos shaded into the fabric of Lakota kinship through wólakȟota,
bringing the population of the multiethnic Lakota realm close to twenty thousand in the early 1860s. "I like them," one Arapaho elder later explained. "They

35. Chief Red Cloud, 1872. Courtesy of National
Anthropological Archives, Smithsonian Institution
(NAA GN 03236).

are what I call 'big friends.' They are a big tribe." Cheyenne chief Turkey Foot
echoed the sentiment: "All the tribes around this country are our relations. They
have intermarried with each other. They are all one flesh." When a Cheyenne
man mistreated an Oglala woman, Red Cloud rode into the offender's village
and whipped him. Cheyennes did not protest the chastisement.[85]

With kinship as its adhesive, the Lakota empire was, at its core, an empire
of equals. Many dispossessed Poncas and countless captives, both Indian and
white, entered the Lakota society coercively and under duress, but hundreds
of Cheyenne and Arapaho families came voluntarily, indeed eagerly. Like any
other imperial power, Lakotas had to find ways to manage the growing diversity within their borders, but unlike most empires, they did not rely on force or
codified hierarchization. There was no social ladder for allied people, only so-

cial niches into which they could slide. Many Dog Soldiers married into Oglala and Sicangu families and formed mixed camps on the Cheyenne-Lakota borderlands, while others gravitated toward Hunkpapas and Sans Arcs farther north. Cheyenne and Arapaho newcomers became part of everyday Lakota life. While retaining their traditional creeds and customs, they participated in Lakota feasts, ceremonies, and councils and used Lakota as a trading language. They were not nations within a nation; they were individuals, families, and bands residing among Lakotas who dealt with diversity by simply accepting it. What mattered to Lakotas most was loyalty, not likeness, and they were comfortable with a realm that bubbled with different habits, ideas, and languages for that also meant new bodies, new skills, and new connections that spelled power."[86]

Lakotas' was an expansive, all-embracing understanding of belonging that recognized no color line. Lakotas had closed their borders to their Yankton relatives after they sold most of their lands to the United States, believing that Yanktons had had no right to sell Sioux lands without their consent. Wašíčus, on the other hand, were welcome as long as they complied with Lakota customs and expectations. Independent traders like Bordeaux and Bissonette who married into Lakota families and learned the language became kin, an absorption that may have secured them a right to attend Lakota councils. And there were others. A mixed-blood trader John Richard brought to the Lakota country many wagonloads of Mexican blankets in the late 1850s, while French-American Joseph Antoine Janis married First Elk Woman, traded with her Oglala kin and Sicangus for over a decade, and knew personally the headmen of both oyátes. Jules Ecoffey supplied Lakotas on the North Platte, served them as an interpreter, and became a confidant of Red Cloud. Traders like Ecoffey were highly valued precisely because they were different. They understood the American mindset and, crucially, could read. A key element of Lakotas' diplomatic prowess was the fact that they had so many literate allies who interpreted and explained wašíču documents for them.

Nothing about these cross-cultural relations was unambiguous. Wašíču traders and trading posts provided Lakotas with food, clothing, tools, and information, but they also supplied them with guns, powder, and ammunition, bolstering their military might that readily translated into extortions along the Oregon Trail, U.S. casualties on battlefields, and treaty-violating raids all across the West. The posts were American in name only. They were critical supply depots that, not unlike U.S. forts, symbolized the power, reach, and prestige of a rising empire.[87]

STRONG DESIRE FOR PEACE AND QUIET

The expanding Lakotas eluded the long arm of the U.S. military-bureaucratic machine by shifting shape and hiding in plain sight. But, at the same time, they also reached out to U.S. agents, knowing that they needed to present themselves in a particular light to keep the military out and the annuities flowing in. The public face Lakotas presented to the Indian Office was that of moderate leaders whose civility concealed the fact that the vast majority of Lakotas had been militants since the Harney massacre.

It is stunning that agent Twiss could write in 1858—a year when Lakota war parties were raiding from the Yellowstone to the Platte and beyond—that "the different bands of this agency observe strictly the conditions and stipulations of the treaty of 1851." The next year Twiss denounced Harney's hard-line policy and advocated the endorsement of akíčhitas—who were almost invariably militants—as preservers of order among Lakotas, a de facto reaffirmation of tribal sovereignty. In a truly extraordinary statement, which seems almost a slippage, he assured the commissioner of Indian affairs that the akíčhitas "will protect any white people whom the war party may chance to meet." The Horse Creek Treaty had specifically obliged Lakotas to live in peace, and here was an agent who reported on ongoing Lakota warfare as a matter of course, virtually rendering the treaty moot. Twiss genuinely liked Lakotas and had married one of them, but similar selective reporting came from Forts Pierre and Union, where agents shunned intimate relations with their nominal subjects. In 1857—a particularly active year of fighting and raiding—agent A. H. Redfield reported how his talks with Two Bears, Iron Nation, and Bear Ribs at Fort Pierre had been "satisfactory; their language and manner indicated, I think, a sincere friendship and a strong desire for peace and quiet, and to observe the stipulations of the [Horse Creek] treaty."[88]

Like all government bureaus, the Indian Office needed basic information to function; it was, in essence, an information-guzzling organization that fueled the United States' imperial metabolism with facts. But the ceaseless inflow of facts and information needed to be processed before it could become useful for policy-makers, and the instrument for that processing was a story. The Indian Office relied on the reports of its field agents, who composed carefully crafted accounts of key events and dutifully sent them in. After a while there was a long narrative of Lakotas in the Indian Office's filing cabinets. Lakotas had manipulated and controlled that narrative to a remarkable degree.

HERE WE ARE

Lakotas cultivated face-to-face relationships with Indian agents and through those intimate relationships they could manage and control them. The image they presented to the agents was a partial one, a moderate minority concealing a militant majority, but it was not a complete fabrication. The Lakotas who visited the agencies—chiefs, warriors, women, children—genuinely enjoyed the visits. They liked most of the officials and treated them with a warmth and candour that won them over.

The U.S. Army was a different matter. In 1859 the secretary of war dispatched a large expedition to explore the "then almost unknown" Yellowstone country for minerals, agricultural prospects, and "the habits and disposition of the Indians inhabiting the country." The army clearly did not trust the accuracy of the Indian Office reports, which would have provided much of the needed information, and the War Department did indeed follow a different agenda. The expedition was to scout the region, now a Lakota domain, for railroads, military operations, and settlement.

Its leader, Captain William F. Raynolds, met with Lakotas at Fort Pierre and informed Bear Ribs of his intention to march past the Black Hills to the west. Next day Bear Ribs addressed the captain. "To whom does this land belong? I believe it belongs to me. . . . Here we are. We are nine nations," he declared, counting the Yanktons and the Yanktonais in. "Here are our principal men gathered together." "It is said I have a father, (the agent), and when he tells me anything I say 'yes'; and when I ask him anything, I want him to say 'yes.'" Bear Ribs was educating Raynolds of the reciprocity and mutuality that had allowed Lakotas and Americans to coexist in the heart of the continent, and he expected him to compromise. Lakota chiefs advised Raynolds to follow the Missouri to the Yellowstone confluence, effectively skirting the Lakota territory, but Raynolds insisted on "the right of transit through their country." If denied, he warned, "the President would send soldiers to wipe out the entire nation from existence." The captain then promised to distribute the annuity goods, which, as a payment for access, diffused the situation.

The headmen withdrew into the fort's trading house where they had been given a large apartment. Raynolds, intrigued, spied on them "'behind the scenes'" and recoiled. The leading men "were lounging about the room literally *au naturel*." Having "discarded their gaudy vestments and barbaric trappings" for loincloths and buffalo robes, "their glory had departed." "They were lying about on the floor in all conceivable postures, their whole air and appearance indicating ignorance and indolence, while the inevitable pipe was being passed from hand to hand." The scene repulsed the impressionable captain, "banishing all ideas of dignity in the Indian character, and leaving a vividly realizing sense of the fact that the red men are savages." Like so many before and after him, Raynolds found it hard to reconcile the carefully constructed public image Lakotas wished to present to the world with the flesh-and-blood human beings behind it. He had no use for the latter.

Raynold's revulsion captures the raw immediacy of cross-cultural accommodation and the delicate artifice of performance and selective myopia that made it possible in the first place. When Raynolds led his men toward the Black Hills several days later, it was the image of the savage Lakotas he carried with him. As the expedition ascended the Cheyenne Valley toward Pahá Sápa, he "could see fires burning around us nightly." It would be a cautious mission. Raynolds skirted the northern fringe of the Black Hills, careful not to draw the wrath of the trailing Lakotas. He could feel Lakotas "watching our movements" until they left their country. Yet, near the Black Hills, he had detected traces of gold.[89]

In that same year agent Twiss, the American who knew the Lakotas best, reported on declining bison herds in the plains. "I must confess, in all candor, that we, the residents of the Indian country, are reposing upon a volcano which may burst forth and overwhelm us in ruin and devastation when we are all least aware of the danger."[90]

7

WAR

Lakotas built worlds on words. There were words that defined social relationships and words that turned biological strangers into kin. There were words that made allies out of enemies and words that preserved good sentiments thereafter. There were sacred words that, when recited and sung with care, appeased spirits, called in the buffalo, and preserved the sacred hoop. There were words that could travel high above with the smoke of the sacred pipe, revealing the purpose of life and keeping the world whole, and there was a word, *škáŋ*, for an all-pervading energy that sustained both life and movement, capturing something essential about Lakota history. There were words for holy women, *wíŋyaŋ wakȟáŋs*, and holy men, *wičháša wakȟáŋs*, who were conduits of sacred powers and made Wakȟáŋ Tȟáŋka understandable.[1]

Words had served Lakotas well. Words had bound them together, keeping them united through numerous transfigurations, and words had helped them make sense of the many worlds they had made before arriving in Pahá Sápa, the place of their creation. Along with numbers, diplomacy had been their most important asset as they shaped the American interior to meet their needs. Sometimes conducted through brusque bargaining, sometimes through unnerving detachment, sometimes through long and eloquent speeches, Lakota diplomacy was a complex affair. Its most potent word was *wólakȟota*, which means bonds of peace grounded in kinship. It had transformed thousands of people into relatives and allies without which Lakotas would have been isolated and vulnerable nothings. Lakotas had words to frighten, overwhelm, and diminish others, and they had words to invoke trust, empathy, and love. Words had brought order and safety because, over and over again, Lakotas had been able to make the wašíčus listen.

ALL THE HORRORS OF INDIAN WAR

Agent Thomas Twiss had listened and he knew more about the Lakotas and their world than any other U.S. official in the mid-nineteenth century. In the summer of 1859 he submitted "a special report on the present condition" of "the wild tribes of the prairies and the mountains, embraced within the limits of the Upper Platte agency." Claiming to be "animated solely with a desire to prevent their utter extinction," he alerted the Indian Office to "certain conditions of things, now in process of rapid development," that threatened to interrupt "this state of repose and tranquility, and involve the scattered white population in all of the horrors and calamities of an Indian war."

It was a last-ditch effort to educate the Indian Office on the desperate conditions that threatened to plunge the West into violence. The report required careful balancing between Twiss's personal affinity with Lakotas and his professional duties as a government agent. "The state of the Indian mind among the wild tribes is one of extreme suspicion in all matters relating to the preservation of game, their only means of subsistence," he wrote. He asked the officials to consider things from a Lakota perspective and have compassion. Lakotas, he admitted, "have stopped white people, and even United States topographical parties, when they have endeavored to penetrate to their hunting grounds," but Lakotas had no choice in the matter because the bison were wasting away. The herds no longer made "the prairie appear black, as formerly, as far as the eye could scan the horizon." Now bison could be found "in small bands only" and "very far distant for the tribes of Indians of this agency." It was a moral challenge hidden behind an unspoken rhetorical question: if your world was dying, would you not fight?[2]

Desperate to prevent bloodshed, Twiss tried to instruct the Indian Office about the Lakota mindset. "These wild tribes have heard that all of the Indian tribes to the eastward of them have ceded their lands to the United States, except small reservations," he wrote, and "by an Indian's reasoning, in a few years these tribes will emigrate further west, and, as a matter of necessity, occupy the hunting grounds of the wild tribes, and cause thereby a rapid decrease in the number of buffalo." He had met with several bands the previous year and had been "most effectually silenced" by the words of one of their chiefs:

> When I was a young man, and I am now only fifty years old, I traveled with my people, through the country of the Sac and Fox tribe, to the great water Minne Tonkah, (Mississippi,) where I saw corn growing, but no white people. Continuing eastward, we came to the Rock River valley, and saw the Winnebagoes, but no white people. We then came to the Fox River valley, and thence to the

Great Lake, (Lake Michigan,) where we found a few white people in the Potta-watomie country. Thence we returned to the Sioux country, at the Great Falls, (Irara or St. Anthony,) and had a feast of green corn with our relations, who resided there. Afterwards, we visited the pipe-clay quarry, in the country of the Yancton Sioux, and made a feast to the "great medicine," and danced the "sun dance"; and then returned to our hunting grounds on the prairie.

The chief's recount of his youthful grand tour served strategic ends: it reminded Americans of the Očhéthi Šakówiŋ's astounding power in the great interior and it announced Lakotas' far-reaching political and kinship connections, warning Americans not to underestimate either. Lakotas, the chief intimated, knew how the Americans operated and would not tolerate the kind of wašíču encroachment that had dispossessed so many tribes around them. "See! The whites cover all these lands that I have just described, and also the lands of the Poncas, Omahas, and Pawnees. On the south fork of the Platte the white people are finding gold, and the Arapahoes and Cheyennes have no longer any hunting grounds."

It is unlikely that Twiss would have missed the angry defiance of the chief's words, but he thought the Lakota reign in the plains was already doomed. "This process of development, this law of Anglo-Saxon progress," he concluded, "is a necessity and a consequence of, and flowing directly from, our free institutions, which, in their strength, purity, and beauty, tend to stimulate and bring forth the vast resources of agriculture, mineral, and commercial wealth, within the boundaries of our great empire." He urged the government to waste no time in starting negotiations to persuade the Lakotas to settle "cordially" in reservations "and devote themselves to labor for their own subsistence."[3]

In mid-September 1859 Twiss held a council with several Lakota, Cheyenne, and Arapaho headmen at his Deer Creek Agency. The well-meaning agent de-livered a chilling speech. After complimenting the Indians for keeping peace along overland trails, he told them that the "white men are settling in every part of your country" and the president "will send his white families to build houses and settle on farms in these valleys. He wishes that the whites shall plant corn and raise herds of cattle where once you had plenty of buffalo; these are now all destroyed."[4]

While Twiss was cajoling Lakotas and their allies to abandon the hunt, fif-teen hundred miles to the east the Indian Office was calculating how much it would cost to hold councils with all the major Plains Indian nations and, at long last, nearly a decade after the 1851 Horse Creek Treaty, arrange their concentra-tion "upon suitable reservations." The cost amounted to more than two hundred thousand dollars, or about "ten dollars per head." The plan was dropped. There were faster and cheaper ways to subjugate the Natives.[5]

ALL THE HIGHER BRANCHES OF MILITARY SCIENCE

As Twiss's reports circulated within the Indian Office, Captain William Raynolds, though having been prevented entering the Black Hills, completed his survey of the Yellowstone and its tributaries. Covering some twenty-five hundred miles, his expedition carefully inspected and mapped the terrain, soil, elevation, weather, fauna, plants, and even mosses and liverworts in this *"terra incognita"* — an exercise in scientific absorption of the land which by American military thinking was a critical step toward possession. As the strategists at West Point saw it, warfare had entered a new era where science was king. Its personification was the army engineer, a renaissance man who, according to one military manual, "requires a knowledge of chemistry, to guide his choice of materials for mortars, cements, and mastics; of mineralogy and geology, for selecting stone; of botany, for timber and the means of preventing its decay; of mathematics, in laying out his work and calculating the thickness and stability of his walls, embankments, &c.; of mechanical philosophy, in constructing his machinery . . . and of all the higher branches of military science."

The scholar-soldier had arrived, and behind him came modern reinforced military forts with "immense" capacity to preserve peace and subdue enemies. In part to compensate for the weak civilian bureaucracy, forts established a constant military presence, provided bases for field operations, served as supply depots, doubled as training grounds, and, crucially, were cheap to maintain. Even their isolation in distant frontiers was a virtue, for there they could "never exert an influence corrupting to public morals, or dangerous to public liberty": since the colonial period, many Americans had seen professional armed forces as a threat to their liberty and democracy. The fort was the perfect tool of conquest, and so Americans came to believe it would be but a matter of time before they speckled the far West, subduing the starving, dying Natives through their sheer presence.

With Native dispossession seemingly imminent, the federal government let the Lakotas be. The War Department's annual report in 1859 included endless accounts of Comanches and a long treatise on the use of camels in the arid Southwest but hardly mentioned the Lakotas. Yet a column of U.S. troops had marched eastward from Fort Laramie across the heart of the Lakota domain, seeking to establish "a correct geographical and local representation of the route with reference to its fitness for the purposes of emigration, and of government in transporting mails, troops, and munitions of war." Its destination was Fort Randall, a new military fort that The Butcher—General Harney—had ordered built on the Missouri to monitor the Lakotas from proper distance.[6]

The U.S. Army received a lesson on the worth of a single fort in the late summer of 1860, when hundreds of Hunkpapas attacked Fort Union on the upper Missouri. The traders managed to shut the gate at the last minute and then watched from the ramparts as the Hunkpapas killed cattle, burned masses of hay and lumber, and destroyed two mackinaw boats. The first casualties were enough to stop the assault, suggesting that it had been less a raid than a message, a denouncement of wašíču farmers, troops, and forts in Lakota lands. Hunkpapas then made a broad southwesterly sweep, recruiting members from Sans Arc and Sihasapa bands, and launched raids along the Oregon Trail. These northern Lakotas would not tolerate any wašíču encroachments and would hold on to the hunt as long as they possibly could. A distressed fur trader complained that they "acted with us more as a people at war with us than otherwise," abusing agents, robbing merchants, and harassing any Americans they might run into.[7]

WE WILL GIVE THEM EARS

In late May 1862 Bear Ribs, the Hunkpapa headman whom Harney had declared as head chief of all Lakotas six year earlier, met with agent Samuel Latta at Fort Pierre. Bear Ribs accepted the annuity goods but told Latta "to bring no more." This would be the last time he would take them. "For eleven years he had been the friend of the white man and the government," he said, hoping that it would send in soldiers to regulate the overland traffic and protect the bison; "yet none had come." His people had had enough and wanted nothing to do with the wašíčus. Accepting annuities after this would put his life in danger. Hunkpapas and other northern Lakotas were turning away from the Americans and their corrupting gifts. Bear Ribs would have to withdraw with them.

It was already too late for him. Ten days later the chief returned to Fort Pierre to face a group of Minneconjous and Sans Arcs who berated the friendly bands and "expressed their determination to kill their five principal men." Bear Ribs faced two Sans Arcs, Mouse and One-That-Limps. Mouse shot Bear Ribs point blank in the chest. Falling, the chief fired his shotgun, killing his killer. His followers killed One-That-Limps. The agent reported to Washington the loss of "the best friend the white man had in the Sioux nation."[8]

Six weeks later a Mr. Garreau delivered to the agent at Fort Berthold on the upper Missouri a letter from nine Hunkpapa headmen. The Hunkpapa attack on Fort Union two years earlier had been a warning; now they relied on written words to get the message through. "We don't want the whites to travel through our country," the letter began. "The Indians have given permission to travel by water, but not by land; and boats carrying passengers we will not allow." The Hunkpapas were severing their ties with the U.S. government to protect their sovereignty and keep their lands inviolate. "We notified the Bear's Rib yearly not to receive your goods; he had no ears, and we gave him ears by killing him. We now say to you, bring us no more goods; if any of our people receive any more from you we will give them ears as we did the Bear's Rib. We acknowledge no agent."[9]

Not long after, Lakotas attacked a steamboat heading upriver to Montana gold-fields, igniting a river war that would see repeated attacks on American steamers, whose insatiable boilers consumed enormous quantities of valuable cottonwood, the main forage that carried Lakota horses through winters. U.S. officials felt powerless in the face of this Indigenous border control. Washington conceived all the lands between the Minnesota and the upper Missouri Rivers as a single jurisdiction which, it soon became clear, was "entirely too large." Lakotas continued to attack and harass the invading boats, asserting their supremacy along the Mníšoše.[10]

THEY ARE TO BE TREATED AS MANIACS

While Lakotas foiled the wašíčus' hegemonic pretensions in the West, their Dakota relatives had collapsed into crippling poverty. Emigrants from the east kept pushing in, settling along the Minnesota Valley, the heart of the Dakota world. In 1851 Dakotas ceded their remaining lands for a reservation and annuities for fifty years. Yet the immigrant encroachment continued. By 1858 the Minnesota Territory had more than 150,000 settlers—mostly Scandinavians, Germans, and Irish—and was about to become a state. Indian agents took a Dakota delegation to Washington and kept it there until the chiefs signed a new treaty that ceded the richest part of their reservation to the United States.[11]

Dakotas grew increasingly dependent on agency traders who, by a federal mandate, managed their treaty annuities, pocketing most of their funds for themselves, their backers in Washington, and select mixed-bloods through complex credit arrangements. The already frayed bonds of amity and reciprocity snapped. Federal agents exacerbated the situation by pressuring Dakotas to give up hunting: only those who showed a willingness to farm could count on government assistance. Dakota villages fractured into self-proclaimed progressives who embraced yeoman farming and Christianity and traditionalists who held on to the collapsing communal world of the hunt and the village. By the time the Civil War erupted in 1861, the little goodwill there had been between the traditionalists and American traders and officials was spent. The harvest failed that year and then the annuities were delayed. When German settlers began encroaching upon their lands, most Dakotas had seen enough. The whites were no longer allies or kin. They had become invaders.[12]

Confederate sympathizers in Minnesota had already informed Dakota chiefs of the many Northern defeats when, in August 1862, a Union recruiter arrived in the reservation to seek volunteers. Dakota warriors saw the desperation in the act and hatched a plan to win their lands back. Agent Andrew Myrick's haughty cynicism aggravated the situation. He refused to sell food to the starving Dakotas on credit and announced through an interpreter, "So far as I am concerned, if they are hungry, let them eat grass." Soon after a Dakota hunting party killed five settlers, prompting a reluctant Mdewakanton chief, Little Crow, to join the rebellion to drive the whites out. They began with their own agency, and one of the first to fall was Myrick. He was found with a tuft of grass in his mouth.

Violence exploded along and around the Minnesota Valley as Dakota warriors killed hundreds of settlers, burned farms, raided stores, and took hostages. Within days twenty-three counties were evacuated, but the rebellion continued, prompting army officers to declare that they now faced "a war of extermination." A preoccupied Abraham Lincoln—busy drafting the preliminary Emancipation Proclamation—created a new Military Department of the Northwest and sent in Major General John Pope, who had just suffered a humiliating defeat at the Second Battle of Bull Run. Mortified by what he took as a demotion and pressured by revengeful Minnesotans, Pope declared that it was his purpose to "utterly to exterminate the Sioux." "They are to be treated as maniacs or wild beasts." But such a glorious campaign was not in the books for Pope. The violence had divided the Dakotas—some still had close ties with whites whom they saw as kin—and the war effectively ended in late September, when the Dakotas released 269 white and mixed-blood captives and Little Crow fled toward the Canadian border.[13]

Pope held nearly two thousand Dakota men, women, and children as prisoners of war and moved most of them to Fort Snelling, where they were kept for nearly a year in a filthy makeshift prison. He put some 400 Dakotas on trial for atrocities against the whites. Military tribunals sentenced 303 to death in hasty superficial trials. Lincoln reviewed the trial records, while Pope and the hardnosed Minnesota governor Alexander Ramsey kept insisting that it would take exactly 303 deaths to balance the approximately 500 dead settlers. Lincoln rejected their demands; he would authorize the execution of only those who had been found guilty of rape or perpetrating massacres. Trying to balance severity against clemency, he ended up blending moral criteria with political ones. The army built a massive collapsible platform on the main street of the town of Mankato and, on December 26, escorted 38 Dakotas and mixed-bloods to it. As the noosed and hooded men shouted their names and tried to lock hands, a man who had lost most of his family sprang the trap. The bodies were buried in a sandbar by the Minnesota River. It was and remains the largest mass execution in American history and is a source of enduring trauma for Dakota people.[14]

Yet for Pope and Congress the war was not over. Congress annulled all treaties with the Dakotas, leaving them without annuity goods at the critical moment when hunting was no longer viable. Hundreds of Dakotas fled north across the border into Canada where they forged ties with Hudson's Bay Company and mixed-race Métis traders who provided them with food, munitions, and sanctuary. Many others sought refuge among Lakotas in the West, and Pope resolved to extend the campaign to chase them down. That decision alone ensured that there would be no decisive victory for him. Instead of chasing down starving, weakened Dakota fugitives, Pope would have to engage the mighty Lakotas on their home terrain.[15]

An opportunity for some sort of closure materialized for Americans in July 1863, when Little Crow, now subsisting on raiding, returned to Minnesota to poach horses and was shot down by a settler. His body was scalped and decapitated and his bones became souvenirs. His skull, scalp lock, and forearms ended up on display in the Minnesota Historical Society and remained public curiosities until the early twentieth century.[16]

Holding bits of dead enemies may have placated some, but the settlers and soldiers in the interior soon realized that real closure would require many more battles and much bloodshed. The United States' war with the Sioux would continue and escalate for several more years. Before the famous Great Sioux War of 1876–77 there was another great Sioux war. That war, starting in Minnesota in 1862 and ending in Montana in 1868, has not found its proper place in the American collective memory because it overlapped with yet another war, a much larger one.

LIKE A COLD BLANKET

The Civil War was a cataclysmic clash over the future of the American republic, over whether it would be defined by slave labor, plantation capitalism, and states' rights or by free labor, industrial capitalism, and broad federal power. But the Civil War was also a continent-wide crisis of authority that saw scores of peoples—not only Southern states but also dozens of Native societies in the West—challenging the explosive growth of Northern state power. The Union—nineteen free and four border slave states—was changing at its very core into an imperial nation-state obsessed with land and authority and intolerant of alien ethnicities and competing sovereignties within its expanding borders. The Civil War both forced and enabled the United States to become a Yankee Leviathan capable of inflicting enormous harm to crush any rebellion, whether domestic or foreign. The most serious foreign rebellion erupted in the Indigenous West, staged by Lakotas and their allies.[17]

Pope's decision to escalate the war was prompted by personal disappointment—there had been no call for him to rejoin the main war—and it was the Union army's biggest misstep in the West. In the spring of 1863 Pope planned an ambitious two-pronged western campaign. One army of three thousand soldiers under Brigadier General Henry Sibley would push from the Minnesota River northwest into the prairies and drive the hostile Dakotas and their rumored Yankton allies into the Missouri Valley. The other force, consisting of twelve hundred cavalrymen under Brigadier General Alfred H. Sully, would move up the Missouri from Fort Randall to trap the Lakotas and cut off the westward-fleeing Dakotas and Yanktonais, ensnaring them between closing jaws. Many of Sibley's troops were Iowan farm boys and mechanics who wanted to fight Southern rebels. The news that they would be fighting the Lakotas instead dropped on them "like a cold blanket."

Pope's pincer movement was one of those attractive abstractions that was all but unattainable in the open grasslands. Sibley's men struggled to find the Sioux, and when they finally did, it was a disaster. In late July they made contact with Dakota and Yanktonai hunting bands some sixty miles east of the Missouri. They bungled the negotiations, and the Indians fled. Large numbers of Dakotas escaped into Canada, where they later became subjects of the British Crown. Yanktonais, more promisingly, fled west toward the Missouri and, as Pope had hoped, ran into a camp full of fighters. But the fighters were not Sully's men. They were Hunkpapas and Sihasapas who had unexpectedly crossed the Missouri to the east to hunt. These united Sioux warriors, numbering over two thousand, engaged Sibley's troops in two battles but had to disengage in the face of ripping artillery fire. They retreated toward the Missouri, moving slowly, burdened by more than a hundred wagons and carts filled with meat and hides. Sibley's troops caught them on the east bank. Hunkpapas and Sihasapas assembled bullboats and, in the dark, began swimming. Holding on to their horses' tails and biting ropes in their teeth, they pulled the boats across the river over and over again, taking nonswimmers and belongings to safety. They were not done when the sun rose, and the troops began firing at them from a bluff. Countless men, women, and children were shot and drowned. Lakotas watched from the opposite bank as the soldiers burned their wagons and winter food. Some of them reportedly recrossed the Missouri to trail the retreating Sibley, "stealing horses from him every night."[18]

Sully had been delayed by a drought that had shallowed the Missouri to the point that steamboat traffic became difficult. When he finally received his supplies in late August, news arrived that hostile Sioux were nearby. He sent out a scouting column that found the Indians in a ravine near Whitestone Hill some fifty miles south of where Sibley had fought his battles. Within moments, the scouts found themselves encircled by what seemed like thousands of warriors. Instead of killing the soldiers, however, the Sioux—Dakotas, Lakotas, Yanktons, and Yanktonais—wanted to talk, explaining that they were only interested in preparing supplies for winter. At sunset Sully arrived and, making his own conclusions of the situation, launched a cavalry charge into the Indian camp; he later claimed that the Sioux had taunted the soldiers by asking "why the whites wanted to come to fight them, unless they were tired of living and wanted to die." The soldiers kept chasing and shooting until they could no longer set apart soldiers from Indians. They killed nearly two hundred, which was not enough for Sully. "It is to be regretted that I could not have had an hour or two more of daylight," he wrote, "for I feel sure, if I had, I could have annihilated the enemy." Burning the lodges and hundreds of thousands of pounds of dried meat took the soldiers two days. Sully, who had married a Yankton woman five years earlier while serving at Fort Pierre, marched the captured Indians across the bone-dry plains to a prison camp on the Missouri below the Great Bend. The Sioux remember it as a death march. The shocked Dakotas believed that "our great father wanted to destroy all his children." Many of them sought safety in the West along and beyond the Missouri.[19]

THE FIRST FIGHT WITH WHITE MEN

The Union army had scored revenge for the Dakota uprising but only by provoking a far more dangerous rebellion in the West where Lakotas were ascending. Their agent's appraisal should have given the army a pause: "A powerful and warlike people, proud, haughty, and defiant; will average six feet in height, strong muscular frames, and very good horsemen." They were, he warned, "capable of doing much harm." A clash on the upper Missouri seemed to prove the agent right. A group of Hunkpapas and Sihasapas had sought safety from the U.S. troops along Burnt Wood Creek, far in the west. Already disgusted with the wašíču tactics, they saw a large mackinaw boat with a dozen or so miners and two women coming downriver. The miners shot an elder who was signaling the travelers to move quickly past them, and Lakotas began firing. The lumber boat lodged on a sandbar, and Lakotas killed all the men in it. They took the women with them, along with some two to three thousand dollars worth of gold nuggets, which they later used to buy munitions and blankets at Fort Berthold.[20]

While their Dakota and Yanktonai relatives were drawn into a deadly conflict with the United States, Lakotas raided the Missouri villagers for horses and fought an on-and-off-again war with the Crows and Assiniboines; they were not at war with the United States. They rendered the Missouri channel unpassable, cutting off the Crows from government annuities. "Our hearts are bad," the

Crow chief Great Bear warned U.S. agents. "The white man is no longer a friend to the Crow Indian."[21]

Much better than the Union generals, Great Bear understood how thoroughly Lakotas now ruled the high plains. And then Dakota refugees from Minnesota began arriving in the Powder River country, seeking asylum among northern Lakotas and alarming them to the new murderous bent of the wašíču soldiers. In the winter of 1863–64 Red Dog, a Hunkpapa who had married into an Oglala band, toured among Lakotas with a Dakota delegation, carrying a war pipe. Everywhere Dakotas asked people to join forces against the wašíčus, finding receptive audiences among nontreaty northern Lakotas. It became the year when "nearly all the Sioux Bands camped together." Moderate voices were silenced, and by the winter of 1864 Lakotas were ready for war—a war the Union was not ready to fight.[22]

Unlike their Dakota relatives, Lakotas and their allies occupied a strategically critical section of the continent where they could disrupt the Union's transportation avenues that supported its war effort in the East. For generations the expansion of the United States had hinged on two mutually reinforcing streams: people flowing west and extracted resources flowing east. The greater the western influx of emigrants, the greater the stream of resources, and the greater the concentration of wealth in the East. The Civil War jeopardized both streams, making their preservation vital for the Union.

Gold was the critical matter. Two new mineral fields—in Colorado and Montana—kept attracting prospectors, whose safety had to be guaranteed. The Union wanted an alternate overland line to the chronically endangered plains routes and moved to make the Missouri Valley secure for steamboats all the way to Fort Benton, where smaller land routes channeled miners into diggings. One look at the map revealed an elemental challenge: whether in the Nebraska and Dakota Territories or along the Missouri, thousands of Lakotas seemed poised to frustrate the plan. Already in August 1862 northern Lakota chiefs had announced to agent Latta that their 1856 treaty with Harney "only gave the right of way on the river for traders; that no emigration was ever contemplated either by land or water; and they would not submit to it, as emigrants brought disease and pestilence into their country." The Missouri Valley, Latta concluded, "would not be safe."[23]

That was how things stood in the spring of 1864. Lakota raiding parties began systematic attacks on overlanders, supply posts, and garrisons along the North Platte. To the south, along the Little Blue and Republican Rivers, Lakotas and Cheyenne Dog Soldiers burned farms and captured horses, cattle, and people across a three-hundred-mile radius: a vast war zone geared to stop American westward expansion in its tracks. Rumors spread among Union soldiers that the Confederate agents were inciting Lakotas and Cheyennes to attack them. Spotted Tail, the resilient Sicangu leader who had learned to speak and read English while imprisoned at Fort Leavenworth, tried to convince the army of his people's commitment to peace in a meeting on the North Platte. Wašíčus were not listening. "There was much unimportant talk not deemed essential," the army interpreter concluded his terse report of the meeting.[24]

While Spotted Tail was trying to assuage American fears, the War Department had already mobilized for battle. The army was keen, though not necessarily prepared, for the task. Pope and Sully—fierce and resentful rivals—were eager to win their way back into the Civil War's eastern theater and everyone around them seemed to clamour for Indian blood. The Sioux, moreover, did not seem to have the stomach for real battle, having caved before Sibley's and Sully's attacks. Forts would be the key to the military campaign. Sully had already built a new one, named after himself, more than a hundred miles up the Missouri and that much closer to Lakotas, and Pope wanted him to build more as he moved up the Missouri toward the Yellowstone. "At present," he wrote, "the Indian trading posts are established at points remote from military posts, so that Indians are offered inducements to keep away entirely from the military forces. The very opposite should be the object of the Government." Without realizing it, Pope was envisioning a policy change that would turn the fort, a colonial institution Lakotas had come to see as essential for their survival, into a menace.[25]

Sully's eighteen hundred men set off in June 1864, pushing up on the east bank of the Missouri and meeting little opposition. A peaceful Lakota contingent, perhaps to intimidate him, had informed Sully of a colossal village of six thousand belligerent warriors somewhere in the upper Heart River country, news that was corroborated by friendly Yanktonais who said the Heart River bands were "eager for a fight." The troops quickly pushed up the east bank of the Missouri to the Cannonball junction, where three fully loaded steamboats waited for them. There they connected with Colonel Minor Thomas's sixteen-hundred-strong Minnesota brigade that had in tow over two hundred settlers heading to Montana goldfields. Sully assigned Thomas's troops to build Fort Rice in a wooded area eight miles above the mouth of the Cannonball. Then his scouts located a village of fifteen to eighteen hundred tipis in the upper Cannonball. In a direct affront to the Lakota policy of territorial integrity, Sully decided to take the emigrants with him and had the steamers ferry everyone to the west bank. The roughly three-thousand-strong procession pushed up the north fork of the Cannonball in scorching heat. But the campsite was empty; the village had moved north. Sully pressed after them across a parched plain. "The water on the east side of the Missouri was a luxury compared to this," one lieutenant complained after having burned his tongue by drinking from a muddy alkali-rich pond. When the village was detected, Sully left the emigrant train behind and pushed north with twenty-two hundred men. The men were "elated."

Lakotas knew to expect them. Earlier, while pushing up the Missouri, Sully's troops had shot three Dakota warriors who had killed one of their engineers. The soldiers had cut off their heads, and Sully had ordered them hung on poles as a warning to other Indians. As he hoped, word had spread quickly across the plains. Sitting Bull, Four Horns, Inkpáduta, and other chiefs had begun to amass Hunkpapa, Sans Arc, Sihasapa, Minneconjou, Yanktonai, and Dakota warriors on the Knife River, and soon they had an army of some sixteen hundred men, ready to punish the wašíčus. When scouts found that the soldiers were coming, they moved the massive village of several thousand people northwest to the base of the rugged, thickly forested Killdeer Mountains, their chosen place to fight.[26]

With the ridges behind them, the Indians watched the soldiers dismount and form a large hollow square to shield their cannons, horses, and wagons. As the phalanx began to advance, they did nothing, allowing the broken dusty terrain in between to do its work. At last they began moving forward, forming a line to confront the wašíčus; "they took a good look at us," one officer reported. Lone Dog, who was "with a ghost" and invincible, rushed forward, "carrying a large war club, gorgeously ornamented." Others followed, testing the flanks of the square with swift, unpredictable mounted charges, but failed to breach it. The square, a lead-spitting fortress of flesh, kept inching ahead, forcing the Indians to retreat toward the village. They broke into small units to deny the wašíču riflemen a clear target. When the square came within cannon range of the lodges and the shelling began, they retreated into wooded ravines next to the village. They shifted into delaying fighting to give their families time to escape. Man Who Never Walked, crippled and eager to fight once in his life, sang his death song and charged toward the soldiers, lying on a horse-pulled travois. He was instantly shot. And then the Indians were gone, leaving robes, masses of pemmican, and nearly sixteen hundred lodges, all of which Sully had promptly burned. The soldiers found and shot a baby that had been left behind. They boasted they had killed more than a hundred warriors.

Behind the mountains began the Little Missouri Badlands, a bone-dry maze of layered, violently convoluted rock that had eroded into pinnacles, spires, cliffs, ridges, slumps, gorges, and ravines. The Indians rode deep into this desolate rocky labyrinth, knowing that they would hold all the advantages there. When the wašíčus came, now with the settler convoy, they set out to ruin the expedition. Wary of their cannons, they avoided battle, shadowing the soldiers for days,

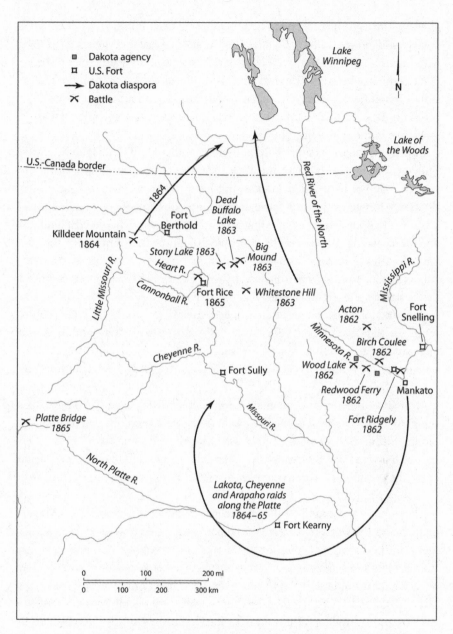

Dakota agency
U.S. Fort
Dakota diaspora
Battle

Lake Winnipeg

Lake of the Woods

N

U.S.-Canada border

Red River of the North

1864

Dead Buffalo Lake 1863

Fort Berthold

Killdeer Mountain 1864

Stony Lake 1863

Big Mound 1863

Heart R.

Little Missouri R.

Cannonball R.

Fort Rice 1865

Whitestone Hill 1863

Mississippi R.

Acton 1862

Fort Snelling

Minnesota R.

Birch Coulee 1862

Cheyenne R.

Wood Lake 1862

Fort Sully

Redwood Ferry 1862

Mankato

Missouri R.

Fort Ridgely 1862

Platte Bridge 1865

North Platte R.

Lakota, Cheyenne and Arapaho raids along the Platte 1864–65

Fort Kearny

0   100   200 mi
0   100   200   300 km

36. The First Great Sioux War, 1862–65, with major battles and movements of Dakota people marked. Map by Bill Nelson.

ghosting through the broken landscape, shooting from buttes and side canyons and stealing horses. Sully called the land "grand, dismal, and majestic," a "hell with fires put out." Only when rock gave way to grass did Lakotas relent. His expedition now reduced to a survival mission, Sully pushed west toward the Yellowstone. When he got there, the water had already fallen too low for steamers to reach the Powder River confluence, the planned site of a fort. Sully embarked downriver without building one.[27]

Impatient, decisive, supremely ambitious, and morally ambiguous, Alfred Sully was an embodiment of the United States' midcentury imperialism. He may or may not have hated Indians, but he certainly did not recognize their rights or sovereignty, looking through them into an infinitely more momentous affair, the real war that was unfolding, so frustratingly close, in the East. For him and for his nation, the Indians had become little more than a nuisance after the United States descended into a life-or-death struggle over its future. His campaign's sordid origins in a personal rivalry with Pope and its ambiguous ending in the badlands were a template for what was to follow.

The attack had been absolutely unnecessary. There would have been other routes to the Yellowstone Valley, but Sully, driven by private ambition and operating in an atmosphere of increasing Indian hating, decided to get there by fighting, by punishing Natives the War Department labeled as hostiles. By doing so, he created an enemy the Union could not afford to have and triggered a war that would continue, on and off, for more than a decade. The Hunkpapas remember Sully's attack as the "first fight with white men," the pictograph depicting Sitting Bull in close combat with a "white who was taking lands." Perhaps as many as three thousand Lakotas and their allies sought refuge in Canada along the Assiniboine River where they spent a humiliating year, stealing food from local farmers.[28]

The unprovoked assault on the Hunkpapas, Sans Arcs, Sihasapas, and Minneconjous was the worst move the War Department could have made at that moment. In the summer of 1864 the northern oyátes were like a tinderbox, which their leaders and Indian agents had so far managed to keep from igniting. They were the most militant of the Lakota oyátes, led by prominent war leaders like Sitting Bull and Gall—adopted brothers—who were deeply suspicious of the wašíčus and suffused by a powerful military ethos that pushed young men to establish themselves through war: Gall had built his reputation by surviving several bayonet stabbings and taking seven scalps in revenge at Fort Berthold. Like all Lakotas, the northern bands could sense that the bison herds were shrinking and they knew that the wašíčus, their inexhaustible reservoir of immigrants, their relentless robe trade, and their voracious steamboats, were to blame. By invading

37. Long Soldier winter count, 1864–65 (detail).
This winter count by an unknown keeper depicts
the "first fight with white men." The Sicangus,
Oglalas, and Minneconjous had clashed violently
with the U.S. Army in the mid-1850s, but for many
northern Lakotas Alfred Sully's attack at the Killdeer
Mountains marked the beginning of a prolonged, on-
and-off-again military conflict with the United States.
Courtesy of National Museum of the American
Indian, Smithsonian Institution (11/6720, detail).
Photo by NMAI Services.

their homelands, Sully set off all those trigger points, radicalizing an entire generation of Lakotas, including the now middle-aged Red Cloud.[29]

THE LITTLE END OF HIS LITTLE FINGER

The late summer and fall brought a retaliation. Lakotas, Cheyennes, and
Arapahos moved the war to the south and raided along the Platte Road for six
weeks, virtually paralyzing overland traffic. The stage line ceased to operate, and
mail to and from California had to travel via Panama. The army failed to engage
the mobile war parties even once. In a routine report, Major General Henry Halleck captured the magnitude of the challenge by penning a brief description of
the Sioux. Their alliance of "several strong and warlike tribes," he wrote, "claims
and roams over the vast region from the western frontier of Minnesota on the

east to the Rocky Mountains on the west, and from the frontier of Iowa and the line of the Platte River on the south to the British possession on the north." He then outlined, without fully realizing the gravity of the situation, the conditions that would frustrate the U.S. Army for more than a decade in the West: "the high latitude of the theatre of war in this department, the immense region of uninhabited country covered by military operations, and the vast distances from the frontier to be traversed before the enemy can be reached." Halleck was a military man preoccupied with logistics. There would have been a pithier way of capturing the challenge the army now confronted: waging a war against a hostile empire on foreign soil.[30]

Major General Samuel Curtis, commander of the Department of the Northwest, devised a plan. In late October, in the midst of a dry spell and southerly winds, Colonel R. R. Livingston, commanding the First Nebraska Cavalry, set that plan in motion at Fort Kearny. He ordered cavalry detachments to follow the south bank of the Platte for two hundred miles, stop at short intervals, and set the grass on fire. Unable to defeat the nomads, the army had decided to burn them out. With favorable winds, Livingston hoped that the fire would consume the grasslands all the way to the Arkansas Valley and deliver a crippling blow to bison herds. While the plan itself was misguided—fires actually stimulate grass growth, and strategic burns had been part of Plains Indians' resource management repertoire for generations—its maliciousness was palpable and unlikely to escape Lakotas. Soon U.S. agents awakened to a shocking reality: Lakotas and their allies had united "to drive the whites away from the Platte, & block the Overland & mail route." It seemed to them that Lakotas, overtaken by a "fiendish disposition," sought to "exterminate all the whites in that country." Lakotas were moving toward war to stop wašíču-induced environmental degradation and to preserve their way of life.[31]

Then, in dead of winter, Cheyenne and Arapaho people from the south began arriving in Lakota villages. Their hands and feet were frozen and their hair was short and many had bloody cuts on their thighs. They put their hands on the heads of Lakota chiefs, asking to be pitied. Hundreds of Colorado Volunteer forces led by Colonel John Chivington had razed their village at Sand Creek, murdering more than 150 of their people, mostly women, children, and the elderly. The wašíčus had killed and scalped pregnant women and cut one of them open, ripped out the fetus, and scalped it. They had destroyed bodies, cutting out arms, legs, fingers, noses, breasts, genitals, and hearts, decorating their hats and uniforms with pieces of humans. Lakotas were horrified and outraged. Cheyennes and Arapahos were allies and kin, and Lakotas took in their pain.[32]

The allies shifted into offensive war. Cheyennes sent war pipes among Lakotas, Yanktons, Yanktonais, and Dakotas, and a Lakota messenger toured all winter camps, rekindling kinship ties and inviting people to fight the wašíčus. It may have been then that Lakotas first danced the Omaha dance, a demonstration of national unity. This may have also been when Red Cloud—a deep thinker and a proficient warrior whose reputation had been damaged by the killing of Bull Bear and who had been frequently passed over for the honor of shirt wearer—began to emerge as a galvanizing leader. In a council among Oglalas he argued for an all-out war that would stop U.S. encroachments. The wašíčus were symbolically fused into the category of thóka, enemy. Thereafter killing and counting coup on them would be as valuable as killing and humiliating Native enemies.[33]

Suddenly, just as the Confederate South was teetering toward collapse, the United States faced another daunting challenge to its authority. A huge Indigenous coalition, bolstered by a moral mandate to avenge, set out to obliterate the Americans. Lakotas and their allies were consumed by anger, but they maneuvered with conspicuous restraint. Although Lakotas had chosen the site of the battle, wašíčus had dictated the tactics at Killdeer Mountain, and it had led to shocking carnage, prompting Lakotas to recalibrate their military strategies. From now on they would hurt the wašíčus with hit-and-run attacks that emphasized mobility over firepower and debilitated the enemy piecemeal. Lakotas would still engage in large open battles but only when they had superior numbers, the advantage of terrain, or no other choice.

And so the alliance struck the United States where it was most visible and vulnerable: the Oregon Trail and the infrastructure that had developed around it. In January the disillusioned Spotted Tail led a large war party on a charge on Julesburg, an important overland station near the South Platte, killing several soldiers. As women led hundreds of packhorses loaded with plunder to a temporary village on the South Platte, war parties descended on the emigrant road, attacking overland columns, driving off entire herds of cattle, pulling down telegraph wires, and torching ranches and stage stations. The offensive culminated in late July on the North Platte where more than a thousand Lakota, Cheyenne, and Arapaho warriors converged around a heavily guarded bridge 130 miles upriver of Fort Laramie. The soldiers' situation was hopeless. Lieutenant Caspar Collins was ordered to lead a detail to escort a wagon column across the bridge. He put on his dress uniform and rode to his death, and the Indians launched a mass attack on the exposed wagon train. Travel and freighting along the Oregon Trail once again ground to a halt, leaving Denver utterly isolated from the East. As they had a decade earlier, the United States' ties to the West became dangerously frail.[34]

Simultaneously in the north a "heavy force" of Hunkpapas, Minneconjous, Sihasapas, Sans Arcs, Two Kettles, Yanktonais, and Cheyennes attacked the U.S. forts. Berthold and Rice fell under siege. Already in January 1865 the commander of the former reported that there were hundreds of Sioux and Cheyenne lodges between his post and Fort Rice. He himself had but forty-nine soldiers in an "ill-constructed stockade, easily fired, hard to defend, cut off from water (in case of an attack), isolated from the rest of the world without the means of communication with any other point, and in the heart of the hostile Sioux country." The garrison's sense of dread was magnified by the arrival of Canadian trading columns. "Bearing the English flag," they brought in "sleigh loads" of ammunition, while urging the Indians "commence by attacking this place." [35]

Sioux needed little prodding. Fueled by disgust over the repeated wašíču atrocities, they harassed the forts for months, attacking loggers and herders and preventing the soldiers from hunting but refraining from risky mass attacks. Sitting on the Mníšoše's west bank, Fort Rice was a flagrant violation of Lakota territorial sovereignty, which revolved around river valleys and other resource domains. Lakotas fixed on starving the soldiers out; many died of scurvy during the winter. But then, in July, alarming news came: General Sully was approaching the fort and had sent runners to warn that he "would make war" on those who continued the siege. Fearing another Killdeer, many lost heart and wanted to give up the fight, but Sitting Bull rode through the different camps, "crying out that he was just from Fort Rice" where Sully had killed "all those that had come in and given themselves up." Sitting Bull's fabrication allowed him to mobilize three hundred warriors for an attack on Fort Rice. For several hours the warriors charged at the fort, only to be repulsed repeatedly by infantry fire and howitzer shelling. Lakotas withdrew west toward the Powder River country, fighting a rearguard action against two thousand trailing soldiers in scorching heat. They retreated high up the Powder where Red Cloud's Oglalas and Little Wolf's Cheyennes had camps. The combined Lakota-Cheyenne force sent the wašíčus into a hasty retreat. [36]

In early fall a Hunkpapa delegation visited Fort Rice. They told the soldiers there that it had been Sitting Bull and The Man That Has His Head Shaved who had led the first wave of attacks on the fort but had then "decamped," retreating behind the lines to tend to stolen horses. Sitting Bull, it seemed, had run away from battle and had been whipped for cowardice in his village. They said he "only lived by the little end of his little finger." [37]

Even if he did, Sitting Bull had a powerful vision for his people and the will and dexterity to see it realized. What mattered at Fort Rice was not so much the outcome but the fact that Lakotas were fighting in the first place. Since Killdeer the peace movement had gathered momentum among the Lakotas. Many were willing to consider farming life in reservations and to give up the hunt and raiding. Sitting Bull believed that this spelled the cultural death of the Lakota people, who constituted the Buffalo Nation, Thathą́ka Oyáte. He needed to maneuver decisively and creatively because the end of the Civil War had ushered in a new continental order.[38]

The United States emerged from the catastrophic war not as a nation but as an empire. The rebelling states remained on maps as before the war, but in reality they were captive territories under military occupation and governance. Acting without any political precedent—how does a failed republican state reunite?— the federal government set out to reconstruct the South after its own image. This was the era of authoritative government agents tasked to impose industrial capitalism, yeoman farming, democracy, and Christian civilization on a vast canvas. "We are to have the charge of this continent," declared the Reverend Henry Ward Beecher. "This continent is to be from this time forth governed by Northern men, with Northern ideas, and with a Northern gospel." It was a for-mula for a comprehensive reconstruction that would simultaneously target both the Southerners and Native Americans. There would two reconstructions, one focused on the rebuilding and reforming the South, the other on pacifying the Indigenous West.[39]

LITTLE HEAPS OF DIRT

The reconstruction of Indigenous America had to start with the rebellious Lakotas and their allies, and the first challenge was to agree how to achieve it. Several generals insisted that force alone would make Indians give up raiding and settle down, but many eastern politicians and philanthropists, sickened by the Sand Creek massacre, argued that moral education was the only justifiable course. Congress sided with the humanitarians and appointed, in March 1865, Senator James R. Doolittle, a staunch Baptist and patriot, to lead a joint special committee to investigate the state of Indian-white affairs in the West. It autho-rized commissions to negotiate new treaties with the plains tribes, including the Sioux. The Sioux commission was headed by Newton Edmunds, governor of the Dakota Territory, who was desperate to put an end to the Indian wars that hindered white settlement in his territory, blocking its path to statehood. Pres-sure came also from Nebraska to the south, where the construction of the Union Pacific Railroad was poised to start in Omaha, making Lakota appeasement a matter of national importance.[40]

Repeatedly humbled by nomad warriors over the years, generals denounced the congressional version of the Indigenous reconstruction as lily-livered and misguided. Sully and Sibley wanted to keep the pressure on the Lakotas, and Pope, in charge of military operations in the Dakota Territory, was deeply cynical of the logic of offering new treaties to the plains tribes. How will they understand treaties and annuities he asked, if "the violation of former treaties and the murder of whites are to be thus compensated?" As he saw it, treaties actually boosted Lakota raids. "It is a common saying with the Sioux, that whenever they are poor, and need powder and lead, they have only to go down to the overland routes and murder a few white men, and they will have a treaty to supply their wants." Pope was not entirely wrong. Since the opening of the Oregon Trail in the mid-1840s, Lakotas had tolerated overland traffic because it yielded resources, whether secured through trading, raiding, extortion, or, as Pope now claimed, through treaty goods.[41]

When Edmunds boarded a steamboat heading up the Missouri into the Lakota country in October 1865, he was thus under a heavy burden to negotiate binding treaties that would domesticate the Lakotas, satisfy the army, and make the West safe for settlers. He had sent runners beforehand, asking different bands to meet the commission along the river. The first stop was among Yanktons on the lower Missouri where the commissioners made their agenda clear. "The President has had a great war with the rebels, secessionist, but the rebels have laid down their arms and that war is over," Major General Samuel Curtis explained through an interpreter. If the Sioux, too, were ready for peace, the president would "give it to them." But he also wanted his Indian allies to join him in a war against tribes that rejected his peace offer. Sidestepping the many unprovoked Union attacks against the Sioux in the previous two years, Curtis laid out a clear choice: you are either friendly or hostile, either for or against the United States.

A Yankton headman Struck by the Ree responded. "I am your friend. . . . In my whole body, I think, I am pure American. It is not to me that you have to tell such things. It is to other nations" — most likely Lakotas — "that you should tell the things you mention about fighting against the whites." The options Curtis had offered were meaningless to Yanktons who nine years earlier had ceded 96 percent of their lands and were now utterly dependent on annuities. "To-day I stand in a situation the same as a hog, ready to take a handful of anything just as it is thrown to him." "My Great Father's young men (agents) trample on me and keep me down." The commissioners granted the starving and "friendly" Yanktons a right to hunt buffalo on their ceded lands and extended them loans of flour, bacon, and hard bread against their annuities. They handed them six peace pipes and asked them if they wanted to be removed elsewhere, a better farmland "where the rain falls." Struck by the Ree said no.[42]

When the commissioners turned to the Sicangus, Hunkpapas, and Two

Kettles, who were also present, Struck by the Ree's angry resignation gave way to the detached confidence of Lakotas. "I do not know," was Sicangu chief Iron Nation's response to the question whether his people were friendly or hostile. And when asked whether he would attend a final peace conference at Fort Sully, he said, "My children are starving, and I cannot be up there." Another chief, The Frog, would represent the Sicangus. But later, when the council commenced at Fort Sully in early October, Iron Nation was there and as elusive as ever. Curtis asked him to name the Sicangu bands and their head chief—crucial information that helped the army control and discipline Indians—and Iron Nation named The Frog, adding that he was "out in the country." When Curtis demanded to know where this mysterious chief lived, Iron Nation deadpanned, "Everywhere; wherever he is." And so, just like that, Iron Nation became the Sicangu nego-tiator, having revealed almost nothing of the people he now represented.[43]

He negotiated hard. When the commissioners introduced an article estab-lishing a universal peace in the plains, Iron Nation outright rejected it, saying that "it is well enough for us to make peace with the whites, but among these dif-ferent tribes of Indians there are many crazy fools." Those people could not think right and embrace Lakotas, and Sicangus would have to fight them. Another article confirmed the well-established government practice of paying Lakotas for rights-of-way through their lands, and the Sicangus received the largest per-capita sum, awarded, bafflingly, for "good behavior." The key article—the estab-lishment of a reservation—conformed to Lakota tradition. The commissioners emphasized that a reservation would not interfere with free movement and the chase. In Lakota thinking hunting rights and unrestricted mobility underwrote sovereignty, and so Iron Nation readily accepted a reservation. When Sibley offered assistance in selecting a site, Iron Nation rebuffed him: "We want to select for ourselves. We know where the corn will grow." He chose two hundred square miles along the White River, the center of the traditional Sicangu do-main.[44]

The commissioners believed that they were remolding the Lakotas into farmers living on confined parcels of land and dependent on American goodwill. Their belief was understandable because Lakotas were indeed transmuting. Since the previous comprehensive treaty talks with the United States fourteen years earlier at Horse Creek, the Lakota world had changed drastically. The wašíčus had in-serted themselves into their lives through agencies, armies, roads, diseases, and war. Bison herds were thinning out and the threat of starvation had become com-monplace. Wašíču presence, many Lakotas realized, had become a fact of life that had to be accommodated. Along with many other Lakota leaders, Iron Na-tion was doing just that but on his own terms. His Sicangus had already taken the radical step of experimenting with corn farming to stave off hunger, and they would accept larger wašíču presence in the form of agents and annuities. Other bands embraced different novelties. Sicangu headman Little Pheasant had accepted the wašíčus' paper and treaty diplomacy and now insisted on having "all my half-breeds with me ... for they can read papers."[45]

Most of the Lakota leaders involved in the negotiations were what U.S. agents called nonmilitants, people who had not fought Sully or Sibley or raided emigrants on overland trails; the openly anti-U.S. chiefs like Sitting Bull, Red Cloud, and Crazy Horse shunned the talks. Americans were negotiating with only a small portion of the Lakotas. Yet, determined to secure the existing overland roads and survey new ones, the commissioners pressured the chiefs to sign treaties that would replace the 1851 Horse Creek Treaty. Claiming control by virtue of technological supremacy, Curtis insisted that the Missouri "was made for steamboats, and they must be allowed to go up and down it." Carefully, he also suggested a new "shorter route through this part of the country" into the Rockies. Throughout the talks Lakotas had been anxiously curious about piles of earth the U.S. soldiers had left behind while moving about. Curtis now revealed that "these little heaps of dirt have been piled up through here to mark where the road may be." They "will do you no harm," he reassured the chiefs.[46]

In the end the commissioners concluded seven treaties with the smaller Lakota bands and two with the Yanktonais. When Iron Nation signed, he touched the pen six times "for each of the charges he had brought against the whites; then casting a withering glance at the commission he turned and left the tent." Like the other chiefs, he resented the talks he had not wanted. The final accords were a compromise that satisfied neither side. They did not involve land cessions but made the tribes "subject to the exclusive jurisdiction and authority of the United States," an abstraction that held little meaning on the ground. A more consequential article obliged the Lakotas and Yanktonais to withdraw from all existing and future overland roads across their lands. The commissioners knew this would bring trouble, but they included the article nonetheless.[47]

ACTIVE AND VIGOROUS HOSTILITIES

The 1865 talks were an exercise in empire building. The American Union, restored through a massive war that had claimed more than six hundred thousand soldiers, was poised to expand again, ready to pick up where it had left off. The northern half of the reunited country was flush with wartime growth—factories, industries, and businesses were all booming—and the 1862 Homestead Act provided a template for orderly westward expansion of settlement, led by handsomely subsidized railroads. Washington, D.C., its population doubled by the war, was now the seat of a supremely confident imperial nation eager to realize its transcontinental future through territorial expansion. As the Civil War gave way to Indian wars, the United States slipped into a state of perpetual war.[48]

By the sheer weight of its population—over thirty million and counting—the United States should have been able to simply shove aside any resisting Natives, but it could not. For all its material prowess, the post–Civil War United States was an administrative and military midget. The war-weary federal government reduced the army from a million to thirty thousand men, rendering westward expansion exceedingly tenuous. From 1862 on the Union Army had been fighting two sprawling wars—one against the Confederate South and the other against the Plains Indians—and when the first war transformed into a full-scale military occupation in 1865, the other raged on. Comanches and Apaches raided across the Southwest borderlands, frustrating the United States' modernizing plans for the region, while Cheyennes and Arapahos killed whites to avenge Sand Creek. But it was Lakotas who posed the gravest threat: with their substantial numbers and extensive range, they held America's westward expansion hostage. Secretary of the Interior James Harlan agonized about how strange and frustrating this persisting Indigenous rebellion appeared from Washington, D.C.:

> The Indians of the plains, who subsist chiefly on buffalo, follow them on their migration toward the north in the early part of the summer, and return in autumn, spreading over the western part of the State of Kansas and the Territories of Nebraska, Dakota, Montana, and Colorado. Influenced by the unfriendly Indians of the southwest, and probably incited by rebel emissaries, they maintained active and vigorous hostilities. Our defenceless frontier settlements were harassed; the communication between the Mississippi Valley and our possessions on the Pacific seriously interrupted; emigrant and government trains assailed; property of great value destroyed, and men, women, and children barbarously murdered.[49]

The downsized army tottered under the pressure. The officers who shifted from the Civil War to Indian wars were, by and large, dedicated and hardened soldiers, but many of them were also very young—the brutal mechanized war had taken a heavy toll among the upper ranks—and they struggled with the transition. Desertions shrunk the enlisted force by up to 20 percent per year, which meant that a considerable part of the force was constantly inexperienced. So prevalent were desertions that commanding officers believed that many were using the army merely as a means of transportation to the West. Yet for all its troubles, the army remained the nation's best safeguard against the "vigorous hostilities" that seemed to be engulfing the plains.[50]

Such was the sense of vulnerability and victimhood among the white Americans that a "policy of the total destruction of the Indians" was being "openly advocated by gentlemen of high position, intelligence, and personal character," Harlan wrote, disapprovingly. It was not only morally repulsive but too expensive: "The attempted destruction of three hundred thousand of these people, accustomed to a nomadic life, subsisting upon the spontaneous productions of the earth, and familiar with the fastnesses of the mountains and the swamps of the plains, would involve an appalling sacrifice of the lives of our soldiers and frontier settlers, and the expenditure of untold treasure." The moment the Confederate South collapsed, an imagined nomad barrier emerged from behind it to block the creation of a single unified nation.[51]

This was the backdrop of General Curtis's little heaps of dirt. Traumatized by the carnage of the Civil War, most Americans had no stomach for wholesale slaughter of Natives, which forced the government to negotiate with the Indians. Washington's paramount ambition was to complete the badly delayed consolidation of a transcontinental nation by stitching its eastern and western halves together by wagon roads and iron bands. Lakotas and their allies would have to allow surveys and roads in their lands; the piles of earth delineated the coordinates of a new infrastructure that would secure America's future. The treaties Lakotas signed in the fall of 1865 thus carried an enormous weight. They would not only allow the United States to fulfill its continental destiny but also save the Lakotas themselves from destruction.[52]

The 1865 treaties also subjected the Lakotas to the age-old imperial strategy of arranging Native peoples into manageable categories. Thereafter, in the minds of U.S. officials, there would be hostile Lakotas and friendly Lakotas. The hostiles were what imperial agents saw as raw savages—wild, backward, inherently violent, and untrustworthy—whereas the friendlies were redeemable savages capable of coexistence and worthy of civilization programs that would deliver them into the fold of Christian agrarianism. The friendly-hostile dichotomy was intentionally crude because it served to simplify things for Indian agents and soldiers who were tasked with navigating the complex world of the Indigenous West. Friendly Lakotas made treaties and negotiated over railroads, overland trails, and land. Hostile Lakotas were legitimate targets, sieved out of good Indians for the army to chase down. During the talks Governor Edmunds left little doubt what this meant: "There is now no middle course for you to pursue. Now is the time for you to state in plain terms whether you will agree to make peace ... or whether you intend to continue the war."[53]

There was a certain kind of brilliance to the American approach to the Lakota problem. For centuries European imperial powers had struggled to control Indigenous powers by identifying accommodating leaders they could co-opt and work with. It was a prodigious challenge destined to fail as the Americans knew so little about the inner workings of the Indigenous societies they meant to control. Now, under the threat of war, Americans transferred the task of sorting out good Indians from bad ones to Lakotas themselves. Lakotas, as both individuals and as groups, would have to decide whether they were friendly or hostile, with the United States or against it. As the Edmunds commission presented it, it was a choice between death and survival.

TENDING TOWARD EXTERMINATION

Montana mines tantalized the post–Civil War United States, yielding millions worth of gold dust and nuggets year after year, a much-needed revenue stream for a nation desperate to rebuild itself. Washington was in a hurry—the success of Reconstruction depended on both momentum and money—and it needed to render the gold stream secure. The main route to Montana was the steamboat line to Fort Benton where wagons took prospectors up to the mountains. Another route followed the Oregon Trail deep into the Rockies and then curved northeast, skirting the Lakota lands that lay east and north of the Bighorn Mountains.

Already in 1863 John Bozeman, a struggling Montana prospector, had led a small group of hopefuls from Fort Laramie to Virginia City in the northern Rockies. It promised to become an exhilarating shortcut to gold, saving hundreds of miles of travel, but it cut straight through the Lakota country and required crossing the Powder, Little Bighorn, Bighorn, and Yellowstone Rivers, the heart of the Lakota world. A Lakota-Cheyenne party forced most of the invaders to turn back, but Bozeman managed to escort a small contingent of men to Virginia City. The next year a party of 150 wagons and 467 men blazed through the Lakota country, managing to fend off an Indian attack with state-of-the-art rapid-fire breechloaders.

Then, in the fall of 1865, as treaty talks were unfolding along the Missouri, the army dispatched 2,500 troops and 179 Pawnee and Omaha Indian scouts to secure the Bozeman Trail—Edmunds's "shorter route through this part of the country." Brigadier General Patrick Connor—who in 1863 had overseen a massacre of some 250 Shoshones on Bear River in Washington Territory—authorized the troops to kill every male Indian over the age of twelve. A joint Lakota-Cheyenne-Arapaho attack near the Little Powder River stopped the main slaughter column and sent it into a miserable retreat through a snowstorm. The retreating soldiers, confounded by the broken terrain, their large slow-moving columns, and the enemy's scorched-earth tactics and guerrilla attacks, lost huge

numbers of horses and mules: Lakotas remembered the encroachment as a bonanza. Yet the army had staked its claim: on the upper Powder Valley a lone post,
soon to be named Fort Reno, now proclaimed the wašíču̇s' intention to have
their road.[54]

Lakotas would not allow it. The Oregon Trail had taught them how wašíču
mass migration harmed the environment, animals, and humans by exhausting
forage, polluting streams, and smuggling in deadly germs. Lakotas had effectively
given up parts of the worn-out Platte Valley, but they would not yield more. Their
vast domain—their empire—was a tapestry of river basins, highlands, lowlands,
and plains, and they needed every part of it intact, as each bestowed on them a
specific source of resources, refuge, and sacred power. Some Americans could
see this but thought it was hopeless, for gold had taken hold of the nation's imagination. Lakotas and their allies, Edmunds wrote a year after his treaty-making
tour, "will not peaceably submit to our intrusion" and thought that no law or
treaty could stop "the diffusion of whites over Indian country, especially if gold is
supposed to exist in any appreciable quantities."[55]

But as long as the diffusion remained limited, peace through wólakȟota was
still possible. In the spring of 1866 Red Cloud sent word that he wanted to talk,
and by late spring two thousand Indians were camping near Fort Laramie. Commissioner Edward Taylor described the negotiations "as important in its results
to the country as any that has ever been effected." Lakotas and Americans had
coexisted in the West for generations, their respective regimes entangling around
each other, infiltrating power into the gaps and blind spots that marked both
regimes. Building on that history, Red Cloud, the very embodiment of a "hostile," formulated a new vision for Lakota-U.S. relations. Together with Oglala
headman They Fear Even His Horses and Sicangu leaders Spotted Tail and
Red Leaf, he let it to be understood that "a treaty could and would be made"
to sanction the Bozeman Trail. If the U.S. government controlled the emigrants
and supplied Lakotas with guns, goods, and food, coexistence could be possible. Rather than a flashpoint, the new overland trail could become what Fort
Laramie had been for decades: a nucleus of common ground where Lakotas and
wašíču̇s could come together as allies and kin. Americans saw a stunning opportunity here, for they believed that the diplomatic Spotted Tail "is always with Red
Cloud, and they two rule the [Lakota] nation."[56]

But then the wašíču̇s botched it, spectacularly so. In June, just as Red Cloud,
They Fear Even His Horses, and Spotted Tail were patiently forging a consensus among Lakotas, Colonel Henry B. Carrington approached the fort on
the Oregon Trail with seven hundred soldiers, wagonloads of construction materials, and a thousand head of beef cattle. He was heading into the Powder River

country to build more forts, and he told Lakotas so: he was introduced to them as the "White Chief going up to occupy Powder River, the Big Horn country, and the Yellowstone." Lakotas were shocked. If Carrington had wanted to provoke them, he succeeded. Appalled by the sheer arrogance of the act, Red Cloud was also baffled by the wašíčus' carelessness with words. "'The Great Father sends us presents and wants us to sell him the road," he said, "but White Chief goes with soldiers to steal the road before the Indians say Yes or No.'" The wašíčus seemed to have ended all dialogue. "Every chief to whom I was thus introduced," Carrington reported, "treated me coldly." Lakotas broke off the talks and left for the Powder River country. They sent a message that they would attack any intruders. Yet the commissioners claimed that they had concluded treaties that satisfied both sides. It was a fabrication. Treaties were signed, but mostly by agency bands who represented a small minority of the Lakotas.[57]

With that the nontreaty Lakotas, the groups of real power, became abstracted into "hostiles," and the army had its war, one that, according to a distressed commissioner of Indian affairs, was "tending toward extermination." Lakotas and their allies retreated far up into the Powder River country where they waited, preparing. The 1866 Oglala Sun Dance on the Tongue River transformed into a war council. There were rumors that Spotted Tail had signed a treaty with the Americans at Horse Creek, and many civil leaders were wavering. They Fear Even His Horses did not want war but, in a display of a refined sense of duty, threw his considerable political weight behind Red Cloud and his hard line. Red Cloud was recognized as supreme war chief, *blotáhuŋka átaya*, the first among equals, and bestowed with the tribal war pipe. His influence and moral authority now began to extend among other nontreaty bands for, as the southernmost oyáte along with the Sicangus, the Oglalas formed a vanguard against an aggressive wašíču frontier that seemed poised to leap into the heart of the Lakota empire and shatter it. In an apocryphal scene, Captain William J. Fetterman allegedly boasted that he could ride through the whole Sioux nation with eighty men.[58]

Lakotas did not have to wait long. Within a month after the Laramie talks, the soldiers were erecting a six-hundred-foot-by-eight-hundred-foot stockade sixty-seven miles northwest of Fort Reno at the east edge of the Bighorn Mountains in the heart of the Lakota territory. They named it Fort Phil Kearny. A month later another fort, C. F. Smith, began to rise where the Bozeman Trail crossed the Bighorn River, ninety miles northwest of Fort Phil Kearny. These were flagrant violations of the Horse Creek Treaty and Red Cloud's warnings; yet Lakotas did not engage. The previous winter had been unusually cold, and they had lost many horses. Rather than attacking the forts themselves, Lakotas raided the army's horse corrals for new mounts.

Lakotas were also seeking new gun markets because arms trade at Fort Laramie had been banned in 1864. Their greatest assets—numbers, diplomatic dexterity, and an ability to transmute—carried them through. In less than two years they had turned the Powder River country into a major commercial hub. Red Cloud drew in Wágluȟes, descendants of Oglala-white marriages, who still received munitions from the Americans at Fort Laramie, and negotiated temporary trade truces with the Crows, who had ties with itinerant traders in Montana Territory, pulling a fiercely determined enemy group on the Lakota orbit; just two years earlier Crow chiefs had "offered the services of all the Warriors of their nation" to the U.S. Army if it helped them drive the Lakotas out of the Powder River country. But the main source of guns was in the north where the independent-minded Métis were building an expansive trading network. Supplied by the Hudson's Bay Company, they sold guns across the unmarked international border and carried back bison robes. Renowned for their martial prowess, they gravitated toward the ascendant Lakotas who could generate a substantial robe output. Soon the Métis operated across the Lakota domain, and many of them became fluent in Lakota. "They come with carts and wagons loaded with goods, powder, and arms to trade with these Indians," Sully complained, "and urge them to commit depredations against our people, so that they may have all the fur trade.... They frequently plant the English flag on the banks of the Missouri in a defiant manner."[59]

The relative quiet along the Bozeman Trail thus concealed an ominous development. Lakotas had responded to the wašíču aggression with an intensive burst of action, expanding their empire into a burgeoning cosmopolitan nexus that transcended international boundaries, amassed state-of the-art weaponry through far-reaching trade links, and harnessed the hostile-friendly taxonomy, a key U.S. colonial tool, to serve their own interests. Americans did not know it yet, but Lakotas had overshadowed them in the deep interior in diplomatic reach and sheer military might. The American mindset seemed at once flippant and hazily concerned. In late fall of 1866 a group of eastern politicians and celebrities witnessed a clash between Lakotas and Pawnees near the Platte Valley. "The shock of meeting was grand and terrific," reported Silas Seymour, a Union Pacific Railroad engineer, who was relieved to see the Pawnees prevail. It was a mock battle, a slice of western exotica intended as an education and entertainment, but it left the engineer uneasy: "What then must be the terrible reality?"[60]

Americans found out soon enough. While stockpiling horses and guns, Lakotas and their allies launched constant raids against the Bozeman Trail forts, their supply and wood details, and their horse and cattle herders; Fort Phil Kearny alone was hit more than fifty times in five months. Lakotas could see how the attacks, interspersed with quiet lulls, agitated the soldiers, prompting them into rash pursuits. A few times they lured troops into ambushes and released brutal violence, but, disappointedly, the wašíčus seemed timid and unwilling to commit to large battles.[61]

While Americans huddled in forts, their horses growing weak for want of grass, most of the Lakotas and their allies moved freely and camped high up in the Powder River country, hunting bison, pasturing horses, and preparing arrows. Elders, chiefs, and warrior societies sent scouting parties to monitor the soldiers, pooled information, and strategized. Women prepared robes, dried meat, and nurtured the moral health of the village, readying the men for battle, and warriors performed ceremonies and sought the proper mindset. Red Cloud and High Backbone, the blotáhuŋka átaya of the Minneconjous, consulted Crazy Horse and other leading warriors. After months of planning, the war council decided to force a mass battle with the wašíčus. They tested the American mettle on December 6, 1866, by attacking a wood train about two miles west of the Fort Phil Kearny. As they had hoped, soldiers poured out of the fort, hot for battle. The Indians retreated up the nearby hills where they stopped and surrounded a cavalry contingent, only to break off the fight at the sight of wašíču reinforcements. They had gathered what they wanted—a sense of the wašíču state of mind—and there was no need for further violence now. They left two mutilated bodies behind, a calculated cruelty bound to incite anger and retribution.[62]

In mid-December Lakotas and their allies began to congregate on the Tongue River, fifty miles north of Fort Phil Kearny. Winter was approaching and time was running out: the Indians needed to fight when their horses were still strong. On the nineteenth, flanked by Red Cloud and a line of blotáhuŋkas, High Backbone began moving up the Tongue with a war pipe, preparing the Lakota nation for war. Behind him rode some fifteen hundred Lakota, Cheyenne, and Arapaho warriors. The next day, as the column approached its target, a wíŋkte, a two-spirit person who possessed potent medicine power, began riding back and forth between the blotáhuŋkas and a range of hills behind which stood Fort Phil Kearny. Three times, riding frantically, the wíŋkte returned with disappointing news: they had seen only ten, then twenty, then fifty wašíču soldiers, not enough for the huge war party to engage. But the fourth return triggered an elation: there had been "a hundred or more." The wíŋkte lay down and was encircled by warriors who struck the ground around their hands, anticipating the coups that waited for them. The column moved forward and made camp ten miles north of the fort. The blotáhuŋkas chose Crazy Horse to lead a decoy party in the battle that would begin at dawn.[63]

The key to High Backbone's plan was the Lodge Trail Ridge, a steep forested range about three miles northwest of Fort Phil Kearny. From there, facing south-west, the Indians could see the frozen Big Piney Creek meandering below, and to the west spread out a cluster of heavy timber, a pinery that wašíču woodcutters visited almost daily. This was where they would engage the soldiers and lure them across the ridge into a flat area where the trap would be sprung. On the morning of the twenty-first the wood train appeared as expected, and a decoy party had it quickly surrounded. An anxious lull ensued, but then the Indians saw what they had hoped for: soldiers filing out of the fort, marching and riding with pur-pose. Auspiciously, the troops did not move toward the besieged wood detail but straight toward the Lodge Trail Ridge. Soon a large contingent was moving up Big Piney Creek. The warriors disengaged from the wood train and rushed north-westward to join the main body behind the Lodge Trail Ridge.[64]

There the trap was being readied. With the main body waiting on the frozen ridge, the decoys below perched on the north bank of the Big Piney. One of the decoys turned himself into a target by wearing a red blanket and sitting against a tree, and Crazy Horse, leading from the front, executed the critical maneuver. Riding hard, he led his decoys up the ridge. The cavalry contingent of the wašíču horde, twenty-seven men, rode after them, followed by a larger group of foot soldiers far back. Crazy Horse wanted as many wašíčus as possible on the ridge and had the decoys yelling taunts and feigning that their horses were worn out. Once all the cavalry had crested the ridge, Crazy Horse ordered his party to speed up and rush downhill toward the flat. When the last wašíču horse soldiers reached the plain, the decoy party split into diverging lines and turned back, riding the opposite direction along both sides of the cavalry. Hidden in the gul-lies and grass on both sides of the flat, pinching their horses' nostrils to silence their neighing, hundreds of Oglala, Minneconjou, Cheyenne, and Arapaho war-riors waited for the decoy lines to converge behind the wašíčus, the moment of attack. In a matter of seconds, an Indigenous army materialized from the broken grassy ground, ensnaring the enemy. Farther back on the ridge, the wašíču foot soldiers saw the ambush and sought cover.

The Bozeman Trail ran across the flat, and the Indians began the killing along the road that had caused the war. They surrounded the cavalry, firing at them below their ponies' necks while riding hard. The fall of a wašíču leader sent the horsemen into a rushed retreat up the ridge, their escape covered by civilian scouts armed with sixteen-shot repeating rifles. Fighting both on horseback and on foot, the Indians chased the fleeing cavalry, slaying them on the run. The horse soldiers rushed past the foot soldiers huddling behind a cluster of boul-ders, and the Indians fell on the exposed infantry. The warriors formed a circle around them and began launching volleys of arrows, killing scores of wašíčus but

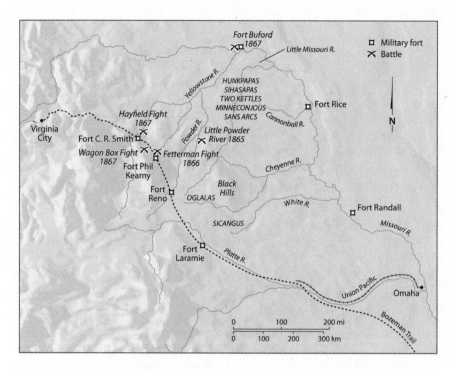

38. The First Great Sioux War, 1866–68, with the major battles along the Bozeman Trail and in the Power River Country marked. Map by Bill Nelson.

also some of their own. Seeing that the wašíču firepower had diminished—the men with repeating rifles had been disposed of—the chiefs ordered the warriors to engage in hand-to-hand combat. Fire Thunder, a sixteen-year-old Oglala warrior, killed six soldiers in a running attack with a pistol and bow. A single officer remained mounted, and Oglala warrior American Horse rode straight toward him, clubbed him down, and, dismounting, slashed his throat. The last foot soldiers were dead in a matter of minutes. The chiefs commanded all the warriors to engage the cavalry on foot. Sensing how things would end, the horse soldiers retreated on a steep narrow crest and cut their mounts loose. The Indians closed in on them, felling them with arrows, clubs, and bullets, and killed them all.[65]

Down at Fort Phil Kearny, Colonel Carrington, the fort commander, had heard the first shots beyond the Lodge Trail Ridge at noon. He dispatched Captain Tenodor Ten Eyck with seventy-six men to bring relief. The fighting stopped at 12:30, and Ten Eyck arrived in the battle site fifteen minutes later. The flat was filled with ecstatic Indians, and Ten Eyck could not see a single American soldier. The warriors signaled him to come down. But then the Indians left to the

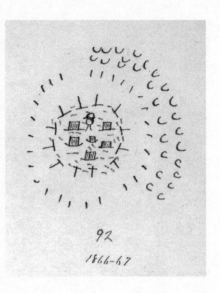

39. The American Horse winter count, 1866–67. "They killed 100 white men at Fort Phil Kearney," notes the pithy caption of this winter count of the Fetterman disaster. Not many counts recorded the fight. Courtesy of National Anthropological Archives, Smithsonian Institution. (NAA INV 08746932, detail).

north, and Ten Eyck entered the battlefield. He found the bodies of Captain Fetterman, the infantry commander, and Captain Frederick H. Brown: the two men seemed to have shot each other in the head. He found a mass of bodies suspended in monstrous shapes, many of them stripped of ears, noses, teeth, chins, fingers, hands, and feet, and he found eyes and brains placed on rocks: their bodies dismantled, these wašíčus would not see, hear, smell, eat, walk, feel, or think in the afterlife. The annihilation had taken place 150 miles north of Fort Laramie—150 invading miles, as Lakotas saw it—into their homelands.[66]

Four days later Oglalas celebrated their victory on the Tongue River. Red Cloud may not have played a role in the battle itself, but he was honored for his moral vision and leadership. A man of pointed words and forceful action, his great strength as a wartime leader was an ability to cut through the noise and focus on the essential. Lakotas and their allies were in a fight for survival, he insisted, but if they remained unified, the war could have a decisive conclusion: the complete and lasting banishment of the wašíčus from the Lakota world. The year 1866 entered an Oglala winter count as the year when "They killed 100 white men at Phil Kearney." The Oglalas and Minneconjous may have lost only eleven warriors. Yet the violence in the heart of the Lakota domain left scars. Black Elk, the influential Oglala wičháša wakháŋ who was three years old at the time, carried troubled memories of the carnage. "I can remember that winter of the Hundred Slain as a man may remember some bad dream," he recounted. "I had never seen a Wasicu then, and did not know what one looked like; but every one was saying that the Wasicus were coming and that they were going to take our country and rub us all out and that we should all have to die fighting." How he felt about the outcome he did not elaborate: "It was the Wasicus who got rubbed out in that battle."[67]

PUNISHED WITH VINDICTIVE EARNESTNESS

The battle had been fought over specific disputes with clear objectives. The U.S. Army wanted to secure free movement along the Bozeman Trail with forts, and the Indians wanted to get rid of both the emigrants and the forts to protect their "last, best hunting grounds." Lakotas and their allies had simply outwitted the army, but Americans immediately exoticized the battle as an atrocity beyond the pale. Fetterman, a Civil War combat veteran, became the symbol of a disaster that became known as the "Fetterman Massacre," a morally charged cry of victimhood that silenced Lakotas' reasons to fight and demonized them as murderous heathens. Humiliated, the army demanded revenge, and the government recognized a grave threat to the westward course of the empire. The forts would stay and the war would continue. Major General Grenville Dodge, one of the Civil War heroes of the Battle of Atlanta two years earlier, was assigned to pacify the Natives. He asked General William Tecumseh Sherman, commander of the vast Military Division of the Missouri, to send ten thousand troops to the West.[68]

The Fetterman Fight, the army's greatest defeat in the West as yet, should have been a lesson, but its emotional aftermath centered more on culpability than tactics. The army's heralded scientific approach to war dissipated into tetchy mudslinging. Carrington claimed that Fetterman, yearning to fight, had disobeyed his orders by crossing the Lodge Trail Ridge, but General Philip St. George Cooke, commander of the Department of the Platte, relieved Carrington from his post, only to be soon relieved himself by Commanding General Ulysses S. Grant who needed a scapegoat. Congress called for an investigation of the Fetterman disaster, and President Andrew Johnson appointed a high-powered special commission to conduct one under the direction of the secretary of the Interior. Careers and reputations were at stake, and emotions ran high.[69]

The search for guilty parties politicized and polarized the United States' Lakota policy, exposing old divisions between federal officials and army officers. One of the commission members, N. B. Buford, described the Fetterman Fight as "horrible," only to ask whether the invasion was "justifiable" and "in accordance with the laws and established customs of our intercourse with the aborigines[.] Have they not been treated as dependent nations?" Starting in April 1867 the commissioners met with Spotted Tail and other treaty chiefs, distributed more than three thousand dollars worth of horses, goods, and provisions, and, stunningly, "assigned them for the present for their hunting grounds all the country south of the Platte and north of the Smoky Hill route." It was a huge swath of land—a startled Spotted Tail declared that not all of it was "ours"—and may well have convinced many Lakotas of a wašíču capitulation. Indeed, anticipating an imminent extension of the Union Pacific Railroad to the base of the Rockies, Buford announced the Bozeman Trail "unnecessary" and insisted that "there is no necessity for an Indian war." Relying on a different arithmetic, Sherman articulated the army's position with ruthless detachment: "Of course, the massacre should be treated as an act of war and should be punished with vindictive earnestness, until at least ten Indians are killed for each white life lost," he wrote. "It is not necessary to find the very men who committed the acts, but destroy all of the same breed."[70]

Concrete practical solutions dissolved into the fault lines of political discord. Lakotas' greatest assets against the United States and its army were their superior mobility and intimate knowledge of the terrain. This should not have posed an insurmountable challenge to the American colossus, but it did. To subdue the nomads the army needed, depending on the estimate, from twenty-five to a hundred thousand soldiers in the northern plains, a commitment the federal government would not make. The long-awaited report of the Doolittle Committee had finally been published, and its message was clear: the Indians were dying and the government was to blame. The committee demanded an immediate reform of Indian policy, and the Johnson administration agreed. Sherman's demands for massive mobilization were ignored, and the army was left to face the Lakotas with what it had, which was far from enough. A week after the Fetterman disaster General Cooke reported that his officers were "not equal to their [Indians'] stratagems in the broken ground they know so well; their numbers, it seems now certain, are so very superior." Given the number and the quality of soldiers available to him, Cooke wrote off the Powder River country. It was necessary to suspend immigration to Montana, "our best new Territory of arable land as well as precious metals," through the Bozeman Trail, "this best route."[71]

Almost all civilian traffic stopped along the trail, which had become "too hot." Only heavily armed military trains moved along it, supplying Forts Phil Kearny, Reno, and C. F. Smith, whose only function now was to protect themselves against Indian attacks. A realization sunk in that forts were all but "worthless" in a war against hypermobile equestrian warriors. The Indians harassed wagon columns and blockaded forts, isolating the cavalry from wood, water, and grass. Hastily arranged peace talks at Fort Laramie failed, foiled by an impromptu U.S. Army attack against a Lakota-Cheyenne village in western Kansas, and Americans descended into bickering, the peace-minded officials blaming the generals for hawkishness, the generals insisting that diplomacy and annuities only financed hostilities. Sherman, increasingly despondent and cynical, began doubting the feasibility of westward expansion itself. "This enemy's country is a land as big as the whole settled United States," he confided in a moment of gloom, "and one may travel weeks, months, years without seeing an Indian, a pony, bush, tree or anything." His conclusion was clear: "We have no interest or desire to produce universal war on the Plains." Americans seemed profoundly uncertain how to run their western empire.[72]

WAR FOR EMPIRE

Lakotas, in the meanwhile, were rapidly expanding their own empire. While Oglalas, Sicangus, and Minneconjous fought the wašíčus and their forts along the Bozeman Trail, northern Lakotas continued to attack steamboats and raid and lay siege to U.S. forts along the upper Missouri where two new unauthorized garrisons, Buford and Stevenson, materialized just as the Powder River War was heating up. Incensed Lakota chiefs threatened to "'destroy all the whites in the country'" and sent messengers among their nonmilitant allies to "'keep out of the way.'" In the south, in the Platte and Republican River countries, Lakotas and their Cheyenne allies attacked all things American. U.S. agents believed that eight to ten thousand Indians might enter the field, wreaking "dreadful havoc," and Sherman wanted to simply assume that "all Indians, not on fixed reservation, are at war." Soon the building of the Union Pacific ground to a halt, its eleven-million-acre federal land grant suddenly rendered useless. In Colorado and Montana governors began preparing for Lakota campaigns, their "citizens clamorous for a war of extermination."

Alarmed army officers reported that Lakotas and Cheyennes were in a state of war and feared that they were cajoling Crows, Blackfeet, Arikaras, and Hidatsas to join them in fighting the Americans. Even Kiowas in the southern plains were reported to be seeking "a compact with the Sioux," gravitating away from the weakened Comanche empire toward the ascending Lakota one. General Christopher C. Augur, commander of the Department of the Platte, made a commiserating plea to Sherman for the protection of overland routes: "You have to look out for the interests of all your departments, and the wants of one, must at times, be made to give way to the needs of another." Sherman, palpably overwhelmed by "thieving bands that come from no one knows where and have gone in like manner," had ordered Augur to move most of his cavalry and infantry to protect Fort Phil Kearny against hostile Lakotas.[73]

All Lakota oyátes, it was clear now, were engaged in a single war against the wašíčus, and they needed synchronized policies to win it. Seen from the Lakota country, the U.S. invasion appeared a giant pincer movement with one flank advancing through the upper Missouri Valley and the other through the Oregon and Bozeman Trails, poised to link up somewhere along the Yellowstone to clasp the Lakotas. Escaping that clasp may have seemed the only judicious thing to do, but Lakotas did the exact opposite. They stayed put. Then they shifted shape.

In the spring of 1867 a massive council took place north of the Powder River forks. Northern Lakotas—Hunkpapas, Minneconjous, Sans Arcs, Two Kettles, and Sihasapas—dominated the meeting ground, but the Oglalas, Yanktonais, and Cheyennes had also sent delegates. Four Hunkpapa shirt wearers carried a stocky, sinuous man on a buffalo robe into the council tipi and laid him down in the place of honor. They said that this man now commanded them in peace and in war. Thirty-six-year-old Sitting Bull had become a transcendent leader who, together with Red Cloud of the Oglalas and High Backbone of the Minneconjous, would guide the Lakota people.[74]

Sitting Bull, Red Cloud, and High Backbone became symbols of Lakota resistance to wašíču invasion. All three boasted impressive records as war leaders and enjoyed wide support in men's societies. Critically, all three were renowned for their unwavering opposition to the wašíču brand of peace, which would have meant reservations, farming, and alien mores and beliefs. This made them inspiring figures among young women and men, who had matured into a world where the hunt, trade, and war were essential for a good life. More pointedly, Red Cloud, High Backbone, and Sitting Bull found themselves at the center of a burgeoning warrior cult fueled by decades of war against American and Native rivals. High Backbone was the mentor and war comrade of Crazy Horse, whose introverted spirituality, single-mindedness, and dazzling performance in the Fetterman Fight made him a venerated figure among his peers, and Sitting Bull, by virtue of his age (he was eleven years younger than High Backbone and Red Cloud) and unassuming charisma, became a model for many aspiring warriors. And Red Cloud was about to have an entire war named after him.[75]

Together, Red Cloud, High Backbone, and Sitting Bull mobilized Lakotas for war not simply as bands and tribes but as an empire. Each drew strength from traditional Lakota principles, allowing power to flow freely from tribal councils to band councils to men's societies to war parties, but now three elevated chiefs served as focal points of Lakota foreign policy, coordinating military and diplomatic operations through their personal gravitas. Red Cloud's Oglalas formed the empire's southern bulwark against wašíču expansionism along the Oregon Trail, the United States' imperial road across the West; Sitting Bull's Hunkpapas led the war effort against the army forts on the upper Mníšoše; and High Backbone's Minneconjous were a fulcrum between the two magnetic poles, joining forces with either as needed. Crucially, the three chiefs could also draw warriors from other oyátes, concentrating awesome force against invaders.

In 1867, during a routine visit to Fort Union trading post, Sitting Bull proclaimed an unyielding campaign against the wašíčus: "I have killed, robbed, and injured too many white men to believe in a good peace. They are medicine"— powerful and confounding— "and I would eventually die a lingering death." Like Red Cloud and High Backbone, Sitting Bull would accept peace only on Lakota terms. Until that came to pass, the war would continue. One of the traders observed how Sitting Bull repeatedly urged the Assiniboines "to join him, telling them not to stick so close to the whites, getting as poor as snakes, eating nothing but bacon and hard-tack." Instead, he offered freedom, prosperity, and personal fulfillment among the Lakotas, whose hunting grounds were still rich and who could raid U.S. forts at will. "Look at me," he challenged the attending Assiniboines, "see if I am poor, or my people either." Soon a U.S. Army officer branded him as "a fierce beast" and "one of the most dangerous and most ill-disposed Indians in Dakota," which had become "the theater for his depredations and assassinations."[76]

It was at that pregnant moment that the contradictions of the U.S. Indian policy finally collapsed into utter dysfunctionality. In late spring of 1867 U.S. commissioners arrived at Fort Laramie, hoping to negotiate truces with Lakotas and their allies. However, by the time the talks began, U.S. troops were already surveying a site for a new garrison, Fort Fetterman, on the North Platte in the Lakota country. The arrogance of the act alienated many pro-treaty Lakotas, who began to gravitate toward Red Cloud and his followers, sharing their powder and lead with them. At a large Sun Dance on the Tongue River Red Cloud announced his intention to continue the war until all the U.S. forts in Lakota lands were dismantled. The war leaders of different tribes divided over targets and agreed to maintain two armies, but all shared Red Cloud's vision: they would eradicate the wašíču presence from the Powder River country once and for all.[77]

Both Native armies avoided the elaborate decoys and ambushes that had brought such spectacular results at the Lodge Trail Ridge a year before. Instead they relied on straightforward shock tactics. Several hundred Cheyennes and Minneconjous rode toward Fort C. F. Smith and attacked an exposed hay-cutting crew, while roughly six hundred Oglalas, Sans Arcs, Minneconjous, and Cheyennes rode toward Fort Phil Kearny and attacked a woodcutting detail six miles west of the garrison. Both armies had an overwhelming advantage in numbers over the enemy, but their confidence dissipated in the astonishingly rapid rifle fire from the wašíču soldiers who had been issued Allin-modified Springfield breechloaders. Both attacks turned into sieges. Fort Smith soldiers retreated into a log corral and held off the Indians. The Fort Phil Kearny troops circled their wagons, punched small holes on their sides, and maintained steady fire through them. After several hours both Indian armies disengaged and disappeared. Casualties were limited and there was little glory to go around for Lakotas and their allies, but Americans hailed the fights as unqualified triumphs.[78]

Lakotas and their allies retreated north into the Rosebud Valley, which, it turned out, was the best thing they could have done. It allowed the United States to claim victory over the allied tribes and consider peace negotiations without losing face. Not coincidentally, the fabricated Native death toll at what became known as the Wagon Box Fight soon swelled into the hundreds, bolstering a necessary narrative of U.S. military power having forced the Lakotas to capitulate. In truth, the United States had lost the war. The Bozeman Trail had become unusable for emigrants, the forts had been locked into a purely defensive campaign, and government officials knew that they could not defeat the superbly mobile Lakota warriors without inordinate material investments and unacceptable human losses.[79]

THE FIRST ONES THAT I WILL WHIP

That realization coincided with a formidable peace movement in Washington. The Indigenous reconstruction had become a sprawling, seething disaster. While the Bozeman Trail turned into a festering wound, Comanches raided across Texas, frustrating the United States' nation-building project in the Southwest. The Apaches tied U.S. troops into a desultory border campaign in Arizona, and the Dog Soldiers kept the central plains in turmoil with raids and gunpowder-spiked "torpedo arrows." Sherman bemoaned that "fifty of these Indians can checkmate three thousand of our soldiers." In California scattered Indian killings and massacres continued, prolonging a decades-long genocide by a state-sanctioned killing machine that enabled U.S. Army soldiers and vigilantes to enslave and slaughter Indians with impunity. The members of the Senate found themselves debating whether the government should integrate or exterminate the Indians and calculating how long the army could keep killing Indians when each kill cost nearly a million dollars. Only two years after the close of the brutal Civil War, Americans faced another spiraling crisis that ate away at their moral fiber. Many among those who knew what was happening found it revolting and disheartening.[80]

And so, already in the summer of 1867—when Lakotas were chasing the army out of the Powder River country—Congress established a high-powered Indian Peace Commission to negotiate with the Lakotas and other plains tribes over grievances, treaties, trails, and reservations. Under the act, Congress named four

civilians to the commission, and President Johnson appointed three generals, creating a politically diverse body that could swing behind peace or war depending
on Native responses. At one end of the spectrum there was Samuel F. Tappan,
a prominent humanitarian crusader who advocated Native self-determination,
and at the other there were General William Harney, the initiator of the killing
of eighty-six Lakotas and Cheyennes in 1855, and the cynical Sherman, who
believed that "hostilities between the races will continue till the Indians are all
killed or taken to a country where they can be watched" and advocated total war
targeting civilians and game as the fastest and thus the most humane solution to
the Indian problem.[81]

In a near repeat of the Edmunds talks three years earlier, the commissioners
ordered Indian agents to gather Sioux leaders for a series of talks along the Missouri, only to be denied. The supposedly friendly Lakotas, Yanktons, and Dakotas
welcomed them not with humility but with demands: guns, powder, blacksmiths, Indian-style clothing, provisions promised in treaties, white farmers to
raise crops for them. Burnt Face, a Sans Arc, wanted a big blanket "as I am a big
bellied man." Some chiefs said they were willing to try farming, but Two Kettle
chief Two Lance gave the envoys a lecture on Lakota sovereignty: "All the men
of my age were born on this side of the River and were raised there. We therefore
claim both sides of the river." If the commissioners did realize how little headway
the U.S. agents had made in domesticating the Lakotas in three years, they did
not report it.[82]

The talks then moved west to the newfound railroad town of North Platte
near the forks of the Platte. In came the moderate Sicangu chiefs Spotted Tail
and Swift Bear, who were now anything but moderate. Both objected fiercely
to the Bozeman Trail and the extension of the Union Pacific west of the Platte
forks because they disturbed the buffalo. The more militant Two Strike pressed
for Sicangu rights to hunt south on the Republican, while Oglala chief The Man
That Walks Under the Ground symbolically turned the tables on commissioners:
"Tell our grandfather that our hands are long and we can almost reach to where
he is." Almost every chief demanded guns and ammunition, presumably for
hunting, and the commissioners, taken aback by the friendlies' assertive stance,
relented. "To give one of these Indians powder and ball is to give him meat," they
rationalized. Sherman would have none of it and asserted the army's uncompromising stance. "The road *must* be built," he thundered, and told the Lakotas to
prepare to become farmers along the Missouri where they would have a reservation. If Lakotas rejected the offer, he warned, they would face "a war that will be
different from any you have ever before had."[83]

Sherman—a remorseless fighter whom an awestruck observer described as cautious and calculating, "with a dash of statesmanship in him"—was preparing the ground for the real showdown. Above all, the commissioners wanted to meet with Red Cloud who more than a year earlier had articulated the rationale for Lakota resistance to U.S. forts, and who had since become something of an obsession for American officials. The architect of the U.S. Army's most shocking defeat in the West, Red Cloud was a study in restraint. Fully aware of his political weight among the wašíčus, he chose the most powerful tactic available to him: he did nothing. For a long time the only thing the Americans knew about him was that he had retired north and was "dissatisfied." Silence did its work, and soon rumors circulated that Red Cloud and his followers "were all determined to make war this summer more actively than last."[84]

Red Cloud waited because the status quo favored him. With the Bozeman Trail soldiers trapped in their forts, Lakotas and their allies extended their raiding sphere south into the Platte Valley, forcing the government to consider suspending the construction of the Union Pacific. When the commissioners arrived in Fort Laramie in the fall of 1867, only Crows were there to meet them. Red Cloud, "the formidable chief of the Sioux," did not show up, the commissioners reported, believing that they had lost an opportunity to secure "a just and honorable peace." Red Cloud—whose outward passivity hid intense inter-oyáte diplomacy in the Powder River country—sent word that "whenever the military garrisons at Fort Phil Kearney and Fort C. F. Smith were withdrawn, the war on his part would cease." "No argument, no presents, no amount of money, no matter how large will ever satisfy these Indians," Commissioner G. P. Beauvais, an old Indian trader, counseled. The forts had to be dismantled. If the government failed to do that, he warned, the commissioners "may as well cease their labors and go home." Having time on his side, Red Cloud announced he would meet the commission next spring or summer.[85]

When spring arrived, the commissioner returned with newly found confidence: late in the previous fall they had signed a series of treaties with the Comanches and other southern plains tribes at Medicine Lodge Creek. But their optimism dissipated soon. Red Cloud's persisting elusiveness forced Americans to start the talks under an acute threat of war. If anything, Lakota resolve seemed to have stiffened. Meeting with both militants and nonmilitans at North Platte and Fort Laramie over several weeks, the commissioners grew anxious as the Lakota list of demands kept growing longer. All the things that anchored U.S. power in the West—roads, rails, steamboats, soldiers, forts, even annuities—fell under threat when Lakota delegates doggedly articulated their key demand: the preservation of their territory, the bison, and the traditional Lakota way of life. Americans could become friends and kin once again through wólakȟota and have peace, but first the forts would have to go. American Horse, who claimed to have killed Fetterman, said he would sign a treaty but left a lingering warning: "If there is anything wrong afterwards I will watch the commissioners, and they will be the first ones that I will whip."[86]

The War Department relented and ordered the forts closed, and President Johnson authorized a larger reservation than the one proposed on the Missouri River. Sitting Bull, perhaps to boost his negotiating position in Red Cloud's shadow, launched a raiding expedition against the upper Missouri forts. Soon after, serving once again as a peace envoy, Father De Smet arrived in Sitting Bull's village on the Powder Valley, escorted by twenty Hunkpapa warriors and carrying the image of the Virgin Mary. Sitting Bull welcomed the Jesuit and that evening spoke to him of war: "I hardly sustain myself beneath the weight of white men's blood that I have shed. The whites provoked the war; their injustices, their indignities to our families, the cruel, unheard of and wholly unprovoked [Sand Creek] massacre shook all the veins which bind and support me." He promised to listen to the wašíčus and stop the war: "As bad as I have been to the whites, just so good am I ready to become toward them."

Next day, in a massive council attended by thousands of men and women, Four Horns and Black Moon, the principal civil leaders, listed their grievances. "The whites are interlacing our country with their highways of transportation and emigration," Black Moon bristled. "They kill our animals, and more than they need." Northern Lakotas would reject any land cessions. Sitting Bull expressed regret over the violence but then, in a flash of passion, demanded that the army abandon its upper Missouri forts. Later, women brought their children to De Smet's lodge and asked the priest to touch the head of each child, legitimizing the proceedings. De Smet escorted a delegation led by Gall — "the most distinguished warrior" — to Fort Rice where, after a daylong gift distribution, twenty lesser chiefs signed a treaty.[87]

While the majority of Lakota chiefs came to Fort Laramie to sign the treaty, Red Cloud still held off, keeping the commissioners in a bind. Then, in late July, high up the Bighorn Mountains, Oglalas and Minneconjous watched the wašíčus filing out of Fort C. F. Smith. Warriors came down and burned it. The scene was repeated at Fort Phil Kearny, and then the soldiers marched out of Fort Reno. And yet Red Cloud waited. In August Lakotas and Cheyennes launched a series of raids against Pawnees and American homesteaders in the central plains, deepening the menace of Red Cloud's elusiveness. Only in early November did Red Cloud lead a large multi-oyáte delegation of 125 headmen to Fort Laramie to make the peace real. Exuding "dignity and disinterestedness," he sat down, forcing the army officers to come to him; he extended the tips of his fingers toward them and said that "his name to the paper would mean peace." Next day he slowly "washed his hands with the dust of the floor," cleaning the land of blood, and signed the treaty. He made all the Americans "touch the pen," ensuring that the wašíčus had listened and understood. It was then and there that the American fetishizing of Red Cloud began.[88]

MUCH MEDICINE MADE

The 1868 Treaty of Fort Laramie—which replaced the 1851 Horse Creek Treaty—was a bafflingly inconsistent compromise that reflected its extraordinary historical circumstances: a comparatively small Indigenous nation had won a war against an aggressive industrial behemoth through strategic deception, concentrated employment of military power, and sheer diplomatic audacity—tactics that often are seen as a Euroamerican prerogative. The treaty allowed the United States to build its railroad along the Platte—now a more tolerable concession as bison hunting in the region was becoming useless—but it set apart a distinct territory for Lakotas' "absolute and undisturbed use and occupation." This was the Great Sioux Reservation that encompassed all the lands west of the Missouri across the Black Hills and extended about two hundred miles from south to north to include the vitally important White, Bad, Cheyenne, Moreau, and Grand Rivers.

Covering more than forty-eight thousand square miles, the new reservation was less than half the size of the Lakota domain recognized in the Horse Creek Treaty, but two articles compensated for the loss. Article 16 designated the lands east of the Bighorn Mountains and north of the North Platte as "unceded Indian territory" where "no white person or persons" could settle. The treaty did not specify the northern border of this territory, effectively leaving the door open for Lakota expansion into the Yellowstone Valley and north of the Missouri—theoretically all the way into Canada. Much of this land had been Crow country; now a treaty tacitly opened it to Lakotas who had been shifting west and north for decades. In the south, Article 11 recognized Lakota hunting rights all the way down to the Republican River, rights which Lakotas had never relinquished. This extensive block of land, which enveloped the Platte Valley and the projected railroad, would be open to Lakota hunters "so long as the buffalo may range thereon in such numbers as to justify the chase." For now, at least, that block seemed to belong to Lakotas who did not make a distinction between using and owning the land.[89]

Far more clearly than the 1851 treaty, the new treaty recognized Lakota sovereignty and established a nation-to-nation relationship between the Lakota nation and the United States. The treaty also quietly acknowledged the Lakota

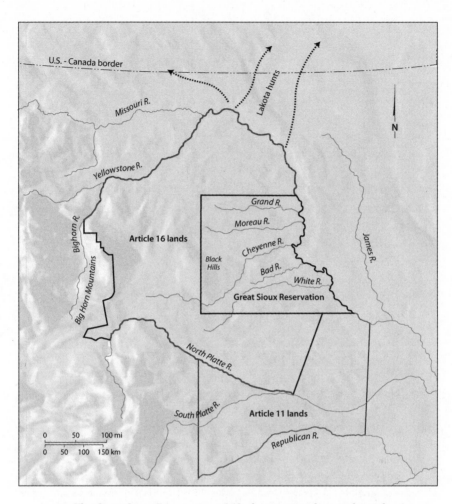

40. The Great Sioux Reservation, 1868, showing Article 11 and Article 16
lands as set by the 1868 Treaty of Fort Laramie. Map by Bill Nelson.

ascendancy over the northern plains. While quietly anticipating further Lakota expansion, the United States seemed to have embraced the Lakotas as equals
and favored allies. The treaty granted them tens of thousands of square miles that
the 1851 treaty had assigned to other tribes, and it pledged the government to
furnish them with several new agencies where crucial goods would be distributed: meat and flour for four years (a pound of both for each person per day),
clothing, farming tools, mills, money (ten dollars per year for hunters, twenty for
farmers), as well as the services of physicians, carpenters, farmers, blacksmiths,
millers, and engineers. They Fear Even His Horses demanded that Bissonnette

41. They Fear Even His Horses and Lone Horse at the 1868 Fort Laramie Treaty council (detail of a group photo, *Interior of Council Chamber, Man Afraid of His Horses* [smoking], by Alexander Gardner). They Fear Even His Horses and Lone Horse were often labeled, simplistically, as moderate or treaty chiefs in contrast to Sitting Bull and other northern Lakotas who shunned treaties with the United States. Courtesy of Newberry Library, Chicago, Edward E. Ayer Digital Collection.

and other mixed-blood traders stay near Lakotas on the Platte: "I consider them all as part of ourselves." Betraying the fear that years of Lakota wars had ingrained in popular consciousness, the treaty listed in detail the things Lakotas should not do to their American allies: disturb their travel, molest their wagon trains, steal their animals, capture them, kill them, scalp them, or shun their schools. The most ominous clause opened the door for future land cessions if three-fourths of adult men consented to it.[90]

Such a conjecture was distant in 1868 when the United States had lost the war and acknowledged Lakotas' right to rule the northern plains as they saw fit. The war, Lone Horn explained, resulted from a failure to communicate: "we do not eat each other when we take each other," he told the commissioners. But now, with the forts dismantled, there would be "plenty of game again," cementing Lakota sovereignty over the northern plains. The wašíčus would have to listen. And with that Lone Horn told the soldiers "to leave as soon as possible." From the Powder River country Sitting Bull sent a more pointed message about Indigenous sovereignty. Only two months after making peace with De Smet, he led a raid on Fort Buford, relieving the garrison of 250 head of beef cattle. Northern Lakotas would accept neither treaties nor reservations.[91]

The winter counts for 1867–68 memorialize the Treaty of Fort Laramie as a happy occasion where Lakotas received many flags and blankets and new denim canvas from the Americans, where many chiefs were recognized, and where much medicine—conciliation and mutual healing—was made. One count mentions that Lakotas made peace with General Harney, the consummate Indian killer become peace emissary; others relate how fifteen Lakotas died in a failed raid into the Crow country. Together, the counts intimate the changing coordinates of Lakota power. In the late 1860s Lakotas needed new hunting grounds in the north and west to compensate for the shrinking bison populations in the south and east, and here was the blueprint for achieving it. The new treaty with the United States would soon bring government agencies into the Lakota realm, furnishing crucial resources that would support Lakota expansion into lands the treaty designated as a kind of Indigenous no-man's-land. Like so many times over the last two centuries, Lakota fortunes would hinge on river valleys. The first among them were Héčhiŋškayapi Wakpá and Pȟežísla Wakpá. The Americans knew them as the Bighorn and the Little Bighorn.[92]

8

SHAPESHIFTERS

The American nation that concluded a treaty with the Lakota nation in 1868 at Fort Laramie had launched itself into a new frontier, beyond the familiar and the safe. That frontier was a real physical place: the United States now brushed against a clearly defined Indigenous domain, the Great Sioux Reservation. Covering a large portion of the northern plains, the Great Sioux Reservation was for Americans a wilderness world beyond U.S. laws and institutions. Like most frontiers, it was a place of prospects and hopes, a fault line where civilization was supposed to triumph over savagery, turning nomads into farmers and heathens into Christians.

The United States that now shared a treaty-sanctioned border with the Lakota nation also existed on a chronological frontier. The late 1860s saw the arrival of the modern. The already ragged old order of the local, the personal, and the improvised would linger on, but the post–Civil War years ushered in, with heated moralistic fury, a new order of professionalism, rationalization, service-centered bureaucracies, and corporate capitalism. Yeoman farmers and rural enterprises lost ground to wage earners and urban factories, and self-sufficiency began to give way to a dependency on faceless institutions. Markets and media became national, industries became mechanized, tuberculosis and other crowd diseases spread aggressively, and life spans became shorter. Fee-based governance—an administrative strategy by which government agents lived not on salaries but on payments for specific services—suffused the federal government with rapacity and corruption, further alienating its citizens from it. The changes were dizzyingly fast, unnerving many Americans who felt rudderless in the shifting world.[1]

But the changes were also exhilarating, intimating renewed national greatness, and they fueled a new kind of arrogance toward the continent's Indigenous peoples. Increasingly mobile, ambitious, and impatient, Americans began to look at the Indians differently. Railroads, the epitome of progress, not only fueled the American ambition but, to a remarkable degree, focused it on Lakotas. In his annual report for 1869 Secretary of the Interior Jacob D. Cox revealed the mental shift:

> The completion of one of the great lines of railway to the Pacific coast has totally changed the conditions under which the civilized population of the country come in contact with the wild tribes. Instead of a slowly advancing tide of migration, making its gradual inroads upon the circumference of the great interior wilderness, the very center of the desert has been pierced. Every station upon the railway has become a nucleus for a civilized settlement, and a base from which lines of exploration for both mineral and agricultural wealth are pushed in every direction. . . . The range of the buffalo is being rapidly restricted, and the chase is becoming an uncertain reliance to the Indian for the sustenance of his family.[2]

Cox must have had the Lakotas in mind when composing the passage. As the Union Pacific and the Central Pacific inched closer to their Utah meeting point in the winter of 1868, it was as if a countdown toward the end of the Lakota reign in the northern plains had begun. Lakotas had been the transcontinentals' greatest obstacle; soon they would become their greatest victims. "The locomotive is the sole solution of the Indian question," argued Senator William Stewart from Nevada. "As the thorough and final solution of the Indian question, by taking the buffalo range out from under the savage, and putting a vast stock and grain farm in its place," railroads would deliver an almost spontaneous dispossession of the Indians. Modernity, it seemed, was finally catching up with the nomads, closing the window to their imagined retrograde barbaric existence. A tidal wave of civilization—of forts, farms, ranches, towns, hotels, banks—was about to wash over them.[3]

By bringing growing numbers of Americans in contact with Natives, railroads also awakened the federal government to the magnitude of its Indian problem. In 1868 the Americans seemed to be fighting Indians all the time, but none challenged them like the Lakotas and their Cheyenne Dog Soldier allies, who raided Pawnees, Poncas, Arikaras, Crows, homesteaders, and railroad crews in the central plains to protect their treaty-sanctioned hunting grounds. Under intense pressure to perform, Major General Philip H. Sheridan, the diminutive, hardened new commander of the Department of Missouri, orchestrated a winter campaign to strike the Indians when they were least mobile and most vulnerable.

To lead it Sheridan picked George Armstrong Custer, a flamboyant lieutenant colonel who seemed unable to avoid controversy and had been court-martialed for ordering deserters to be shot without trial and for leaving his post. Custer could be volatile and insufferable, but he could fight. At dawn on November 27 he delivered the ruthless, calculated effectiveness Sheridan knew he was capable of. With the cheerful drinking song "Garry Owen" filling the air, nearly eight hundred soldiers of the Seventh Cavalry converged on a sleeping Cheyenne village on the Washita River. Within two hours they had killed dozens of men, women, and children, burned the tipis, and slaughtered nearly nine hundred horses. It was a crippling blow to Cheyenne power in the middle country and an atrocity that evoked the infamy of Sand Creek four years earlier. The next summer Sheridan sent Major Eugene Carr, the Fifth Cavalry, fifty-four supply wagons, and 150 Pawnee scouts to finish off the business by attacking a Dog Soldier camp near the South Platte. It was a rout. When the retreating Cheyennes saw their tipis and food reserves burning, they knew they had become refugees in their own country.[4]

The Cheyenne village Custer had crushed at the Washita was the village of the well-known peace chief Black Kettle. Army offices, on the whole, had resigned themselves to the fact that the subjugation of the plains nomads necessitated targeting noncombatants, but President Ulysses S. Grant had not. He thought that the nation's Indian policy had degenerated into a hideous failure. He appointed his former military aide, Ely S. Parker of the Seneca nation, as the first Native American commissioner of the Indian Office and, with him, launched a new Indian policy. Under the "Peace Policy," the Indians would be appeased until there would be so many whites and so few resources that armed resistance became impossible. Reservations would rid the Natives of nomadism, polygamy, and "barbarous dialects," and tribal nations would dissolve into "one homogenous mass" of Christian, English-speaking homesteaders. When Congress prevented Grant from putting the army in charge of the new policy, he chose the Quakers, effectively subcontracting them to implement the United States' Indian policy.

This was the federal government's attempt to shift into softer and more mature imperialism: rather than fighting and killing the Indians, it would manage and mold them. The Peace Policy was designed to do to Indigenous America what Reconstruction was to do to the South: swiftly modernize its people and absorb them into a single national body. Deemed inherently incompetent and inclined to succumb to "the lower and baser elements of the civilized society," the Indians themselves were not consulted on how this was to be achieved.[5]

In the Great Sioux Reservation, Lakotas could immediately feel the government's new managerial approach. Winter counts for 1868–69 focus on white men's cattle and beef: the first treaty annuities had materialized as herds of Texas cattle, a not-so-subtle attempt to detach Lakotas from the bison and the chase.

Indian Office agents in Washington worked diligently to erase corruption and earn Lakotas' trust; transparency and orderliness would define life in the Great Sioux Reservation. Annuities were to be handed out at three new Missouri River agencies—Whetstone Creek, Cheyenne River, and Grand River—and under the army's supervision; they were to be delivered in the original package, against receipts, and in the presence of the chiefs and an interpreter. Indian agents and army officers carefully monitored the mood of Lakotas and their leaders. When General Alfred Terry heard of an attempt by American citizens to survey the Black Hills for a settlement in the summer of 1868, he immediately ordered a detail to chase them out. By the fall J. R. Hanson, the head agent of the Lakotas, had reason to be hopeful. The lower Sicangus' attitude toward farming was "very cheering" and they had some five hundred acres under cultivation, a "progress" that "ought to satisfy any body familiar with the peculiarities of these wild people, very many of whom never before attempted to raise a hill of corn, or even thought until within the past year, that they would ever have to depend upon any other mode of gaining a living than the chase."[6]

But Hanson's sample was not representative. Most of the lower Sicangus were Wágluhes, who had lived near Fort Laramie for years, experimenting with farming in the unforgiving northern plains conditions and gradually adopting elements of the American culture. These Lakotas were already moving toward what the Americans understood as civilization when Grant launched his grand experiment in accelerated assimilation. The great majority of Lakotas accepted annuities but vehemently rejected their civilized trappings. They demanded specific goods—guns and ammunition, not plows and seeds—and insisted that beef cattle be delivered to them on the hoof so they could hunt them down on horseback in imitation of the bison chase. Government agents labeled them as traditionalists hopelessly out of sync with the historical momentum, which was half true. These Lakotas had little use for American modernity because they had already forged one of their own.[7]

I WILL GO SLOWLY

Far removed from the destructive power of railroads, the Powder River country was the heart of the Lakota world. There, with their Cheyenne and Arapaho allies, Lakotas lived in great tipi villages that dwarfed most wašíču settlements for hundreds of miles in any direction. Often including more than a thousand lodges—a thousand complex households—they moved in warmer seasons leisurely from one river valley to another, and stretched out dozens of miles along the Yellowstone, Powder, Rosebud, Tongue, and Bighorn, periodically accommodating over ten thousand people. The tipis were larger than ever, often made of more than twenty buffalo hides, and filled with imported goods. It took six horses to move just one of those big lodges. Government agents supplied Lakotas with annuities, and independent American traders were eager to trade with the wealthiest Native nation in the interior. Finely honed protocols structured the booming commerce. Red Cloud welcomed prominent traders by erecting a lodge for them next to his own and had their goods placed within it and their wagons corralled around it. He then offered a great feast.

The inflow of merchandize was both voluminous and varied. In came wagon-loads of state-of-the art Remingtons and Colt six-shooters, powder, lead, saddles, swords, iron axe heads, iron arrow and lance points, awls, files, knives, hide scrapers, scissors, cast-iron kettles and skillets, spoons, red and blue Navajo blankets, clothing, fabrics, buttons, beads, bells, bracelets, earbobs, German silver rings, pipe tomahawks, brass and glass adornments, dried Mexican pumpkins, sweet Mexican cornmeal, coffee, and whiskey, for which Lakotas bartered buffalo robes and meat. Lakota villages abounded with objects, both necessities and luxuries, which brought their owners joy, status, spiritual contentment, and, when shared, respect and power. These modern Lakota villages were centers of intensive and fulfilling consumption.

This commercial prowess was fueled by Lakotas' greatest modernizing engine: the still relatively new horse-powered bison hunt that could yield massive quantities of hides, meat, fat, and sinew in a matter of minutes. By the late 1860s Lakotas had built prodigious horse herds: an average household probably owned around twenty animals, some of them trained for hunting and war, the rest used as beasts of burden. A specialized labor force of young boys and enemy captives tended to the herds, watering, pasturing, grooming, and protecting the treasured beasts. When the mobile villages struck camp, cottonwood-studded riverbanks and floodplains became blanketed by enormous herds, the pulsating, organic engine of the Lakota economy.

Contemporary Americans saw the Powder River country as an Indigenous retreat, an insular world intentionally cut off from the rapidly expanding American empire of cities, railroads, settlers, farms, ranches, and capitalism—a perception that has dominated outsider views of the Lakotas ever since. In reality, the Powder River country under the Lakota rule was a safe and dynamic cosmopolitan world of its own where transnational commercial circuits converged, where Indians enjoyed many comforts and advantages of the industrial age, and where new ideas about being in the world were constantly debated. Lakotas knew full well that they lived in a transitional period of innovation, quickening change, and questioning of old conventions. But contrary to the tired old stereotype of obstinate, tradition-bound Indians, they embraced this radical regeneration of their world.[8]

Lakotas had lived with wašíčus in their midst for two centuries, and they had had U.S. forts and agencies in their lands and on their borders for two generations. This had become accepted and normal. Close wašíču presence had given them access to new markets, technologies, foods, peoples, and ideas. Some of the novelties—such as Christianity—they approached with deep scepticism, some with relish. By the late 1860s Lakotas had entered—irreversibly, it seemed— a new technological age where life without guns, metal, horses, and textiles was unimaginable. Ready-made utensils and tools rendered daily chores immeasurably faster and easier, while horses and guns kept them safe. The introduction of the 1866 Winchester lever-action repeating rifle alone nearly revolutionized their ability to inflict harm on their enemies. Colonel Richard Irving Dodge could but marvel at the speed and scope of the change. Repeating rifles, he wrote, had transformed "the Plains Indian from an insignificant, scarcely dangerous adversary into as magnificent a soldier as the world can show."[9]

Men and women alike relied on foreign goods for safety, comfort, and status, and families measured their wealth and social standing in the horses and trade goods they possessed. From cooking to keeping warm to feeling beautiful to feeling powerful, everyday life now necessitated access to and consumption of imported products. Many families included captives whose labor was essential for the managing of horse herds and the production of bison robes, which kept the all-important export economy running. Lakotas were still Lakotas and in control of their world, even though that world had changed fundamentally. Thus far they had adapted ingeniously to it.

The creation of the Great Sioux Reservation magnified that sense of newness, a rupture between the past and the present. In 1869 along the Powder River both Crazy Horse and Sitting Bull addressed a council deliberating Lakota policy toward the wašíčus. Crazy Horse—a man who believed he was only good for war and was widely celebrated for his uncompromising position toward the wašíčus—now emerged as the very embodiment of Lakota capacity to change. "This tribe will slowly be living with white men," he said, "but whereas I fear the land will be taken under duress without payment, you should go on home. Soon I shall come. If I were present I would not sell it to the whitemen. So take the message: I will go slowly." Sitting Bull echoed the eminent warrior: "I shall make peace with whitemen slowly."

This was *iwáštegla*, a new political philosophy that recognized that Lakotas would have to gradually learn to live with the wašíčus, whose presence in their world had become an irrevocable fact. In the long run, this could mean farming and settling in reservations. In the short run, it meant accepting whatever material and political support the Americans could offer while thwarting any

American attempts to civilize and remold them. Lakotas still expected wašíčus to compromise more than they did: after all, most of their interactions took place in Lakota territory. In this charged moment one can glimpse something essential about Lakotas' ability to accept new realities, adjust to changing governing conditions, and yet remain entirely Indigenous. Confident as Lakotas may have been about their place in the world, they remained flexible and receptive. They would survive the wašíču version of modernity by selectively embracing it.[10]

Lakotas rejected the wašíčus' reformist zeal so forcefully because they knew its dangers intimately. On the eastern side of the Mníšoše they could see how unrestrained civilization programs played out. There their Yankton, Yanktonai, and Dakota kin had lived on small reservations for years, suffering a sharp decline. Pressured into farming, their crops tended to fail while government rations fell repeatedly short. Deprived and often starving, they had become horribly diminished. Those reservations were a warning. The Yankton agent worked hard to secure enough supplies for his wards, but his superior saw in Yanktons little more than a useful tool for pacifying the Lakotas. "Located as they are," he wrote in 1869, "directly between the wild and warlike bands of their great nation and the frontier settlements of the irresistible advance of civilization, they are the practicable medium for reclaiming from savage life their roving and bloodthirsty brothers, by transmitting to them, and inducting and disseminating among them, the modes of life and the rules of law and order of their white brothers on the other side."[11]

Repulsed by such wašíču schemes and certain of their ability to adapt to changing circumstances, Lakotas set out to mold the Great Sioux Reservation to meet their needs. Federal agents envisioned the reservation as a tightly controlled space of cultural engineering where Lakotas would be stripped of their savage habits. Lakotas, however, saw the reservation as an Indigenous domain where government officials operated under their auspices. What mattered to them most were the American resources—rations, clothing, guns, tools, and vaccines—that buttressed their power and ambitions in the great interior. They had few illusions about the agents' intentions—primarily because the agents were so effusive about their plans to Americanize them—and they refused to become wards. Instead, they meant to transform the agencies into stepping stones in their ongoing quest to keep their world prosperous and inviolate. The result was a prolonged contest over the standing of the Lakota nation within the American one and over the very meaning of the reservation itself.

THE NON-RESERVATION

U.S. Indian agents had two major incentives to make the Lakota reservation experiment work. The first was personal and humanitarian: many of them genuinely cared for Indians and wanted to help them survive in the rapidly changing world. The second was money. The Indian wars burdened the federal government, their employer. It was calculated that wars with Native Americans since the early 1840s had cost the United States more than $750 million dollars. In the late 1860s the government was spending an estimated $144,000 dollars a day to fight the Lakotas and other Plains Indians, more than 8 percent of the total annual government expenditure. A military solution to the Lakota problem simply was not fiscally viable.[12]

The agents of the Great Sioux Reservation were responsible for a lot, and they soon felt the pressure. Agent Hanson regretted how the peace policy placed different Lakotas in unequal positions. The few Lakotas who were willing to try farming, he reported, were suffering unjustly because the government had not offered enough support to facilitate the difficult transition: "The peace they have been influenced to maintain has saved the government millions of dollars, but has entailed misery and semi-starvation upon themselves." Most of the funds, Hanson seethed, went to appeasing the militant chiefs and bands that categorically rejected farming and lived in the Black Hills and the Powder River country, far from the Missouri agencies. The government, he wrote, "appropriates liberal sums—more liberal than were ever before granted to the Indians—to the benefit of the miserable devils besmeared with the blood of white men, women, and children, whose hostility has cost the government millions of dollars." This, Hanson insisted, was not only morally wrong but financially unsustainable. He could feel the reservation experiment floundering even before it had gotten off the ground.[13]

The agents had to refine their tactics. Just making rations available would not be enough to domesticate the Lakotas who came to the agencies to collect goods and food, only to immediately return to their homelands in the west or north. The agents had to render Lakotas both visible and accountable, which meant, at its most basic, naming and counting them. The agents began compiling lists that identified individual Lakotas and their relatives, bands, leaders, camping grounds, and character. Soon there were files detailing misconducts and what under U.S. law were crimes. Lists became means of monitoring behaviors, assigning culpability, meting out punishments, and fixing nomads in place. Hunger became an instrument of power and food a reward: dispensing and withholding rations became the agents' principal means to enforce compliance. The Great Sioux Reservation was in danger of turning into an alien world where simply being known could be perilous: it spelled the loss of individual autonomy and the dissolution of Lakota sovereignty. It spelled subjecthood.[14]

Lakotas fought back with the most effective tactic at their disposal: they shifted shape. While earlier they had resolutely rejected the U.S. government practice of dividing them into "friendlies" and "hostiles" as a damaging misrepresentation, they now accepted it for tactical purposes. Friendly chiefs and bands lived near the Missouri agencies, regularly collected their annuities—a pound of "'tame buffalo meat'" and a pound of flour per lodge per day—and kept experimenting with farming, even if half-heartedly, to gratify the agents. As instructed, they traded only along the river and rarely ventured west to hunt. Their leaders—Swift Bear of the Sicangus, They Fear Even His Horses of the Oglalas, Bone Necklace of the Yanktonais, and other moderates—developed close personal ties with the agents, who in turn supplied them with plows, threshing machines, gristmills, sawmills, and rations.[15]

But most Lakotas lived far away from the agencies. They remained as mobile as ever, their operations covering a vast arc from the Republican Valley in the south beyond the Bighorn Mountains and the Yellowstone and Missouri Valleys in the west and north in the search of bison to hunt and rival Indians' crops to pillage. Both the bison and the rivals were becoming scarce, forcing Lakotas to range wider and deeper. Led by chiefs who had fought the United States for years, these Lakota bands appeared to Indian agents as distant, elusive, and menacing. They would not trade along the Missouri and expected traders to come to them, and they demanded to have their agencies built in the west, nearer to the Black Hills and the Powder River country. How they lived and how they interacted with the agents made them appear as unreconstructed "hostiles"—indignant, vengeful, and insulated. The label would serve them well.[16]

The two divisions—hostiles and friendlies—appeared definite and fixed, and the Lakota nation seemed to be splintering. Many oyátes and thióšpayes were genuinely distraught, and some of them split permanently over their position toward the American state. At the Whetstone Agency militant Lakotas seemed to possess an "over-awing influence" over "the friendly and peacefully disposed," keeping them "in constant terror" and preventing "any improvement in civilization." But the friendly-hostile dichotomy was also a useful screen that allowed Lakotas to maneuver in ways that, if fully visible, would have been unacceptable to wašíču agents. While entrenched in the Black Hills and the Powder River country in the west, most nonagency bands regularly visited the agency bands in the east, sharing information and resources and reaffirming the kinship ties that bound them together. The Lakota nation became a labyrinthine nexus of people and networks that straddled the outwardly fixed East-West, friendly-hostile configuration.

That nexus was largely hidden from U.S. agents, who could glimpse only fragments of it. Without entirely realizing why, they saw their aspirations of administrative control dissolving into a shapeshifting Lakota regime. A flummoxed army officer complained about how "there is one class of Indians which has been friendly for four or five years, and are nearly permanent residents, only leaving from time to time to hunt or pick wild fruits. With this class there is no trouble. There is another class passing half their time at these agencies and half in the hostile camps. They abuse the agents, threaten their lives, kill their cattle at night, and do anything they can to oppose the civilizing movement, but eat all the provisions they can get." An equally confounded army officer at the Grand River Agency complained how there were "Indians constantly coming and going from and to the hostile camps, who while here are fed and clothed by the government" and "who pay the government" with raids and killings. The Cheyenne River agent reported how Two Kettles, Sans Arcs, and Minneconjous spoke of the U.S. president "as 'a white fool and a dog, without eyes or brains.'" He could not tell whether his wards were hostiles or friendlies. By simply making themselves illegible to U.S. agents, Lakotas were able to keep the wašíču state at a distance.[17]

For nearly a decade after the Treaty of Fort Laramie Lakota bands continued to hunt, raid, trade, and visit one another largely as they pleased. Bands gathered together to formulate policies and launch war expeditions against encroaching wašíču and Native neighbors. The villages of recognized "friendly" chiefs became sanctuaries for "hostile" nonagency bands, and the western villages of nonagency chiefs became refuges for dissatisfied agency bands. The friendly label shielded militant nonagency bands against U.S. reprisals, and the hostile label allowed agency bands to conceal their less-than-friendly activities. Such relentless transfiguration, the recurring congregating and disbanding and moving about, rendered the agents increasingly impotent. They struggled to even name the Lakotas, the necessary first step in an effort to individualize and control them, and their lists of friendlies and hostiles became symbols of their own weakness and failure. When a "hostile" warrior, "displaying the scalp of a white woman dangling at his breast," faced an army officer and "deliberately stated that his hands were dyed fresh with the white man's blood," all that the officer could do was to report the affront to Washington.[18]

The large multiethnic villages in the unceded territory were the most visible manifestation of enduring Lakota autonomy and power. There Sitting Bull emerged as the focal point of a widening intertribal resistance to American imperialism. The Hunkpapa headman's staunch opposition to the U.S. military forts on the upper Missouri had made him an inspiring figure among young men across band and tribal lines. He epitomized the principal Lakota virtues of bravery, fortitude, generosity, and wisdom, and carried himself modestly and at times reservedly: he suffered from bouts of severe depression that made him turn inward. He won the support of the quiet and reclusive Crazy Horse, widely considered the greatest Lakota warrior, who shared his deep ambivalence toward the wašíčus. Crazy Horse refused to visit agencies and lived in the Powder River country year-round, personifying the pure, uncorrupted ideals of what it meant to be Lakota and how to remain Indigenous. Countless Lakotas, Cheyennes, and Arapahos found hope, perhaps even fate, in his vision, and emulated his example. Many others chose to do so more selectively, traveling to the Missouri agencies to visit relatives or leaving the agencies in the summer to visit the Powder River country and join in Sun Dances and communal hunts, the foundation of Lakota existence.[19]

It may have been in the summer of 1869 when Lakotas from several oyátes came together to implement a radical political reform to boost their capacity to repel wašíču expansionism. Some four thousand people were present, probably on Rosebud Creek, when Four Horns, the visionary Minneconjou shirt wearer, asked the Lakotas to change. The shirt wearers, "the owners of the tribe," he proposed, would step aside to make room for a supreme war chief, *okíčhize ithán-čhan*, who would lead the Hunkpapas, Minneconjous, Sihasapas, and Yanktonais in the increasingly volatile world. Four Horns orchestrated an elaborate ceremony that elevated Sitting Bull, his nephew, into the role. "When you tell us to fight, we shall fight, when you tell us to make peace, we shall make peace," Four Horns declared. Whether mostly a symbolic honor or not, Sitting Bull's elevation signaled a concerted Lakota effort to meet the wašíču threat with centralized military and political action if necessary.

Sitting Bull's election was a dramatic departure from tradition: no such leadership position had existed among the Sioux. After the ceremony the new chief was raised on a horse. He paraded around the campground, singing: "Ye Tribes / behold me / The chiefs (of old) are no more / Myself Shall take Courage." He had chosen his words carefully. He would lead people not by an institutional mandate but through example and persuasion. His power would be situational rather than institutional: he could negotiate with outsiders on behalf of multiple bands and, in times of crisis, lead them in war through his personal charisma and spiritual prowess. He would be the gravitational center of a broad on-and-off-again alliance that, when necessary, could wield power on a massive scale.[20]

The Powder River villages of Sitting Bull, Gall, and Crazy Horse were an open rejection of the reservation system, but perhaps the most pointed symbol of the creative Lakota maneuvering under the shifting conditions was Spotted Tail's single village in the interior of the Great Sioux Reservation. Spotted Tail, a man who invariably evoked strong passions, had flatly refused to settle near the Whetstone Agency on the Missouri where, just across the river, wašíču squatters were already staking claims and where whiskey peddlers smuggled their product into

42. Sitting Bull in battle, 1870. Sitting Bull was a civil leader whose authority rested on his vision for the Lakota people and his military record. Here he pictures himself counting coup on a soldier with his bow, after having rescued Jumping Bull, an Assiniboine whom he had adopted as his brother. The image is Four Horns's copy of Sitting Bull's original drawing. Courtesy of National Anthropological Archives, Smithsonian Institution (NAA MS 1929A 08585600).

Lakota camps in relabeled tomato and peach cans, causing "terrible debauchery." He located his thousands-strong village tens of miles to the west and refused to travel to the agency to collect annuities. His village became a gathering place for both militant and nonmilitant bands, confounding the agents who were careful not to alienate the formidable leader whose influence seemed to transcend all political fault lines. Humbled, they began to freight annuities directly to Spotted Tail's village, leaving extra coffee, bacon, and sugar in the chief's tipi. Soon the village boasted more than three hundred lodges that clung to "their nomadic habits." Spotted Tail rode to the Whetstone Agency once a fortnight or so to socialize with the agents and watch the annuity goods being unloaded from steamboats. He inspected a government school where many Wágluȟes sent their children and did not object to its existence. He did not think it could pose a threat to Lakota sovereignty.[21]

Sitting Bull and Spotted Tail offered Lakotas two alternatives on how to protect their autonomy in a world where U.S. presence had become an irreversible fact. While Spotted Tail straddled Lakota and wašíču worlds, living within the reservation boundaries where bison were increasingly scarce, Sitting Bull's vision was imbued with the kind of unfaltering confidence that had sustained the Očhéthi Šakówiŋ through two centuries of wašíču infringements. But not all Lakotas shared his optimism. A more cynical mindset had begun to take root among a growing number of Lakotas who could sense that their way of life was doomed and would have to be refitted to new realities. They looked for leadership in a man who had exemplified uncompromising Lakota resistance to U.S. expansionism for years. When Red Cloud warned Lakotas that they would have to change to survive, many listened. He wanted them to focus not on who they were or what they had been but on what was happening to them. A passionate and pragmatic man, he may have loathed what Lakotas had to do, how they would have to compromise, but he was determined to see it through. In his mind, there was no alternative.[22]

In the late 1860s and early 1870s Red Cloud held an ambiguous place in the minds of U.S. government agents, an uncertainty that reflected his shifting position in Lakota politics. Spotted Tail's resolve to live in the west crumbled in a hard winter in 1869–70 when the agents failed to deliver adequate rations to his village and more than a hundred children and elders died. The chief moved on the Missouri's west bank where his village—and his political stature—actually swelled as other struggling bands sought food and goods under his auspices. But Red Cloud unequivocally rejected a Missouri agency. He refused to live among wašíču agents and give up the chase, a stance that made him an essential leader among the Oglalas despite the uncertainty of his official status: he had a superb record as a war leader and a spokesman of the Oglalas, but it was not clear whether he was an itháŋčhaŋ, band leader, or wakíčuŋzA, camp administrator. But unlike Sitting Bull, Red Cloud was willing, even eager, to secure government rations and munitions for his people. He was willing to welcome Americans and their annuities to preserve the traditional life of the hunt in the high plains; he would bring Lakotas closer to the wašíču world in order to preserve their independence. He was becoming the very essence of the age-old Lakota tradition of embracing outsiders and their resources while rejecting their alien ideas and institutions.[23]

YOU WOULD HAVE CUT YOUR THROAT LONG AGO

On June 6, 1870, President Grant and his wife Julia, members of the cabinet with their wives, officials of the Indian Office and the Interior Department, and British and Russian ministers joined Red Cloud, Spotted Tail, and other

Lakota emissaries for an evening reception in the State Dining Room of the White House. Lakotas had sent three separate delegations to the capital, hoping to resolve outstanding issues with thuŋkášila—grandfather—the president of the United States. They still trusted in face-to-face diplomacy with the wašíčus, but it became a troubled summit. A few days later Red Shirt, one of the Oglala delegates, threatened to commit suicide in the capital.[24]

Rumors of war had brought the chiefs to Washington. In the previous summer the U.S. Army, assisted by Pawnee scouts, had clashed with the already weakened Cheyenne Dog Soldiers at Summit Springs in northwestern Colorado, killing and capturing some fifty men and women. Demoralized, the Dog Soldiers dispersed, some seeking refuge in Indian Territory, others among Lakotas in the north. American bison hunters swarmed into the suddenly vacant central plains, spurred by the westward-inching Kansas Pacific Railroad that would soon carry their bulky products to eastern markets. The Union Pacific already stretched across the plains along the Platte, preventing the bison's north-south migrations and undermining their reproductive capacity. The range of the smaller northern herd, *pté wazíyata*, began contracting north and westward, and soon the thick bison populations of old could be found only in the Powder River country and the far northern plains. And in January 1870, roughly half a year after Summit Springs, the U.S. Army had attacked a peaceful Blackfoot Indian village on the Marias River, killing some two hundred men, women, and children, one of the bloodiest Indian massacres in U.S. history.[25]

Some Lakotas advocated caution in the heated atmosphere, while others, including Red Cloud, insisted that Lakotas needed to protect their interests with force. He led a raiding expedition to the south, and soon Lakota war parties swarmed into the upper North Platte Valley to steal horses and mules and to attack soldiers, mail patrols, and hunters. And then, in December 1869, word began to spread across the Lakota country that a large expedition was being prepared in the town of Cheyenne to explore the agricultural and mineral potential of the newly formed Wyoming Territory. The word was that the expedition would head north, which meant that it would enter the heart of the unceded territory between the Black Hills and the Bighorn Mountains and "drive out the Indians." Lakotas readied themselves for an invasion. In the spring stories of Lakota unrest began appearing in western newspapers, their editorials demanding that the federal government adopt more forceful measures to keep the Lakotas within their reservation. Caught between western hard-liners and eastern humanitarians, Grant grew nervous. He ordered the prospecting expedition aborted—earning the Board of Indian Commissioners' praise for his "wise consideration"—and authorized a meeting with Lakota chiefs.[26]

As the most prominent moderate headmen—leaders who had sway among both the friendlies and the hostiles—Red Cloud and Spotted Tail were the obvious heads of the Lakota embassy, representing the Oglalas and Sicangus. Put off by Red Cloud's eminence among Americans, They Fear Even His Horses, the hereditary chief of the Oglalas, refused to go. Agents persuaded both chiefs to accept the government's invitation and authorized each to assemble a personal delegation. Although in broad agreement over Lakota policy toward the United States, Red Cloud and Spotted Tail would not presume to speak for all Lakotas: the northern nontreaty Lakotas led by Sitting Bull shunned all talks with wašíčus. In the end, Lakotas organized three delegations—the third came from the Grand and Cheyenne River Agencies, representing the Minneconjous, Sans Arcs, and Two Kettles. With twenty-one members, Red Cloud's delegation was by far the largest, and the army took special measures to impress the formidable chief. Red Cloud asked to be received at Fort Laramie where Brigadier General John E. Smith welcomed him with pomp and deference that evoked the wašíču capitulation to his demands two years earlier. Smith escorted Red Cloud's delegation not to Cheyenne, the nearest railway station, but to Pine Bluff, a small station forty miles to the east; Red Cloud did not need to see how the Wyoming capital was booming, and the residents of Cheyenne did not need to see how the government was catering to the notorious architect of the Fetterman massacre. Red Cloud and his delegates arrived in Washington a week later, after stops in Omaha and Chicago, and were taken to the Washington House on Pennsylvania Avenue, where they met Spotted Tail and his three delegates. The meeting was emotionally charged and cautious: the previous fall Spotted Tail had killed, in self-defense, Big Mouth, an Oglala-born Wágluȟe chief who was his passionate opponent and Red Cloud's relative, in a liquor-fueled feast in Spotted Tail's growing Missouri village. Spotted Tail and Red Cloud may have despised each other, but they quickly established a working relationship that allowed each to maneuver independently and according to his political and personal preferences.[27]

Spotted Tail's Sicangus had been in the capital more than a week, and they were already exhausted and eager to return home. Their hosts had exposed them to a string of visitors—photographers, sculptors, amateur linguists, and even a Cherokee delegation from Indian Territory—and they had taken them to the theater, the botanical garden, the Smithsonian Institution, the Patent Office, Mount Vernon, and General Sherman's residence, where they were offered strawberries and ice cream and shown "Indian curiosities from all parts of the country." Palpably disgusted with the tactlessness, Spotted Tail refused to sit down to be photographed. In a final meeting the Secretary of the Interior Jacob D. Cox urged him to teach his followers to farm so that they would not starve after the bison had died off. When Cox then moved to inform the chief that "he must expect some trouble in his life; that white men had trouble," Spotted Tail could or would no longer contain his disdain: "If you had had as much trouble in your life as I have had in mine," he said, "you would have cut your throat long ago."[28]

Whereas Spotted Tail grew cynical and withdrew, Red Cloud became more confident and assertive. He was a sensation. Americans wanted their most formidable Indigenous adversaries imposing and inspiring, for in their might they could see a reflection of that of their own, and Red Cloud fit the bill. The *New York Times* heralded him as "a perfect Hercules," "a man of brains, a good ruler, an eloquent speaker, and able general and fair diplomat," "undoubtedly the most celebrated warrior living on the American Continent," who commanded ten thousand people and two thousand warriors. It was imperative, the paper insisted, to "create in his mind a favorable impression" of the Americans. Red Cloud's and Spotted Tail's delegations met with the secretary of the Interior and were escorted on tours of the Capitol, the Arsenal, and the Washington Navy Yard, a clumsy attempt to impress the chiefs with U.S military and administrative prowess. Red Cloud seemed to have seen right through it. He observed from the gallery the Senate debating the Indian Appropriation Bill—a momentous piece of legislation that would abolish the treaty system and drastically curb Indigenous sovereignty—without uttering a word. At the Arsenal the women of the Lakota delegations prepared for an exhibition of cannon fire by covering their ears to make known that they were familiar with such guns, and Red Cloud calmly examined a fifteen-inch coastal defense gun, measuring the diameter of its barrel with his hand and face. At the navy yard Lakotas inspected an ironclad monitor with some interest after they had been invited to try to cut its deck with their knives, but Red Cloud flatly declined the commandant's lunch invitation. He had come to Washington for business, not pleasure, he said.[29]

The following day came the festivities and proceedings at the White House. The evening dinner reception was a sumptuous affair under massive chandeliers, and it prompted Spotted Tail to observe that "the white man had a great many more good things to eat and drink than they sent to the Indians." Someone saw here a didactic opportunity and told the chief that this was because "the white man has quit the war path and gone to farming." Spotted Tail quipped that he would be happy to take on farming if "you will always treat me like this and let me live in as big [a] house."[30]

Spotted Tail's grim sarcasm gave way to Red Cloud's hard bargaining the next day when official talks began in the Indian Office. Like Tiyoskate in Montreal 175 years earlier, Red Cloud expected the wašíčus to treat him and his people as equals and kin, but his methods could hardly have been more different. Where Tioyskate had pleaded to be loved and pitied, Red Cloud simply insisted on being respected. He sat on the floor, underlining his intimate connection to the earth and mocking the Americans for having been raised on chairs, and bombarded Secretary Cox and Commissioner Parker with demands and harangues. "The Great Father says he is good and kind to us," he announced, adding: "I can't see it." "I came here to tell my Great Father what I do not like in my country." Fort Fetterman sat in Oglala land and had to be abandoned, he insisted, and no roads would be allowed into the Black Hills. The Oglala agency could not stay in the Missouri Valley, and trade in guns and ammunition had to be reinstated. "Tell the Great Father to move Fort Fetterman away and we will have no more troubles." Red Cloud came across as angry and impatient, but beneath his bluster there was a carefully considered political agenda, one that had a distinct spatial manifestation.[31]

Red Cloud and the other Lakota chiefs understood well what would later become known as the tyranny of distance, the struggle of people and nations to extend their authority and power over remote places. The United States had already begun compressing time and space in the northern Great Plains with steam power—with boats along the Missouri and a railroad along the Platte— but the far recesses of the vast grasslands were still beyond its effective reach. That was where Red Cloud needed to live. He insisted on having his agency built in the West in the unceded territory where hunting was still viable and where U.S. agents and American whiskey traders could not reach and corrupt them. In a public audience with President Grant in the White House, Red Cloud was adamant that the Oglalas would never settle on the Mníšoše. "I have said three times that I would not go to the Missouri," he said, "and now I say it here for the fourth time." Grant had already suffered a similar harangue from Spotted Tail. Stymied, he quickly ended the meeting.[32]

Unable to persuade the Lakotas or dictate terms to them, U.S. officials relied on the most effective negotiation instrument available to them: printed word. The next day Cox and Parker produced a map of the Indian country and a copy of the 1868 Treaty of Fort Laramie and had interpreters and traders read out its key sections line by line. It was a shock: the treaty was not the same one that had been read to Lakotas a year and a half earlier. Back then interpreters had provided a more cursory—perhaps a purposely selective—reading of the terms to Lakota chiefs who had accepted their words as facts. Lakotas transmitted, received, and preserved knowledge orally; to them spoken words were the all-important thing. The words they had heard in 1868 *were* the treaty. But now they were shown a radically different version with several disturbing clauses. The printed version authorized the United States to build new roads through Lakota lands, retain its existing forts near the borders of the reservation, and build the Lakota agencies on the Missouri and there only. Then came the bombshell: the unceded lands did not belong to Lakotas in perpetuity, but only as long as hunting remained viable. This was the first time Red Cloud and Spotted Tail learned about the critical clause that stipulated that the unceded territory would be available to Lakota hunters "so long as the buffalo may range thereon in such numbers as to justify the chase." What made things indefinitely more menacing now was that the bison herds were shrinking fast, drained by the Union Pacific and wašíču hunters. With a few new words, the Lakota sovereignty was put on a timer.[33]

Red Cloud retorted immediately. Denouncing the government's maneuver in its entirety, he said that he had agreed to the 1868 treaty "merely to show that he was peaceable, and not to grant their lands." That treaty was a peace treaty that pledged the United States to provide Lakotas with resources and nothing more. The treaty Cox and Parker now introduced meant nothing to him. Reasserting the primacy of spoken words, he said, "I never heard of it and do not mean to follow it." Other delegates accused the interpreters and traders, many of whom were mixed-bloods, for fraudulence at the Fort Laramie talks and said that they could not bring news of this kind to their villages at home. It was later that night in the Washington House that Red Shirt announced that "he wanted to commit suicide, saying that he might as well die here as elsewhere, as they had been swindled." A disgusted Red Cloud demanded to be taken home at once.[34]

Desperate to improve their negotiating leverage, U.S. officials had tried to find and fuel jealousies between Spotted Tail and Red Cloud, openly catering to the Oglala chief over his Sicangu counterpart. But the two chiefs faced similar challenges and were in agreement on key issues, especially Lakotas' right to determine the location of their agencies. All the talks took place under intense scrutiny—the *New York Times* and other major newspapers ran several detailed features on the negotiations and individual Lakotas—which turned the talks into a kind of performative contest. With their exotic customs, wittiness, charm, and sense of drama, Red Cloud and Spotted Tail dominated that contest. The press loved the projected image, which put enormous pressure on the American government to deliver an honorable outcome. The last thing Grant's administration—which had committed itself to the Peace Policy and its humanitarian ethos—needed was Lakota suicides in the capital.

A new war with the Lakotas suddenly seemed a real possibility, and Grant yielded. Lakotas were told that thuŋkášila had agreed to modify the Laramie treaty. Red Cloud could locate his Oglala agency on the upper Cheyenne River near the Black Hills, far from the Missouri, and Spotted Tail could move his Sicangu agency to his chosen spot near the upper White River more than two hundred miles west of the Whetstone Agency—or so the already weary chief chose to understand the somewhat vague promises. James Bordeaux, Joseph Bissonnette, and other familiar traders would follow him there. Lakotas had won the central dispute. With the agency issue resolved to their satisfaction, the other building blocks of their sovereignty would fall into place by default, for western agencies implied other government concessions: that Lakotas could continue to live in the unceded territory, near the last great bison herds of the Powder River country but removed from the U.S. military forts along the Missouri, for thirty-five years; that they could receive annuities in the heart of their domain and away from the corrupting influences of wašíču settlers and whiskey peddlers; that they would determine who was fit to trade in their country; and that the Black Hills and all the resources and riches they might contain were inviolate and belonged to Lakotas.[35]

Red Cloud and Spotted Tail had prevailed, but the Friends of the Indian, a group of Indian reform advocates, worried over their state of mind in the aftermath of the arduous negotiations. Red Cloud seemed agitated and insisted on returning home immediately. The famous Oglala chief's real and rumored ties to the hostiles in the Powder River country now became a concern: what would happen if a frustrated and angered Red Cloud returned home and denounced the Americans and their Lakota policy? The Friends hatched an emergency plan: they would take the Lakota delegations to New York and Philadelphia to mass meetings with pro-Indian humanitarians. Red Cloud agreed reluctantly and began preparing the ground once more for his diplomatic maneuvering. In a departing meeting with Cox, he stated that a council of thirty-two Lakota "nations" had elected him to negotiate on their behalf and that he himself was but a conduit of their collective will. He would say and do what he had to. He could not be swayed.

And so it would be. In Philadelphia Red Cloud and the other Lakota delegates were so palpably irate that Colonel Smith decided to take them straight to New York. There, at Cooper Institute, Red Cloud addressed a capacity crowd made up of Quakers, various humanitarians, and the generally-interested. He may have known his audience only superficially, but he could read a room. He delivered a triumphant performance. Standing on a platform with the other chiefs and dressed in a waistcoat and a high crowned silk hat, he prayed in silence, raising his hands toward the skies and then down toward the earth. Then, "drawing his blanket around him majestically," he spoke—of the battles he had fought for his people and of the injustices his people had suffered, accentuating the power of his words with his hands and standing perfectly motionless while a translator conveyed the meaning of his statements. "The magnetism which he evidently exercises over an audience," the *New York Times* enthused, "produced a vast effect over the dense throng." The chief reminded his audience of the elemental human traits they shared—"You have children. We, too, have children, and we wish to bring them up well. We ask you to help us do it"—and his "refreshing, simple, and unaffected utterances ... went right into the home to the hearts and consciences of the great multitude." Not even Oglala chief Red Dog's cutting remarks could dampen the buoyant mood that had been generated. "When the Great Father first sent out men to our people, I was poor and thin; now I am large and stout and fat," Red Dog announced. "It is because so many liars have been sent out there, and I have been stuffed full with their lies."[36]

Red Cloud's reluctant appearance in New York turned out to be vital. The leading generals of the army strongly opposed the talks with Lakotas, whom they saw as wards of the government, people they should manage, not parley with. Lakotas, Sherman had insisted in the spring of 1870, "should be told plainly and emphatically that they are expected to occupy that Reservation north of Nebraska and to trade on the Missouri River." Along with most top officials, Sherman wanted the Lakotas anchored in the Missouri Valley, where the army could monitor and, if necessary, suppress them with steam-powered military force. Western newspapers echoed the army's stance, mocking the eastern humanitarians as naïve do-gooders who had been duped by Red Cloud and whose gullibility would expose settlers to a new and devastating Sioux war: with the U.S. government on their side, supplying them with goods and guns, Lakotas would be more dangerous than ever before. But the army's and the westerners' protests had little traction in the East after Red Cloud's triumph in New York, which the humanitarians leveraged for all it was worth. The public opinion swung on Lakotas' side, and the Grant administration reacted accordingly. When Red Cloud left for the West, Cox sent a commission to Fort Laramie to welcome the chief home with a trainload of presents.[37]

Back in Washington, government agents had tried to offer Red Cloud a carriage as a present—an all too obvious attempt to civilize and emasculate the celebrated warrior—but Red Cloud had insisted on having horses instead. When he arrived in Fort Laramie, he accepted the gifts waiting him there: saddles, horses, and ammunition. After brief festivities at the fort, which with its large Wágluȟe population resembled as much a Lakota village as it did a U.S. military establishment, Red Cloud rode out. He headed neither to the east toward the Missouri, nor toward the Black Hills, but into the Powder River country where the vast majority of Oglalas, Sicangus, Hunkpapas, Minneconjous, Two Kettles, Sihasapas, and Sans Arcs lived. There he would find his true constituency, which would determine the merits of his diplomatic efforts.[38]

I AM RED CLOUD

Lakota politics shifted from the frantic Washington–New York interlude back into Lakota mode and rhythm. Red Cloud spent the summer in busy diplomacy, patiently building a national consensus for peace and securing Chey-

enne and Arapaho backing for the iwáštegla policy. He spoke of the spreading
web of railroads that would channel unprecedented numbers of settlers into the
West and gained supporters, but his signature achievement—the relocation of
the Oglala agency west of the Black Hills—faced fierce opposition from many
Lakotas who believed that government presence near Pahá Sápa would draw un-
wanted wašíču attention to the region "where there was much gold" and feared
that "their country would be overrun with adventurous white men in search of
the precious metal." Thus Red Cloud informed U.S. agents that they wanted a
different location, which opened the door for another wašíču attempt to keep the
agencies within the reservation.[39]

What followed was an exasperating wrangling prolonged by the Americans' singular negotiating advantage—Lakotas needed their rations and goods
because the bison herds were shrinking—and the consensus-driven, time-
consuming Lakota politics. In a series of meetings near Fort Laramie, U.S. agents
proposed various locations north of the Platte, eager to draw the Lakotas into
the reservation and determined to protect the existing and expected American
settlements along the valley. Lakotas insisted that the Platte Valley was theirs and
demanded to have the agency farther south and outside the reservation boundaries. The Americans, even the highly sympathetic Board of Indian Commissioners, struggled to understand them. Lakotas, the baffled commissioners reported, "are extremely sensitive in regard to the slightest encroachment upon
their reservation, or the hunting grounds allotted to them in the treaty of 1868,
and have objected even to the establishment of an agency for their own benefit
within its limits." In reality, Lakotas had a number of strategically critical reasons
to insist on a southern location outside the reservation. There, near the North
Platte, the agency would not only be close to Fort Laramie, their favored place
to trade, but it would also serve as an entryway into the contested Article 11 lands
where Lakotas needed to maintain a hunting existence in order to retain them.
The agency location had direct and momentous consequences for Lakota sovereignty.[40]

The talks became a drawn-out exercise in assigning blame and asserting moral
obligations, which played into Lakota hands. When one of the agents asked
whether the buffalo were scarce, They Fear Even His Horses told him that "he
ought to know as he had been through the country scaring them away." Red
Cloud cornered the agents by declaring that President Grant had assured him in
Washington that Fort Fetterman "was there to watch my interests as well as his."
"I told my Great Father," he said, "that he did not need any more of these lands.
The Great Father's houses in Washington are full of money stolen from the pro-
ceeds of our lands." The talks deadlocked. Months later the agents threatened to

withdraw government annuities if Lakotas did not comply; Red Cloud said he would himself kill any Lakotas who received annuities at sites unauthorized by Lakota councils. While the dispute dragged on, the House of Representatives, determined not to cede sole control of Indian affairs to the Senate and resolved to move more tribal lands in the public domain and for railroads, declared that no new treaties would be made, ever. Lakotas did not know it, but the United States had ceased to consider them—along with hundreds of Indigenous societies—as a sovereign nation.[41]

After a year of bitter dispute, in June 1871, Red Cloud rode into Fort Laramie to resolve the agency issue, the "grand leading object" of Lakota-U.S. relations. He was taken into a building known as the Theater where a council would be held. He named his desired interpreters among the post traders, faced his audience—the post commandant Colonel Smith, a new Lakota agent John W. Wham, the Board of Indian Commissioners chairman Felix Brunot, and thirty-two Lakota chiefs—and began:[42]

> I am Red Cloud. The Great Spirit raised both the white man and the Indian. I think He raised the Indian first. He raised me in this land and it belongs to me. The white man was raised over the great waters, and his land is over there. Since they crossed the sea, I have given them room. There are now white people all about me. I have but a small spot of land left. The Great Spirit told me to keep it. I went and told the Great Father so. Since I came back, I have nothing more to say. I told all to the Great Father.... Whatever I do, my people will do the same. Whatever the Great Spirit tells me to do I will do. I have not yet done what the Great Father told me to do. God raised us Indians. We are two nations. Whatever we decide to do, we want to do together. I must ask you to wait. I am trying to live peaceably.[43]

Red Cloud had perfected his negotiating tactics with the wašíčus: he would be nothing if not unpredictable. Shifting from assertive to accommodating, from moralizing to pitiable, from spiritual to practical, he reassured the wašíčus while subtly threatening an all-out war if denied. Such posturing had become necessary, even expected, because both Red Cloud and the U.S. officials were under intense pressure to deliver. Both represented large, divided, and vocal interest groups, and both negotiated on the razor's edge of violence, acutely aware that failure to reach an acceptable solution could well lead to carnage only three years after the celebrated Laramie treaty that had officially ended the bloody Powder River War. U.S. officials had to appease the noisy eastern humanitarian lobby that claimed the president as their champion and the equally assertive politicians and army officers who wanted the Lakotas confined and tamed. Red Cloud spoke for both the agency-dwelling Lakota minority and the great majority that resolutely rejected agency life, balancing between cooperation and militant defiance and seeking, all at once, a way to secure American material aid and American guarantees for enduring Lakota sovereignty.

Responding to Red Cloud's speech, the American agents tried to overwhelm the chief by lacing kindness with threats. General Smith reassured him that "when the Great Father sees that your hearts are good, he will send you plenty of all that you wish," and went on to lecture how young Lakota men "cannot shoe a horse, or build a house; they must have someone to teach them." Betraying his anxiety, Brunot threatened occupation: "If trouble come, war houses will go into your country." Holding his ground, Red Cloud retorted, "I have given my friends" the Americans "a good deal. I have only a little of my country left; and I gave the railroad to my friends, and I want to be paid for it." Smith warned that rations would be withheld if Oglalas did not designate a site for their agency; Red Cloud, having boasted complete command over his people just moments ago, retreated behind traditional consensus politics, insisting that he would have to confer with Crazy Horse, Black Twin, Charging Shield, and Little Big Man, the most defiant of the Powder River Lakotas, men who were "wild, like the antelope." "I am afraid if I open an agency some of my friends will jump over me," he said. While he himself was "willing to go over the river"—to move north of the Platte—he would have to convince "all the rest to agree to it."[44]

Later, in a private meeting with Smith and Brunot, Red Cloud provided the Americans an education on Lakota politics. "I am here alone to-day, away from my council-men," who numbered twenty-six, he explained. "That is why I could not name a place for my agency." "We will meet on the Cheyenne River," he promised, "I will get men of sense, and will try and decide where to put the post." As for Lakotas' Cheyenne and Arapaho allies, they "are like lost children, they will agree with me at any time." Yet he was uncomfortable with the American efforts to elevate him above other Lakota chiefs: "I do not want to be the only chief; at the treaty of 1851, we made one great chief"—Mato Oyuhi—"and the white men killed him." The following day Smith pressured Red Cloud to speed things up. "The earth will not move away," the chief responded, "it will be here for a long time, and there need be no hurry. I am trying to persuade my people all to go, and it takes time to bring them all to it." They were in the Lakota country now, and things evolved differently there. Red Cloud rode out north the next day to attend a Sun Dance and council, promising to keep the agents informed.[45]

As in 1867 Red Cloud simply disappeared, unsettling the agents. After an anxious wait, word arrived that the Oglala councillors had rejected the site north of the Platte and wanted an agency outside the reservation, within a day's ride east of Fort Laramie. The news triggered rounds of heated debate during which the easily agitated agent Wham bombarded Commissioner Parker in Washington with telegrams and letters, urging him to consent and send in goods. With Red Cloud ominously absent, Parker relented. In the late summer a string of Oglala bands came to draw rations at the new agency, which soon became known as the Red Cloud Agency. They stayed only briefly. By the early fall the agents knew only vaguely where they were. Red Cloud seemed to have vanished.[46]

The location of the Oglala agency was a bitter disappointment to a number of American groups with a stake in the nation's Indian and Lakota policies: to western settlers and ranchers because it bolstered Lakota claims to a massive block of land; to the humanitarians, missionaries, and Indian Office agents because it undermined their reservation-centered civilization schemes; to the army because clashes between settlers and Lakotas were now more likely; to railroad companies and land speculators whose western profits hinged on a peace with the Lakotas; to the Grant administration because Red Cloud's stature as a liaison capable of reaching both agency and militant Lakotas seemed to have plummeted. The small window of accommodation that had opened with Fetterman's demise began to close.[47]

WE SHALL BE STARTLED BY A MASSACRE

Without Red Cloud, the Sitting Bull we know — purist, stunningly victorious, pivotal — would not have been possible. Red Cloud's personal charm, emotional suppleness, and ability to shift seemingly at will from boastful to subtle to decisive to cagy captivated U.S. policymakers, making him the essential Lakota in the American mind. His outsized diplomatic presence tricked the Americans into believing that he could influence most if not all Lakotas, an impression Red Cloud variously cultivated and denied. During the rambling Laramie talks a thoroughly frustrated agent Wham had told him flatly that the Americans wanted him to "say where the agency shall be, and be the big chief after it is fixed." Like many other U.S. policymakers, Wham wanted to cut through the labyrinthine Lakota politics by placing a single individual on the top. Red Cloud rejected the title but embraced the role. By doing so he became essential also to Sitting Bull and the northern nonagency Lakotas who found a surprising sanctuary in the Oglala chief's long shadow. Together, Red Cloud and Sitting Bull embodied the two broad foreign political options available to Lakotas — delicate accommodation and violent resistance — as they faced the expansionist U.S. empire.[48]

In the early 1870s railroads became a burning issue in Lakota-American relations. Transcontinentals threatened to crush the Lakota realm like a vice. The tracks for the Northern Pacific were being laid from Minnesota toward North Dakota and the Lakota territory, while in the south the Union Pacific kept siphoning in settlers whose ranches crowded the North Platte Valley. The Red Cloud Agency stood in the middle of this ranching frontier, blocking American expansion around the valley and aggravating the railroad companies that wielded outsized influence over the federal government through lobbying and bribing. Indian Office agents saw the writing on the wall: the Oglala agency, only a few months in operation, would have to be moved. This was a stinging personal blow to Red Cloud as an Oglala and Lakota spokesman. His nimble and audacious scheming in Washington and at Fort Laramie had made him a galvanizing leader who symbolized Indigenous resilience to thousands of Indians beyond the Oglalas. But now, with the all-important agency under attack and with railroads poised to envelop the Lakotas, he faced a kind of crisis that, like the U.S. military posts in the Powder River country five years earlier, endangered the very survival of his people.[49]

He improvised. Although diminished now, he was still looked to by many for guidance, and he soon regained his centrality in the eyes of U.S. policymakers. He realized that the long-standing Lakota strategy—keeping military forts out of Lakota lands and keeping the Oglala agency in Article 11 lands—was not enough in the overheated situation where wašíču expansion threatened bison herds and Lakota existence. He now merged spatial politics with temporal ones and adopted a distinctly delaying stance on the agency issue that served both national and personal interests: the longer he could postpone a decision, the longer Lakotas could claim their unceded hunting ranges and the longer he himself could stay in power.

Red Cloud walked a thin line between impatient government agents and uncompromising northern Lakotas. The continuing erosion of bison herds in the Powder River country and the growing American presence around it fueled fierce resentment among young warriors who had come of age there and knew no other home. Northern warrior societies emerged as forceful political players that categorically denounced government agencies, agency chiefs, and farming, gravitating toward leaders committed to uncompromised Lakota autonomy. Alarmed Indian agents reported how "the hostile Sioux out north"—bands led by Sitting Bull, Black Twin, Crazy Horse, and other chiefs with robust military records—exerted a strong influence across the realm, drawing in thousands of people from the agencies during the warm months. James Daniels, a new Oglala agent, warned that while the government officials "slumber in the belief" that Lakotas' "savage prejudices are to be overcome by generous acts, fatherly care, and kindness, we shall be startled by a massacre." For his own and for his people's sake, Red Cloud needed to become a conduit between northern warriors and U.S. agents. Neither was willing to compromise, and both had to be conciliated. It would take time, and that was what Red Cloud set out to create.[50]

An opportunity presented itself in the spring of 1872 when Lakota and U.S. envoys met at the Red Cloud Agency to decide whether it should be moved within the reservation boundaries. After a nine-month sojourn in the Powder River country, Red Cloud resurfaced. Although his standing among the Oglalas was already crumbling—many of his followers had left his thióšpaye to join those of American Horse and They Fear Even His Horses the Younger, who boasted more prestigious lineages—he began a prolonged maneuvering that left both Lakotas and Americans uncertain of his goals, motivations, and role. He presided over the meeting as the Oglala spokesman but deferred to warriors and the head shirt wearer They Fear Even His Horses the Younger who reproached the president for failing to supply guns and protect his peoples' right to hunt and live in the unceded territories. Balancing between Lakota factions and burning political capital at an alarming rate, Red Cloud observed how the talks collapsed into an impasse. Brigadier General Edward O. C. Ord, baffled that Lakotas "should be allowed to plunder so near the post and to kill whites with apparent impunity," demanded harder measures, and agent Daniels insisted that the agency be moved on the upper White River within the reservation, a demand that drew the immediate reproach of Oglala traditionalists who insisted that the agency should stay on the North Platte, allowing them to "go all over the country." "I never saw Chiefs and Head men who had so little control over their young men," a flustered Daniels complained. The resulting deadlock was an opening for Red Cloud who offered to revisit Washington with an Oglala delegation.[51]

U.S. policymakers sought to reduce the perplexingly complex Lakota politics to the person of Red Cloud who, they hoped, could generate a consensus for peace and expedite the process of bringing all the Lakotas into the Great Sioux Reservation. In late May he dictated an ambiguous peace-promoting letter to the nonagency northern Lakotas, his "friends." "You must carry on the war yourself, I am done," he announced—and then left for the capital with agent Daniels and twenty-six Oglala delegates. The hastily organized visit was a shorter and plainer reiteration of the 1870 one and its results were scantier. The secretary of the Interior promised Lakotas lead and powder, and Red Cloud flatly rejected the president's naïve proposition that the Lakotas move into Indian Territory. He did, however, formally accept the relocation of the Oglala agency to the White River. Returning home, Red Cloud must have known that it was far from enough to appease the Oglala warriors who despised agencies and the very idea of a reservation. He waited three months to inform Daniels that Oglala councils had rejected the White River site. Daniels blamed Red Cloud for the turnabout and labeled the "perfect Hercules" cowardly.[52]

The controversy descended into posturing in which threats of violence seemed a primary means of communication. Army officers wanted to cancel Oglala rations and bring in troops to enforce the agency relocation but were blocked by the Indian Office. Oglala warriors threatened to kill Daniels at his agency and said they would go into the Republican River to hunt bison "whether they got permission or not," thus reasserting their rights to the Article 11 lands. Sheridan declared that those rights had "always been a matter of regret to me" and "productive of great injury to the reservation system." Once again Red Cloud remained elusive through all this, and his reappearance at the North Platte agency in November 1872 was a shock to Daniels. The chief arrived with young warriors and told the agent that they had been fighting whites somewhere in the north. He announced that he would now come every month to collect rations, which he expected to receive on the North Platte—only to soon demand an agency nearer the Black Hills on a site where farming was utterly impossible. Daniels feared that Red Cloud, the essential intermediary, had joined forces with the warrior societies.[53]

The American plans for Lakota domestication seemed to be sliding backwards. It was already clear that the Oglalas, running out of supplies, would have to yield, but Red Cloud kept delaying and pushing the agents for better terms for half a year more. It was a risky gamble. Pressured by a rapidly growing white population—nearly half a million settlers would call Nebraska home by 1880—the federal government began surveying the unceded Lakota lands between the North Platte and the Nebraska state line and placing those lands on the market. The Red Cloud Agency, a veritable village that could balloon to hold as many as thirteen thousand Indians, stood directly in the path of America's westward march. "It is very doubtful whether Red Cloud and his followers can be induced to give up a part of this unceded territory, which is by them claimed as much as any portion of their permanent reservation," a Wyoming daily correctly predicted. By simply staying put, Red Cloud forced the U.S. government to treat his people with care. All the while thousands of Oglalas and Sicangus hunted, raided, and camped in the North Platte and Republican Valleys, keeping the unceded territory unceded.[54]

When the Oglalas finally accepted the White River site, they did so on their own terms. It was Oglalas who put the agency there, Red Cloud insisted, and announced that "*they* would regulate affairs here." The warriors paraded around the new grounds to "intimidate and show their power." A plan to build a mission near the agency was quickly shelved. Red Cloud established his own camp away from the agency in a spot where it was concealed by a chain of grassy hills but monitored the agents from a distance. Together with the other chiefs, he set "limits to the range of travel of the agent and employés," had a post trader discharged for selling whiskey, and brushed off the agents' warnings that Oglalas should no longer travel south of the Platte to hunt. When the new agent, John J. Saville, a Denver physician chosen by the Episcopalian Church, organized his first distribution of annuities in the fall of 1873, he was shocked by the arrival of large numbers of "exceedingly vicious and insolent" northern Lakotas who camped around the agency, made "unreasonable demands for food, and supplemented their demands with threats." When Saville tried to count and identify them, he was promptly arrested by hundreds of "these wild fellows and returned to the agency for trial." Lakotas were systematically inflating their numbers to secure enough rations from the seemingly stingy U.S. government, and now they turned the wašíčus' apparent advantage—institutional record keeping—against the hapless agent. "The Indians in council constantly refer to previous treaties with which I am not conversant," Saville complained. "It would aid me in getting a correct understanding of their ideas to have all the treaties which have been made with them." Lakotas were making it plain how they saw the agency: it was a sovereign Indigenous space as well as a supply base that helped the Lakota nation preserve its steppe dominion as long as possible.[55]

Red Cloud's delaying tactics served Oglala interests by buying his followers time—years—to prepare themselves to the iwáštegla mindset, the inevitability of living with the wašíčus and sharing "the good road" with them. But Red Cloud's maneuvering also became a screen that shielded the larger Lakota nation against the United States' hegemonic pretensions. By drawing attention to himself, he had created a massive blind spot in the federal government's field of vision where Sitting Bull and the other northern Lakotas could operate almost unobstructed, pushing rival tribes out of bison domains and even raiding government agencies. He did so by keeping the controversy over the Oglala agency at the forefront of Lakota-U.S. relations year after year; his meetings with local agents and his much-publicized visits to the capital lulled American policymakers into believing that they could control a critical segment of the Lakota nation through him.[56]

They could not. The U.S. government expected three things from Lakotas: that they live in peace with their neighbors, that they accept American education programs, and that they stay within the bounds of the greater Sioux Reservation, which included the unceded territories. Northern Lakotas—the Powder River country oyátes—defied all those expectations. While Red Cloud held the center stage, keeping the U.S. policymakers on their toes, northern Lakotas stealthily kept reshaping the American West to meet their needs. Much of their maneuvering—raids, wars, transnational diplomacy and commerce—unfolded in the deep interior, beyond the reach and sight of the American state, leaving the agents uninformed and nervy. It did not help that the Grant administration had found itself mired in a sprawling corruption scandal over the Crédit Mobilier, the construction and finance company of the Union Pacific Railroad, distracting the federal government from the challenges to its authority in the West. On the ground, half a continent away from Washington, Agent Saville lived in mortal fear of the northern Lakotas who entered the Red Cloud Agency as they pleased, claiming vastly inflated numbers to maximize their rations. Soon Saville was handing out eight hundred thousand pounds of beef each month.[57]

For half a decade Red Cloud had forced the wašíčus to notice him and the needs and demands of his people. He paid a heavy personal price for this. A descendant of a middling lineage, he had stirred up the Oglala politics and was branded as a usurper, but he kept at it. Through sheer determination and personal charisma, he distracted the U.S. government to the point that it neglected a far greater threat that had been brewing for years.[58]

BUFFALO IMPERIALISM

A lush highland basin tucked between the Black Hills and the Bighorn Mountains, the Powder River country had once been a superb hunting ground filled with seemingly inexhaustible bison herds. By the late 1860s that was no longer the case. Some ten thousand Lakotas—Hunkpapas, Oglalas, Sicangus, Minneconjous, Two Kettles, Sihasapas, and Sans Arcs—and thousands of their Cheyenne and Arapaho allies had lived there for more than a decade, hunting the buffalo for robes and meat and gradually draining the herds. The largest herds now existed farther away, in the far northwestern plains along and beyond the Yellowstone Valley, drawing Lakotas in. It meant, once again, war.

In the winter of 1869–70 two Hunkpapa youths ran into a party of thirty Crows in a deep snow. Crows killed one but only wounded the other, who made it to the village of Sitting Bull. The Hunkpapa chief organized a large revenge party that immediately pushed after the Crows who were fleeing on foot. When caught, they sought protection behind a massive boulder, and the Hunkpapas launched an uncharacteristic frontal attack. The battle lasted until all the Crows were dead. Sitting Bull counted three coups, but lost thirteen warriors, including his uncle, Looks-for-Him-in-a-Tent. A winter count shows deadly projectiles—bullets, not arrows—flying toward the Crows, one of the first counts showing Lakotas using guns in combat. The battle was symptomatic in its intensity, anticipating what was to come. Long-standing enmities blended with new anxieties over subsistence and survival to fuel unforgiving and inescapable violence.[59]

In the summer of 1870, possibly at Mathó Pahá northeast of the Black Hills, an Oglala tribal council of hundreds of headmen, elders, and warriors came together to appoint a new war chief for their oyáte, a consolidation of execu-

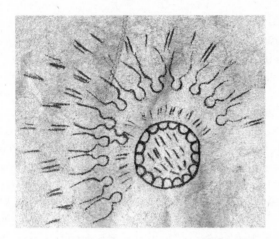

43. Lone Dog winter count, 1870–71 (detail). This winter count depicts the Hunkpapa-Crow fight, showing how the Hunkpapas converged around the Crows and kept firing at them through the night. The winter count illuminates how declining hunting opportunities intensified rivalries and hardened attitudes. Courtesy of National Museum of the American Indian, Smithsonian Institution (01/0617, detail). Photo by NMAI Services.

tive power that mirrored Sitting Bull's and Gall's elevation earlier among the Hunkpapas. Three senior chiefs—They Fear Even His Horses, Bad Wound, and Big Road—were assigned to make the decision. The person they chose was led from the circle of warriors to them, and they held a pipe to his lips and placed a three-foot war club in his hands. Crazy Horse, recently deposed as a shirt wearer for having eloped with Black Buffalo Woman, reentered the military core of the Oglala nation as its most renowned warrior. An intensely private man, he paraded the council grounds as a Thunder Dreamer, his exposed body painted yellow and with members of warrior societies behind him, liberated to do what he did best: protect his people on the battlefield.[60]

Crazy Horse knew that it would take a national war to secure enough bison for the Lakota people, and he set out to generate one. That fall, with some fifty Oglala tipis, he rode north into the Yellowstone country to meet with Sitting Bull. While Red Cloud was operating as a highly visible conduit between Lakotas and Americans during the years following the 1868 Laramie treaty, Sitting Bull had solidified his role as the foremost war leader of the northern malcontents who denounced the treaty as irrelevant and dangerous: it may have removed U.S. military forts from the Powder River country, but it also left the detested upper Missouri forts intact and did not ban steamboat traffic along the river. From a northern Lakota perspective the United States continued to violate Lakota sovereignty, and Sitting Bull insisted that there was no peace between his people and the Americans. When Crazy Horse came to him, the two warrior-leaders formulated a new policy. Neither accepting nor rejecting Red Cloud's temporizing strategy, they pledged to shun the wašíčus whose very existence threatened the bison and Lakota survival. They would wage a defensive war against the United States—a war that was sustained by munitions secured from independent American and Métis traders—while focusing their military might on enlarging their hunting domains. In the fall of 1870 Sitting Bull masterminded a devastating cattle-butchering raid against Fort Buford. It turned out to be his last attempt to clear the upper Mníšoše of the wašíčus. With Crazy Horse, he shifted his ambitions on buffalo ranges.[61]

At a time when the United States was starting to emerge as a global power by extending its imperial reach to the Pacific, and when Congress was moving to abolish the century-old treaty system with the Indians, responding to ever-louder demands that there was no room for sovereign Native nations in the modern United States, northern Lakotas spearheaded an explosive expansion in the heart of the continent. War parties from all seven oyátes, augmented by Cheyenne and Arapaho allies, fanned out of the Powder River country, waging simultaneous wars against Crows, Utes, Shoshones, and Flatheads. Lakota foreign policy was crystallizing into a quest to command *all* the northern grasslands where bison still existed in adequate numbers. Although aimed at saving the traditional Lakota way of life, it was a forward-looking campaign that would turn a vast segment of the interior into a buffalo reserve where Lakota power and sovereignty would endure.

For a long while it seemed possible. Ranging across a widening belt, Lakota war parties carved out a new bison domain beyond the Bighorns and the Yellowstone raid by raid, victory by victory. Women piled up new reserves of meat, fat, and hides; men accumulated horses, captives, and war honors; families flourished and grew. The newly thriving northern Lakota villages became gravitational points for Cheyennes, Arapahos, Yanktonais, and Yanktons who sought protection and relief under their auspices. While almost all Native societies were struggling to maintain their numbers in the face of starvation, disease, cultural loss, and sheer despair, the northern Lakota communities burgeoned: their combined population may have exceeded fifteen thousand. By 1871 several thousands of them were reported to be living in what U.S. maps called the Montana

Territory, curbing the ambitions of some of the most vociferous settlers in the American West. That meant nothing to Lakotas. Any claims the settlers might put forward were worthless because there were still bison, whose very existence underwrote Lakota claims to the unceded territory. And there were millions of beasts left.[62]

Northern Lakotas were rectifying the glaring loophole in the Laramie treaty: it did not specify the northern boundary of the unceded territory. By pushing into the Montana Territory, Sitting Bull, Crazy Horse, and their thousands of followers were finally creating a boundary—and making the lands within it theirs, literally and legally. By tying the ownership of the land to the viability of the chase in 1868, the federal government had created a paradoxical situation in which Lakotas could preserve their sovereignty only by expanding and dispossessing other Native nations. To survive, Lakotas had to overlap, almost perfectly, with the bison, which in the early 1870s demanded constant warfare: there was not enough game to go around, and Crows, Utes, Shoshones, and Flatheads would have to make room so that Lakotas could have enough. The Laramie treaty had geared a massive swath of the American West toward violence.

As so often before Lakotas held a singular advantage in war: they could mobilize far more warriors than their enemies could. But to fully capitalize on their numbers, they needed guns, powder, and lead; they needed to pair territorial expansion with a commercial one. Ever since the wašíču show of firepower in the Battle of Killdeer in 1864, Sitting Bull and other northern leaders had built up their gun reserves. While distancing themselves from the American government, they continued to trade with American merchants along the upper Missouri. They also tightened their ties with the Métis who, threatened by the Canadian annexation of Rupert's Land in 1869, had mounted a failed rebellion under Louis Riel. Disaffected Métis moved farther west, specialized in bison-robe trade, and made "overtures to the Sioux for an alliance." Commercial gravity, together with a shared abhorrence of modern states, pulled Métis and Lakotas together. The upper Missouri Valley became a site for a seasonal rendezvous where Lakotas and their allies traded buffalo meat and hides for Canadian guns, munitions, and whiskey. A Hunkpapa winter count for 1870–71 captures the routinization of the practice: "Another party of 10 Frenchmen came and traded with Indians." An anxious Indian agent believed that Lakotas could "procure all they desire from the Red River Half Breeds."[63]

Lakota hunters, raiders, and traders had ventured north for decades, but now their sojourns began to coalesce into occupation. Drawn by the Métis markets and a relative absence of wašíčus, more and more Lakotas, Yanktons, Yanktonais, and Dakotas gravitated north and stayed there longer. Quietly, keeping their distance from the string of U.S. forts on the upper Missouri, they began turning the far reaches of the Great Plains into a Sioux domain. They forged diplomatic ties with their long-standing Assiniboine enemies whom Sitting Bull and other northern Lakota chiefs had been cajoling for years. Trading, hunting, and camping with their new allies, they built thickening kinship networks that anchored them to the land. What official maps showed as the U.S.-Canada border area began to transform into a de facto Sioux-Assiniboine borderland.[64]

Stunned by the rapid transformation of political geography, Isaac Cowie, a Hudson's Bay Company trader, fretted how the new Sioux-Métis-Assiniboine alliance "would be able to overcome the Saulteaux [Sauteurs] and their friends, the Crees, and capturing Forts Qu'Appelle and Ellice on the way with the munitions therein, raid the settlement of Portage la Prairie, and massacre the inhabitants of Winnipeg, while besieging Fort Garry." Not long after Cowie received a gift of tobacco from Lakotas, who stated they "wished to send a strong delegation to arrange that Fort Qu'Appelle should become their trading post." The local Indians were horrified: that the Lakotas would "now be made more formidable by the invasion of the tribe under the notorious depredator Sitting Bull, was not to be thought of." Undeterred, Lakotas sent "some of their best speakers and ablest men" to negotiate with the Canadians, who were exposed to classic Sioux diplomacy that blended historicity, selective remembering, arrogance, and accommodation into a mix that left the wašíčus both baffled and buoyant. The ambassadors "went back to ancient history to prove that they had always been the friends of the British against the Americans, and showed a silver medal of King George in evidence." One of the ambassadors, Cowie reported, "stated that they had been for years spying out the land as one they wished to obtain possession of and therein to become good and loyal British Indians, supporting and trading with the Hudson's Bay Company."[65]

With its strong commercial undertones and diplomatic maneuvering, the Canadian-bound expansion seemed distinct from the aggressive bison-driven expansion around the Powder River country, but in truth the two expansions were closely linked. A good portion of the guns and munitions Lakotas secured from Canada surely circulated among Powder River bands during the communal gatherings in and around Pahá Sápa, allowing Lakotas to monopolize bison grounds and market outlets across a vast arc beyond their core territory. Improbably, Lakotas were still operating on an imperial scale, seizing viable hunting ranges from western Wyoming and central Montana across the southern Canadian plains. Only a triangle-shaped chunk of land between the lower Yellowstone and the Milk River, a tributary of the Missouri, separated the two Lakota expansions from one another.[66]

THEY HAVE COME TO STAY

It may have been the worst possible location for a new Sioux agency, but there it stood, not far from the Missouri-Milk confluence. The old government agency at the site had served Assiniboines, Crows, and Gros Ventres for years, and the agents were hopeful that their wards would soon become farmers. But in the spring of 1871 several thousand Lakotas, Yanktons, Yanktonais, and Dakotas had suddenly come in, telling the stunned agents that they expected to be fed. Many of them were refugees from Canada where they had lived since the U.S.-Dakota War of 1862. "Every effort in my power has been made to induce them to go to the Sioux agencies east," agent Andrew J. Simmons reported, "but without effect. They close their ears to my words."[67]

Then bands of Lakotas began arriving, filling Simmons with dread: "They are superior to the neighboring people in equipments for warfare, and I think are braver and better warriors: their horses are numerous and of good quality and they keep constantly on hand a large supply of ammunition which they can always [obtain] from the Half breeds of the British possessions. They have become the great terror of the whites on the upper Missouri River." Simmons focused on all things masculine, ignoring the crucial point: hundreds of Lakota women had arrived with the men, signaling permanence and possibly occupation. Simmons may have missed the clues, but he got the message: "they come in force with their whole encampment asserting '*they have come to stay*.'" He also understood what pulled Lakotas in: they pursued the contracting bison herds, "which now appear to be almost surrounded and cornered" in the Milk River country. The area was known as "the Indians 'Paradise,' owing to the immense amount of buffalo."[68]

Simmons asked for permission to provide supplies for Lakotas at the Milk River, and the Indian Office complied, though not without apprehensions over their "disposition for evil." The resident Crows and Gros Ventres, longtime U.S. allies, fled upriver, and the Milk River agency became a Sioux agency. A nearby trading post, Fort Peck, became a Sioux post where bison robes could be traded for guns, powder, and bullets. Firmly positioned in the Milk Valley, Lakotas and their allies promptly took over the swath of land between the Milk and lower Yellowstone, consolidating their expansions into one great realm that seemed to underwrite their sovereignty for the foreseeable future: they now controlled access to the bulk of the remaining bison. In the fall Sitting Bull visited Fort Peck and told its traders that he was willing to open peace talks with the Americans. He promised to prevent any raids until he heard back from the government.[69]

Washington officials seized the startling opening. Sitting Bull and a Minneconjou chief Black Moon spent the spring of 1872 near Fort Peck with seven hundred lodges and had several meetings with U.S. agents. Sitting Bull accepted government rations for the first time, stirring hopes that this elusive leader of the northern "hostiles" might be softening. Commissioner Francis A. Walker urged Congress to allocate five hundred thousand dollars to feed and clothe the Lakotas at Fort Peck, intimating that "the submission of the whole tribe will result." Few in Washington seemed to have noticed two sentences the agent of the Montana Superintendency had put in the middle of his annual report: "Of these Teton Sioux, there are probably 1,000 lodges, under the control of Sitting Bull. These Indians occupy and range over a section of country which covers the proposed route of the Northern Pacific Railroad for several hundred miles, and from all I can learn it is their intention to resist the survey of that country, and the road itself." Sitting Bull took government rations not because his resolve was melting but because the supplies helped expand and consolidate the Lakota empire in the far north—just as the U.S. empire was gearing up for an invasion.[70]

In June 1872, without warning, U.S. surveyors and soldiers entered the Yellowstone valley from both east and west, probing it for the Northern Pacific. Fear of Lakota resistance had created an engineering gap of more than two hundred miles along the river, and the army assigned more than eleven hundred officers, soldiers, scouts, and beef-herders to escort survey teams that were scheduled to meet at the Powder confluence. The expeditions were more than an outrage; they breached the sanctity of the unceded territory, which Lakotas thought included the Yellowstone Valley, and signaled a rejection of the budding conciliation northern Lakotas and wašíčus had been forging along the Milk. Lakotas learned about both expeditions early on—Spotted Eagle had told the agents in early April that "he would fight the rail road people as long as he lived"—but the Americans knew little about Lakota whereabouts. Commander of the westbound prong, Colonel David S. Stanley, was not aware that more than ten thousand Lakotas, Cheyennes, and Arapahos had gathered on the Powder, preparing for a Sun Dance and a summer excursion against the Crows. The gathered Indians heard about the surveyors, and sent more than a thousand warriors up the Yellowstone.[71]

They found the intruders camping along Pryor Creek on the Yellowstone, and immediately launched a surprise night attack that failed to penetrate wagon-enforced infantry pickets. Lakotas took a position on the bluffs above the wašíčus, firing down on them as morning broke. Crazy Horse, dressed in white buckskin and his face painted white, charged at a dead run across the picket line, taunting the wašíčus. Sitting Bull walked down toward the camp, sat down within firing range, and lit his pipe. Four warriors joined him. Ignoring the bullets whining by, he passed the pipe around, then carefully cleaned it, walked back up the ridge, and announced the fight over. The soldiers, for their part, ended the fight by throwing the body of Hunkpapa Plenty Lice onto a campfire. The survey expedition continued downriver for a few days, unnerved and apprehensive of its sporadically drunk commander, before turning back west. When the eastern survey expedition later reached the Powder River, it was received there not by fellow Americans but by the tall, bulky, and gloriously audacious Gall. He faced the wašíčus alone, painted for war, his Hunkpapa warriors behind him, and told them to leave.[72]

Oddly, while the two heavily armed survey expeditions had pushed into the Yellowstone Valley, ready for bloodshed, the secretary of the Interior had dispatched a high-powered peace commission to Fort Peck to parley with the Lakotas. Arriving in late July, the commissioners found nearly three thousand Lakotas and Yanktonais but not Sitting Bull nor any other prominent chiefs: they were busy shadowing and fighting U.S. soldiers along the Yellowstone. The intended goal—bringing Sitting Bull and other noted "hostiles" to Washington— had to be abandoned. Instead, the commissioners received a lesson on the new geopolitical realities in the far northern plains. It was only now, facing minor chiefs at the edge of an active war zone, that U.S. agents began to realize the immensity of the blunder they had made by opening Fort Peck and the Milk River to Lakotas.

Assistant Secretary of the Interior Benjamin R. Cowen reported a burgeoning anti-wašíču Lakota empire that "had embraced those members of various tribes"—Dakotas, Yanktons, Yanktonais, Cheyennes, Arapahos, and even Kiowas—"who had become dissatisfied with the conduct of those tribes which had assumed treaty relations with the Government, and who were opposed to peace on any terms with the whites. Such a confederation, bound together solely by a common and implacable hatred toward the whites, as may be supposed, exercise a reign of terror in the country through which they roam." Cowen identified Sitting Bull and Black Moon as the leaders of this multitribal coalition, and went on to depict Fort Peck, a U.S. garrison, as Sitting Bull's seat of power: "When he has visited the post his control of his braves is said to have been more complete than is usual among Indians, and other chiefs showed their respect for him by removing their koo [coup] feathers from their heads in his presence."

Much of Cowen's information was secondhand, but his account captured the sudden burst of Lakota power that the opening of the Milk River agency had made possible: Sitting Bull and his followers could now range from the North Platte through the Powder River country and Yellowstone and Milk Rivers into Canada all the way to the South Saskatchewan River and Lake Winnipeg, the bison hunters' fault line where grasslands begin to give way to woodlands.

Cowen's recommended course of action confirmed just how extensive the Lakota dominance had become. Fort Peck should be opened to Assiniboines and Dakotas who could "mingle" there with Lakotas, while the relocated Crows formed "a barrier between these hostile Indians and settlers of Eastern Montana." Fort Peck, he asserted, was "simply a trading-post, in a good location, near good timber, water, and grass." In truth it was a missing piece that allowed Sitting Bull and northern Lakotas to consolidate their steppe hegemony. By the end of the year more than eight hundred Lakota tipis stood around Fort Peck, receiving traders and amassing guns. Only much later would U.S. officials realize how Lakotas and their allies had come to occupy "the greater portion of a territory which extended from the Mississippi River to the Rocky Mountains and from the British possessions to the northern boundary of Kansas."[73]

Outmaneuvered and cut down to size, U.S. policymakers rationalized. Sitting Bull may have refused to visit Washington, but Red Cloud had not. In his annual report Commissioner Walker—who knew very little about the Indians but wanted peace with them regardless of the means—recounted how Red Cloud's visit had been "particularly influenced by the desire to impress the Ogallalas with a sense of the power of the Government, in view of the approach of the Northern Pacific Railroad to the rich hunting-grounds of these Indians upon the Powder River." He declared the effort a success: "The Red Cloud Sioux form the nearest and most natural re-enforcement, in case of war, to the 'hostile camps' of the Upper Missouri." This was wishful thinking. Burdened by a stinging failure to keep the Lakotas out of the Northern Pacific's way, Walker had retreated to what had by now become the Indian Office's default position: he minimized the Lakota threat to the nation's future and maximized the government's successes with the supposedly friendly Red Cloud.[74]

THE SIOUX ARE ON THE WAY AND YOU ARE AFRAID OF THEM

In an 1872 government report on the Northern Pacific Railroad—still stuck east of the Missouri—the author drew attention to a rarely considered perspective: "The agent for the Crows, who are the true allies of the Government in this matter, desiring the construction of the railroad as a barrier against their inveterate enemies, the Sioux, reports that this has caused great depression among that people, being taken as an indication of the weakness of the Government."[75]

It was. In the early 1870s, when there were not supposed to be any sovereign Indigenous nations left within the U.S. borders, Lakotas were still expanding, sometimes at the expense of their Native neighbors, sometimes that of the United States. The expansion now had a desperate streak to it—Lakotas were racing to control the remaining viable hunting grounds around them to stave off starvation and the collapse of their autonomy—but it was an expansion nonetheless. Americans were acutely aware of the blows they suffered at Lakota hands, but many of the blows that found Native targets were either unnoticed or brushed aside. Out of weakness and callousness, Americans allowed the Lakota expansion to continue.[76]

In August 1873 perhaps as many as one thousand Oglalas and Sicangus left their agency to hunt in the Republican Valley. They ran into a four-hundred-strong Pawnee hunting party. There had been constant clashes between Lakotas and Pawnees over hunting rights in previous years, and Oglalas and Sicangus were desperate to keep competitors out of the Republican, their last good bison domain in the south. The Platte Valley was already devoid of game, and the Republican herds were their last tie to the ancient hunting life. Warriors charged at the Pawnees, forcing a hasty retreat. The Pawnees escaped into a ravine, seeking cover in trees and scrub. The canyon became a death trap. Shooting down from the bluffs, Lakotas killed more than seventy men, women, and children. They returned to the agency with Pawnee captives, more than a hundred Pawnee horses, and masses of stolen hides and meat.

The battered and diminished agent Saville tried to persuade Lakotas to return the stolen property to Pawnees, but he was silenced by chief Little Wound who said that Oglalas had not made peace with the Pawnees and would treat their enemies as they pleased. Two months later nearly five hundred Pawnees, led by prominent warriors defying traditional chiefs, left their Loup Valley reservation to relocate four hundred miles south to Indian Territory, their new home. Rather than punishing the Lakotas, Saville pleaded the Indian Office to send in more rations to keep them content; he wanted to "give a feast," the only way he could bring them together and count them. Not long after he ordered five kegs of powder, five hundred pounds of lead, and seventy-five hundred rounds of ammunition for Lakotas. In the meanwhile, the remaining Pawnees on the Loup were forbidden to hunt and were soon starving. By the fall of 1875 they, too, had moved south.[77]

Lakota winter counts trace this violent history with the Pawnees in unusual detail, reflecting how high the stakes had become. Lakotas needed to preserve bison populations in the south not only for survival but because viable bison herds validated their claim to the Article 11 lands. This also meant that the smaller tribes in the region—the Poncas, Otoe-Missourias, and Omahas—had to either leave or stay within their reservations. Cut off from game by Lakotas, Poncas stopped making formal hunts in 1871, only to realize that they could not tend their fields properly, fearing that the Sicangus would "exterminate the tribe if they separated." "Here they must stay, with no food but parched corn or roots," one missionary lamented, while Lakotas, "who have given the government so much trouble, receive plenty of food and clothing" — "steamboats going up the river freighted with stores for these wild Indians." Demoralized, Poncas became "prisoners" of Sicangus, and moved to Indian Territory in 1876. The four hundred or so Otoe-Missourias had their last successful communal hunt in 1872 and a final symbolic one in 1875; a year later nearly half of them lived in Indian Territory. Omahas managed to hold on to their reservation, perhaps because their chiefs made a concerted effort to placate Lakotas with gifts of corn.[78]

The wars over bison and territory also intensified in the west. Crows, Shoshones, and Utes launched small raids to contain the westbound Lakota hunting and war parties, but they had neither the numbers nor the matériel to stop the expansion. Lakotas lost warriors and horses to enemy raiders, but they could absorb the damage: buoyed by good hunts, their numbers were still growing, and their raiding parties created a steady flow of mounts. By the early 1870s, moreover, Lakotas had accumulated a substantial mass of repeating rifles, which gave them a decisive advantage over the western tribes, whose impoverished villages attracted few white traders. Crows, after a humiliating flight that lasted several days, confronted their agents on the rationale of the government policy. "When we fought the Sioux this last time, we found them loaded with flour that our Great Father had given them, and what was worse for us, plenty of good guns and ammunition, and lots of good horses that the white people let them steal.... Give us these things, and you shall see we can fight." It is telling that one of the largest battles between Crows and Lakotas took place at Pryor Creek, deep in traditional Crow territory.[79]

And so the western border of the Lakota empire kept shifting westward, eventually reaching the clear, twisting, sporadically cottonwood-lined Bighorn River, the Yellowstone's largest tributary. In the fall of 1872 Lakota-Arapaho war parties twice attacked the Crow agency on Mission Creek, more than a hundred miles west of Bighorn, prompting U.S. agents to seek to relocate the agency. They struggled to find a spot that would be safe from Lakota incursions, leaving the Crows in a limbo and disgusted with the American weakness in the face of the Lakota onslaught. "You say the railroad is coming up the Yellowstone; that is like the whirlwind and cannot be turned back. I do not think it will come," the Crow chief Blackfoot admonished U.S. commissioners a year later. "The Sioux are on the way and you are afraid of them; they will turn the whirlwind back. If you whip the Sioux, and get them out of its way, the railroad may come, and I will say nothing."

The railroad did eventually come, ushering in U.S. troops and U.S. authority, but well before it came Lakotas. Raids into the Crow country and American

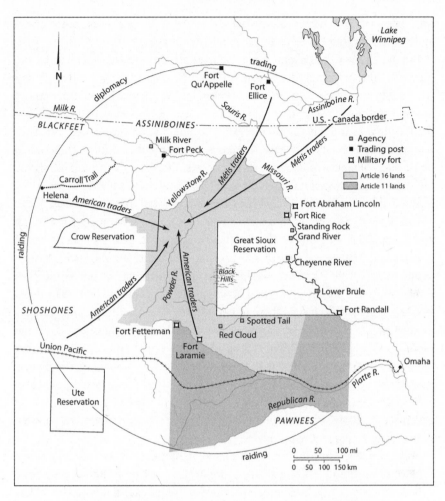

44. Lakota ascendancy in the early 1870s. Map by Bill Nelson.

settlements in the Gallatin Valley became a routine with Sitting Bull serving as a gravitational force. After wintering at Fort Peck, Hunkpapa bands moved west "with no worse intentions than to visit and hunt," one agent observed, "but once there, they are restrained and overawed by Sitting Bull, his associate chiefs, and his formidable warrior soldier lodge." Lakotas came across as "a different class of people," recognizing "no obligation to the white people," and thrust their raiding domain deep into the West, creating chaos only they could navigate. Suddenly all American settlements "within the reach of the Sioux hunting-grounds" were in danger. The Carroll Trail, a crucial transportation line connecting Helena to the Missouri River, was in risk of being cut off. At times it seemed it was Crows who protected Americans against Lakotas rather than vice versa. Both settlers and soldiers saw the Crows as an extra "regiment of cavalry."

But the Crows were Lakotas' primary target, for they stood between them and the bison. Crows were at times forced to flee their reservation in the face of massive Lakota war parties seeking game, horses, mules, and cattle, and their powerless agent seemed to accept "the annual Sioux invasion" as a fact of life. Such was the Lakota pressure that Crow chiefs were rumored to be considering "an offensive and defensive alliance with the Sioux as against the whites." There could be no such alliance, of course—the game was too scarce and the hatreds ran too deep—and Crows remained close allies of the United States. Before long, Lakotas occupied "the larger and most fertile portion of their reservation."[80]

Like Crows, Shoshones looked to Americans for protection against Lakotas and their allies. But unlike Crows, they managed to put distance between Lakotas and themselves. Decades of fighting over hunting rights had left them debilitated, and they had accepted a reservation in the lee of the Wind River Range, far to the southwest of the Lakota sphere of operations. Yet, even there, fear of Lakota attacks forced them to periodically flee. Eventually, they ceded a mineral-rich section of their reservation to secure the government's goodwill and protection. This, in the minds of U.S. agents, was a sign of supreme wisdom: they "are among the most intelligent and best disposed of any Indians on the plains," gushed the governor of the Wyoming Territory. "Wash-a-kie, their chief, is in all respects a superior Indian." Their agents reported a growing consumption of government rations—beef, bacon, flour, and sugar—which indicated that Shoshones were giving up the hunt.[81]

So were Utes. They had secured a large eighty-seven-thousand-square-mile reservation in the new Colorado Territory in 1861, but in 1868 they were compelled to accept a much-reduced domain. Five years later the government imposed another reduction, which broke Ute power. Lakota-Arapaho-Cheyenne war parties pushed deep into Ute territory, and growing numbers of Ute hunters began to frequent Denver, expecting to be fed, much to the exasperation of the city's inhabitants and the territory's Indian agents: "Even were they ever so well able to pay for hotel accommodations, they are not a desirable class of customers to the proprietors of any of our public-houses." In the summer of 1873 Ute hunters wished to parade enemy scalps on the streets of Denver: they had killed three Lakota warriors while hunting along the Republican. The Indian agent banned the parade, and Utes celebrated their surprising victory outside the city for a week. It was clear that there would not be many more. Agents reported "improved industrial habits," larger crops, and a growing willingness to live in houses.[82]

Establishing control over shrinking bison herds was the paramount motive of Lakota warfare in the early 1870s, and it spawned a sprawling raiding hinterland that extended from the Canadian plains into the Rockies and deep into the American Southwest. Closer to home, Lakotas waged a sporadic raiding war against the Arikaras, Hidatsas, and Mandans who now shared a reservation along the Missouri and Little Missouri Rivers. Lakota war parties raided the reservation for horses and corn with growing confidence, sometimes coming with women and often informing their agents of their intentions and successes. Arikaras retaliated by raiding Lakotas at their Grand River and Cheyenne River Agencies, but their agent wanted to move them to Indian Territory, farther away from Lakotas. He was promptly rebuffed: "they fear that it is too warm for them. . . . Besides they love their own country; their dead are buried here; the Government probably would not redeem its promises better there than here." For Arikaras the U.S. Indian policy was a demoralizing exercise in hypocrisy. "'The hostile Sioux have all they want from the Government without removal from their country,'" their chiefs protested. "'Why cannot the Rees, who have been so friendly and faithful these many years?'" The Arikaras stayed put, their numbers slowly declining in the shadow of an overpowering Lakota-U.S. alliance.[83]

As their rivals yielded ground, Lakotas emerged, in many ways, more powerful than ever. Never before had they ranged over more territory or reached so far. Their core area—their homeland—exceeded the Great Sioux Reservation by tens of thousands of square miles, and their hunting and raiding domain stretched from Lake Winnipeg in the north to the Republican Valley in the south and from the Missouri Valley in the east to the Continental Divide in the west. They had thousands of Indigenous allies on their orbit and diplomatic and commercial ties to Canada and Washington, D.C. They had several handsomely stocked government agencies at their disposal, and they went to war with cutting-edge military technology. Formidable, flexible, and ubiquitous, they commanded the attention of the U.S. government like no other Indigenous nation.

The power Lakotas wielded in the early 1870s was at once immediate and astonishing. The United States was emerging as a global colossus whose "monstrous contiguous economic territories" inspired awe and fear across the Atlantic and the Pacific; suddenly "America" became coupled with danger, invasion, and menace. Closer by, in the central Great Plains, the U.S. Army and government agents had unilaterally eradicated the sovereignty of the southern Cheyennes and Arapahos and moved them to Indian Territory. Spurred by railroads, steamboats, and the telegraph, American settlers were spreading rapidly across the continent, appropriating space on a vast scale. But whereas the Germans, French, Italians, or Japanese fretted over the American danger, Lakotas seemed unperturbed and composed. On December 25, 1873, after having been treated to a Christmas Day feast at his agency, Red Cloud reprimanded agent Saville for unfulfilled promises. "When the Great Spirit made us," he said, "he gave us the bow and arrow. He gave you the gun. We are trying to do good, and are still waiting for the guns for our people." Saville, he made clear, was there to serve, not govern, the Lakotas: "All we want is the guns and ammunition, and we want you to get them for us."[84]

9

Upside-Down Soldiers

These are some of the things that happened, according to Lakota winter counts, in the early 1870s: Lakotas clashed with Crows, Arikaras, and Pawnees a number of times. They lost horses to Ute raiders and floods, but they also found horses with spotted hooves. They traded with the Métis. Shoshones killed and scalped High Backbone, the celebrated Minneconjou headman, and Arikaras killed The Flame's second son. Anus-On-Both-Sides killed two Crows. John Richard, a wašíču trader, killed Yellow Bear, an Oglala, and the Oglalas killed Richard. Two prostitutes were killed. Fool Bull died hunting bison. Bull Head gave a ceremony. One year the sun turned dark. The winter counts also record events directly related to the United States and its agents—an adobe house built in the Red Cloud Agency, a Dakota scout Bad Bird killed by soldiers, Rain in the Face imprisoned at Fort Abraham Lincoln on the Missouri, goods issued—but it was the Indigenous context that dominated the Lakota collective memory of the early part of the decade that would end in a cataclysmic collision with the American state.[1]

Lakotas had stopped a large railroad survey expedition on the Yellowstone, visited Washington, D.C., and negotiated hard with the U.S. president and his cabinet. They had stared down local government agents across their domain, making certain that they knew their role, which was to ensure that the United States honored its promises to the Lakotas. In the spirit of the distinctly modern iwáštegla policy, Lakotas were gradually adjusting to a reality where coexistence with the wašíčus was a fact of life. And yet their most pressing concerns centered on issues that were fundamentally Indigenous: securing access to bison, protecting vital riverine habitats, and preserving a technological edge over rivals through trade. Lakotas had grown to depend on American support—goods, guns, political backing—in their struggles with Native rivals, but that did not make the Americans essential: Americans were to them as much a solution as they were a problem. Americans would abandon the Lakotas only gradually, one betrayal at a time, but when they finally did, the shock of it was all the more terrible.

THE GREAT SIOUX PROBLEM

He had just arrived in the West and was already dreaming of the East—of its familiar cultured comforts, of New York and its cosmopolitan buzz, of the adulation his rugged frontier exoticism never failed to inspire in more genteel climes. A passionate and devoted soldier, he was nonetheless uncomfortable with the professional culture of the regular army, which rejected his individualism, grandiosity, and hunger for recognition. A man suspended between America's frontier past and its modernist corporate future, George Armstrong Custer was nothing if not inconsistent.

In early spring 1873 Custer resumed active command of ten companies of the Seventh Cavalry in Yankton, the capital of the vast Dakota Territory, which no more than eleven thousand white people called home, their presence dwarfed by the thirty thousand Lakotas and their allies who dominated the northern Great Plains. He would be part of an expedition that would change that and much more. America's westward expansion had been thwarted by Lakotas and their allies the previous summer when they forced the army to abandon the survey for the Northern Pacific. "This railroad is a national enterprise," Sheridan had since announced, "and we are forced to protect the men during its survey and construction, through, probably, the most warlike nation of Indians on this continent, who will fight for every foot of the line." To avoid another humiliation, General Sherman had assembled a massive force. Custer's Seventh Cavalry formed but one component of a body that included 79 officers, 1,451 men, 353 civilian engineers, 27 Indian scouts, 275 wagons and ambulances, and more than 2,000 horses and mules. They carried enough rations to stay on the field for two months and enough scientific expertise to identify mining opportunities. As in the previous year, Colonel David Stanley, a functioning alcoholic who had Sheridan's friendship and trust, was in charge.[2]

The Yellowstone Expedition of 1873 was expected to do much more than to complete the survey of the river basin for the railroad; it would also launch the long overdue subjugation of the Lakotas, "the most determined, the ablest, and the most dangerous Indian tribes upon this continent." "If we are to allow these Indians to stop this work," one member of the House of Representatives had declared a few months earlier, "we might as well give up our Government at once." After years of futile attempts to break the military power of Lakotas, Comanches, and other Plains Indians, the railroad had come to signify a cure-all solution to the Indian problem. By allowing quick troop deployments and by ushering in settlers, railroads would dramatically accelerate the dispossession of the Native Americans. The commissioner of Indian affairs predicted that "the progress of two years more, if not of another summer, on the Northern Pacific Railroad will of itself completely solve the great Sioux problem, and leave the ninety thousand Indians ranging between the two transcontinental lines as incapable of resisting the Government as are the Indians of New York or Massachusetts."[3]

But even if war was needed to complete the railroad and Lakota dispossession, government agents were confident that they had co-opted enough "friendlies" to dilute Lakota military might. "The working on the proposed line of the Northern Pacific Railroad will meet with no opposition from any of these Indians," promised the agent of the Grand River Agency who watched over six thousand Lakotas and Yanktonais. By 1873 roughly half of the Lakotas lived more or less permanently near agencies, which suggested to U.S. officials that their military capacity had become decisively compromised. In his annual report Commissioner Edward P. Smith urged the nation to abandon its "fiction" in "our Indian relations" and forgo "as rapidly as possible, all recognition of Indians in any other relation than strictly as subjects of the Government." Federal officials with deep ties to the railroads had already divested the Wahpeton-Sisseton Sioux of five million acres between the Red and Missouri Rivers, and the Lakotas would have to yield next. "If it should become necessary to reduce the hostile portion of these Sioux to submission by military force," Smith was confident it could be done, for the Lakotas were surrounded by Native enemies: "The Government will find faithful and efficient allies in the several Indian tribes around, the Crows, Black Feet, Gros Ventres, and Arickarees. From these Indians a sufficient number of scouts can be enlisted to break the power of the Sioux Nation."[4]

Saddled with heavy expectations but confident of success, the prodigious Yellowstone Expedition moved west from Fort Rice on the Missouri in late June. Lakotas knew they were coming, but they waited until the wašíču reached the Yellowstone-Tongue junction in early August, far from U.S. military forts on the Missouri. They saw an opportunity in an advance detachment of horse soldiers riding on the north bank, and decided to bait them into a pursuit. Six warriors charged in to stampede the wašíču horse herd; as expected, the soldiers rushed after their mounts—and toward some three hundred warriors hiding in a cottonwood grove. The warriors charged "in perfect line," and the soldiers formed a skirmish line. The warriors kept shooting and charging at the line for three hours in 110°F heat and eventually set the grass on fire to burn the wašíčus out. The soldiers retreated, and the warriors chased them downriver until they saw a dust cloud: it was the main wašíču column. Lakotas swung around and withdrew up-river, the wašíčus now chasing them, marching hard to the tune of "Garry Owen." Custer—Pȟehíŋ HáŋskA, Long Hair, to Lakotas—had realized that there was a whole Lakota village nearby with women and children and rushed to "make short work" of it to sap the enemy's morale. When Lakotas neared the mouth of the Bighorn, they packed their possessions into bull boats and swam their horses across the fast-running Yellowstone to its south bank. Custer, burdened with the heavy army horses, failed to do the same and set up camp.[5]

At night the soldiers woke up to the sound of rifle fire: Sitting Bull had brought Minneconjou, Oglala, Sans Arc, and Cheyenne reinforcements, and now they shot at the wašíču camp on the far bank. The distance was nearly five hundred yards, but the fire was shockingly accurate: many Lakota warriors now carried Winchester magazine rifles; Henry and Spencer repeaters; and Springfield, Enfield, and Sharps breechloaders. There was a short duel between an expert U.S. sharpshooter and a Lakota marksman, which the latter won. Then some three hundred Indians crossed the river above and below the wašíču camp and Gall led a band of mounted warriors on its flank, releasing concentrated carbine fire and forcing Custer to form a new line of defense. It could have been a rout, three years early, if Colonel Stanley had not moved downriver with unusual speed. Once he brought his infantry and four Rodman guns on the scene and began shelling Sitting Bull and the warriors across the river, the battle was over. Lakotas moved south along the Bighorn, and Americans pushed northeast to the Mussel-shell River and turned back.[6]

And then the wašíčus vanished from the Yellowstone basin, their railroad seemingly abandoned: after two failed surveying expeditions in consecutive years it seemed there would be no more. Lakotas appeared to have stopped U.S. expansion in its tracks. They did not know—could not have known—that the United States had been gripped by financial panic. Jay Cooke and Company, the financier of the Northern Pacific, had defaulted its loans, triggering a sprawling financial crisis. Fifty-eight railroads went bankrupt within a year, and half of the nation's iron foundries failed. Credit tightened, prices fell, wages plummeted, and jobs melted away. The United States stood economically paralyzed, and the gigantic enterprise that was the Northern Pacific Railroad lay dead on the Missouri near Bismarck, its untouched, pointless rails covered with grass.[7]

That same year a Lakota boy had a vision in the Little Bighorn Valley. He was a sensitive child who heard voices and communicated with spirits. Now two men asked him to follow them into the clouds: his grandfather was calling him. He was circled by millions of horses—"a sky full of horses"—and a bay horse guided him into a cloud tipi of Thunder Beings where he saw the six grandfathers who were the six directions: west, north, east, south, above, and below, the whole

45. The Red Cloud Agency in 1876. Courtesy of the Collections of
History Nebraska, Nebraska State Historical Society, RG5895.

of the universe. The grandfathers showed him sick children, emaciated horses, wailing men and women, people dying—"it looked like a dying nation"—and they showed him herds of buffalo and dancing horses. They said they would take him to the center of the earth, and then he was on top of Pahá Sápa where he could see all the earth. Black Elk saw "what is good for humans and what is not good for humans." He knew what his people had to do.[8]

FORTS AND FRICTION

"The Oglalas killed the Indian agent's (Seville's) clerk," reads an 1874 winter count. The long-suffering Saville had struggled from the start in his post at Red Cloud Agency. Red Cloud and other chiefs had made sure the agent knew his place: he was there to serve, to make sure that Lakotas got what the United States had promised them in 1868. Saville was also unnerved by the animosity of the hundreds of northern nontreaty Lakotas who came in to draw food and goods as the weather turned cold, and refused to be counted and identified. Saville caved in to their demands for rations, believing, accurately, that the agency chiefs could not guarantee his safety. Things came to a head in February 1874. Saville panicked and called in troops, and a Minneconjou warrior walked into the clerk's building and shot Saville's nephew, Frank Appleton, at point blank, likely mistaking the young man for Saville himself. Saville asked again for troops, and now Sheridan sent more than nine hundred men to the White River. They built Camp Robinson to oversee Red Cloud Agency and Camp Sheridan to watch over Spotted Tail's site. Ever since its humiliating defeat in the Powder River War, the U.S. Army treated any Lakota threat as a potential national emergency.

The forts were a blatant violation of Lakota sovereignty—both were in the unceded Article 11 lands that extended all the way south to the Republican Valley—and they hardened the uncompromising stance of the nontreaty oyátes. Yet thousands of northerners came to the Red Cloud Agency in the summer to collect rations and guns: whatever misgivings they may have harbored, the agencies were Lakota agencies and designed to deliver rations, tools, and other crucial resources guaranteed in the 1868 treaty.[9]

MAKE IT A LITTLE HOT

Shiny, seductive, and finite, gold could remake lives and worlds. The soft, heavy metal with little utilitarian value did that simply because people believed it could. People believed in that metaphysical quality in regular times—it was taken for granted—and they believed in it with fervent, desperate urgency when times were bad. In 1874 the times were bad, spectacularly so, and when news arrived that rich veins of gold had been found in the Black Hills, it galvanized the nation. Gold had helped lift the nation from the material and moral ruins of the Civil War; now it could lift it from a debilitating depression.[10]

The news came from one of the many small expeditions that the U.S. Army had sent in to find a suitable site for a fort near the Black Hills to protect the tracklayers of the blocked Northern Pacific Railroad. The fort, Sherman thought, would allow the army to deliver a crippling blow to the seemingly invincible Lakotas whom the national media now conflated with rebellious blacks, Chinese immigrants, disaffected farmers, and labor activists as an acute threat to the fragile industrial order. Sheridan, who had orchestrated total war against Native civilians during Cheyenne, Arapaho, and Comanche campaigns in 1868–69, believed that Lakota hostility now amounted to "a general Indian war" and proposed to President Grant that military forts in the Black Hills would "make it a little hot for the [Lakota] villages and stock if these Indians attempted to raid on the settlements south." Grant agreed, and Sheridan picked Custer, whose conduct during the Yellowstone Expedition had much enhanced his professional standing, to lead the Black Hills Expedition: one hundred covered wagons; more than nine hundred cavalry and infantry; sixty-one Arikara scouts; several guides, engineers, and "practical miners"; three Gatling machine guns; three journalists; a photographer; and a geologist, Newton H. Winchell from the University of Minnesota, all moving out of Fort Abraham Lincoln, skirting the Great Sioux Reservation and entering the hills from the north. In mid-August, after six weeks of travel, the convoy found traces of gold. Custer exaggerated the discovery, and the expedition delivered what he had geared it up for: it created a national event. Reporters dispatched excited press releases, newspapers picked up and magnified the story, and in the late fall of 1874 the Black Hills gold rush was a reality.[11]

46. Panoramic view of the camp at Hidden Wood Creek during Custer's Black Hills expedition, photograph by W. H. Illingworth, 1874. The picture was taken near the site where the expedition discovered gold. Camouflaged as a scientific endeavor, Custer's Black Hills Expedition was an exercise in settler colonialism aimed at dispossessing Native inhabitants to make room for white colonists and entrepreneurs. Courtesy of National Archives, photo no. 519425.

A feared attack by Sitting Bull never materialized—Lakotas were hunting in the West—but when the homebound expedition approached the Grand River, it entered a "thoroughly burned" prairie. Lakotas, the expedition's chief engineer William Ludlow concluded, had fired the grass to "embarrass our march." In his report Ludlow adopted the army line on the Black Hills and Lakotas: "In case, at any future time, complications with the Sioux or the advancing needs of bordering civilization should make it necessary to establish military posts upon this Indian reservation, indications all pointed to the Black Hills as the suitable point, both on account of their geographical position and of the abundance of wood, water, and grass to be found there." The hills, he concluded, provided Lakotas "a ready refuge in time of war."[12]

The specter of war descended over the West. Sheridan, who privately wanted to see the Black Hills settled by Americans, issued harsh orders to keep trespassers out of Lakota lands. He ordered officers to detain prospector parties in Sioux City and Yankton, to have their wagons burned and their leaders arrested for violating the ban. Sharing Sheridan's stated stance, General Alfred Terry thought the Black Hills were absolutely closed to intruders. But the draw of gold was uncontainable. Western newspapers generated fervor and fear to bring in the army to open the Black Hills. "The greatest excitement prevails among the Indians," the *Bismarck Tribune* had reported while Custer was still in the field, "and Four-Horns, who led off for war, said there was no excuse for any of the Indians to remain at peace with the treacherous whites. For his part, he would intercept Custer if he lost half of the braves of the nation." The Dakota territorial legislature pressured the government to open the Black Hills and found passionate supporters in Congress. The army continued to patrol the hills and evict trespassers, protecting the Indians and the settlers from one another, but there was no stopping the hopeful, desperate trespassers.[13]

Custer's Black Hills Expedition triggered unfiltered anger across the Lakota realm. When Saville tried to fly a U.S. flag at the Red Cloud Agency to mark the Sabbath, Lakota warriors were enraged. The flag symbolized to them the power of the U.S. Army and threatened to turn the agency into a military fort. Some two hundred warriors, "painted and ready for war," broke the flagpole into pieces as agents stood by helplessly. Saville was in his office with Red Cloud, pleading with him to intervene, but the chief casually told him that a Lakota council had decided to destroy the pole. Saville sent a messenger to Camp Robinson to bring in troops, and soon Lieutenant Emmet Crawford rode in with twenty-five cavalrymen. He was promptly stopped by mounted warriors and forced to back down. It was Oglala leaders Sitting Bull, They Fear Even His Horses the Younger, Red Dog, and other chiefs, not Saville or Crawford, who finally restored order. Women prepared a feast to restore normalcy. It was now clear to everyone who ran the agency. Saville estimated that there were nearly ten thousand Lakotas—large numbers of "hostile" northerners had once again come in—and he struggled to put a positive spin on things in his reports. He could not. "The Indians don't try to deceive me so much," was one of his better efforts. The War Department decided not to arrest and prosecute the Minneconjous implicated in the killing of Appleton, fearing that such action could start a war.[14]

Quietly Americans began preparing for a showdown. Sheridan wanted to "take the hostile backbone out of these unruly savages," while the Indian Office agents worked hard to keep the friendly Lakotas receptive. They urged the government to send in more beef, pork, flour, sugar, and coffee, hoping that the goods would fortify the agency bands against the militancy of Sitting Bull and other northern chiefs. Sheridan put his hope in strategically placed forts. There was Fort Abraham Lincoln "on the north of the Reservation, Forts Sully, Rice and Randall on the east," he strategized, "and if I could get a fort in the Black Hills on the west, and one on the Niobrara on the south . . . these wild Indians would be somewhat hemmed in." If such an isolation was achieved "the Indians might be sufficiently intimidated to keep, at least a portion if not all, on the side of friendship and peace." Knowing that a war with the mobile nomads would be chaotic, Sheridan wanted clear categories that distinguished friendlies from hostiles and civilians from targets.[15]

That the U.S. government was determined to subjugate the Lakotas became clear soon. White professional bison hunters had intensified their operations in the aftermath of the financial collapse—a low-capital industry, hunting was largely immune to the panic—and the U.S. government did nothing to stop the slaughter. On the contrary, knowing that Indigenous sovereignty in the plains rested on the bison, Secretary of the Interior Columbus Delano welcomed the destruction as a way to accelerate the nomads' domestication, and army officers provided protection and ammunition to hunting squads. Between 1872 and 1874 white hunters may have shipped more than three million hides to the East from the southern and central plains—close to three thousand animals per day—plunging the herds into a terminal decline. Just north of the main killing field, the Republican Valley was soon affected: the primary hunting domain of Oglalas and Sicangus began to fail.[16]

Already in March 1874 Congress had allocated funds for purchasing Lakota hunting rights in the Republican Valley, an action that would cancel the Lakota title to the Article 11 lands, and in the fall commissioners appeared at the Spotted Tail and Red Cloud Agencies. Spotted Tail had juggled deep schisms at his Whetstone Agency for years, accommodating traditionalists and those who were willing to give up the hunt, while simultaneously placating U.S. officials. Now, desperate to preserve his agency's unique position as a functioning nexus of conflicting interests, he relinquished his followers' hunting rights in return for fifty thousand dollars worth of goods and agreed to move to a new location where farming would be possible. Commissioner Smith promptly argued that Spotted Tail's decision to give up hunting rights had annulled almost *all* Lakota rights to Article 11 lands.[17]

Red Cloud's Oglalas, however, were a rude awakening to the commissioners: "They utterly refused to listen to any terms suggested by us." Red Cloud insisted that the Republican belonged to Lakotas because there were still bison there and flatly refused to discuss hunting rights. The commissioners were baffled because they did not know the deeper backstory. They had unknowingly stepped into a long-festering power struggle among agency Lakotas, nontreaty Lakotas, the Indian Office, the army, and Congress—a struggle that was vastly intensified by "gigantic" corruption that revolved around the "Indian ring," a conglomeration of political bosses, kickback-seeking Indian Office agents, and government contractors who sold the agency rotten pork, inferior flour, and overpriced beef cattle. It was there that the Peace Policy and the iwáštegla mindset first began to dissolve into resentment, disgust, and violence.[18]

Just how bad things had become dawned on the Indian Office in the winter of 1874–75 when annual reports from different Lakota agencies were compiled in Washington. The long winter sojourns of northern Lakotas had fueled friction at the Whetstone Agency on the Missouri, as they had at the Red Cloud Agency. Agent E. A. Howard blamed young warriors: "Much of the trouble caused by Indians on this reservation is caused by young men, who are difficult to manage in any part of the world. Many of these were children here when the late treaty was made. They know nothing, care nothing about its stipulations, and while the older men of the tribe are peaceable, they find it difficult to control the young men." Howard captured the generational dynamic at the core of the strife, but he missed the widespread conviction among the Lakotas, the young as well as the old, that the 1868 Laramie treaty, whatever its exact stipulations, had reaffirmed Lakota sovereignty in the face of the wašíču state. For Lakotas the building of Camps Robinson and Sheridan and Custer's invasion of Pahá Sápa amounted to a declaration of war.

Lakotas were being corralled and domesticated, and they had to find a way out of the bind. Like the Americans, they sought a radical spatial reorganization to defuse the danger. Whereas the U.S. Army wanted to encircle the Sioux reservation with forts, many nontreaty Lakotas wanted to rid the Great Sioux Reservation of government agencies and forts altogether. They saw them as instruments of conquest and cultural degradation, and they sought uncompromised sovereignty over the land.

Unnerved by an influx of "troublesome" and "well armed" Minneconjou bands from the north, Howard called in the army to keep peace at Whetstone. The situation was similarly explosive at the Cheyenne River Agency. "The excitement occasioned by the report of the late expedition to the Black Hills country has reached this agency," wrote its agent, "and I am sorry to say has done visible harm in causing dissatisfaction and discontent. I find the Indians irritable, and even in those who have been hitherto most friendly and appreciative I have discovered signs of incipient hostility and insubordination." Only at the Standing Rock Agency (previously the Grand River Agency) did the agents believe that they could manage the Lakotas without troops, and even there the Lakotas seemed "not very tractable" and wholly averse to Christianity, schools, and farming. Lakotas responded to the wašíču invasion not as agency Indians but as a nation.[19]

SITTING BULL'S SOLDIERS

The wašíču assaults seemed relentless in 1874. One particular group of intruders came from the west and called themselves the Yellowstone Wagon Road and Prospective Expedition. Like the others before them, they were lethal. They were trappers, wolfers, buffalo hunters, scouts, and Civil War veterans, some 150 in all, and they had left Bozeman in late February, armed with repeating rifles and cannons and more than forty thousand cartridges. They had said they would be scouting a wagon road down the Yellowstone Valley but mostly they were after gold. Sitting Bull's Hunkpapas detected them in late March, as they were approaching the Rosebud junction. Hunkpapas attacked them twice but suffered heavy losses against the seasoned frontiersmen. At last, a hundred warriors slipped into a ravine near the wašíčus and began dropping their big American mounts with long-range rifles. The wašíčus retreated to the west, but not before leaving behind provisions laced with strychnine and a booby-trapped fake grave. An inquisitive Lakota warrior flew thirty feet in the air but survived.[20]

The Yellowstone Wagon Road and Prospective Expedition was symptomatic of a larger flaw with wašíčus that crystallized in the invasion of Pahá Sápa: they lied. They made treaties and broke them. They embraced people as kin then treated them like strangers. Although northern Lakotas shunned close interactions with government agents, they believed that the United States had recognized their sovereignty over the northern plains in 1868. As 1874 unfolded it became clear to Sitting Bull and other northern leaders that the Americans no longer respected that agreement. Almost anywhere they looked — east, west, south — they saw wašíču encroachments that brought death and disturbed the bison. They started preparing for war.

At first it was an internal matter. Lakotas could anticipate a challenge similar to the one they had faced and neutralized eight years earlier in the Powder River country. Then they had consolidated decision-making in the hands of Sitting Bull, Red Cloud, and High Backbone, whose collective authority had drawn the all-important but faction-ridden warrior societies behind the war effort. Sitting Bull now set in motion a similar shapeshifting. He recruited a personal bodyguard — "Sitting Bull's Soldiers" — that drew prominent devoted supporters from several societies, crisscrossing and softening the political fault lines: he wanted men and their loyalties to converge around him. Mirroring Sitting Bull, Crazy Horse, too, formed a personal bodyguard to foster warrior solidarity. He recruited more than forty rising warriors into his Last-Born Child Society: he wanted younger sons of renowned families because he believed that they were more competitive and tenacious than the privileged older sons. With Sitting Bull's un-compromising gravitas and Crazy Horse's burgeoning military fame, northern Lakotas had two focal points around which to marshal when the wašíčus came.[21]

I AM NO DOG

War was not yet inevitable. In fact, there were no insurmountable reasons for a seismic conflict between Americans and Lakotas in the 1870s. The bank-ruptcy of the Northern Pacific had delayed the opening of the northern plains for settlers, the plains cattle industry was already heading toward overexpansion, and the lands west of the 98th meridian—including the entire Lakota domain— were not suitable for farming. Moreover, Lakotas and Americans had managed to communicate and cooperate for several years, preventing violent clashes from escalating into all-out war. Both seemed committed to peace and coexistence.

But the will to compromise was dissipating fast. Before the 1874 Black Hills Expedition the two expanding powers had managed to coexist in the northern plains; afterwards they found it overwhelmingly difficult to do so. One empire had invaded the vital center of the other, forcing a grotesque imbalance. On both sides there were still those who wanted to avoid carnage, but the human mo-mentum was against them. The year 1875 became a year of missed opportunities to preserve peace.

In early spring, while Grant's cabinet explored ways to extinguish Lakota title to the Black Hills, the army made an intense effort to keep miners out of the hills, patrolling a huge swath of land to the east and often commissioning Lakota guides. An Indian agent reported that Sicangus and Oglalas "are fully aware of the Black Hills excitement, and depend entirely upon the government to watch their interests." Sheridan declared that the "integrity of the treaty with the Sioux will be maintained at all hazards," and stated that cavalry detachments could "occupy the two or three gaps in the Black Hills and effectually exclude tres-passers." But they could not. There were too many jobless wanderers, too many men hypnotized by gold, and too much ground to cover. In a council with gov-ernment agents, Red Cloud was at once disillusioned and disgusted, but he had lost none of his capacity to impress. "Look at me!" he exploded. "I am no Dog. I am a man. This is my ground, and I am sitting on it. You tell me about the Great Fathers Troops. He has troops all over the world, and I do not believe that the Great Father has not Troops enough to keep white men away from the Black Hills."

Soon Pahá Sápa teemed with wašíčus. Spotted Tail, thoroughly cynical now, admonished the agents for looking after "their own good, not ours. If they only came here to gather money for a short time—but they gather here it all, which makes us poorer and poorer." Then, in late spring, the government dispatched Lieutenant Colonel Richard Irving Dodge with more than 450 soldiers and scientists to the Black Hills to determine just how much gold there was. The scientists found a decent amount, enough to "yield a good return," though much of it was sprinkled widely. Dodge promptly declared that "the Black Hills have never been a permanent home for any Indians"; they were mere sojourners, "depraved" nomads who had failed to find the gold under their feet. Custer's route to the hills—"the thieves' road" for the Lakotas—would become a highway.[22]

Gold and corruption prompted the government to bring yet another Lakota delegation to the capital in late May. The winter had been harsh, many Lakotas were hungry, and some, it was believed, contemplated rebellion. Rampant corruption, an upshot of fee-based governance and the plague of the Grant administration, had gripped the Red Cloud Agency. A pioneering Yale paleontologist Othniel March—he would uncover the evolution of the horse that made the Lakotas so formidable—had become aware of the situation while collecting fossils in Nebraska and put together a report detailing substandard annuities of putrid pork, rotten tobacco, and inferior flour, coffee, and sugar. Secretary of the Interior Delano would eventually have to resign, but in the short run the administration tried to leverage hunger for concessions. Red Cloud, Spotted Tail, and Lone Horn met briefly with Grant, but the substantial talks were with Delano and Commissioner of Indian Affairs Smith. Smith told the chiefs that the government was under enormous pressure to take possession of the seemingly gold-laden Black Hills and the unceded territories, and Delano pressed the issue. "The President," he said, "has no money. I have no money, and the Commissioner of Indian Affairs has none, except if Congress gives it to us." It was a thinly veiled threat. "Now, if you don't do what is right," he said, "Congress will refuse to give any more aid, so I want you to think about it, and do what is best for yourselves and children."

What the government thought would be best for Lakotas was simple: accept the inevitable, sell their lands, get out of the way, and move to Indian Territory. It was an insult and a gross miscalculation. Red Cloud, Spotted Tail, and other agency Lakotas were already preparing themselves for the idea that the Black Hills would have to be sold, but now all hope of a dialogue evaporated. "You speak of another country, but it does not concern me," Spotted Tail retorted. "I want nothing to do with it. I was not from there; but, if it is such a good country, you ought to send the white men now in our country there and let us alone."

All that the chiefs wanted to discuss was the quantity and quality of rations, the material foundation of the U.S.-Lakota accommodation. Red Cloud said "he had come to Washington, expecting to get something; but he found everybody poor." He still expected the Great Father to listen and preserve the delicate coexistence, but he did not. In an edgy final meeting with Grant and Delano, the president announced that Lakotas would have to relinquish the remaining Article 11 lands because bison herds no longer supported profitable hunts there. White settlers, he explained, "were rapidly spreading over the Western country" and the land "was now needed by them." He offered twenty-five thousand dollars for it all. Spotted Tail may have relinquished *his* hunting rights, but Red Cloud would have none of it. Upon leaving, he refused to pose for the customary group photograph. Three weeks later Grant authorized the Allison Commission — named for its chairman, Iowa senator William B. Allison — to visit the Lakotas and negotiate the relinquishment of the Black Hills. On site in the West, General George Crook had begun forging a peaceful council ground by ordering the miners to leave the Black Hills by August 15 or face forced removal. A large cavalry force began scouring the hills, and the miners began moving out "under protest."[23]

While the U.S. government prepared for the momentous talks, northern Lakotas gathered for a Sun Dance on Rosebud Creek. It was at once a religious and political affair: there were Hunkpapas, Oglalas, Sans Arcs, Minneconjous, and Cheyennes, thousands of them, and they all shared a deep concern over growing American presumption. After the Sun Dance arbor had been raised, Sitting Bull emerged, riding a black war horse, his body covered with shining yellow clay, his lower face black and black bands circling his ankles and wrists, his chest a black disk, the sun. He dismounted and began dancing toward the arbor, carrying a Lakota and a Cheyenne calumet, his horse behind him, approaching and retreating with him as the Sun Dance pole came closer. "I have nearly got them," he cried three times as he drew his enemies toward him, only to pull back three times. He threw his arms out and brought the pipes to his chest. He had surrounded his enemies and had them in his power. Then he talked. He spoke of Pahá Sápa, the "food pack" that sustained life, and of the importance of a transcending Indigenous alliance that alone could keep the wašíčus out. When an envoy of agency Oglalas arrived in Rosebud in early August to persuade the northerners to meet the Allison Commission, Sitting Bull could witness his vision of Indigenous unity taking bodily form. Both nontreaty and agency Lakotas gave about one hundred speeches, arguing for two radically contrasting visions for their nation without breaking it. They had reaffirmed their solidarity and their resilience.[24]

When the Allison Commission finally reached the meeting ground near the Red Cloud Agency in late September, it was received by thousands of exasperated Lakotas, Yanktons, Dakotas, Cheyennes, and Arapahos: the miners were still in the Black Hills. Crook's deadline had passed but he had done little to expel them. The commissioners had been instructed to consider the Indians' "interests not less than those of the Government" and "secure the best interests of both parties, so far as practicable": his cherished Peace Policy already in ruins, Grant still clung to his grand vision for a morally rigorous Indian policy. But what had been conceived as a bid to secure mining rights in the Black Hills had escalated into an attempt to absorb much of the Lakota domain. Dispensing pleasantries, Allison proposed to buy most of the Black Hills "for mining uses." That much Lakotas could have expected. But Allison also offered to buy much of the unceded territory west and north of the Black Hills. That was the Powder River country, the heart of the northern Lakota domain where hunting was still possible. "It does not seem to be of very great value or use to you," argued the either callous or clueless Allison.

Four hundred northern Lakota warriors had come down for the council, intermingling among the massive crowd and urging their allies to reject Allison's proposal. When their resolve appeared to be crumbling, Little Big Man, a shirt wearer in Crazy Horse's band, rode into the council ground and threatened to shoot the first chief who signed away Lakota lands. When the talks resumed the chiefs stood the commissioners down with demands that were clearly unacceptable. They insisted on being supported "for seven generations ahead," and Spotted Tail announced that the interest from leasing the Black Hills should support his people "until the land falls to pieces." Spotted Bear wanted seventy million dollars. "Our Great Father has a big safe, and so have we," he said. "This hill is our safe."

The "exorbitant" sums were a de facto rejection of the government proposal, but the unpracticed commissioners pushed ahead and offered to buy the hills for six million dollars or lease mining rights for four hundred thousand dollars per year. They were roundly rejected. Stymied and humiliated, they recommended exacting measures. To receive annuities in the future, Lakotas would have to "perform labor," send their children to schools, embrace private property, and move into areas where farming was possible. The commissioners also recommended the abolition of all agencies and proposed that Congress simply fixed a price for the Black Hills. "The plan here suggested," they wrote, "should be presented to the Indians as a finality": its rejection should cancel all government support. The plan revealed the commission's stupendous naïveté and inability to grasp the realities. There were, at that time, some thirteen thousand Lakotas, Cheyennes, and Arapahos at the Red Cloud Agency expecting rations. They could not be denied.[25]

On November 1 Commissioner of Indian Affairs Smith wrote in his annual report that "a general Indian war is never to occur in the United States." Two days later an Indian war was on the White House agenda. Grant had invited Smith, Secretary of War William Belknap, Secretary of the Interior Zachariah Chandler, and Generals Crook and Sheridan to a secret meeting. He saw no other option than war to solve the struggle over the Black Hills, but reluctant to abandon his Peace Policy, he was unwilling to declare one. Instead, he announced, the army was to stand down and let things flow spontaneously into bloodshed. The orders banning whites from the Black Hills would remain in effect but they would not be enforced. The miners would flood the hills and Lakotas would start a war they would lose. To ensure a rapid unfolding of events, Smith was assigned in early December to order all Lakotas living outside the reservation boundaries to report to an agency by the end of January. Those who did not would be hunted down.[26]

WHIP THEM INTO SUBJECTION

The deadline was unreasonable. Even if the nontreaty Lakotas had wanted to meet it—which they did not—it would have been physically next to impossible to do so. It was winter, travel was slow, and most bands were camping deep in the Powder River and Yellowstone countries. Key people in Grant's cabinet knew this, and so did Generals Crook and Terry, who were responsible for the immediate military operations. Both reported before 1876 dawned that they were ready to attack.[27]

The U.S. officials also knew that most nontreaty Lakotas despised agency life. Northern Lakotas did visit agencies to draw rations and munitions, sometimes spending weeks near them if conditions were harsh, but for them agencies could never be home: they were a resource base and a conduit that allowed the United States to honor its treaty obligations to them. Earlier, at the Rosebud council, Sitting Bull had articulated this anti-agency ideology. "He would not sell his land," he said, and "had never been to an agency." He had never accepted rations and "was no agency Indian"; he and his followers would not be counted, catalogued, and disciplined by wašíču agents. Sitting Bull associated agency life with cultural death and loss of land—the latter would follow from the first because Lakotas needed to hunt to retain the unceded territories—so the ultimatum from the United States spelled hot war. The wašíčus had turned themselves into an existential threat. Lakotas had clashed with them again and again, but now they would be fighting for cultural survival. The wašíčus meant to eliminate them not only as a political power but as a people. They would have to fight.[28]

But the United States was forcing a war it was not ready for. The Americans were still desperately unfamiliar with the northern plains geography and hardly knew the people they meant to fight. "A man about 45 years old, and possessed of more than ordinary intelligence and ability for an Indian. He is said to wield great power and influence over his followers," was all that the agent at the Standing Rock Agency could gather about Sitting Bull in November 1875. Agent Saville at the Red Cloud Agency had to clarify to Commissioner Smith that there were two Sitting Bulls, an Oglala and a Hunkpapa; Smith then reported officially—and recklessly—that the nontreaty Lakotas numbered but a few hundred. "I am led not only to repeat with increased confidence the statement made last year," he put in print, "that a general Indian war is never to occur in the United States, but also to the opinion that conflict with separate tribes will thereafter be of rare occurrence, and only in the nature of skirmishing." He expected that Sitting Bull's "outlaws," who "have never yet in any way recognized the United States Government," would have to be compelled into a reservation, but he thought it would not require a war.[29]

The agents were even less aware of how thoroughly Lakotas now commanded the interior. They had expanded their range explosively to the west and north, and now, as the United States set out to break them, they were still expanding. In the summer of 1875 a Lakota village of some two thousand warriors fought a climactic three-day battle with the Crows at the mouth of the Bighorn River and forced them to retreat far into the west. The Crow agency was relocated southeast in the Stillwater Valley, where it stood directly in the path of Lakota war parties. Lakota raids only increased, and the U.S. Army seemed utterly powerless to stop them. Soon Lakotas were raiding the Nez Perces and Bannocks far in the west.[30]

Indian Office inspector Erwin C. Watkins, who toured the northern plains in the fall of 1875, gained a rare glimpse into this changing world and failed to make sense of it. Northern Lakotas, he reported "occupy the center, so to speak, and roam over Western Dakota and Eastern Montana, including the rich valleys of the Yellowstone and Powder Rivers, and make war on the Arickarees, Mandans, Gros Ventres, Assinaboines, Blackfeet, Piegans, Crows, and other friendly tribes on the circumference. . . . They are rich in horses and robes, and are thoroughly armed. . . . From their central position they strike to the east, north, and west, steal horses, and plunder from all the surrounding tribes, as well as frontier settlers, and luckless white hunters, or emigrants who are not in sufficient force to resist them."

Watkins had captured something of the imperial scope of the Lakota power, and yet he seemed astonished that these people would "claim to be the sovereign rulers of the land," the 1871 prohibition of treaty making echoing in the background. "They are still as wild and untamable, as uncivilized and savage, as when

Lewis and Clark first passed through their country," he protested. "Surrounded by their native mountains, relying on their knowledge of the country and powers of endurance, they laugh at the futile attempts that have thus far been made to subjugate them." "The true policy," he proposed, "is to send troops against them in the winter—the sooner the better—and whip them into subjection." Watkins expected it to be easy, assuming that the hostiles could mobilize a few hundred warriors at best. Custer disagreed. In Chicago, on his way west, he told a reporter, with a "melancholy sigh," that he expected to face eight to ten thousand warriors, "enough to do a vast amount of damage to the country up there." The American state was going to war half-blind.[31]

After the November meeting at the White House, the Indian Office and the Department of the Interior had effectively handed over the nation's Lakota policy to General Sheridan. He had a small window of opportunity to deliver the desired subjugation and he knew it: "Unless they are caught before early spring they cannot be caught at all," he wrote to Sherman in early February 1876. Custer's attack at the Washita in the winter eight years earlier had broken Cheyenne power in the central plains, and Sheridan thought it provided a template for the Lakota war. He formulated a winter campaign of three converging columns that would push into the heart of the Lakota stronghold in the Yellowstone and Powder River countries from western Montana, Fort Fetterman, and Fort Abraham Lincoln on the upper Missouri. General Terry, in charge of the Dakota column, knew that defeating the superbly mobile Lakotas depended on strong cavalry, and he put his trust in Custer: "I think my only plan will be to give Custer a secure base well up on the Yellowstone from which he can operate, at which he can find supplies, and to which he can retire at any time the Indians gather in too great numbers for the small force he will have." Terry seemed to anticipate a war of attrition in which American matériel and strong supply lines would decide the outcome.[32]

It was a skeleton plan, and it did not play out well. Crook, pushing north into the Powder Valley from Fort Fetterman in early March with nearly nine hundred men, ordered Colonel Joseph J. Reynolds to attack a Lakota camp on the river bottom in bitter cold. It turned out to be a mixed Oglala-Cheyenne village. The Indians sought shelter in the cracks of the bluffs, firing at the soldiers who worked frantically to burn and destroy the village and everything in it—tipis, tools, ammunition, gunpowder, robes, horses, and tons of dried meat. The Indians recaptured some of their horses at night, and then headed downriver to the north. They were taken in by Crazy Horse and then by Sitting Bull who organized a massive sharing of food, tipis, blankets, robes, and horses. The army had lost the element of surprise, and its winter campaign would have to become a spring campaign. From then on every day—every warmer day—reduced the American chances of victory. Crook, "disgusted with the terrible blunders," brought charges against Reynolds, accusing him of dereliction of duty.[33]

Just as Crook and Reynolds botched the crucial opening battle, Custer was in Washington, having been called in to testify before Congress on corruption charges against the Grant administration. He had little desire to join the war in the West and hoped to stay in the East for a while. He liked the politics, the parties, the salons, the theater, the fame. He wanted to be a man of substance, not war.[34]

TWO MARCHES TO ROSEBUD

If the war was on, the Americans did not seem to want to fight it. The January 31 deadline passed, most Lakotas were still in the open plains, and the army had done almost nothing to force them into agencies. The most immediate threat the nonagency Lakotas faced in the spring of 1876 was not the U.S. military, but a group of Montana opportunists who had built a small settlement, Fort Pease, on the Yellowstone opposite the mouth of the Bighorn. Hunkpapas, Sans Arcs, and Cheyennes wintered near the fort, keeping it under a casual siege and eventually forcing the interlopers out. Mostly Lakotas focused on their Indigenous neighbors. They clashed with Crows and Utes in the west and with Hidatsas on the Little Missouri. Sicangu raiding parties from a seemingly tranquil Spotted Tail Agency roved along the Missouri. Sitting Bull was reported to have no plans to attack the Americans.[35]

But the destruction of the Powder River village made it plain that war would come, and Lakotas knew what to expect: Ash Hollow, Whitestone Hill, Killdeer, Sand Creek, Powder River, and Washita had taught them that the wašíčus killed indiscriminately. Quietly, skirting the official gaze, Lakotas started preparing. Mostly they sought guns. The army had banned all weapons trade with the Lakotas, but in late March and April army officers and local newspapers began complaining about how Sitting Bull's followers were amassing guns from Fort Peck and from friendly Hidatsas and Assiniboines and Métis traders who ranged all the way south in the Black Hills. A Montana paper warned of a rapidly changing balance of power: "Instead of meeting poorly armed bands of Indians, as was expected, the troops in the field during this campaign will have to contend against well prepared and well armed hordes of ruthless and blood-thirsty savages. The Sioux under Sitting Bull are better armed to day than the troops who are to oppose them." An Indian Office agent reported how the "hostiles under Sitting Bull" solicited Arikaras, Mandans, and Hidatsas to "join them against the whites." He thought that some of his wards "believe the Sioux are to be the victors by virtue of superiority of numbers." Gros Ventres visited Sitting Bull's village and "left there all the arms and ammunition they had."[36]

The highly mobile Lakotas had a tactical advantage over the U.S. Army in their homelands, but to fully capitalize on that advantage they needed to condense the theater of war. The moment they knew the entry points of the wašíču invasion, they could concentrate warriors in those points and deliver devastating blows with swift mounted attacks. The focal point of this defensive war would be Sitting Bull's village, which already hosted hundreds of Cheyenne exiles. In April the Hunkpapa chief sent out messengers, and soon bands began arriving, turning his village into a moveable procession of Indigenous power. Sitting Bull had wintered east of the Powder River but began now shifting west and north toward better grass and larger bison herds, drawing in bands from all directions. Crazy Horse came from the south, and Dakota and Yankton refugees led by Inkpáduta came from Canada. Oglalas, Sicangus, Sans Arcs, Minneconjous, Sihasapas, and Cheyennes came from all across the Powder River country. And then, as the plains greened, relatives from the agencies began streaming in.

They all came because North America's Indigenous space was shrinking dizzyingly fast. Almost everywhere railroads, settlers, miners, ranchers, and hunters were staking claims, shoving off Natives, and hoarding resources—minerals, robes, skins, water, and grass. Lakotas represented the Natives' last best hope, a still-expanding Indigenous power that had repeatedly denied and humiliated the American empire—and might do so again. The swelling village—in the core of which was the reunited Sioux alliance, Očhéthi Šakówin—became a hive of activity. Large bison herds could be still be found in the Powder River country and around the Yellowstone Valley. Men hunted and scouted, women processed the meat and made robes, and boys tended to horses, fattening them on spring grass. Everybody talked, pooling information about wašíču soldiers, agency policies, traders, Crows. The village crossed the Powder and then the Tongue, still absorbing people, eventually moving in six separate tribal circles, Cheyennes in the front, Hunkpapas guarding the rear. By mid-May the village was on lower Rosebud Creek and contained more than four hundred lodges and eight hundred warriors, many of them armed with pistols, Springfield carbines, Winchester repeaters, and other state-of-the-art weapons. It was a prodigious concentration of military power that was only potentially belligerent. "We supposed that the combined camps would frighten off the soldiers," remembered Cheyenne warrior Wooden Leg.[37]

It was during the long march to Rosebud in the spring of 1876 that Sitting Bull and the Hunkpapas emerged as the central protagonists of Indigenous resistance to white encroachment. Although Americans vilified Sitting Bull as the ultimate hostile, the Hunkpapas were for most Indians mysterious hunter-nomads who shunned outsiders; the Cheyennes who had now attached themselves to Sitting Bull's village thought they were "almost strangers." They saw in Sitting Bull and Hunkpapas not militants but isolationists: "These people kept mostly at peace by staying away from all white settlements," believing that withdrawal offered the best chance for survival. That changed during the march. The chiefs from all tribal circles met at "each place of camping," debating how to respond to the American threat. They counseled restraint. "Our combination of camps was simply for defence," remembered Wooden Leg, a Cheyenne. "We were within our treaty rights as hunters." But young warriors demanded immediate action, and attitudes began to change. They were traveling with their families and wanted to stop the whites with force. Finely echoing their unease, Sitting Bull said he did not want war but would fight if attacked.[38]

A westbound Lakota scouting party had detected the approaching wašíčus on the upper Yellowstone in early May and promptly stole more than thirty horses from the army's new Crow scouts. Lakotas kept shadowing the large wašíču-Crow column, staging decoy attacks and waving "an immense war bonnet," brashly announcing themselves to the soldiers and Crows, and leaving them palpably anxious. Soon after a Cheyenne hunting party detected soldiers to the south on the Tongue, moving toward the village with Indian scouts. The allies knew now for certain that the Americans meant war. These soldiers were not protecting railroad crews; they came to kill Indians. Yet the council chiefs commanded the warriors to wait.[39]

This was Sitting Bull's moment. He came "into admiration by all Indians as a man whose medicine was good," Wooden Leg recounted, "as a man having a kind heart and good judgment as to the best course of conduct. He was considered as being altogether brave, but peaceable. He was strong in religion—the Indian religion." He was also the last long-serving northern Lakota leader, for High Backbone had died in 1870 on a raid. Never before had Sitting Bull had so many looking to him for guidance; never had so much depended on what he would do next.[40]

The first vision—the "terrible dream"—came to him near the mouth of Rosebud. He "felt that something or somebody was prompting him to go up the top of the butte nearby and commune with the Great Mysterious," Wakȟáŋ Tȟáŋka. He prayed and meditated and descended into a dream. From the east came a high wind, raising a dust cloud that collided with a white cloud that was an Indian village "sailing smoothly against the gale." As the gale drew near, he saw behind it "countless soldiers with shining guns, swords, brass and nickel plated trimmings on harnesses, saddles and bridles and spurs." When the gale and the cloud collided, there was a dreadful crash: "Nothing was left of the threatening gale." The cloud sailed east and then north "and was soon out of sight." Sitting Bull returned to the village and told the other chiefs to anticipate "a glorious victory for the Indians." Sadness washed over him. It had come to this. Only terrible carnage could bring deliverance from violence.[41]

Burdened by an enormous pressure, Sitting Bull reached out to Wakȟáŋ Tȟáŋka. In late May he asked three comrades to see and hear him as he climbed up on a hill to pray. Facing the sun, he performed a pipe ceremony, asking Wakȟáŋ Tȟáŋka to pull him through trouble: "Save me and give me all my wild game animals and have [them] close enough so my people will have food enough this winter and also the good men on earth have more power." If Wakȟáŋ Tȟáŋka did this for him, he would dance for two days and two nights and give the Great Spirit a whole buffalo.[42]

The village alliance moved up the Rosebud Valley and spread out on both sides of the creek, Cheyennes in the south and Hunkpapas in the north. Hunkpapas sponsored a Sun Dance. On June 4 two women and a man cut down a cottonwood trunk and carried it into an arbor for holy men to paint. The next day pledgers, those who had vowed to dance, entered the arbor. Two had their breasts pierced with skewers. Holy men brought each of them a rope that was attached to the Sun Dance pole and tied the ropes to the skewers. They grasped the pledgers by the waist and pulled hard until blood began to flow. The ceremonial decider asked the sun to accept their sacrifice, have pity on them, and fulfill the bleeding men's hopes. The pledgers yanked themselves backward, tearing their skin to free themselves of the skewers. On June 6 Sitting Bull gave flesh and stepped outside time. He sat down against the central pole, and Jumping Bull, an Assiniboine whom he had captured as a boy and adopted as a brother, took his left arm and removed a piece of flesh with an awl and a knife. He did this fifty times, moving up the arm, and then repeated the process on the right. Covered with blood, Sitting Bull began to dance, staring at the sun as he moved around the pole. He danced for hours until, suddenly, he stopped, wobbling but refusing to fall. When he finally collapsed a sea of hands caught him.

When he came to, Sitting Bull asked Black Moon, a Minneconjou, to announce the vision he had received. He had heard a voice from above saying that "these have no ears," and he had seen soldiers on horseback "coming down like grasshoppers, their heads down and hats falling off." He had learned what would happen to the soldiers and what the Indians should do: "These are to die but you are not supposed to take their spoils." On June 15 the village packed up its possessions and marched farther west, tracking bison. That night they found out who the upside-down soldiers were. Cheyenne scouts brought word of a massive

American army that was approaching fast from the south. Many of these wašíčus would die.[43]

Sheridan had, at long last, gotten the Lakota campaign off the ground. Colonel John Gibbon had led some 450 men of the Seventh Infantry and the Second Cavalry out of Fort Ellis in western Montana Territory in late March with pointed objectives: find the hostiles east of the Bighorn River, "strike them unawares," and prevent them from fleeing north of the Yellowstone and the Missouri. While Lakotas and their allies had marched west to the Rosebud, Gibbon had marched east along the Yellowstone; it had been Gibbon's troops the Lakota scouts had tracked in May. Although Gibbon had failed to engage the enemy—his Crow scouts were "mortally afraid" of Lakotas, and he could not move his heavy columns across the torrential Yellowstone in springtime—he had at least penetrated deep into enemy territory, within sight of the "immense Indian camp" on the Rosebud. On June 9, at the mouth of the Rosebud, he united with Terry, who had pushed west from Fort Abraham Lincoln into the Yellowstone with more than 900 men and 150 wagons.[44]

While Gibbon struggled on the Yellowstone, Crook had begun his second attempt to penetrate the Powder River country from the south: this would be the third component of the hammer-and-anvil offensive Sheridan had envisioned months ago, an operation that had morphed from a winter campaign into a summer one. Crook's column left Fort Fetterman on May 29, pushing north in a "long black line." Stories of the Fetterman fiasco were fresh in the minds of the soldiers thanks to the reminiscences of the mercurial Frank Grouard, the son of a Hawaiian woman and a Mormon missionary and Sitting Bull's adopted brother, who had left the Lakotas to become Crook's head scout. It was a difficult, nerve-racking march. Crook's Crow and Shoshone scouts had failed to materialize—they had their own reasons to fight the Lakotas and their own schedule—and he was advancing all but blind. Moreover, the soldiers believed that Crazy Horse had sent a warning that the Americans would be attacked as soon as they "touched the waters of the Tongue." On June 6, in a raging downpour, the column lost its way; the next day it reached the Tongue and made camp. The camp was awakened at midnight by Indians walking on the bluffs on the opposite bank, threatening destruction. The attack came in the afternoon of the ninth when the Indians "rained down a severe fire" across the river. When the size of the wašíču army—more than a thousand men—dawned on them, they quickly disengaged and retreated north. Shortly, the invaders turned south.[45]

But on June 16 the soldiers reemerged near the head of the Rosebud: Crook had finally secured his Indian scouts, more than 200 altogether, and was "spoiling for a fight." When the news of Crook's return reached them, the great Lakota-

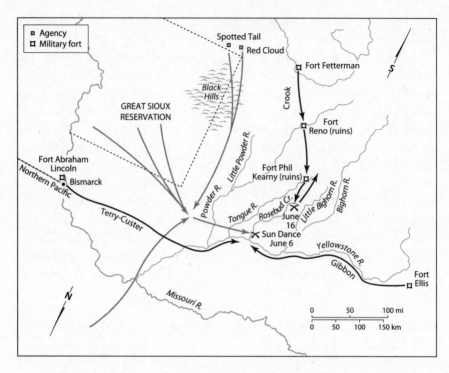

47. Mobilizations, a view from the north, spring and early summer 1876.
Map by Bill Nelson.

Cheyenne village was thrown into confusion. This was clearly a massive invading army, but it was coming from the south and not the east as Sitting Bull had predicted. Elders urged restraint, but warriors began preparations. A rushed council elected Crazy Horse to lead a preemptive strike. He invoked an ancient ritual, "Gathering the Warriors," and at night pushed south with an army of 750 warriors. Rather than waiting for Crook to bring the war to the Lakotas, Crazy Horse meant to take the war to the wašíčus.

When the Lakota-Cheyenne army drew near the Rosebud in the morning, Crazy Horse, occupying high ground, divided the warriors into two prongs and sent them down the bluffs to fall on the enemy. Crook's Shoshone and Crow auxiliaries pushed back the western prong, and the soldiers repulsed the eastern one. In a master stroke, Crazy Horse changed tactics, shifting into fluid and mobile battle. Retreating northwest, he regrouped and launched quick raids into enemy positions, his mounted warriors releasing deadly fire with Winchesters and Henrys, only to retreat, regroup, and attack again. As he gradually shifted the battlefront northeast, American lines extended to near the snapping point.

Crook canceled an attempt to find and attack the Lakota-Cheyenne village, consolidated his forces in the center, and, although clearly thwarted and spent, declared victory. The Indians disengaged, and Crook retreated south. On the way the soldiers passed the ruins of the abandoned Bozeman Trail forts, "feeling the loss of just such depots."[46]

Without knowing it, Crazy Horse had neutralized Sheridan's pincer plan. Terry, having discovered an Indian trail, had planned to chase the Indians into the Bighorn Valley and Crook was supposed to drive the Indians toward Terry. But Crook did not drive any Indians anywhere: the Indians drove *him* out, neutralizing his massive column as an invasion force.[47]

MOBILIZATIONS

The Battle of the Rosebud had ruined Sheridan's grand strategy, but the general stayed the course. He needed a clear target and relied on the federal bureaucracy to create one. The Indian Office, through its many agencies, was supposed to sift hostile Lakotas from friendly ones, thereby marking out a distinct war zone for the army to operate in. That zone was the Powder River country, the home of Sitting Bull, Crazy Horse, and their irredeemable militants. In the winter and spring of 1876 it seemed that the plan might work. At the Red Cloud Agency, the vital testing ground for the clash between Lakota sovereignty and federal authority, Oglalas and Sicangus seemed unusually quiet. The new agent, James Hastings, noted how "the occupation of the Black Hills" and "the military operations against the hostile Indians" had been "sources of constant uneasiness" among his wards, but he was happy to report having "succeeded in gaining their confidence and keeping them quiet." He thought that a growing number of Lakotas was warming up to the idea of farming, which gave him confidence that the government "will find little trouble in persuading them to go south"—to leave their homelands for Indian Territory.[48]

Lakotas did shift shape, but not in the way Hastings and the government officials expected. The repeated violations—the prospector invasion of Pahá Sápa, Crook's unprovoked attacks, Gibbon's Yellowstone march—aggravated the supposedly peaceful agency Lakotas. Nontreaty chiefs sent runners to call in warriors from the Red Cloud, Spotted Tail, and Standing Rock Agencies, and the hostile-friendly screen dissolved as the outwardly divided Lakota nation snapped into collective action. Behind it emerged the Lakota empire.[49]

There were early warnings that went ignored for too long. In early 1876 the various branches of the government were bombarded with increasingly anxious reports from the northern plains. Crazy Horse and Black Twin, "leaders of hostile Sioux," were rumored to be heading toward the Red Cloud Agency in mid-

February. "Sioux scout from Standing Rock reports all young men are leaving reservation with best ponies. They report going to fight Crow Indians, but he says they are going to join Sitting Bull," Major Marcus Reno wired in late April. On May 30 a now-worried Sheridan wired Sherman that "all the agency Indians capable of taking the field are now, or will be, on the war-path," adding the next day that Red Cloud Agency stood almost deserted and about "fifty lodges from Spotted Tail [had] also gone, some with families." Four days later Captain J. S. Poland wrote that Kill Eagle, a Sihasapa chief, had left Standing Rock with twenty lodges, apparently to join "the hostile Sitting Bull." More alarmingly, Poland also reported that the agency population had been twenty-five hundred lower than the average for some time. Rumors circulated that "all able-bodied male Indians had left Red Cloud Agency," and on June 8 a telegram reached the capital, informing Sherman that Sitting Bull's village had swollen into nearly thirteen hundred lodges, which translated into roughly two thousand warriors.[50]

These were crucial shreds of information that should have alerted the high command to a stunning concentration of Indigenous power around the northern Lakotas and Sitting Bull, but the shreds never cohered into a clear picture. This was partly because most officials on the ground reported grossly inflated numbers on their agencies: they received government rations in proportion to the number of their wards, and they needed all the rations they could get to keep the Indians content. Not surprisingly, many agency chiefs, too, exaggerated the number of their followers. A more elemental cause was the top military officials' failure to understand the Indians and their ways. Contemplating the perceived obstinacy of Lakotas a year earlier, Sheridan had written: "Indians are the most clannish people in existence. Their government is clannish, their wild, warlike education is clannish, their social character and customs are clannish." The frustrated general had actually captured something essential about the Lakota society, but blinded by preconceived notions of what counted as organization, he could not see how kinship, a shared sense of connectedness, had allowed Lakotas to forge a common front against an overpowering enemy. Like most Americans, he thought that Lakotas—like all Indians—fought as individuals and for personal glory. Blinded by ethnocentrism, Sheridan and the U.S. Army had missed a sweeping national mobilization Lakotas had implemented in plain sight.[51]

And so Sheridan pressed ahead with *his* mobilization, confident of the enemy's organizational inferiority. The army had contracted the paddle steamer *Far West* to move supplies from the railhead in Bismarck into the Yellowstone, the army's main entryway into hostile territory. The *Far West* also served as Terry's headquarters, and on June 21 it sat at the mouth of the Rosebud with no Indians in sight. It was there that Terry held a pivotal meeting with Gibbon and Custer to finalize plans for a decisive attack on the Lakotas.

The presence of Custer seemed like a small miracle to all three. Not only did it seem he had lost his appetite for war while sojourning in the East, but his testimony against Grant, his former commanding general, had rankled the army chain of command, making him persona non grata. Equally distastefully, Custer seemed to have planted a story in the *New York World* saying that Grant had sidelined the army's best Indian fighter out of spite, thereby endangering the entire Sioux campaign. But many of his commanders still saw in Custer a superior soldier and wanted him reinstated. Grant relented but insisted that Custer lead the Seventh Cavalry, 750 soldiers and 31 Arikara and Crow scouts, under Terry's direct supervision. On board the *Far West* was a man desperate to redeem himself.[52]

Terry expected the Indians to shift westward and sketched a reduced two-arm pincer maneuver—he had no word from Crook and his southern arm. Custer was to move south along the Rosebud, find the Indian trail, and follow it west, while Terry and Gibbon would push up the Yellowstone and, on the morning of the twenty-sixth, strike south along the Little Bighorn. Custer would scoop up the Indians from the south and drive them north toward Gibbon and Terry's infantry and cavalry anvil. The maneuver's success hinged on Custer's speed— he had a lot of distance to cover—and so he had his regiment shed sabers, Gatling guns, and wagons. Mules would carry his supplies. He raced south on the twenty-second, and Terry and Gibbon embarked up the Yellowstone on the *Far West*. Custer soon found the trail, deep and clear. On the twenty-fourth his officers noticed that the trail had suddenly grown messier and broader, eventually becoming three hundred yards wide and heading west: the trails had either converged or diverged, and the mobile Indian village was either swelling or breaking up. Custer seemed to have thought the latter was the case and pushed forward— in haste.[53]

The trails had in fact converged, leading toward the Greasy Grass, a narrow, shallow, and wildly meandering tributary of the Bighorn. More agency Indians had arrived from the south and followed the trail to the stream the Americans knew as the Little Bighorn; an Indigenous empire was coalescing, preparing itself for massive collective action. On the twenty-fourth Lakotas and Cheyennes spread their great village of about one thousand lodges, six to eight thousand people, and some twenty thousand horses along the Greasy Grass, the many tribal circles forming an elongated archipelago of clustered tipis. The village was sheltered by steep bluffs to the east and bounded by a lush rolling floodplain to the west, a natural luxuriant pasture for the massive horse herd. But, more immediately, the Greasy Grass was a good place to fight the great battle the Indians knew was coming.[54]

Lakotas had learned early on about the growing steamer traffic and the concentration of soldiers and supplies on the Yellowstone; they were certain that the soldiers were coming and they knew to expect the dust storm Sitting Bull had predicted. Lakotas had adapted to the U.S. way of fighting them and knew that there would be a large cavalry attack soon after they stopped moving. This meant that they could choose the place and, to a degree, the time of the battle. In late afternoon of the twenty-fourth Lakota scouts arrived with intelligence from a fifty-mile ride. They had followed a large column of mounted soldiers heading up the Rosebud and could see that the lodge-pole tracks would lead the wašíčus to the Greasy Grass. Chiefs gathered for an intertribal council. Some thought that an attack was imminent, and a number of young Cheyenne warriors took suicide vows, pledging to fight to the death. Others believed that the wašíčus wanted to parley, having just been humiliated on the Rosebud, or were still far away. Some socialized and danced deep into the night. Sitting Bull climbed up the bluffs and asked Wakȟáŋ Tȟáŋka to have pity on his people.[55]

Simultaneously, the combined Terry-Gibbon column approached the Greasy Grass from the north. "We are now en route to the Indian village, which is supposed to be on the Little Big Horn," Lieutenant James Bradley reported to his journal. He felt buoyant. "It is undoubtedly a large one, and should Custer's command and ours unite, we, too, will have a large force numbering all told about one thousand men, armed with the splendid breech-loading Springfield rifles and carbines, caliber forty-five, and strengthened by the presence of Low's battery of three Gatling guns. Should we come to blows it will be one of the biggest Indian battles ever fought on this continent, and most decisive in its results." He had no doubt about what was going to happen: "The utter destruction of the Indian village, and overthrow of Sioux power will be the certain result."[56]

I WIPED HIM OUT

A dust cloud, rising with the midafternoon heat, gave the wašíčus away. They were riding hard across the long flat, charging directly toward them. There was no time for a council; returning scouts said that the whole wašíču army was coming. Criers ran and rode from camp to camp, and Sitting Bull, certain of his people's spiritual primacy and military superiority, urged restraint, saying that the soldiers might want to negotiate; he knew that the wašíču horse soldiers preferred to attack before dawn, charging into sleeping camps. But then two bullets hit Sitting Bull's mount. "Now my best horse is shot, it is like they have shot me," he said. "Attack them."

Men collected their weapons and war horses and rushed toward the closing wall of flesh and lead, buying time for women, children, and the old to find cover. There were terrible volleys of carbine fire ripping through tipi covers, shattering tipi poles, killing horses. There were herders hurrying horses to safety, and there were women packing for flight, carrying children out of harm's way, painting their faces for war, singing death and strong-heart songs, and watching their sons, husbands, and fathers ride toward the rising smoke. The wašíču charge lost momentum. Bizarrely, the soldiers dismounted and formed a skirmish line nearly half a mile away from the first tipi circle. They simply stayed there, shooting, mostly inaccurately. Only the Indian scouts pushed toward the village. They captured some horses and killed several women and children before disengaging.

Lakotas and Cheyennes seized the initiative. The warriors maintained a steady fire at the wašíču horde—perhaps a half of them carried firearms, many of them repeaters—while One Bull, Black Moon, Big Road, and Crazy Horse orchestrated a series of mounted charges, bringing some two hundred warriors into battle. The wašíču line melted away. The soldiers retreated into the woods along a loop of dry riverbed, but there would be no respite. Warriors shouted that the wašíčus should have brought more Indians to do their fighting for them. They routed the visibly panicked soldiers out of the trees and chased them over a twelve-foot bank into the river as if they were buffalo, unhorsing them with quick-slashing tomahawks and filling them with horror that made them shoot at the sky. The water turned red. The warriors stripped the dead of pistols, guns, ammunition, and scalps, and drove the living up a steep bluff on a hill where they hunkered down. It had all been strangely straightforward. They turned back and headed toward the village, singing victory songs. For a moment they feared that the soldiers would move along the ridge into the village's rear, but they did not. They just stood there, apparently having exhausted their ammunition. The fight had now lasted an hour.[57]

Down on the valley floor Sitting Bull inspected the carnage, which was staggering in its extent and intimacy. Dozens of bodies lay on the plain, some dead, some dying. Men went through them, searching for guns and cartridges, while women and boys finished off wounded enemies, rendering their bodies useless in the next world. They found the corpse of Bloody Knife, the son of a Hunkpapa father and an Arikara mother, who had moved to live among the Arikaras and later served in several U.S. military campaigns against the Lakotas; he was Custer's favorite scout. Two women, sisters, cut off his destroyed head—it had taken a bullet—and paraded it on a pole in the village. Their mother recognized the face: it was her brother's. The women worked hard on the body of Teat, or Isaiah Dorman, an African-American man who had married a Hunkpapa woman and then served the U.S. Army and Custer as a scout and an interpreter. They ensured his body would be useless in the world after.[58]

That necessary work was interrupted by a sickening realization. The warriors had banished the wašíču invaders up on a hill to the south, but now there was another, even larger, mass of horse soldiers on the hills, advancing toward the village's rear. The warriors knew the wašíčus would target women and children to distract combatants—the Washita and other battles had made that plain—and these soldiers were already dangerously close. Gall saw other wašíčus descending a coulee toward the Greasy Grass and the village center. Crossing the river would not be difficult because the water was low there. Runs the Enemy saw men waving blankets in warning. Then he saw a wašíču horde that, like Sitting Bull's grasshoppers, "seemed to fill the whole hill." Crazy Horse and Sitting Bull realized that the decisive battle would take place there and rushed toward the village; others did the same. They found the village safe but in a state of feverish flight. Women, children, and old men were evacuating, and Dull Knife and Runs the Enemy thought they were losing the battle. Sitting Bull, riding along the village perimeter, was desperate to shield the village and its noncombatants. He urged the warriors to take the fight to the wašíčus.

They did. At some point the Indians realized that the wašíčus had made a critical mistake in splitting their forces and not attacking simultaneously. With a large number of the wašíču soldiers incapacitated in the south, the warriors could now concentrate overwhelming numbers against the attacking horse soldiers. Warriors discharged volleys across the river, covering others who forded the Greasy Grass. They pushed up the ridge through its maze of coulees, gulches, and ravines, absorbing fire from above, shooting down soldiers and horses with bullets and arrows, slowly driving them up the ridge. The battle zone shifted to high ground and away from the village, and the wašíču soldiers formed a skirmish line, each man five yards from another. Yellow Nose, a Ute captive who had taken the identity of his captors and become a Cheyenne warrior, charged at the soldiers five times. He grabbed a guidon from a trooper and counted coups on the enemy with it, galvanizing his comrades. Gall, who had not seen action yet, was still in the village, searching for his family. His lodge was empty. He found his two wives and three children in the woods. They were dead. For some time he did not know what he was supposed to do. Then he took his hatchet and rode up the hill toward the wašíčus. When he killed them, they would see his face.[59]

The fighting became increasingly fluid, fragmented, and confined because the Indians willed it so. Badly outnumbered, the wašíčus began to retreat along the ridgeline, looking for openings to attack. Most of the warriors pursued them while some moved parallel to the Greasy Grass, keeping between the soldiers and the village, firing from a distance. When the warriors saw a large contingent stop and form a skirmish line, they launched a mass charge but were stopped by heavy fire. The warrior body dissolved almost instantly, reverting to individual and small group fighting. The Indians maintained pressure through long-range firing and felled exposed soldiers with arrows. They crept upon them through the sagebrush and gullies and stampeded remaining wašíču horses with blankets. In a pivotal creative move, Crazy Horse raced nearly a mile downstream with a band of warriors, rushed up a deep ravine into the enemy's rear and began delivering deadly flanking fire to pin the wašíčus down. It was a singular tactical maneuver in a battle that was effectively uncontrollable. Still farther downriver warriors saw soldiers storming down the ridge toward the Greasy Grass near a ford where thousands of noncombatants had sought refuge. The warriors had anticipated such a move, and they sent the wašíčus back with a storm of arrows and bullets. The battle was entering its third hour, and Lakotas had thwarted the enemy's most effective strategy: this time the wašíčus could not target civilians. From there onward the Indians' superior numbers would determine the outcome.[60]

Repulsed and outflanked, the wašíčus still commanded a long stretch of the ridgetop, but their situation was rapidly deteriorating. More and more Indians kept pushing up the hillside, "swarming like ants." Using the uneven terrain to conceal themselves, they converged around the wašíčus, shooting and stampeding their horses. Gall, axing down soldiers with controlled rage, led a mass attack of mounted and foot warriors that forced the wašíčus to yield a critical position, creating an opening for Crazy Horse. He launched a charge through heavy crossfire and cut the enemy line in two, and his warriors rushed in to dispatch the confused, isolated soldiers. Others joined in, shooting and clubbing them down. Then Cheyenne suicide warriors rode straight toward the soldiers to shield their charging comrades from bullets. Wašíču maneuvers turned from offensive to defensive to reactionary. Some still fought on horseback—poorly, it seemed—others on foot. Their lines crumbled and their cohesion dissolved, and the warriors surged in to engulf the isolated units like a rising tide. Seeing that the wašíčus were unraveling, they closed in to axe and club them down. Every wašíču killed meant that another one became exposed. The soldiers made several brief stands but each lasted but minutes. They could not stop the onslaught. "We circled around and around," Two Moons remembered. "We had them surrounded."

Soon there were fewer than one hundred wašíčus left. The Indians slowed down for a moment, repositioned, and then pressed on again. The wašíčus scrambled toward a small round hill on the far end of the ridge, killed their horses in a semicircle, and crouched behind the still-heaving bodies. They had only moments to live, and they fired wildly or not at all. Some shot themselves. There was no military structure left. The Indians thought the wašíčus "became foolish,

48. The Battle of the Greasy Grass (pictographic account, 1881). Red Horse,
a Minneconjou who fought in the Battle of the Greasy Grass, made forty drawings
of the combat. Contrary to the mythic Custer-centric images of the Last Stand,
this pictographic account shows the battle's claustrophobic messiness and carnage.
Courtesy of National Anthropological Archives, Smithsonian Institution
(NAA MS 2367A 08570700).

many throwing away their guns and raising their hands," begging for mercy that
would not be offered. A group of soldiers found a small gap in the cordon and
started toward the river. They made "their arms go as though they were running,
but they were only walking": they were dead within minutes. The Indians descended on the surviving soldiers, who could hardly be seen behind the smoke
and dust. Crazy Horse produced a shrieking scream with his eagle-bone whistle
and made another mounted run between the remaining wašíču positions. The
soldiers released a volley but missed; the warriors knew the wašíčus were spent.
They charged, and the soldiers and the Indians became a single, uneven jumble.
No shots could be heard for they had blended into an unceasing roar. The killing,
the Indians would later remember, became methodical. They "did not take a
single soldier prisoner, but killed all of them; none were left alive for even five
minutes." It was as if "they were driving buffalo to a good place to slaughter,"

remembered Julia Face. Down at the village women captured riderless wašíču horses.[61]

There were no celebrations, just more work to be done. Dozens of dead kin had to be collected, mourned, and sung to. Women had to see to the mass of wašíču corpses, among them the remains of Pȟehíŋ HáŋskA, the ubiquitous wašíču chief who had slaughtered Cheyennes on the Washita, attacked Lakotas on the Yellowstone, and led prospectors to Pahá Sápa. It was a ghostly scene that stirred reflection. "I wasn't a bit sorry," thought Black Elk. "I knew beforehand that this was going to happen." "They came to fight us and we had to fight. . . . I went among them and met the soldiers," remembered Iron Hawk. "These white men wanted it, they called for it and I let them have it."[62]

There was also more fighting to do. The battered horse soldiers who had retreated to the hilltop in the early stages of the battle were still entrenched there, in the hundreds. They had to be banished or killed. "As soon as we had killed all the different soldiers"—Custer's troops—"the Sioux all went back to kill the soldiers on the hill" in the south, remembered Red Horse. After collecting guns and ammunition—repeaters and saddlebags full of cartridges—from the dead wašíčus, the Indians rode south. They found the wašíču soldiers utterly exposed on the hilltop that provided almost no natural cover. They circled around the elevation and began long-range sniping from hills and ridges, taking shifts to maintain constant pressure on the dug-in soldiers. They made several quick charges at them, keeping them agitated and preventing them from getting water. They stopped only when darkness fell, starting again at sunrise. At midafternoon the following day scouts returned from downriver with word of an approaching wašíču column of horse and foot soldiers. Lakotas and Cheyennes were wary of facing infantry and its "big guns," and the chiefs thought there had been enough fighting. They broke camp and began moving south.[63]

As Terry's column approached the battlefield, fleeing Crow scouts from Custer's command came to it, informing the general of the annihilation. Most of his men found it impossible to accept, and scouts were sent toward the Indian village to "communicate with Custer should he prove to be in possession." The soldiers found a village "in motion, retreating before us" and shielded by horsemen "maneuvering like a body of cavalry." They thought it was Custer commanding his unit. A hail of bullets quickly destroyed the fantasy. When Terry and his column reached the hilltop to which the soldiers had retreated in the early stages of the battle, all the Indians were gone. The battered officers there were utterly unable to offer a coherent report. No one knew what exactly had happened to Custer's five companies and the more than two hundred men who had ridden into battle with him along the ridge. Terry dispatched Captain Frederick Benteen—who despised Custer and believed that he was somewhere grazing horses—to find out. Benteen's detachment found the bodies in clusters that told to the experienced soldier a story of several last stands. Nearly all the bodies had been mutilated, leaving their owners with various combinations of incapacities in the spirit world. Pȟehíŋ HáŋskA had been sent there whole. He had a gash on his thigh, and an arrow had been rammed into his penis. He had left this world diminished, and he would enter the next diminished.[64]

So complete was their victory that Lakotas and Cheyennes put only sixteen miles between themselves and the wašíčus before repitching the village beside the Greasy Grass. Women erected tipis and boys took the massive herd of more than fifteen thousand horses to the cottonwoods by the stream. Messengers were sent to carry news to the agencies. The next day the camp moved along Lodge Grass Creek at the foot of the Bighorn Mountains. But that night panic swept through the village. Soldiers in blue were coming, riding side by side. It was a prank: they were Indians dressed in soldiers' uniforms. Then the Indians celebrated, dancing victory dances and singing victory songs. They sang about Pȟehíŋ HáŋskA, thanking him for leaving them so many "holy irons"—guns—which he was not worthy to carry. "A charger, he is coming. I made him come," they sang. "When he came, I wiped him out. He did not like my ways; that is why." They sang and danced all night. After a few days they scattered. Some Cheyennes looped back toward the battlefield, looking for stray horses. They did not even get close. The stench of rotting flesh and blood was too sickening.[65]

WHAT ARE THE FACTS IN THIS CASE?

In the aftermath of their triumph many Lakotas thought that they should press the advantage. Crazy Horse and He Dog believed that an attack was the best defense and urged Lakotas and Cheyennes to rejoin in a great coalition and attack Forts Fetterman and Laramie on the same day to banish the wašíčus. Others, mostly agency Lakotas, argued that they should simply wait and allow the wašíčus to open peace talks. Practical considerations interfered, too: munitions were low, horses needed pasture, and summer hunts awaited. The agency Lakotas began peeling off, and the moment passed. The plans for a concentrated campaign dissolved into a series of small offensives. A party attacked the *Far West* on the Yellowstone below the Powder, and Crazy Horse led a band of warriors to the Black Hills to raid the miners. In early fall Lakota scouts saw wašíču soldiers streaming out of Fort Fetterman, wearing buffalo-hide coats and fur caps. They were riding into winter, their best ally.[66]

The news of the annihilation reached Washington in the midst of the nation's centennial celebrations. First there was shock and disbelief. The only explana-tion to the Natives' triumph, it was suggested, was that they had been led by "Bison," a tawny youth who had attended West Point. Others saw in Sitting Bull an archdemon who had schemed Custer's defeat and death. There were cries of immediate retaliation, but there were also those who thought Lakotas had had every right to defend their homes and lives. Lewis H. Morgan, a pioneer of sci-entific anthropology who saw Indians as savages with potential for progress, pub-lished a letter in *The Nation*, asking, "What are the facts in this case? General Custer, at the head of three hundred cavalry, rode into an Indian encampment, men, women, and children, and killed all who resisted without hesitation and without remorse. Unfortunately for General Custer and his men, they encoun-tered the bravest and most determined Indians now living in America. They were surrounded and defeated, so that not a man escaped. They experienced the pre-cise fate they intended for the Indians."[67]

In shorter supply than sympathy were clear-eyed assessments of why things had turned out the way they did. An Army Corps of Engineers lieutenant ac-knowledged that "Sitting Bull has displayed the best of generalship in this campaign," but his was a minority view. On July 8, Secretary of War J. Donald Cameron gave his appraisal to the president. The Lakotas, he began, "have for centuries been pushed westward by the advancing tide of civilization," getting it wrong from the start. His was but one of many acts of misrepresentation that, over generations, have diminished the Lakota people as historical actors. The sec-retary could have written about the Lakotas' vast capacity to determine their own destiny, about their diplomatic and military sophistication, about their founda-tional role in shaping the course of American history, but he did not. The United States was gearing up to crush the Lakotas as a sovereign nation, and the presi-dent and the American people needed a different kind of Lakotas: primitive, treacherous, weak, and controllable. At the very moment the Americans awoke to the reality that there was an unyielding, seemingly unconquerable Indigenous power in their midst, they began a systematic erasing of the Lakotas and their re-markable history—the creation of Lakota America—from memory.[68]

THE AFTERMATH

The corpses had lain there for too long before the soldiers got to them, and it took still longer to clean up the field. Finding, collecting, and moving the bodies was hard and hideous work and there were so many of them. The dead did not re-ceive proper burials, and the photographs that reached the East outraged the na-tion. It was a massacre and an atrocity, a product of horrible errors and misjudg-ments and hate. People demanded answers from those who were responsible.

The symmetry was striking, indeed overwhelming, for the dead were not Custer's men but Lakotas. The place was not the Little Bighorn River but Wounded Knee Creek, and the year was not 1876 but 1890. Yet there was a direct link between the two killing fields. One flowed from the other and, to some, demanded the other.[69]

The United States' response to the Little Bighorn had been decisive and overwhelming; of the roughly sixteen hundred military engagements with Native Americans, this one hurt most. Humiliated, government officials snapped into action. Having learned from their mistakes in the spring and summer of 1876, Congress and the army mounted a comprehensive campaign to defeat and dispossess the Lakotas. Custer was elevated into an exemplary Christian knight, and the hill of his Last Stand became "a Golgotha" of America's "frontier settlements." There would be a reckoning.[70]

In early September, six weeks after Custer's fall, the wašíču emissary George W. Manypenny arrived in the Red Cloud Agency with a group of commissioners. One of them, Henry B. Whipple, a bishop and an advocate of Native Americans, opened the talks with a prayer and told Lakotas that the Great Father did not "wish to throw a blanket over your eyes, and to ask you to do anything without first looking at it." What he asked Lakotas to look at, and accept, was cultural death. Much of their land—the foundation of their identity and sovereignty— would need to become the property of white settlers. "I never want to leave this country," protested Wolf Necklace at Standing Rock. "All my relatives are lying here in the ground, and when I fall to pieces I am going to fall to pieces here."

A vengeful Congress had already passed legislation compelling the Lakotas to relinquish all their lands outside the Great Sioux Reservation, including the Black Hills, which were producing two million dollars in gold a year. Whipple announced this as a fait accompli. The only other option presented was to move south to Indian Territory, now the Territory of Oklahoma. If Lakotas agreed, they would have the Great Father's largesse: food, clothing, and tools. A number of chiefs present signed an agreement. Fire Thunder, an Oglala, held a blanket before his eyes and touched the pen. Satisfied, Manypenny's commissioners continued their tour of Lakota agencies, collecting a total of 230 signatures, roughly 10 percent of men living in the agencies. The 1868 Treaty of Fort Laramie stipulated that at least three-fourths of adult Lakota males had to sign any future land cession, so Manypenny was about 1,500 signatures short. Congress did not care. It ratified the agreement in February 1877 by an overwhelming majority. The Lakotas lost 7.3 million acres—an enormous windfall of grass and land for white ranchers and farmers—and found themselves hemmed in. By wašíču law Pahá Sápa now belonged to the United States.[71]

Red Cloud, American Horse, Little Wound, They Fear Even His Horses the Younger, Spotted Tail, and others had signed the agreement because their people were under siege. In the wake of the Little Bighorn the army took control of what was now understood as the nation's "Sioux problem." The Indian Office simply capitulated, abdicating authority to the men in blue. Sheridan placed Lakota agencies under military control and ordered all horses and guns in them confiscated. The Lakota society could not function without its mounts. It could not feed itself, defend itself, or maintain its unity. The ties between agency bands and nontreaty holdouts crumbled, leaving the latter critically weakened. Sheridan ordered four thousand troops into the Powder River country, and General Crook and Colonel Nelson A. Miles launched a war of attrition. They found neither triumph nor redemption in it. The few fights they managed to force were unsavory affairs, marked by desultory attacks, futile chases, assaults on peace delegations and sleeping villages, and a near defeat to Crazy Horse's and Two Moons's Lakota-Cheyenne force. Crook and Miles—ferocious, prickly rivals—dispatched inflated reports of Indian casualties, and the press elevated the skirmishes into battles, but a proper victory eluded the army. Stunned by the apparent loss of Pahá Sápa and starving to the point they had to sell their horses for food, northern Lakotas began moving into agencies in early 1877.

By then Sitting Bull, the quintessential "hostile," had already taken his followers to the Great Mother's country across the "medicine line," a hundred-mile stretch of the U.S.-Canadian border that seemed to stop U.S. troops like a spell. Crook had to ask Red Cloud and Spotted Tail to help him bring Crazy Horse in. The two chiefs agreed on the condition that Crazy Horse be given his own agency near the Black Hills. In May the chief rode into the Red Cloud Agency with twelve hundred men, women, and children, more than two thousand horses, and loads of brand-new breechloaders, the building blocks for a new life in Pahá Sápa where the northern Lakota oyátes could be united. But Crook never proposed a northern agency—Sheridan and Sherman would never have allowed it—alienating the Oglala chief who now had to find a space for himself and his followers in an agency that carried another chief's name. Army officers were disappointed when he became "extremely reticent" when they probed him for the various battles he had fought against them. Four months later, fearing that he was plotting an uprising, government officials ordered him detained and taken to Fort Robinson. It was only when he saw the tiny jail that Crazy Horse realized he would be arrested. He recoiled, a scuffle erupted, and a bayonet thrust killed him. The U.S. Army's tenure in charge of the "Sioux problem" was effectively over.[72]

INVASIONS

The army's withdrawal only opened the door for another assault by the federal government, now in the form of assertive agents, missionaries, school teachers, and "civilization" programs. The agents no longer sought to reform the Lakota society; that policy had expired the moment Custer died. They now aimed to hollow out Lakota society and fill the void with white American values, norms, words, customs, and thoughts. Once tribalism was pulverized, so went the logic, Lakotas could be absorbed into the American society as individuals and nuclear families.

Some Lakotas accepted and actively embraced farming and schools, but most were horrified by the assimilationist zeal. After all, Lakotas had possessed an extensive reservation and dominated the vast northern plains only a year earlier; their fall from power had been shockingly fast and complete. The acreage under the plow increased across the reduced reservation, but so too did resentment and despair. Chiefs struggled to maintain their status in a strange world where government agents incited rivalries among them, mobilized the akíčhitas to control them, and withheld rations to weaken them. Former hunters and warriors were reduced to eking out a living by driving wagons, hauling freight, and cutting wood. Women's traditional roles narrowed in the male-dominated reservation milieu and their standing as providers deteriorated as men took up farming and secured wage jobs. Children were removed from their families and taken to boarding schools where, separated from what was traditional and safe, they received an education geared to extinguish the Lakota culture.

The Great Sioux Reservation became a battleground for competing visions of the Lakota future. In 1881 Spotted Tail was killed by Crow Dog, a captain of the Indian police, who could not accept the old chief's defiant traditionalism, persisting popularity, and multiple wives. That same year Sitting Bull, no longer able to hold on to his starving followers, crossed the medicine line again and formally surrendered at Fort Buford with Crow King. He gave his rifle to his six-year-old son who handed it over to an army officer. "I wish it to be remembered that I was the last man of my tribe to surrender my rifle," the fifty-year-old chief said. "This boy has given it to you, and now wants to know how he is going to make a living," he said, intimating the struggles his son and others of his generation would face in the alien world the wašíčus imposed on the Lakotas. Crow King asked a *Chicago Tribune* correspondent for two dollars to buy dolls for his girls.

Sitting Bull was taken to Fort Randall on the Missouri River where he was held as a prisoner of war for nearly two years. He then settled in the Standing Rock Agency where James McLaughlin, a ruthlessly effective assimilation crusader, was tearing the fabric of the Lakota society apart by recruiting "boss" farmers,

49. Ration day at the Pine Ridge Agency, photograph by C. G. Morledge.
The distribution and withholding of rations were the Indian Office's most effective
method of making the Lakotas visible, accountable, and controllable. Courtesy
of the Denver Public Library, Western History Collection (X-31388).

policemen, and judges among the Lakotas to educate, monitor, and punish other
Lakotas. The rift between the Indian police and traditional spiritual leaders became particularly corrosive.[73]

Sitting Bull suffered in this upside-down world where chiefs, dances, feasts,
ceremonies, and societies were under assault, where federal agents openly detested their wards, and where his adopted brother Gall became a boss farmer.
McLaughlin harbored a near-pathological hatred for Sitting Bull, denouncing
him as obstinate and dangerous, and geared up efforts to stamp out the traditional Lakota culture. The year 1883 was a good one for him. "Col. McLaughlin
went out hunting buffalo with Indians," reads a Hunkpapa winter count: it was
the last communal hunt by the Standing Rock people. The herds were all but
gone, and the Cheyenne River, Rosebud, and Pine Ridge people also had their
last hunts around the same time. A vast emptiness fell in the center of the Lakota
world. Wičháša wakháŋs continued to perform buffalo-calling ceremonies to
keep the people on the "right road," and Lakota families raised their cattle com-
munally, trying to preserve their traditional family and band structures. In 1885
Sitting Bull joined William F. Cody's Wild West Show for a few months. It was
almost as if Buffalo Bill's lurid re-creation of the West—in his rendition, at least,

50. Sioux Indian police line up on horseback in front of the Pine Ridge Agency buildings, Dakota Territory, 1882. The Indian police was a key government institution aimed at monitoring, controlling, and disciplining the Lakotas and other Native Americans in their own homelands. Courtesy of National Archives, photo no. 519143.

the Indians got to defeat Custer over and over again—possessed more authenticity than the wretchedness of the aggressively modernized Standing Rock.

It was much the same in the other agencies. At Pine Ridge the edgily passionate agent Valentine T. McGillycuddy clashed with Red Cloud over schools, funds, land policies, religion, treaty obligations, and sheer primacy. Red Cloud had not lost any of his political shrewdness. When Secretary of the Interior Carl Schurz visited the agency in 1879, it was Red Cloud, not McGillycuddy, who received him. Sitting on a chair in the center of a semicircle of Lakotas, he faced Schurz directly, making it clear to whom Pine Ridge belonged. The frustrated agent promoted They Fear Even His Horses the Younger over the older chief, but Red Cloud schemed a visit to Washington to meet President Grover Cleveland. Dressed in wašíču clothes—an astute move calculated to assuage the Great Father—Red Cloud made his case. It triggered an investigation that covered almost all Indian reservations in the western United States. McGillycuddy was removed, a rare victory for Lakotas during the brutal early years of reservation existence.[74]

The Indian Office pressured the Lakotas so hard because it was pressured by the government which in turn was pressured by liberal reformers, evangelicals, and western settlers, ranchers, and railroad boosters who wanted Indian reservations gone. The Great Sioux Reservation was to them a massive barrier blocking not only U.S. progress but also the uplift of Lakotas themselves. In 1887 Congress passed the General Allotment Act—also known as the Dawes Severalty Act—and two years later approved the Sioux Agreement, which called for the breakup of the Great Sioux Reservation into five smaller units, the cession of eleven million acres to the United States, and the allotment of the remaining lands to individual families. Red Cloud, American Horse, and other prominent chiefs categorically rejected the bill—it required the consent of three-quarters of adult males to pass—but many acquiesced when General Crook, a soldier many Lakotas had come to know and trust, warned them that if they did not sign, the Great Father would simply seize the lands he needed and leave the Lakotas on their own, depriving them of his rations, annuities, and protection. To hinder collective resistance, Crook had Lakotas sign the bill serially, as individuals, and returned to Washington with enough signatures to have the Great Sioux Reservation carved up into five isolated islands of controllable size. In a year the Great Father would open the ceded lands, half of the Lakota domain, to wašíču colonization, but at least Lakotas could now count on his continued care.[75]

But already, in a routine economizing move, Congress had reduced the Sioux appropriation to nine hundred thousand dollars, and things fell apart. Lakotas learned that their rations had been cut by 20 to 25 percent—a mere one hundred thousand annual saving for Congress but a catastrophic reduction for Lakotas who were trying to adjust to farming and new economic realities. The winter of 1889–90 was severe and Lakotas suffered extensive crop failures. Whooping cough and influenza spread explosively among the starving population, taking a particularly heavy toll on children.

In the midst of the death and despair arrived a message of hope, rebirth, and deliverance from Nevada where the Paiute Indian holy man and prophet Wovoka spoke of a new religion that promised the resurrection of the dead and the return of the old, seemingly lost, Indigenous world. Wovoka's message was a complex one—he urged Indians to be industrious and to work with and for the whites— but it was the prophetic vision of restored earth and a better world that gripped the Lakotas. Lakota emissaries rode the trains west to hear Wovoka's message and brought it home where it flowed into the hole left by the Sun Dance, which was now practiced in secret. Lakotas began dancing and singing, holding hands in a circle while turning clockwise around a tree. Some women and men wore special dresses and shirts to protect themselves against bullets. Step by step, their anger over the wašíču betrayals and arrogance became politicized. By the fall of

1890 nearly one-third of the Lakotas — about four thousand men and women — had become Ghost Dancers, receiving visions of resurrected kin, of restored bison and horse herds, of a world without disease, poverty, and wašíčus. One of the dancers was Sitting Bull, an alleged skeptic whose prayer tree became a focal point of the movement. Soon there would be a great transformation that would destroy the present world and usher in an unblemished one that only the dancers could enter.[76]

Indian agents and army officers saw malice, even a vast anti-white conspiracy, in the movement and refused to issue rations as long as the dancing continued. At Pine Ridge, the new agent, D. F. Royer, a fragile and excitable man, wired to Washington that the "Indians are dancing in the snow & are wild & crazy," and asked for troops. Lakotas moved the dance deep into the Badlands. General Miles, who desired to restore army control over Indian affairs in a warless world, declared that the most serious Indian war in history was at hand. President Benjamin Harrison's cabinet authorized an armed response — the Republicans wanted to show strength toward the Lakotas to win votes in the critical state of South Dakota — and six to seven thousand fighting men, nearly one-third of the entire U.S. Army, descended on the Lakota country in mid-November. It was an invasion. Miles sent Buffalo Bill Cody to detain Sitting Bull. A flabbergasted McLaughlin, desperate to reassert his primacy in the agency affairs, had Cody stopped and ordered the Standing Rock Indian Police to arrest Sitting Bull. The chief seemed to want to surrender but then changed his mind. He was shot in the back and then in the head. He died in front of his log cabin.[77]

Some of Sitting Bull's followers sought refuge in the camp of Spotted Elk, the son of Lone Horn, the architect of the Lakota-Crow truces in the 1850s. Like his father, Spotted Elk (also known as Big Foot) was a pragmatist who defended the Ghost Dancers' right to worship but took care not to provoke wašíču soldiers. The army officers misread the situation and branded Spotted Elk as Sitting Bull's successor and as the key hostile outside the Badlands. The man they had targeted was incapacitated by pneumonia and was on his way to Pine Ridge to find a place to rest. Instead of allowing him to come in, Miles ordered Spotted Elk and his followers arrested, disarmed, and detained.

Miles assigned the Seventh Cavalry to escort Spotted Elk's people to the Wounded Knee Creek. There Colonel James W. Forsyth ordered the Indians rounded up for the night and had four Hotchkiss cannons placed on a hill overlooking their camp. The soldiers began drinking whiskey secured from a local trader. Next morning Forsyth positioned three lines of troops on the other side of the Indian camp and ordered the soldiers to search the Indians for weapons. When a Lakota man resisted — he wanted to be paid for his gun — a struggle broke out, and the gun went off. It was all it took for the Seventh to begin general firing. The Hotchkiss guns poured down heavy explosive shells from the hill, killing most of the men almost instantly. Those still alive retreated toward a ravine behind the camp, shooting at the soldiers to provide cover for women and children. Whatever fight there had been was over within minutes, but the firing continued for over half an hour and was followed by point-blank executions. At least 270 Indians died, and at least 170 of them were women and children. Like people, army units remember. Some members of the Seventh Cavalry openly celebrated the massacre as revenge for the Little Bighorn. Twenty soldiers who participated in the killing were awarded the Congressional Medal of Honor.

Due to a blizzard, a burial detail from Pine Ridge did not reach the killing field for several days. The bodies had frozen into grotesque shapes and were spread across the valley, with a woman and three children killed three miles away: the Seventh's hunt had been relentless and ruthless. The burial party loaded the dead into wagons, took them atop the hill where the Hotchkiss guns had been, and threw the corpses into a mass grave. The party did not find all the bodies, but it did get most of them. Each fetched two dollars, and the party made a small fortune.[78]

The Wounded Knee Massacre was an atrocity, a betrayal, and a human catastrophe. "A people's dream died there," the poet and ethnographer John G. Neihardt had Black Elk say, "the nation's hoop is broken and scattered." The words, invented by Neihardt, were not Black Elk's, but they capture the enormity of the pain and loss. The past and the present had been torn violently apart, and history itself seemed to have ended. With the Lakota men, women, and children, America's Indigenous civilization seemed to have died at Wounded Knee, turning more than two hundred thousand Indians into relics.[79]

Less than three years later, at the World's Fair in Chicago, Frederic Jackson Turner, a young Wisconsin historian, delivered one of America's most influential scholarly lectures ever. He argued that the American West, a wilderness, had been conquered with the ax and the plow, not armies and violence. Turner was already writing the Lakotas—and the Wounded Knee Massacre—out of history. In the exposition fairground, visitors could study reconstructed Indian villages "as an illustration of the primitive life of the aborigines" as well as reproduced boarding schools that would process the very Indianness out of Indians.[80]

Yet Lakotas would survive as a people. The sacred hoop would be mended and the Lakota nation would rise again. Not all was lost and buried at Wounded Knee.

Epilogue: The Lakota Struggle for Indigenous Sovereignty

There is a tangible change in winter counts during and after the painful years between 1877 and 1890. Several counts stopped in the late 1870s, ending with Crazy Horse's death, with the U.S. Army confiscating horses, or with children sent to boarding schools. "Big Foot killed," reads one of the few winter counts that refers to the Wounded Knee Massacre, the silence capturing the enormity of the shock and trauma.

For two decades thereafter the counts are a catalogue of suicides, murders, killings, hangings, and domestic violence—a record of Indigenous dispossession, dysfunction, and subjugation, and of colonialism working exactly as intended. By 1877—the same year the American Museum of Natural History in New York put up exhibits of Native Americans alongside reptiles and fishes—Senator Henry Dawes had already proposed a severalty act that rationalized an old piece-meal policy of splitting up tribal landholdings into individual parcels of land, thus sieving individuals out of the tribal mass and supposedly saving them from dispossession and destitution by turning them into property owners.

Allotment did not begin in the Sioux reservations until the 1890s, but then it proceeded rapidly and disastrously. At the Pine Ridge and Lower Brule Reservations mixed-blood families clustered together in the best farming lands and began separating from their full-blood kin who were pushed out of tribal governments. A large portion of the Rosebud Reservation was sold to the government and then to wašíču homesteaders. Whites secured enough of Pine Ridge's "surplus land" so that they could organize Bennett County in 1909 in what had once been the core of Red Cloud's and the Oglalas' domain. The chief, shrunken and nearly blind, died that year. In one of his last interviews, thinking of his "poor and worthless" land, he spoke of the sense of loss and the lack of dignity of it all: "Think of it! I, who used to own rich soil in a well-watered country so extensive

51. Preparing to hunt cows, c. 1895. Striving to preserve their traditions under the
Indian Office's authoritarian supervision, Lakotas tried to replicate their age-old
hunting life by demanding that the government issued beef rations "on the hoof"
so that men could chase the steers and shoot them down on horseback.
Women then skinned and cut the meat. These occasions allowed Lakota women
and men to reinforce their identities and social roles. Courtesy of John A. Anderson
Collection, Nebraska State Historical Society, RG2969-PH-2-216.

that I could not ride through it in a week on my fastest pony, am put down here.
. . . Now I, who used to control 5000 warriors, must tell Washington when I am
hungry. I must beg for that which I own."[1]

The federal government had abandoned its obligation to protect Indigenous
property for a distinctively colonial land policy. This was the dark side of the
post–Civil War liberal order: the anxious, relentless impulse to absorb nonwhite
people—blacks, Mexicans, Chinese, Indians—into the nation's racial fabric as
individuals detached from their native cultures, while silencing the dispossessed
in the name of progress. Lakotas had become captive people, divided, weakened,
and confined to reservations that often seemed less homelands than prisons. In
the long aftermath of Wounded Knee, the federal government no longer considered the Lakotas a military threat, and the Indian Office received a broad mandate to manage them as wards. Lakotas soon felt its hard, paternalistic grip: the
agents sought to turn reservations into total institutions where almost every as-

pect of human behavior was supervised, recorded, and disciplined. As the Indian Office awakened to its prodigious power to shape human life, the personal, political, and public space of the Lakota people grew alarmingly narrow.[2]

During their more than century-long dealings with the United States, Lakotas had learned that the wašíču state was nothing if not changeable: full of moralistic indignation one moment, willing to negotiate the next, seemingly indifferent now, and then once again accommodating. This newest version was at once quieter and more intrusive than any previous one. By 1902 the United States had acquired new colonial possessions in Cuba and the Philippines—and a newly galvanized martial ethic that fueled both external and internal empires. In the heightened imperial milieu, the Indian Office continued to attack the Lakotas' religious traditions, pressure them to dress and talk like white Americans, and limit their rations to force them to lease and sell their land to white farmers and cattle raisers. Christian churches proliferated, and Wakȟáŋ Tȟáŋka became associated with the Christian God. In 1924 a congressional act granted automatic citizenship to all existing and future Native Americans—in part to recognize the service of thousands of Indians in World War I—but it did little to bring them rights or respect. The Indians remained subordinate people, subject to the whims of a foreign empire. Three years later the wašíčus began carving gigantic heads of four of their presidents into the granite of the Six Grandfathers, a spiritually vital part of the Black Hills that many Lakotas believed had been taken from them illegally. The initial plans of including Red Cloud, Sacagawea, and Crazy Horse in that American pantheon were dropped.[3]

Lakotas knew that they had entered a new era of enormous complexity. They had to accept a larger wašíču presence in their lives—they were deeply dependent on government support—while finding ways to keep the U.S. state at a distance. They would have to embed their nation within a much larger nation and somehow remain Lakotas. To do this, to preserve the core of their being, they would have to push much of what made them Lakotas out of sight. While farming, raising cattle, and working for wages, they continued to live near kin to preserve the traditional thióšpaye organization against the imposed wašíču model of family life. They continued to meet, worship, dance, and celebrate life more or less as they always had, but they moved the full Sun Dance out of the public eye, to remote, hard-to-access corners of their reservations where government agents could not reach them. They continued to perform the outlawed Ghost Dance and other rituals that, if made visible, would have drawn wašíču wrath. Quietly in the margins, the spiritual and political core of their world endured. That core, hardened by centuries of colonial intrusion, proved extraordinarily resilient, sustaining the principle of indissoluble Lakota sovereignty. It also proved transcending, for the

52. Sioux giveaway ceremony. A large number of Lakota women gathering in a circle at the Rosebud Reservation to perform the giveaway ceremony in memory of departed family members. Ceremonies like this one helped preserve and protect the traditional Lakota culture under the U.S. government assimilation programs. Courtesy of John A. Anderson Collection, Nebraska State Historical Society, RG2969-PH-2–143.

Lakota struggle for self-determination would become closely intertwined with the larger Indigenous struggle for sovereignty and rights.[4]

"As we entered the 1930s, we thought conditions were about as bad as they could be," remembered Oglala spiritual leader Frank Fools Crow. The U.S. government was "changing our way of life so rapidly we could hardly keep up with what they were doing." And then, suddenly, the assimilationist pressure slackened. In 1934 Congress passed the Indian Reorganization Act (IRA), which disallowed future allotments, aimed to strengthen tribal identities, and lodged significant power in tribal governments in the hope of fostering self-sufficiency and self-determination. A part of the larger New Deal reforms, the IRA was the centerpiece of an Indian New Deal that would make possible modern tribalism, a hybrid of Indigenous traditions and U.S.-type democracy and entrepreneurship. The brainchild of Indian Affairs Commissioner John Collier, a passionate and headstrong idealist, the reform emanated from Washington, D.C., with a strong whiff of paternalism and disregard for traditional governing practices.

53. Snow on the ground, c. 1900. A tipi stands next to a log cabin in the
Rosebud Reservation, capturing how Lakotas blended the traditional and the
new into a dynamic Indigenous way of life that lost none of its indigeneity
when becoming modern. Courtesy of John A. Anderson Collection,
Nebraska State Historical Society, RG2969-PH-2–207.

Many recoiled at Collier's radical multiculturalism and, shockingly to Collier,
many of them were Indians. Fools Crow was one of them.

In the Lakota country Collier learned what Indigenous modernity looked
like in practice. Many Lakotas had adapted to the new circumstances and had
no desire to go back. George White Bull from the Standing Rock Reservation
said he liked owning his own land—his allotment—and that most of the Indian
New Deal advocates were educated mixed-bloods who had already sold their
lands and would dominate leadership positions. The Rosebud chairman doubted
that there was any one person on the reservation who could take charge of self-
government. Placing someone in a fixed leadership position, he explained, was
not the Lakota way: "In every critical crisis point in history there has always been
the rise of the man of the hour." Lakota politics were fluid and ever-adaptable,
and Collier's design of constitutional governments and majority vote was too
rigid. Only Pine Ridge and Rosebud people adopted the Reorganization Act,

and the consequences were alarming. The IRA divided and factionalized the Oglalas and Sicangus at a time when the Lakotas faced a renewed wave of colonial assaults. Rather than turning the Lakotas into modern-traditional hybrids, it threatened to separate them into town and rural dwellers, traditionalists and progressives, full-bloods and mixed-bloods.[5]

The U.S. state was a many-sided organism with voracious appetites and seemingly unlimited means. The Sioux Bill had already fragmented the Lakota territory, the foundation of Lakota sovereignty and nationhood, and in the mid-1940s Lakotas faced another federal assault on their independence. The Pick-Sloan project, a colossal joint endeavor of the Army Corps of Engineers and the Bureau of Reclamation, built five flood-control dams on the Missouri River as well as reservoirs and irrigation structures on its tributaries. Lakotas, who were not consulted, lost 6 percent of their land base—mostly fertile bottomlands, the center of their economic and cultural life—as dams inundated reservations. Six hundred families, one-third of the Lakota population, became refugees and relocated with minimal government support. Fort Peck Dam dispossessed 350 Sioux and Assiniboine families, and the Standing Rock Reservation lost its most valuable land to Lake Oahe, a 370,000-acre reservoir. In all, the Pick-Sloan project absorbed 550 square miles of Indian land, half the size of Rhode Island. That thousands of Sioux men had voluntarily joined the military during World War II, serving on submarines and as code talkers in the Pacific, on destroyers in the Atlantic, and in dangerous reconnaissance missions in infantry, mattered little to policymakers. As Indians, their rights and their well-being were disposable.[6]

Lakotas seemed unable to stop the federal intrusions into their lands and lives but, as the vanquishers of Custer and the victims at Wounded Knee, they still wielded unparalleled moral power. When disgust with imposed federal policies erupted into forceful urban and reservation activism in the 1960s, many Lakotas emerged as key figures in pan-Indian protest movements that sought to dismantle the Bureau of Indian Affairs (BIA)—the successor of the Indian Office—which they denounced as a colonial agency that meant to turn the first Americans into white Americans whether they wanted it or not.

In a long tradition stretching back to Tiyoskate, Black Bull, and Red Cloud, Vine Deloria, Jr., a theologian and intellectual from the Standing Rock Reservation, relied on words, wit, and biting irony to expose U.S. hegemonic pretensions. His 1969 book, *Custer Died for Your Sins*, was a rousing, acerbic, and funny manifesto of Indian rights in which he condemned, among other things, the federal government's abysmal record in honoring its more than four hundred treaties with Native American nations. Alongside the Black Power movement, Deloria insisted, there should be a Red Power movement with a distinct

agenda centered on Indigenous sovereignty under attack: here was the intellectual foundation for the American Indian Movement (AIM) that was gathering
momentum in the United States and Canada. While cohering into a genuine
pan-Indian struggle for self-determination, AIM revolved to a striking degree
around Lakota protagonists, Lakota issues, and Lakota action.[7]

The once-dominant Lakotas knew how to command attention. As the Red
Power movement gathered momentum, they seemed to be everywhere, now a
part of a group of Native activists claiming the closed prison island of Alcatraz
as abandoned federal land; soon after protesting on Mount Rushmore against
the U.S. capture of Pahá Sápa and other treaty violations; then staging a massive
multitribal demonstration in Gordon, Nebraska, where authorities had failed to
mount a proper investigation into the death of an Oglala man, Raymond Yellow
Thunder, by local Indian haters, suffusing the town with fury and fear. That fear
emboldened AIM leaders to organize a remarkable pan-Indian delegation, the
Trail of Broken Treaties, that caravanned from the West Coast to Washington,
D.C., to deliver a list of demands, which included the restoration of treaty relations between the United States and Indian tribes, the return of 110 million acres
of Native land, and the abolition of the widely despised Bureau of Indian Affairs.
Poor planning and federal indifference at the capital stymied the mission, and
five hundred Indians occupied the BIA headquarters for seven days in a surreal
standoff with the U.S. government.[8]

The absurd, disquieting saga of the Trail of Broken Treaties brought to the
surface a widening rift between the pan-Indian radicals and the old-line tribal
leaders, a discord that came to a head in the Lakota country. Since the 1930s,
the Lakota reservations had been home to progressives, often mixed-bloods, and
traditionalist, often full-bloods. Recently elected tribal chairman of the Pine
Ridge Reservation, Dick Wilson, a mixed-blood and a BIA favorite, was a totali-
tarian who suffused Oglala politics with nepotism, fraud, and fear, exacerbating
internal divisions. Pine Ridge was one of the poorest places in the United States
with 50 percent unemployment and collapsing education and health care systems, and Wilson's corruption threatened to plunge it into an abyss: AIM accused him of fixing elections, facilitating sales of Oglala land to non-Indians, and
allowing strip-mining in the reservation. Wilson's armed enforcer-bodyguards
brutalized opponents, neutralizing any efforts to remove the chairman. When
AIM brought its dramatic activism to Pine Ridge in February 1973, Wilson was
ready. Seventy-five federal marshals, all members of an elite rapid response strike
force, had arrived to protect the Pine Ridge tribal office building. On the roof of
the militarized building stood a .50-caliber machine gun, a modern version of
Hotchkiss gun. Its purpose was to keep AIM out of Pine Ridge.[9]

54. Indians stand outside the Sacred Heart Catholic Church at Pine Ridge, 1973.
A conflict over civil rights, self-determination, and sovereignty, Wounded Knee
1973 was as much a media struggle as it was a political one. Images like this
brought the AIM to the world's notice as a modern-day warrior society.
Courtesy of Getty Images. Photo by Bettmann.

Joining forces with traditional spiritual healers, political leaders, and local
activists, AIM now fulfilled its vision of becoming a modern-day warrior society,
leading the Oglala oyáte—and, symbolically, all Indians—into a fight against
an alien, aggressive foreign power. About two hundred Indians, many of them
women and children, some of them armed with shotguns and hunting rifles,
caravanned to Wounded Knee, a hamlet of roughly one hundred residents. The
U.S. government mobilized and dispatched heavily armed FBI agents, U.S. marshals, National Guard soldiers, and BIA police officers to seal off Wounded Knee
with roadblocks and armored personnel carriers, while Air Force phantom jets
made reconnaissance flights over the site. News images of a war zone in the
heart of the United States entered homes around the world. Tensions mounted
and sporadic shots were exchanged. Another massacre at Wounded Knee, now
against U.S. citizens, seemed possible. When the BIA categorically refused to
remove Wilson, the negotiations faltered, and the Indians at Wounded Knee
seceded from the United States. They revived the 1868 Fort Laramie Treaty and
declared that Wounded Knee had become the Independent Oglala Nation.

When Assistant Attorney General Harlington Wood visited Wounded Knee, two young mounted Indians escorted him in like a foreign dignitary to meet Oglala activist Russell Means, Carter Camp of the Ponca tribe, and Leonard Crow Dog, a Sicangu wičháša wakháŋ.[10]

The besieged Indians held out for seventy-one days, weathering a Dakota winter storm, ten thousand rounds of gunfire, being labeled as criminals by the secretary of the Interior, and White House neglect. But they were not alone. Antiwar groups, Chicanos, and Black Panthers supported them, as did numerous demonstrations in the United States and abroad. On March 19 the Independent Oglala Nation received a delegation from the Six Nations of Iroquois Confederacy, which shared Lakotas' struggle for sovereignty and nationhood. And then the Indians danced, wearing special shirts and making the Ghost Dance visible after eighty-three years. Wounded Knee began to seem like a place where everything happened twice. When machine-gun fire killed Buddy Lamont, an Oglala Vietnam veteran, the White House promised to investigate the AIM complaints. The Indians disengaged on May 8. At noon the FBI began a criminal investigation, and agents "leaped into their rented Plymouths and Fords and sped down the dusty hill to the town."[11]

The aftermath of the Wounded Knee occupation may seem like a defeat for AIM and Lakotas. Federal agents arrested nearly twelve hundred people nationwide in relation to the occupation, and in Pine Ridge the FBI persecuted AIM members for years while Wilson continued to serve as tribal chairman. But the occupation caught national and international attention, drawing unprecedented interest in Native American struggles. Many non-Indians received an education when an AIM member announced: "Our people are sovereign, each tribe unto itself, and have been like that for thousands of years.... Sovereignty means the ability to guide our own lives, the ability to even make mistakes if that's what it takes. We know how to live with the world, instead of on it, or off it, or against it."[12]

Suddenly there was genuine momentum at both national and grassroots levels. "Real soon, now," said Wallace Black Elk, a Lakota wičháša wakháŋ, "this is a turning point. The hoop, the sacred hoop was broken at Wounded Knee, and it will come back again." The Native American sovereignty movement was energized and national politicians took notice. In 1975 Congress passed the Self-Determination and Education Assistance Act, which instituted a contractual relationship between Indian tribes and federal agencies. After a century and a half of federal paternalism, Lakotas could now negotiate over specific programs and they could say no. One of the agencies they could now say no to was the Bureau of Indian Affairs.[13]

Lakotas could also make demands. They had never accepted the loss of the Black Hills, had filed several lawsuits to recover them, and had refused any form of monetary compensation. In 1974 they tried again, and succeeded. The Indian Claims Commission, a temporary judicial arbiter, decided that the 1877 government takeover of the hills had violated the 1868 treaty as well as the Fifth Amendment. The Court of Claims confirmed the ruling and awarded the Lakotas, with retroactive interest, $122 million. In 1980 the Supreme Court upheld the decision in a landmark ruling that underscored Native Americans' inviolate rights to land. As expected, Lakotas refused the millions and pressed on with the fight to recover the hills themselves. By holding on to the land, they made a stance for treaty rights, religious integrity, and larger Indigenous struggle for sovereignty. Today, the award for the Black Hills would be more than $1.3 billion, but Lakotas refuse the money which would legalize the seizure of their sacred land. "It's always been ours," said Jane Spotted Tail about Pahá Sápa in 2011. "It will always be ours."[14]

In a way, the victory of the Black Hills case took Lakotas back to the mid-nineteenth century, a time when the U.S. government treated them as a sovereign nation—not because it chose to but because it had to—and negotiated treaties that reflected Lakota interests as much as they did those of the United States. Emboldened, Lakotas intensified their efforts to protect their sovereignty on the ground. This encompassed tribal courts, tribal colleges, language revitalization, Lakotanized curricula, infrastructure and housing programs, renewable energy projects, and reviving traditional arts and rituals. It meant proclaiming and performing sovereignty in daily life, grounding sovereignty in specific places and specific cultural practices; at its most basic level, it meant dignity in one's personal life. It also involved drastic political reforms. Lakotas made concerted efforts to replace the externally imposed top-down governing system with more inclusive and indigenized models that transfer power from tribal councils to local leaders. The nimbler regimes were less susceptible to factionalism and better positioned to respond to external threats, which from the 1980s on came increasingly and in many forms from their white neighbors and the state of South Dakota: in the recurrent attempts to open more of the Black Hills for development and resource extraction; in the 11,000 cans of beer sold every day in Whiteclay, a tiny community just south of Pine Ridge whose only function was to sell alcohol to Indians; in the white flour, refined sugar, and other cheap and unhealthy government-aid commodities; in the New Age "culture vultures" who entered sacred Lakota sites to perform bastardized versions of Lakota religious ceremonies.[15]

Since Wounded Knee II, however, the Lakotas have carried unprecedented symbolic weight as persecuted minority people, and it has brought them the attention of human rights activists, federal agents, and even presidents. In the summer of 1999 the Lakota country was shaken by yet another AIM demonstration over yet more killings of Lakota men. With Wounded Knee II echoing in the background, a thousand protestors squared off with the Nebraska State Patrol and the Pine Ridge tribal police. In the midst of this, President Bill Clinton arrived in Pine Ridge, becoming the first U.S. president to visit an Indian reservation in more than six decades. Harold Salway, the president of the Oglala Sioux Tribe, received Clinton as one head of a sovereign nation receives another and then, with leaders from more than a hundred tribes present, educated him on the realities of Indian country: Pine Ridge's crushing unemployment, its life expectancy of forty-five, its lack of public transportation, banks, or industry. He expected the United States to do more.[16]

Lakotas needed more because the legacies of conquest ran so deep. Poverty still gripped their reservations, and alcoholism, drugs, diabetes, depression, and suicides kept claiming lives. Racial prejudice, both overt and hidden, manifested itself in the hiring practices, funding allocation, and judicial system of the states of South Dakota and Nebraska, and many Lakotas did not feel welcome in Rapid City, Bismarck, and other nearby cities. Lakotas had to find Lakota solutions to Lakota problems, and they did. They founded dynamic community centers, built revenue-generating casinos, and litigated the closing of Whiteclay beer stores, ending the decades-long "liquid genocide." By protesting and litigating and by simply refusing to be neglected, they won the attention of powerful allies. A 2012 United Nations investigation advocated the return of the Black Hills to them, and two years later President Barack Obama visited the Standing Rock Reservation where, facing eighteen hundred Native Americans, he announced that nation-to-nation relationship should now be considered the rule, not an exception. The president proposed that Congress could return part of the Black Hills to the Očhéthi Šakówiŋ. A new era of Indigenous sovereignty beckoned.[17]

People started arriving in the summer of 2016, carrying water. They came from all over the country and then from all over the world: Native Americans, Maoris, Mongolians, Muslims, Sami, Hindus, environmentalists, clergy, veterans, and Water Wookie Warriors. Thousands of them came to protest, pray, and offer solidarity to the Lakota people of the Standing Rock Reservation, which was under threat. The Standing Rock Sioux Tribe had filed a lawsuit against Dakota Access, a subsidiary of Energy Transfer Partners, which had secured a permit from

North Dakota Public Service Commission to proceed with the construction of a projected 1,772-mile underground pipeline that would move 470,000 barrels of crude oil a day from northwestern North Dakota to Illinois. The Dakota Access Pipeline would pass under the Mníšoše half a mile north of the Standing Rock Reservation, crossing sacred lands and burial sites and threatening to contaminate the reservation's water reservoir if it ever ruptured or leaked—something that pipelines do with alarming frequency. The original plan had the pipeline cross the Missouri near Bismarck, but the risk to the capital's drinking water had been considered too grave. The rationale seemed clear: Indians matter less.

As in 1973, the world took notice. People flocked in, defying National Guardsmen, local police, and Energy Transfer Partners' security guards and their bulldozers, sound cannons, tear gas, and rubber bullets. LaDonna Brave Bull Allard, Phyllis Young, Joye Braun, and many other women—elders, teachers, activists, healers, intellectuals—rose up, leading protests and prayers and drawing global attention to the Lakota struggle for water rights and sovereignty. The overpowering show of solidarity prompted the Obama administration to review the pipeline. The president pledged that federal agencies would liaise with the Indians as "sovereign to sovereign," and the Army Corps of Engineers halted construction to conduct an environmental review. But only days after taking office in 2017, President Donald Trump cleared the way for the construction of the Dakota Access Pipeline.[18]

It became a standoff. The main protest camp, called Oceti Sakowin, at the confluence of the Cannonball and Missouri Rivers, swelled to hold as many as ten thousand people, animated by a disgust with the Trump administration's anti-environmental policies and galvanized by solidarity for the Lakota people whose struggle against colonial aggression had become nearly synonymous with the larger Indigenous struggle for rights and recognition. As Native, national, and global concerns converged, protests erupted in New York, Washington, and elsewhere in the country. Lakotas argued that the pipeline violated the United Nations Declaration on the Rights of Indigenous Peoples, and the United Nations criticized the U.S. government for failing to consult Native Americans over the pipeline. The Trump administration did not seem to care, and North Dakota state officials closed the protest site. The pipeline had already leaked before its completion in May 2017, and six months later it suffered a 210,000-gallon leak in South Dakota.[19]

In the spring of 2018 thousands of Lakotas and representatives from other Native nations gathered at Fort Laramie National Historical Site in Wyoming to commemorate the 150th anniversary of the signing of the 1868 Treaty of Fort Laramie. Considering the treaty an active and living document that continues to underwrite not only Lakota but broader Indigenous sovereignty in North America, Native communities came together to honor the spirit of the treaty signers, reflect on their ever-evolving relationship with the United States, and re-assert their self-determination by evoking an era when they could not be ignored. The Treaty of Fort Laramie was a product of a seemingly implausible historical sequence that saw the Lakotas, a relatively small Native nation, defeat the United States, an industrial giant, in the battlefield, forcing it to acknowledge the power and sovereignty of the Lakota people.

It is that history of violence, coexistence, and persistence that will help Lakotas survive the oil leaks, the arrogance of foreign powers, the attacks on their sover-eignty, the misappropriation of their rituals, the misuses of their history, and the weight of being the quintessential Indigenous people whose choices, actions, and very existence seem to carry heightened symbolic significance. Lakotas will endure because they are Iktómi's people, supple, accommodating, and abso-lutely certain of their essence even when becoming something new. There will be other governments, other regimes, and other epochs, but the Lakotas will prevail. They will always find a place in the world because they know how to be fully in it, adapting to its shape while remaking it, again and again, after their own image.

Abbreviations

AAAG	Acting Assistant Adjutant General.
AAG	Assistant Adjutant General.
AGO	National Archives and Records Service, Washington, DC. Records of the Adjutant General's Office. Record Group 94. Selected Letters Received by the Office of the Adjutant General, Main Series, 1871–1880. M666.
ARC	R. Eli Paul, ed., *Autobiography of Red Cloud: War Leader of the Lakotas.* Helena: Montana Historical Society, 1997.
ARCIA	*Annual Report of the Commissioner of Indian Affairs.* U.S. Department of the Interior. Washington, DC: GPO. University of Wisconsin–Madison Libraries Digital Collections. Available at http://digicoll.library.wisc .edu/cgi-bin/History/History-idx?type=browse&scope=HISTORY .COMMREP.
BKWC	"Ben Kindle's Winter Count," in Martha Warren Beckwith, "Mythology of the Oglala Sioux," *Journal of American Folklore* 43 (Oct.–Dec. 1930), 349–67.
BLC	A. P. Nasatir, ed., *Before Lewis and Clark: Documents Illustrating the History of the Missouri, 1785–1804.* 2 vols. 1952; rprt. Lincoln: University of Nebraska Press, 1990.
BMWC	Roberta Carkeek Cheney, *The Big Missouri Winter Count.* Happy Camp, CA: Naturegraph, 1979.
BTWC	Dakota Goodhouse, "Blue Thunder Winter Count." Available at http:// thefirstscout.blogspot.com/2015/12/the-blue-thunder-or-yellow-lodge -winter.html.
CC	Walter Stanley (Stanley Vestal) Collection, Western History Collections, University of Oklahoma Library.
CMCF	Richard G. Hardorff, ed., *Cheyenne Memories of the Custer Fight.* Lincoln: University of Nebraska Press, 1995.
CoIA	Commissioner of Indian Affairs.

CPWC   Dakota Goodhouse, "The Chandler-Pohrt Winter Count Revisited."
            Available at http://thefirstscout.blogspot.co.uk/2016/01/the-chandler
            -pohrt-winter-count.html.
DCB   *Dictionary of Canadian Biography*, University of Toronto/Université Laval.
            Available at http://www.biographi.ca/.
DÉ   Pierre Margry, ed., *Découvertes et établissements des Français dans l'ouest
            et dans le sud de l'Amérique Septentrionale (1614–1754).* 6 vols. Paris:
            Imprimerie Jouaust at Sigaux, 1886.
DGWC   Dakota Goodhouse, "The Drifting Goose Winter Count: John K. Bear
            Winter Count Revisited." Available at https://drive.google.com/file/d
            /1qz8c_dNmZcNqetandW7P96zJlz8Ju9Hc/view.
DWC   Alexis Praus, *The Sioux, 1798–1922: A Dakota Winter Count, Cranbrook
            Institute of Science Bulletin* 44 (1962).
EDA   Ella Deloria Archive, Dakota Indian Foundation, Chamberlain, SD.
            Available at http://zia.aisri.indiana.edu/deloria_archive/browse.php.
FIT   Edwin Thompson Denig, *Five Indian Tribes of the Upper Missouri: Sioux,
            Arickaras, Assiniboines, Crees, Crows,* ed. John C. Ewers. Norman:
            University of Oklahoma Press, 1961.
FTUM   Raymond J. DeMallie, Douglas Parks, and Robert Vézina, trans. Mildred
            Mott Wedel, Raymond J. DeMallie, and Robert Vézina, eds., *A Fur
            Trader on the Upper Missouri: The Journal and Description of Jean-
            Baptiste Truteau, 1794–1796.* Lincoln: University of Nebraska Press, 2017.
GPO   Government Printing Office.
GRA   Grand River Agency.
HAC   R. Cole Harris, ed., *Historical Atlas of Canada,* vol. 1: *From the Beginning
            to 1800.* Toronto: University of Toronto Press, 1987.
HB   Patricia C. Albers, *The Home of the Bison: An Ethnographic and
            Ethnohistorical Study of the Wind Cave National Park,* unpub. ms.
            Submitted in fulfillment of Cooperative Agreement CA606899103
            between the U.S. National Park Service and the Department of
            American Indian Studies, University of Minnesota, 2003. Available at
            http://npshistory.com/publications/wica/home-of-the-bison-v1.pdf.
HDWC   Dakota Goodhouse, "The High Dog Winter Count." Available at http://
            thefirstscout.blogspot.co.uk/2015/12/the-high-dog-winter-count.html.
HHWC   High Hawk's winter count. In Edward S. Curtis, *The North American
            Indian,* ed. Frederick Webb Hodge. 20 vols. Cambridge, MA: University
            Press, 1908, vol. 3: 159–82.
HNAI   William C. Sturtevant, gen. ed., *Handbook of North American Indians.*
            17 vols. Washington, DC: Smithsonian Institution, 1978.
Hostilities *Letter of the Secretary of the Interior, Communicating, in Compliance
            with a Resolution of the Senate of the 8th Instant, Information Touching
            the Origin and Progress of Indian Hostilities on the Frontier, July 13, 1867,*
            Sen. Ex. Doc. 13, 40th Cong., 1st Sess.

IALT	Charles J. Kappler, comp. and ed., *Indian Affairs: Laws and Treaties*, vol. 2. Washington, DC: GPO, 1904.
IHC	*Collections of the Illinois State Historical Library*. 34 vols. Springfield: Trustees of the Illinois State Historical Library, 1940.
IVCF	Richard G. Hardorff, ed., *Indian Views of the Custer Fight*. Norman: University of Oklahoma Press, 2005.
JJM	Kenneth P. Bailey, ed. and trans., *Journal of Joseph Marin, French Colonial Explorer and Military Commander in the Wisconsin Country, August 7, 1753–June 20, 1754*. n.p.: published by the editor, 1975.
JLCE	Gary E. Moulton, ed., *Journals of the Lewis and Clark Expedition*. 13 vols. Lincoln: University of Nebraska Press, 1983–2001.
JLV	Lawrence J. Burpee, ed., *Journals and Letters of Pierre Gaultier de Varennes de la Vérendrye and His Sons*. Toronto: Champlain Society, 1927.
JR	Reuben Gold Thwaites, ed., *The Jesuit Relations and Allied Documents*. 73 vols. Cleveland: Burrows Bothers, 1896–1901.
LAC	Library and Archives Canada. Online at Library and Archives of Canada.
LBR	Herman J. Viola, *Little Bighorn Remembered: The Untold Story of Custer's Last Stand*. New York: Crown, 1999.
LC	Jerome A. Greene, ed., *Lakota and Cheyenne: Indian Views of the Great Sioux War, 1876–1877*. Norman: University of Oklahoma Press, 1994.
LLCE	Donald Jackson, ed., *Letters of the Lewis and Clark Expedition with Related Documents, 1783–1854*. Urbana: University of Illinois Press, 1962.
LR	Letters Received.
LROIA	National Archives and Records Service, Washington, DC. Bureau of Indian Affairs. Record Group 75. Records of the Office of Indian Affairs, Central Office, Letters Received, 1824–1881. M234.
MBWC	Dakota Goodhouse, "The Medicine Bear Winter Count." Available at http://thefirstscout.blogspot.co.uk/2015/08/the-medicine-bear-winter-count.html.
MBWCV	Dakota Goodhouse, "The Medicine Bear Winter Count Variant." Available at http://thefirstscout.blogspot.co.uk/2016/09/a-medicine-bear-winter-count-variant.html.
MMSC	National Archives and Records Service, Washington, DC. Bureau of Indian Affairs. Record Group 75. "Minutes of Meetings of the Special Commission, Mar. 4–June 12, 1867," Records Relating to the Investigation of the Fort Philip Kearney (or Fetterman) Massacre, 1866–1867. M740, roll 1.
MPHC	*Michigan Pioneer Historical Society: Collections and Researches*. 40 vols. Lansing, MI: The Society, 1877–1929.
NSHS	Nebraska State Historical Society.
NYCD	E. B. O'Callaghan, ed., *Documents Relative to the Colonial History of*

	the State of New York; Procured in Holland, England, and France, by Romeyn Brodhead. 15 vols. Albany, NY: Parsons, Weed, 1853–87.
PBC	*Proceedings of a Board of Commissioners to Negotiate a Treaty or Treaties with the Hostile Indians of the Upper Missouri, 1865.* Beinecke Rare Book and Manuscript Library. Yale University.
PSP	Philip Henry Sheridan Papers: General Correspondence, 1853–1888, Library of Congress.
RCA	Red Cloud Agency.
RCF	George E. Hyde, *Red Cloud's Folk.* 1937; rprt. Norman: University of Oklahoma Press, 1975.
RHO	*Red Horse Owner's Winter Count: The Oglala Sioux 1786–1968,* ed. Joseph S. Karol. Marin, SD: Booster, 1969.
SASDHS	State Archives of the South Dakota Historical Society, Pierre.
SDHC	*South Dakota Historical Collections.* 38 vols. Pierre: South Dakota Historical Society, 1902–76.
SF	National Archives and Records Service. Record Group 393. "Special Files" of Headquarters, Created by the Military Division of the Missouri, Relating to Military Operations and Administration, 1863–1885. M1495. Roll 2: "Citizen Expeditions" to the Black Hills, Feb. 1874–Oct. 1875; roll 4: Sioux War, Sept. 1876–Dec. 1877; roll 7: Indian War (Hancock's War), Jan.–July 1867.
SG	Raymond J. DeMallie, ed., *The Sixth Grandfather: Black Elk's Teachings Given to John G. Neihardt.* Lincoln: University of Nebraska Press, 1984.
SI	Secretary of the Interior.
SOJ	John Ordway, "Sergeant Ordway's Journal," in Milo M. Quaife, ed., *The Journals of Captain Meriwether Lewis and Sergeant John Ordway.* Madison: State Historical Society of Wisconsin, 1916.
SRM	Louis Houck, trans. and ed., *The Spanish Regime in Missouri: A Collection of Papers and Documents Relating to Upper Louisiana Principally within the Present Limits of Missouri during the Dominion of Spain.* 2 vols. Chicago: R. R. Donnelley, 1909.
STF	George E. Hyde, *Spotted Tail's Folk.* 1961; rprt. Norman: University of Oklahoma Press, 1974.
TINA	Alexander Philipp Maximilian, Prince of Wied, *Travels in the Interior of North America, 1832–34.* Vols. 22–24 of Reuben Gold Thwaites, ed., *Early Western Travels, 1748–1846.* Cleveland: Arthur H. Clark, 1904–7.
TN	Annie Heloise Able, ed., *Tabeau's Narrative of Loisel's Expedition to the Upper Missouri.* Norman: University of Oklahoma Press, 1939.
TP	Clarence Edwin Carter, comp. and ed., *The Territorial Papers of the United States.* 28 vols. Washington, DC: GPO, 1934–75.
UMA	Upper Missouri Agency.
UPA	Upper Platte Agency.

WHC   *Collections of the State Historical Society of Wisconsin*, ed. Reuben Gold Thwaites. 20 vols. Madison: State Historical Society of Wisconsin, 1855–1911.

YSF   Candace S. Greene and Russell Thornton, *The Year the Stars Fell: Lakota Winter Counts at the Smithsonian*. Lincoln: University of Nebraska Press, 2007.

NOTES

1. For the year 1776, the United States, and Lakotas, see Claudio Saunt, *West of the Revolution: An Uncommon History of 1776* (New York: W. W. Norton, 2014), 149–51.

2. For the enduring fascination and changing meanings of Custer, the Indian wars, and the Battle of the Little Bighorn, see Michael A. Elliott, *Custerology: The Enduring Legacy of the Indian Wars and George Armstrong Custer* (Chicago: University of Chicago Press, 2007).

3. Dee Brown, *Bury My Heart at Wounded Knee: An Indian History of the American West* (New York: Holt, Rinehart and Winston, 1970).

4. For a transformative study of Lakota expansion, see Richard White, "The Winning of the West: The Expansion of the Western Sioux in the Eighteenth and Nineteenth Centuries," *Journal of American History* 65 (Sept. 1978), 319–43.

5. While there are hundreds of studies on late nineteenth-century Lakota history, there have been only a handful of substantive works focusing on the Lakotas in the seventeenth, eighteenth, and early nineteenth centuries. This has resulted in a stunted historiography that suggests that Lakotas were somehow inherently and instantly primed to conquer the American West.

6. This book is part of a larger continental turn in American history, a sustained scholarly effort to nudge the field out of its Atlantic and Anglo-centric trenches. For a sample of representative studies, in addition to the works listed in the next footnote, see James Axtell, *Beyond 1492: Encounters in Colonial North America* (New York: Oxford University Press, 1992); Colin G. Calloway, *New Worlds for All: Indians, Europeans, and the Remaking of Early America* (Baltimore: Johns Hopkins University Press, 1997); Daniel K. Richter, *Facing East from Indian Country: A Native History of Early America* (Cambridge: Harvard University Press, 2001); Alan Taylor, *American Colonies* (New York: Viking, 2001); John Smolenski and Thomas J. Humphrey, eds., *New World Orders: Violence, Sanction, and Authority in the Colonial Americas* (Philadelphia: University of Pennsylvania Press, 2005); Paul Mapp, "Imperial History from

Atlantic, Continental, and Pacific Perspectives," *William and Mary Quarterly* 63 (Oct. 2006), 713–24; Peter C. Mancall and James H. Merrell, eds., *American Encounters: Natives and Newcomers from European Contact to Indian Removal, 1500–1850* (New York: Routledge, 2007); Anne F. Hyde, *Empires, Nations, and Families: A New History of the North American West* (Lincoln: University of Nebraska Press, 2011); Juliana Barr and Edward Countryman, eds., *The Contested Spaces of Early America* (Philadelphia: University of Pennsylvania Press, 2014); Saunt, *West of the Revolution*; Kathleen DuVal, *Independence Lost: Lives of the Edge of the American Revolution* (New York: Random House, 2015); and Alan Taylor, *American Revolutions: A Continental History, 1750–1804* (New York: W. W. Norton, 2016).

7. As with many Indigenous people, Lakotas are often portrayed as passive foreign political actors who reacted to rather than initiated change and were driven by needs and conventions rather than strategy or geopolitical ambitions. I have tried in this book to challenge such simplifications as this: "The seven divisions of the Teton Sioux [Lakotas] had no central political authority capable of binding them to a peace agreement. Thus there was no grand strategy, but the same basic needs prompted expansion of all seven divisions." See Thomas W. Dunlay, *Wolves for the Blue Soldiers: Indian Scouts and Auxiliaries with the United States Army, 1860–1890* (Lincoln: University of Nebraska press, 1982), 112.

8. In spite of their formative role in shaping American history, Lakotas are still neglected as real foreign political actors. Consider, for example, the definitive work on U.S. foreign relations, George C. Herring's *From Colony to Superpower: U.S. Foreign Relations since 1776* (New York: Oxford University Press, 2008). Lakotas merit one passing mention as "hostile Sioux" (p. 112) in the context of the Lewis and Clark expedition.

9. The assumptions mentioned here do not necessarily reflect the exact arguments of the authors but rather the ways in which scholars have interpreted and applied those arguments and how the models, through replication in new contexts, have accrued new meanings. For key works and discussions of the concepts, see David J. Weber, "Turner, the Boltonians, and the Borderlands," *American Historical Review* 91 (Feb. 1986), 66–81; Patricia Nelson Limerick, *The Legacy of Conquest: Unbroken Past of the American West* (New York: W. W. Norton, 1987); Richard White, *The Middle Ground: Indians, Empires, and Republics in the Great Lakes Region, 1650–1815* (New York: Cambridge University Press, 1991); Richard White, *"It's Your Misfortune and None of My Own": A New History of the American West* (Norman: University of Oklahoma Press, 1991); Jay Gitlin, "On the Boundaries of Empire: Connecting the West to Its Imperial Past," in *Under an Open Sky: Rethinking America's Western Past*, ed. William Cronon, George Miles, and Jay Gitlin (New York: W. W. Norton, 1991), 71–89; Daniel H. Usner, Jr., *Indians, Settlers, and Slaves in a Frontier Exchange Economy: The Lower Mississippi Valley before 1783* (Chapel Hill: University of North Carolina Press, 1992); Mary E. Young, "The Dark and Bloody but Endlessly Inventive Middle Ground of Indian Frontier Historiography," *Journal of the Early Republic* 13 (Summer 1993), 193–205; R. David Edmunds, "Native Americans, New Voices: American Indian History, 1895–1995," *American Historical Review* 100 (July 1995), 717–40; Kerwin Lee Klein, *Frontiers of Historical Imagination: Narrating European Conquest of Native*

America, 1890–1990 (Berkeley: University of California Press, 1997); Andrew R. L. Cayton and Fredrika J. Teute, eds., *Contact Points: American Frontiers from the Mohawk Valley to the Mississippi, 1750–1830* (Chapel Hill: University of North Carolina Press, 1998); Jeremy Adelman and Stephen Aron, "From Borderlands to Borders: Empires, Nation-States, and the Peoples in between in North American History," *American Historical Review* 104 (June 1999), 814–41; Juliana Barr, "Geographies of Power: Mapping Indian Borders in the 'Borderlands' of the Early Southwest," *William and Mary Quarterly* 68 (Jan. 2011), 5–46; Pekka Hämäläinen and Samuel Truett, "On Borderlands," *Journal of American History* 98 (Sept. 2011), 338–61; James H. Merrell, "Second Thoughts on Colonial Historians and American Indians," *William and Mary Quarterly* 69 (July 2012), 451–512; and Brian Delay, ed., *North American Borderlands* (New York: Routledge, 2013).

10. The Native-centered historical scholarship, commonly known as the "new Indian history," is vast and growing. Since the 1990s, its gold standard has been a regional study that places Native peoples at the front and center of major historical developments. For a selection, see Francis Jennings, *The Invasion of America: Indians, Colonialism, and the Cant of Conquest* (Chapel Hill: University of North Carolina Press, 1975); William Cronon, *Changes in the Land: Indians, Colonists and the Ecology of New England* (New York: Hill and Wang, 1983); James Axtell, *The Invasion Within: The Contest of Cultures in Colonial North America* (New York: Oxford University Press, 1985); James H. Merrell, *The Indians' New World: Catawbas and Their Neighbors from European Contact through the Era of Removal* (Chapel Hill: University of North Carolina Press, 1989); Timothy Silver, *A New Face on the Countryside: Indians, Colonists, and Slaves in South Atlantic Forests, 1500–1800* (New York: Cambridge University Press, 1990); White, *Middle Ground*; Gregory Evans Dowd, *A Spirited Resistance: The North American Indian Struggle for Unity, 1745–1815* (Baltimore: Johns Hopkins University Press, 1992); Daniel K. Richter, *The Ordeal of the Longhouse: The Peoples of the Iroquois League in the Era of European Colonialism* (Chapel Hill: University of North Carolina Press, 1992); Usner, *Indians, Settlers, and Slaves*; Elliott West, *The Contested Plains: Indians, Goldseekers, and the Rush to Colorado* (Lawrence: University Press of Kansas, 1998); James F. Brooks, *Captives and Cousins: Slavery, Kinship, and Community in the Southwest Borderlands* (Chapel Hill: University of North Carolina Press, 2002); Alan Gallay, *The Indian Slave Trade: The Rise of the English Empire in the American South, 1670–1717* (New Haven: Yale University Press, 2002); Colin G. Calloway, *One Vast Winter Count: The Native American West before Lewis and Clark* (Lincoln: University of Nebraska Press, 2003); Gilles Havard, *Empire et mètissage: Indiens et Français dans le Pays d'en Haut, 1660–1715* (Paris: Septentrion, 2003); Jeffrey Ostler, *The Plains Sioux and U.S. Colonialism from Lewis and Clark to Wounded Knee* (New York: Cambridge University Press, 2004); Alan Taylor, *The Divided Ground: Indians, Settlers, and the Northern Borderland of the American Revolution* (New York: Alfred A. Knopf, 2005); David J. Weber, *Bárbaros: Spaniards and Their Savages in the Age of Enlightenment* (New Haven: Yale University Press, 2005); Kathleen DuVal, *The Native Ground: Indians and Colonists in the Heart of the Continent* (Philadelphia: University of Pennsylvania Press, 2006); Ned Blackhawk,

Violence over the Land: Indians and Empires in the Early American West (Cambridge: Harvard University Press, 2006); Hampton Sides, *Blood and Thunder: An Epic of the American West* (New York: Doubleday, 2006); Juliana Barr, *Peace Came in the Form of a Woman: Indians and Spaniards in the Texas Borderlands* (Chapel Hill: University of North Carolina Press, 2007); Brian DeLay, *War of a Thousand Deserts: Indian Raids and the U.S.-Mexican War* (New Haven: Yale University Press, 2008); Pekka Hämä-läinen, *The Comanche Empire* (New Haven: Yale University Press, 2008); Christina Snyder, *Slavery in Indian Country: The Changing Face of Captivity in Early America* (Cambridge: Harvard University Press, 2010); Lance R. Blyth, *Chiricahua and Janos: Communities of Violence in the Southwestern Borderlands, 1680–1880* (Lincoln: University of Nebraska Press, 2012); Brett Rushforth, *Bonds of Alliance: Indigenous and Atlantic Slaveries in New France* (Chapel Hill: University of North Carolina Press, 2012); Michael Witgen, *An Infinity of Nations: How the Native New World Shaped Early America* (Philadelphia: University of Pennsylvania Press, 2012); Elizabeth A. Fenn, *Encounters in the Heart of the World: A History of the Mandan People* (New York: Hill and Wang, 2014); Natale A. Zappia, *Traders and Raiders: The Indigenous World of the Colorado Basin, 1540–1859* (Chapel Hill: University of North Carolina Press, 2014); Andrew Lipman, *The Saltwater Frontier: Indians and the Contest for the American Coast* (New Haven: Yale University Press, 2015); Michael McDonnell, *Masters of Empire: Great Lakes Indians and the Making of America* (New York: Hill and Wang, 2015); Joshua L. Reid, *The Sea Is My Country: The Maritime World of the Makahs* (New Haven: Yale University Press, 2015); and Tiya Miles, *The Dawn of Detroit: A Chronicle of Slavery and Freedom in the City of Straits* (New York: New Press, 2017). Also see Susan Sleeper-Smith, Juliana Barr, Jean M. O'Brien, Nancy Shoemaker, and Scott Manning Stevens, eds., *Why You Can't Teach United States History without American Indians* (Chapel Hill: University of North Carolina Press, 2015). For American identity, see Jill Lepore, *The Name of War: King Philip's War and the Origins of American Identity* (New York: Alfred A. Knopf, 1998); Peter Silver, *Our Savage Neighbors: How Indian War Transformed Early America* (New York: W. W. Norton, 2007); and Carroll Smith-Rosenberg, *This Violent Empire: The Birth of an American National Identity* (Chapel Hill: University of North Carolina Press, 2010).

11. For a magnificent collection that brings together fourteen Lakota winter counts with comments provided by nineteenth-century Lakota recorders, see Candace S. Greene and Russell Thornton, *The Year the Stars Fell: Lakota Winter Counts at the Smith-sonian* (Lincoln: University of Nebraska Press, 2007). I have also relied on several un-published winter counts translated and transcribed by Dakota Goodhouse and wish to acknowledge my gratitude for his willingness to share his work with me.

12. For shapeshifting and trickster stories as concepts and as models for writing Indige-nous history, see Richard Erdoes and Alfonso Ortiz, eds., *American Indian Myths and Legends* (New York: Pantheon, 1984); Philip J. Deloria, "The Twentieth Century and Beyond," in *The Native Americans: An Illustrated History*, ed. Betty Ballantine and Ian Ballantine (Atlanta: Turner Publishing, 1993), 461–62; Alfred A. Cave, *Prophets of the Great Spirit: Native American Revitalization Movements in Eastern North America* (Lincoln: University of Nebraska Press, 2006); Margaret Connell Szasz, *Scottish*

Highlanders and Native Americans: Indigenous Education in the Eighteenth-Century Atlantic World (Norman: University of Oklahoma Press, 2007); Witgen, *Infinity of Nations*; and Karl Jacoby, "Indigenous Empires and Native Nations: Beyond History and Ethnohistory," in Pekka Hämäläinen, "The Comanche Empire," *History and Theory* 52 (Feb. 2013), 60–66.

1. A PLACE IN THE WORLD

1. "Extrait de la Relation des événements passés en Canada de 1694 à 1695," *DÉ* 6: 55–56. On their way to Montreal, the convoy was ambushed by the Iroquois, who killed one and wounded three. See "An Account of the Most Remarkable Occurrences in Canada from the Month of September 1694 to the Sailing of Vessels in 1695," *NYCD* 9: 603, 609. For the volume and extent of the French slave trade, see Rushforth, *Bonds of Alliance*, 135–92. "Sauteur" is a French designation for the Anishinaabe people who lived on the shores of Lake Superior.

2. "Account of the Most Remarkable Occurrences," 609. For a forceful argument about the centrality of guns in Native American warfare, trade, and diplomacy, see David J. Silverman, *Thundersticks: Firearms and the Violent Transformation of Native America* (Cambridge: Harvard University Press, 2016).

3. Claude Charles Le Roy, Bacqueville de La Potherie, *Histoire de l'Amérique Septentrionale*, 4 vols. (Paris: Nyon fils, 1753), 4: 30–31 ("came to cry" [est venu pleuerer avec nous], "Father" [Pere, laissez-nous venger], 30; "a bellicose Nation" [une Nation bellicqueuse], 31).

4. La Potherie, *Histoire*, 4: 32–33 ("All the Nations" [Toutes les Nations ont un Pere qui leur donne sa protection, & qui ont le fer, mais moi je suis un bâtard qui cherche un Pere]; "a Village" [un Village de sa Nation]; "master of iron" [le maître du fer], 32; "Take courage" [Prends couarage, grand Capitaine, ne me rejette pas, ne me méprise pas, encore bien que je paroisse malheureux à ses yeux. Toutes les Nations qui sont ici presentes savent que je suis riche, & que le peu qu'ils t'offrent se prend sur mes terres], 33).

5. La Potherie, *Histoire*, 4: 33 ("compelled" [m'a obligé d'abandonner mon corps pour venir demander sa protection]).

6. "Extrait de la Relation," 57 ("on condition" [à condition qu'il n'escouteroit que la voix de son père]); La Potherie, *Histoire*, 4: 33–34 ("take pity" [ayez pitié de moi; je sçai bien que je suis incapable de vous parler, n'étant encore qu'un enfant], 33; "could do" [pourront faire lors qu'elles auront la protection d'un si bon Pere qui leur envoyera des François leur porter du fer, dont ils ne commencent qu'à avoir la connoissance], 33–34). For Onontio, see White, *Middle Ground*, 36, 40; and Havard, *Empire et métissage*, 215–39.

7. Jean-Baptiste Bénard de la Harpe, "Voyage up the Mississippi in 1699–1700 by Mr. Le Sueur as given by Benard de la Harpe from Le Sueur's Journal," in *Early Voyages Up and Down the Mississippi, by Cavelier, St. Cosme, Le Sueur, and Guignas*, ed. John Gilmary Shea (Albany: Joel Munsell, 1861), 91.

8. For technology, trade goods, and wašíčus, see Bruce M. White, "Encounters with Spirits: Ojibwa and Sioux Theories about the French and Their Merchandise," *Ethno-*

history 41 (Summer 1994), 381–89; and Arthur J. Ray, *The Indians in the Fur Trade: Their Role as Trappers, Hunters, and Middlemen in the Lands Southwest of Hudson Bay, 1660–1870* (Toronto: University of Toronto Press, 1974), 81.

9. For Wyandots and early fur trade, see Conrad E. Heidenreich, *Huronia: A History and Geography of the Huron Indians, 1600–1650* (Toronto: McClelland and Stewart, 1971), 219–50; and Bruce G. Trigger, *The Children of Aataentsic: A History of the Huron People to 1660* (Montreal: McGill-Queens University Press, 1976), 246–664.

10. *JR* 23: 225 ("Their Villages"); *HAC*, pl. 35. In quoting passages from *The Jesuit Relations*, I have not retained the italics in the original.

11. *JR* 23: 225 ("of a certain," "eighteenth," "have never"). For the Sioux-Assiniboine split, see Brenda Farnell, *Do You See What I Mean? Plains Indian Sign Talk and the Embodiment of Action* (1995; rprt. Lincoln: University of Nebraska Press, 2009), 337, fn 8; and Pierre-Jean De Smet, *Life, Letters and Travels of Father Pierre-Jean De Smet, S.J., 1801–1873*, 4 vols., ed. Hiram Martin Chittenden and Alfred Talbot Richardson (New York: Francis P. Harper, 1905), 4: 1382. The split may have been more gradual than oral traditions suggest. See Raymond DeMallie and David Reed Miller, "Assiniboine," *HNAI* 13, Part 1: 572–73. For "na·towe·ssiwak," see Raymond J. DeMallie, "Sioux until 1850," *HNAI* 13, Part 2: 749. According to Sioux oral traditions, the Assiniboines splintered off from the Yanktonais, and linguistic evidence suggests that the split occurred sometime after 1500. See Stephen Return Riggs, "Dakota Grammar, Texts and Ethnography," *Contributions to North American Ethnology* 9 (Washington, DC: GPO, 1893), 164; and Douglas R. Parks and Raymond J. DeMallie, "Sioux, Assiniboine, and Stoney Dialects: A Classification," *Anthropological Linguistics* 34, nos. 1–4 (1992), 2: 247–48.

12. For population estimates, see Pierre-Esprit Radisson, *Voyages of Peter Esprit Radisson: Being an Account of His Travels and Experiences among the North American Indians, from 1652 to 1684* (Boston: Prince Society, 1885), 219–20; and Nicolas Perrot, *Memoir on the Manners, Customs, and Religion of the Savages of North America*, in *The Indian Tribes of the Upper Mississippi Valley and Region of the Great Lakes*, 2 vols., ed. Emma H. Blair (Cleveland: Arthur H. Clark, 1911–12), 1: 170. All estimates of Sioux numbers are educated guesses. Gary Clayton Anderson argues that the total Sioux population may have reached 38,000 in 1650. See Gary Clayton Anderson, *Kinsmen of Another Kind: Dakota-White Relations in the Upper Mississippi Valley, 1650–1862* (1984; rprt. Lincoln: University of Nebraska Press, 1997), 16–19.

13. For wakȟáŋ, see *SG*, 81, 89; and Philander Prescott, "The Dacotahs or Sioux of the Upper Mississippi," in *Information Respecting the History, Condition, and Prospects of the Indians of the United States*, 6 vols., comp. and ed. Henry R. Schoolcraft (Philadelphia: Lippincott, Grambo, 1853), 3: 227–29. For Siouan and Sioux migrations, see John R. Swanton, "Siouan Tribes and the Ohio Valley," *American Anthropologist* 45 (Jan.–Mar. 1943), 49–66; Dale R. Henning, "The Oneota Tradition," in *Archaeology on the Great Plains*, ed. Raymond W. Wood (Lawrence: University of Kansas Press, 1998), 360–64; Guy Gibbon, *Sioux: The Dakota and Lakota Nations* (Malden, MA: Blackwell, 2003), 33–46; and Beth R. Ritter, "Piecing Together the Ponca Past: Re-

constructing Degiha Migrations to the Great Plains," *Great Plains Quarterly* (Fall 2002), 272–75. For the cold and wet cycle, known as the Neo-Atlantic episode, see Jim Daschuk and Greg Marchildon, "Climate and Aboriginal Adaptation in the South Saskatchewan River Basin, A.D. 800–1700," IAAC Working Paper No. 7, 5 (cited with permission of Jim Daschuk); and David A. Baerreis and Reid A. Bryson, "Climatic Episodes and the Dating of the Mississippian Cultures," *Wisconsin Archaeologist* 46 (Dec. 1965), 215–16. For Cahokia, see Timothy R. Pauketat, *Cahokia: Ancient America's Great City on the Mississippi* (New York: Viking, 2009).

14. For Mde Wakan, the seven oyátes, and Lakota mobility, see James R. Walker, *Lakota Society*, ed. Raymond J. DeMallie (Lincoln: University of Nebraska Press, 1982), 14–17. For Teton/thítȟuŋwaŋ, see DeMallie, "Sioux until 1850," 755; and Edward S. Curtis, *The North American Indian*, 20 vols., ed. Frederick Webb Hodge (Cambridge, MA: University Press, 1908), 3: 31. "Ecotone" is a scientific term for the transitional zone where the Lakotas settled. For ecotones, see B. A. Nicholson, "Modeling Subsistence Strategies in the Forest/Grassland Transition Zone of Western Manitoba during the Late Prehistoric and Early Historical Periods," *Plains Anthropologist* 33 (Aug. 1988), 351–65; and Paul G. Risser et al., "Special Issue: Ecotones," *Ecological Applications* 3 (Aug. 1993), 367–445. For the woodland-grassland ecotone, see Anthony M. Davis, "The Prairie-Deciduous Forest Ecotone in the Upper Middle West," *Annals of the Association of American Geographers* 67 (June 1977), 204–13. For the Little Ice Age and bison, see Douglas M. Bamforth, "Climate, Chronology, and the Course of War in the Middle Missouri Period of the North American Great Plains," in *The Archaeology of Warfare: Prehistories of Raiding and Conquest*, ed. Elizabeth Arkush and Mark W. Allen (Gainesville: University Press of Florida, 2006), 84–87; and Judith Rose Cooper, "Bison Hunting and Late Prehistoric Human Subsistence Economies in the Great Plains" (Ph.D. diss., Southern Methodist University, 2008), 145–52. For the food yield of bison, see Robert Michael Morrissey, "The Power of the Ecotone: Bison, Slavery, and the Rise and Fall of the Grand Village of the Kaskaskia," *Journal of American History* 102 (Dec. 2015), 685. For Lakota myths and traditions, see Ella Deloria, *Dakota Texts*, Publications of the American Ethnological Society 14 (New York: G. E. Stechert, 1932), 99–106, 114–20; James R. Walker, *Lakota Myth*, ed. Elaine A. Jahner (1983; rprt. Lincoln: University of Nebraska Press, 2006), 51–52, 109–18, 185–86; and Walker, *Lakota Society*, 13–14. For Pipestone Quarry, Sioux movements, and early communal bison hunts, see Leonard Rufus Bruguier, "The Yankton Sioux Tribe: People of Pipestone, 1634–1888" (Ph.D. diss., Oklahoma State University, 1993), 7–30; Theodore L. Nydahl, "The Pipestone Quarry and the Indians," *Minnesota History* 31 (Dec. 1950), 193–208, and HHWC, 160–62. The information on western gatherings comes from Kinsley Bray (personal communication).

15. Raymond J. DeMallie, *Teton Dakota Kinship and Social Organization* (Chicago: University of Chicago, 1971), 99–102, 107–8; DeMallie, "Sioux until 1850," 718; Raymond J. DeMallie, "Kinship and Biology in Sioux Culture," in *North American Indian Anthropology: Essays on Society and Culture*, ed. Raymond J. DeMallie and Alfonso Ortiz (Norman: University of Oklahoma Press, 1994), 130–33. Some Sioux traditions

may suggest a notion of the Očhéthi Šakówiŋ as "a kind of confederacy," but oral traditions also emphasize that the Očhéthi Šakówiŋ was first and foremost an alliance among people who considered one another kin. See Walker, *Lakota Society*, 15.

16. DeMallie, *Teton Dakota Kinship and Social Organization*, 11–12, 42, 118–19; Perrot, *Memoir*, 1: 166; Radisson, *Voyages*, 220.

17. Louis Hennepin, *A New Discovery of a Vast Country in America*, ed. Reuben Gold Thwaites (Chicago: A. C. McClurg, 1903), 471–72 ("I am going," 472); R. P. Louis Hennepin, *Description de la Louisiane: Nouvellement decouverte au sud'oüest de la Nouvelle France, par ordre du roy* (Paris: Sebastien Hure, 1683), 66; Rushforth, *Bonds of Alliance*, 37–38.

18. Radisson, *Voyages*, 149 ("very strong"). For the metaphorical equation of eating and domestication and slavery, see Rushforth, *Bonds of Alliance*, 35–51.

19. Walker, *Lakota Society*, 15–16 ("center," 16); André Pénicaut, *Relation of M. Penicaut*, ed. Edward D. Neill, trans. A. J. Hill (Minneapolis, n.d), 8–9; Hennepin, *New Discovery*, 1: 224 ("without any Culture"); Hennepin, *Description de la Louisiane*, 201–2; Claude Allouez, "Father Allouez's Journey to Lake Superior, 1665–1667," in *Early Narratives of the Northwest, 1634–1699*, ed. Louise Phelps Kellogg (New York: Charles Scribner's Sons, 1917), 132 ("marsh rye"); Samuel W. Pond, *The Dakota or Sioux in Minnesota as They Were in 1834* (St. Paul: Minnesota Historical Society Press, 1986), 26–31; Raymond J. DeMallie, "The Sioux at the Time of European Contact: An Ethnohistorical Problem," in *New Perspectives on Native North American Cultures, Histories, and Representations*, ed. Sergei Kan and Polly Strong (Lincoln: University of Nebraska Press, 2006), 239–60. For muskellunge, see J. V. Brower, *Kathio: Memoirs of Explorations in the Basin of the Mississippi* (Saint Paul: H. L. Collins, 1901), 48.

20. For farming, see Radisson, *Voyages*, 220; *JR* 23: 225; and *JR* 55: 169. See also Gibbon, *Sioux*, 63–65.

21. For corn harvesting and the centrality of lakes, see Radisson, *Voyages*, 215, 226 ("wandring nation," 226). For the importance and construction of canoes, see Hennepin, *New Discovery*, 1: 228, 236, 246–47.

22. *JR* 15: 41–43 ("men who already feel," 41; "I am obliged," 43).

23. David S. Jones, *Rationalizing Epidemics: Meanings and Uses of American Indian Mortality since 1600* (Cambridge: Harvard University Press, 2004), 31; John Winthrop to Sir Simonds D'Ewes, July 21, 1634, *The Winthrop Papers*, 3 vols., ed. Allyn Bailey Forbes (Boston: Massachusetts Historical Society, 1943), 3: 171–72 ("I am still").

24. For Native American immune systems, colonialism, and disease mortality, see David S. Jones, "Virgin Soils Revisited," *William and Mary Quarterly* 60 (Oct. 2003), 703–42; Elizabeth A. Fenn, *Pox Americana: The Great Smallpox Epidemic of 1775–82* (New York: Hill and Wang, 2001), 26–27; and Catherine Cameron, Paul Kelton, and Alan C. Swedlund, eds., *Beyond Germs: Native Depopulation in North America* (Tucson: University of Arizona Press, 2012).

25. *HAC*, pl. 35; Daniel K. Richter, *Before the Revolution: America's Ancient Pasts* (Cambridge: Harvard University Press, 2011), 145–47; Daniel K. Richter, *The Ordeal of the Longhouse: The Peoples of the Iroquois League in the Era of the European Colonization* (Chapel Hill: University of North Carolina Press, 1992), 58–59.

26. Richter, *Ordeal of the Longhouse*, 56–65; Jon Parmenter, *The Edge of the Woods: Iroquoia, 1534–1701* (East Lansing: Michigan State University Press, 2010), 62–105; Trigger, *Children of Aataentsic*, 789–97; White, *Middle Ground*, 1–5, 10–14; Witgen, *Infinity of Nations*, 99; Colin C. Calloway, *One Vast Winter Count: The Native American West before Lewis and Clark* (Lincoln: University of Nebraska Press, 2003), 225–34; *JR* 34: 197 ("the people"); *JR* 55: 103; *HAC*, pl. 35; Stephen Warren and Randolph Noe, "'The Greatest Travelers in America': Shawnee Survival in the Shatter Zone," in *Mapping the Mississippian Shatter Zone: The Colonial Indian Slave Trade and Regional Instability in the American South*, ed. Robbie Ethridge and Sheri M. Shuck-Hall (Lincoln: University of Nebraska Press, 2009), 165–67; Sami Lakomäki, *Gathering Together: The Shawnee People through Diaspora and Nationhood, 1600–1870* (New Haven: Yale University Press, 2014), 25–26. While many Great Lakes Indians retreated westward to escape Iroquois violence, many Anishinaabe villagers stayed put, repeatedly turning back Iroquois war parties. See McDonnell, *Masters of Empire*, 35–36.

27. Richter, *Ordeal of the Longhouse*, 50–74.

28. *JR* 41: 79 ("the fury," "the very end").

29. For refugees, resident Indians, nindoodemag, and intermarriage, see Heidi Bohaker, "*Nindoodemag*: The Significance of Algonquian Kinship Networks in the Eastern Great Lakes Region, 1600–1701," *William and Mary Quarterly* 63 (Jan. 2006), 23–52; Sarah M. Pearsall, "Native American Men—and Women—at Home in Plural Marriages in Seventeenth-Century New France," *Gender & History* 27 (Nov. 2015), esp. 591–610; Rushforth, *Bonds of Alliance*, 26–27; and McDonnell, *Masters of Empire*, 8–13, 34–36. The calumet ceremony probably originated in the West among the Wichitas, Pawnees, and Arikaras. See Donald L. Blakeslee, "The Origin and Spread of the Calumet Ceremony," *American Antiquity* 46 (Oct. 1981), 759–68; and Gene Weltfish, *The Lost Universe: Pawnee Life and Culture* (1965; rprt. Lincoln: University of Nebraska Press, 1977). See also Ian W. Brown, "The Calumet Ceremony in the Southeast as Observed Archaeologically," in *Powhatan's Mantle: Indians in the Colonial Southeast*, ed. Gregory A. Waselkov, Peter H. Wood, and Tom Hatley (1989; rprt. Lincoln: University of Nebraska Press, 2006), 371–420.

30. White, *Middle Ground*, 10–23; Helen Hornbeck Tanner, ed., *Atlas of the Great Lakes Indian History* (Norman: University of Oklahoma Press, for the Newberry Library, 1987), 30–31. Since the publication of Richard White's *The Middle Ground* in 1991, an intense and seemingly inexhaustible scholarly debate has simmered over the exact social and political makeup of the pays d'en haut in the aftermath of the Iroquois onslaught. A number of scholars have criticized White's depiction of the western Lakes Indians as refugees with shattered societies and insignificant territorial attachments and argued for the persistence of Indigenous social and political formations throughout the Iroquois invasions and French imperial impositions. Still others have criticized White for underestimating the role of French imperial power in shaping the pays d'en haut while some have made a case for a Native-controlled world. The debate has been one of the most stimulating in recent American historiography, but it is also partially misguided. The debate has not sufficiently reckoned with the regional

differences in the Great Lakes world. The cohering, kinship-based Anishinaabe world centered on eastern Lake Superior, but things were radically different farther west and south, especially around Green Bay where the largest numbers of refugees resided. These western Lakes people needed and relied extensively on French mediation— White's "imported imperial glue"—to stabilize their world. This was the nucleus of French-Indian accommodation and the site where a middle ground emerged, matured, and survived. For key works of the debate, see Anderson, *Kinsmen of Another Kind*, xiii; Bohaker, *"Nindoodemag"*; Susan Sleeper-Smith, "The Middle Ground Revisited: Introduction," *William and Mary Quarterly* 63 (Jan. 2006), 4–5; Richard White, "Creative Misunderstandings and New Understandings," *William and Mary Quarterly* 63 (Jan. 2006), 9–14; Havard, *Empire et mètissage*; Rushforth, *Bonds of Alliance*, esp. 24–27; Witgen, *Infinity of Nations*; Michael A. McDonnell, "Rethinking the Middle Ground: French Colonialism and Indigenous Identities in the Pays d'en Haut," in *Native Diasporas: Indigenous Identities and Settler Colonialism in the Americas* (Lincoln: University of Nebraska Press, 2014), 79–108; and Andrew Lipman, "No More Middle Grounds?" *Reviews in American History* 44 (March 2016), 24–30.

31. White, *Middle Ground*, 104–9; McDonnell, *Masters of Empire*, 36–39; Calloway, *One Vast Winter Count*, 230–34; José António Brandão, *"Your Fyre Shall Burn No More": Iroquois Policy toward New France and Its Native Allies to 1701* (Lincoln: University of Nebraska Press, 1997), 107–8.

32. White, *Middle Ground*, 5–185. For Jesuits, see Richter, *Before the Revolution*, 42–43.

33. For fur trade, see McDonnell, *Masters of Empire*, 38–39. For Lakes Indians and the Sioux, see Perrot, *Memoir*, 1: 164 ("so rash").

34. Radisson, *Voyages*, 154 ("terror," "a cruell warre," "never"); Perrot, *Memoir*, 1: 159–63 ("have pity," 161; "people far inferior," 162; "so terrified," 163). For the psychological effect of guns and gunshot wounds, see Hennepin, *New Discovery* 1: 235.

35. Perrot, *Memoir*, 1: 163 ("loaded," "humiliating"); and Radisson, *Voyages*, 226 ("for men"). For Great Lakes military culture, see Antoine Laumet de la Mothe Cadillac, "Relation de la Sieur de la Motte Cadillac," Edward E. Ayer Collection, MS 130, Special Collections, Newberry Library. For ceremonial weeping, see White, "Encounters with Spirits," 385–86.

36. Radisson, *Voyages*, 149 ("companys"); Claude Charles Le Roy, Sieur de Bacqueville de La Potherie, *History of the Savage People Who Are Allies of New France*, in *Indian Tribes of the Upper Mississippi Valley*, ed. Blair, 2: 32; *JR* 54: 191.

37. DeMallie, "Sioux until 1850," 720; Wilfred Mott Wedel, "Iowa," *HNAI* 13, Part 1: 432; La Potherie, *History*, 1: 281; Perrot, *Memoir*, 1: 163.

38. Radisson, *Voyages*, 154; Perrot, *Memoir*, 1: 166–67.

39. W. J. Eccles, *French in North America, 1500–1783* (East Lansing: Michigan State University Press, 1998), 32–80; Richter, *Before the Revolution*, 256–58; Gilles Havard, *Histoire des coureurs de bois: Amérique du Nord, 1600–1840* (Paris: Indes Savantes, 2016), 57–58; *HAC*, 86.

40. Radisson, *Voyages*, 201–2; Witgen, *Infinity of Nations*, 59–61.

41. Ibid., 154–57, 205 ("eye by an arrow," "his courage," 154; "seeing," 155; "wound," 157; "very Image," 205).

42. Ibid., 207–9 ("After this," "tobbacco," 207; "more elevated," "appeare," 208).

43. Ibid., 209–12 ("to take," 211).

44. Ibid., 213–15 ("a speech," 213; "Yee," 215). For an insightful discussion of women, diplomacy, and cross-cultural communication, see Juliana Barr, "A Diplomacy of Gender: Rituals of First Contact in the 'Land of the Tejas,'" *William and Mary Quarterly* 61 (July 2004), 393–434.

45. Radisson, *Voyages*, 216–17 ("We weare," "an universall," 216; "lead," 217).

46. Ibid., 218–19 ("two redoubted," 218; "most exquisite," "according to," 219). According to Jean-Baptiste Bénard de la Harpe, a French officer in Louisiana, the Sioux called Indians who were not Sioux "strangers." See Harpe, "Voyage up the Mississippi," 104.

47. Radisson, *Voyages*, 219 ("This feast").

48. Ibid., 207 ("Nation"); 219.

49. Ibid., 213, 219–20 ("for not to," 213; "seaven small," 219; "cabbans," "there weare," "a kind of Stone," "retire," "in the whole," "far better," "loaden," 220).

50. *JR* 50: 297, 301 ("Babylon," 301); *JR* 54: 165 ("More than"); Witgen, *Infinity of Nations*, 65–67.

51. *JR* 51: 47; *JR* 54: 185–91 ("in order to," 191). For the rise of Kaskaskia and slave traffic, see Robert Michael Morrissey, *Empire by Collaboration: Indians, Colonists, and Governments in Colonial Illinois Country* (Philadelphia: University of Pennsylvania Press, 2015), 52–59.

52. *JR* 49: 241; *JR* 51: 53 ("They speak"); *JR* 54: 167, 191–93 ("only," 167; "the Iroquois," "manners," 191; "when," 193).

53. Allouez, "Father Allouez's Journey," 132 ("in extreme"); *JR* 54: 193 ("They have," "message," "I could wish," "Christianity," 193); François-Marc Gagnon, Nancy Senior, and Réal Ouelette, *The Codex Canadensis and the Writing of Louis Nicolas* (Montreal: McGill-Queen's University Press, 2011), 15.

54. For the rise of the Odawas, see McDonnell, *Masters*, 38–44.

55. Perrot, *Memoir*, 1: 187–88 ("sung," 187); *JR* 54: 193. For Sinagos, see Rushforth, *Bonds of the Alliance*, 39.

56. Perrot, *Memoir*, 1: 188–90; *JR* 55: 169–71 ("a general," 169–71); *JR* 58: 67 ("fully resolved").

57. Perrot, *Memoir*, 1: 164–66 ("give prompt," 166); *JR* 54: 167; *JR* 55: 169 ("made themselves," "with such skill"); *JR* 58: 257 ("exceedingly"). For Chequamegon, see also Robert E. Bieder, *Native American Communities in Wisconsin, 1600–1800: A Study of Tradition and Change* (Madison: University of Wisconsin Press, 1995), 66–67. For the diaspora, see *JR* 54: 217, 229–33; *JR* 55: 97–101; *JR* 56: 115–17; *JR* 57: 203, 209 ("almost," "show Them," 203; "praying," 209); *HAC*, pl. 38. For the Sioux anvil, see White, *Middle Ground*, 11. Some Odawas were relocating south also to counter Iroquois claim to Lakes Erie and Ontario. See McDonnell, *Masters of Empire*, 47–48.

58. Perrot, *Memoir*, 1: 188–90 ("intending," 188; "a body," "slew," "by climate," "the disorder," 189).

59. Perrot, *Memoir*, 1: 189–90 ("unwilling," "he might," 190).

60. *JR* 55: 203–5 ("seemed," "You have," 203; "They have," 203–5; "but the weak," 205).

61. E. E. Rich, *The History of the Hudson's Bay Company, 1670–1870*, 3 vols. (London: The Hudson's Bay Record Company, 1958–60), 1: 533–55; Ann M. Carlos and Frank D. Lewis, *Commerce by a Frozen Sea: Native Americans and the European Fur Trade* (Philadelphia: University of Pennsylvania Press, 2010), 57.

62. *JR* 55: 105–13 ("territories," 107; "You know," "Beyond the sea," 111; "all the affairs," "enough hatchets," "The Father," 113).

63. *JR* 57: 207 ("This place"); *JR* 58: 277 ("blackened"). For the centrality of the Sioux in French designs in the interior, see also *JR* 58: 257.

64. "Mémoire du sieur Greyselon Du Lhut adressé à Monsieur le Marquis de Seignelay," *DÉ* 6: 22 ("to make peace" [faire la paix avec les Nadouesioux, leurs communs ennemis]); "Lettre du sieur Du Lhut à M. le Comte de Frontenac, April 5, 1679," *DÉ* 6: 27–30. For an incisive reconstruction of the peace process, see Witgen, *Infinity of Nations*, 143–48. For the peace process as product of Dulhut's engineering, see Bieder, *Native American Communities*, 67. Dulhut wrote about "all the other Nations of North," which almost certainly meant Crees and Assiniboines. For Dulhut's strategic designs, see "Mémoire du sieur Greyselon Du Lhut," 22; "Lettre du sieur Du Lhut à M. le Comte de Frontenac," April 5, 1679, *DÉ* 6: 30–32; and "de Greyselon Du Lhut à M. De la Barre escrite au-dessus du Portage de Teiagon, Sept. 10, 1684," *DÉ* 6: 50–51. See also "Greysolon Dulhut, Daniel," *DCB* (accessed Sept. 21, 2016).

65. For travel times, see Carolyn Podruchny, *Making the Voyager World: Travelers and Traders in the North American Fur Trade* (Lincoln: University of Nebraska Press, 2006), 101; and Timothy J. Kent, *Rendezvous at the Straits: Fur Trade and Military Activities at Fort De Buade and Fort Michilimackinac, 1669–1781*, 2 vols. (Ossineke, MI: Silver Fox Enterprises, 2004), 1: 39.

66. Havard, *Histoire des coureurs de bois*, 61–112; James Pritchard, *In Search of Empire: The French in the Americas, 1670–1730* (Cambridge: Cambridge University Press, 2004), 153–54; Claiborne A. Skinner, *The Upper Country: French Enterprise in the Colonial Great Lakes* (Baltimore: Johns Hopkins University Press, 2008), 36.

67. Du Lhut to Frontenac, Apr. 5, 1679, *DÉ* 6: 30 ("a nursery of beavers" [une pépinière de castors]); "Lettre du Père Enjalran à Lefèvre de la Barre, gouverneur de la Nouvelle-France," Aug. 26, 1683, *DÉ* 5: 5; *JR* 65: 239; Rushforth, *Bonds of Alliance*, 224; *HAC*, pl. 38; Tanner, *Atlas*, map 6; "The Voyage of St. Cosme, 1698–99," in *Early Narratives*, ed. Kellogg, 344; "Greysolon Dulhut, Daniel," *DCB* (accessed Sept. 28, 2016). For gun trade, see White, *Middle Ground*, 136.

68. La Potherie, *History*, 1: 354–66 ("I have learned," "father," 354; "Vomit," "Nothing," 355); "Lettre du Jésuite Henri Nouvel à la Barre," Apr. 23, 1684, LAC, MG1-C11A, C-2376, F-6, fols. 523–523v; "Dulhut letter," Apr. 12, 1684, *WHC* 16: 114–17; White, *Middle Ground*, 78–82; Witgen, *Infinity of Nations*, 157–59, 200–210. La Potherie's history gives two different accounts of Perrot's council with Mesquakies but in both Perrot offers his body to restore peace. A Yanktonai winter count may refer to Perrot as the first white person to visit them. See DGWC.

69. La Potherie, *History*, 1: 369–72 ("they should," 370; "give suck," 372). See also Witgen, *Infinity of Nations*, 227–29.
70. La Potherie, *History*, 1: 372.
71. DeMallie, "Kinship and Biology in Sioux Culture," 130–33. For a broader context, see Patricia Albers and Jeanne Kay, "Sharing the Land: A Study in American Indian Territoriality," in *A Cultural Geography of North American Indians*, ed. Thomas E. Ross and Tyrel G. Moore (Boulder: Westview, 1987), 47–91; and Juliana Barr, "Geographies of Power: Mapping Indian Borders in the 'Borderlands' of the Early Southwest," *William and Mary Quarterly* 68 (Jan. 2011), 5–46.
72. E. D. Neill, "Early French Forts and Footprints in the Valley of the Upper Mississippi," in *Collections of the Minnesota Historical Society* (1860–67; rprt. St. Paul: Minnesota Historical Society, 1889) 2: 90–92; Jacques Nicolas Bellin, *Remarques sur la carte de l'Amérique Septentrionale: Comprise entre le 28e et le 72e degree de Latitude* (Paris: De l'Imprimerie de Didot, 1775), 123; Anderson, *Kinsmen of Another Kind*, 33; James H. Howard, "Yanktonai Ethnohistory and the John K. Bear Winter Count," *Plains Anthropologist* 21 (Aug. 1976), 21 ("The very first").
73. La Potherie, *History*, 2: 52–96.
74. Perrot, *Memoir*, 1: 109–10; La Potherie, *History*, 1: 276–78 ("their native," 278); John H. Moore, *The Cheyenne* (Cambridge, MA: Blackwell, 1996), 14–18.
75. Richter, *Ordeal of the Longhouse*, 133–36; Timothy J. Shannon, *Iroquois Diplomacy on the American Frontier* (New York: Penguin, 2008), 38–44.
76. Gilles Havard and Cecile Vidal, *Histoire de l'Amérique française* (2003; rev. ed., Paris: Flammarion, 2014), 105; Parmenter, *Edge of the Woods*, 160–61; Stephen Warren, *The Worlds the Shawnees Made: Migrations and Violence in Early America* (Chapel Hill: University of North Carolina Press, 2014), 107–8, 111–12; Calloway, *One Vast Winter Count*, 235, 247. The French maintained a small overwintering post at Green Bay, Fort de la Bai-des-Puants, but the post was all but insignificant militarily. Robert Michael Morrissey points out that most of the captives taken by the Iroquois were slaves, which lessened the blow, allowing a speedier recovery. See Morrissey, *Empire by Collaboration*, 57–58.
77. Jacques-René de Brisay de Denonville to Jean-Baptiste Colbert de Seignelay, Sept. 9, 1686, *NYCD* 9: 296–303 ("on all sides," "the Colony," 298). For French attempts to encourage western Indians to fight the Iroquois, see Perrot, *Memoir*, 1: 246–49, 266–68; La Potherie, *History*, 2: 52–53, 60, 64, 67, 77, 83, 89; and "Observations on the State of Affairs in Canada," Nov. 18, 1689, *NYCD* 9: 431–44. For Lakes Indians as shield, see Gilles Havard, *The Great Peace of 1701: French-Native Diplomacy in the Seventeenth Century* (Montreal: McGill-Queen's University Press, 2001), 88. For protests against French trading with and favoring the Sioux, see La Potherie, *History*, 2: 104, 111.
78. La Potherie, *History*, 2: 97, 101 ("implacable," "with all," "cut," "practiced," 97); "Prise de Possession par Nicolas Perrot," *DÉ* 5: 33–34 ("all the places" [tous lęs lieux, oú is a cy devant esté et oú il ira], 33; "proprietors" [propriétaires], 34). Perrot's attempt to establish French sovereignty in the West by piggybacking on Sioux power is an

example of what some historians have called shared or quasi-sovereignty. For quasi-sovereignty, see Lauren Benton, *A Search for Sovereignty: Law and Geography in European Empires, 1400–1900* (Cambridge: Cambridge University Press, 2010), esp. 222–78.

79. La Potherie, *History*, 2: 97–102 ("God allows," 99; "whom I will" 100; "swore," 102).

80. Ibid., 100–105 ("funeral calumets," 100; "no longer," 104.) For Perrot's fortunes, see "Perrot, Nicolas," *DCB* (accessed Sept. 7, 2016).

81. For the eastward retreat of Sioux enemies, see R. David Edmunds and Joseph L. Peyser, *The Fox Wars: The Mesquakie Challenge to New France* (Norman: University of Oklahoma Press, 1993), 22; and Witgen, *Infinity of Nations*, 251. For Seuer, see Richard Weyhing, "Le Sueur in the Sioux Country: Rethinking France's Indian Alliances in the Pays d'en Haut," *Atlantic Studies* (2013), 38–40; Havard, *Histoire des coureurs de bois*, 123; Roy W. Meyer, *History of the Santee Sioux: United States Indian Policy on Trial* (1967; rev. ed. Lincoln: University of Nebraska Press, 1993), 10; and Louise Phelps Kellogg, *The French Régime in Wisconsin and the Northwest* (Madison: State Historical Society of Wisconsin, 1925), 252.

82. "Ordinance for Maintaining the Frontenac, Michilimackinac and St. Joseph of the Miamis posts, Versailles, April 28, 1697," in *Letters from New France: The Upper Country, 1686–1783*, ed. and trans. Joseph L. Peyser (Urbana: University of Illinois Press, 1992), 61–62; Havard, *Empire et mètissage*, 71–72; Kellogg, *French Régime*, 257.

83. Pénicaut, *Relation*, 8; M. de Champigny, "Licenses to Trade Are Evoked," Oct. 13, 1697, in *Collections and Researches Made by the Michigan Pioneer and Historical Society* (Lansing, MI: Robert Smith Printing Co., State Printers and Binders, 1904), 33: 75; "An Account of the Most Remarkable Occurrences in Canada, from the Departure of the Vessels in 1696 to the 15th of October 1697," *NYCD* 9: 672–75 ("Sciou," 674).

84. Neill, "Early French Forts," 96; Havard and Vidal, *Histoire de l'Amérique française*, 120–23; Weyhing, "Le Sueur in the Sioux Country," 39, 42. For the importance of the Sioux for the French, see Louis-Hector de Callière au ministre, Oct. 31, 1701, LAC, MG1-C11A, C-2381, fols. 123–24.

85. Pénicaut, *Relation*, 4–8; Harpe, "Voyage up the Mississippi," 89–109 ("a good supply," 102; "thou must," 109); Callière to Jérôme Phélypeaux, comte de Pontchartrain, Oct. 17, 1700, *NYCD* 9: 713; "Mémoire donné par le sieur d'Iberville des costes, qu'occupe l'Angleterre dans l'Amérique septentrionale, depuis la rivière Saint-Mathieu jusqu'à la rivière Saint-Georges," *DÉ* 4: 549; DGWC; Howard, "Yanktonai Ethnohistory," 24; Weyhing, "Le Sueur in the Sioux Country," 42–43; Martha Royce Blaine, *The Ioway Indians* (Norman: University of Oklahoma Press, 1979), 25–26.

86. For Indigenous power and perseverance, see Daniel K. Richter, *Facing East from Indian Country: A Native History of Early America* (Cambridge: Harvard University Press, 2003); Juliana Barr, "The Red Continent and the Cant of the Coastline," *William and Mary Quarterly* 69 (July 2012), 521–26; and Pekka Hämäläinen, "The Shapes of Power: Indians, Europeans, and North American Worlds from the Seven-

teenth to the Nineteenth Century," in *Contested Spaces of Early America*, ed. Barr and Countryman, 31–68.

87. For frontier posts, see D. W. Meinig, *The Shaping of America: A Geographical Perspective on 500 Years of History*, Vol. 1: *Atlantic America, 1492–1800* (New Haven: Yale University Press, 1986), esp. 3–278; and Jay Gitlin, "Empires of Trade, Hinterlands of Settlement," in *The Oxford History of the American West*, ed. Clyde A. Milner II, Carol A. O'Connor, and Martha Sandweiss (New York: Oxford University Press, 1994), 96–108. Read together, Richard White's *Middle Ground* and David Weber's *The Spanish Frontier in North America* (New Haven: Yale University Press, 1992) capture the transformative power of trading posts in North American history.

88. Cadillac, "Relation."

89. Harpe, "Voyage up the Mississippi," 102.

90. Hennepin, *New Discovery*, 1: 223 ("Nations *Tintonha*"); Harpe, "Voyage up the Mississippi," 102–3 ("the prairies," 103); Raymond J. DeMallie, "Afterword: Thinking Ethnohistorically," in *Transforming Ethnohistories: Narrative, Meaning, and Community*, ed. Sebastian Felix Brown (Norman: University of Oklahoma Press, 2013), 249.

91. For exchange rates, see Jessica Dawn Palmer, *The Dakota Peoples: A History of the Dakota, Lakota, and Nakota through 1863* (Jefferson, NC: McFarland, 2008), 122; and Roland Bohr, *Gifts from the Thunder Beings: Indigenous Archery and European Firearms in the Northern Plains and the Central Subarctic, 1670–1870* (Lincoln: University of Nebraska Press, 2014), 137–38. For the possible Lakota-Arikara clashes on the Missouri, see Fenn, *Encounters*, 42–46.

92. HHWC, 160.

2. FACING WEST

1. For illuminating overviews of the Pueblo Revolt, see Andrew L. Knaut, *The Pueblo Revolt of 1680: Conquest and Resistance in Seventeenth-Century New Mexico* (Norman: University of Oklahoma Press, 1997); David J. Weber, *What Caused the Pueblo Revolt of 1680?* (Boston: Bedford/St. Martin's, 1999); and "Declaration of Pedro Naranjo of the Queres Nation," Dec. 19, 1681, in *Revolt of the Pueblo Indians of New Mexico and Otermin's Attempted Reconquest, 1680–1682*, ed. Charles Wilson Hackett (Albuquerque: University of New Mexico Press, 1942), 2: 245–49 ("swiftest," 246).

2. For the anti-Spanish and anti-Christian character of the revolt, see Ramón Gutiérrez, *When Jesus Came, the Corn Mothers Went Away: Marriage, Sexuality, and Power in New Mexico, 1500–1846* (Stanford: Stanford University Press, 1991), 134–36; and Matthew J. Liebmann, *Revolt: An Archeological History of Pueblo Resistance and Revitalization in 17th Century New Mexico* (Tucson: University of Arizona Press, 2012), 29–82.

3. Liebmann, *Revolt*, 83–206; Weber, *Spanish Frontier in North America*, 137–41.

4. John C. Ewers, *The Horse in Blackfoot Indian Culture: With Comparative Material from Other Western Tribes* (Washington, DC: Smithsonian Institution, 1955), 2–12; William R. Swagerty, "Indian Trade in the Trans-Mississippi West to 1870," *HNAI* 4:

History of Indian White Relations (Washington, DC: Smithsonian Institution, 1988), 351–53; Pekka Hämäläinen "The Western Comanche Trade Center: Rethinking Plains Indian Trade System," *Western Historical Quarterly* 29 (Winter 1998), 489–93.

5. Pita Kelekna, *The Horse in Human History* (Cambridge: Cambridge University Press, 2009), 21–91, 333–79.

6. Alice Marriott and Carol K. Rachlin, *Plains Indian Mythology* (New York: Thomas Y. Crowell, 1975), 90; Ewers, *Horse in Blackfoot Indian Culture*, 306–9. In 1804, Patrick Gass, a member of the Lewis and Clark expedition, noted that Lakota dogs were small but could haul about a load of roughly seventy pounds. See Patrick Gass, *A Journal of the Voyages and Travels of a Corps of Discovery* (Philadelphia: Mathew Carey, 1810), 47.

7. For horse and gun frontiers, see Frank Raymond Secoy, *Changing Military Patterns in the Great Plains (17th Century through Early 19th Century)*, Monographs of the American Ethnological Society 21 (New York: J. J. Augustin, 1953); and *HAC*, pl. 57.

8. For the changing Iroquois fortunes, see Richter, *Ordeal of the Longhouse*, 105–213; and Parmenter, *Edge of the Woods*, 181–249.

9. For the Great Peace of 1701, see White, *Middle Ground*, 39–40, 142–49; and Havard, *Great Peace of 1701*, 59–159.

10. Jon Parmenter, "After the Mourning Wars: The Iroquois as Allies in Colonial North American Campaigns, 1676–1760," *William and Mary Quarterly* 64 (Jan. 2007), 50–57; White, *Middle Ground*, 149–52; Witgen, *Infinity of Nations*, 266–78. White and Witgen offer different views on the long-term effects of the Great Peace in the pays d'en haut, the former writing that peace resulted in an expansion of the French-Indian middle ground, the latter arguing that the peace began fracturing the middle ground almost immediately. See Witgen, *Infinity of Nations*, 416–17, fn 52. Seen from Sioux's perspective, the Great Peace signalled their exclusion from an evolving middle ground that, whether crumbling or not, had turned eastward.

11. Harpe, "Voyage up the Mississippi," 108 ("it is for thee"). For mutual accommodation and kinship ties, see Anderson, *Kinsmen of Another Kind*, 36–38.

12. Pénicaut, *Relation*, 10–11; M. de la Mothe Cadillac, "Report of Detroit," Aug. 31, 1703, *MPHC* 33: 173; "Pierre Le Sueur," *DCB* (accessed Feb. 27, 2017).

13. Pénicaut, *Relation*, 8; Havard, *Histoire des coureurs de bois*, 119–26, 137–39; Callière to Pontchartrain, Nov. 4, 1702, *NYCD* 9: 737.

14. "Conference between M. de Vaudreuil and the Indians," Nov. 14, 1703, *NYCD* 9: 746–54; Philippe de Rigaud de Vaudreuil au ministre, Oct. 19, 1705, LAC, MG1-C11A, F-22, fol. 238 ("the freedom" [la liberté de faire la guerre aux Scioux, afin de leurs donner de l'occupation . . . de faire la guerre a l'iroquois que je regarde comme la seulle nation quil mimporte de conserver]). For Detroit, anti-Sioux rhetoric, and French efforts and struggles to build an anti-Sioux front, see M. de la Mothe Cadillac, "Report on Detroit," Aug. 31, 1703, *MPHC* 33: 161–81; and "Rapport de Clairambault d'Aigremont au ministre," Nov. 14, 1708, LAC, MG1-C11A, C-2382, fols. 47v–48v; White, *Middle Ground*, 150–54.

15. *YSF*, 72–75 ("camped," 72). Yanktonai winter counts mention "many wild horses"

already in 1692 and horses were reported along the lower Missouri Valley by 1700. Yanktonai counts also report horse trading in 1707. See DGWC; Howard, "Yanktonai Ethnohistory," 22, 24; Gilbert J. Garraghan, S.J., "The Emergence of the Missouri Valley into History," *Illinois Catholic Historical Review* 9 (Apr. 1927), 312. According to High Hawk's winter count, Sicangus were using horses in hunting in the late 1680s. See HHWC, 161.

16. For climate and game, see Michael C. Stambaugh et al., "Drought Duration and Frequency in the U.S. Corn Belt during the Last Millennium (AD 992–2004)," *Agricultural and Forest Meteorology* 151 (Feb. 2011), 159; John R. Bozell, "Culture, Environment, and Bison Populations in Late Prehistoric and Early Historic Central Plains," *Plains Anthropologist* 40 (May 1995), 145–63; and Brad Logan, "The Protohistoric Period on the Central Plains," in *Archaeology and Paleoecology of the Central Plains*, ed. Jack L. Hoffman (Fayetteville: Arkansas Archaeological Survey, 1996).

17. York Fort Journals, Aug. 3, 1716, Hudson's Bay Company Archives, Archives of Manitoba, B239/a/2; Ray, *Indians in the Fur Trade*, 11–14; Silverman, *Thundersticks*, 254; Toby Morantz, "Northern Algonquian Concepts Status and Leadership Reviewed: A Case Study of the Eighteenth-Century Trading Captain System," *Canadian Review of Sociology and Archaeology* 19 (1982), 482–500.

18. Anderson, *Kinsmen of Another Kind*, 24–28; RCF, 5–7; Kingsley M. Bray, "Before Sitting Bull: Interpreting Hunkpapa Political History, 1750–1876," *South Dakota History* 40 (Summer 2010), 99–100; RCF, 7–9.

19. Lakota traditions suggest that oyátes developed more distinctive identities as they migrated and expanded westward from the Mde Wakan. See Walker, *Lakota Society*, 13–14. For the prairie Indians and hunting, see Dale R. Henning, "Plains Village Tradition: Eastern Periphery and Oneota Tradition, *HNAI* 13, Part 2: 222–33; and Blaine, *Ioway Indians*, 12–15.

20. DGWC ("chased"). For the importance of river valleys in grasslands environments, see Elliott West, *The Way to the West: Essays on the Central Plains* (Albuquerque: University of New Mexico Press, 1995), esp. 13–50. See also John H. Moore, *The Cheyenne Nation: A Social and Demographic History* (Lincoln: University of Nebraska Press, 1987), 127–67.

21. The possibility for peace through common rituals was evident in 1715, when Yanktons and Mandans shared the calumet, trying to quell the violence. See Howard, "Yanktonai Ethnohistory," 27.

22. J. Owen Dorsay, "Migrations of Siouan Tribes," *American Naturalist* 20 (March 1886), 212–19; Howard, "Yanktonai Ethnohistory," 21; James H. Howard, "Notes on the Ethnogeography of the Yankton Dakota," *Plains Anthropologist* 17 (Nov. 1972), 283–85; David J. Wishart, *An Unspeakable Sadness: The Dispossession of the Nebraska Indians* (Lincoln: University of Nebraska Press, 1994), 4–6; RCF, 8–12, 14; Raymond J. DeMallie, "Joseph N. Nicollet's Account of the Sioux and Assinoboin in 1839," *South Dakota History* 5 (1975), 348; Margot P. Liberty, W. Raymond Wood, and Lee Irwin, "Omaha," *HNAI* 13, Part 2: 399; David Miller, Dennis Smith, Joseph R. McGeshick, James Shanley, and Caleb Shields, *The History of the Assiniboine and Sioux Tribes of the Fort Peck Indian Reservation, Montana, 1800–2000* (Helena: Fort

Peck Community College and Montana Historical Society, 2008), 30; Moore, *Cheyenne Nation*, 83, 117–18; Moore, *Cheyenne*, 23–29; *RCF*, 18.

23. For Missouri villagers, see Donald J. Lehmer, "Plains Village Tradition: Postcontact," *HNAI* 13, Part 1: 247–48.

24. *YSF*, 72–76 ("on horseback," 76; "Came," 77).

25. Howard, "Yanktonai Ethnohistory," 24 ("annihilated"); *YSF*, 76–79 ("among the lodges," "camped alone," 79). Yanktonai winter counts mention clashes with Missouri villagers already around the turn of the century, but they probably referred to Lakotas who had pushed deeper west. See DGWC; and Howard, "Yanktonai Ethnohistory," 23–24.

26. For the fragility of guns, see Wayne E. Lee, "Military Revolution of Native North America," in *Empires and Indigenes: Intercultural Alliance, Imperial Expansion, and Warfare in the Early Modern World*, ed. Wayne E. Lee (New York: New York University Press, 2011), 66; and Ann M. Carlos and Frank D. Lewis, *Commerce by the Frozen Sea: Native Americans and the European Fur Trade* (Philadelphia: University of Pennsylvania Press, 2010), 10. For corn, see *YSF*, 74.

27. R. Cole Harris, *The Reluctant Land: Society, Space, and Environment in Canada before Confederation* (Vancouver: UBC Press, 2008), 105–14; Ray, *Indians in the Fur Trade*, 51–54.

28. There is an enduring belief that the Lakotas were well-armed and militarily dominant already in the early eighteenth century and could thus defeat and push aside their enemies with relative ease, a view that glosses over the struggles, uncertainties, and the sheer slowness of their westward expansion, resulting in a teleological reading of their rise to power. But, in contrast, a number of scholars have argued that Lakotas were simply pushed into the West by militarily overpowering Assiniboines, Crees, and Ojibwes, a view that obscures the multitude of pull-and-push factors that fueled Lakota migrations. For a small sample of the debate, see Gary Clayton Anderson, "Early Dakota Migration and Intertribal War," *Western Historical Quarterly* 11 (Jan. 1980), 17–36; James O. Gump, *The Dust Rose Like a Smoke: The Subjugation of the Zulu and the Sioux* (Lincoln: University of Nebraska Press, 1994), 29–30; Secoy, *Changing Military Patterns*, 66–67; and Robert W. Larson, *Gall: Lakota War Chief* (Norman: University of Oklahoma Press, 2007), 19.

29. White, *Middle Ground*, 82–90, 149–54; Richter, *Ordeal of the Longhouse*, 223–24; Joseph Marest to Philippe de Rigaud, Marquis de Vaudreuil, June 4, 1708; Vaudreuil and Jacques Raudot, "Report," Nov. 14, 1708; "Letter from Sr. d'Aigremont," Nov. 14, 1708, *MPHC* 33: 383–87, 404, 432–33.

30. White, *Middle Ground*, 154–59; Edmunds and Peyser, *Fox Wars*, 64–72.

31. Edmunds and Peyser, *Fox Wars*, 72–76; Claude de Ramezay to the Minister, Sept. 18, 1714; Ramezay and Claude Michel Bégon de la Cour to the French Minister, Sept. 13 and 16, 1715, *WHC* 16: 300–303, 311–22; Vaudreuil and Bégon to the Minister, Sept. 20, 1714, *WHC* 16: 306; "Relation du Sieur de Lamothe Cadillac" [1718], *DÉ* 5: 122–23.

32. For the terms and various geopolitical ramifications of the Treaty of Utrecht in North America, see *HAC*, 88, pl. 40; and Richter, *Ordeal of the Longhouse*, 235.

33. Harold A. Innis, *The Fur Trade in Canada: An Introduction to Canadian Economic History* (1970; rprt. Toronto: University of Toronto Press, 2001), 106–7; W. J. Eccles, "French Exploration in North America, 1700–1800," in *North American Exploration: A Continent Defined*, ed. John Logan Allen (Lincoln: University of Nebraska Press, 1997), 1: 159. François Furstenberg uses the concept of "hot spots" to great effect in his essay on "the Long War for the West" from 1754 to 1815 and identifies the Ohio Country as the first of the constantly shifting hot spots. I borrow the term here with a provision that the Ohio Country had become a hot spot already in the early years of the eighteenth century. See François Furstenberg, "The Significance of the Trans-Appalachian Frontier in Atlantic History," *American Historical Review* 113 (June 2008), esp. 650–52.

34. For French geopolitics, see White, *Middle Ground*, 146–47, 159–60; Morrissey, *Empire by Collaboration*, 123–46; and Ramezay and Bégon to the French Minister, Nov. 7, 1715, *WHC* 16: 331–32. For chemin de voyageurs, see Jacob Van der Zee, "Episodes in the Early History of the Western Iowa Country," *Iowa Journal of History and Politics* 11 (July 1913), 325; and William J. Petersen, "Historical Setting of the Mound Region in Northeastern Iowa," *Iowa Journal of History and Politics* 31 (Jan. 1933), 54–55.

35. For the French and the Mesquakie-Iroquois-British connection, see White, *Middle Ground*, 159.

36. For the Mesquakie-Sioux alliance and the French, see "Charlevoix's *Journal historique*," *WHC* 16: 417–18 ("great damage," 417). For the French struggles to balance between their loyal allies and Mesquakies, see Edmunds and Peyser, *Fox Wars*, 90–109; and White, *Middle Ground*, 159–64. For the search of the Sea of the West and its centrality to French imperial designs, see Lawrence J. Burpee, *The Search for the Western Sea: The Story of the Exploration of North-Western America* (New York: D. Appleton, 1908); and Paul W. Mapp, *The Elusive West and the Contest for Empire, 1713–1763* (Chapel Hill: University of North Carolina Press, 2011), 5–6, 31, 149–62, 166–67, 195–96, 203, 369, 372–74.

37. For the marginalization and extermination of the Mesquakies, see "Résumé d'une lettre de Vaudreuil," Oct. 6, 1721, LAC, MH1-C11A, F-43, fols. 325v–326v ("to hold back" [retenir ceux qui voudront faire la guerre aux Renards], fol. 326; "destroy them entirely" [detruire entierement], fol. 326v); "Resumé of French Relations with the Foxes, from 1715 to 1726," Apr. 27, 1727, *WHC* 17: 3–5; and "Extract of a Memoir from the King to the Governor and Intendant of New France," May 14, 1728, *WHC* 17: 21. For the French-Sioux reconciliation, French plans and efforts to break the Mesquakie-Sioux alliance, and Fort Beauharnois, see Vaudreuil to the commandant Pierre Dugué Boisbriant, May 20, 1724, *WHC* 16: 441–42 ("succor," 442); "Memoir Concerning the Peace Made by Monsieur De Lignery with the Chiefs of the Foxes (Renards), Sauks (Sakis), and Winnebagoes (Puans a la Baie)," June 7, 1726, *WHC* 3: 148–50; "Letter of the Marquis De Beauharnois," Oct. 1, 1726, *WHC* 3: 159; "Memorandum about the Sioux," Apr. 29, 1727, *WHC* 17: 7–9; "Relation du voyage chez les Sioux par le père Guignas," Sept. 19, 1728, LAC, MG1-C11A, F-51, fols. 442–45; Charles de la Boische, Marquis de Beauharnois au ministre, July 21, 1729, LAC, MG1-C11A, C-2389, fols. 125–26; and Beauharnois et Gilles Hocquart au ministre, Oct. 25, 1729, LAC, MG1-

C11A, C-2389, fol. 25v ("to win" [pour s'attirer le coeur des Sioux qui rejetterons toujours leurs propositions tant qu'ils verront le françois chés eux]).

38. "Paroles d'un chef renard adressées à Coulon de Villiers," LAC, MG1-C11A, F-49, fols. 521–521v; M. le marquis de Beauharnois par le R. P. Guignas, missionnaire de la Compagnie de Jésus, May 29, 1728, *DÉ* 6: 558; Constant le Marchand de Lignery to Beauharnois, Aug. 30, 1728, *WHC* 17: 33–34; "Narrative of de Boucherville," *WHC* 17: 36–37 ("hearts," 37); Beauharnois to the French Minister, May 19, 1729, July 21, 1729, and Oct. 1, 1731, *WHC* 17: 62–63, 139–41; Beauharnois and Hocquart to the French Minister, Nov. 2, 1730, *WHC* 17: 113 ("total destruction"); Beauharnois, "Traité de la nouvelle Compagnie des Sioux," June 6, 1731, *DÉ* 6: 563–67; Charles des Champs de Boishébert to Beauharnois, Feb. 28, 1732, *WHC* 17: 148–52; "Report of Trade for 1732," *MPHC* 34: 97–98 ("great satisfaction," 97); Beauharnois to the French Minister, Oct. 15, 1732, *WHC* 17: 167–69 ("caused," 167); Hocquart to the French Minister, Oct. 26, 1735, *WHC* 17: 230 ("very good"). For the collapse of Mesquakies, see Edmunds and Peyser, *Fox Wars*, 128–201. The size of the Lakota band was calculated in men—about sixty—which probably translates close to three hundred people.

39. Beauharnois and Hocquart to the Minister, Aug. 12, 1736, *NYCD* 9: 1051 ("appeared"). For Jesuits, see *JR* 68: 281–85. For the concept of Native ground, see Duval, *Native Ground*.

40. Pierre Gaultier de Varennes et de La Vérendrye, "Report," June 2, 1737, *JLV*, 211–13; Jos. Fr. Lafitau to Father General, Apr. 4, 1738, in *The Aulneau Collection, 1734–1745*, ed. Arthur E. Jones (Montreal: Archives of St. Mary's College, 1893), 93–96 ("decked out," 94); "Anonymous Report to Charles de la Boische, Marquis de Beauharnois, 1736," *JLV*, 262–66. See also Bill Moreau, "The Death of Père Aulneau, 1736: The Development of Myth in the Northwest," *CCHA Historical Studies* 69 (2003), 54–60.

41. For the Cree and Assiniboine expansion, see Beauharnois to Jean-Frédéric Phélypeaux, comte de Maurepas, Oct. 15, 1732, *JLV*, 93–94; and Harold Hickerson, "Land Tenure of the Rainy Lake Chippewa and the Beginning of the 19th Century," *Smithsonian Contributions to Anthropology* 2, no. 4 (Washington, DC: Smithsonian, 1967), 44–45. For the Treaty of Utrecht and French designs, see Mapp, *Elusive West*, 132–67, 196–98.

42. W. J. Eccles, "La Mer de l'Ouest: Outpost of an Empire," in Eccles, *Essays on New France* (Oxford: Oxford University Press, 2007), 96–109; Mapp, *Elusive West*, 195–96; Antoine Champagne, "The Vérendryes and Their Successors, 1727–1760," *Transactions of the Manitoba Historical Society*, ser. 3 (1968–69), available at http://www.mhs.mb.ca/docs/transactions/3/verendryes.shtml (accessed Dec. 25, 2015).

43. Beauharnois to the French Minister, Oct. 1, 1731, *WHC* 17: 139–40; Burpee, *Search for the Western Sea*, 237–44; Fenn, *Encounters in the Heart of the World*, 79–85, 90; John S. Milloy, *The Plains Cree: Trade, Diplomacy, and War, 1790–1870* (Winnipeg: University of Manitoba Press, 1988), 41–42. For Sioux disinterest in French missionaries, see L. F. Nau to Father Bonin, Oct. 2, 1735, in *Aulneau Collection*, ed. Jones, 65–66.

44. La Vérendrye to Beauharnois, May 21 and 25, 1733; "Report of Beauharnois," Sept. 28, 1733, *JLV*, 95–110. For the legalization of Indian slavery in New France, see Brett

Rushforth, "'A Little Flesh We Offer You': The Origins of Indian Slavery in New France," *William and Mary Quarterly* 60 (Oct. 2003), 777–808.

45. La Vérendrye to Beauharnois, *JLV*, May 21 and 25, 1733, 95–102; La Vérendrye, "Journal," May 27, 1733, to July 12, 1734, *JLV*, 173–86 ("bitter," 175; "dearest," 180); Beauharnois to Maurepas, Oct. 14, 1736, *JLV*, 208–13; Rushforth, *Bonds of Alliance*, 229–31.

46. La Vérendrye, "Report," 249–62. For the commercial dominance of Crees, see Ray, *Indians in the Fur Trade*, 59–60; and *HAC*, pl. 57. Sicangu winter counts for the 1730s record repeated clashes with Assiniboines, listing both losses and victories. See *YSF*, 80–81.

47. La Vérendrye, "Report," and Beauharnois to Maurepas, Oct. 1, 1838, *JLV*, 238, 288; Ray, *Indians in the Fur Trade*, 18; Eileen M. McMahon and Theodore J. Karamanski, *North Woods River: The St. Croix in Upper Midwest History* (Madison: University of Wisconsin Press, 2009), 24–25; Witgen, *Infinity of Nations*, 307–12.

48. Jean-Baptiste Gaultier de La Vérendrye, "Journal," July 20, 1838, to May 1739, *JLV*, 297–335; "Journal of the Expedition of the Chevalier de la Verendrye and One of His Brothers to Reach the Western Sea," *JLV*, 406–32.

49. "Relation du sieur St. Pierre, commandant au poste des Sioux, jointe à la lettre de M. le Marquis de Beauharnois," Oct. 14, 1737, *DÉ* 6: 575–76; Beauharnois to Maurepas, Oct. 14, 1736, *JLV*, 211–12.

50. "Relation du sieur St. Pierre," 576–77 ("ripped," [arracha ce cachet avec l'oreille] "with reflection," [avec reflexion et dessein], 577]). I have not retained the italics in the original.

51. McMahon and Karamanski, *North Woods River*, 26; "Relation du sieur de St. Pierre," 579–80.

52. Beauharnois to the French Minister, Oct. 14, 1737, *WHC* 17: 268 ("nearly died," "It would be"); and Aulneau to Father Bonin, Apr. 30, 1736, in *Aulneau Collection*, ed. Jones, 76; *HAC*, pl. 39.

53. La Vérendrye, "Report," 257–58; "Relation du sieur de St. Pierre," 578; Louis Denys, Sieur de la Ronde to Beauharnois, June 28, 1738, July 22, 1738, and Feb. 17, 1739, *WHC* 17: 277–79, 310; "Speeches of the Foxes, Sauk, Winnebago, Ottawa, and Menominee, to Governor-General Beauharnois," June 20, 1740, *WHC* 17: 325; Beauharnois to the French Minister, Oct. 12, 1742, *WHC* 17: 426–28; Ray, *Indians in the Fur Trade*, 14–16; Beauharnois to the French Minister, June 30, 1739, *WHC* 17: 315–18.

54. *RCF*, 13–14; Judith A. Boughter, *Betraying the Omaha Nation, 1790–1916* (Norman: University of Oklahoma Press, 1998), 24.

55. *YSF*, 82.

56. Sicangu winter counts, our best source for the 1730s and 1740s, record almost constant horse raids along the Missouri Valley. See *YSF*, 80–84.

57. For the 1741 attack, see "Paroles des Sioux, Sakis, Renards, Puants, Sauteux de la pointe de Chagüamigon, et folles avoines," July 1742, LAC, MG1-C11A, C-2394, fol. 213v; Beauharnois and Hocquart to the French Minister, Sept. 24, 1742, *WHC* 17: 418; and Beauharnois to Maurepas, Oct. 12, 1742, *JLV*, 384 ("create," "were only"). The sources give different numbers for the slain Sioux; 160 was given by Sioux themselves

and thus used here. For Indian slavery in New France, the Montreal slave markets, and the centrality of the Sioux in the slave traffic, see Rushforth, *Bonds of Alliance*, 174–92, 229–36. See also Havard and Vidal, *Histoire de l'Amérique française*, 238–41. For La Colle, see Beauharnois to the French Minister, Sept. 26, 1741, WHC 17: 361–62; La Vérendrye, "Journal," July 20, 1838, to May 1739, 294–95; and Beauharnois to Maurepas, Sept. 24, 1742, *JLV*, 380.

58. For Sioux restraint, see "Paroles des Sioux," fol. 213v. For the attack against the Illinois, see "Memoir on the Indians and Their Relations," WHC 17: 336–37.

59. "Paroles des Sioux," fols. 213–213v ("the other" [de l'autre côté de la moitié de la terre], fol. 213; "we came" [nous sommes (venus) nous en plaindre a vous], fol. 213v).

60. "Paroles des Sioux," fol. 214 ("started to cry" [ont pleuré en nous voyant], "though I am" [quoique je sois chef, les jeunes gens ne font pas toûjours ma volonté], "that is why" [c'est pourquoy je vous prie d'avoir pitié de moy], "Mon Pere" ["My Father"], "this is the reason" [c'est la raison qui m'Engage de vous prier de nous accorder un officier dans nos villages, pour nous donner de l'Esprit]). For Sioux slaves in Montreal, see Rushforth, *Bonds of Alliance*, 193–94.

61. "Réponse de Beauharnois aux paroles des Sioux, Sakis, Renards, Puants, Sauteux de la Pointe de Chagüamigon et Folles-Avoines," July 28, 1742, LAC, MG1-C11A, C-2394, fols. 235–236v ("to make" [pour vous faire connoître combien je veux que la paix et la tranquillité regnent parmy les Nations de Mes Enfants], fol. 235; "if you" [si vous faites encore quelque mauvais coûp . . . je lâcheray tous mes François et les nations qui me demandeut pas mieux que de fonceur sur tes villages, pour se renger de tout ce que vous a les fait par le passé], fol. 235v; "reconcile" [concilier toutes choses], fol. 236; "I have to" [il faut auparavant que je voye de quelle façon v(ous) vous comporterés], "My Children" [Mes Enfans, comme je vous vois nûs, je vous donne de quoy vous couvrir], "milk" [lait], "Listening" [en Ecoutant ma parole], fol. 236v).

62. Beauharnois to the French Minister, Oct. 28, 1745, WHC 17: 447–51; "Diary of Events for the Year 1747, Sent by the Governor and Intendant of New France to the French Minister," WHC 17: 456–69; Memoir of Raymond to the French Minister," Nov. 2, 1747, WHC 17: 475–76 ("who have"); "Diary of Events for the Year 1747 Sent by the Governor and Intendant of New France to the French Minister," WHC 17: 478–92; Beauharnois to Maurepas, Oct. 28, 1746, NYCD 10: 37 ("chiefs," "bound"). For the loosening of the French-Indian alliance in the pay's d'en haut in the 1740s, see White, *Middle Ground*, 189–201.

63. White, *Middle Ground*, 210–11; "Enumeration of the Indian Tribes Connected with the Government of Canada: Warriors and Armorial Bearings of Each Nation, 1736," WHC 17: 248; W. J. Eccles, *The Canadian Frontier, 1534–1760* (1969; rev. ed. Albuquerque: University of New Mexico Press, 1983), 151–58.

64. Pierre-Jacques de Taffanel de La Jonquière et Bigot au ministre, Oct. 9, 1749, DÉ 6: 636–37; La Jonquière to the French Minister, Aug. 18, 1750, and Sept. 16, 1751, WHC 18: 63–67, 76–79 ("The young man," 78); Kellogg, *French Régime*, 379–81; *JJM*, 72; Grace Lee Nute, "Marin versus La Verendrye," *Minnesota History* 32 (Dec. 1951), 227–28; Cynthia L. Peterson, "Historical Tribes and Early Forts," in *Frontier*

Forts of Iowa: Indians, Traders, and Soldier, 1682–1882, ed. William E. Whittaker (Iowa City: University of Iowa Press, 2009), 15–16; Douglas A. Birk, "French Presence in Minnesota: The View from Site M020 near Little Falls," in *French Colonial Archaeology: The Illinois Country and the Western Great Lakes,* ed. John A. Walthall (Urbana: University of Illinois Press, 1991), 254.

65. At midcentury the Sioux began to figure prominently in French strategic calculations. See, for example, Jean-Baptiste Benoist to Charles de Raymond, Feb. 11, 1750, La Jonquière to Antoine Louis Rouillé, Oct. 15, 1750, "Order of Command for Macarty," Aug. 8, 1751, and Macarty to Vaudreuil, Sept. 2, 1752, *IHC* 29: 165, 239–41, 316–17, 654–55. For the search of the Sea of the West, see La Jonquière et Bigot au ministre, Oct. 9, 1749, *DÉ* 6: 637.

66. For Joseph Marin, see "Marin de la Malgue, Joseph," *DCB* (accessed Feb. 9, 2016).

67. *JJM,* 62–77 ("Prairie Sioux," 63; "well all winter," 65); White, *Middle Ground,* 140–41. See also La Jonquière to Rouillé, Sept. 1, 1751, *IHC* 29: 342–46.

68. Kenneth P. Bailey, "Introduction," *JJM,* ix; Kellogg, *French Régime,* 381; Anderson, *Kinsmen of Another Kind,* 52–53.

69. *JJM,* 77–103 ("The Sioux played," 77); "Extrait de Mémoire de M. Marin fils, capitaine et chevalier de l'ordre militaire de Saint-Louis," *DÉ* 6: 653–54 ("of the greatest consequence," [de la dernière conséquence], 654).

70. *JJM,* 93–95 ("completely changed," 93; "want," 95).

71. *JJM,* 95 ("Here is a map").

72. *JJM,* 93–97; Marin to Monsieur Deschambeau, June 1, 1754, *JJM,* 151 ("The Mississippi belongs").

73. For the Indian rebellion in the Ohio Country and the situation in the early 1750s, see White, *Middle Ground,* 202–42. For a contrasting view of the Sioux-French alliance and France's imperial prospects, see Rushforth, *Bonds of Alliance,* 236–37.

74. McDonnell, *Masters of Empire,* 132–59.

75. Fred Anderson, *Crucible of War: The Seven Years' War and the Fate of Empire in British North America, 1754–1766* (New York: Vintage Books, 2000), 59–65.

76. YSF, 85–88 ("Went," 87). Lakota winter counts were not meant to be comprehensive histories, and we cannot pinpoint the first mounted raid to the winter of 1757–58: it may have taken place sometime earlier or later. However, read as a whole, the Battiste Good winter count, which begins in 1700, strongly suggests that the shift to mounted warfare did not happen until the 1750s: horses are mentioned frequently in the winter counts for the 1740s, but there are no hints of riding.

77. Doane Robinson, "A History of the Dakota or Sioux Indians: From Their Earliest Traditions and First Contact with White Men to the Final Settlement of the Last of Them upon Reservations and the Consequent Abandonment of the Old Tribal Life," *South Dakota Historical Collections* 2 (Aberdeen: News Printing, 1904), 23–24; Jean-Baptiste Truteau, "Journal of Truteau on the Missouri River, 1794–1795," *BLC* 1: 299; *RCF,* 16–17; Lehmer, "Plains Village Tradition," 247. For Arikaras and the Missouri, see Douglas R. Parks, "Bands and Villages of the Arikara and Pawnee," *Nebraska History* 60 (Summer 1979), 215–16.

78. Moore, *Cheyenne*, 13–19; West, *Contested* Plains, 68–75; W. Raymond Wood, "Biesterfledt: A Post-Contact Coalescent Site on the Northeastern Plains," *Smithsonian Contributions to Anthropology* 15 (Washington, DC: Smithsonian Institute, 1971), 60–68; George F. Will and George F. Hyde, *Corn among the Indians of the Upper Missouri* (St. Louis: William Harvey Miner, 1917), 43–44.

79. John D. Speth and Katherine A. Spielmann, "Energy Source, Protein Metabolism, and Hunter-Gatherer Subsistence Mechanisms," *Journal of Archeological Anthropology* 2 (1983), 1–31.

80. For Iktómi, see Martha Warren Beckwith, "Mythology of the Oglala Dakota," *Journal of American Folklore* 43 (Oct.–Dec. 1930), 339–442; James R. Walker, *Lakota Belief and Ritual*, ed. Raymond J. DeMallie and Elaine A. Jahner (Lincoln: University of Nebraska Press, 1980), 51, 53, 72, 101, 106–7, 112, 128–29; J. R. Walker, "The Sun Dance and Other Ceremonies of the Oglala Division of the Teton Dakota," *Anthropological Papers of the American Museum of Natural History* 16, Part 2 (New York: American Museum of Natural History, 1917), 90; Zitkala-Za, *Old Indian Legends* (1901; rprt. Lincoln: University of Nebraska Press, 1985), vi, 2–3; and Amos E. Oneroad and Alanson B. Skinner, *Being Dakota: Tales and Traditions of the Sisseton and Wahpeton*, ed. Laura L. Anderson (St. Paul: Minnesota Historical Society Press, 2003), 123–42.

81. DeMallie, "Kinship and Biology in Sioux Culture," 130–33.

82. For a critical discussion of the westward shift of the Očhéthi Šakówiŋ's eastern border, see Anderson, *Kinsmen of Another Kind*, 19–28, 44–48, 55. Anderson seeks to debunk the "myth" of Chippewa imperialism, which revolves around an alleged three-day battle of "Kathio" in which the Chippewas defeated the Sioux so thoroughly that they abandoned their homelands around Mille Lacs. Instead, Anderson emphasizes pull factors, especially new commercial opportunities, behind Dakota relocations. Yet, while the battle of "Kathio" is likely a myth, it seems clear that the *combined* pressure of Assiniboine, Cree, and Sauteur raids took a heavy toll on the Dakotas, probably forcing them to yield ground in the north and east. The Dakota relocations, in short, are best understood as a product of both push and pull factors.

83. "Extract from Memoir of Legardeur de Saint-Pierre, May–Aug. 1753," *WHC* 18: 133 ("Sioux of the Prairies," "Sioux of the Rivers," "desired").

3. THE IMPERIAL CAULDRON

1. For Omahas, Poncas, Otoes, and Iowas, see J. Owen Dorsey, "Omaha Sociology," in *3d Annual Report of the Bureau of Ethnology, 1881–1882* (Washington, DC: GPO, 1884), 212–13; Alice C. Fletcher and Francis La Flesche, "The Omaha Tribe," *27th Annual Report of the Bureau of American Ethnology, 1905–06* (Washington, DC: GPO, 1911), 81, 86; Donald N. Brown and Lee Irwin, "Ponca," *HNAI* 13, Part 2: 416; Vaudreuil to French Minister, July 20, 1757, *WHC* 18: 195–97; Vaudreuil to Rouillé, Aug. 26, 1749, *IHC* 29: 101–3; and Boughter, *Betraying the Omaha Nation*, 24–25. For Bourgmont, see *BLC* 1: 12–22; and Elliott West, *The Essential West: Collected Essays* (Norman: University of Oklahoma Press, 2012), 137–41. For the Spanish expedition,

see Weber, *Spanish Frontier in North America*, 168–71. For Missouri River trade, see French Minister to Beauharnois, Apr. 28, 1745, and "Memoir of Bougainville [1757]," *WHC* 18: 5–7, 177–78. For larger context, see White, "Creative Misunderstandings and New Understandings."

2. Stanley A. Ahler, "Reflections and Future Suggestions," in "Archaeology of the Mandan Indians at On-a-Slant Village (32Mo26), Fort Abraham Lincoln State Park, Norton County, North Dakota," ed. Stanley A. Ahler (Flagstaff: Office of Research and Graduate Studies, Northern Arizona State University, submitted to the North Dakota Parks and Recreation Department, 1997), 432; PaleoCultural Research Group, "Prehistory on First Street, NE: The Archaeology of Scattered Village in Mandan, North Dakota," ed. Stanley A. Ahler (2002); Craig M. Johnson, "A Chronology of Middle Missouri Plains Village Sites," *Smithsonian Contributions to Anthropology* 10 (Washington, DC: Smithsonian Institution Scholarly Press, 2007), 191–97; Fenn, *Encounters in the Heart of the World*, 143–45.

3. For the deterioration of the middle ground in the pays d'en haut, see White, *Middle Ground*, 202–22. For the French and Indian War, see Anderson, *Crucible of War*, 185–204.

4. Anderson, *Crucible of War*, 400–409.

5. *RCF*, 17–18; George E. Hyde, "The Mystery of the Arikaras," *North Dakota History* 19 (Jan. 1952), 30–33.

6. An Oglala winter count for 1759–60 records how "Bands separated in winter," possibly indicating that some Oglala thióšpayes had left the Oglala winter camp to live with Arikaras. Indeed, the winter is the first entry of the No Ears calendar, suggesting that a split had occurred among the Oglalas. See *YSF*, 88. For Marin, see *JJM*, 104. For Seven Years' War and the Sioux, see Anderson, *Crucible of War*, 453–55, 470–71; and Anderson, *Kinsmen of Another Kind*, 58. Some coureurs de bois and British traders seem to have visited Sioux in the early 1760s, but without posts and regular supply trains, the trade fell woefully short of satisfying Sioux needs. See "Lieut. James Gorrell's Journal," *WHC* 1: 25–26. For the scarcity of goods among Oglalas, see *BKWC*, 351.

7. For the Oglalas who sided with Arikaras, see *TN*, 104. Two winter counts mention the civil war. See *BKWC*, 351; and *YSF*, 91 ("They who").

8. For abandonment of farming and village life, see *TN*, 104. For bison populations, see Dan Flores, "Wars over Buffalo: Stories versus Stories on the Northern Plains," in *Native Americans and the Environment: Perspectives on the Ecological Indians*, ed. Michael E. Harkin and David Rich Lewis (Lincoln: University of Nebraska Press, 2007), 156–57.

9. "Lieut. James Gorrell's Journal," 25–37 ("certainly," "They can," "regular," "wished," 36; "send," 36–37).

10. For a broad overview of the Treaty of Paris and North America, see Colin C. Calloway, *The Scratch of a Pen: 1763 and the Transformation of North America* (New York: University of Oxford Press, 2006). For the anti-British rebellion, commonly known as Pontiac's Rebellion, see Gregory Evans Dowd, *War under Heaven: Pontiac, the Indian Nations, and the British Empire* (Baltimore: Johns Hopkins University Press,

2002). For the collapse of Indian trade, see Marjorie Gordon Jackson, "The Beginning of British Trade at Michilimackinac," *Minnesota History* 11 (Sept. 1930), 239–45. For Fort Augustus, see Jonathan Carver, *Travels through the Interior Parts of North America in the Years 1766, 1767, and 1768* (London: C. Dilly, H. Payne, and J. Phillips, 1781), 21–22.

11. Carver, *Travels,* 59–63 ("swallow," 60); Paul L. Stevens, "Wabasha Visits Governor Carleton, 1776: New Light on a Legendary Episode of Dakota-British Diplomacy on the Great Lakes Frontier," *Michigan Historical Review* 16 (Spring 1990), 24–26; Moore, *Cheyenne Nation,* 132–35.

12. YSF, 92–94 ("great mystery," 94).

13. YSF, 95 ("They burnt"); Howard, "Yanktonai Ethnohistory," 37; HHWC, 121; Robert W. Galler, Jr., "Sustaining the Sioux Confederation: Yanktonai Initiatives and Influence on the Northern Plains, 1680–1880," *Western Historical Quarterly* 39 (Nov. 2008), 473.

14. YSF, 95–96, 99; Esteban Rodriguez Miró to Antonio Rengel, Dec. 12, 1785, *BLC,* 1: 126; DeMallie, "Sioux until 1850," 731; Douglas W. Owsley, Hugh E. Barryman, and William M. Bass, "Demographic and Osteological Evidence for Warfare at the Larson Site, South Dakota," *Plains Anthropologist* 22 (Nov. 1977), 119–31.

15. For the drought, see Charles W. Stockton and David M. Meko, "Drought Recurrence in the Great Plains as Reconstructed from Long-Term Three-Ring Records," *Journal of Applied Meteorology* 22 (Jan. 1983), 23. For drowned bison, see YSF, 94–95.

16. For horse care in general among the Plains Indians, see Ewers, *Horse in Blackfoot Indian Culture,* 33–58. For horses in winter counts, see YST, 95–100; BKWC, 353–54; and HHWC, 166.

17. White, *Middle Ground,* 305–22; Susan Sleeper-Smith, *Indian Women and French Men: Rethinking Cultural Encounter in the Western Great Lakes* (Amherst: University of Massachusetts Press, 2001), 65; Thomas Gage to Earl of Shelburne, Feb. 22, 1767, in *The Correspondence of General Thomas Gage with the Secretaries of State, 1762–1775,* 2 vols., ed. Clarence E. Carter (New Haven: Yale University Press, 1931–33), 1: 121–24.

18. "The Narrative of Peter Bond," in *Five Fur Traders of the Northwest: Being the Narrative of Peter Pond and the Diaries of John Macdonell, Archibald N. McLeod, Hugh Faries, and Thomas Connor,* ed. Charles M. Gates (St. Paul: University of Minnesota Press, 1993), 45–51 ("Drid & Grean," "I Perseaved," "had not Hit," "on the Counter," "found," 46; "Excited," 49).

19. Jay Gitlin, *The Bourgeois Frontier: French Towns, French Traders, and American Expansion* (New Haven: Yale University Press, 2010), 13–22; "Captain Gordon's Journal," Aug. 31, 1766, and Thomas Gage to William Johnson, Jan. 19, 1767, *IHC* 11: 330–31, 498; "Narrative of Peter Pond," 45, 47; Francisco Cruzat to Don Luis de Unzaga y Amezaga, Nov. 21, 1776, in *Spain in the Mississippi Valley, 1765–1794,* 4 vols., ed. Lawrence Kinnaird, Annual Report of the American Historical Association, 1945 (Washington, DC: GPO, 1949), Vol. 1, Part 1: 235–36.

20. "Narrative of Peter Pond," 45–46, 58 ("Grate Number," "Kill," 58).

21. For western excursions, see YSF, 96–97, 99, 101; and HHWC, 166–67. For the Black

Hills and Lakotas, see *SG*, 309–10; Ronald Goodman, *Lakota Star Knowledge: Studies in Lakota Stellar Theology* (Rosebud Sioux Reservation: Sinte Gleska University Press, 1992), 1–2; Jeffrey Ostler, *The Lakotas and the Black Hills: The Struggle for Sacred Ground* (New York: Penguin, 2004), 3–6; Alexandra Witkin-New Holy, "The Heart of Everything That Is: Paha Sapa, Treaties, and Lakota Identity," *Oklahoma City University Law Review* 23 (Spring–Summer 1998), 317–52; and Alexandra Witkin-New Holy, "Black Elk and the Spiritual Significance of Paha Sapa (the Black Hills)," in *The Black Elk Reader*, ed. Clyde Holler (Syracuse: Syracuse University Press, 2000), 188–208.

22. *YSF*, 97. For the timing of Lakota discovery of the Black Hills, see Saunt, *West of the Revolution*, 149–51, 162; and Ostler, *Lakotas and the Black Hills*, 9–10. In the 1970s Fools Crow, a Lakota spiritual and civil leader, related how he was taught "that small hunting parties made journeys as far west as the Rocky Mountains long before our entire nation migrated to buffalo country, and that it was during one of these trips that the original Sacred Calf Pipe and instruction for its use in prayer was given." See Thomas E. Mails, *Fools Crow* (Lincoln: University of Nebraska Press, 1979), 55.

23. For supply problems and British overtures, see Colin G. Calloway, *The American Revolution in Indian Country: Crisis and Diversity in Native American Communities* (New York: Cambridge University Press, 1995), 38–42. For Wabasha, see A. S. De Peyster to Frederick Haldimand, June 1, 1779, and Patrick Sinclair to Diedrick Brehm, Feb. 15, 1780, *WHC* 11: 132, 145 ("uncommon," 145); and Stevens, "Wabasha Visits Governor Carleton," 35–46 ("a prince," 35; "the most distant," 44).

24. "Memoir of Charles de Langlade," *WHC* 7: 176; Cruzat to Bernardo de Galvez, Dec. 19, 1780, *WHC* 18: 413–15 ("One cannot," 413); Jean Baptiste Malliet to Cruzat, Jan. 9, 1781, in *Spain in the Mississippi Valley*, ed. Kinnaird, Vol. 2, Part 1: 414 ("This party"). For the battle of St. Louis, see Calloway, *American Revolution in Indian Country*, 42. For British trade on the Des Moines, see Galvez to Fernando de Leyba, Jan. 13, 1779, *SRM* 1: 166; and "Report of the Indian Tribes Who Receive Presents at St. Louis," Nov. 15, 1777, *SRM* 1: 145. For marriages, see Anderson, *Kinsmen of Another Kind*, 66–69.

25. Fenn, *Pox Americana*, 126–31; Fenn, *Encounters in the Heart of the World*, 163; John McNeill, *Mosquito Empires: Ecology and War in the Greater Caribbean, 1620–1914* (New York: Cambridge University Press, 2010), 197–234; Ashley Jackson, *The British Empire: A Very Short Introduction* (Oxford: Oxford University Press, 2013), 72.

26. Fenn, *Pox Americana*, 215–20; Hämäläinen, *Comanche Empire*, 111.

27. For Arikaras and Mandans, see Fenn, *Encounters in the Heart of the World*, 216–19. Smallpox appears in a Sicangu winter account for 1779–80, but three other counts date the pox between the winters of 1780–81 and 1782–83. An Oglala account for 1782–83 reports measles, although the disease may well have been smallpox. See *YSF*, 101–4. For weather, see *YSF*, 100, 102, 105; and Adam R. Hodge, "'In Want of Nourishment for to Keep Them Alive': Climate Fluctuations, Bison Scarcity, and the Smallpox Epidemic of 1780–82 on the Northern Great Plains," *Environmental History* 17 (Apr. 2012), 365–403.

28. Miró to Rengel, Dec. 12, 1785, *BLC* 1: 126; "Extract from the Journals of the Voyage of

J-Bte Trudeau," in *FTUM*, 177–79; Parks, "Arikara," 387–88; Fenn, *Encounters in the Heart of the World*, 164–65; W. Raymond Wood and Lee Irwin, "Mandan," *HNAI* 13: Part 1: 349–50, 352; Frank Henderson Stewart, "Hidatsa," *HNAI* 13, Part 1: 329; West, *Contested Plains*, 71; Moore, *Cheyennes*, 89.

29. *TINA* 23: 318 ("were not"); Miró to Rengel, Dec. 12, 1785, *BLC* 1: 123, 126–27 ("dryness," 127); William Clark, Aug. 18, 1806, *JLCE* 1: 28 ("Old Indian Village"). For the Mandan retreat, see Fenn, *Encounters in the Heart of the World*, 166. For the Arikara-Mandan attack, see *YSF*, 105.

30. For the location of Arikara villages, which marked the northern limit of Lakotas' Missouri domain, see Miró to Rengel, Dec. 12, 1785, *BLC* 1: 123, 126–27 ("dominating," 127). For the Mandan story, see *TINA* 23: 306–7 ("all is level," 306; "See here," 306–7).

31. For the crossing of the Missouri, see DeMallie, "Sioux until 1850," 731.

32. *YSF*, 98, 100–101, 107–14 ("Came," 103). For smallpox among the Assiniboines and Crees, see Fenn, *Pox Americana*, 193.

33. *TN*, 152–53 ("always wandering," "abandoned," 152; "over the prairies," 153); *JLCE* 3: 421; "Extract from the Journals of the Voyage of J-Bte Trudeau," 199. It seems clear that oral histories of Missouri River villagers informed the accounts of fur traders and explorers like Jean-Baptiste Truteau, Pierre-Antoine Tabeau, and Lewis and Clark who penned brief histories of the Lakota-Cheyenne conflict. For Masikotas, see Moore, *Cheyenne*, 89. For clashes with Cheyennes and Crows, see *YSF*, 107–12, 114.

34. *YSF*, 110–14 ("froze," 113).

35. Lakota winter counts for 1792–94 record several clashes with Arikaras intercepted with brief truces. See *YSF*, 116–18. For Arikaras, see "Extract from the Journals of the Voyage of J-Bte Trudeau," 177 ("This nation"); "Trudeau's [Truteau's] Description of the Upper Missouri," *BCL* 2: 379; Zenon Trudeau to Manuel Gayoso de Lemos, Dec. 20, 1797, *BLC* 2: 527; and *TN*, 123–24.

36. Three Lakota counts for different winters—1791–92 and 1792–93—mention the Mandan peace, but given that winter counts cover the period from first snow to first snow, they probably refer to the same event. See *YSF*, 115, 117. For the Omaha peace, see *YSF*, 115. For wintering in the Arikara village, see *YSF*, 116. For the flag, American traders, and the white woman, see *YSF*, 113–15; *BKWC*, 354; and Harry Anderson, "An Investigation of the Early Bands of the Saone Group of Teton Sioux," *Journal of the Washington Academy of Science* 46 (March 1956), 91–92.

37. Joseph Henry Taylor, *Sketches of Frontier and Indian Life on the Upper Missouri and Great Plains* (Bismarck: J. H. Taylor, 1897), 128 ("a great," "From").

38. Ibid., 128 ("pumpkins").

39. Ibid., 128–30 ("She was winsome," 128; "a stranger," 129; "With the light," 130). Running Face's account does not mention Lakotas, but winter counts for 1793–94 suggest that they were present at the council. Moreover, the destruction of the fifty-eight lodges probably refers to the sacking of the Mandan village. The winter counts for 1794–95 also record Lakotas camping and fighting Mandans. See *YSF*, 118–19; *BTWC*.

40. Parks, "Arikara," 366; Fenn, *Encounters in the Heart of the World*, 171–72, 195; Frank Henderson Stewart, "Hidatsa," *HNAI* 13, Part 1: 329; "Extract from the Journals of the Voyage of J-Bte Trudeau," 177.

41. For the collapse of Arikara and Mandan coexistence, see Fenn, *Encounters in the Heart of the World*, 195–96. For the Grand River Arikara villages, see *JLCE* 3: 146–47, 150–52, 400. For new alliances and wars, see *TINA* 23: 229–30; Thomas Miller, Brandon House Post Journal, Aug. 4, 1797, Hudson's Bay Company Archives, Archives of Manitoba, B22/a/5, fol. 10; *JLCE* 3: 331; and *YSF*, 120. For Lakota captives among Mandans around this time, see Albert L. Hurtado, "When Strangers Met: Sex and Gender on Three Frontiers," in *Writing the Range: Race, Class, and Culture in the Women's West*, ed. Elizabeth Jameson and Susan Armitage (Norman: University of Oklahoma Press, 1997), 131.

42. Saone Lakotas seem to have taken over the lands around Beaver Creek, between the Mandan and Hidatsa villages to the north and the now vacant Arikara villages to the south. For an early record of the Saones along the upper Missouri, see *TN*, 103, 106, fn 27.

43. "Extract from the Journals of the Voyage of J-Bte Trudeau," 199 ("same character," "visit"). For Missouri villagers' corn harvests, see George F. Will and George E. Hyde, *Corn among the Indians of the Upper Missouri* (1917; rprt. University of Nebraska Press, 1964); and Fenn, *Encounters in the Heart of the World*, 69–71.

44. While among Arikaras in 1795, Truteau wrote about a "village called Chaony, which will soon be coming here, usually roam the land to the northeast of the Missouri, but, lacking buffalo bulls and cows in those regions, they are forced to cross to the western side of the river where these animals are found in large numbers." The Chahony were Saones, and they seemed to be ranging widely from their core region that was not far to the northeast from Arikara villages. See "Extract from the Journals of the Voyage of J-Bte Trudeau," 199. Reflecting the situation around 1800, Tabeau associated the Hunkpapas with the Saones. See *TN*, 104. For the Saones as a multi-oyáte organization, see *RCF*, 12–13; Bray, "Before Sitting Bull," 99–100; and Anderson, "An Investigation of the Early Bands of the Saone Group of Teton Sioux," 87–94.

45. J.-Bte Trudeau, "Abridged Description of the Upper Missouri," *FTUM*, 333 ("As soon as").

46. For early St. Louis, see Gitlin, *Bourgeois Frontier*, 13–17. For early Missouri trade, see "Report of Indian Traders Given Passports by Don Francisco Cruzat," Nov. 28, 1777, and "Report of Indian Tribes Who Receive Presents at St. Louis," Nov. 15, 1777, *SRM* 1: 138–45; and Miró to Rengel, Dec. 12, 1785, *BLC* 1: 121.

47. "Extract from the Journals of the Voyage of J-Bte Trudeau," 205 ("much more"). For the Chouteaus and Osages, see DuVal, *Native Ground*, 120–27, 150–51, 169–73; Anne F. Hyde, *Empires, Nations, and Families: A History of the North American West, 1800–1860* (Lincoln: University of Nebraska Press, 2011), 33–37; and William E. Foley and C. David Rice, *The First Chouteaus: River Barons of Early St. Louis* (Urbana: University of Illinois Press, 1983), 13–86. For British activities, see Fenn, *Encounters*, 179–81; Havard, *Histoire des coureurs de bois*, 358; *BLC* 1: 58–81; and A. P. Nasatir,

"Anglo-Spanish Rivalry on the Upper Missouri," *Mississippi Valley Historical Review* 16 (Dec. 1929), 378–82. For profit margins, see Stephen Aron, *American Confluence: The Missouri Frontier from Borderland to Border State* (Bloomington: Indiana University Press, 2005), 86. The Spanish officials also worried that British traders could penetrate the Missouri River from the east via the Iowa and Des Moines Rivers. See Luis de Las Casas to François Luis Hector Carondelet, Feb. 17, 1792, and Carondelet to Las Casas, Jan. 10, 1793, *SRM* 1: 332, 343–44. For the Missouri trade, see Miró to Rengel, Dec. 12, 1785, *BLC* 1: 124–26.

48. For Spanish exploration, see *BLC* 1: 71–78. For d'Eglise, Arikaras, and Lakotas, see Trudeau to François Luis Héctor Carondelet, Oct. 20, 1792, and June 8, 1794, *BLC* 1: 160–61, 233 ("kept him," 233).

49. For Spanish and French visions for the Missouri trade, see Carondelet to the Duque de la Alcudia, Jan. 8, 1796, *BLC* 2: 389–93 ("line of forts," 393); and "Report of Carondelet," 1793, *SRM* 2: 10. In his 1796 letter the governor of Louisiana wrote that, alongside the British challenge from the north, the greatest obstacle to the development of the Missouri trade "consists in securing passage through the nations established on the Lower Missouri." See Carondelet to Alcudia, Jan. 8, 1796, *BLC* 2: 388.

50. "Clamorgan's Instructions to Truteau, St. Louis, June 30, 1794," *BLC* 1: 243–53 ("fix," 244); "Extract from the Journals of the Voyage of J-Bte Trudeau," 77–91 ("all the nations," 77–79). For a portrayal of Clamorgan, see Julie Winch, *The Clamorgans: One Family's History of Race in America* (New York: Hill and Wang, 2011), 7–39.

51. "Extract from the Journals of the Voyage of J-Bte Trudeau," 95 ("extreme," "as much to").

52. Ibid., 95–97 ("several," "called," "On this occasion," "of the Yankton," 95; "fairly," 97).

53. Ibid., 99–101 ("like a pack," "fierce," 99; "loud," "Great," "knowing," "had taken," "find," 101).

54. Ibid., 103–7 ("bad men," "would only," 103; "open up," "called," "This was," 105; "a proportionate," 107).

55. Ibid., 105–9 ("My distress," 105; "once alerted," "remain," "having," 107; "would come," 107–9).

56. Ibid., 107–9 ("had no," 107).

57. Douglas R. Parks, "Introduction," *FTUM*, 29; *BLC* 1: 88, 273–94.

58. "Extract from the Journals of the Voyage of J-Bte Trudeau," 103–7, 125 ("gladdened," 103; "diabolical," 107; "all the Indians," 125).

59. Ibid., 103 ("well received").

60. "Clamorgan's Report of the Operations of the Commercial Company, 1795," *SRM* 2: 173–78 ("flatter," 178); "Extracts from McKay's Journal—and Others," in *Proceedings of the State Historical Society of Wisconsin* 63 (1915), 193–94; "Mackay's Journal," *SRM* 2: 189 ("silk flags"); Jacques Clamorgan to Carondelet, Sept. 20, 1796, *BLC* 2: 458 ("with reservation"); David Williams, "John Evans' Strange Journey, Part 2: Following the Trail," *American Historical Review* 54 (Apr. 1949), 511–26.

61. "Extracts from the Journal of M. Truteau, Agent for the Illinois Trading Company, Residing at the Village of Ricara, up the Missouri," in Thomas Jefferson to Meriwether Lewis, Nov. 16, 1803, from *Thomas Jefferson and Early Western Explorers*, transcribed

and edited by Gerard W. Gawalt, Manuscript Division, Library of Congress, available at http://www.loc.gov/resource/mtj1.029_0512_0513 ("greatest," "abound") (accessed Feb. 12, 2018); Trudeau, "Abridged Description of the Upper Missouri," *FTUM*, 261 ("roam").

62. "Trudeau's Report Concerning the Settlements of the Spanish Illinois Country," 1798, *SRM* 2: 255 ("The goods"). For the North West Company and expansion of Canadian fur trade, see Ray, *Indians in the Fur Trade*, 125–30. For the revival of Dakota trade, see Anderson, *Kinsmen of Another Kind*, 66–74.

63. Carondelet to Las Casas, Nov. 24, 1794, *BLC* 1: 255 ("commerce," "many settlers").

64. Carondelet to Prince of Peace, Mar. 20, 1797, *BLC* 2: 503–6 ("English companies," 505; "to conserve," 506); "Trudeau's Report Concerning the Settlements," 255 ("His Majesty's"). Governor Carondelet wrote that the Canadian companies were inciting "the Sioux and other Indian nations," but the Sioux were clearly the group he was most concerned about. See Carondelet to Prince of Peace, 505.

65. Truteau, "Journal," *BLC* 1: 296 ("they were feared"). For the North West gun, see Charles E. Hanson, Jr., "The North West Gun," *Nebraska State Historical Society Publications in Anthropology* 2 (Lincoln, 1955); and Secoy, *Changing Military Patterns*, 96–98.

66. Pierre Chouteau to Albert Gallatin, Nov. 7, 1804, *BLC* 2: 759 ("beaucoup"); Kinsley M. Bray, "Teton Sioux Population History, 1655–1881," *Nebraska History* 75 (Summer 1994), 176.

67. For trading and camping, see "Extract from the Journals of the Voyage of J-Bte Trudeau," 259–60; "Trudeau's [Truteau's] Description," 379; and Clamorgan to Carondelet, Apr. 10, 1796, *BLC* 2: 418. In 1806 Cheyennes owned large herds of superior horses, and that growth of equine wealth must have been well under way in the late 1790s. For Cheyenne horse numbers, see Elliott Coues, ed., *New Light on the Early History of the Greater Northwest: The Manuscript Journals of Alexander Henry and David Thompson, 1799–1814*, 3 vols. (New York: Francis P. Harper, 1897), 1: 377–78. The sharing of horse wealth with Lakotas is ingrained in Cheyenne traditions. See Moore, *Cheyenne Nation*, 117. The rebuilding of the Lakota-Cheyenne alliance was not without difficulties. An Oglala winter count for 1798–99 record how an Oglala war party "brought home many Cheyenne scalps." See *YSF*, 124.

68. "Captain McKay's Journal," *BLC* 2: 495 ("so that," "principal," "tiresome"); James McKay to de Lemos, June 8, 1797, *BLC* 2: 562 ("to Traffic"). For Blackbird and Omahas, see Truteau, "Journal," 282–94; and Boughter, *Betraying the Omaha Nation*, 20–22.

69. Zenon Trudeau, "Examination of Derouin," May 14, 1797, *BLC* 2: 516–17 ("in order to," 517).

70. *YSF*, 119, 123, 126, 128–30 ("The first white man ever seen," 126; "the first white man to trade," 128; "A trader," 130).

71. For the Lakota woman, see *YSF*, 126 ("who had been"). See also *YSF*, 136, for an Oglala winter count for 1804–5 that states that "an Indian woman, married to a white man, was unfaithful; she was killed by a man named Ponka." Tabeau commented, mockingly, the benefits of intermarriage for fathers by highlighting the case of Mato-

kokipabi, an old soldier who offered his daughter to Loisel in "the hope of rolling in the wealth of the son-in-law." See *TN*, 106–7 ("the hope," 107). For intermarriage in the North American interior, see Jennifer Brown, *Strangers in Blood: Fur Trade Company Families in Indian Country* (Vancouver: University of British Columbia Press, 1980); Sylvia Van Kirk, *Many Tender Ties: Women in Fur Trade Society, 1670–1870* (Norman: University of Oklahoma Press, 1993); John Mack Faragher, "The Custom of the Country: Cross-Cultural Marriage in the Far Western Fur Trade," in *Western Women: Their Land, Their Lives*, ed. Lillian Schlissel, Vicki L. Ruiz, and Janice Monk (Albuquerque: University of New Mexico Press, 1988), 199–225; Michael Lansing, "Plains Indian Women and Interracial Marriage in the Upper Missouri Trade, 1804–1868," *Western Historical Quarterly* 31 (Dec. 2000), 413–33; and Sleeper-Smith, *Indian Women and French Men*.

72. For northern raids, see "David Thompson's Journal," in *Early Fur Trade on the Northern Plains: Canadian Traders among the Mandan and Hidatsa Indians, 1738–1818*, ed. W. Raymond Wood and Thomas D. Thiessen (Norman: University of Oklahoma Press, 1985), 102, 108, 111–12. For Lakotas and Arikaras, see "Extract from the Journals of the Voyage of J-Bte Trudeau," 199 ("to avoid," "out of fear"). For the Lakota colony, see Truteau, "Journal," *BLC*, 1: 310 ("to obtain"). For raids, see Truteau, "Journal," 295; and *YSF*, 120, 122–25 ("while," 122; "the God Woman," "I am," 123; "holy," 124). For the release of the Arikara woman, see *YSF*, 125.

73. For Crow wars, see *YSF*, 127–28; and Truteau, "Journal," 308–10. Some Lakotas also clashed with Cheyennes, but the conflict seems to have been brief and more personal than communal. See *YSF*, 120–21, 124. For the annual cycle, see "Trudeau's [Truteau's] Description," 382. For declining game, see Truteau, "Journal," 269, 310. The James River rendezvous was first mentioned by Truteau in 1795. See Truteau, "Journal," 301. For the James River rendezvous, see *TN*, 121–23 ("This concourse," 122–23).

74. *TN*, 123 ("Although," "become mediators," "treat," "a terrible").

75. D. W. Meinig, *The Shaping of America: A Geographical Perspective on 500 Years of History*, Vol. 1: *Atlantic America, 1492–1800* (New Haven: Yale University Press, 1986), 323–25; George Washington to Secretary of State, July 1, 1796, in *Writings of George Washington*, 39 vols., ed. John C. Fitzpatrick (Washington, DC: GPO, 1931–39), 35: 112 ("short"). "Spanish lake" is from Arthur Preston Whitaker, *The Spanish-American Frontier, 1783–1795: The Westward Movement and the Spanish Retreat in the Mississippi Valley* (1927; rprt. Lincoln: University of Nebraska Press, 1969), 3.

76. This notion draws from François Furstenberg's brilliant analysis of the contingencies of North American history in the late eighteenth and early nineteenth centuries. Furstenberg identifies New Orleans and, more broadly, the Southeast as hot spots of imperial rivalry in the 1780s and 1790s, focusing on the eastern half of the Mississippi watershed. See Furstenberg, "Significance of the Trans-Appalachian Frontier," 662–68. My discussion here brings the western half of the Mississippi watershed into the frame, introducing new protagonists—especially the Lakotas—as shapers of continental developments.

77. "Report of Carondelet," 12, *SRM* 2: 12 ("Thus they are," "the rich"). For 1790 British

invasion plan, see Frederick Jackson Turner, "The Policy of France toward the Missis-sippi Valley in the Period of Washington and Adams," *American Historical Review* 10 (Jan. 1905), 258. For Spanish anxieties, also see Carondelet to Alcudia, Jan. 8, 1796, *BLC* 2: 393.

78. For French plans, see Turner, "Policy of France toward the Mississippi Valley," 258–59. For Saint-Domingue, see Edward E. Baptist, *The Half Has Never Been Told: Slavery and the Making of America Capitalism* (New York: Basic Books, 2014), 44. For Genet and Rogers, see Alan D. Gaff, *Bayonets in the Wilderness: Anthony Wayne's Legion in the Old Northwest* (Norman: University of Oklahoma Press, 2004), 212–16; Frederick J. Turner, "The Origin of Genet's Projected Attack on Louisiana and the Floridas," *American Historical Review* 3 (July 1898), 653–71; and Furstenberg, "Sig-nificance of the Trans-Appalachian Frontier," 667–68.

79. For Spanish policies in Louisiana and West Florida, see Gilbert C. Gin, "The Immi-gration Policy of Governor Esteban Miro in Spanish Louisiana," *Southwestern His-torical Quarterly* 73 (Oct. 1969), 164–75; Weber, *Spanish Frontier in North America*, 271–81; and Francis Andrew McMichael, *Atlantic Loyalties: Americans in Spanish West Florida, 1785–1810* (Athens: University of Georgia Press, 2008), 16–53. For back-country separatism and independent colonies, see Turner, "Origin of Genet's Attack," 652–53; Andrew R. L. Cayton, "'Separate Interests' and the Nation-State: The Wash-ington Administration and the Origins of Regionalism in the Trans-Appalachian West," *Journal of American History* 79 (1992): 39–67; Eric Hinderaker, *Elusive Em-pires: Constructing Colonialism in the Ohio Valley, 1673–1800* (New York: Cambridge University Press, 1997), 236–67; and Patrick Griffin, *American Leviathan: Empire, Nation, and Revolutionary Frontier* (New York: Hill and Wang, 2007), 212–39.

80. For British agents, see Prideaux Selby to Peter Russell, Jan. 23, 1799, *WHC* 18: 460–61 ("a nation," "all mounted," 461). The British were clearly thinking about Lakotas for their scheme: only Lakotas were fully mounted among the Sioux. For American emigrants, see Weber, *Spanish Frontier in North America*, 281–82; and Alan Taylor, "Remaking Americans: Louisiana, Upper Canada, and Texas," in *Contested Places of Early America*, ed. Barr and Countryman, 16–17. For Boone, see John Mack Fara-gher, *Daniel Boone: Life and Legend of an American Pioneer* (New York: Henry Holt, 1992), esp. 264–89. For Austin, see Gregg Cantrell, *Stephen F. Austin: Empresario of Texas* (New Haven: Yale University Press, 1999), 20–30.

4. THE LAKOTA MERIDIAN

1. Napoleon's overseas empire remains an unstudied topic. For an illuminating recent contribution, see Bernard Gainot, "The Empire Overseas: The Illusion of Restora-tion," in *Napoleon's Empire: European Politics in Global Perspective*, ed. Ute Planert (New York: Palgrave Macmillan, 2016), 142–56.

2. Stanley Elkins and Eric McKitrick, *The Age of Federalism: The Early American Re-public, 1788–1800* (New York: Oxford University Press, 1995), 406–30.

3. Furstenberg, "Significance of the Trans-Appalachian Frontier," 658, 668–71; Walter Johnson, *River of Dark Dreams: Slavery and Empire in the Cotton Kingdom* (Cam-

bridge: Harvard University Press, 2013), 23. France offered to buy Louisiana from Spain in 1795, and the Spaniards considered the possibility several times in the late 1790s. See Frederick Jackson Turner, "The Policy of France toward the Mississippi Valley in the Period of Washington and Adams," *American Historical Review* 10 (Jan. 1905), 266; and Weber, *Spanish Frontier*, 289–91.

4. Quote from Thomas Jefferson to Robert R. Livingston, Apr. 18, 1802, Thomas Jefferson Papers, ser. 1, General Correspondence, 1651–1827, Library of Congress, Washington, DC, available at https://www.loc.gov/item/mtjbib011277/ (accessed Nov. 12, 2017).

5. Furstenberg, "Significance of the Trans-Appalachian Frontier," 671–72; David Brion Davis, *The Problem of Slavery in the Age of Revolution, 1770–1823* (New York: Oxford University Press, 1975), 150–51; Baptist, *Half Has Never Been Told*, 45; Havard and Vidal, *Histoire de l'Amérique française*, 707–11; Greg Grandin, *The Empire of Necessity: Slavery, Freedom, and Deception in the World* (New York: Metropolitan Books/ Henry Holt, 2014), 283.

6. Robert L. Paquette, "Revolutionary Saint Domingue in the Making of Territorial Louisiana," in *A Turbulent Time: The French Revolution and the Greater Caribbean*, ed. David Barry Gaspar and David Patrick Geggus (Bloomington: Indiana University Press, 1997), 204–25; Gainot, "Empire Overseas"; Jürgen Osterhammel, *The Transformation of the World: A Global History of the Nineteenth Century* (Princeton: Princeton University Press, 2014), 400.

7. Curtis M. Geer, *Louisiana Purchase and the Westward Movement* (Philadelphia: G. Barrie, 1904), 205–15 ("You have," 215).

8. For smallpox and cold winter, see *YSF*, 129–31 ("Smallpox," 131); *BMWC*, 13; *RHO*, 59; *BTWC*; and Howard, "Yanktonai Ethnohistory," 41–42. For trade, see *HDWC*.

9. For Loisel and Fort Aux Cèdres, see Regis Loisel to Charles Dehault Delassus, Lieutenant Colonel of the stationary regiment of Louisiana, and Lieutenant Governor of Upper Louisiana, Mar. 20, 1800, in *American State Papers: Documents of the Congress of the United States, in Relation to the Public Lands, From the First Session of the Twenty-Fourth to the Second Session of the Twenty-Fourth Congress, Commencing December 8, 1835, and Ending February 28, 1837*, 8 vols., ed. Asbury Dickins and John W. Forney (Washington, DC: Gales and Seaton, 1861), 8: 117–18; *BLC* 1: 114–15; *TN*, 20–31; *JLCE* 3: 100–102; and Patrick Gass, *A Journal of the Voyages and Travels of a Corps of Discovery* (Philadelphia: Mathew Carey, 1810), 42. For Heney, see *TN*, 73, 80; Meriwether Lewis, "The Ethnology of in Eastern Indians," in *Original Journals of the Lewis and Clark Expedition, 1804–1806*, 8 vols., ed. Reuben Gold Thwaites (New York: Dodd, Mead, 1904–5), 6: 97; *BLC* 1: 114; and Daniel Royot, *Divided Loyalties in a Doomed Empire: The French in the West from New France to the Lewis and Clark Expedition* (Newark: University of Delaware Press, 2007), 157–58. For shod horses, see *YSF*, 131–33. For trade goods, see *TN*, 170–71; and Jacques Clamorgan, "Account of the Indian Trade," *FTUM*, 393–97.

10. *TN*, 106–7 ("old soldier," 106; "as they," 107); *HDWC*.

11. *TN*, 107–8.

12. *TN*, 107 ("founded upon," "reason"). For the competitive nature of Lakota society at this time, see *TN*, 104–6.

13. *TN*, 130–31, 136 ("upon the faith," "Vengeance," "interests," 131; "known," 136).

14. *TN*, 131 ("In this season," "which they openly," "They steal").

15. *TN*, 131–33 ("forming," "assured," "fix," "a ruinous," "surrounded," 131).

16. *TN*, 130, 138 ("a certain," 130; "announce," 138).

17. *TN*, 138–45, 150 ("customary," "seen," 139, "not a fit," 150).

18. For the vilification of the Arikaras, see Roger L. Nichols, "The Arikara Indians and the Missouri River Trade," *Great Plains Quarterly* 2 (Spring 1982), 77–93.

19. *TN*, 164–66 ("A post," 165).

20. *YSF*, 132–37, 144 ("woolly," 134); BKWC, 356–57; *BMWC*, 15; HDWC; BTWC; *TN*, 100. The alliance with the Mandans paved the way for significant cultural and technological exchanges. For example, Lakotas taught the villagers how to craft heavy-soled moccasins. See Fenn, *Encounters in the Heart of the World*, 76.

21. *TN*, 108–11 ("elevated," 109; "urgently," "envious," "who is seen," "fidgety, 111"). Tableau called Black Buffalo "Black Bull," but Black Buffalo is the more common version and therefore used here.

22. *TN*, 99–101, 108–10 ("formerly," 99; "fierce," "very mild," 101; "reduced," 110); *YSF*, 132, 136; White, "Winning of the West," 326. For nomadism, see *JLCE* 3: 399. For Omahas and Poncas, see Wishart, *Unspeakable Sadness*, 25–37; Liberty, Wood, and Irwin, "Omaha," 400; and Brown and Irwin, "Ponca," 418. For a vacated Missouri, see *JLCE* 3: 37–49.

23. *TN*, 104.

24. The emergence of new Lakota oyátes remains conjectural since sources are scarce and fragmentary. In 1804 Tableau listed Oglalas ("Okondanas"), Sicangus ("Sitchanrhou-Titons") Minneconjous ("Minican-hojou"), Hunkpapas ("Hont-papas"), Sans Arcs ("Hitasiptchone"), and Two Kettles ("Waniwacteonillas"), which suggests that these oyátes had begun to develop distinct identities. See *TN*, 104; DeMallie, "Sioux until 1850," 748; and Ostler, *Plains Sioux and U.S. Colonialism*, 22. Lewis and Clark recorded five oyátes—Sicangus, Oglalas, Minneconjous, Two Kettles, and Hunkpapas—as well as the multi-oyáte Saone cluster. See *JLCE* 3: 415–18, 420. The first Hunkpapa and Minneconjou winter counts are from 1798–99 and 1801–2, respectively, suggesting that these oyátes were already splintering off at that time, but the emergence of the Hunkpapas and Sihasapas may have been under way already in the 1760s. See *YSF*, 124, 128; Howard, "Yanktonai Ethnohistory," 34–36; Robinson, "History of the Dakota or Sioux Indians," 2: 26; and Bray, "Before Sitting Bull," 98–102, 106–7. For Minneconjous, see also "A Map of Lewis and Clark's Track, across the Western Portion of North America from the Mississippi to the Pacific Ocean," in *History of the Expedition under the Command of Captains Lewis and Clark*, 2 vols. (Philadelphia: Bradford and Inskeep; and New York: Abm. H. Inskeep, 1814), 1: frontispiece.

25. *YSF*, 128, 130 ("Time people were on prairie," 128; "Time people had no horses," 130). For oral histories, see Walker, *Lakota Society*, 18 ("allies"); and SG, 307–8 ("expanded," "We are seven," 307; "The Mysterious," "other people," 308). It is impossible to pinpoint Lakota oral histories to exact moments in time. Lakotas did not understand time as a linear sequence of events but rather as a cyclical repetition of experiences and processes that do not necessarily have clear beginnings and ends. Time

for Lakotas is not a precisely quantifiable element but rather a set of relationships and qualities that allows an endless repetition of patterns and possibilities. Time for them is a matter of being and belonging, not progression. The emergence of the seven Lakota oyátes may have happened once and it may have happened many times over. The fact that several Lakota winter counts begin at the time when Lakotas lived along the Missouri is significant: they etched on the land stories and experiences that gave Lakotas a moral title on the land. For Lakota and broader Native American concepts of time and belonging, see Walker, *Lakota Society*, 110–15; and Vine Deloria, Jr., *God Is Red: A Native View of Religion* (1973; rprt. Golden, CO: Fulcrum, 2003), 61–75.

26. YSF, 133–37; BTWC ("in praise"); BKWC, 356 ("a wand"); HDWC. The calumet features prominently in the early nineteenth-century winter counts, suggesting intensifying interactions and cooperation among Lakota oyátes and with non-Lakotas. Yanktons maintained a foothold on the upper Missouri where they hunted bison, but they also migrated seasonally east to trap beaver, sojourning along the Minnesota, Des Moines, and James Rivers. See *TN*, 84–85, 102.

27. For the workings of Jefferson's mind, see Joseph J. Ellis, *American Sphinx: The Character of Thomas Jefferson* (New York: Vintage, 1998). For Jefferson's ideal geography, John Seelye, *Beautiful Machine: Rivers and the Republican Plan, 1755–1825* (New York: Oxford University Press, 1991), 199.

28. "The Journal of Patrick Cass, May 14, 1804—September 23, 1806," JLCE 10: 1 ("to pass"). Jefferson had predicted in the mid-1780s that the American takeover of North America would take place within forty years. See Ellis, *American Sphinx*, 97. For preparations, see Gary E. Moulton, "Introduction," *JLCE* 2: 3–71; and Kevin C. Witte, "In the Footsteps of the Third Spanish Expedition: James Mackay and John T. Evans' Impact on the Lewis and Clark Expedition," *Great Plains Quarterly* 26 (Spring 2006), 89–94. Jefferson was well aware that Louisiana was neither empty nor unclaimed but rather a home for numerous Native peoples. Lewis and Clark added much detail to Jefferson's base knowledge at Camp Dubois. The Sioux, however, figured surprisingly little in Clark's Camp Dubois notes considering their political power along the Missouri. See *JLCE* 2: 133–226.

29. For Jefferson's instructions, see Jefferson to Lewis, June 20, 1803, LLCE, 61–66. For maps, see W. Raymond Wood, "The Missouri River Basin on the 1795 Soulard Map: A Cartographic Landmark," *Great Plains Quarterly* (Summer 1996), 183–98; and W. Raymond Wood, *Prologue to Lewis and Clark: The Mackay and Evans Expedition* (Norman: University of Oklahoma Press, 2003), 133–51. For Jefferson's plans for Indian removal, see Nicholas Guyatt, *Bind Us Apart: How Enlightened Americans Invented Racial Segregation* (New York: Basic, 2016), 223–33. Jefferson also contemplated a removal of free blacks and emancipated slaves to Louisiana, but he recoiled at the idea of a black colony in the West, fearing, apparently, southern opposition and revolutionary influences from Saint Domingue. See Guyatt, *Bind Us Apart*, 253–57; and Robert J. Miller, *Native America, Discovered and Conquered: Thomas Jefferson, Lewis & Clark, and Manifest Destiny* (Westport, CT: Praeger, 2006), 90–91. Jefferson's source for Lakota numbers was probably Jacques Clamorgan who had earlier

written that their number "surpasses thirty to forty thousand men." See Jacques Clamorgan, "Account of the Indian Trade," *FTUM*, 401.

30. Jefferson to Lewis, Nov. 16, 1803, and Jan. 22, 1804, *LLCE*, 138–39, 165–66 ("from 30. to 60.000[?]," 138; "Although," 166); James P. Ronda, *Lewis and Clark among the Indians* (Lincoln: University of Nebraska Press, 1984), 12, 29–30.

31. *JLCE* 2: 221 ("a Mr. *Teboux*"); Ernest Staples Osgood, ed., *The Field Notes of Captain William Clark, 1803–1805* (New Haven: Yale University Press, 1964), 21 ("probability"). For gift bundles, see "Bailing Invoice of Indians Sundries for Indians Presents," in *Original Journals*, ed. Thwaites, 6: 270–77 ("foreign Nations," 273); Ronda, *Lewis and Clark among the Indians*, 14–15; and *JLCE* 2: 206–11.

32. Ellis, *American Sphinx*, 247 ("ten"); "Recapitulation of Purchases by The Purveyor for Capt. Lewis," *LLCE*, 93–96; James B. Garry, *Weapons of Lewis and Clark Expedition* (Norman: University of Oklahoma Press, 2012), 18–19, 41–54, 91–104; Donald L. Carr, *Into the Unknown: The Logistics Preparation of the Lewis and Clark Expedition* (Fort Leavenworth, KS: Combat Studies Institute Press, n.d.).

33. Jefferson to Robert Smith, July 13, 1804, Thomas Jefferson Papers, ser. 1, General Correspondence, 1651–1827, Library of Congress, Washington, DC, available at https://www.loc.gov/resource/mtj1.030_1058_1058/.

34. For Jefferson's vision and its contradictions, see Ellis, *American Sphinx*, 247–53; Seelye, *Beautiful Machine*, 193–209; and William F. Willingham and Leonoor Swets Ingraham, eds., *Enlightenment Science in the Pacific Northwest: The Lewis and Clark Expedition* (Portland: Lewis and Clark College, 1984). For Jefferson's views of the government power and the West, see Ellis, *American Sphinx*, 240–70.

35. *JLCE* 2: 438–41, 487–93 ("happy," 441; "I came," 491; "a Spoon ful," 492). For the misunderstanding between Americans and Otoes and Missourias, see Ronda, *Lewis and Clark among the Indians*, 21–23.

36. *TN*, 127–28 ("wearied," 127; "with open," 128).

37. *JLCE* 3: 21–28.

38. *JLCE* 3: 29–30 ("Listen," 29; "we open," 30).

39. *JLCE* 3: 40–104 ("great Smoke," 104).

40. *JLCE* 3: 104–9 ("all things," "were not afraid," 108).

41. *JLCE* 3: 111–13 ("the Grand Chief," 111; "Such," "¼ a glass," "verry fond," 113). For Cruzatte, see Osgood, *Field Notes*, 148. For Tranquil Water, see "Trudeau's [Truteau's] Description," 378.

42. For contemporary accounts that capture the competitive nature of Lakota politics but misinterpret it as lack of order, see Truteau, "Journal," 270–72; and *TN*, 104–16.

43. *JLCE* 3: 111–13 ("as a Cloake," 113); Gass, *Journal of the Voyages and Travels*, 44 ("were poor," "they had"). "Partisan" signifies a war leader or a war-party leader, blotáhuŋka in Lakota. See *JLCE* 3: 114, fn 3.

44. *JLCE* 3: 112–13 ("So personal," "walked," "Spoke," "pointing," "in verry," 112; "warm," 113); SOJ, 138–39 ("must and would," "he had warriers," "their great father," "have them," 139); Gass, *Journal of the Voyages and Travels*, 44 ("his soldiers").

45. SOJ, 139 ("requested," "loaded"); Joseph Whitehouse, "The Original Journal of Pri-

vate Joseph Whitehouse," in *Original Journals of the Lewis and Clark Expedition*, ed. Thwaites, 7: 63; *JLCE* 3: 112–14 ("Brave," "anchored," "I call," 114).

46. *JLCE* 3: 117 ("great anxiety," "generally ill looking"); Whitehouse, "Original Journal," 63.

47. *JLCE* 3: 115–19 ("permited," "put down," 118); SOJ, 140.

48. *JLCE* 3: 116–19 ("great Chief," "to the Same," "Came forward," "Staid," 116; "Sacrifise," 118). Tabeau also recorded the Lakota practice of offering women to traders. See *TN*, 180. As James P. Ronda has observed, where Lewis and Clark gloried in all the new things they encountered along the Missouri, the Natives tried to soften the edges of the new practices and things the Corps presented, trying to fit them into their expectations and worldview. See James P. Ronda, "Exploring the Explorers: Great Plains Peoples and the Lewis and Clark Expedition," in *Lewis and Clark and the Indian Country: The Native American Perspective*, ed. Frederick E. Hoxie and Jay T. Nelson (Urbana: University of Illinois Press, 2007), 119.

49. *JLCE* 3: 121–23 ("take her," 121; "to Stop," 123); Gass, *Journal of the Voyages and Travels*, 45–46.

50. *JLCE* 3: 123–25; Whitehouse, "Original Journal," 7: 65; Gass, *Journal of the Voyages and Travels*, 46; "The Nicholas Biddle Notes," Apr. 1810, *LLCE*, 51 ("you have told us"); SOJ, 142 ("did not mean," "he was mad"); Osgood, *Field Notes*, 151.

51. *JLCE* 3: 124 ("I am verry").

52. Ronda's *Lewis and Clark among the Indians* has a superb chapter on the Corps of Discovery and Lakotas. My interpretation differs from Ronda's in that it places the Lewis and Clark expedition in longer historical and broader geopolitical context. Ronda concludes that the captains' "Sioux talks had failed. The Sioux were no closer to becoming part of the St. Louis trade network" (p. 40). As this and the previous chapter show, Lakotas and especially Sicangus were in 1804 already well integrated in the St. Louis–Missouri Valley trade system and were maneuvering to preserve their central position. Moreover, Lakotas not only dominated much of the upper Missouri by the time of the expedition but actually consolidated their power along the valley even as Lewis and Clark were trying to assert American power and sovereignty.

53. *JLCE* 3: 126–62 ("prepared," 138; "close together," 161; "the Different," "compelled," 163); *TN*, 123–26 ("captains," 124; "tower," "insubordination," 126).

54. *JLCE* 3: 156–57 ("made," "Shot," "Sioux," "to interceed," 156).

55. *JLCE* 3: 161–63, 401 ("great influence," 163; "Though," 401).

56. *JLCE* 3: 159–63 ("Can you," "When you," 159; "his great father," "a Doubt," 162).

57. *TN*, 128–29 ("terror," "leaguing," "the slavery," 128); *JLCE* 3: 169 ("those people").

58. *JLCE* 3: 218–19. Clark penned a description of Mandan trade during the Corps winter sojourn. See *JLCE* 3: 403. See also John C. Ewers, "The Indian Trade of the Upper Missouri before Lewis and Clark: An Interpretation," *Bulletin of the Missouri Historical Society* 10 (1954), 429–46; and Fenn, *Encounters in the Heart of the World*, 179–204.

59. *TN*, 128–34 ("would become," 130; "By this," "closed," 132; "horses," "an eye," 133).

60. The attempt to create satellite villages was thwarted by Lakotas, but the notion was also rejected by the villagers themselves. Ronda's *Lewis and Clark among the Indians*

offers an insightful discussion of the Corps of Discovery, Lakotas, and Arikaras. My interpretation departs from Ronda's conclusion that the Lakota-Arikara relations were essentially peaceful and cooperative, "an uneasy symbiosis" (p. 48). A long-term view of the Lakota-Arikara relations leaves little doubt that the relationship was coercive and asymmetrical. For Arikara views of the Lewis and Clark expedition, see Christopher Steinke, "'Here Is My Country': Too Né's Map of Lewis and Clark in the Great Plains," *William and Mary Quarterly* 71 (Oct. 2014), 589–610.

61. *JLCE* 3: 196–97, 233–34, 243–46, 304–5, 418 ("the Smallpox," "the Sioux," 233; "an army," 243; "join," 304; "Kill everry," 304–5); *TN*, 129–30; François-Antoine Larocque, "Missouri Journal," in *Early Fur Trade*, ed. Wood and Thiessen, 140; SOJ, 181, 184–85 ("Souix Savages," 181).

62. *JLCE* 3: 332 ("the arrival"); *JLCE* 4: 7, 10–11; Lewis to Jefferson, Apr. 7, 1805, *LLCE*, 233 ("well armed," "fired on").

63. For Jefferson's designs for the western Indians and the Corps of Discovery, see Miller, *Native America*, 99–114.

64. *JLCE* 3: 418 ("the vilest"); "The Nicholas Biddle Notes," Apr. 1810, *LLCE*, 517 ("a cunning"); Gass, *Journal of the Voyages and Travels*, 47 ("It appears").

65. Clark's emotional denigration of the Lakotas had a long legacy. In 1952, in an influential assessment of the encounter between the Corps of Discovery and Lakotas, Bernard DeVoto dubbed Lakotas as "bully boys" who relied on "storm trooper tactics" and whom Lewis and Clark had nonetheless chastised and reduced to "women" with skillful and determined diplomacy. It was an uncritical and uncontextualized reading of the Lewis and Clark's journals that diminished Lakotas as historical actors, reducing them to the pervasive stereotype of simple savages easily awed by agents of civilization. See Bernard DeVoto, *The Course of Empire* (1952; rprt. Boston: Houghton Mifflin, 1998), 445, 448 ("storm-trooper," 445; "bully boys," "women," 448). For the impact of Clark's appraisal, see also Craig Howe, "Lewis and Clark among the Tetons: Smoking Out What Really Happened," *Wicazo Sa Review* 19 (Winter 2004), 47–72. My formulation of a Lakota Meridian is inspired by Stephen H. Lekson, *The Chaco Meridian: Centers of Political Power in the Ancient Southwest* (Walnut Creek, CA: Altamira, 1999).

66. Charles McKenzie, "Fourth Expedition to the Missouri," in *Early Fur Trade*, ed. Wood and Thiessen, 282–83; Elliott Coues, ed., *New Light on the Early History of the Greater Northwest: The Manuscript Journals of Alexander Henry and David Thompson, 1799–1814*, 3 vols. (New York: Francis P. Harper, 1897), 1: 375–77 ("The neighing," "posted," 377). For the flag, see Ronda, *Lewis and Clark*, 110–11.

67. Coues, ed., *New Light*, 1: 378.

68. Ibid., 404, 408 ("as the time," "make," 404).

69. McKenzie, "Some account," 230–31 ("a remarkable," 230); Coues, ed., *New Light*, 1: 314 ("in hopes"); François-Antoine Larocque, "Yellowstone Journal," in *Early Fur Trade*, ed. Wood and Thiessen, 198; David Thompson, *David Thompson's Narrative of His Explorations in Western America, 1784–1812*, ed. J. B. Tyrrell (Toronto: Champlain Society, 1916), 214–15, 218–19.

70. Treaty 7 Elders and Tribal Council with Walter Hildebrandt, Dorothy First Rider, and

Sarah Carter, *The True Spirit and Original Intent of Treaty 7* (Montreal and Kingston: McGill-Queen's University Press, 1997), 7. These early nineteenth-century northern operations of Lakotas have received little if any scholarly attention.

71. *JLCE* 8: 300–303. For whooping cough, see Fenn, *Encounters in the Heart of the World*, 247–48.

72. *JLCE* 8: 298–306 ("his Great," 298; "Certainly," 299; "one minit," "kill them," 306). For Sheheke and Jusseaume, see Fenn, *Encounters in the Heart of the World*, 250; Royot, *Divided Loyalties*, 184–87; and *BMWC*, 16.

73. *JLCE* 8: 329–31 ("bad people," "Sufficiently," 330; "put them," 331); *SOJ*, 394–95.

74. Andro Linklater, *An Artist in Treason: The Extraordinary Double Life of General James Wilkinson* (New York: Walker, 2009), 62–237; David O. Stewart, *American Emperor: Aaron' Burr's Challenge to Jefferson's America* (New York: Simon and Shuster, 2011), 65–306; Julie M. Fenster, *Jefferson's America: The President, the Purchase, and the Explorers Who Transformed a Nation* (New York: Crown, 2016), 222–25.

75. B. Parks to William Henry Harrison, May 1805, RG 107, LR, Secretary of War Papers, Main Series, National Archives and Records Service, Washington, DC ("handsome"); Anderson, *Kinsmen of Another Kind*, 78–79. For Dakotas' eastbound push, see Anderson, "Early Dakota Migration," 32–33.

76. Wilkinson to the Secretary of War, July 27, Aug. 10 and 24, 1805, Wilkinson to the Officers of the Territory, Aug. 22, 1805, and Wilkinson to Zebulon M. Pike, July 30, 1805, *TP* 13: 164–72, 182–85, 188–91 ("perilous," Wilkinson to the Officers of the Territory, 188). For Wilkinson, British traders, and McClallan, see Wilkinson to the Secretary of War, Sept. 8, 1805, *TP* 13: 196–200 ("somewhat," 196; "Small," 199); and John Bakeless, *Lewis and Clark: Partners in Discovery* (Mineola, NY: Dover, 1974), 372. Wilkinson was busy. In 1805, urged by the secretary of war, he authorized a trading post built on the lower Missouri Valle near St. Louis. See David Andrew Nichols, *Engines of Empire: Indian Trading Factories and the Negotiation of American Empire* (Chapel Hill: University of North Carolina Press, 2016), 58–59.

77. For Dakota-British relations in the upper Mississippi Valley at the turn of the century, see Anderson, *Kinsmen of Another Kind*, 74–76.

78. White, *Middle Ground*, 512 ("confront," "the White Devil"). For Osages as target of Indigenous warfare, see Secretary of War to Governor Harrison, June 20, 1805, *TP* 7: 296.

79. Jared Orsi, *Citizen Explorer: The Adventurous Life of Zebulon Pike* (New York: Oxford University Press, 2014), 95–103; "General Wilkinson's Proclamation," Aug. 24, 1805, M222, LR, Secretary of War, Unregistered Series, 1789–1860, roll 2, Unregistered File, National Archives and Records Service.

80. Anderson, *Kinsmen of Another Kind*, 79–84; Orsi, *Citizen Explorer*, 104–10 ("many and strong," "large boats," 106); "Treaty with the Sioux, Sept. 23, 1805," *IALT* 2: 1031.

81. "Treaty with the Sioux," Sept. 23, 1805, *IALT* 2: 1031. For a multifaceted discussion of Pike's western exploration, see the various essays in Matthew L. Harris and Jay H. Buckley, ed., *Zebulon Pike, Thomas Jefferson, and the Opening of the American West* (Norman: University of Oklahoma Press, 2012).

82. *JLCE* 3: 418 ("their trade"); Meriwether Lewis to Thomas Jefferson, Sept. 23, 1806,

cited in Paul Russell Cutright, A *History of the Lewis and Clark Journals* (Norman: University of Oklahoma Press, 1976), 16 ("richer"); Wishart, *Fur Trade*, 19–20.

83. Wishart, *Unspeakable Sadness*, 39; Hiram Martin Chittenden, *History of the American Fur Trade of the Far West*, 3 vols. (New York: Francis P. Harper, 1902), 1: 120; "Arrival of Lewis and Clark at St. Louis," *Western World* (Oct. 1, 1806), in James P. Ronda, "St. Louis Welcomes and Toasts the Lewis and Clark Expedition: A Newly Discovered Newspaper Account," in *Explorations into the World of Lewis & Clark*, 3 vols., ed. Robert A. Saindon (Scituate, MA: Digital Scanning, 2003), 3: 1280–81 ("The friend").

84. Larry E. Morris, *The Perilous West: Seven Amazing Explorers and the Founding of the Oregon Trail* (Lanham, MD: Rowman and Littlefield, 2013), 13 ("there was no"). For Jefferson's speech, see Jefferson to the Indian Delegation, Jan. 4, 1806, and Jefferson to the Arikaras, Apr. 11, 1806, *LLCE*, 280–83, 306 ("all gun-men," 306); and *JLCE* 8: 357.

85. For Lisa, see William H. Goetzmann, *Exploration and Empire: The Explorers and Scientist in the Winning of the American West* (1966; rprt. Austin: Texas State Historical Association, 1993), 17–18. For Pryor's party, see Clark to Henry Dearborn, May 18, 1807, RG 107, LR, Secretary of War Papers, Main Series, roll 5. For Sheheke's visit to Washington, see Fenn, *Encounters in the Heart of the World*, 252–57.

86. Nathaniel Pryor to Clark, Oct. 16, 1807, in Elliott Coues, "Letters of William Clark and Nathaniel Pryor," *Annals of Iowa* 1 (1895), 616 ("about half"); *YSF*, 142 ("Many people").

87. *TN*, 151 ("almost"); Pryor to Clark, Oct. 16, 1807, in Coues, "Letters of William Clark and Nathaniel Pryor," 616–19 ("chewing," "the storm," 616; "even," 619). Lakota winter counts for 1806–10 depict repeated conflicts between Lakotas and Arikaras, suggesting that Lakotas were bending the villagers under their will. See *YSF*, 140–47.

88. Wishart, *Fur Trade*, 42–45; *YST*, 144–47; James P. Ronda, *Astoria and Empire* (Lincoln: University of Nebraska Press, 1990), 131.

89. Lewis to Pierre Chouteau, June 8, 1809, *TP* 14: 348–49 ("for the reputation," 348; "exterpate," 349). For Sheheke in St. Louis, see Fenn, *Encounters in the Heart of the World*, 259–60.

90. Chouteau to the Secretary of War, Dec. 14, 1809, and Lewis to Chouteau, June 8, 1809, *TP* 14: 343–51 ("I shall," 345; "Form a body," 349). For Shekeke's death, see Fenn, *Encounters in the Heart of the World*, 265.

91. Ronda, *Astoria and Empire*, 151–54; John Bradbury, *Travels in the Interior of America in the Years 1809, 1810, and 1811* (London: Sherwood, Neely, and Jones, 1817), 82–89; Henry M. Brackenridge, *Views of Louisiana; Together with a Journal of a Voyage up the Missouri River in 1811* (Pittsburgh: Cramer, Spear, and Eichbaum, 1814), 236–38; Nicholas Boilvin to the Secretary of War, Aug. 2, 1809, *TP* 14: 288 ("command").

92. *YSF*, 149–50. For the Mandan and Hidatsa post, see Fenn, *Encounters in the Heart of the World*, 262. For Lakota power in the early 1810s, see Jervis Cutler, *Topographical Description of the State of Ohio, Indian Territory, and Louisiana* (Boston: Charles Williams, 1812), 126–27, 131–32.

93. For a reinterpretation of the War of 1812 as a conflict over still unsettled loyalties rather than between two coherent nations, see Alan Taylor, *The Civil War of 1812: American Citizens, British Subjects, Irish Rebels, and Indian Allies* (New York: Alfred A. Knopf,

2010). For an American assessment of the Dakota Sioux as "the most formidable" of the western tribes that were gravitating toward the British, see Boilvin to the Secretary of War, Feb. 11, 1811, *TP* 14: 439.

94. Some contemporaries, emphasizing the ambitions and actions of American and British agents, thought that the War of 1812 had become a civil war between pro-American Lakotas and pro-British Dakotas. See, for example, Aaron Woodward, "Divide and Conquer: Manuel Lisa Splits the Sioux in the War of 1812," *Heritage of the Great Plains* 46 (Winter 2014), 40–41.

95. Anderson, *Kinsmen of Another Kind*, 84–87 ("abandon," 87); Boilvin to the Secretary of War, Aug. 30, 1810, Feb. 11, 1811, *TP* 14: 410–11, 439 ("shut," 411; "their Old," "His beloved," 439). For the spread of Tecumseh's message, see John Sugden, *Tecumseh: A Life* (New York: Henry Holt, 1997), 145, 149, 189.

96. Sandy Antal, *Wampum Denied: Procter's War of 1812* (Ottawa: Carleton University Press, 1997), 71–74, 251–52; Maurice Blondeau to Benjamin Howard, Apr. 3, 1813, and "Maurice Blondeau's Report of a Council at Fort Madison," Mar. 27, 1813, *TP* 14: 658–62.

97. Anderson, *Kinsmen of Another Kind*, 87–91; Antal, *Wampum Denied*, 261–67, 383–84; Robert S. Allen, *His Majesty's Indian Allies: British Indian Policy in the Defence of Canada, 1774–1815* (Toronto: Dundurn Press, 1992), 123–44 ("Pahinshashawacikiya," 142); La Feuille to Charles Roberts, Feb. 5, 1813, Jos Rolette and others to Roberts, Feb. 10, 1813, Richard Bullock to Henry Proctor, Sept. 25, 1813, *MPHC* 15: 244–46, 391. For St. Louis in the War of 1812, see Julius W. Pratt, "Fur Trade Strategy and the American West Flank in the War of 1812," *American Historical Review* 40 (Jan. 1935), 258–73. For Sioux ambitions, see Blondeau to Howard, Apr. 3, 1813, *TP* 14: 659. For Blue Eyes Woman, see HDWC. From the fall of 1813 onward only small numbers of Dakotas continued to fight with the British. See Robert Malcomson, *Historical Dictionary of the War of the 1812* (Lanham: Scarecrow Press, 2006), 478, 521–22, 526–27.

98. For British activities in the upper Missouri, see Chittenden, *American Fur Trade*, 553–56. For Mandans and Hidatsas, see Fenn, *Encounters in the Heart of the World*, 264–65, 270. For fur trade and Lisa, see *BMWC*, 18; Clark to William H. Crawford, Sept. 20, 1815, *American State Papers* 6, *Indian Affairs*, Vol. 2, 14th Cong., 1st Sess., 76; Clark to the Secretary of War, Dec. 11, 1815, *TP* 15: 95–96; Manuel Lisa to Clark, July 1, 1817, quoted in Aaron Woodward, "Divide and Conquer," *Heritage of the Great Plains* 46 (2013–14), 42–43; and Robinson, "A History of the Dakota or Sioux Indians," 92–93. Lisa traded with Lakotas near the Big Bend and the Arikara villages in the summer of 1812 before retreating downriver to Council Bluffs. See John C. Luttig, *Journal of a Fur-Trading Expedition on the Upper Missouri 1812–1813*, ed. Stella Madeleine Drumm (St. Louis: Missouri Historical Society, 1920), 54–56, 73–82. For larger context, see Jay H. Buckley, *William Clark: Indian Diplomat* (Norman: University of Oklahoma Press, 2008), 89–113.

99. For capturing of wild horses, see YSF, 151–53; and *BMWC*, 19. For mustangs, see Dan Flores, "Bringing Home All the Pretty Horses: The Horse Trade and the Early American West, 1775–1825," *Montana: The Magazine of Western History* 58 (Summer

2008), 3–8. For evolving horse cultures and competition, see Patricia C. Albers, "Symbiosis, Merger, and War: Contrasting Forms of Intertribal Relationships among Historical Plains Indians," in *The Political Economy of North American Indians*, ed. John H. Moore (Norman: University of Oklahoma Press, 1993), 93–132; West, *Contested Plains*, 71–78; Hämäläinen, *Comanche Empire*, 149–50, 182–96; and Moore, *Cheyenne*, 79–93. For Lakota warfare and diplomacy, see YSF, 153–57.

100. *RCF*, 33–34; *HB*, 63–64; *YSF*, 155–57.

101. *YSF*, 157–61; *BKWC*, 357; Ostler, *Lakotas and the Black Hills*, 10–12; Moore, *Cheyenne*, 93.

102. Antal, *Wampum Denied*, 263–309; Taylor, *Civil War of 1812*, 412–44.

103. Clark to Mr. Turcotte, Edward E. Ayer Collection, MS 173, Special Collections, Newberry Library; *IALT* 2: 112–15, 128–30; Anderson, *Kinsmen of Another Kind*, 92–93 ("final extinction," 93).

104. Benjamin O'Fallon to Clark, May 20, 1818, *TP* 15: 407–12 ("ferocious," 409; "be always," "the Great Spirit," "I cannot," "Yes," 410; "Sioux," 411; "we see," 412).

105. Anderson, *Kinsmen of Another Kind*, 103–25; Robinson, "History of the Dakota or Sioux Indians," 2: 155–56. According to the Blue Thunder winter count, starving Dakotas "ate their own" in the winter of 1827–28. See BTWC.

106. Chester L. Guthrie and Leo L. Gerald, "Upper Missouri Agency: An Account of Indian Administration on the Frontier," *Pacific Historical Review* 10 (Mar. 1941), 47–56. For expeditions, see *National Intelligencer*, Oct. 9 and Oct. 15, 1818; Francis Freeling to Charles Bagot, Nov. 2, 1818, Foreign Office FO/133, fols. 225–26, National Archives of United Kingdom; Roger L. Nichols, ed., *The Missouri Expedition, 1818–1820: The Journal of Surgeon John Gale with Related Documents* (Norman: University of Oklahoma Press, 1969); and Cardinal Goodwin, "A Larger View of the Yellowstone Expedition, 1819–1820," *Mississippi Valley Historical Review* 4 (Dec. 1917), 299–313.

107. J. C. Calhoun to Thomas H. Benton, Feb. 18, 1824, In Senate of the United States, Mar. 18, 1824, Graff Collection, MS 1611, Special Collections, Newberry Library; Edwin James, *Account of an Expedition from Pittsburgh to the Rocky Mountains, Performed in the Years 1819 and '20*, 2 vols. (Philadelphia: H. C. Carey and I. Lea, 1823), 1: 180 ("under"); Paul Wilhelm, Duke of Württemberg, *Travels in North America, 1822–1824*, trans. W. Robert Nitske, ed. Savoie Lottinville (Norman: University of Oklahoma Press, 1973), 363 ("the treacherous," "the more"). For American plans, see, for example, Henry Atkinson to the Secretary of War, Nov. 24, 1820, *TP* 15: 674. For settlers, see Aron, *American Confluence*, 158–72. For posts and bison herds, see *YSF*, 159–67, 169, 171–72; *BMWC*, 20; *HDWC*; and *RHO*, 60. One trading post is often recorded in more than one count. The posts listed here seem to have been different ones. Most of them were probably small structures run by a few independent traders.

108. Wishart, *Fur Trade*, 46–56; Chittenden, *American Fur Trade*, 1: 321–27. Along with Sicangus and Oglalas, Saones, Hunkpapas, Sans Arcs, Yanktons, and Yanktonais also traded regularly at Fort Tecumseh. See Anonymous, "Fort Tecumseh and Fort Pierre Journal," *SDHC* 9 (1918), 93–167.

109. *YSF*, 160, 167; *BTWC*; Wilhelm, *Travels in North America*, 391; Wishart, *Unspeak-*

able Sadness, 43. For Crows, see Colin G. Calloway, *Pen and Ink Witchcraft: Treaties and Treaty Making in American Indian History* (New York: Oxford University Press, 2013), 171.

110. "Mr. Pilcher's Answers to Questions Put to Him by the Committee of the Senate on Indian Affairs," Sen. Doc. 56, 18th Cong., 1st Sess., 14; Henry Leavenworth to Atkinson, Oct. 20, 1823, in "Official Correspondence of Leavenworth Expedition of 1823 into South Dakota for the Conquest of the Ree Indians," ed. Doane Robinson, *SDHC* 1 (1902), 210–13; William R. Nester, *The Arikara War: The First Plains Indian War, 1823* (Missoula, MT: Mountain Press, 2001), 137–47, 160–69.

111. For fighting and talks, see Leavenworth to Atkinson, Oct. 20, 1823, in "Official Correspondence of Leavenworth Expedition," ed. Robinson, 214–33; Nester, *Arikara War*, 169–81; *FIT*, 54–57 ("whole pieces," 55); and Dale L. Morgan, *Jedediah Smith and the Opening of the West* (Lincoln: University of Nebraska Press, 1964), 42–77. For Arikaras' flight and sojourn among Mandans, see *TINA* 23: 223–26; and O'Fallon to Atkinson, July 15, 1824, in *The West of William H. Ashley: The International Struggle for the Fur Trade of the Missouri, the Rocky Mountains, and the Columbia, with Explorations beyond the Continental Divide, Recorded in the Diaries and Letters of William H. Ashley and His Contemporaries, 1822–1838*, ed. Dale Lowell Morgan (Denver: Old West Publishing, 1964), 83. For Lakota views, see CPWC; HDWC; *RHO*, 60; and *YSF*, 173–75 ("abundance," 174).

112. For a Lakota view of the Leavenworth expedition, see T. P. Moore to Thomas H. Harvey, Sept. 21, 1846, *ARCIA 1846–47*, 78. For the 1825 expedition and treaties, see H. Atkins to Major General Brown, Nov. 23, 1825, H. Doc. 117, 19th Cong., 1st Sess., 5–16; *IALT* 2: 227–32, 235–36; and John Quincy Adams, *A Treaty between the United States of America and the Teton, Yancton, and Yanctonies Bands of the Sioux Indians*, June 22, 1825, Edward E. Ayer Collection, folio E95.U69, 1825, Special Collections, Newberry Library.

113. *YSF*, 180, 182–83, 185; BTWC; Anonymous, "Fort Tecumseh and Fort Pierre Journal," 107; John Dougherty to John A. Eaton, July 1, 1830, Dougherty to Clark, Nov. 29 and 30, 1832, Clark to Cass, Dec. 10, 1832, and Dougherty to William Clark, Nov. 12, 1834, LROIA, UMA, roll 883; *TINA* 22: 335; J. F. A. Sanford to Clark, July 17, 1832, LROIA, St. Louis Superintendency, roll 750; "Hugh Evans' Journal of Colonel Henry Dodge's Expedition to the Rocky Mountains in 1835," ed. Fred S. Perrine, *Mississippi Valley Historical Review* 14 (Sept. 1927), 203 ("poverty"); "Report on the Expedition of Dragoons, under Colonel Henry Dodge, to the Rocky Mountains in 1835," *American State Papers* 21, *Military Affairs*, Vol. 6, 24th Cong., 1st Sess., 133; Wishart, *Unspeakable Sadness*, 80–81.

114. *YSF*, 193, 196–97 ("killed many," 193); *FIT*, 34; *TINA* 23: 305–6. For Norway rats, see Fenn, *Encounters in the Heart of the World*, 290–94, 305–8.

115. *Journal of the House of Representatives of the United States*, 22d Cong., 1st Sess. (Washington, DC: Duff Green, 1831), 705 ("the destructive"); "Statement of the Fund for Extending the Benefits of Vaccination to the Indian Tribes," *ARCIA 1832*, 174–75; Cass to Dougherty, May 9, 1832, Letters Sent, Office of Indian Affairs, Record Group 75, M21, roll 8, National Archives and Records Service; Dougherty to the Secretary of

War, June 6, 1832, LROIA, UMA, roll 883; Meriwether Martin to Cass, Nov. 27, 1832, LROIA, UPA, roll 750; J. Diane Pearson, "Lewis Cass and the Politics of Disease: The Vaccination Act of 1832," *Wicazo Sa Review* 18 (Fall 2003), 9–22; Andrew C. Isenberg, "An Empire of Remedy: Vaccination, Natives, and Narratives in the Early American West," *Pacific Historical Review* 86 (Feb. 2017), 84–113.

116. William H. Keating, comp., *Narrative of an Expedition to the Source of the St. Peter's River, Lake Winnepeek, Lake of the Woods, &c. &c. Performed in the Year 1823*, 2 vols. (Philadelphia: H. C. Carey and I. Lea, 1824), 1: 380–81; Wilhelm, *Travels in North America*, 366; James, *Account of an Expedition from Pittsburgh to the Rocky Mountains*, 1: 179 ("fine," "very prominent," "more attentive"). See also George Davenport to Pierre Chouteau & Co, Nov. 22, Edward E. Ayer Collection, MS 215, Special Collections, Newberry Library. For Sioux population, see Bray, "Teton Sioux Population History," 176.

117. Wishart, *Fur Trade*, 56; Geo. Catlin, *Letters and Notes on the Manners, Customs, and Condition of the North American Indians*, 2 vols. (London: Egyptian Hall, 1841), 1: 14, 209, 226–31 ("an immense," 209; "*medicine-canoe*," 229).

118. For Fort Pierre and Pierre Dorion, Jr., see *TINA* 22: 317–18, fn 181 ("From the roof," 317; "Indians," "old interpreter," "scalps," 318); Havard, *Histoire des coureurs de bois*, 391; and Larry E. Morris, *The Perilous West: Seven Amazing Explorers and the Founding of the Oregon Trail* (Lanham, MD: Rowman and Littlefield, 2013), 173–74. In 1832 George Catlin counted six to seven hundred Lakota and Yankton tipis around Fort Pierre. See Catlin, *Letters and Notes*, 1: 209.

5. THE CALL OF THE WHITE BUFFALO CALF WOMAN

1. There are numerous variations of the story of the White Buffalo Calf Woman. I have not prioritized any one version, drawing instead from many with the understanding that the story changes and adapts over time with Lakota people. For representative versions, see Richard Erdoes and Alfonso Ortiz, eds., *American Indian Myths and Legends* (New York: Pantheon, 1984), 48–52 ("the circle," 49; "walk," "a living," "earth," 50); *SG*, 283–85 ("With visible," 284), reproduced from *The Sixth Grandfather: Black Elk's Teachings Given to John G. Neihardt*, ed. Raymond J. DeMallie, by permission of the University of Nebraska Press, copyright 1984 by the University of Nebraska Press; Walker, *Lakota Belief and Ritual*, 109–12; Elaine A. Jahner, "Lakota Genesis: The Oral Tradition," in *Sioux Indian Religion: Tradition and Innovation*, ed. Raymond J. DeMallie and Douglas R. Parks (Norman: University of Oklahoma Press, 1987), 51–52; and Joseph Epes Brown, ed., *The Sacred Pipe: Black Elk's Account of the Seven Rites of the Oglala Sioux* (Norman: University of Oklahoma Press, 1953), 3–9. For broader discussions of Lakota religion and ceremonies, see Marla N. Powers, *Oglala Women: Myth, Ritual, and Reality* (Chicago: University of Chicago Press, 1986), 35–52; Raymond J. DeMallie and Robert H. Lavenda, "Wakan: Plains Siouan Concepts Power," in *The Anthropology of Power: Ethnographic Studies from Asia, Oceania, and the New World*, ed. Richard Adams and Raymond D. Fogelson (New York: Academic Press, 1977), 153–65; Rani-Henrik Anderson, *The Lakota Ghost*

Dance of 1890 (Lincoln: University of Nebraska Press, 2008), 48–54; and Albert White Hat, Sr., *Life's Journey—Zuya: Oral Teachings from Rosebud*, comp. and ed. John Cunningham (Salt Lake City: University of Utah Press, 2012).

2. Jahner, "Lakota Genesis," 52 ("There was nothing sacred," "There was no"); Vera Louise Drysdale, *The Gift of the Sacred Pipe* (Norman: University of Oklahoma Press, 1995), 6 ("With this pipe"); Frances Densmore, *Teton Sioux Music and Culture* (1918; rprt. Lincoln: University of Nebraska Press, 1992), 65–66 ("I represent," 65; "When," "By this pipe," 66); DeMallie, "Kinship and Biology in Sioux Culture," 127–30.

3. The key source on the ethnic landscape of the late eighteenth- and early nineteenth-century Black Hills is TN, 154–55. See also HB, 63–64; and Ostler, *Lakotas and the Black Hills*, 10–11. John H. Moore argues that Cheyennes were in full possession of the mountain range still in 1840, while other scholars argue for more layered occupation of the Hills. See Moore, *Cheyenne*, 93; HB, 64; and Ostler, *Lakotas and the Black Hills*, 9–13. Many Native people, including the Poncas, claimed long-term presence at and ownership of the Black Hills. See "Ponca Delegates in the Indian Office," Jan. 5, 1858, in *Ratified Treaty No. 306, Documents Relating to the Negotiation of the Treaty of March, 1858, with the Ponca Indians*, Digital Collections, University of Wisconsin–Madison Libraries, available at http://digicoll.library.wisc.edu/cgi-bin/History/History-idx?type=article&did=History.IT1858no306.i0001&id=History.IT1858no306&isize=M (accessed June 25, 2017). For rock art, see Linea Sundstrom, *Storied Stone: Indian Rock Art in the Black Hills Country* (Norman: University of Oklahoma Press, 2004).

4. TINA 22: 325–27 ("frequently," 327). An 1824 U.S. Army report designated the upper Missouri Valley as the western boundary of the Očhéthi Šakówiŋ. See Keating, comp., *Narrative of an Expedition*, 1: 377. In 1823 the Sicangus sold twenty-seven or twenty-eight horses to a group of American trappers, which suggests that they had more horses than they needed for moving and hunting. See Charles L. Camp, ed., *James Clyman, Frontiersman: The Adventures of a Trapper and Covered-Wagon Emigrant as Told in His Own Reminiscences and Diaries* (San Francisco: California Historical Society, 1928), 23. In the late 1840s at least some Lakota bands were reported to possess, on average, roughly ten horses per lodge. See David M. Potter, ed., *Trail to California: The Overland Journal of Vincent Geiger and Wakeman Bryarly* (New Haven: Yale University Press, 1945), 99.

5. "Mr. Pilcher's Answers," 15; Atkinson, "Expedition up the Missouri," 9; RCF, 39, 115; Camp, ed., *James Clyman*, 22–24; HB, 64–65, 71–72. For the Teton and White Rivers, see Moore, *Cheyenne Nation*, 172–73. For portrayals of Bull Bear, see Parkman, *Oregon Trail*, 127–28, 135; and RCF, 53.

6. For horse nomads' reliance on riparian forests, see Moore, *Cheyenne Nation*, 149–67. See also Philip V. Wells, "Scarp Woodlands, Transported Grassland Soils, and Concept of Grassland Climate in the Great Plains Region," *Science* 148 (Apr. 9, 1965), 246–49. Euro-American visitors often noted the high saline content of the small plains lakes. See, for example, Coues, ed., *New Light on the Early History of the Greater Northwest*, 316.

7. Isenberg, *Destruction of the Bison*, 13–19; Norman J. Rosenberg, "Climate of the

Great Plains Region of the United States," *Great Plains Quarterly* 7 (Winter 1986), 22–32. For the persisting importance of the Missouri Valley for Lakotas, see Andrew Dripps to Harvey, Aug. 27, 1845, *ARCIA 1845*, 543.

8. For the Black Hills climate, the bison, and paintings, see Moore, *Cheyenne Nation*, 69–71, 147; and Saunt, *West of the Revolution*, 158–64. For Lakota presence in the Black Hills, see *YSF*, 184, 188–89, 191; James H. Howard, "Dakota Winter Counts as a Source of Plains History," *Smithsonian Institution Bureau of American Ethnology Bulletin* 173, Anthological Papers, No. 61, 368; and *HB*, 63–64, 72–73. Oglalas and Sicangus had spearheaded the move into the Black Hills and were the first oyátes to settle there.

9. Alan J. Osborn, "Ecological Aspects of Equestrian Adaptations in Aboriginal North America," *American Anthropologist* 85 (Sept. 1983), 568–70; West, *Contested Plains*, 70–71; Pekka Hämäläinen, "The Rise and Fall of Plains Indian Horse Cultures," *Journal of American History* 90 (Dec. 2003), 846–48; *FIT*, 17 ("the wild").

10. George Catlin reported already in 1832 that Lakotas could muster "at least eight to ten thousand warriors, well mounted and well armed." Catlin exaggerated the Lakota numbers, but there is no reason to doubt his remarks on full-fledged equestrianism. See Catlin, *Letters and Notes*, 1: 208. For the benefits of the equestrian shift, see West, *Contested Plains*, 50–52; Dan Flores, *Caprock Canyons: Journeys into the Heart of the Southern Plains* (Austin: University of Texas Press, 1990), 82–83; and Hämäläinen, *Comanche Empire*, 25–30. For plant and animal biomass, see Vaclav Smil, *Energy in Nature and Society: General Energetics of Complex Systems* (Cambridge: Massachusetts Institute of Technology, 2008), 80.

11. Ella Cara Deloria, *Speaking of Indians* (1944; rprt. Lincoln: University of Nebraska Press, 1998), 55; Walker, "Sun Dance," esp. 60–62.

12. For grasses, horses, bison, droughts, and winters, see Osborn, "Ecological Aspects of Equestrian Adaptations in Aboriginal North America," 563–91; Flores, "Bison Ecology and Bison Diplomacy," 481; James E. Sherow, "Workings of the Geodialectic: High Plains Indians and Their Horses in the Region of the Arkansas Valley, 1800–1870," *Environmental Historical Review* 16 (Summer 1992), 69–70; West, *Way to the West*, 21–22; and Moore, *Cheyenne Nation*, 163.

13. For Lakota annual cycle, see Royal B. Hassrick, *The Sioux: Life and Customs of a Warrior Society* (1964; rprt. Norman: University of Oklahoma Press, 1988), 171–76, 202–11; *BMWC*, 26; and "Thirteen Lakota Moons," Akta Lakota Museum and Cultural Center, available at http://aktalakota.stjo.org/site/News2?page=NewsArticle&id=8911 (accessed Feb. 21, 2018). For horse medicines, see Clark Wissler, "Societies and Ceremonial Associations in the Oglala Division of the Teton-Dakota," *Anthropological Papers of the American Museum of Natural History* 11, ed. Clark Wissler (New York: Trustees, 1916), 95–98. For the size of mobile villages, see Catlin, *Letters and Notes*, 1: 44–45.

14. Walker, *Lakota Society*, 28–29, 32–34, 74–84 ("overhauling," 82); Deloria, *Speaking of Indians*, 40–42; *ARC*, 113–15; Raymond J. DeMallie and Robert H. Lavenda, "Wakan: Plains Siouan Concepts of Power," in *The Anthropology of Power: Studies from Asia, Oceania, and the New World*, ed. Richard Adams and Raymond D. Fogelson (New

York: Academic Press, 1977), 154–66; DeMallie, "Kinship and Biology in Sioux Culture," 132–33; Hassrick, *Sioux*, 198–200, 279–87; JoAllyn Archambault, "Sun Dance," *HNAI* 13, Part 2: 984; Arthur Amiotte, "The Lakota Sun Dance: Historical and Contemporary Perspectives," in *Sioux Indian Religion*, ed. Raymond J. DeMallie and Douglas R. Parks (Lincoln: University of Nebraska Press, 1987), 77–79; *FIT*, 13–14; Kingsley M. Bray, "The *Itazipcho* Hoop: Sans Arc Lakota Tribal Organization," *English Westerners' Society* 46, no. 2 (2013), 22–23; Isenberg, *Destruction of the Bison*, 98–99; Chittenden, *American Fur Trade*, 2: 865 ("one continuous"); *SG*, 144; Wissler, "Societies and Ceremonial Associations," 13–14; Jeffrey Ostler, "'They Regard Their Passing as Wakan': Interpreting Western Sioux Explanations for the Disappearance for the Bison's Decline," *Western Historical Quarterly* 30 (Winter 1999), 481–82; Bettelyoun and Waggoner, *With My Own Eyes*, 20–21. For Lakota values, see Walker, *Lakota Society*, 65; and Hassrick, *Sioux*, 32–40.

15. *YSF*, 186–89, 193, 196–97, 200–207; *BMWC*, 23–25, 27; *ARC*, 44–47; Dougherty to William Clark, Nov. 12, 1834, LROIA, UMA, roll 883; Daniel Miller to D. D. Mitchell, Aug. 18, 1843, *ARCIA 1843*, 398–401 ("resolved," 401); Daniel Miller to Harvey, Sept. 16, 1844, *ARCIA 1844*, 139–40; John Miller to Harvey, Sept. 10, 1847, LROIA, Council Bluffs Agency, roll 217; *FIT*, 21–30; Richard White, *The Roots of Dependency: Subsistence, Environment, and Social Change among the Choctaws, Pawnees, and Navajos* (Lincoln: University of Nebraska Press, 1983), 197; Wishart, *Unspeakable Sadness*, 47. Colonel Henry Dodge recorded the decline of bison population near the Pawnee villages as early as in 1833. See "Report on the Expedition of Dragoons," 133.

16. White, "Winning of the West," 334–35; West, *Way to the West*, 61–64; Flores, "Wars over the Buffalo," 159–62; William Medill, "Report," Nov. 30, 1848, *ARCIA 1848*, 389; Francis T. Bryan to J. J. Abert, Feb. 19, 1857, Sen. Ex. Doc. 11, Part 2, 35th Cong., 1st Sess., 461 ("settle"); "Explorations in the Dacota Country in the Year 1855 by Lieut. G. K. Warren, Topographical Engineer of 'Sioux Expedition,'" Sen. Ex. Doc. 76, 34th Cong., 1st Sess., 9. William Clark recognized the phenomenon of the buffer zones in 1806: "I have observed that in the country between the nations which are at war with each other the greatest numbers of wild animals are to be found." See *JLCE* 8: 328. Colonel Richard Irving Dodge identified the plains around the Niobrara and White Rivers a long-standing "debatable land," where Lakotas contested hunting ranges with Pawnees. See R. I. Dodge, *Chicago Inter Ocean*, Aug. 5, 1875, quoted in William Duncan Strong, "An Introduction to Nebraska Archaeology," *Smithsonian Miscellaneous Collections* 93 (Washington, DC: Smithsonian Institution, 1935), 37.

17. Bray, "Teton Sioux," 174; *YSF*, 168–202.

18. Joshua Pilcher to Clark, July 18, 1835, LROIA, UMA, roll 883; Mitchell to W. N. Fulkerson, June 10, 1836, Clark to Elbert Herring, July 13, 1836, and Pilcher to Clark, Sept. 15, 1838, LROIA, UMA, roll 884 ("keen," "a state," Mitchell to Fulkerson); *FIT*, 36; *DWC*, 14–15; BTWC; De Smet, *Life*, 1: 189–90; *HB*, 72, 77; Atkinson, "Expedition up the Missouri," 8–9; Ostler, *Plains Sioux and U.S. Colonialism*, 24.

19. Wishart, *Unspeakable Sadness*, 75–77 ("they would," 76); Dougherty to Thomas McKenney, Sept. 14, 1827, LROIA, UMA, roll 883 ("prowl"); Pilcher to Clark, Sept. 15,

1838, LROIA, UMA, roll 884; Harvey to Medill, Sept. 5, 1846, *ARCIA 1846*, 72 ("exceedingly").

20. Joseph N. Nicollet, *Joseph N. Nicollet on the Plains and Prairies: The Expeditions of 1838–1839 with Journals, Letters, and Notes on the Dakota Indians*, ed. and trans. Edmund C. Bray and Martha Coleman Bray (St. Paul: Minnesota Historical Society, 1976), 147, 261; James H. Howard, *The Ponca Tribe, Smithsonian Institution Bureau of American Ethnology Bulletin* 195 (Washington, DC: GPO, 1965), 28–29; Wishart, *Unspeakable Sadness*, 83–84; Ostler, *Plains Sioux and U.S. Colonialism*, 25. For a later observation of the Wazhazhas, see G. K. Warren, *Preliminary Report of Explorations in Nebraska and Dakota, in the Years 1855–'56–'57* (Washington, DC: GOP, 1875), 48.

21. White, *Roots of Dependency*, 201–5; Wishart, *Unspeakable Sadness*, 75, 80–81; Fred W. Voget, "Crow," *HNAI* 13, Part 1: 714; *YSF*, 187–97.

22. William Laidlaw to Jonathan L. Bean, Sept. 21, 1831, Fort Tecumseh and Fort Pierre Letterbooks, 1830–32, Chouteau Collection, Missouri Historical Society, St. Louis; *YSF*, 183–85, 188, 190; Charles E. Hanson, Jr., and Veronica Sue Walters, "The Early Fur Trade in Northwestern Nebraska," 1985 Nebraska State Historical Society reprint of *Nebraska History* 57 (Fall 1976), 4. For Lakota robes, see Dale R. Morgan and Eleanor Towles Harris, eds., *The Rocky Mountain Journals of William Marshall Anderson: The West in 1834* (San Marino, CA: Huntington Library, 1967), 179.

23. David Lavender, *Fort Laramie and the Changing Frontier* (1985), 18–34; LeRoy R. Hafen and Francis Marion Young, *Fort Laramie and the Pageant of the West, 1834–1890* (1938; rprt. Lincoln: University of Nebraska Press, 1984), 24–31; Wishart, *Fur Trade*, 62–63; White, "Winning of the West," 334; *HB*, 75.

24. Joseph Bissonette to John Sybille and David Adams, July 25, 1843, and Bissonette to Sibille Adams & Co, Dec. 19, 1843, in *The David Adams Journals*, ed. Charles E. Hanson, Jr. (Chadron, NE: Museum of the Fur Trade, 1994), 48–49, 55–56; Kingsley Bray, "The Lakotas and the Buffalo Robe Trade: The Season of 1838–1839," *Museum of the Fur Trade Quarterly* 49 (Spring 2013), 3–12; Wishart, *Fur Trade*, 72–74. For Lakota relations with and attitudes toward the Americans, see John B. Dunbar to David Greene, May 5, 1836, *Collections of the Kansas State Historical Society* 14 (1915–18) (Topeka: Kansas State Printing Plant, 1918), 623 ("said"); and Pilcher to Clark, Sept. 15, 1838, LROIA, UMA, roll 884. The Lakota share of the total robe production is difficult to estimate. Forks of the Cheyenne, a Lakota-Cheyenne post, collected 4,360 robes in 1829–30 when the total number of robes shipped down the Missouri was in the low thousands. In 1831–32 Fort Pierre, largely a Lakota post, collected 13,000 robes, which seem to have counted for at least one-third of the total plains production; Father De Smet estimated the total American Fur Trade Company traffic at 45,000 robes in 1839 by which time the total output was considerably larger than six years earlier. For estimates, see Wishart, *Fur Trade*, 58–59; De Smet, *Life*, 1: 179; and Parkman, *Oregon Trail*, 354, fn 133. The revolutionary impact of steamboats was captured by the president of the American Fur Company Ramsay Crooks who congratulated Pierre Chouteau for pioneering the new technology, "You have brought the Falls

of the Missouri as near as comparatively, as was the River Platte in my younger days." See Ramsay Crooks to Pierre Chouteau, Jr., Nov. 16, 1832, Fort Tecumseh and Fort Pierre Letterbooks.

25. Wishart, *Unspeakable Sadness*, 45–48; Daniel Miller to Mitchell, Aug. 18, 1843, *ARCIA 1843*, 400; Daniel Miller to Harvey, Sept. 16, 1844, *ARCIA 1844*, 138–42; Dunbar, "The Pawnee Indians: Their Habits and Customs," *Magazine of American History* 5 (Nov. 1880), 321–22.

26. For the upper Missouri fur trade as a system, see Wishart, *Fur Trade*, 79–109. My formulation draws and builds on Wishart's conceptualization by highlighting the system's two-partite logic around steam- and horsepower and St. Louis merchant elite and Lakotas.

27. Anderson, *Kinsmen of Another Kind*, 130–76; Patricia C. Albers, "Santee," *HNAI* 13, Part 2: 769–70; MBWC.

28. Catlin, *Letters and Notes*, 1: 16, 118, 249 ("melting," "domestic," 16; "Amongst," 118; "in the heart," 249). For the contradictions in Catlin's views about Native Americans, see John Hausdoerffer, *Catlin's Lament: Indians, Manifest Destiny, and the Ethics of Nature* (Lawrence: University Press of Kansas, 2009).

29. Deloria, *Speaking of Indians*, 39–41; Powers, *Oglala Women*, 73–74, 81–87; Luther Standing Bear, *My People the Sioux*, ed. E. A. Brininstool (1928; rprt. Lincoln: University of Nebraska Press, 1975), 13 ("Our home"); Emil Her Many Horses, "Remembering Lakota Ways," in *A Song for the Horse Nation: Horses in Native American Cultures*, ed. George P. Horse Capture and Emil Her Many Horses (Washington, DC: National Museum of the American Indian, Smithsonian Institution, 2006), 11–13; EDA, Ethnography, box 1, The Dakota Way of Life, ch. 12, Relatives and Social Kinship; Deloria, *Speaking of Indians*, 38–39; Hassrick, *Sioux*, 214–15 ("women's arms," 215); Robert M. Utley, *The Lance and the Shield: The Life and Times of Sitting Bull* (New York: Henry Holt, 1993), 70, 252; Barbara Tedlock, "The Clown's Way," in *Teachings from the American Earth: Indian Religion and Philosophy*, ed. Dennis Tedlock and Barbara Tedlock (New York: Liveright, 1975), 105–8; Wissler, "Societies and Ceremonial Associations," 75–80; Walker, *Lakota Society*, 43, 56; Beckwith, "Mythology of the Oglala Dakota," 346–47, 419; BKWC, 352; Powers, *Oglala Women*, 73–74. That men consulted women for political matters and decisions is a theme that consistently emerged in my discussions with Lakota elders and scholars.

30. Catlin, *Letters and Notes*, 1: 118–19, 249. For Lakota women's work and responsibilities, see Jeannette Mirsky, "The Dakota," in *Cooperation and Competition among Primitive Peoples*, ed. Margaret Mead (New York: McGraw-Hill, 1937), 385; Gibbon, *Sioux*, 72–75; and Raymond J. DeMallie, "Teton," *HNAI* 13, Part 2: 808. For robe processing, see Edwin Thompson Denig, "Indian Tribes of the Upper Missouri," ed. J. N. B. Hewitt, *Forty-Sixth Annual Report of the Bureau of American Ethnology to the Secretary of the Smithsonian Institution, 1928–1929* (Washington, DC, 1930), 541. For robe-gun exchange rate, see Rudolph Friederich Kurz, *Journal of Rudolph Friederich Kurz: An Account of His Experiences among Fur Traders and American Indians on the*

Mississippi and the Upper Missouri Rivers during the Years 1846 to 1852, ed. J. N. B. Hewitt (Washington, DC: GPO, 1937), 176.

31. Walker, *Lakota Society*, 50; Raymond J. DeMallie, "Male and Female in Traditional Lakota Culture," in *The Hidden Half: Studies of Plains Indian Women*, ed. Patricia C. Albers and Beatrice Medicine (Washington, DC: University Press of America, 1983), 243–45; Mirsky, "Dakota," 417; Isenberg, *Destruction of the Bison*, 99–101; *TINA* 22: 327 ("wealthy"); ARC, 78–80; James C. Olson, *Red Cloud and the Sioux Problem* (Lincoln: University of Nebraska Press, 1965), 23.

32. Catlin, *Letters and Notes*, 1: 118–19 ("the brave"). For women's social position, privileges, and roles, see Deloria, *Speaking of Indians*, 39–41; Walker, *Lakota Society*, 40–43; Mirsky, "Dakota," 384–85, 410–11; Gibbon, *Sioux*, 74; and Catherine Price, *The Oglala People: A Political History, 1841–1879* (Lincoln: University of Nebraska Press, 1996), 18–19. For a broader view of the negative impact of the fur trade on Plains Indian women, see Alan M. Klein, "The Plains Truth: The Impact on Colonialism on Indian Women," *Dialectical Anthropology* 7 (Feb. 1983), 299–313.

33. Mirsky, "Dakota," 385–86; Hassrick, *Sioux*, 132; Isenberg, *Destruction of the Bison*, 101–3; Walker, *Lakota Society*, 62–63; Walker, *Lakota Belief and Ritual*, 231–32; DeMallie, "Teton," 808–9; Utley, *Lance and the Shield*, 20; Clark Wissler, "Societies and Ceremonial Associations in the Oglala Division of the Teton-Dakota," *Anthropological Papers of the American Museum of Natural History* 11, Part 1 (New York: American Museum of Natural History, 1912), 76–77; DeMallie, "Male and Female in Traditional Lakota Culture," 253. Captives were considered Lakotas when they learned the language and proper behavior. See Walker, *Lakota Society*, 55. For an overview of the negative effects of equestrianism on Plains Indian women, see Margot Liberty, "Hell Came with Horses: Plains Indian Women in the Equestrian Era," *Montana: The Magazine of Western History* 32 (Summer 1982), 10–19.

34. DeMallie, "Male and Female in Traditional Lakota Culture," 251–52; Isenberg, *Destruction of the Bison*, 101. For a rare example of a failed courtship by a middling young suitor, see Richard Irving Dodge, *Our Wild Indians: Thirty-Three Years of Personal Experience among the Red Men of the Great West* (Hartford, CT: A. D. Worthington, 1883), 321–22.

35. They Fear Even His Horses is often mistranslated as Man Afraid of His Horses.

36. For examples that cover the period from the 1830s into the 1860s, see "Songs by Sitting Bull," box 104, folder 18, CC; ARC, 39, 107–11; Joseph M. Marshall III, *The Journey of Crazy Horse: A Lakota History* (New York: Viking Penguin, 2004), 14–22, 59, 139; Bray, *Crazy Horse*, 5–13, 24–26, 121; Kingsley M. Bray, "Lone Horn's Peace: A New View of Sioux-Crow Relations, 1851–1857," *Nebraska History* 66 (Spring 1985), 30; RCF, 34, 40, 87; Francis Parkman, *The Oregon Trail*, ed. Ottis B. Sperlin (New York: Longmans, Green, 1910), 127, 129, 132–38; Standing Bear, *My People the Sioux*, 11–12; Thaddeus A. Culbertson, *Journal of an Expedition to the Mauvaises Terres and the Upper Missouri in 1850*, ed. John Francis McDermott (Washington, DC: GPO, 1952), 78; Joseph Agonito, "Young Man Afraid of His Horses: The Reservation Years," *Nebraska History* 79 (Fall 1998), 116; Olson, *Red Cloud and the Sioux Problem*, 16–

24; Utley, *Lance and the Shield*, 6–7, 10–22, 28–29, 100; Stanley Vestal, *Warpath: The True Story of the Fighting Sioux Told in a Biography of Chief White Bull* (1934; rprt. Lincoln: University of Nebraska Press, 1984), 3–49; Gary C. Anderson, *Sitting Bull and the Paradox of Lakota Nationhood* (New York: Pearson/Longman, 2007), 37–63; and Robert W. Larson, *Gall: Lakota War Chief* (Norman: University of Oklahoma Press, 2007), 16. See also Walker, *Lakota Belief and Ritual*, 74, 193–239; Walker, *Lakota Society*, 53–55; and Gibbon, *Sioux*, 103. For raising of boys, see DeMallie, "Male and Female in Traditional Lakota Culture," 247–50.

37. *YSF*, 196–97; *FIT*, 18 ("the successful").

38. *YSF*, 198, 200–201 ("went," 198; "on the ice," 201); Rufus B. Sage, *Rocky Mountain Life: or, Startling Scenes and Perilous Adventures in the Far West during an Expedition of Three Years* (Boston: Thayer and Eldridge, 1859), 196; *RCF*, 49; John Dougherty, "Report," *ARCIA 1838*, 503–4. For Red Cloud, see *ARC*, 34–37.

39. For smallpox, see Pilcher to William Clark, Feb. 27, 1838, LROIA, UMA ("one great grave yard"); Dunbar to Greene, June 8, 1838, *Collections of the Kansas Historical Society*, vol. 14, ed. William E. Connelley (Topeka: Kansas State Printing Plant, 1918), 630–32; White, *Roots of Dependence*, 155; and Fenn, *Encounters in the Heart of the World*, 316–25. For Pawnees, see Dunbar, "Journal," May 27, 1835, *Collections of the Kansas State Historical Society* 14, 602; and Dunbar, "Pawnee Indians," 331, 334 ("position," 334). The commissioner of Indian affairs estimated that 17,200 Sioux, Mandans, Hidatsas, Arikaras, Assiniboines, and Blackfeet died during the 1837–38 epidemic, which does not include the thousands of Pawnees, Omahas, Otoes, Poncas, Crees, and others who perished. See T. Hartley Crawford to J. R. Poinsett, Nov. 25, 1838, *ARCIA 1838*, 453; Fenn, *Encounters in the Heart of the World*, 323, 325; Wishart, *Unspeakable Sadness*, 77–81; and *FIT*, 125. Several winter counts reported smallpox in 1837–38, suggesting that, along with Oglalas, some Sicangu, Hunkpapa, and Yanktonai bands contracted the disease. See *YSF*, 202–3; and MBWC.

40. Dougherty, "Report," *ARCIA 1838*, 504 ("They think," "The day"); *YSF*, 207. For positive reports on Pawnee condition, see Dunbar to J. V. Hamilton, Oct. 19, 1839, RG 4302, MS 0480, Correspondence, box 1, folder 1, NSHS; and "Manuscript of John Dunbar, Missionary to the Indians," John Dunbar, RG 4302, MS 0480, Manuscripts, folder 4, NSHS. For the attack, see James Henry Carleton, *The Prairie Logbooks: Dragoon Campaigns to the Pawnee Villages in 1844, and to the Rocky Mountains in 1845*, ed. Louis Pelzer (Chicago: Caxton Club, 1943), 108–9 ("returned," 108); Dunbar to Greene, July 10 and Nov. 14, 1843, *Collections of the Kansas Historical Society* 14, 656–59; Daniel Miller to Mitchell, Aug. 18, 1843, *ARCIA 1843*, 402–3 ("declared"); "Manuscript by Samuel Allis, Missionary and Teacher to the Indians," RG 2628, box 1, folder 1, NSHS; and Wishart, *Unspeakable Sadness*, 91–92. For horses in Pawnee villages, see "Report on the Expedition of Dragoons," 133.

41. The story of the stolen sacred arrows comes from Pawnee oral histories. See George A. Dorsey, "How the Pawnee Captured the Cheyenne Medicine Arrows," *American Anthropologist* 5 (Oct. 1903), 644–58. For the Lakota capture of the arrows, see *YSF*, 214–15 ("In the fight," 214); and *BMWC*, 27. For Sweet Medicine and sacred arrows, see Moore, *Cheyenne Nation*, 102–5.

42. Harvey to Medill, Oct. 29, 1847, *ARCIA 1847–1848*, 102–3; (?) Hamilton to T. H. Henry, July 5, 1844, and Andrew Drips to Harvey, Apr. 6, 1845, LROIA, UMA, roll 884; White, *Roots of Dependency*, 201–9; Wishart, *Unspeakable Sadness*, 92–93.

43. Harvey to Crawford, Sept. 10, 1845, *ARCIA 1845*, 537; Dunbar to Greene, June 30 and Oct. 12, 1846, *Collections of the Kansas Historical Society* 14, 683–89; Harvey to Medill, Oct. 29, 1847, *ARCIA 1847–48*, 101 ("everything"); *Daily Missouri Republican*, May 28, 1847; John Miller to Harvey, Sept. 15, 1848, *ARCIA 1848*, 466; Wishart, *Unspeakable Sadness*, 92–93; George E. Hyde, *The Pawnee Indians* (1951; rprt. Norman: University of Oklahoma Press, 1974), 226–29.

44. Daniel Miller to D. D. Mitchell, July 1, 1843, *ARCIA 1843*, 406; Harvey to Crawford, Oct. 8, 1844, *ARCIA, 1844–1845*, 136; Richard S. Elliott to Crawford, July 24, 1845, *ARCIA 1845*, 553; Harvey to Medill, Oct. 29, 1847, *ARCIA 1846*, 100–101. For drought, see Connie A. Woodhouse, Jeffrey J. Lukas, and Peter M. Brown, "Drought in the Western Great Plains, 1845–1845," *American Meteorological Society* (Oct. 2002), 1485–93; and West, *Way to the West*, 79–81. For winter counts, see *YSF*, 217–18 ("much feasting," 217; "immense," 218).

45. Wishart, *Unspeakable Sadness*, 79, 86–88; John Miller to Harvey, Sept. 10, 1847, LROIA, Council Bluffs Agency, roll 217; G. C. Matlock to Harvey, Sept. 25, 1848, *ARCIA 1848*, 469 ("will soon"); Harvey to Crawford, Sept. 10, 1845, *ARCIA 1845*, 532–33; De Smet, *Life*, 2: 628; Kurz, *Journal of Rudolph Friederich Kurz*, 66.

46. Wishart, *Unspeakable Sadness*, 88–90; John Miller to Harvey, Sept. 10, 1847, LROIA, Council Bluffs Agency, roll 217; John E. Barrow to Mitchell, Oct. 1, 1849, *ARCIA 1849–50*, 140.

47. John Miller to Harvey, Sept. 10, 1847, LROIA, Council Bluffs Agency, roll 217 ("determined"). For robes and tongues, see De Smet, *Life*, 2: 635; and Matlock to Harvey, Sept. 25, *ARCIA 1848*, 468. Fort Pierre, predominantly a Sioux post, took in 75,000 robes in 1849, a year when 110,000 robes were again collected from the upper Missouri, suggesting an overwhelming Sioux dominance of the trade. See Alexander Ramsey, "Report," Oct. 13, 1849, *ARCIA 1849*, 85; and William S. Hatton to Mitchell, Oct. 5, 1849, *ARCIA 1849*, 135.

48. Fulkerson to William Clark, Oct. 1, 1837, and Pilcher to Clark, Sept. 15, 1838, LROIA, UMA, roll 884 ("will cease," Pilcher to Clark); Fenn, *Encounters in the Heart of the World*, 323–35; Stewart, "Hidatsa," 331; Parks, "Arikara," 367; Bettelyoun and Waggoner, *With My Own Eyes*, 45; Annie Heloise Abel, ed., *Chardon's Fort Clark Journal, 1834–1839* (Pierre, SD: Lawrence K. Fox, 1932), 181 ("I beheld").

49. Abel, ed., *Chardon's Fort Clark Journal*, 181 ("20 Skins").

50. For Fort Berthold, see G. Hubert Smith, *Like-a-Fishhook Village and Fort Berthold, Garrison Reservoir North Dakota* (Washington, DC: National Park Service, 1972), 5–7.

51. *FIT*, 15, 28–29 ("extremely fond," 29); Bray, "Teton Sioux," 182–83.

52. Nicollet, *Joseph N. Nicollet*, 259–62.

53. Describing the situation in the 1830s, Denig noted how Lakotas, Yanktons, and Yanktonais were "fond of corn" and "in want of provisions." See *FIT*, 35. For Black Hills ecology, see Douglas B. Bamforth, *Ecology and Human Organization on the Great*

Plains (New York: Plenum Press, 1988), 7–8; 112–13; and George R. Hoffman and Robert R. Alexander, *Forest Vegetation of the Black Hills National Forest of South Dakota and Wyoming: A Habitat Type Classification*, Research Paper RM, 276, June 1987 (Fort Collins, CO: U.S. Dept. of Agriculture, Forest Service, Rocky Mountain Forest and Range Experiment Station, 1987), available at https://www.biodiversity library.org/item/177483#page/53/mode/1up (accessed Jan. 23, 2017).

54. For the cultural centrality and religious significance of the Black Hills for Lakota people, see Witkin-New Holy, "Heart of Everything That Is," 317–23; Charlotte Black Elk, "Children of the Four Relations around the Heart of Everything That Is," in *Lakota Star Knowledge: Studies in Lakota Stellar Theology*, ed. Ronald Goodman (Rosebud, SD: Sinte Gleska University, 1992), 44–45; Mario Gonzales, "The Black Hills: The Sacred Land of the Lakota and Tsistsistas," *Cultural Survival Quarterly* 19 (Jan. 1996), 63–69; and Sundstrom, *Storied Stone*, 42–43, 81–83 ("visible," 83). For bison numbers, see Isenberg, *Destruction of the Bison*, 23–28.

55. For the Sun Dance and the social dynamics around it, see Ella Deloria, "The Sun Dance of the Oglala Sioux," *Journal of American Folklore* 42 (Oct.–Dec. 1929), 354–413; Walker, *Lakota Belief and Ritual*, 176–91; James R. Walker, "The Sun Dance and Other Ceremonies of the Oglala Division of the Teton Dakota," *Anthropological Papers of the American Museum of Natural History* 16, Part 2: 94–121; Ostler, *Lakotas and the Black Hills*, 17–19; and Bray, "Lakotas and the Buffalo Robe Trade," 11.

56. DeMallie and Parks, *Sioux Indian Religion*, 34–42: HB, 76–77.

57. YSF, 189–91.

58. For animal bounty, battles, and raids, see BKWC, 359–60 ("Black-face," 360); and FIT, 21, 139–41, 144, 154.

59. FIT, 149, 154–55 ("cunning," 149; "The warrior," 154–55); Fulkerson to Clark, Oct. 1, 1837, and Pilcher to Clark, Sept. 15, 1838, LROIA, UMA, roll 884; Wishart, *Fur Trade*, 30–31, 57–58; Voget, "Crow," 697.

60. YSF, 197.

61. FIT, 21 ("the Crows," "exterminating").

62. YSF, 204–13 ("carried the pipe," 204; "killed an entire village," 205; "killed," 206; "killed a Crow," 207; "Sitting-Bear," 208; "30 spotted," 209; "a feast," "Lone Feather," 212; "Killed four," 213); BKWC, 360. See also HDWC; RCF, 51–52; and FIT, 19–20.

63. For an early high-yield raid, see ARC, 48–54.

64. RCF, 40, 45–57; ARC, 67–70; Parkman, *Oregon Trail*, 136–37; Price, *Oglala People*, 23–26; Olson, *Red Cloud and the Sioux Problem*, 20–22; Bray, "Teton Sioux," 181; YSF, 210; Mario Gonzalez and Elizabeth Cook-Lynn, *The Politics of Hallowed Ground: Wounded Knee and the Struggle for Indian Sovereignty* (Urbana: University of Chicago Press, 1999), 30. For liquor trade, see Hafen and Young, *Fort Laramie*, 71–77. Oglalas were introduced to whiskey in the winter of 1821–22 when they "had all the mni wakhan (spirit water or whiskey) they could drink." See YSF, 170. Red Cloud's father was said to have died of alcoholism, around 1825. See Hyde, RCF, 36.

65. For the Oglala range and population, see FIT, 19–21; RCF, 57–58; and Bray, "Teton Sioux," 174, 181. Overland travel, which the contemporaries identified as the main culprit of bison decline in the central Great Plains, was not yet as significant as market

hunting and drought in depressing bison numbers. See Isenberg, *Destruction of the Bison*, 107–10.

66. *YSF*, 216–18 ("said his prayers," 216); Kingsley M. Bray, *Crazy Horse: A Lakota Life* (Norman: University of Oklahoma Press, 2006), 8–10.

67. Parkman, *Oregon Trail*, 94–213 ("the whole," 106; "within," "five," 107; "horsemen," 130; "as if," "a miniature," 131; "farther," 181; "immense," 201; "rich," 202; "gigantic," 204).

68. Parkman, *Oregon Trail*, 175 ("Superb"). For a slightly different interpretation of the 1846 expedition, see White, "Winning of the West," 335–36.

69. *FIT*, 204 ("Situated"); Parkman, *Oregon Trail*, 113 ("blew").

70. *YSF*, 221; "War Record of Chief Makes Room," box 104, folder 12, pp. 1–2, CC; Ray, *Indians in the Fur Trade*, 104–7, 156–70; *FIT*, 68–72.

71. *FIT*, 89–90 ("In a few," 89–90). See also Charles Larpenteur, *Forty Years a Fur Trader on the Upper Missouri: The Personal Narrative of Charles Larpenteur, 1833–1872*, ed. Elliott Coues, 2 vols. (New York: Francis P. Harper, 1898), 212.

72. *FIT*, 24–25 ("a point," "Here," 25). The 1847 Assiniboine attack may have also been prompted by an earlier battle. In 1846 Parkman learned of a recent clash between Lakotas and Assiniboines on the upper Missouri: Lakotas were said to have "exterminated" an entire village. See Parkman, *Oregon Trail*, 115.

73. *FIT*, 23 ("seldom"). Denig wrote about Minneconjous, but his portrayal is applicable, with minor adjustments, to Hunkpapas, Sans Arcs, and Sishapas as well. See, for example, Melfine Fox Everett, "Why the Mandans Fought for Custer and the Seventh Cavalry," *LBR*, 135; and Nicollet, *Joseph N. Nicollet*, 261. For Sitting Bull, see Utley, *Lance and the Shield*, 14–37; Anderson, *Sitting Bull and the Paradox of Lakota Nationhood*, 61–71; and "The Young Eagle Statement," *IVCF*, 130. For Gall, see Larson, *Gall*, 35, 236.

74. For Lakota territory, see Pilcher to Clark, Sept. 15, 1838, LROIA, UMA, roll 884; and *FIT*, 3–14. Denig described the situation in the early 1850s, but the Lakota domain had assumed its scope several years earlier. For Lakota population, see Bray, "Teton Sioux Population," 176. For Comanches, see Hämäläinen, *Comanche Empire*, 292–303.

75. Walker, *Lakota Belief and Ritual*, 115 ("are more").

76. For adoption, see Walker, *Lakota Belief and Ritual*, 200–203.

77. Walker, *Lakota Belief and Ritual*, 82–83 ("The spirit," 83); DeMallie, "Kinship and Biology in Sioux Culture," 29.

78. For the political organization of thióšpayes, see *SG*, 320–21; Wissler, "Societies and Ceremonial Associations," 7–11, 36–41; *STF*, 26–27; Mirsky, "Dakota," 390–92; DeMallie, "Teton," 801–2; DeMallie, "Sioux until 1850," 734–35; Price, *Oglala People*, 2, 6–17; *ARC*, 150; and EDA, Dakota Ethnography, box 3, Notes on Law, Election of Indian Councilors. While still useful, Wissler's description misses the dynamic and flexible nature of Lakota political organization, assuming mistakenly, for example, that itháŋčhaŋs were elected in office for life. For kinship as the foundation of society, see Walker, *Lakota Society*, 15–18; and DeMallie, "Kinship and Biology in Sioux Culture," 125–43.

79. For tribal circle or the sacred hoop, see Walker, *Lakota Society*, 13–14. For načás, see EDA, Dakota Ethnography, box 3, Notes on Law, Election of Indian Councilors; DeMallie, "Teton," 802. Lakotas did not come into sustained contact with Arapahos until the late 1820s and 1830s, which suggests that the borrowing of "načá" happened around that time. For references to powerful, well-established tribal or multiband leaders in the 1830s and 1840s, see *FIT*, 20–21, 23–26, 28–29; Culbertson, *Journal of an Expedition to the Mauvaises Terres*, 136; and Parkman, *Oregon Trail*, 131–36.

80. Powers, *Oglala Women*, 48–51, 64; Walker, *Lakota Belief and Ritual*, 195–240; Nicollet, *Joseph N. Nicollet*, 271–72; DeMallie, "Teton," 807; Price, *Oglala People*, 4–5. Huŋká ceremony is often portrayed as a male institution, but it was available to women as well. See Bettelyoun and Waggoner, *With My Own Eyes*, 22.

81. The history of shirt wearers is indefinite, but many scholars think the institution was well established by the midcentury. Among the Oglalas, the shirt wearer institution dates back in the early decades of the nineteenth century. See Marshall, *Journey of Crazy Horse*, 138; Bray, "The Oglala Lakota," 153, fn 13; and Kingsley M. Bray, "Lakota Statesmen and the Horse Creek Treaty of 1851," *Nebraska History* 98 (Fall 2017), 159. There are also differing views on whether shirt wearers' authority extended beyond their respective oyátes. For a range of views, see Wissler, "Societies and Ceremonial Associations," 7, 39–40; Vestal, *Warpath*, 51; DeMallie, "Teton," 802; Price, *Oglala People*, 12–13, 17; Hassrick, *Sioux*, 26–29; SG, 300; and Curtis, *North American Indian*, 3: 12. George F. Hyde's notes that the Sicangus had four "war shirt wearers." See STF, 26. Oglalas may have chosen their first four shirt wearers in 1851. See Larsson, *Gall*, 36. Dearth of sources make it difficult to determine when exactly the more centralized Lakota political culture took shape. For example, Jeffrey Ostler notes that "there is little evidence of large multiband councils before the 1850s." See Ostler, *Plains Sioux and U.S. Colonialism*, 23. It seems clear, however, that the centralizing thrust was tangible well before 1850 in form of načás, powerful tribal or multiband leaders, and the institution of shirt wearers.

82. SG, 321–22, 389–90; Curtis, *North American Indian*, 3: 16; Bray, *Crazy Horse*, 119–22. The description of the initiation ceremony is based on Oglala traditions.

83. For generational dynamics, see Walker, "Sun Dance," 75; and DeMallie, "Teton," 802. For Crazy Horse, see Bray, *Crazy Horse*, 130–31, 143–47, 172–73.

84. For societies in general, see Walker, *Lakota Belief and Ritual*, 260–70; SG, 323; Mirsky, "Dakota," 408–10; Wissler, "Societies and Ceremonial Associations," 7–75; DeMallie, "Teton," 803–4; and Vestal, *Warpath*, 25–26, 51–53. For horse and wife stealing, see Parkman, *Oregon Trail*, 137 ("gallant," "would always"); Culbertson, *Journal of an Expedition to the Mauvaises Terres*, 78–79; and Utley, *Lance and the Shield*, 29. The prevalence of wife stealing is captured by the Oglala huŋká codes, which stated that huŋká should "steal women from other Indians than the Oglalas." See Walker, *Lakota Belief*, 205. This interpretation of men's societies differs from standard studies that tend to portray—indeed systematize—the Lakota political organization as a largely harmonious whole whose different bodies complemented one another, ensuring extensive political participation and smooth governance at different levels—local, band,

tribal, and multitribal or national. Social tensions and conflict are typically discussed under a separate heading. Bringing political and social spheres together draws attention to the deep, mostly generational tensions that unsettled Lakota politics as well as to political innovations that helped diffuse those tensions.

85. The reconstruction of the shifting authority has been pieced together from the following sources: ARC, 150–51; Walker, "Sun Dance," 73–78; Mirsky, "Dakota," 391–92; SG, 326; Walker, *Lakota Society*, 29, 31, 60–61, 79, 84, 86–87, 94; DeMallie, "Teton," 805–6; and Price, *Oglala People*, 14–15. For an early glimpse into akíčhitas' authority, see TN, 117 ("the soldier's right").

86. For examples of how collective hunts and ceremonies, especially the Sun Dance, doubled as crucial political assemblies for tribal and multitribal affairs, see Bray, *Crazy Horse*, 19, 87, 119–23, 150–52, 310–13; Stanley Vestal, *Sitting Bull, Champion of the Sioux: A Biography* (Boston: Houghton Mifflin, 1932), 150–53; Bill Yenne, *Sitting Bull* (Yardley, PA: Westholme, 2008), 20–27; Larsson, *Gall*, 82–83; and SG, 108. There has been considerable confusion about centralization, and the lack thereof, in Lakota politics. In an otherwise admirable study, Gary Clayton Anderson notes that Lakotas constituted "a nation that lacked permanent political structure and definition." See Anderson, *Sitting Bull and the Paradox of the Lakota Nationhood* (New York: Pearson, 2007), 71. I am making a case for a different way to understand political power. The Lakota political organization did have both structure and definition; the difference was that it was built on movement and fluidity. Decision-making power and authority shifted constantly from one body to another, moving from group to group and place to place in an endless on-and-off-again pattern. That political power was transient and not spatially fixed or divided into clearly defined functions—executive, legislative, judicial, policing—does not automatically mean lack of structure. On the contrary, should we not see an arrangement in which power and authority flowed smoothly, predictably, and perpetually among numerous constituents as a finely-tuned sophisticated structure?

87. For kinetic empires, see Pekka Hämäläinen, "What's in a Concept? The Kinetic Empire of the Comanches," *History and Theory* 52 (Feb. 2013), 81–90.

6. EMPIRES

1. For the Bureau of Indian Affairs, see Francis Paul Prucha, *The Great Father: The United States Government and the American Indians* (Lincoln: University of Nebraska Press, 1984), 164; and Ronald N. Satz, *American Indian Policy in the Jacksonian Era* (Norman: University of Oklahoma Press, 1957), 151–54. For the Bureau of Indian Affairs as a colonial office, see Brian Delay, "Indian Politics, Empire, and the History of American Foreign Relations," *Diplomatic History* 39 (Nov. 2015), 935.

2. Joshua D. Rothman, *Flush Times and Fever Dreams: A Story of Capitalism and Slavery in the Age of Jackson* (Athens: University of Georgia Press, 2012), 3–4; Johnson, *River of Dark Dreams*, 1–45, 245–302; Baptist, *Half Has Never Been Told*, 3–38, 175–85; Sven Beckert, *Empire of Cotton: A Global History* (New York: Alfred A. Knopf, 2014), 102–4.

3. For early treaties, see Francis Paul Prucha, *American Indian Treaties: The History of a Political Anomaly* (Berkeley: University of California Press, 1994), Appendix B, "Ratified Indian Treaties"; and Stuart Banner, *How the Indians Lost Their Land: Law and Power on the Frontier* (Cambridge: Harvard University Press, 2005), 112–90. For Jackson, see Michael. D. Green, *The Politics of Indian Removal: Creek Government and Society in Crisis* (Lincoln: University of Nebraska Press, 1982), 42–48; and Steve Inskeep, *Jacksonland: President Andrew Jackson, Cherokee Chief John Ross, and a Great American Land Grab* (New York: Penguin, 2015), 38–50. For the changing status of Native nations, see Philip J. Deloria, "From Nation to Neighborhood: Land, Policy, Culture, Colonialism, and Empire in U.S. Indian Relations," in *The Cultural Turn in U.S. History: Past, Present, and Future*, ed. James W. Cook, Lawrence B. Glickman, and Michael O'Malley (Chicago: University of Chicago Press, 2008), 350–56; Richard White, *"It's Your Misfortune and None of My Own": A New History of the American West* (Norman: University of Oklahoma Press, 1991), 87–89; and Daniel Walker Howe, *What God Hath Wrought: The Transformation of America, 1815–1848* (New York: Oxford University Press, 2007), 368. For northern removal, see John P. Bowes, *Land Too Good for Indians: Northern Indian Removal* (Norman: University of Oklahoma Press, 2016).

4. Satz, *American Indian Policy in the Jacksonian Era*, 155–210; Prucha, *Great Father*, 218–42; Prucha, *American Indian Treaties*, 156–82; Stephen J. Rockwell, *Indian Affairs and the Administrative State in the Nineteenth Century* (New York: Cambridge University Press, 2010), 32, 132–45; Guyatt, *Bind Us Apart*, 288, 292–303; Christina Snyder, "The Rise and Fall and Rise of Civilizations: Indian Intellectual Culture during the Removal Era," *Journal of American History* 104 (Sept. 2017), 386–409. For the "logic of elimination," see Patrick Wolfe, "Settler Colonialism and the Elimination of the Native," *Journal of Genocide Research* 8 (June 2006), 387–409.

5. For the scale and scope of the Indian Removal, see Theda Perdue and Michael D. Green, eds., *The Columbia Guide to American Indians of the Southeast* (New York: Columbia University Press, 2001), 97; Gary Clayton Anderson, *Ethnic Cleansing and the Indian: The Crime That Should Haunt America* (Norman: University of Oklahoma Press, 2014), 151–72; Prucha, *Great Father*, 214; and Robert M. Utley, *The Indian Frontier of the American West, 1846–1890* (Albuquerque: University of New Mexico Press, 1984), 37. For a recasting of Indian Removal as a campaign of ethnic cleansing, see Christopher D. Haveman, *Rivers of Sand: Creek Indian Emigration, Relocation, and Ethnic Cleansing in the American South* (Lincoln: University of Nebraska Press, 2016). For slave capitalism—or what Walter Johnson calls the "slave racial capitalism"—see Johnson, *River of Dark Dreams*; Matthew A. Axtell, "Toward a New History of Capitalism and Unfree Labor: Law Slavery, and Emancipation in the American Marketplace," *Law & Social Inquiry* 40 (Winter 2015), 270–300; and Andrew J. Torget, *Seeds of Empire: Cotton, Slavery, and the Transformation of the Texas Borderlands, 1800–1850* (Chapel Hill: University of North Carolina Press, 2016), esp. 137–217. "Perfect settler sovereignty" refers to a situation in which a settler society rejects legal pluralism and asserts both territorial and legal jurisdiction over Indige-

nous peoples, assuming a right to dissolve their polities and remove them. See Lisa Ford, *Settler Sovereignty: Jurisdiction and Indigenous People in America and Australia, 1788–1836* (Cambridge: Harvard University Press, 2010), 183–203.

6. Andres Stephanson, *Manifest Destiny: American Expansion and the Empire of Right* (New York: Hill and Wang, 1995), 3–47; Nicholas Guyatt, *Providence and the Invention of the United States, 1607–1876* (New York: Cambridge University Press, 2007), 216–19; Andrew C. Isenberg and Thomas Richards, Jr., "Alternative Wests: Rethinking Manifest Destiny," *Pacific Historical Review* 86 (Feb. 2017), 4–17.

7. Thomas R. Hietala, *Manifest Design: American Exceptionalism and Empire* (1985; rev. ed. Ithaca: Cornell University Press, 2003).

8. Brian Delay, *War of a Thousand Deserts: Indian Raids and the U.S.-Mexican War* (New Haven: Yale University Press, 2008), esp. 61–296; D. W. Meinig, *The Shaping of America*, Vol. 2: *Continental America, 1800–1867* (New Haven: Yale University Press, 1993), 146–51.

9. There is considerable interest in and debate over the character of the nineteenth-century United States: was it first and foremost an imperial nation-state, an administrative state, a military-fiscal state, a settler empire, or something else? What matters here is how the American state appeared to the Native Americans who clashed with it, went to war with it, allied with it, and were dispossessed by it. For many Native peoples, the American state appeared a remote force with an astounding ability to effect change from a distance through the deployment of soldiers and government agents. For an example of recent, conceptually oriented works, see George C. Herring, *From Colony to Superpower: U.S. Foreign Relations since 1776* (Oxford: Oxford University Press, 2008); Walter Nugent, *Habits of Empire: A History of American Expansion* (New York: Alfred A. Knopf, 2008); Mark R. Wilson, *The Business of Civil War: Military Mobilization and the State, 1861–1865* (Baltimore: Johns Hopkins University Press, 2006); Brian Baloch, *A Government Out of Sight: The Mystery of National Authority in Nineteenth-Century* (Cambridge: Cambridge University Press, 2009); Rockwell, *Indian Affairs and the Administrative State in the Nineteenth Century*, 217–45; William H. Bergmann, *The American National State and the Early West* (New York: Cambridge University Press, 2012); Max Edling, *Hercules in the Cradle: War, Money, and the American State* (Chicago: University of Chicago Press, 2014); Gary Gerstle, *Liberty and Coercion: The Paradox of American Government from the Founding to the Present* (Princeton: Princeton University Press, 2015); Steven Hahn, *A Nation without Borders: The Unites States and Its World in an Age of Civil Wars, 1830–1910* (New York: Viking, 2016); and Richard White, *The Republic for Which It Stands: The United States during Reconstruction and the Gilded Age, 1867–1896* (New York: Oxford University Press, 2017).

10. For the permanent Indian frontier, see Utley, *Indian Frontier of the American West*, 37.

11. William M. Meigs, *The Life of Thomas Hart Benton* (Philadelphia: J. P. Lippincott, 1904), ("the white," 309; "Civilization," "I cannot," 310).

12. See, for example, Medill to W. L. Marcy, Nov. 30, 1847, *ARCIA 1847–1848*, 12; Medill

to Marcy, Nov. 30, 1848, *ARCIA 1848*, 389; and C. G. Matlock to Harvey, Sept. 25, *ARCIA 1848*, 469.

13. *YSF*, 215–25 ("man eaters," 218); HDWC; *RHO*, 61.

14. For peaceful encounters on the Oregon Trail, see, for example, Potter, ed., *Trail to California*, 97, 99; Keith F. Fleury, "Journal of Crossing the Platte in 1850," Special Collections, Harold B. Lee Library, Brigham Young University, Provo, UT, available at http://contentdm.lib.byu.edu/cdm/compoundobject/collection/Diaries/id/1179 /rec/4 (accessed Dec. 12, 2017); and Edward Jackson, "Journal," 33, Special Collections, Harold B. Lee Library, Brigham Young University, Provo, UT, available at http://contentdm.lib.byu.edu/cdm/compoundobject/collection/Diaries/id/7658 /rec/12 (accessed Dec. 12, 2017). For Native Americans and overland trail soundscape, see Sarah Keyes, "'Like a Roaring Lion': The Overland Trail as a Sonic Conquest," *Journal of American History* 96 (June 2009), 19–43. Things were not altogether tranquil. Lakotas did complain already in 1845 that the bison were being "wantonly killed and scared off" by overlanders, prompting Indian agent Thomas H. Harvey to warn that "an unpleasant collision, if not bloodshed" was imminent. See Harvey to T. Hartley Crawford, Sept. 10, 1845, *ARCIA 1845*, 536. For They Fear Even His Horses, see Bray, "Lakota Statesmen," 159–63.

15. Howard Stansbury, *An Expedition to the Valley of the Great Salt Lake of Utah including a Description of Its Geography, Natural History, and Minerals, and an Analysis of Its Waters with an Authentic Account of the Mormon Settlement* (Philadelphia: Lippincott, Crambo, 1855), 42–46 ("richly," 43); *YSF*, 227 ("having").

16. Louise Amelia Knapp Clappe, *The Shirley Letters from the California Mines in 1851– 52* (San Francisco: Thomas C. Russell, 1922), 322 ("boundless"); Stansbury, *An Expedition to the Valley of the Great Salt Lake of Utah*, 44–45 ("melancholy," 44; "fled," 44; "a little," 44–45; "very sick," "with great," 45); *YSF*, 226 ("Many"); Josephine Waggoner, *Witness: A Hunkpapa Historian's Strong-Heart Song of the Lakotas*, ed. Emily Levine (Lincoln: University of Nebraska Press, 2013), 69 ("Whole villages"); West, *Way to the West*, 87–88; Ostler, *Plains Sioux and U.S. Colonialism*, 33–34. For emigrant numbers, see John D. Unruh, Jr., *The Plains Across: The Overland Emigrants and the Trans-Mississippi West, 1840–60* (Urbana: University of Illinois Press, 1979), 119–20. For Sicangu losses, see Bray, "Teton Sioux," 180.

17. *YSF*, 228–29; *BMWC*, 29; *RHO*, 61; Unruh, *Plains Across*, 120, 438; Thomas Fitzpatrick to D. D. Mitchell, May 22, 1849, LROIA, UPA, roll 889; Fitzpatrick to Mitchell, Sept. 24, 1850, *ARCIA 1850*, 24–25 ("what then," 25). For the decline of the bison and its influence on U.S. Indian agents, see White, "Winning of the West," 340; and West, *Way to the West*, 52.

18. John Phillip Reid, *Policing the Elephant: Crime, Punishment, and Social Behavior on the Overland Trail* (San Marino, CA: Huntington Library, 1996); Keith Heyer Meldahl, *Hard Road West: History and Geology along the Gold Rush Trail* (Chicago: University of Chicago Press, 2007), 13–17; Michael L. Tate, *Indians and Emigrants: Encounters on the Overland Trail* (Norman: University of Oklahoma Press, 2006), 134.

19. Robert M. Utley, "Indian–United States Military Situation, 1848–1891," *HNAI* 4, *History of Indian-White Relations*, 165; Merrill J. Mattes, *The Great Platte River Road:*

The Covered Wagon Mainline via Fort Kearny to Fort Laramie (Lincoln: University of Nebraska Press, 1969), 172–91.

20. Mitchell to Luke Lea, Nov. 11, 1851, *ARCIA 1851*, 27; Percival G. Lowe, *Five Years a Dragoon and Other Adventures on the Great Plains* (Kansas City, MO: Franklin Hudson Publishing, 1906), 78; LeRoy R. Hafen and W. J. Ghent, *Broken Hand: The Life of Thomas Fitzpatrick, Mountain Man, Guide and Indian Agent* (1931; rprt. Lincoln: University of Nebraska Press, 1981), 279–83; Prucha, *American Indian Treaties*, 237–38; Bray, "Lakota Statesmen," 162.

21. Bray, "Lakota Statesmen," 165–68; Kingsley M. Bray, "Sitting Bull and Lakota Leadership," *Brand Book* 43 (Summer 2010), 18–19; Lowe, *Five Years a Dragoon*, 78–79 ("grand," "dignified," 78).

22. Lowe, *Five Years a Dragoon*, 78–85 ("at their own," 78; "They did not," 78; "They were rich," 78–79; "moving," "howled," 80; "had 'boots and saddles,'" 80); Marshall, *Journey of Crazy Horse*, 32–33.

23. Orlando Brown to Fitzpatrick, Aug. 16, 1849, Letters Sent, Office of Indian Affairs, Record Group 75, M21, roll 42, National Archives and Records Service ("to impress"); Lowe, *Five Years a Dragoon*, 87–88; De Smet, *Life*, 2: 675–79; Hafen, *Broken Hand*, 292–93; Prucha, *American Indian Treaties*, 237–39; Raymond J. DeMallie, "Touching the Pen: Plains Indian Treaty Councils in Ethnohistorical Perspective," in *Ethnicity in the Great Plains*, ed. Frederick C. Luebke (Lincoln: University of Nebraska Press, 1980), 40–42; "Treaty of Fort Laramie with Sioux etc., 1851," *IALT* 2: 594–96 ("provisions," 595).

24. Brown to Thomas, Aug. 16, 1849, Letters Sent, Office of Indian Affairs, Record Group 75, M21, roll 42, National Archives and Records Service. For the permanent Indian Territory (or Frontier), see Russell F. Weigley, *The American Way of War: A History of the United States Military Strategy and Policy* (Bloomington: Indiana University Press, 1973), 70–71, 154–55. For the idea of colonies, see Medill, "Report," Nov. 30, 1848, *ARCIA 1848*, 388–90 ("an ample," 390); Lea, "Report," Nov. 27, 1850, *ARCIA 1850*, 3–5 ("wild," 4); and Orlando Brown to Thomas Ewing, Nov. 30, 1849, *ARCIA 1849–1850*, 11–12. See also White, *"It's Your Misfortune and None of My Own,"* 89–92.

25. Bray, "Lakota Statesmen," 169.

26. *Missouri Republican*, Nov. 2, 1851 ("we have," "We are"). For a pioneering reinterpretation of the Laramie conference, see White, "Winning of the West," 340–41.

27. *Missouri Republican*, Nov. 9, 1851 ("If there is," "These lands"). In 1849 the Platte River was generally considered as the boundary between Lakota and Pawnee domains. See unknown, "Tour to California," 1849, 21, Special Collections, Harold B. Lee Library, Brigham Young University, Provo, UT, available at http://contentdm.lib .byu.edu/cdm/compoundobject/collection/Diaries/id/7678/rec/3 (accessed Dec. 12, 2017).

28. "Treaty with the Sioux—Sisseton and Wahpeton Bands, 1851," "Treaty with the Sioux—Mdewakanton and Wahpakoota Bands, 1851," and "Treaty of Fort Laramie with Sioux, Etc., 1851," *IALT* 2: 588–96; *Missouri Republican*, Nov. 2, 1851 ("We are").

29. *Missouri Republican*, Nov. 23, 1851; Bray, "Lakota Statesmen," 169–71. For Mato Oyuhi, see *STF*, 53; and Ostler, *Lakotas and the Black Hills*, 40.

30. De Smet, *Life*, 2: 682–83; Lowe, *Five Years a Dragoon*, 88–89; Hafen and Young, *Fort Laramie*, 193–95. For gifts, see Waggoner, *Witness*, 70; YSF, 221, 230–31; and BMWC, 29 ("the Big Issue"). For signatories, see "Treaty of Fort Laramie with Sioux, etc., 1851," *IALT* 2: 596.

31. *Daily National Intelligencer* (Washington, DC), Jan. 7, 1852 ("one of us"); Stan Hoig and Paul Rosier, *The Cheyenne* (New York: Chelsea House, 2006), 43; Kurz, *Journal of Rudolph Friederich Kurz*, 221 ("the news").

32. "Treaty of Fort Laramie with Sioux, etc., 1851," 594–96. It is a common misunderstanding that *each* Native nation received an annuity of $50,000 at the Horse Creek Treaty. In reality the Native nations that signed the treaty shared a total annuity of $50,000. See Mitchell to Lea, Nov. 11, 1851, *ARCIA 1851*, 28. According to Jeanne Oyawin Eder and Michael Her Many Horses, the 1851 treaty "in no way implied surrender of sovereignty or lands." See Jeanne Oyawin Eder, "A Dakota View of the Great Sioux War, with Stories Collected by Michael Her Many Horses," *LBR*, 58. The 1851 treaty was known at the time as the Horse Creek Treaty but was later renamed the Treaty of Fort Laramie.

33. Lea to A. H. H. Stuart, Nov. 27, 1851, *ARCIA 1851*, 6 ("to throw"); YSF, 231 ("Great distribution"); BKWC, 361; Marshall, *Journey of Crazy Horse*, 34 ("Holy Road").

34. Mitchell to Lea, Nov. 11, 1851, *ARCIA 1851*, 28–29 ("The different," 28; "the country," "fully," 29); De Smet, *Life*, 2: 675, 681; YSF, 221, 229–31; RHO, 61; DWC, 17. For Indian-Indian talks at the Horse Creek, see Mitchell to Lea, Nov. 11, 1851, *ARCIA 1851*, 29; and Bray, "Lone Horn's Peace," 29–30.

35. For Bordeaux and Bissonnette, see John Dishon McDermott, "James Bordeaux," in *French Fur Traders and Voyageurs in the American West*, ed. LeRoy Reuben Hafen and Janet Lecompte (1965; rprt. Lincoln: University of Nebraska Press, 1997), 42–52; Waggoner, *Witness*, 73–74; Hanson and Walters, "Early Fur Trade," 12–16; Charles Hanson, Jr., "Reconstruction of the Bordeaux Trading Post," *Nebraska History* 53 (1972), 137–39; Bettelyoun and Waggoner, *With My Own Eyes*, 143–44, fn 12; Stansbury, *An Expedition to the Valley of the Great Salt Lake of Utah*, 45–47; and ARC, 142. For Smoke and the Oglala council, see Bray, "Lakota Statesmen," 164–65. Similar overlapping of military authority and commercial interests took place on the Missouri at Fort Pierre, which doubled as a trade depot, military fort, and Indian agency. See Mitchell to P. Chouteau, May 3, 1853, LROIA, UMA, roll 885.

36. For emigrant numbers, see Unruh, *Plains Across*, 120. For the decline of bison herds, see Alfred J. Vaughan to Alfred Cumming, Oct. 19, 1854, *ARCIA 1854*, 79, 82–83; Thomas S. Twiss to Cumming, Oct. 10, 1855, *ARCIA 1855*, 83; and West, *Way to the West*, 57.

37. Alfred J. Vaughn to Alfred Cumming, Sept. 20, 1853, *ARCIA 1853*, 118 ("exterminated"); YSF, 232, 234–36; RCF, 70.

38. Parkman, *Oregon Trail*, 133 ("the breath"); YSF, 231–32 ("was not killed," 231). Several winter counts mention the impromptu peace council at Lone Horn's lodge. One count identifies the party as Nez Perces, another as Crows, and two others simply refer to "enemy" or "enemies." Given the proximity of Crows to Minneconjous and the subsequent events, it is very likely that the party in question was a Crow one.

39. BKWC, 362; Bray, "Lone Horn's Peace," 32–37.

40. For the joint agency, see Twiss to CoIA, Sept. 22, 1856, *ARCIA 1856*, 98. For Spanish blankets, see *YSF*, 233, 244.

41. Vaughan to Cumming, Mar. 21, 1854, LROIA, UMA, roll 885 ("full," "scalps," "drew"); Vaughan to Cumming, Oct. 19, 1854, *ARCIA 1854*, 88–89 ("good," 89).

42. Bettelyoun and Waggoner, *With My Own Eyes*, 43 ("rich"). For smell and bison, see Twiss to A. B. Greenwood, Aug. 16, 1859, Sen. Ex. Doc. 35, 36th Cong., 1st Sess., 3; and Ostler, "'They Regard Their Passing as *Wakan*,'" 482–84.

43. Fitzpatrick to Cumming, Nov. 19, 1853, *ARCIA 1853*, 126–27 ("the soldiers," 127); Mitchell to Lea, Oct. 17, 1852, *ARCIA 1852*, 67 ("very proper"). For Lakota attitudes, also see Vaughan to Cumming, Mar. 6, 1854, LROIA, UMA, roll 885. For the amendment of the treaty, see Prucha, *American Indian Treaties*, 239–40, 440–41.

44. *RCF*, 72–73 ("crack," 72); Charles Page to W. Hoffman, May 28, 1855, Sen. Ex. Doc. 91, 34th Cong., 1st Sess., 11 ("with thirty"); Ed. Johnson to Hoffman, Oct. 10, 1855, ibid., 22–26; Vaughan to Cumming, Mar. 21, 1854, LROIA, UMA, roll 885 ("easily"); Waggoner, *Witness*, 74 ("Every"); Marshall, *Journey of Crazy Horse*, 40.

45. "Statement of Mr. Bordeau, a Trader Living at the Place Where the Affair Occurred," Sen. Ex. Doc. 91, 34th Cong., 1st Sess., 5–6 ("he would," "their custom," 5); copy of a letter of James Bordeaux, Aug. 29, 1854, *ARCIA 1854*, 93–94; *RCF*, 73–76; George W. Manypenny to R. McClelland, Nov. 25, 1854, *ARCIA 1854*, 16–17; Paul N. Beck, *The First Sioux War: The Grattan Fight and Blue Water Creek, 1854–1856* (Lanham, MD: University Press of America, 2004), 47–61; Gump, *Dust Rose Like Smoke*, 60–61; Douglas C. McChristian, *Fort Laramie and the U.S. Army on the High Plains, 1849–1890*, National Park Service, Historical Resources Study, Fort Laramie Historic Site, February 2003, 61–74, available at https://www.nps.gov/parkhistory/online_books /fola/high_plains.pdf (accessed 31 Dec. 2016). Fleming claimed that Mato Oyuhi promised to give up High Forehead, prompting him to send Grattan to "receive the offender." The army investigation painted the fight as an unprovoked and premediated Lakota attack on Grattan and his men, but they do provide a picture of the general progress of the fight. See H. B. Fleming to L. Thomas, Aug. 20, 1854, and the various reports in *Engagement between United States Troops and Sioux Indians*, H. Report 63, 33d Cong., 2d Sess., 1–27 ("receive," 2).

46. *YSF*, 235–37.

47. Hoffman to S. Cooper, Nov. 29, 1854, Jan. 18, 1855, H. Ex. Doc. 36, 33d Cong., 2d Sess., 3–5; W. Whitfield to A. Cumming, Sept. 27, 1854, *ARCIA 1854*, 94–95; *BMWC*, 30 ("Plenty"); Vaughan to Cumming, Oct. 19, 1854, *ARCIA 1854*, 88 ("next"); Beck, *First Sioux War*, 80–81; Robert M. Utley, *Frontiersmen in Blue: The United States Army and the Indian, 1848–1865* (Lincoln: University of Nebraska Press, 1967), 114–15; R. Eli Paul, *Blue Water Creek and the First Sioux War, 1854–1856* (Norman: University of Oklahoma Press, 2004), 32–33.

48. Elliott West, "Reconstructing Race," *Western Historical Quarterly* 34 (Spring 2003), 6–26; Meinig, *Shaping of America*, 2: 175, 193–94.

49. Jefferson Davis, "Report of the Secretary of War," Dec. 4, 1854, Sen. Ex. Doc. 1, Part 2, 33d Cong., 2d Sess., 5 ("a deliberately"); "Extract of a Letter Submitted to the De-

partment (January 15) by the Hon. D. R. Atchison, United States Senate, from Major Dougherty," H. Ex. Doc. 36, 33d Cong., 2d Sess., 7 ("A prompt"). Representative Thomas Hart Benton had denounced the Grattan affair as "a heavy penalty for a nation to pay for a runaway Mormon cow, and the folly of and juvenile ambition of West Point fledgling." For the size of the army, Paul, *Blue Water Creek*, 28.

50. Cumming to Manypenny, Feb. 14, 1856, H. Ex. Doc. 65, 34th Cong., 1st Sess., 4, 7 ("great," 4); George Rollie Adams, *General William S. Harney: Prince of Dragoons* (Lincoln: University of Nebraska Press, 2001), 8–119; Beck, *First Sioux War*, 80 ("whip").

51. Twiss to CoIA, Oct. 1, 1855, *ARCIA 1855*, 80–81 ("act," "hostile," "drive," 80; "about 4,000," 81); Twiss to Cumming, Oct. 10, 1855, *ARCIA 1855*, 82 ("whole"); William S. Harney to Lorenzo Thomas, June 2, 1855, Adjutant General's Office, War Department, LR, roll 517 ("must be," "destroy"). For state power, see Jack P. Greene, *Peripheries and Center: Constitutional Development in the Extended Polities of the British Empire and the United States, 1607–1788* (Athens: University Press of Georgia, 1986); and William J. Novak, "The Myth of the 'Weak' American State," *American Historical Review* 113 (June 2008), 763–69.

52. William Harney to Secretary of War, Nov. 10, 1855, Adjutant General's Office, War Department, LR, roll 518; Beck, *First Sioux War*, 90–92 ("By God," 92); Richmond L. Clow, "Mad Bear: William S. Harney and the Sioux Expedition of 1855–1856," *Nebraska History* 61 (1980), 136–38; Tony R. Mullis, *Peacekeeping on the Plains: Army Operations in Bleeding Kansas* (Columbia: University of Missouri Press, 2004), 79; Ray H. Mattison, ed., "The Harney Expedition against the Sioux: The Journal of Capt. John B. S. Todd," *Nebraska History* 43 (1962), 110 ("that if").

53. Nathan Augustus Monroe Dudley to Robert Harvey, Jan. 29, 1909, in R. Eli Paul, "Battle of Ash Hollow: The 1909–1910 Recollections of General N. A. M. Dudley," *Nebraska History* 62 (1981), 380–84 ("holding," 381); Mattison, ed., "Harney Expedition against the Sioux," 111–14 ("depredations," "he himself," "he could not," 112; "a battle," 113; "poured," "and for five," "as the field," 114); Waggoner, *Witness*, 477; Davis, "Report of the Secretary of War," Dec. 3, 1855, Sen. Ex. Doc. 1, 34th Cong., 1st Sess., 4; Clow, "'Mad Bear,'" 138–41.

54. William Harney to Secretary of War, Nov. 10, 1855, Adjutant General's Office, War Department, LR, roll 518 ("begged," "prestige"); Bettelyoun and Waggoner, *With My Own Eyes*, 60–61; STF, 75–77; Lt. G. K. Warren's 1855 Journal," in *Little Chief's Gatherings: The Smithsonian Institution's G. K. Warren 1855–1856 Plains Indian Collection and the New York State Library's 1855–1857 Warren Expeditions Journals*, ed. James A. Hanson (Crawford, NE: Fur Press, 1996), 110 ("worst," "their buffalo, "would be"); Doreen Chaky, *Terrible Justice: Sioux Chiefs and U.S. Soldiers on the Upper Missouri, 1854–1868* (Norman: University of Oklahoma Press, 2012), 38–39, 46–47.

55. S. Harvey, "Minutes of the Council Held at Fort Pierre, Nebraska Territory, on the First Day of March, 1856," Sen. Ex. Doc. 94, 34th Cong., 1st Sess., 1–28 ("cultivating," "any band," 5; "To fight," 10); Vaughan to CoIA, Oct. 27, 1856, *ARCIA 1856*, 85; Parmenas Taylor Turnley, *Reminiscences of Parmenas Taylor Turnley: From the Cradle to Three Score and Ten* (Chicago: Donohue and Henneberry, 1892), 169–73; Chaky,

Terrible Justice, 55–67; Utley, *Frontiersmen in Blue*, 118–19 ("The Butcher," 119); Marshall, *Journey of Crazy Horse*, 109 ("Woman Killer"); YSF, 237–39 ("white beard," 237; "Putinska," 239); Alban W. Hoopes, "Thomas S. Twiss, Indian Agent on the Upper Platte, 1855–1861," *Mississippi Valley Historical Review* 20 (Dec. 1933), 358–60; Richmond L. Clow, "William S. Harney," in *Soldiers in the West: Biographies from the Military Frontier*, ed. Paul Andrew Hutton and Durwood Ball (Norman: University of Oklahoma Press, 2009), 81.

56. Vaughan to Cumming, Sept. 10, 1856, ARCIA *1856*, 77–85 ("to see," 77–78; "it is truly," "The affair," 85). Yanktons had, in fact, began experimenting with farming earlier to compensate for the declining hunts. See Vaughan to Cumming, Sept. 12, 1855, ARCIA *1855*, 71.

57. YSF, 239–57. Vaughan himself had had a forewarning in the winter of 1856, when Yanktonais paid cold and threatening visits to him. See Chester L. Guthrie and Leo L. Gerald, "Upper Missouri Agency: An Account of Indian Administration on the Frontier," *Pacific Historical Review* 10 (Mar. 1941), 53–54.

58. For Indian Territory, see Elias Rector to J. W. Denver, Sept. 24, 1857, ARCIA *1857*, 191–207.

59. Hahn, *Nation without Borders*, 114–91; Meinig, *Shaping of America*, 2: 170–96; Benjamin Madley, *The American Genocide: The United States and the California Indian Catastrophe, 1846–1873* (New Haven: Yale University Press, 2016); David L. Bigler and Will Bagley, *The Mormon Rebellion: America's First Civil War, 1857–1858* (Norman: University of Oklahoma Press, 2011); Hämäläinen, *Comanche Empire*, 310–13.

60. A. Cumming to Denver, Aug. 20, 1857, ARCIA *1857*, 117 ("is of unusual"); "Treaty with the Yankton Sioux, 1858," IALT 2: 776–81; A. H. Redfield to A. M. Robinson, Sept. 1, 1858, ARCIA *1858*, 84–86 ("their entire," 84); Twiss to Charles E. Mix, Sept. 23, 1858, ARCIA *1858*, 95 ("exceedingly," "into effect"); Raymond DeMallie, "Yankton and Yanktonai," HNAI 13, Part 2: 779.

61. For a comprehensive synthetic view, based on a large volume of secondary literature, that pinpoints the decline of Lakotas to the early 1850s, see HB, esp. 88.

62. RCF, 82; Hyde, STF, 90.

63. For Little Bear, see FIT, 26 ("hatred," "destruction"). For Four Horns, see YSF, 239–41; and HDWC. For Sitting Bull, see Utley, *Lance and the Shield*, 36–37. For High Backbone, see Bray, *Crazy Horse*, 56. Soon after the council, the Sans Arcs, led by Crow Feather, were reported to be "in open hostility against the United States." See Kintzing Pritchette to Mix, Aug. 22, 1858, ARCIA *1858*, 69.

64. George W. Kingsbury, *History of Dakota Territory*, 5 vols. (Chicago: S. J. Clarke, 1915), 1: 862 ("any").

65. G. K. Warren, *Preliminary Report of Explorations in Nebraska and Dakota in the Years 1855-'56-'57* (Washington, DC: GPO, 1875), 18–19.

66. Ibid., 19–21 ("privilege," "no white," "these Black Hills," 19; "if the presents," 20).

67. Ibid., 19 ("encamped," "Their feelings").

68. Ibid., 20 ("to induce," "General," "knew").

69. Ibid., 51–52 ("sufferance," 51; "They are," 51–52; "Under," 52).

70. Ibid., 52 ("for the region," "disease," "The present," 52).

71. Vaughan to Cumming, Sept. 10, 1856, *ARCIA 1856*, 85; Warren, *Preliminary Report*, 50 ("Their country"). For the myth of the vanishing Indian, see Brian W. Dippie, *The Vanishing American: White Attitudes and U.S. Indian Policy* (Middletown, CT: Wesleyan University Press, 1982). For bison, see Vaughan to Cumming, Oct. 19, 1854, *ARCIA 1854*, 79; Vaughan to Cumming, Sept. 10, 1855, *ARCIA 1855*, 77; Vaughan to Cumming, Sept. 10, 1856, *ARCIA 1856*, 82–83; Redfield to John Haverty, Sept. 9, 1857, *ARCIA 1857*, 133–34; *HB*, 94; and William A. Dobak, "Killing the Canadian Buffalo, 1821–1881," *Western Historical Quarterly* 27 (Spring 1996), 51. For robes, see Chaky, *Terrible Justice*, 68. Dan Flores estimates that each Lakota ate, on average, six buffalos per year. See Flores, "Bison Ecology," 479.

72. *YSF*, 240 ("half"); Yenne, *Sitting Bull*, 22–23.

73. Twiss to CoIA, July 6, 1857, LROIA, UPA, roll 890; Redfield to Haverty, Sept. 9, 1857, *ARCIA 1857*, 131–32; Twiss to Mix, Sept. 23, 1858, *ARCIA 1858*, 95; *YSF*, 240–56; J. F. Kinney to N. G. Taylor, June 4, 1867, *Hostilities*, 127; BKWC, 362–64; Frederick E. Hoxie, *Parading through History: The Making of the Crow Nation in America, 1805–1935* (New York: Cambridge University Press, 1995), 78; *RCF*, 93–94; Leslie Shores, "A Look into the Life of Thomas Twiss, First Indian Agent at Fort Laramie," *Annals of Wyoming* 77 (Winter 2005), 11; Amos Bad Heart Bull and Helen H. Blish, *A Pictographic History of the Oglala Sioux* (Lincoln: University of Nebraska Press, 1968), 116–68, 172–81, 185–87. For the Crow trail, see Bray, *Crazy Horse*, 61. Oglalas initially objected the westward move of their agency, complaining that the new location was too close to Crow country and dangerous to visit. But the agency soon became a base for Lakotas' westward expansion. For protests, see C. A. May to AAAG, Oct. 6, 1858, LROIA, UPA, roll 890.

74. *YSF*, 249 ("an unusual," "Buffalo"). For Lakota reaction to disease and declining game, see *FIT*, 19, 22 ("sends," 19). For Crazy Horse, see Bray, *Crazy Horse*, 60–63.

75. *FIT*, 27; *ARC*, 153; Redfield to Haverty, Sept. 9, 1857, *ARCIA 1857*, 125; Redfield to A. M. Robinson, Sept. 1, 1858, *ARCIA 1858*, 87; Twiss to Mix, Sept. 23, 1858, *ARCIA 1858*, 91, 95 ("insolent," 95); Twiss to Mix, Feb. 1861, LROIA, UPA, roll 890; *YSF*, 240, 242, 244; *RCF*, 90–92, 96. For Crow leaders, Blackfoot raids, and traders, see *FIT*, 161–85, 201–4 ("infested," 201); *ARC*, 148; Hoxie, *Parading through History*, 80–82; and Paul, "Battle of Ash Hollow," 380. For Crow goods ending in Lakota hands, see "Report of First Lieutenant John Mullins, 2d dragons, on Route from Fort Benton to Fort Union, between the Missouri and Yellowstone Rivers, 1860," Sen. Ex. Doc., 40th Cong., 2d Sess., 77, 167.

76. Samuel N. Latta to William P. Dole, Aug. 27, 1862, *ARCIA 1862*, 193; Bray, *Crazy Horse*, 67–69; Curtis, *North American Indian*, 4: 91–96. According to Crow oral traditions, Lakotas "made the first serious attempt to conquer our tribe" in around 1860. See Joseph Medicine Crow, "Custer and His Crow Scouts," *LBR*, 107.

77. William P. Dole, "Report," Nov. 15, 1864, *ARCIA 1864*, 29 ("waiting"); Henry H. Reed to Dole, [n.d.], *ARCIA 1864*, 271 ("dare," "but in this"); Vaughan to Cumming, Sept. 12, 1855, *ARCIA 1855*, 74–75; *YSF*, 255–69; *DWC*, 21.

78. *FIT*, 139–42, 160–61; *YSF*, 255–56, 267.

79. Twiss to Mix, Sept. 23, 1858, *ARCIA 1858*, 95 ("insolent"). For wars and clashes, see *YSF*, 236, 251, 253; *ARC*, 124, 143–46; Vaughan to Cumming, Sept. 12, 1855, *ARCIA 1855*, 75; and Twiss to CoIA, July 13, 1858, LROIA, UPA, roll 890.

80. *YSF*, 232 ("the pipe"); *RHO*, 61; West, *Contested Plains*, 256; Haverty to Manypenny, Oct. 18, 1855, *ARCIA 1855*, 69–70; Cumming to Manypenny, Feb. 14, 1856, H. Ex. Doc. 65, 34th Cong., 1st Sess., 8; John Robertson to Mix, Mar. 14, 1858, J. Shaw Gregory to Mix, Mar. 23 and Aug. 27, 1859, LR, Omaha Agency, roll 604; Geo. B. Graff to A. M. Robinson, Oct. 1, 1860, *ARCIA 1860*, 92; J. L. Gillis to A. M. Robinson, Oct. 1860, *ARCIA 1860*, 93–94; Charles E. Mix, "A Memorandum for the Secretary of Interior," Jan. 11, 1858, in *Ratified Treaty No. 306, Documents Relating to the Negotiation of the Treaty of March, 1858, with the Ponca Indians*, Digital Collections, University of Wisconsin-Madison Libraries, available at http://digicoll.library .wisc.edu/cgi-bin/History/History-idx?type=article&did=History.IT1858no306 .i0001&id=History.IT1858no306&isize=M (accessed June 25, 2017). Also see "Manuscript by Samuel Allis, Missionary and Teacher to the Indians," MS 2628, box 2, NSHS.

81. West, *Contested Plains*, 230–35, 273–75.

82. For the Cheyenne-Arapaho treaty, see "Treaty with the Arapahoe and Cheyenne, 1861," *IALT* 2: 807–11. For the central plains, see West, *Contested Plains*, 280–97. For Lakota activities and prosperity during the early Civil War years, see *YSF*, 248–52. Lakotas are barely mentioned in the annual reports of the Indian Office in 1861 and 1862, suggesting minimal federal awareness and interference with their affairs.

83. "Special Report of Thomas S. Twiss, Aug. 16, 1859," Sen. Ex. Doc. 35, 36th Cong., 1st Sess., 7 ("council-lodge," "a large"). For raids, see *YSF*, 145.

84. *YSF*, 240, 242, 244; *BMWC*, 30–31; Vaughan to Cumming, Sept. 12, 1855, *ARCIA 1855*, 75; Redfield to A. M. Robinson, Oct. 17, 1860, *ARCIA 1860*, 89. For captives, see Walker, *Lakota Society*, 36, 54–55, 137, 144; and John Loree to H. B. Branch, Sept. 1, 1862, *ARCIA 1862*, 130. For guns, see "Report of the Secretary of War, Communicating . . . the Report of Brevet Brigadier General W. F. Raynolds, on the Exploration of the Yellowstone and the Country Drained by That River," Sen. Ex. Doc. 77, 40th Cong., 1st Sess., 16; Harold L. Peterson, *The Great Guns* (New York: Grosset and Dunlap, 1971), 175–85; and Loretta Fowler, *Arapahoe Politics, 1851–1978: Symbols in Crises of Authority* (Lincoln: University of Nebraska Press, 1982), 35.

85. "Council with Arapahoes and Cheyennes," Aug. 12, 1875, in *Report of the Special Commission Appointed to Investigate the Affairs of the Red Cloud Indian Agency, July, 1875* (Washington, DC: GPO, 1875), 376 ("I like"); Henry M. Stanley, *My Early Travels and Adventures in America and Asia*, 2 vols. (New York: Charles Scribner's Sons, 1895), 1: 205–6 ("All the tribes"); *ARC*, 116–17. For numbers, see Newton Edmunds to Dennis N. Cooley, Oct. 1, 1865, *ARCIA 1865*, 189; Bray, "Teton Sioux," 176; Fowler, "The Arapaho," 857; and John H. Moore, Margot P. Liberty, and A. Terry Straus, "Cheyenne," *HNAI* 13, Part 2: 880.

86. Moore, *Cheyenne Nation*, 198; Moore, *Cheyenne*, 97; Bray, *Crazy Horse*, 93; *HB*, 90–93. For Cheyenne concepts of kinship, nationhood, and alliance, see Christina Gish Hill, *Webs of Kinship: Family in Northern Cheyenne Nationhood* (Norman: University of Oklahoma Press, 2017), 74–82.

87. Warren, *Preliminary Report*, 20–21; *Report of the Secretary of War Communicating*, 19; Paul L. Hedren, *Fort Laramie and the Great Sioux War* (Norman: University of Oklahoma Press, 1988), 45; *The Indian Interviews of Eli S. Ricker, 1903–1919*, ed. Richard E. Jensen, *Voices of the American West*, Vol. 1 (Lincoln: University of Nebraska Press, 2005), 367; *RCF*, 95–97; *YSF*, 244; Twiss to Cumming, Oct. 10, 1855, *ARCIA 1855*, 82; Price, *Oglala People*, 20. For a rare document acknowledging the Indigenous makeup of the trading posts, see Twiss to CoIA, Sept. 22, 1856, *ARCIA 1856*, 98.

88. Twiss to Mix, Sept. 23, 1858, *ARCIA 1858*, 95 ("the different," 95); Redfield to A. M. Robinson, Sept. 1, 1858, *ARCIA 1858*, 86, 91; Twiss to Greenwood, Sept. 1, 1859, *ARCIA 1859*, 135 ("will protect"); Redfield to A. M. Robinson, Nov. 5, 1858, LROIA, UMA, roll 885; Redfield to Haverty, Sept. 9, 1857, *ARCIA 1857*, 126 ("satisfactory"); *YSF*, 238–43; *DWC*, 18–19; Cumming to Manypenny, Sept. 25, 1856, *ARCIA 1856*, 68; Wishart, *Unspeakable Sadness*, 127, 133; Bray, *Crazy Horse*, 46–47.

89. *Report of the Secretary of War Communicating*, 1–34 ("then almost," 3; "habits," 4; "To Whom," "It is said," 20; "the right," "the President," "behind," "were lounging," "discarded," "their glory," "They were lying," "banishing," 21; "could see," 27; "watching," 34).

90. Twiss to Greenwood, Sept. 26, 1859, Sen. Ex. Doc. 35, 36th Cong., 1st Sess., 12 ("I must").

7. WAR

1. Walker, *Lakota Belief*, 35–37, 82–83, 87–90; Raymond J. DeMallie, "Lakota Belief and Ritual in the Nineteenth Century," in *Sioux Indian Religion*, ed. DeMallie and Parks (Lincoln: University of Nebraska Press, 1987), 27–31.

2. Twiss to Greenwood, Aug. 16, 1859, Sen. Ex. Doc. 35, 36th Cong., 1st Sess., 3 ("a special," "animated," "certain," "this state," "The state," "have stopped," "the prairie," "in small," "very far"). Characteristically, there were local and regional variations in the decline of the bison herds. A Yanktonai winter count reported "much pemmican" for 1859. See MBWC.

3. Twiss to Greenwood, Aug. 16, 1859, Sen. Ex. Doc. 35, 36th Cong., 1st Sess., 4–6 ("These wild," "most effectually," "When I," "see!," 4; "This process," 4–5; "cordially," 5).

4. Twiss, "Proceedings of a Council," Sept. 18, 1859, Sen. Ex. Doc. 35, 36th Cong., 1st Sess., 7–11 ("white men," 7).

5. Greenwood to J. C. Breckinridge, Apr. 12, 1860, Sen. Ex. Doc. 35, 36th Cong., 1st Sess., 1–2 ("arrange," "ten," 2).

6. "Report of the Secretary of War, Communicating . . . the Report of Brevet Brigadier General W. F. Raynolds, on the Exploration of the Yellowstone and the Country Drained by That River," Sen. Ex. Doc. 77, 40th Cong., 1st Sess., 10 ("*terra incognita*"); H. Wager Halleck, *Elements of Military Art and Science* (New York: D. Appleton, 1846), esp. 135–54, 300–341 ("immense," "never," 151; "requires," 301–2); C. D. Anderson to John Munroe, Aug. 22, 1859, Sen. Ex. Doc. 2, 36th Cong., 1st Sess., 441–48 ("a correct," 447). For scientific approach to war in the United States, see Ian C. Hope, *A Scientific Way of War: Antebellum Military Science, West Point, and the Ori-*

gins of American Military Thought (Lincoln: University of Nebraska Press, 2015). For Fort Randall, see Jerome A. Greene, Fort Randall on the Missouri, 1856–1892 (Pierre: South Dakota Historical Society Press, 2005). For American fears of a standing army, see Gordon S. Wood, Empire of Liberty: A History of the Early American Republic, 1879–1815 (New York: Oxford University Press, 2009), 262–67.

7. B. S. Schoonover to A. M. Robinson, Aug. 23, 1860, LROIA, UMA, roll 885; Latta to William P. Dole, Aug, 27, 1862, ARCIA 1862, 193; John E. Sunder, The Fur Trade on the Upper Missouri, 1840–1865 (Norman: University of Oklahoma Press, 1965), 215; Charles Primeau to CoIA, June 20, 1862, ARCIA 1862, 373 ("acted").

8. Latta to Dole, Aug, 27, 1862, ARCIA 1862, 192–93 ("for eleven," "yet," 192; "to bring," 193); Primeau to CoIA, June 20, 1862, ARCIA 1862, 373–74 ("expressed," 374); Charles E. De Land, "Old Fort Pierre and Its Neighbors," SDHC 1: 366–68, fn 68.

9. "Message of Chiefs of Unepapa Band of Sioux to Their Agent," July 25, 1862, ARCIA 1862, 372.

10. Robert M. Utley, The Lance and the Shield: The Life and Times of Sitting Bull (New York: Henry Holt, 1993), 51; Greg Gordon, "Steamboats, Woodhawks, and War on the Upper Missouri River," Montana: Magazine of Western History 61 (June 2011), 30–47; J. B. S. Todd to William Jayne, Dec. 11, 1861, LROIA, UMA, roll 885 ("entirely").

11. "Treaty with the Sioux—Sisseton and Wahpeton Bands, 1851," "Treaty with the Sioux—Mdewakanton and Wahpakoota Bands," "Treaty with the Sioux—Mendawakanton and Wahpahoota Bands, 1858," "Treaty with the Sioux—Sisseeton and Wahpaton Bands, 1858," IALT 2: 588–93, 781–89. For the 1858 treaty and treaty negotiations, see Barbara T. Newcombe, "'A Portion of the American People': The Sioux Sign a Treaty in Washington in 1858," Minnesota History 45 (Fall 1976), 82–96.

12. For a detailed discussion of these developments, see Andersson, Kinsmen of Another Kind, 177–260. For a contemporary Dakota perspective, see Wamditanka, A Sioux Story of the War: Chief Big Eagle's Story of the Outbreak of 1862 (St. Paul: Minnesota Historical Society, 1894), 384–88. See also Waziyaṭawiŋ Angela Wilson, Remember This! Dakota Decolonization and the Eli Taylor Narratives (Lincoln: University of Nebraska Press, 2005), 5–6; Kathryn Zabelle Derounian-Stodola, The War in Words: Reading the Dakota Conflict through the Captivity Literature (Lincoln: University of Nebraska Press, 2009), 21–22; and Karen V. Hansen, Encounter on the Great Plains: Scandinavian Settlers and the Dispossession of Dakota Indians, 1890–1930 (New York: Oxford University Press, 2013), 36–38.

13. Wamditanka, Sioux Story, 388–94; Winifred W. Barton, John P. Williams: A Brother to the Sioux (New York: Fleming H. Revell, 1919), 49–50 ("So far," 49); H. H. Sibley to Alex Ramsey, Aug. 20, 1862, and John Pope to Sibley, Sept. 28, 1862, in Minnesota in the Civil and Indian Wars, 2 vols., comp. and ed. The Board of Commissioners (St. Paul: Pioneer Press, 1893), 2: 165 ("a war"), 257 ("utterly"); Steven Hahn, "Slave Emancipation, Indian Peoples, and the Projects of a New American Nation-State," Journal of the Civil War Era 3 (Sept. 2013), 307–9; Robert M. Utley, Frontiersmen in Blue: The United States Army and the Indian, 1848–1865 (Lincoln: University of Nebraska Press, 1967), 264–69. For evolving attitudes and internal tensions among the Dakotas, see Andersson, Kinsmen of Another Kind, 226–76.

14. Alvin M. Josephy, *The Civil War in the American West* (New York: Viking, 1991), 133–39; Eric Foner, *The Fiery Trial: Abraham Lincoln and American Slavery* (New York: W. W. Norton, 2010), 261; David Martinez, "Remembering the Thirty-Eight: Abraham Lincoln, the Dakota, and the U.S. War on Barbarism," *Wicazo Sa Review* 28 (Fall 2013), 5–29; *New York Times*, Jan. 11, 1863.

15. Roy W. Meyer, "The Canadian Sioux: Refugees from Minnesota," *Minnesota History* 41 (Spring 1968), 13–15; Robert Werner, "Dakota Diaspora after 1862," *Minnesota Heritage* 6 (2012), 38–59; David G. McCrady, *Living with Strangers: The Nineteenth-Century Sioux and the Canadian-American Borderlands* (Toronto: University of Toronto Press, 2006), 17–24.

16. Josephy, *Civil War in the American West*, 138–40; Walter N. Trenerry, "The Shooting of Little Crow: Heroism or Murder?" *Minnesota History* 38 (Sept. 1962), 150–53; Gary Clayton Anderson, *Little Crow: Spokesman for the Sioux* (St. Paul: Minnesota Historical Society Press, 1986), 181.

17. This formulation of the American state and the Civil War era draws in particular on Elliott West, "Reconstructing Race," *Western Historical Quarterly* 34 (Spring 2003), 6–26; Hahn, "Slave Emancipation"; Hahn, *Nation without Borders*; Ari Kelman, *A Misplaced Massacre: Struggling over the Memory of Sand Creek* (Cambridge: Harvard University Press, 2013), esp. xi; and Richard Franklin Bensel, *Yankee Leviathan: The Origins of Central State Authority in America* (New York: Cambridge University Press, 1990).

18. Sibley to J. F. Meline, Aug. 7 and 16, 1863, in *Minnesota in the Civil and Indian Wars*, comp. and ed. The Board of Commissioners, 2: 297–305; Josephy, *Civil War in the American West*, 139–43 ("like," 141); *New York Times*, Oct. 18, 1863 ("stealing"). For a detailed map of the Dakota diaspora, see "Map of the Dakota Diaspora, 1862–1870," available at http://www.usdakotawar.org/history/aftermath (accessed May 12, 2018).

19. "Report of Brig. Gen. Alfred Sully, United States Army, Commanding Expedition, September 3, 1863, Battle of White Stone Hills, Dakota Territory," in George W. Kingsbury, *History of Dakota Territory*, 2 vols. (Chicago: S. J. Clarke, 1915), 1: 291–95 ("tired," 293; "It is," 294). See also Paul N. Beck, *Columns of Vengeance: Soldiers, Sioux, and the Punitive Expeditions, 1863–1864* (Norman: University of Oklahoma Press, 2013), 153–63; Josephy, *Civil War in the American West*, 144–46; Hansen, *Encounter on the Great Plains*, 43–45; and Standing Buffalo's letter, in *Through Dakota Eyes: Narrative Accounts of the Minnesota Indian War of 1862*, ed. Gary Clayton Anderson and Alan R. Woolworth (St. Paul: Minnesota Historical Society Press, 1988), 294 ("our great").

20. Latta to Dole, Aug. 27, 1862, ARCIA *1862*, 193–97 ("A powerful," 193; "capable," 197); Waggoner, *Witness*, 71–72.

21. YSF, 249–54; HDWC; CPWC; Henry W. Reed to Dole, Jan. 4, 1863, LROIA, UMA, roll 885; Jayne to Dole, Oct. 8, 1862, ARCIA *1862*, 176; John Hutchinson to Dole, Sept. 23, 1863, and Latta to Dole, Aug. 27, 1863, ARCIA *1863*, 155, 170–71; "Report of First Lieutenant John Mullins, 2d Dragoons, on Route from Fort Benton to Fort Union, between the Missouri and Yellowstone Rivers, 1860," Sen. Ex. Doc. 77, 40th

Cong., 2d Sess., 166–67 ("Our hearts," 167). The Sicangus and Oglalas were considered to be at peace with the United States before the Sully campaign. See "Minutes of a Council Held with Brule and Ogalalla Sioux, June 8, 1864, Held at Cottonwood Springs, Nebr. Ter.," *SDHC* 8: 296–99.

22. *BMWC*, 32 ("nearly all"); Bray, *Crazy Horse*, 76.

23. For gold, Lakotas, and the Civil War, see Josephy, *Civil War in the American West*, 147; Latta to Dole, Aug. 27, 1862, *ARCIA 1862*, 196 ("only," "would not"); and Michael Clodfelter, *The Dakota War: The United States Army versus the Sioux, 1862–1865* (Jefferson, NC: McFarland, 2006), 80–82.

24. For raids, see Bettelyoun and Waggoner, *With My Own Eyes*, 83; and Bray, *Crazy Horse*, 77–78. For the Lakota threat to the Union, see G. S. Benson to Sibley, May 10, 1864; Sibley to Pope, June 9, 1864, and Pope to Newton Edwards, June 30, 1864, *SDHC* 8: 261–62, 292–93, 306. For Confederate agents, see Eugene F. Ward, *The Indian War of 1864: Being a Fragment of the Early History of Kansas, Nebraska, Colorado, and Wyoming* (Topeka, KS: Crane, 1911), 194–95. For the North Platte meeting, see "Minutes of a Council Held with Brule and Ogalalla Sioux, June 8, 1864," *SDHC* 8: 296–99 ("There was much," 299).

25. Pope to Henry W. Halleck, Apr. 29, 1864, *SDHC* 9: 247; Pope to Halleck, May 12, 1864; Pope to Sully, May 25 and 26, 1864, *SDHC* 8: 263–65, 276–79 ("At present," 264); Clodfelter, *Dakota War*, 83.

26. The year 1864 was remembered as the winter when "nearly all the Sioux Bands camped together." See *BMWC*, 32.

27. For the Sully expedition and the Battle of the Killdeer Mountain, see Sully to AAG, Department of the Northwest, July 7, 1864, and Sully, "Report," Aug. 13, 1864, *SDHC* 8: 309–10, 313–21 ("eager," 310; "grand," 314); John Pattee, "Dakota Campaigns," *SDHC* 5: 306–15 ("they took," "carrying," 308); July 31, 1864, Sully to AAG, Department of the Northwest, July 31 and Aug. 13, 1864, John Pattee to John H. Pell, Aug. 2, 1864, A. B. Brackett to Pell, Aug. 1, 1864, Nelson Miner to Sully, Aug. 2, 1864, in *The War of the Rebellion: A Compilation of the Official Records of Union and Confederate Armies*, 55 vols. (Washington, DC: GPO, 1896), Series 1, Vol. 41, Part 1: 141–48, 160–63; Halleck to Pope, Nov. 3, 1864, *SDHC* 8: 352; David L. Kingsbury, "Sully's Expedition against the Sioux in 1864," *Collections of the Minnesota Historical Society* 8 (St. Paul: Minnesota Historical Society, 1898), 449–60 ("the water," 453; "elated," 454; "hell," 457); Nicholas Hilger, "General Alfred Sully's Expedition of 1864," *Contributions to the Historical Society of Montana* 2 (Helena: State Publishing Company, 1896), 314–28; Louis Pfaller, "Sully Expedition of 1864, Featuring the Killdeer Mountain and Badlands Battles," *North Dakota History* 31 (Jan. 1964), 1–59; Utley, *Lance and the Shield*, 54–59; and Beck, *Columns of Vengeance*, 202–46. For a Lakota perspective, see "White Bull Interview," box 105, folder 24, pp. 1–16, CC ("with a ghost," 2). Also see Fanny Kelly, *Narrative of My Captivity among the Sioux* (Cincinnati: Wilstach, Baldwin, 1871), 92–105.

28. *YSF*, 255 ("first," "white"); Meyer, "Canadian Sioux," 15–16. Later, during the campaigns against the Cheyennes in the central plains, Sully would suddenly become

cautious, slow, and dithering. See Robert M. Utley, *Frontier Regulars: The United States Army and the Indian, 1866–1891* (1973; rprt. Lincoln: University of Nebraska Press, 1984), 147.

29. For Gall, see *DWC*, 21; and HDWC. For Red Cloud, see Bettelyoun and Waggoner, *With My Own Eyes*, 78.

30. Halleck to Pope, Nov. 3, 1864, *SDHC* 8: 348–49 ("several," 348–49; "The high," 349); *STF*, 102–4.

31. *RCF*, 107–8; James E. Potter, *Standing Firmly by the Flag: Nebraska Territory and the Civil War, 1861–1867* (Lincoln: University of Nebraska Press, 2012), 154–55; Twiss to CoIA, Jan. 23, 1865, LROIA, UPA, roll 891 ("to drive," "fiendish"). For intentional fires, see Isenberg, *Destruction of the Bison*, 72; and James, *Account of an Expedition*, 1: 405.

32. Kelman, *Misplaced Massacre*, 22–24, 149; Stan Hoig, *The Sand Creek Massacre* (Norman: University of Oklahoma Press, 1961), 145–92; Ostler, *Plains Sioux and U.S. Colonialism*, 45; *STF*, 104–5; Olson, *Red Cloud and the Sioux Problem*, 11–12.

33. Bray, *Crazy Horse*, 79; DeMallie, "Sioux," 796; Mario Gonzalez and Elizabeth Cook-Lynn, *The Politics of Hallowed Ground: Wounded Knee and the Struggle for Indian Sovereignty* (Urbana: University of Illinois Press, 1999), 30; *RCF*, 97; Cooley to James Harlan, Oct. 31, 1865, *ARCIA 1865*, 25. For the Omaha dance, see *BMWC*, 32.

34. *STF*, 106–8; Bray, *Crazy Horse*, 79, 84–86; George Bird Grinnell, *The Fighting Cheyennes* (New York: Charles Scribner's Sons, 1915), 211–16; Utley, *Frontiersmen in Blue*, 301–22; Price, *Oglala People*, 55; Steven C. Haack, "'This Must Have Been a Grand Sight': George Bent and the Battle of the Platte Bridge," *Great Plains Quarterly* 30 (Winter 2010), 6–8; John Hart, ed., "A New Account of the Battle of Platte Bridge, July 28, 1865: The Recollections of John Benton Hart," *Kansas History* 38 (Spring 2015), 50–51.

35. A. B. Moreland to Sully, Jan. 31, 1865, in *War of the Rebellion* 48, Part 1: 700–701 ("bearing," "sleigh," 700; "ill-constructed," 701); Pope to U. S. Grant, June 14, 1865, *ARCIA 1865*, 196 ("heavy"); George E. Hyde, *Life of George Bent: Written from His Letters* (Norman: University of Oklahoma Press, 1968), 168–73.

36. *Frontier Scout*, June 15, 1865; Sully to AAG, Department of the Northwest, Aug. 8, 1865, Sully to Pope, July 17, 1865, Sully to AAG, Department of the Northwest, July 22, 1865, in *War of the Rebellion* 48, Part 2: 1090–91, 1109–10, 1172–73 ("would make," "crying," 1173); Utley, *Lance and the Shield*, 67–70.

37. *Frontier Scout*, Oct. 12, 1865 ("decamped," "only lived").

38. This is essentially Robert Utley's assessment of Sitting Bull as a man and a leader in his magisterial *Lance and the Shield*. See in particular p. 68.

39. Meinig, *Shaping of America*, 2: 516–28; Eric Foner, *Reconstruction: America's Unfinished Revolution, 1863–1877* (New York: Harper and Row, 1988), 228–45; Sidney E. Mead, "American Protestantism since the Civil War," *Journal of Religion* 36 (Jan. 1956), 7 ("We are"). Elliott West has made a compelling case for a Greater Reconstruction, or a pair of parallel reconstructions, in *The Last Indian War: The Nez Perce Story* (New York: Oxford University Press, 2009).

40. For the Doolittle Committee and treaty initiatives, see Donald Chaput, "Generals,

Indian Agents, and Politicians: The Doolittle Survey of 1865," *Western Historical Quarterly* 3 (July 1972), 269–72; Prucha, *American Indian Treaties*, 270–72; Price, *Oglala People*, 55–57; and Utley, *Frontiersmen in Blue*, 309–15.

41. Pope to Grant, June 14, 1865, ARCIA 1865, 197 ("the violation," "It is").

42. *PBC*, 2–7 ("The President," "give," "I am," 2; "To-day," "My Great Father's," 3; "starving," "where," 7).

43. *PBC*, 9, 37 ("I do not know," "My Children," 9; "out," "Everywhere," 37).

44. *PBC*, 38–39 ("it is," "good behavior," 38; "We want," 39).

45. *PBC*, 47 ("all my").

46. *PBC*, 102 ("was made," "shorter," "these little," "they will").

47. Granville Stuart, *Forty Years on the Frontier as Seen in the Journals of Granville Stuart*, 2 vols., ed. Paul C. Philips (Cleveland: Arthur H. Clark, 1925), 2: 68–73 ("for each," 71); Michael A. Sievers, "Westward by Indian Treaty: The Upper Missouri Example," *Nebraska History* 56 (1975), 85–86; "Treaty with the Sioux—Minneconjou Band, 1865"; "Treaty with the Sioux—Lower Brulé Band, 1865"; "Treaty with the Blackfoot Sioux, 1865"; "Treaty with the Sioux—Two-Kettle Band, 1865"; "Treaty with the Sioux—Sans Arcs Band, 1865"; "Treaty with the Sioux—Hunkpapa Band, 1865"; "Treaty with the Sioux—Yanktonai Band, 1865"; "Treaty with the Sioux—Upper Yanktonai Band, 1865"; "Treaty with the Sioux—Oglala Band, 1865," *IALT* 2: 883–89, 896–908 ("subject to," 883); Newton Edmunds, S. R. Curtis, Orrin Guernsey, and Henry W. Reed, "Report of the Northwestern Treaty Commission to the Sioux of the Upper Missouri," *ARCIA 1866*, 168–76.

48. The notion of perpetual war refers, of course, to the sequence that saw the Cold War evolving into the war on terror. The situation in the late nineteenth-century North America bears many similarities to that later dynamic, the most obvious parallel being the sheer length of the wars: the partly overlapping Civil War and the Indian wars lasted from the 1850s into the late 1870s or, arguably, to 1890. For the United States as an imperial nation, see Hahn, *Nation without Borders*.

49. Meinig, *Shaping of America*, 2: 532–33; Gregory P. Downs, *After Appomattox: Military Occupation and the Ends of War* (Cambridge: Harvard University Press, 2015); Pekka Hämäläinen, "Reconstructing the Great Plains: The Long Struggle for Sovereignty and Dominance in the Heart of the Continent," *Journal of the Civil War Era* 6 (Dec. 2016), 488–94; "Extract from the Report of the Secretary of the Interior Relative to the Report of the Commissioner of Indian Affairs," *ARCIA 1865*, iii ("The Indians").

50. For the post–Civil War army, see Utley, *Frontier Regulars*, 10–43; Edward M. Coffman, *The Old Army: A Portrait of the American Army in Peacetime, 1784–1898* (New York: Oxford University Press, 1986), 372–75; Downs, *After Appomattox*, 102; and White, *Republic for Which It Stands*, 115–16.

51. "Extract from the Report of the Secretary of the Interior," iii–iv ("policy," iii; "the attempted," iii–iv).

52. The 1865 treaties do not figure prominently in U.S. or Lakota/Sioux historiography, eclipsed by the 1851 Horse Creek and 1868 Fort Laramie treaties, which involved more Indians and government agents. Yet the 1865 treaties were enormously significant, setting the stage for the political and geographical arrangements and misunder-

standings (both real and fabricated) that sparked off the great "Sioux Wars" of the 1860s and 1870s.

53. *PBC*, 22 ("There is").

54. For the Bozeman Trail and clashes with Lakotas and Cheyennes, see *RCF*, 129–33, 137; Grinnell, *Fighting Cheyennes*, 195–206; H. D. Hampton, "The Powder River Expedition," *Montana: The Magazine of Western History* 14 (Autumn 1964), 6–15; John Dishon McDermott, *Circle of Fire: The Indian War of 1865* (Mechanicsburg, PA: Stackpole Books, 2003), 83; Susan Badger Doyle, "Indian Perspectives on the Bozeman Trail," *Montana: The Magazine of Western History* 40 (Winter 1990), 56–67; and Nelson Cole to Grant, Feb. 10, 1867, and Samuel Walker to Geo F. Price, Sept. 25, 1865, in *Powder River Campaigns and Sawyers Expedition of 1865*, ed. LeRoy R. Hafen and Ann W. Hafen (Glendale, CA: Arthur H. Clark, 1961), 60–100. For the Bear River Massacre, see David Haward Bain, *Empire Express: Building the First Transcontinental Railroad* (New York: Penguin, 1999), 229.

55. The Lakota resistance to U.S. encroachment manifested itself in late 1865 and early 1866 in a burst of raids and verbal protests. See Henry E. Maynadier to Cooley, Jan. 25, 1866, and Newton Edmunds, Curtis, Guernsey, and Henry W. Reed to Harlan, Aug. 25, 1866, *ARCIA 1866*, 171–73, 205–6 ("will not," "the diffusion," 172). For Lakota disposition in general, see E. B. Taylor to Cooley, Mar. 29, 1866, LROIA, UPA, roll 891; and Marshall, *Journey of Crazy Horse*, 141–42. For Lakota population, see Bray, "Teton Sioux," 176.

56. E. B. Taylor to Cooley, Mar. 17, 1866 ("as important"); E. B. Taylor to CoIA, June 9, 1866 ("a treaty"), LROIA, UPA, roll 891; Maynadier to Cooley, Mar. 9, 1866, *ARCIA 1866*, 206–7 ("is always," 207); N. B. Buford to E. M. Stanton, June 6, 1867, SF, roll 7.

57. Henry B. Carrington, "History of Indian Operations on the Plains," Sen. Ex. Doc. 33, 50th Cong., 1st Sess., 5–6 ("White chief," "every chief," 6); Marshall, *Journey of Crazy Horse*, 143–44; *RCF*, 139–41; John S. Gray, *Custer's Last Campaign: Mitch Boyer and the Little Bighorn Reconstructed* (Lincoln: University of Nebraska Press, 1991), 39–48; Robert W. Larson, *Red Cloud: Warrior-Statesman of the Lakota Sioux* (Norman: University of Oklahoma Press, 1997), 91–93; Bray, *Crazy Horse*, 91–93; Frances C. Carrington, *My Army Life and the Fort Phil. Kearny Massacre on the Plains* (Philadelphia: J. B. Lippincott, 1910), 46–47 ("The Great Father"). Mrs. Carrington was not present at the encounter and was paraphrasing what she learned later, most likely from her husband. For treaties, see E. B. Taylor and Henry E. Maynadier, "Report of the Commissioner Appointed by the President of the United States to Treat with the Indians at Fort Laramie," *ARCIA 1866*, 208–9; and "Articles of a Treaty Made and Concluded at Fort Laramie in the Territory of Dakota, by and between Edward B. Taylor, Superintendent of Indian Affairs, Robert N. McClarren, Thomas Wistar, and Col. Henry E. Maynadier, June 27, 1866," in *Papers Relating to Talks and Councils Held with the Indians in Dakota and Montana Territories in the Years 1865–1869* (Washington, DC: GPO, 1910), 19–20.

58. Cooley to Harlan, Oct. 31, 1865, *ARCIA 1865*, 51 ("tending"); Maynadier to Frank Wheaton and E. B. Taylor, Apr. 5, 1866, LROIA, UPA, roll 891; Bray, *Crazy Horse*, 93. For the abstraction of Lakotas as "hostiles," see M. T. Patrick to E. B. Taylor, Sept.

20, 1866, *ARCIA 1866*, 209; E. B. Chandler to H. B. Denman, Jan. 13, 1867, *Hostilities*, 11–13; Carrington, "History of Indian Operations on the Plains," 15; Sully to E. B. Taylor, Apr. 22, 1867, and Sully to Commanding Officer, Apr. 25, 1867, MMSC. For Fetterman, see Shannon Smith Calitri, "'Give Me Eighty Men': Shattering the Myth of the Fetterman Massacre," *Montana: The Magazine of Western History* 54 (Autumn 2004), 44–59; and Kinsley Bray, personal communication.

59. I. V. D. Reeve to E. W. Smith, Jan. 7, 1867, LR, Headquarters, Department of Dakota, 1866–1877, M1734, National Archives and Records Service, roll 1; Carrington, "History of Indian Operations on the Plains," 20–21; Marie Caroline Post, *The Life and Mémoirs of Comte Régis de Trobriand, Major-General in the Army of the United States* (New York: E. P. Dutton, 1910), 367; James Bridger to the Editor, May 4, 1867, *Army and Navy Journal*, June 29, 1867, 715; Sully to O. H. Browning, Apr. 4, 1867, MMSC ("offered"); Frank Rzeczkowski, *Uniting the Tribes: The Rise and Fall of Pan-Indian Community on the Crow Reservation* (Lawrence: University Press of Kansas, 2012), 52–61; Bray, *Crazy Horse*, 95; McCrady, *Living with Strangers*, 11–15, 24–26; Michael Hogue, *Metis and the Medicine Line: Creating a Border and Dividing a People* (Chapel Hill: University of North Carolina Press, 2015), 75. The temporary truces with the Crows were delicate because violent clashes alternated with trade fairs. See N. C. Kinney to AAAG, Feb. 9, 1867, SF, roll 7; *YSF*, 255–56, 258; and Sully to Curtis, Feb. 25, 1865, in *War of the Rebellion* 48, Part 1: 979–80 ("They come," 980). For horse losses, see *YSF*, 296–98.

60. Even as Lakotas and their allies were mobilizing for war, U.S. Army officers believed that the Indians would and could not launch a general war. See Olson, *Red Cloud and the Sioux Problem*, 48–50; and Silas Seymour, *Incidents of a Trip through the Great Platte Valley, Rocky Mountains and Laramie Plains in the Fall of 1866* (New York: D. Van Nostrand), 89–90 ("The shock," 89; "What then," 90).

61. Carrington, "History of Indian Operations on the Plains," 14–26, 49; Report of the Special Commissioner, July 8, 1867, *Hostilities*, 60–62; Gray, *Custer's Last Campaign*, 49–51; Larson, *Red Cloud*, 98. Frances Carrington, the wife of Henry B. Carrington, commander of Fort Phil Kearny, provides a frank account of the events and the mood in the fort during the summer and fall of 1866. See Carrington, *My Army Life and the Fort Phil. Kearney Massacre*, 293–94.

62. J. W. Vaughn, *Indian Fights: New Facts on Seven Encounters* (Norman: University of Oklahoma Press, 1966), 32–42; Grinnell, *Fighting Cheyennes*, 223; John B. Sanborn to Browning, July 8, 1867, *Hostilities*, 63–64. The literature on what became known as the "Fetterman Massacre" is vast. There were no American survivors, and the battle became a focus of national debate in the United States for years. Here I have imagined the battle from an Indigenous viewpoint, focusing on what Lakotas and their allies wanted, what they may have seen and known, and how they organized for war. By December 6, Carrington had adopted a policy of attacking the "hostiles" at every opportunity. See Dee Brown, *The Fetterman Massacre* (London: Pan Books, 1974), 170–74.

63. Bray, *Crazy Horse*, 96–97; Grinnell, *Fighting Cheyennes*, 228–29 ("a hundred," 229); Brown, *Fetterman Massacre*, 186–88.

64. "Enid Neihardt's Transcription of Fire Thunder's Account," in *Eyewitnesses to the Fetterman Fight: Indian Views*, ed. John E. Monnett (Norman: University of Oklahoma Press, 2017), 51; Marshall, *Journey of Crazy Horse*, 146–47; Grinnell, *Fighting Cheyennes*, 223–24; Vestal, *Warpath*, 53–54; Report of the Special Commissioner, 63–66. The troops may have headed directly toward the Lodge Trail Ridge in order to cut off the retreat of the warriors surrounding the woodcutting detail. See Bray, *Crazy Horse*, 98. Vestal's *Warpath* is centered on the biography of Minneconjou chief White Bull who in 1932 related his life story to historian Stanley Vestal who cross-checked it with other historical sources. The biography and the historical events it describes are generally considered accurate, but the biography's true value is in that reveals a rare Indian perspective on a long stretch of Lakota history.

65. For Native accounts, see "Enid Neihardt's Transcription of Fire Thunder's Account," 51–52; "Two Moons' Story," in Hyde, *Life of George Bent*, 343–46; Grinnell, *Fighting Cheyennes*, 225–35; *Warpath*, 56–69; and Marshall, *Journey of Crazy Horse*, 149–50. *Warpath* provides the accounts of White Bull, a Minneconjou warrior, and White Elk, a Cheyenne elder, related decades later. Further information on how the battle unfolded can be gleaned from contemporary military reports and correspondence and an 1887 congressional investigation. See Henry B. Carrington, "Report," Jan. 3, 1867, Sen. Ex. Doc. 97, 49th Cong., 2d Sess., 2–4; Carrington, "History of Indian Operations on the Plains," 2–41; Henry B. Carrington, "In the Matter of Fort Philip Kearny Massacre," LROIA, UPA, roll 892; and Sanborn to Browning, July 8, 1867, in *Hostilities*, 64–65. For scholarly discussions, see Bray, *Crazy Horse*, 97–102; Brown, *Fetterman Massacre*, 187–99; and Vaughn, *Indian Fights*, 44–90. For an argument that U.S. officers and troops were unaware of the vast numbers of allied warriors behind the Lodge Trail Ridge and that High Backbone's ruse had worked, see John H. Monnett, *Where a Hundred Soldiers Were Killed: The Struggle for the Powder River Country in 1866 and the Making of the Fetterman Myth* (Albuquerque: University of New Mexico Press, 2008), 134–35.

66. Carrington, "Report," 4–5; Monnett, *Where a Hundred Soldiers Were Killed*, 144–51; William Murphy, "The Forgotten Battalion," *Annals of Wyoming* 7 (1930), 390. For the cultural context of mutilations, see Douglas D. Scott, "Archaeological Perspectives on the Battle of the Little Bighorn: A Retrospective," in *Legacy: New Perspectives on the Battle of the Little Bighorn*, ed. Charles R. Rankin (Helena: Montana Historical Society, 1996), 178–79.

67. "Two Moons' Story," 346; *RCF*, 159; Bray, *Crazy Horse*, 102; *YSF*, 239 ("They killed"); Black Elk account, in *Eyewitnesses to the Fetterman Fight*, ed. Monnett, 47 ("I can remember," "It was"). There is considerable disagreement about Red Cloud's role in the Fetterman Fight. See Larson, *Red Cloud*, 99–100; Vestal, *Warpath*, 68; Buford to Stanton, June 6, 1867, SF, roll 7; and John R. Brennan to Doane Robinson, Feb. 23, 1904, Doane Robinson Papers, 1880–1946, box 3359A, folder 5: Correspondence, 1904, SDHS.

68. Buford to Stanton, June 6, 1867, SF, roll 7 ("last"); Bain, *Empire Express*, 312.

69. Carrington, "Report," 3; Olson, *Red Cloud and the Sioux Problem*, 51–56; Shannon D.

Smith, *Give Me Eighty Men: Women and the Myth of the Fetterman Fight* (Lincoln: University of Nebraska Press, 2008), 128–34; Browning to Sully et al., Feb. 18, 1867, *Hostilities*, 55–56.

70. Sully to N. G. Taylor, Apr. 22, 1867, Sully, letter, May 6, 1867, Sanborn, letter, May 8, 1867, and Sanborn to S. T. Bulkley, May 9, 1867, MMSC; Sully to C. C. Augur, May 19, 1867, LROIA, UPA, roll 892; Buford to Stanton, June 6, 1867, SF, roll 7 ("horrible," "justifiable," "assigned," "unnecessary," "there is no"); Speech of Spotted Tail, Apr. 20, 1867, MMSC ("ours"); William Tecumseh Sherman to George Cooke, Dec. 28, 1867, quoted in Olson, *Red Cloud and the Sioux Problem*, 52 ("Of course," "It is not necessary"). For the hard army line, see also Sully to Browning, Apr. 4, 1867, MMSC. General Sully reported that the extension of Lakota hunting grounds south of the Platte Valley was "only a temporary arrangement during existing difficulties with the military and the Sioux and other Indians in this section." See Sully to Commanding Officer, Apr. 25, 1876, MMSC.

71. Sanborn to Browning, July 8, 1867, *Hostilities*, 67; Cooke to J. A. Rawlings, Dec. 27, 1866, Sen. Ex. Doc. 15, 39th Cong., 2d Sess., 6–7 ("not equal," 6; "our best," "this best," 7); RCF, 158; Utley, *Indian Frontier*, 105–7.

72. Sully to L. V. Bogy, Mar. 9, 1867, *Hostilities*, 76 ("too hot"); Augur to W. T. Sherman, May 22, 1867, and Sherman to Grant, June 11, 1867, SF, roll 7 ("this enemy's," "we have no" in Sherman to Grant); Stanley, *My Early Travels*, 1: 131–33 ("worthless," 131); J. F. Kinney to N. G. Taylor, June 4, 1867, *Hostilities*, 127; RCF, 157–58; Granville Stuart, *Forty Years on the Frontier as Seen in the Journals and Reminiscences of Granville Stuart*, 2 vols., ed. Paul C. Phillips (Cedar Rapids, IA: Torch Press, 1925), 2: 62–66; George W. Webb, *Chronological List of Engagements between the Regular Army of the United States and Various Tribes of Hostile Indians Which Occurred during the Years 1790 to 1892, Inclusive* (St. Joseph, MO: Wing, 1939), 28–29; Bray, *Crazy Horse*, 103–4; RCF, 154; Utley, *Frontier Regulars*, 133–55; Prucha, *Great Father*, 549–56.

73. Philippe Régis Denis de Trobriand, *Army Life in Dakota: Selections from the Journal of Philippe Régis Denis de Keredern de Trobriand*, ed. Milo Milton Quaife, trans. George Francis Will (Chicago: Lakeside Press, 1941), 26–27, 45, 102, 157–58, 231; Reeve to Smith, Dec. 29, 1866, and Feb. 24, 1867, and J. R. Hansen to D. S. Stanley, May 24, 1867, LR, Headquarters, Department of Dakota, 1866–1877, M1734, roll 1 ("destroy all," "keep out," "dreadful havoc" in Reeve to Smith, Feb. 24, 1867); Sherman to George K. Leet, July 1, 1867, H. Ex. Doc. 1, 40th Cong., 2d Sess., 65–68 ("all Indians," 67); Sully to Browning, Mar. 23 and May 3, 1867, MMSC; *New York Times*, June 22 and 25, 1867 ("citizens," June 25); N. C. Kinney to AAAG, Feb. 9, 1867, SF, roll 7; Winfield S. Hancock to J. H. Leavenworth, Mar. 11, 1867, *Hostilities*, 81 ("a compact"); Augur to Sherman, May 22, 1867, and Sherman to Grant, June 11, 1867, SF, roll 7 ("you have to," Augur to Sherman; "thieving bands," Sherman to Grant); Sherman to Augur, Apr. 14, 1867, LR, Headquarters, Department of Dakota, 1866–1877, M1734, roll 2; Sully to Browning, Mar. 25, 1867, MMSC; N. G. Taylor et al., "Report to the President by the Indian Peace Commission," Jan. 14, 1868, H. Ex. Doc. 97, 40th Cong., 2d Sess., 14; Sully to N. G. Taylor, Apr. 28, 1867, *Hostilities*, 93. For the

Union Pacific, see Richard White, *Railroaded: The Transcontinentals and the Making of Modern America* (New York: W. W. Norton, 2011), 24.

74. I have refrained from specifying Sitting Bull's exact status and position because, in the end, we simply do not know for certain. There is considerable debate about the issue, interpretations ranging from the maximalist view—that Sitting Bull became supreme chief of all Lakota oyátes—to the minimalist view that Sitting Bull's authority did not reach beyond the Hunkpapas. I have relied mostly on Sitting Bull's own words as well as the testimony of One Bull, Sitting Bull's nephew and adopted son. See "Songs by Sitting Bull," box 104, folder 18, CC; "One Bull Interview," box 104, folder 11, vi, CC; and "Information in Sioux and English with Regard to Sitting Bull Given by His Nephew Chief One Bull," box 104, folder 11, CC. For key scholarly works, see Stanley Vestal, *Sitting Bull, Champion of the Sioux: A Biography* (Boston: Houghton Mifflin, 1932), 91–95; Utley, *Lance and the Shield*, 84–89; Ostler, *Plains Sioux and U.S. Colonialism*, 52; Anderson, *Sitting Bull*, 68–71; James Macfarlane, "'Chief of All the Sioux': An Assessment of Sitting Bull and Lakota Unity, 1868–1876," *American Nineteenth Century History* 11 (Sept. 2010), 299–320; and Kingsley M. Bray, "Before Sitting Bull: Interpreting Hunkpapa Political History, 1750–1867," *South Dakota History* 40 (Summer 2010), 97–135. I have relied on Kingsley Bray's conclusion on the timing of Sitting Bull's inauguration. See *Crazy Horse*, 105–6, 420, fn 8.

75. For the credentials, reputations, and supporters of the three leaders, see Marshall, *Journey of Crazy Horse*, 87–91, 183–86; RCF, 97, 139–40; Olson, *Red Cloud and the Sioux Problem*, 23–26; Utley, *Lance and the Shield*, 86–89; Anderson, *Sitting Bull*, 64–71; and Yenne, *Sitting Bull*, 62–64.

76. Larpenteur, *Forty Years a Fur Trader on the Upper Missouri*, 359 ("I have," "to join," "Look"); Trobriand, *Army Life in Dakota*, 292 ("a fierce").

77. Browning to Sully, Sanborn, Buford, E. S. Parker, J. F. Kinney, and G. P. Beauvais, Feb. 18, 1867, Sanborn to N. G. Taylor, June 16, 1867, and J. F. Kinney to N. G. Taylor, June 4, 1867, *Hostilities*, 55–56, 115–16, 126; Denman to N. G. Taylor, July 16, 1867, and Patrick to Denman, July 28, 1867, LROIA, UPA, roll 892; Paul L. Hedren, *Powder River: Disastrous Opening of the Great Sioux War* (Norman: University of Oklahoma Press, 2016), 21. In the spring of 1867 the army was also making plans to fortify Fort Laramie, punish hostile Lakotas, and keep the Bozeman Road open, even though there was a growing realization that the war was unwinnable. See Sherman to Augur, Apr. 14, 1867, LR, Headquarters, Department of Dakota, 1866–1877, M1734, roll 2.

78. Vestal, *Warpath*, 71–79; Monnett, *Where a Hundred Soldiers Were Killed*, 194–201; Jerome A. Green, "The Hayfield Fight: A Reappraisal of a Neglected Action," *Montana: The Magazine of Western History* 22 (Autumn 1972), 35–41.

79. For estimates of Native casualties at the Wagon Box Fight, see Vestal, *Warpath*, 79–82.

80. For the situation in 1866 and 1867, see Karl Jacoby, *Shadows at Dawn: An Apache Massacre and the Violence of History* (New York: Penguin, 2008), 78–90; West, *Contested Plains*, 309–10; Madley, *American Genocide*, esp. 330–34; White, *Republic for Which It Stands*, 108–15; Hämäläinen, "Reconstructing the Great Plains," 491–94, 499–500; *Congressional Globe*, 40th Cong., 1st Sess., July 1867, 667 ("fifty"); and

Kerry O. Oman, "The Beginning of the End: The Indian Peace Commission of 1867–1868," *Great Plains Quarterly* 22 (Winter 2002), 37.

81. Oman, "Beginning of the End," 35–38; Prucha, *American Indian Treaties,* 279–80; Sherman to Grant, June 11, 1867, SF, roll 7 ("hostilities").

82. "Council with the Minneconjou, Oglalla, Onk-Pah-Pas, Brules, Two Kettles, and Blackfeet Sioux Tribes," "Council with the Yanktons," and "Council with the Santees," in *Proceedings of the Great Peace Commission of 1867–1868,* with an introduction by Vine Deloria, Jr., and Raymond J. DeMallie (Washington, DC: Institute for the Development of Indian Law, 1975), 32–47, 51–54 ("All the men," 33; "as I am," 36).

83. "Meeting with Chiefs and Headmen," and "Council with Spotted Tail's Camp," in *Proceedings of the Great Peace Commission,* 57–66 ("Tell our," 59; "the road," 61; "a war," 63); Stanley, *My Early Travels,* 1: 199–207 ("our trade," 205); "Report of Indian Peace Commissioners," H. Ex. Doc. 97, 40th Cong., 2d Sess., 4 ("To give"); "Council with the Cheyennes, Brulés, Ogallalahs, etc., at North Platte, September 18, 1876," in *Papers Relating to Talks and Councils,* 48–55; Denman to CoIA, Aug. 24, 1867, LROIA, UPA, roll 892. There has been a strong tendency in the scholarship to essentialize the hostile-friendly division in Lakota politics. For Sicangu maneuvering, see Kingsley M. Bray, "Spotted Tail and the Treaty of 1868," *Nebraska History* 83 (Spring 2002), esp. 23–25.

84. Buford to Stanton, June 6, 1867, *Hostilities,* 59 ("dissatisfied"); Patrick to Denman, July 28, 1867, LROIA, UPA, roll 892 ("were all"); Bettelyoun and Waggoner, *With My Own Eyes,* 105. For Sherman, see Stanley, *My Early Travels,* 1: 153 ("with a dash"); and Ron Chernow, *Grant* (London: Head of Zeus, 2017), 353.

85. Hyde, *Life of George Bent,* 346; "Report of Indian Peace Commissioners," 5 ("the formidable," "a just," "whenever"); Beauvais to SI, Sept. 29 and Dec. 14, 1867, LROIA, UPA, roll 892 ("may as well," Sept. 29; "no argument," Dec. 14); Marshall, *Journey of Crazy Horse,* 152–55. For Red Cloud's stature among Americans, see Price, *Oglala People,* 67–68, 76–77, 82; and Oman, "Beginning of the End," 38–39. For the Union Pacific, see Larson, *Red Cloud,* 108. For Red Cloud's elusiveness, see also Sully to N. G. Taylor, Apr. 22, 1867, MMSC. For inter-oyáte diplomacy, see Beauvais to SI, Dec. 14, 1867, LROIA, UPA, roll 892; and Trobriand, *Army Life in Dakota,* 256–57.

86. "Proceedings of Council with the Brule at Fort Laramie, April 28 and 29, 1868, at Which a Treaty Was Signed," "Proceedings of Council with Spotted Tail of the Brules and Others of His Hand, at North Platte, April 4, 1868," "Proceedings of Preliminary Council at Laramie, April 13," and "Council of the Indian Peace Commission with the Oglala Sioux Indians at Fort Laramie, Dak. T., May 24, 1868," in *Papers Relating to Talks and Councils,* 5–15, 85–89 ("if there," 88); "Council with One Horn, Elk That Bellows Walking, and the Minneconjous," in *Proceedings of the Great Peace Commission,* 119–20. For the Medicine Lodge Creek treaties, see Utley, *Frontier Regulars,* 133.

87. Sherman to Grant, May 8, 1868, H. Ex. Doc. 239, 40th Cong., 2d Sess., 1–3; Denman to N. G. Taylor, Nov. 6, 1868, ARCIA 1868, 230–31; Utley, *Lance and the Shield,* 78. For De Smet and treaty talks, see De Smet, *Life,* 3: 911–21 ("I hardly," 912; "the whites," 816; "most distinguished," 918); and "Statement by the Rev. P. J. De Smet,

S.J., of His Reception by and Council with the Hostile Unkpapa Indians," in *Papers Relating to Talks and Councils*, 108–13.

88. Charles Geren to N. G. Taylor, July 1, 1868, *ARCIA 1868*, 252–54; "Account of Red Cloud Signing the Treaty, Nov. 29, 1868," in *Proceedings of the Great Peace Commission*, 173–76 ("dignity," "his name," "washed," 174; "touch," 175); Bettelyoun and Waggoner, *With My Own Eyes*, 105; Red Cloud, *Autobiography*, 190; Ostler, *Lakotas and the Black Hills*, 62. For the raids in the central plains, see Bray, "Spotted Tail and the Treaty of 1868," 29–30.

89. "Treaty with the Sioux—Brulé, Oglala, Miniconjou, Yanktonai, Hunkpapa, Blackfeet, Cuthead, Two Kettle, Sans Arcs, and Santee—and Arapaho, 1868," *IALT* 2: 998–1007 ("absolute," 998; "unceded," "no white," "so long," 1002). For incisive discussions of the treaty terms, see Ostler, *Plains Sioux and U.S. Colonialism*, 48–51; Ostler, *Lakotas and the Black Hills*, 63–67; and Edward Lazarus, *Black Hills/White Justice: The Sioux Nation versus the United States, 1775 to Present* (New York: Harper Collins, 1991), 268–69. My reading of the 1868 Fort Laramie Treaty and its meaning to Lakotas differs somewhat from previous interpretations by emphasizing the multiple—and often unintentional—ways in which the articles of the treaty facilitated Lakota expansion at the expense of their Indigenous neighbors and rivals. While the treaty did create a legal framework for later imposition of U.S. sovereignty over the Lakotas, in the immediate aftermath it underwrote Lakota power. For the Union Pacific, Utah, and Montana, see Robert G. Athearn, *Union Pacific Country* (1971; rprt. Lincoln: University of Nebraska Press, 1976), 204–5.

90. "Council of the Indian Peace Commission with the Oglala Sioux Indians at Fort Laramie," 85 ("I consider"); "Treaty with the Sioux—Brulé, Oglala, Miniconjou, Yanktonai, Hunkpapa, Blackfeet, Cuthead, Two Kettle, Sans Arcs, and Santee—and Arapaho, 1868," *IALT* 2: 999–1002. The Lakota gravitation northward into what became designed as "unceded Indian territory" was already under way and known to U.S. officials in 1865. See Sully to AAG, Department of Missouri, Aug. 13, 1865, *War of the Rebellion* 48, Part 2: 1181–82.

91. "Council of the Indian Peace Commission with the Oglala Sioux Indians at Fort Laramie," 88–89 ("we do not," 88; "plenty," "to leave," 89); Utley, *Lance and the Shield*, 84.

92. *YSF*, 260–62; *BMWC*, 33; *DWC*, 21; James H. Howard, "Dakota Winter Counts as a Source of Plains History," *Smithsonian Institution, Bureau of American Ethnology Bulletin* 173, Anthropological Papers No. 61, 391–92. See also Bettelyoun and Waggoner, *With My Own Eyes*, 80.

8. SHAPESHIFTERS

1. For fee-based governance, see Nicholas R. Parrillo, *Against the Profit Motive: The Salary Revolution in American Government, 1780–1940* (New Haven: Yale University Press, 2013), esp. 15–21, 121–24; Richard White, *The Republic for Which It Stands: The United States during Reconstruction and the Gilded Age, 1867–1896* (New York: Oxford University Press, 2017).

2. For post–Civil War years and the emergence of modern America, see Alan Trachtenberg, *The Incorporation of America: Culture and Society in the Gilded Age* (New York: Hill and Wang, 1982); Heather Cox Richardson, *West from Appomattox: The Reconstruction of America after the Civil War* (New Haven: Yale University Press, 2007), 78–93; White, *Republic for Which It Stands*, esp. 23–252; and T. J. Stiles, *Custer's Trials: A Life on the Frontier of a New America* (New York: Vintage, 2015), xvi–xxi; "Report of the Secretary of the Interior," Nov. 15, 1869, H. Ex. Doc. 1, Part 3, 41st Cong., 2d Sess., vii–ix.

3. William Stewart, "Report," Feb. 19, 1869, S. Report 219, 40th Cong., 3d Sess., 15–16 ("The locomotive," 15; "As the thorough," 16). See also Robert G. Angevine, *The Railroad and the State: War, Politics, and Technology in the Nineteenth-Century America* (Stanford: Stanford University Press, 2004), 171–73; and Stanley, *My Early Travels*, 173–77.

4. For Lakota raids, see J. A. Potter to J. R. Hanson, May 5, 1868, Upper Missouri Agency Records, 1863–1870, MS 17, box 1, folder 1, Agency Correspondence, January–June, 1868, SASDHS; DeWitt C. Poole to E. S. Parker, Oct. 1, 1869, LROIA, UPA, roll 894; Charles H. Whaley to Denman, Aug. 20, 1868, *ARCIA 1868*, 234–35; Wm. H. Hugo to Parker, Nov. 13, 1869, LROIA, Ponca Agency, roll 671; Stuart, *Forty Years*, 2: 84–85; and Bray, "Spotted Tail," 28–30. For Sheridan, see Paul Andrew Hutton, *Phil Sheridan and His Army* (Lincoln: University of Nebraska Press, 1985), esp. 20–27. For Custer and the Washita, see Stiles, *Custer's Trials*, 283–305, 310–16; Jerome A. Greene, *Washita: The U.S. Army and the Southern Cheyennes, 1867–1869* (Norman: University of Oklahoma Press, 2004), 116–38. For Dog Soldiers, see West, *Contested Plains*, 311–16. For a comprehensive study of Pawnee scouts, see Mark Van de Logt, *War Party in Blue: Pawnee Scouts in the U.S. Army* (Norman: University of Nebraska Press, 2010).

5. For Grant's vision, see Ulysses S. Grant, "First Annual Message," Dec. 6, 1869, in *A Compilation of the Messages and Papers of the Presidents*, 20 vols., comp. James D. Richardson (New York: Bureau of National Literature, 1897), 9: 3993. For Peace Policy, see "Report to the President by of the Indian Peace Commission, January 7, 1868," *ARCIA 1868*, 27–50 ("barbarous dialects," "one homogenous," 44); Francis A. Walker, *The Indian Question* (Boston: James S. Osgood, 1874), 63 ("The lower"); Francis Paul Prucha, *American Indian Policy in Crisis: Christian Reformers and the Indian, 1865–1900* (Norman: University of Oklahoma Press, 1964), 30–56; and Mark Wahlgren Summers, *The Ordeal of Reunion: A New History of Reconstruction* (Chapel Hill: University of North Carolina Press, 2014), 181–82.

6. YSF, 262–63; Parker to Hanson, June 11, 1869, Upper Missouri Agency Records, 1863–1870, MS 17, box 1, folder 3, Agency Correspondence, January–June, 1869, SASDHS; Hanson to Parker, July 9, 1869, and W. Hill to D. S. Stanley, Oct. 3, 1869, Upper Missouri Agency Records, 1863–1870, MS 17, box 1, folder 4, Agency Correspondence, July–December, 1869, SASDHS; Alfred Terry to Col. Alexander Chambers, July 13, 1868, Upper Missouri Agency Records, 1863–1870, MS 17, box 1, folder 1, Agency Correspondence, January–June, 1868, SASDHS; Hanson to A. J. Faulk, Sept. 16, 1868, Upper Missouri Agency Records, 1863–1870, MS 17, box 1, folder 12, Agent's

Monthly Reports to the Superintendent of Indian Affairs, 1868–1869, SASDHS ("very cheering," "progress," "The peace," "appropriates").

7. For cattle on the hoof, see D. C. Poole, *Among the Sioux of Dakota: Eighteen Months' Experience as an Indian Agent*, 1869–70 (New York: D. Van Nostrand, 1881), 94–95; and Walker, *Indian Question*, 32.

8. For Lakota villages, traders, and trade goods, see Standing Bear, *My People the Sioux*, 13; N. C. Kinney to AAAG, Feb. 9, 1867, SF, roll 7; J. A. Campbell to Parker, Aug. 5, 1870, LROIA, UPA, roll 896; Cole to Grant, Feb. 10, 1867, in *Powder River Campaigns*, 81; De Smet, *Life*, 3: 911–14; A. J. Simmons to B. R. Cowen, Dec. 8, 1872, LROIA, Montana Superintendency, roll 495; J. W. Daniels to CoIA, LROIA, RCA, roll 717; *RCF*, 153; and "Official Report of General Custer," Aug. 15, 1873, in Ami Frank Mulford, *Fighting Indians in the 7th United States Cavalry: Custer's Favorite Regiment* (Corning, NY: Paul Lindsley Munford, n.d.), 139; and Brown, *Fetterman Massacre*, 186, 81. For a Hunkpapa account of village movements in the early and mid-1870s, see Joseph White Bull statement in Stanley Vestal, *New Sources of Indian History, 1850–1891* (Norman: University of Oklahoma Press, 1934), 159–63. For Red Cloud and trade protocols, see ARC, 153–54. For weapons and imported goods, see James A. Hanson, *Metal Weapons, Tools and Ornaments of the Teton Dakota Indians* (Chadron, NE: Museum of the Fur Trade, 2001), 22–110; and Hanson and Walters, "Early Fur Trade," 16–17. For horse herds, see Ewers, *Horse in Blackfoot Indian Culture*, 32; and Pekka Hämäläinen, "The Rise and Fall of the Plains Indian Horse Culture," *Journal of American History* 90 (Dec. 2003), 861. Until the late 1840s, the Comanches had been the wealthiest Native nation in the interior by a conformable margin, but by the late 1860s their economy and power had collapsed precipitously. See Hämäläinen, *Comanche Empire*, esp. 239–330.

9. Richard Irving Dodge, *Our Wild Indians: Thirty-Three Years' Personal Experience among the Red Men of the Great West* (Hartford, CT: A. D. Worthington, 1883), 450 ("the Plains Indian").

10. Eugene Buechel and Paul I. Manhart, *Lakota Tales and Texts*, 2 vols. (Chamberlain, SD: Tipi Press, 1998), 2: 624, 629 ("This tribe," "I shall," 629); Bray, *Crazy Horse*, 132–33.

11. DeMallie, "Yankton and Yanktonai," 779–81; P. H. Conger to Faulk, Sept. 7, 1868, and Benjamin Thompson to N. G. Taylor, Oct. 31, 1868, ARCIA 1868, 186–87, 193–96; John A. Burbank to Parker, Oct. 1, 1869, ARCIA 1869, 302 ("located"); P. H. Conger to Burbank, ibid., 306–8; *STF*, 162.

12. David E. Wilkins, *American Indian Sovereignty and the U.S. Supreme Court: The Masking of Justice* (Austin: University of Texas Press, 1997), 52.

13. Hanson to Faulk, Sept. 16, 1868, Upper Missouri Agency Records, 1863–1870, MS 17, box 1, folder 12, Agent's Monthly Reports to the Superintendent of Indian Affairs, 1868–1869, SASDHS ("The peace," "appropriates"). See also Memorial and Petition to His Excellency U. S. Grant President of the United States and to the Senate and House of Representatives in Congress Assembled, 1870, and J. M. Flemming to Campbell, Apr. 19, 1870, LROIA, UPA, roll 896.

14. Ostler, *Lakotas and the Black Hills*, 71; Matthew G. Hannah "Space and Social Con-

trol in the Administration of the Oglala Lakota ('Sioux'), 1871–1879," *Journal of Historical Geography* 19 (Oct. 1993), 412–32; *RCF*, 194–95; *Report of the Special Commission Appointed to Investigate the Affairs at the Red Cloud Indian Agency*, 13, 97, 282, 382, 572, 603. Hannah sees in the government attempts to control the Lakotas a systematic policy of spatial fixation aimed at rendering the Lakotas visible, accountable, and civilized.

15. *STF*, 146–69; "Treaty with the Sioux—Brulé, Oglala, Miniconjou, Yanktonai, Hunkpapa, Blackfeet, Cuthead, Two Kettle, Sans Arcs, and Santee—and Arapaho, 1868," *IALT* 2: 1001; J. C. O'Connor to H. R. Clum, Sept. 18, 1871, *ARCIA 1871*, 526 ("tame"); Hanson to AAG, Sept. 16, 1868, Upper Missouri Agency Records, 1863–1870, MS 17, box 1, folder 12, Agent's Monthly Reports to the Superintendent of Indian Affairs, 1868–1869, SASDHS; Burbank to Parker, Oct. 1, 1869, *ARCIA 1869*, 302–6; Chambers to George D. Ruggles, Aug. 2, 1870, LROIA, UPA, roll 895; Poole, *Among the Sioux of Dakota*, 115–16; DeMallie, "Yankton and Yanktonai," 782.

16. "Hostile" is a derogatory non-Indigenous term for the nonagency Lakotas who, broadly speaking, included the northern Lakota oyátes led by such renowned chiefs as Sitting Bull and Crazy Horse. In this and the next chapter I argue, however, that the hostile-friendly dichotomy was a simplification that obfuscated U.S. government agents' understanding of the Lakota nation and politics and seriously undermined their efforts to control and domesticate the Lakotas. While the agencies and the government policies did cause friction among different thióšpayes and oyátes, Lakotas preserved their sense of solidarity and continued to function as a unified nation. This unity largely escaped the U.S. agents who consigned the Lakotas into rigid preconceived administrative categories. It has also tended to elude later historians who, in general, have focused on either the agency or nonagency Lakotas, rarely placing both in the same frame. Keeping *all* the Lakota oyátes in the same frame is precisely my goal in chapters 8 and 9.

17. D. S. Stanley to CoIA, Aug 17, 1869, LROIA, UPA, roll 894 ("over-awing"); D. S. Stanley to O. D. Greene, Aug. 20, 1869, *ARCIA 1869*, 330–31 ("there is," 331); W. Harmon to Sheridan, Dec. 9, 1869, and Stanley to Greene, Feb. 12, 1870, LROIA, UPA, roll 895 ("Indians constantly" in Harmon to Sheridan); Stanley to E. S. Parker, May 7, 1870, and George M. Randall to E. S. Parker, Sept. 1, 1870, LROIA, UPA, roll 896; Burbank to Parker, Sept. 30, 1870, *ARCIA 1870*, 207–8 ("white fool," 208); Walker, *Indian Question*, 30–31; Pekka Hämäläinen, "Reconstructing the Great Plains: The Long Struggle for Sovereignty and Dominance in the Heart of the Continent," *Journal of the Civil War Era* 6 (Dec. 2016), 500–502. Lakota strategies of managing the distance between themselves and the United States are an example of what James Scott had called "the art of not being governed." See James C. Scott, *The Art of Not Being Governed: An Anarchist History of Upland Southeast Asia* (New Haven: Yale University Press, 2009).

18. For the struggles of government officials, see Burbank to E. S. Parker, Aug. 31, 1869, and Chambers to Ruggles, May 1 and 6, 1870, LROIA, UPA, roll 894; S. S. Turner to Burbank, Mar. 9, 1870, Sheridan to Sherman, May 14, 1870, Sherman to Sheridan, May 18, 1870, Sherman to Tho. M. Vincent, July 13, 1870, and N. H. French to S. B.

Hayman, July 6, 1870, LROIA, UPA, roll 895; and Randall to Burbank, Apr. 5, 1870, Randall to Parker, Apr. 23, 1870, Poole to Burbank, Apr. 28, 1870, and J. A. Hearn to Burbank, June 29, 1870, LROIA, UPA, roll 896 ("displaying," "deliberately," Randall to Parker).

19. For Sitting Bull, see Utley, *Lance and the Shield*, 85–89; and Peter Cozzens, *The Earth Is Weeping: The Epic Story of the Indian Wars of the American West* (New York: Alfred A. Knopf, 2016), 192. According to DeMallie, in 1869 most Lakotas lived in the unceded territory. See DeMallie, "Teton," 797.

20. "Songs by Sitting Bull," box 104, folder 18, CC ("Ye tribes"); Typescripts by Robert Higheagle, box 104, folder 24, CC. There are multiple views on Sitting Bull's exact title and authority. See, for example, Utley, *Lance and the Shield*, 85–86; Ostler, *Plains Sioux and U.S. Colonialism*, 52–53; Anderson, *Sitting Bull*, 68–71; and Mac-farlane, "'Chief of All the Sioux.'" My interpretation emphasized the dual nature of power in the Lakota society: it was at once fluid and fixed to a person, both hori-zontal and hierarchical. One Bull says that Crazy Horse was elected here as the head war chief of the Oglalas, but he may have conflated two processes of political reform among the Lakotas.

21. N. G. Taylor to Sherman, July 29, 1868, and Patrick to Denman, Sept. 16, 1868, LROIA, UPA, roll 893; Poole to CoIA, July 21 and 27, 1869, LROIA, UPA, roll 894; Poole to Burbank, Feb. 24, 1870, LROIA, UPA, roll 895; Poole to Augur, Jan. 8, 1870, Poole to Burbank, Apr. 28, 1870, and Burbank to CoIA, Sept. 1, 1870, LROIA, UPA, roll 896; Burbank to Parker, Sept. 30, 1870, ARCIA 1870, 206–7 ("their nomadic," 206); Susan Bordeaux Bettelyoun and Josephine Waggoner, *With My Own Eyes: A Lakota Woman Tells Her People's History*, ed. Emily Levine (Lincoln: University of Nebraska Press, 1998), 5, 90 ("terrible debauchery," 5); Poole, *Among the Sioux of Dakota*, 117–20; STF, 152–69; Bray, "Spotted Tail," 30–33; STF, 161–64; RCF, 170–71.

22. For Red Cloud and Spotted Tail, see STF, 146–69; and Olson, *Red Cloud and the Sioux Problem*, 24–26, 130–54. For Sitting Bull, see Utley, *Lance and the Shield*, 84–89.

23. Price, *Oglala People*, 86, 96; Bray, "Spotted Tail," 31; RCF, 172; STF, 172. Impressed by what they understood as Sitting Bull's patriotism and Spotted Tail's adaptability, some historians have tended to portray Red Cloud as an uncouth and stubborn "non-progressive" who clung "stubbornly to the old roving and hunting life and never to give it up" and failed to formulate coherent policies. "For an Indian," concluded George E. Hyde, "Red Cloud was an able man, but it is to be doubted whether he ever had the breadth of vision that Spotted Tail sometimes exhibited." See RCF, 172 for all quotes.

24. John E. Smith to E. S. Parker, July 15, 1870, LROIA, UPA, 1870, roll 896; Poole, *Among the Sioux of Dakota*, 181–87. For the U.S. president as tȟuŋkášila, grandfather, see DeMallie, "Touching the Pen," 50–51; and Ostler, *Plains Sioux and U.S. Colo-nialism*, 112.

25. West, *Contested Plains*, 313–16; J. P. Cooper to Denman, Aug. 27, 1868, LROIA, UPA, roll 893; O' Connor to Clum, Sept. 9, 1871, LROIA, GRA, roll 305; Warren A. Beck and Ynez D. Haase, *Historical Atlas of the American West* (Norman: University of

Oklahoma Press, 1989), map 10; Andy R. Graybill, *The Red and the White: A Family Saga in the American West* (New York: W. W. Norton, 2013), 121–29.

26. *RCF*, 171–73; *STF*, 172–73; Bray, *Crazy Horse*, 132–34; Sheridan to Sherman, Apr. 27, 28, and 29, 1870, Sherman to Sheridan, May 4, 5, and 18, 1870, John Evans et al. to E. D. Townsend, May 17, 1870, and A. M. Robinson to J. C. B. Davis, May 30, 1870, LROIA, UPA, roll 895; Sherman to W. W. Belknap, Apr. 21, 1870, Chambers to Ruggles, May 1, 1870, and John E. Smith to Parker, July 15, 1870, LROIA, UPA, roll 896; *Daily Alta California*, June 2, 1870 ("drive out"); "Third Annual Report of the Board of Indian Commissioners," Dec. 12, 1871, *ARCIA 1871*, 13 ("wise"). For western attitudes, see "Petition of Citizens of Carbon County Wyoming to His Excellency U S Grant, Pres. of U.S.," June 4, 1870, LROIA, UPA, roll 896.

27. Poole to Burbank, Nov. 24, 1869, and Burbank to E. S. Parker, Nov. 29, 1869, LROIA, UPA, roll 894; Price, *Oglala People*, 90; Poole, *Among the Sioux of Dakota*, 164–66; *New York Times*, June 2 and 3, 1870; John E. Smith to Parker, July 15, 1870, LROIA, UPA, roll 896; *RCF*, 174–75; *STF*, 166–69, 173–74. While recognizing the broad and transcending influence of both Spotted Tail and Red Cloud, U.S. officials tended to associate Spotted Tail with the friendlies and Red Cloud with the hostiles. See Olson, *Red Cloud and the Sioux Problem*, 96–99.

28. Poole, *Among the Sioux of Dakota*, 151–63, 188–89 ("Indian curiosities," 160; "must expect," "if you had," 189); *New York Times*, June 2, 1870.

29. *New York Times*, June 1, 2, 4, and 5, 1870 ("a man of brains," "create," June 1; "a perfect," June 2); Olson, *Red Cloud and the Sioux Problem*, 98–103.

30. *New York Times*, June 7, 1870 ("the white man," "you will"); *STF*, 177–78; Ostler, *Lakotas and the Black Hills*, 72.

31. Transcript of interviews with Red Cloud in Washington, June 7, 1870, LROIA, UPA, roll 895 ("The Great Father," "I came," "Tell"); Olson, *Red Cloud and the Sioux Problem*, 104–5.

32. *New York Times*, June 8, 1870 ("I have said"); *RCF*, 176–77.

33. *New York Times*, June 11, 1870; "Treaty with the Sioux—Brulé, Oglala, Miniconjou, Yanktonai, Hunkpapa, Blackfeet, Cuthead, Two Kettle, Sans Arcs, and Santee—and Arapaho, 1868," *IALT* 2: 998–1007 ("so long," 1002). It is possible that the interpreters and traders had left many clauses unclear unintentionally in 1868, for many of them were not fully literate. See Ostler, *Lakotas and the Black Hills*, 65.

34. *New York Times*, June 11 and 12, 1870 ("merely," "I never," June 11; "he wanted," June 12).

35. *New York Times*, June 12, 1870; transcript of interviews with Red Cloud, June–July 1870; Poole to Burbank, July 4, 1870, and Burbank to Parker, Sept. 1, 1870, LROIA, UPA, roll 896; *RCF*, 190; Hanson and Walters, "Early Fur Trade," 17–18.

36. *RCF*, 178–80; *New York Times*, June 17, 1870 ("drawing," "You have," "When the Great"); *New York Herald*, June 17, 1870 ("refreshing"); Robert G. Hays, *A Race at Bay: New York Times Editorials on "the Indian Problem," 1860–1890* (Carbondale: Southern Illinois University Press, 1997), 101 ("The magnetism"); transcript of interviews with Red Cloud, June–July.

37. Sherman to Sheridan, Mar. 23 and Apr. 29, 1870, LROIA, UPA, roll 895 ("should be told," Apr. 29); *RCF*, 180; R. L. Smith to Clum, Aug. 18, 1871, LROIA, RCA, roll 715.

38. *RCF*, 181; Franklin Flint to Ruggles, July 15, 1870, and Chambers to Ruggles, Aug. 2. 1870, LROIA, UPA, roll 895.

39. Chambers to Parker, July 8 and 14 and Aug. 2, 1870, Flint to Ruggles, July 15 and Aug. 1, 1870, and "Report of United States Special Indian Commission," Aug. 22–Oct. 18, 1870, LROIA, UPA, roll 895; Flint to Parker, Aug. 6 and 29, 1870, LROIA, UPA, roll 896; R. L. Smith to Ruggles, Mar. 22, 1871, LROIA, RCA, roll 715; J. W. Wham to CoIA, Oct. 26, 1871, *ARCIA 1871*, 697–98 ("where," "their country," 698); Bray, *Crazy Horse*, 150–53. The 1871 ARCIA is one of the first official reports to mention Black Hills gold. It did not spark a rush; knowing what a rush would have meant to their wards, the Indian agents may well have decided not to spread the news.

40. "Third Annual Report of the Board of Indian Commissioners," Dec. 12, 1871, *ARCIA 1871*, 13 ("are extremely").

41. "Report of United States Special Indian Commission," John E. Smith to Parker, July 15, 1870, Augur to Townsend, Aug. 29, 1870, Felix Brunot to C. C. Cox, Oct. 29, 1870, and Flint to Ruggles, Dec. 18, 1870, LROIA, UPA, roll 895 ("was there," "I told," "Report"); Parker to Clum, Apr. 4, 1871, Wham to Parker, Mar. 24, Apr. 11, 12, and 14, and May 12 and 26, 1871, John E. Smith to Parker, Mar. 24 and May 19, 1871, Brunot to Secretary of the Interior, May 22, 1871, John E. Smith to Ruggles, Mar. 22, 1871, and John E. Smith to Parker, May 19, 1871, LROIA, RCA, roll 715; Wham to CoIA, Oct. 26, 1871, *ARCIA 1871*, 698–99; Price, *Oglala People*, 97–98. For the end of treaty making, see Prucha, *American Indian Treaties*, 295–310; and White, *Railroaded*, 59–61. The appropriations bill that ended treaty making declared that while no new treaties would be made, existing treaties would be honored.

42. Wham to CoIA, Oct. 26, 1871, *ARCIA 1871*, 698 ("grand"); Brunot to Columbus Delano, June 12, 1871, LROIA, RCA, roll 715.

43. Thos. K. Cree, "Report of a Council Held at Fort Laramie, Wyoming Territory, June 12, 1871," *ARCIA 1871*, 23.

44. Ibid., 23–26 ("when the Great Father," "cannot shoe," 24; "if trouble," "I have given," "I am afraid," 25; "willing," 26; "wild").

45. Ibid., 26–27 ("I am here," "that is," "We will meet," "are like small," 26; "I do not want," "The earth," 27); Brunot to Delano, June 14 and 15, 1871, LROIA, RCA, roll 715.

46. Wham to Parker, July 1, 2, 7, 8, 10, 12, 13, and 14, 1871, Vincent to Sheridan, July 5, 1871, Parker to Clum, July 7, 1871, William D. Whipple to Sheridan, July 8, 1871, Brunot to Delano, Oct. 21, 1871, and John E. Smith to Clum, Nov. 21, 1871, LROIA, RCA, roll 715; Price, *Oglala People*, 100; Olson, *Red Cloud and the Sioux Problem*, 138–47.

47. Wham to Clum, Aug. 4, Sept. 18, 20, and 25, Oct. 4, and Nov. 3, 1871, and R. L. Smith to Clum, Aug. 8, 1871, LROIA, RCA, roll 715.

48. Cree, "Report of a Council Held at Fort Laramie," 28 ("say").

49. For Lakota resistance of railroads, see "The Indians and the Railroads," *ARCIA 1872*, 75–76; Daniels to Francis A. Walker, July 6, 1872, LROIA, RCA, roll 716; and

O'Connor to CoIA, June 17, 1872, LROIA, GRA, roll 305. For demands to remove the agency, see John E. Smith to Clum, Nov. 21, 1871, LROIA, RCA, roll 715. For railroad companies' influence over the federal government, see White, *Railroaded.*

50. Daniels to Francis A. Walker, Sept. 15, 1872, ARCIA *1872*, 268–69 ("the hostile," "slumber," 268); O'Connor to Francis A. Walker, LROIA, GRA, roll 305; "Report of Hon. B. R. Cowen, Assistant Secretary of the Interior, Hon. N. J. Turney, and Mr. J. W. Wham, Commissioners to Visit the Teton Sioux at and near Fort Peck, Montana," *ARCIA 1872*, 456–57; Edward P. Smith to AAG, Mar. 21, 1872, LROIA, RCA, roll 716. For Black Twin, see Edward P. Smith to AG, Mar. 21, 1872, LROIA, RCA, roll 716; and John J. Saville to Edward P. Smith, Jan. 8, 1874, LROIA, RCA, roll 719.

51. Daniels to Francis A. Walker, Sept. 15, 1872, ARCIA *1872*, 268; Daniels to Francis A. Walker, Feb. 1, Mar. 25 and 30, and Apr. 11 and 14, and May 1, 1872 ("I never saw," "go all over," Apr. 14); John E. Smith to AG, Mar. 21, 1872, John E. Smith to Townsend, Apr. 13, 1872, E. O. C. Ord to Sheridan, Apr. 14, 1872, and Ord to AAG, HQ, Military Division of the Missouri, Apr. 14, 1872 ("should be allowed"), LROIA, RCA, roll 716. For American Horse and They Fear Even His Horses the Younger, see Price, *Oglala People*, 89–90.

52. Daniels to Francis A. Walker, July 6, 1872, LROIA, RCA, roll 716 ("friends," "you must"); *RCF*, 196–98; Daniels to Francis A. Walker, Sept. 11, and 22, 1872, LROIA, RCA, roll 716; Olson, *Red Cloud and the Sioux Problem*, 150–52. Spotted Tail, too, visited Washington in 1872, mainly to discuss the relocation of his agency east near the Missouri. See "Indian Delegations to Washington during the Year," *ARCIA 1872*, 97.

53. John E. Smith to Francis A. Walker, Sept. 22, 1872, Francis A. Walker to John E. Smith, Sept. 26, 1872, John E. Smith to AAG, Sept. 27, 1872, and Daniels to Francis A. Walker, Oct. 24 and 25, 1872, Nov. 11 and 16, and Dec. 12, 1872, LROIA, RCA, roll 716; Daniels to Francis A. Walker, Feb. 28, 1873, Sherman to AAG, Mar. 7, 1873, and Sheridan to Townsend, Dec. 27, 1872, LROIA, RCA, roll 717 ("always," Sheridan to Townsend).

54. J. J. Reynolds to AAG, Dept. of Platte, Jan. 28, 1873, Daniels to CoIA, Feb. 24 and 28, Mar. 25, Apr. 15, May 17, June 12, and Aug. 1, 1873, Brunot to Edward P. Smith, Apr. 11, 1873, John F. Coad to CoIA, May 27, 1873, E. Kemble to Edward P. Smith, June 2, 1873, Henry E. Alvord to CoIA, June 25, 1873, and J. Russell to Post Adjutant, Fort McPherson, Neb., LROIA, RCA, roll 717; Wishart, *Unspeakable Sadness*, 187; *Cheyenne Daily Leader*, June 6, 1873 ("it is very").

55. Alvord to CoIA, June 23, 1873, Saville to Edward P. Smith, Aug. 14 and Sept. 22, 1873, Daniels to Edward P. Smith, Aug. 23, 1873, and Edward P. Smith to SI, Nov. 14, 1873, LROIA, RCA, roll 717 ("*they* would," Saville to Smith, Aug. 14; "intimidate," Daniels to Smith, Aug. 23; "the Indians in council," Saville to Smith, Sept. 22); "Early History of the Pine Ridge Mission, 1874–1892," Woksape Tipi—Academic/Public Library and Archives, Pine Ridge Indian Reservation; Charles W. Allen, *From Fort Laramie to Wounded Knee: In the West That Was* (Lincoln: University of Nebraska Press, 1997), 17; Saville to Edward P. Smith, Aug. 31, 1874, ARCIA *1874*, 251–52 ("limits," "exceedingly vicious," "unreasonable," "these wild," 251). I am using "institutional" advisedly

here. Lakotas achieved through oral dissemination a cross-generational transfer of information that could be as effective as what nineteenth-century states achieved through bureaucratic machineries.

56. "Red Cloud's Message to the Great Father," Oct. 26, 1873, LROIA, RCA, roll 717 ("the good road"). For Red Cloud's maneuvering, see, for example, Daniels to Francis A. Walker, Mar. 25, 1872, and John E. Smith to AG, Mar. 21, 1872, LROIA, RCA, roll 716; and Daniels to CoIA, Apr. 15, 1873, LROIA, RCA, roll 717. The annual reports of the commissioner of Indian affairs give an idea of the magnitude of the blind spot. The report for 1871 was typical. "Very little is known of these Indians except as to their general character of being a nervous and hostile band" was all the superintendent of the Montana Superintendency could offer on Sitting Bull and his followers. See J. A. Viall to CoIA, Sept. 15, 1871, ARCIA 1871, 416.

57. Saville to Edward P. Smith, Dec. 11, 1873, LROIA, RCA, roll 717. For the Crédit Mobilier scandal, see White, Railroaded, 63–66.

58. ARC, 32; Omaha Daily Herald, Sept. 17, 1875; Marshall, Journey of Crazy Horse, 164.

59. DWC, 21; YSF, 266–67; Utley, Lance and the Shield, 97–99.

60. Bray, Crazy Horse, 153. For Thunder Dreamers, see Lee Irwin, The Dream Seekers: Native American Visionary Traditions of the Great Plains (Norman: University of Oklahoma Press, 1994), 53–54; and Hassrick, Sioux, 271–73.

61. Bray, Crazy Horse, 153–54; Utley, Lance and the Shield, 82, 90–91. Sitting Bull's stance that Lakotas and wašíčus were at war did not go unnoticed in the East: on June 3, 1870, the New York Herald ran a story of Lakota operations along the Missouri under the heading "Open Declaration of War upon the Whites—Fort Buford to Be Attacked."

62. For Lakota population, see Bray, "Teton Sioux," 175–76. For wars, see BTWC; CPWC; and DGWC. For the Montana Territory, see Census Bulletin 33 (Jan. 17, 1901), available at https://www2.census.gov/library/publications/decennial/1900/bulletins/demographic/33-population-mt.pdf (accessed June 13, 2018).

63. Isaac Cowie, The Company of Adventurers: A Narrative of Seven Years in the Service of the Hudson's Bay Company during 1867–1874 (Toronto: William Briggs, 1913), 444 ("overtures"); YSF, 268 ("Another party"); John E. Tappan to CoIA, Sept. 10, 1871, ARCIA 1871, 522; Vestal, Warpath, 154–55; Randall to Parker, Sept. 1, 1870, LROIA, UPA, roll 896 ("procure").

64. McCrady, Living with Strangers, 24–32; Cowie, Company of Adventurers, 205, 257.

65. Cowie, Company of Adventurers, 444–47 ("would be," 444; "wished," 445; "now," 446; "some," "went back," "stated," 447). For Crees, see Regna Darnell, "Plains Cree," HNAI 13, Part 1: 641; and Anthony R. McGinnis, Counting Coup and Cutting Horses: Intertribal Warfare on the Northern Plains, 1738–1889 (Evergreen, CO: Cordillera, 1990), 142–43.

66. Bison herds shrunk rapidly in the Canadian plains in the 1870s, but good hunts were still possible in the early years of the decade. See Dobak, "Killing the Canadian Buffalo," 47–52.

67. Cowen to Secretary of War, May 18 and June 8, 1871, and Viall to E. S. Parker, May

12, 1871, AGO, roll 16; Simmons to Viall, Aug. 31, 1871, *ARCIA 1871*, 430–31 ("Every,"
430).

68. Simmons to E. S. Parker, May 12, 1871, AGO, roll 16 ("They are," "they come in force,"
"which now appear"); A. S. Reed to Sully, Aug. 31, 1870, *ARCIA 1870*, 200 ("the
Indians 'Paradise'").

69. Simmons to Parker, May 12, 1871, and Clum to Cowen, June 7, 1871, AGO, roll 16
("disposition"); Viall to CoIA, Sept. 15, 1871, and W. H. Lewis, "Report," July 18, 1871,
ARCIA 1871, 411–12, 433; Utley, *Lance and the Shield*, 93–94. For trade, see "White
Bull Interview," box 105, folder 24, p. 78, CC.

70. Durfee and Peck to CoIA, Jan. 5, 1872, and Simmons to Francis A. Walker, June 9,
1872, LROIA, Montana Superintendency, roll 492; Viall to CoIA, Sept. 15, 1871,
ARCIA 1871, 416–17 ("Of these," 416); Simmons to Viall, Sept. 1, 1872, *ARCIA 1872*,
276–78; Walker to Delano, Jan. 23, 1872, H. Ex. Doc. 96, 42d, Cong., 3d Sess., 8–10
("the submission," 10); Simmons to Peck, Dec. 8, 1872, LROIA, Montana Superintendency, roll 495. The U.S. agents' misreading of the situation is captured by the superintendent of Indian affairs of Montana Territory who had "no apprehensions that the
surveying parties of the Northern Pacific Railroad will meet with opposition from the
Tetons, with proper escort." See Viall to Francis A. Walker, June 13, 1872, LROIA,
Montana Superintendency, roll 493. But the Board of Indian Commissioners had
warned already in 1871 that "the privilege which may be deemed necessary for the
Northern Pacific Railroad Company may be had by negotiation at a moderate cost,
whereas the attempt to seize it without will probably occasion a renewal of the war."
See "Third Annual Report of the Board of Indian Commissioners," 13.

71. Lakotas had known about the expeditions at least since March 1872. See Theo.
M. Koues to Francis A. Walker, Mar. 30, 1872, and Stanley to CoIA, Apr. 7, 1872,
LROIA, Cheyenne River Agency, roll 127 ("he would fight"); and O'Connor to CoIA,
Jan. 30, 1872, LROIA, GRA, roll 305. Also see Daniels to Francis A. Walker, July 6,
1872, LROIA, RCA, roll 716; and O'Connor to CoIA, June 17, 1872, LROIA, GRA,
roll 305. Black Moon stated that the village consisted of two thousand lodges and that
fourteen hundred warriors took part in the fight. See Simmons to Cowen, Dec. 8,
1872, LROIA, Montana Superintendency, roll 495.

72. For the Northern Pacific survey and Lakota attacks, see M. John Lubetkin, *Jay Cooke's
Gamble: The Northern Pacific Railroad, the Sioux, and the Panic of 1873* (Norman:
University of Oklahoma Press, 2006), 114–46; Bray, *Crazy Horse*, 162–63; Larson,
Gall, 81–85; and Utley, *Lance and the Shield*, 108–9. For Lakota accounts of the
battle, see Vestal, *Warpath*, 137–44, and Simmons to Cowen, Dec. 8, 1872, LROIA,
Montana Superintendency, roll 495. There had been a preliminary survey party in the
Yellowstone Valley in the summer of 1871. See Lubetkin, *Jay Cooke's Gamble*, 80–113.

73. "Report of Hon. B. R. Cowen, Assistant Secretary of the Interior, Hon. N. J. Turney,
and Mr. J. W. Wham, Commissioners to Visit the Teton Sioux at and Near Fort Peck,
Montana," 456–59 ("who had become," 456; "When he," 457; "mingle," 458; "simply,"
459); Viall to Francis A. Walker, Sept. 25, 1872, *ARCIA 1872*, 274 ("a barrier"); Delano
to CoIA, Dec. 11, 1872, LROIA, Montana Superintendency, roll 492; Simmons to

Turney, Dec. 15, 1872, LROIA, Montana Superintendency, roll 495; Manypenny et al. to J. Q. Smith, Dec. 9, 1876, Sen. Ex. Doc. 9, 44th Cong., 2d Sess., 9 ("the greater"). For gun trade, see "White Bull Interview," box 105, folder 8, p. 30, and "White Bull Interview," box 105, folder 24, p. 78, CC.

74. "Indian Delegations to Washington during the Year," 97 ("particularly," "The Red Cloud"). For Walker, see White, *Republic for Which It Stands*, 292–95.

75. "Indians and the Railroads," *ARCIA 1872*, 76 ("The agent").

76. For the scarcity of bison, see Simmons to Viall, Aug. 31, 1871, *ARCIA 1871*, 431; Koues to Francis A. Walker, Jan. 20, 1872, LROIA, GRA, roll 127; Daniels to Francis A. Walker, Oct. 24, 1872, LROIA, RCA, roll 716; and Simmons to Cowen, Dec. 8, 1872, LROIA, Montana Superintendency, roll 495.

77. Samuel M. Janney to Clum, Sept. 26, 1871, *ARCIA 1871*, 437; Barclay White to Francis A. Walker, Sept. 24, 1872, *ARCIA 1872*, 213–14; Jacob M. Troth to Janney, Oct. 6, 1870, Clum to White, Feb. 22, 1873, William Burgess to White, Aug. 9, 1873, White to Edward P. Smith, Aug. 11, 1873, and J. W. Williamson to Burgess, Aug. 12, 1873, LROIA, Pawnee Agency, roll 662; Saville to Edward P. Smith, Sept. 24 and 27, Oct. 27, and Dec. 11, 1873, and J. W. Dear to SI, Dec. 16, 1873, LROIA, RCA, roll 717; Saville to CoIA, Dec. 29, 1873 (two letters), LROIA, RCA, roll 718 ("give a feast"); Pawnee chiefs to Edward P. Smith, Aug. 21, 1874, LROIA, Pawnee Agency, roll 663; Garland James Blaine and Martha Royce Blaine, "Pa-Re-Su A-Ri-Ra-Ke: The Hunters That Were Massacred," *Nebraska History* 58 (Fall 1977), 342–58; Wishart, *Unspeakable Sadness*, 190–201; White, *Roots of Dependency*, 210–11. Reflecting an old trope of warlike, instinctively violent Lakotas, one scholar of the Plains Indian wars writes, without any evidence, that Lakotas were "thirsting for blood." See McGinnis, *Counting Coup*, 125. The collapsing bison herds and the fierce competition over remaining game, together with the long-standing enmities between the two nations, are the real explanations for the carnage.

78. YSF, 267, 269–73; *BMWC*, 35–36; Hugo to Parker, Sept. 18, 1870, *ARCIA 1870*, 216–17; Burbank to E. S. Parker, June 27 and Aug. 13, 1870, LROIA, Ponca Agency, roll 671; J. Owen Dorsey, "Ponka Mission," May 6, 1872, LROIA, Ponca Agency ("exterminate," "here"); Edward P. Smith, June 9, 1873, LROIA, Ponca Agency, roll 672; Birkett to Edward P. Smith, Oct. 18, 1873, *ARCIA 1873*, 241–42; Saville to Edward P. Smith, Aug. 7, 1874, LROIA, RCA, roll 718; A. J. Carrier to Edward P. Smith, Oct. 7, 1875, *ARCIA 1875*, 248–50; Wishart, *Unspeakable Sadness*, 202–34 ("prisoners," 205).

79. RHO, 62; E. M. Camp to Sully, Aug. [n.d.], 1870, and Sully to E. S. Parker, Sept. 20, 1870, H. Ex. Doc. 1, Part 4, 41st Cong., 3d Sess., 656–63 ("When we fought," Camp to Sully, 663); Simmons to Francis A. Walker, May 18, 1872, LROIA, Montana Superintendency, roll 492; F. D. Pease to Viall, Sept. 1, 1872, *ARCIA 1872*, 280; Stanley to CoIA, Apr. 7, 1872, LROIA, Cheyenne River Agency, roll 127; Thomas H. Leforge, *Memoirs of a White Crow Indian as Told by Thomas B. Marquis* (1928; rprt. Lincoln: University of Nebraska Press, 1974), 84–96. For Lakota accounts of Crow wars, see Vestal, *Warpath*, 131, 145–53.

80. Pease to CoIA, Sept. 28, 1873, *ARCIA 1873*, 248–49; "Report of the Commission to Negotiate with the Crow Tribe of Indians," Aug. 11, 1873, *ARCIA 1873*, 113–43 ("You

say," 133); Wm. W. Anderson to Edward P. Smith, Sept. 1, 1874, *ARCIA 1874*, 267 ("with no worse"); James Wright to Edward P. Smith, July 14, 1874, and B. F. Potts to Edward P. Smith, Aug. 24, 1874, LROIA, Montana Superintendency, roll 500 ("a different class," "no obligation," Potts to Smith); McGinnis, *Counting Coup*, 138 ("regiment"); Dexter E. Clapp to Edward P. Smith, Sept. 10, 1875, *ARCIA 1875*, 301–4 ("within the reach," "The annual," 302; "the larger," 303); J. V. Bogert to D. W. Benham, June 18, 1875, AGO, roll 221 ("an offensive"); Hoxie, *Parading through History*, 100–107.

81. Campbell to E. S. Parker, Oct. 1, 1870, and G. W. Fleming to Campbell, July 1, 1870, *ARCIA 1870*, 174–75, 178–80 ("are among the most," 175); "The Indian Legislation of the Last Session and the Action of This Office Thereon," *ARCIA 1872*, 90; Campbell to Delano, Aug. 9, 1873, LROIA, RCA, roll 717; James Irvin to Edward P. Smith, Sept. 23, 1874, *ARCIA 1874*, 271.

82. Ned Blackhawk, *Violence over the Land: Indians and Empires in the Early American West* (Cambridge: Harvard University Press, 2006), 210–24; J. S. Littlefield to Edward P. Smith, Sept. 30, 1873, and James B. Thompson to CoIA, Sept. 1, 1873, *ARCIA 1873*, 257, 262–63; James B. Thompson to CoIA, Sept. 1, 1874 ("Even were they"), and J. J. Critchlow to Edward P. Smith, Sept. 22, 1874, *ARCIA 1874*, 271–73, 276–77 ("improved," 276). For Ute raids, see also *YSF*, 274.

83. Stanley to E. S. Parker, Feb. 20, 1870, LROIA, UPA, roll 896; Burbank to Parker, Sept. 30, 1870, *ARCIA 1870*, 209–10; O'Connor to Parker, May 17 and June 12, 1871, LROIA, GRA, roll 305; Edmond Palmer to Edward P. Smith, Sept. 8, 1874, *ARCIA 1874*, 247–48; L. B. Sperry to Edward P. Smith, Aug. 31, 1874, *ARCIA 1874*, 245 ("they fear," "'The hostile Sioux,'"); Melfine Fox Everett, "Why the Arikara Fought for the Seventh Cavalry," in *LBR*, 135, 138; Mary Jane Schneider, "Three Affiliated Tribes," *HNAI* 13, Part 1: 391; Parks, "Arikara," 387.

84. "Red Cloud Speech," in *Report of the Special Commission*, 436–37 ("When," 436; "all we want," 437); Sven Beckert, "American Danger: United States Empire, Eurafrica, and the Territorialization of Industrial Capitalism," *American Historical Review* 122 (Oct. 2017), 1137–70. For administrative saturation of space, see Charles S. Meier, "Consigning the Twentieth Century to History: Alternative Narratives for the Modern Era," *American Historical Review* 105 (June 2000), 807–31. For Cheyennes and Arapahos, see Hämäläinen, "Reconstructing the Great Plains," 487–89.

9. UPSIDE-DOWN SOLDIERS

1. *YSF*, 268–74; HDWC; MBWC: MBWCV; BTWC.

2. D. S. Stanley, *Report of the Yellowstone Expedition of 1873* (Washington, DC: GPO, 1874), 3; *Army and Navy Journal* 11, no. 7, Sept. 27, 1873, 99; Anderson, *Ethnic Cleansing and the Indian*, 291–92; *Congressional Globe*, 42d Cong., 3d Sess., Mar. 3, 1873, 2096 ("This railroad"); D. S. Stanley, *Personal Memoirs* (Cambridge: Harvard University Press, 1917), 244–45. For Stanley and Sheridan, see M. John Lubetkin, ed., *Before Custer: Surveying the Yellowstone, 1872* (Norman: University of Oklahoma Press, 2015), 34. For numbers, see Bray, "Teton Sioux," 176; "Table Showing Number

of Indians within the United States," *ARCIA 1873*, 336–40; and Moore, *Cheyenne Nation*, 325. For an illuminating study of Custer, see Stiles, *Custer's Trials*, esp. 376–80.

3. *Congressional Globe*, 42d Cong., 3d Sess., Mar. 3, 1873, 2096 ("the most determined," "if we were"); CoIA, "Report," *ARCIA 1872*, 9 ("the progress").

4. O'Connor to F. A. Walker, Aug. 31, 1872, Koues to Francis A. Walker, Aug. 15, 1872, and Henry F. Livingston to Francis A. Walker, Sept. 1, 1872, *ARCIA 1872*, 261–63 ("The working," 261); Palmer to Clum, Aug. 14, 1873, LROIA, GRA, roll 306; CoIA, "Report," Nov. 1, 1873, Livingston to Edward Parker, Sept. [n.d.], 1873, and J. W. Daniels to CoIA, Aug. 28, 1873, *ARCIA 1873*, 3–6, 233, 243–44 ("fiction," "as rapidly," 3; "If it should," "the Government," 6); "Table Showing Number of Indians," 336. For Wahpeton-Sissetons, see White, *Railroaded*, 60–62; and G. Edward White, *Law in American History: From Reconstruction through the 1920s* (New York: Oxford University Press, 2016), 76–77.

5. *New York Tribune*, Aug. 25, Sept. 8, and Sept. 9, 1873 ("make short work," Sept. 9); "Official Report of General Custer," 134–37 ("in perfect," 135); Stanley, *Report of the Yellowstone Expedition*, 5–6; "Yellowstone Expedition of 1873," *Journal of the United States Association* 16 (Oct. 1905), in *Eyewitnesses to the Indian Wars, 1865–1890: The Long War for the Northern Plains*, 4 vols., ed. Peter Cozzens (Mechanicsburg, PA: Stackpole, 2004), 4: 135–36; Joe De Barthe, *The Life and Adventures of Frank Grouard* (St. Joseph, MO: Combe, c. 1894), 114–15.

6. *New York Tribune*, Aug. 25 and Sept. 9, 1874; "Official Report of General Custer," 138–44; Larson, *Gall*, 89–92; "Interview with John Henley," in *Custer & Company: Walter Camp's Notes on the Custer Fight*, ed. Bruce R. Liddic and Paul Harbaugh (1995; rprt. Lincoln: University of Nebraska Press, 1998), 45–49. For repeaters, see Dorsey, "Ponca Mission"; *New York Tribune*, Sept. 9, 1874; Addison M. Quivey, "The Yellowstone Expedition of 1874," *Contributions to the Historical Society of Montana* 1 (1876), 281; Donovan, *Terrible Glory*, 188; Bray, *Crazy Horse*, 179; and Utley, *Lance and the Shield*, 102.

7. White, *Railroaded*, 77–84; Stiles, *Custer's Trials*, 402–6.

8. SG, 114–35, 163 ("sky," 115; "it looked like," 128; "what is good," 135).

9. YSF, 272 ("The Oglalas killed"); Saville to Edward P. Smith, Feb. 14, 1874, in *Report of the Special Commission*, 437–38; STF, 210–11; Frank N. Schubert, *Outpost of the Sioux Wars: A History of Fort Robinson* (Lincoln: University of Nebraska Press, 1993), 5–7; Joe Jackson, *Black Elk: The Life of an American Visionary* (New York: Farrah, Straus and Giroux, 2016), 70; Saville to Edward P. Smith, Dec. 29, 1873, Feb. 14 and 16, 1874, and Mar. 5, 1874, H. W. Moore to Edward P. Smith, Jan. 9, 1874, and Delano to CoIA, Nov. 13, 1874, LROIA, RCA, roll 718; Saville to Edward P. Smith, Aug. 31, 1874, *ARCIA 1874*, 251. For northern Lakota sojourns at Red Cloud Agency and difficulties in counting the Indians at the agency, see "Red Cloud's Speech," Dec. 25, 1873, Saville to Edward P. Smith, Dec. 29, 1873, Feb. 2, 1874, and Nov. 30, 1874, LROIA, RCA, roll 718; and Thomas R. Buecker, *Fort Robinson and the American West, 1874–1899* (Norman: University of Oklahoma Press, 1999). For Lakota responses to Camps Robison and Sheridan, see, for example, Jno. E. Smith to AAG, Dept. of the Platte, LROIA, RCA, roll 718.

10. For an incisive analysis of how gold shaped human perceptions of the land in the Great Plains and the American West, see West, *Contested Plains*.

11. Letter of Philip Henry Sheridan, Nov. 23, 1874, and Sheridan to Jonathan Wheeler, Nov. 24, 1874, PSP ("a general," "make," Nov. 24; Sheridan's Nov. 24 letter recounted his thinking and talks with Grant in the summer of 1874); Anderson, *Ethnic Cleansing and the Indian*, 293–94; Catharine R. Franklin, "Black Hills and Bloodshed: The U.S. Army and the Invasion of the Lakota Land, 1868–1876," *Montana: The Magazine of Western History* 63 (Summer 2013), 33–36. For Custer's standing, see Stiles, *Custer's Trials*, 399. For larger context, see Richard Slotkin, *The Fatal Environment: The Myth of the Frontier in the Age of Industrialization, 1800–1890* (Norman: University of Oklahoma Press, 1985), 338–70.

12. William Ludlow, *Reconnaissance of the Black Hills of Dakota, Made in the Summer of 1874* (Washington, DC: GPO, 1875), 6, 22 ("thoroughly," "embarrass," "a ready," 22).

13. *Bismarck Tribune*, Aug. 19, 1874 ("The greatest"); Pinkney Lugenbeel to AAG, Sept. 23, 1874, SF, roll 2; Franklin, "Black Hills and Bloodshed," 36–38; Anderson, *Ethnic Cleansing and the Indian*, 295–96.

14. "Testimony of Major William H. Jordan," and Saville to CoIA, Oct. 24, 1874, in *Report of the Special Commission*, 310–12, 441–42 ("painted," 310); Saville to Edward P. Smith, Aug. 13 and 31, 1874, L. P. Bradley to AG, Dept. of the Platte, Oct. 25, 1874, Jordan to AAG, District of the Black Hills, Oct. 23, 1874, Jordan to Ruggles, Oct. 29, 1874, and Saville to Cox, Dec. 16, 1874, LROIA, RCA, roll 718 ("hostile," "The Indians don't," Saville to Cox); Allen, *From Fort Laramie to Wounded Knee*, 22–23; Price, *Oglala People*, 135–37. For the decision not to prosecute, see Jordan to AAG, Dept. of the Platte, Oct. 23, 1874, and Ord to Commanding Officer, District of the Black Hills, Oct. 28, 1874, LROIA, RCA, roll 718.

15. Letter of Sheridan, Nov. 23, 1874, and Sheridan to Wheeler, Nov. 24, 1874, PSP ("take the hostile," Nov. 23; "on the north," "the Indians might be," Nov. 24); Saville to Edward P. Smith, Aug. 3, 7, 15, 24, and 31, 1874, LROIA, RCA, roll 718.

16. Isenberg, *Destruction of the Bison*, 136–37, 151–52.

17. Kingsley, "Spotted Tail," esp. 32–33; Samuel D. Hinman to W. H. Hare, Nov. 10, 1874, *ARCIA 1874*, 95–96; STF, 223–24; Edward P. Smith, "Report," Nov. 1, 1875, *ARCIA 1875*, 5–6. Serious plans to abrogate Lakota hunting rights south of the reservation proper had been under preparation for months. See CoIA to Delano, Nov. 14, 1873, LROIA, RCA, roll 717.

18. "Report of the Sioux Commission," Nov. 28, 1874, *ARCIA 1874*, 87–97 ("they utterly," 96). For corruption, see Saville to Edward P. Smith, June 6, 1875, O. C. Marsh to Edward P. Smith, June 25, 1875, and CoIA to A. H. Bullock et al., July 1, 1875, LROIA, RCA, roll 719; Ulysses S. Grant to Marsh, July 16, 1875, in *The Papers of Ulysses S. Grant*, 26 vols., ed. John Y. Simon (Carbondale: Southern Illinois University Press, 2003), 212–14; *Report of the Special Commission*, 2, 8, 10, 20, 47, 113 ("gigantic," 10); and White, *Republic for Which It Stands*, 357–60.

19. E. A. Howard to CoIA, Sept. 30, 1874, *ARCIA 1874*, 253–54 ("troublesome," "well armed," 253; "much of the trouble," 254); H. W. Bingham to Saville to E. P. Smith, June 6, Sept. 14, 1874, *ARCIA 1874*, 240 ("The excitement"); Delano to CoIA, Apr. 27,

1874, and Saville to Edward P. Smith, Sept. 28, 1874, LROIA, RCA, roll 718; Palmer to Edward P. Smith, Sept. 8 and Nov. 9, 1874, and William Pound to George H. Williams, Nov. 30, 1874, LROIA, GRA, roll 306 ("not very tractable," Palmer to Smith, Nov. 9, 1874); Howard, letter, Jan. 16, 1875, LROIA, Spotted Tail Agency, roll 840. In 1871 the agents at Grand River had expected slow progress in Christianization due to their persisting attachment to the hunting life. See O'Connor to Clum, Sept. 9, 1871, LROIA, GRA, roll 305. In April 1874 a hopeful Saville reported that twenty Lakota families at Red Cloud Agency wanted "assistance to commence farming," which in fact captures how little interest there was for agriculture. See Saville to CoIA, Apr. 1, 1874, LROIA, RCA, roll 718.

20. Quivey, "Yellowstone Expedition of 1874," 268–84; Mark H. Brown, *Plainsmen of the Yellowstone: A History of the Yellowstone Basin* (New York: G. P. Putnam's Sons, 1961), 216–19; French L. MacLean, *Sitting Bull, Crazy Horse, Gold, and Guns: The Yellowstone Wagon Road and Prospective Expedition and the Battle of Lodge Grass Creek* (Atglen, PA: Schiffer, 2016); Utley, *Lance and the Shield*, 118–19.

21. Bray, *Crazy Horse*, 177–78.

22. Franklin, "Black Hills and Bloodshed," 36–39; Anderson, *Ethnic Cleansing and the Indian*, 295–96; *New York Times*, Nov. 12, 1875 ("yield"); John S. Collins to Grant, Apr. 4, 1875, LROIA, Spotted Tail Agency, roll 841 ("are fully," "their own"); *New York Times*, Mar. 13, 1875 ("integrity"); Sheridan to Sherman, Mar. 25, 1875, in *Eyewitnesses to the Indian Wars*, ed. Cozzens, 188–91 ("occupy," 191); Grant to the Senate of the United States, Mar. 17, 1875, and John S. Collins to Grant, Mar. 28, 1875, in *Papers of Ulysses S. Grant*, ed. Simon, 26: 84–89, 122 ("Look at me," 122); "Proceedings of a Council with the Indians at Red Cloud Agency," LROIA, RCA, roll 719; W. D. Whipple to AG, Jan. 12, 1875, and Saville to Edward P. Smith, Mar. 2, 1875, LROIA, RCA, roll 719; Terry to AAG, Mar. 9, 1875, and John S. Collins, letter, Mar. 24, 1875, SF, roll 2; Howard to CoIA, June 2 and Aug. 14 and 27, 1875, LROIA, Spotted Tail Agency, roll 840; Richard Irving Dodge, *The Black Hills: A Minute Description of the Routes, Scenery, Soil, Climate, Timber, Gold, Geology, Zoölogy, Etc.* (New York: James Miller, 1876), 72–73, 78, 94, 118, 151, 136–38 ("the Black Hills," 136); Edward P. Smith, "Report," 8; Ostler, *Lakotas and the Black Hills*, 88–89 ("depraved," 88). Lakotas showed considerable restraint in the face of the wašíču invasion. Writing in late September, Sheridan reported that "Indian affairs in the Dept. of Dakota has been remarkably quiet." See letter of Sheridan, Sept. 25, 1874, PSP; and "Report of the Commission Appointed to Treat with the Sioux Indians for the Relinquishment of the Black Hills," ARCIA 1875, 189 ("thieves' road").

23. G. A. Custer to AAG, Mar. 3, 1875, and Terry to AAG, Mar. 9, 1875, SF, roll 2; Saville to Edward P. Smith, Apr. 8, 1875, LROIA, RCA, roll 719; RCF, 228–29; "Council with Sioux Delegation," June 2, 1875, in *Papers of Ulysses S. Grant*, ed. Simon, 26: 138–47; *Daily Alta California*, May 28, 1875 ("The President," "Now," "he had come," "You speak"); *New York Times*, June 3, 1875 ("were rapidly"); "Report of the Commission Appointed to Treat with the Sioux Indians," 184; Anderson, *Ethnic Cleansing and the Indian*, 298; *New York Herald*, Aug. 16, 1875 ("under protest"). For Grant and Marsh, see *Report of the Special Commission*; and Chernow, *Grant*, 830–31. Marsh's

key study on the evolution of the horse is O. C. Marsh, "Fossil Horses in America," *American Naturalists* (May 1874), 288–94.

24. Peter J. Powell, *People of the Sacred Mountain: A History of the Northern Cheyenne Chiefs and Warrior Societies, 1830–1879*, 2 vols. (San Francisco: Harper and Row, 1981), 2: 928–29 ("I have," 929); SG, 163–64, 171–72 ("food pack," 163); De Barthe, *Life and Adventures of Frank Grouard*, 173–75; Saville to Edward P. Smith, Aug. 16, 1875, LROIA, RCA, roll 719.

25. "Report of the Commission Appointed to Treat with the Sioux Indians," 184–200 ("interests," 184; "secure," 185; "for mining uses," "It does not," "exorbitant," 187; "for seven," "until the land," "Our Great Father," 188; "perform labor," "The plan," 199); Saville to Edward P. Smith, Sept. 23, 1875, LROIA, RCA, roll 719; SG, 172; Bray, *Crazy Horse*, 190–91; Paul Magid, *The Grey Fox: George Crook and the Indian Wars* (Norman: University of Oklahoma Press, 2015), 153–55. For Red Cloud Agency, see Saville to Edward P. Smith, Oct. 25, 1875, LROIA, RCA, roll 719. For hunting, see Saville to Edward P. Smith, Oct. 11, 1875, LROIA, RCA, roll 719.

26. CoIA, "Report," Nov. 1, 1875, ARCIA 1875, 7 ("a general"); John Stephens Gray, *Centennial Campaign: The Sioux War of 1876* (Norman: University of Oklahoma Press, 1988), 30–31; J. Q. Smith to SI, Jan. 21, 1876, H. Ex. Doc. 184, 44th Cong., 1st Sess., 12–13.

27. George Crook to AAG, Division of Missouri, Dec. 22, 1875, and Terry to AAG, Division of Missouri, Dec. 28, 1875, H. Ex. Doc. 184, 44th Cong., 1st Sess., 15–16. The government's ultimatum reached the Lakotas unevenly. Johnson Holy Rock, a Lakota elder, stated that "there was no such request [to report to the agencies], just the military assault that took place along the Little Bighorn. They [Lakotas] were forced to fight." See Jeanne Oyawin Eder, "Dakota View of the Great Sioux War," 68.

28. For Lakota attitudes and views of agencies, see Daniels to Francis A. Walker, LROIA, RCA, roll 716; and Howard to CoIA, Jan. 3 and 8, 1875, LROIA, Spotted Tail Agency, roll 840. For Sitting Bull, see De Barthe, *Life and Adventures of Frank Grouard*, 174 ("he would not"). While sojourning near Fort Peck, Sitting Bull categorically refused to accept rations. See Simmons to Cowen, Dec. 8, 1872, LROIA, Montana Superintendency, roll 495.

29. Edward P. Smith, "Report," and John Burke to Edward P. Smith, Sept. 1, 1875, ARCIA 1875, 3–5, 244 ("I am led," "outlaws," 5; "a man," 244); Edward P. Smith to SI, Nov. 27, 1875, H. Ex. Doc. 184, 44th Cong., 1st Sess., 7–8; Saville to CoIA, Nov. 13, 1874, LROIA, RCA, roll 718; Walker, *Indian Question*, 220–21.

30. Benham to AAAG, District of Montana, June 23 and 29 and July 7, 1875, Potts to Delano, July 8, 1875, Columbus Delano to the President, July 8 and 19, 1875, George L. Browning to AAAG, July 8, 1875, Terry to AAG, Aug. 8, 1875, Philip Sheridan to AG, July 1, 1875, N. Healey to Secretary of the Interior, July 15, 1875, and Edward P. Smith to AAG, Aug. 6, 1875, AGO, roll 221; Clapp to Edward P. Smith, July 5, 1875, LROIA, Montana Superintendency, roll 501; James S. Brisbin to AAG, Department of Dakota, Mar. 21, 1876, LR, Montana Superintendency, roll 505; Hoxie, *Parading through History*, 108.

31. E. C. Watkins to Edward P. Smith, Nov. 9, 1875, Sen. Ex. Doc. 52, 44th Cong., 1st

Sess., 3–4 ("occupy," "claim," "The United States," "surrounded," 3; "They are still," "The true policy," 4); *Chicago Daily Tribune*, Feb. 14, 1876 ("melancholy," "enough"). Writing mainly of pre-modern states, James Scott has noted how they were often "partially blind," lacking an accurate map of its claimed realm and the people in it. See James Scott, *Seeing Like A State: How Certain Schemes to Improve the Human Condition Have Failed* (New Haven: Yale University Press, 1998), esp. 2.

32. Carl F. Day, *Tom Custer: Ride to Glory* (Norman: University of Oklahoma Press, 2002), 221–22 ("unless," 221); Gray, *Centennial Campaign*, 40 ("I think").

33. Powell, *People of the Sacred Mountain*, 2: 937–45; George Ruhlen to AAG, Department of Dakota, Apr. 19, 1876, SF, roll 2; Thomas B. Marquis, *A Warrior Who Fought Custer* (Minneapolis: Midwest Company, 1931), 170–72; "The Two Moons Interview," in *Lakota Recollections of the Custer Fight: New Sources of Indian-Military History*, ed. Richard G. Hardorff (1991; rprt. Lincoln: University of Nebraska Press, 1997), 132; "The Bull Hump and White Bird Interview," CMCF, 84, 87; Vestal, *Warpath*, 182–83; Bray, *Crazy Horse*, 194–200. For a comprehensive study of what became known as the Big Horn Expedition, see Paul L. Hedren, *Powder River: Disastrous Opening of the Great Sioux War* (Norman: University of Oklahoma Press, 2016), 261 ("disgusted").

34. Stiles, *Custer's Trials*, 433–38.

35. Utley, *Lance and the Shield*, 119–20, 129; Hoxie, *Parading through History*, 108; YSF, 276; *Bismarck Weekly Tribune*, Jan. 19, 1876; Howard to CoIA, Mar. 15, 1876, LROIA, Spotted Tail Agency, roll 840; C. W. Darling to CoIA, Sept. 8, 1876, ARCIA 1876, 29; J. Q. Smith to SI, Feb. 21, 1877, H. Ex. Doc. 184, 44th Cong., 1st Sess., 26.

36. DWC, 22; Reno to AAG, Mar. 3, 1876, William Courtenay to Daniel Huston, Mar. 27, 1876, and Ruhlen to AAG, Department of Dakota, Apr. 19, 1876, SF, roll 2; *Fort Benton Record*, Apr. 1, 1876 ("Instead"); Darling to CoIA, Sept. 8, 1876, ARCIA 1876, 29–30 ("hostiles," "join," 29; "believe," 30); Fox Everett, "Why the Arikara Fought for the Seventh Cavalry," 138.

37. Marquis, *Warrior Who Fought Custer*, 177–86 ("We supposed," 179); Joseph White Bull statement, in Stanley Vestal, *New Sources of Indian History, 1850–1891: The Ghost Dance, the Prairie Sioux—a Miscellany* (Norman: University of Oklahoma Press, 1934), 163; Ruhlen to AAG, Department of Dakota, Apr. 19, 1876, J. S. Poland to AAG, Department of Dakota, 1876, and Wesley Merritt, telegram, June 7, 1876, SF, roll 2; Utley, *Lance and the Shield*, 133–35; Bray, *Crazy Horse*, 201; Silverman, *Thundersticks*, 4. For a reconstruction of Indian movements in the spring of 1876, see Gray, *Centennial Campaign*, 321–36. In June 1874 Lakotas reported at Red Cloud Agency that there was little game left south of the Yellowstone: the best remaining hunting grounds were to the north and west of the valley. See Saville to Edward P. Smith, July 18, 1874, LROIA, RCA, roll 718.

38. Marquis, *Warrior Who Fought Custer*, 177–78, 185 ("almost strangers," 177; "These people," 178; "each," "Our combination," 185); "White Bull Interview," box 105, folder 24, pp. 70–71, CC.

39. James H. Bradley, *The March of the Montana Column: A Prelude to the Custer Disaster*, ed. Edgar I. Stewart (Norman: University of Oklahoma Press, 1961), 7–129 ("an immense," 122); Marquis, *Warrior Who Fought Custer*, 193–97; Utley, *Lance and the*

Shield, 135–36. For Crow scouts, see Colin G. Calloway, "'The Only Way Open to Us': The Crow Struggle for Survival in the Nineteenth Century," *North Dakota History* 53 (Summer 1986), 25–34.

40. Marquis, *Warrior Who Fought Custer*, 178–79 ("into admiration," 178).

41. One Bull account, box 110, folder 8, pp. 1–2, CC ("felt," "sailing," "countless," "nothing," "and was soon" 1; "terrible dream," 2).

42. "White Bull Interview," box 105, folder 24, pp. 80–82, CC ("Save me," 81). Sitting Bull's prayers and political maneuvering have often been portrayed as stemming from visionary revelations and pure altruism. I have also emphasized here the daunting personal pressures Sitting Bull was facing in the spring of 1876.

43. Buechel and Manhart, *Lakota Tales*, 2: 379–83; Marquis, *Warrior Who Fought Custer*, 191–92; SG, 173–74; Joseph White Bull statement, 163; "White Bull Interview," box 105, folder 24, p. 83; "One Bull Interview," box 105, folder 19, pp. 47–49, 77, CC ("these have," "coming," "These are," 77); "White Bull Interview," box 105, folder 8, p. 54, CC; Vestal, *Sitting Bull*, 151–53.

44. Gibbon to Terry, Mar. 8, 1876, SF ("strike"); Bradley, *March of the Montana Column*, 122–37 ("immense," 124; "mortally," 129); Sheridan to Sherman, May 29, 1876, H. Ex. Doc. 184, 44th Cong., 1st Sess., 53–54; Fred Dustin, *George Armstrong Custer and Custer's Trial: The Aftermath; Review by Judge Advocate General Holt and Final Action by General Grant* (London: Westerners Publications, 2000), 10; John S. Gray, *Custer's Last Campaign: Mitch Boyer and the Little Bighorn Reconstructed* (Lincoln: University of Nebraska Press, 1993), 131–32.

45. John G. Bourke, *On the Border with Crook* (New York: Charles Scribner's, 1891), 291–96 ("long," 291; "touched," "rained," 296); Reuben Briggs Davenport, "The Skirmish at Tongue River Heights, June 9, 1876," in *Battles and Skirmishes of the Great Sioux War, 1876–1877: The Military View*, ed. Jerome A. Greene (Norman: University of Oklahoma Press, 1993), 21–25; Gray, *Centennial Campaign*, 110–16. The identity and the number of the Indians was unclear, but it is likely that they were Cheyennes and Lakotas.

46. Bourke, *On the Border with Crook*, 311–20 ("feeling," 320); Bray, *Crazy Horse*, 205–6; Marshall, *Journey of Crazy Horse*, 219–22; Gray, *Centennial Campaign*, 117–24 ("spoiling," 118); Davenport, "The Battle of Rosebud Creek, June 17, 1876," in *Battles and Skirmishes*, ed. Greene, 26–40; "Two Moons Interview," 134; Sheridan to Sherman, May 29, 1876, H. Ex. Doc. 184, 44th Cong., 1st Sess., 54. Johnson Holy Rock stated that Crazy Horse "whipped" the Americans on the Rosebud. See Jeanne Oyawin Eder, "A Dakota View of the Great Sioux War," 68.

47. For Terry's plans, see "The George W. Glenn Narrative Account," *IVCF*, 192. Crow oral traditions state that, from a military point of view, the battle was a draw. See Joseph Medicine Crow, "Custer and His Crow Scouts," *LBR*, 109.

48. Jas. S. Hastings to CoIA, Aug. 10, 1876, *ARCIA 1876*, 33 ("the occupation," "succeeded," "will find").

49. For calls, see Young Two Moon account, *LC*, 70; Joseph White Bull statement, 163; Grinnell, *Fighting Cheyennes*, 343–44. For the close ties between agency and nontreaty Lakotas, see Waggoner, *Witness*, 127.

50. J. Chandler to SW, Feb. 17, 1876, SF ("leaders"); Reno to AAG, Apr. 27, 1876, H. Ex. Doc. 184, 44th Cong., 1st Sess., 52 ("Sioux scout"); Sheridan to Sherman, May 30, 1876, ibid., 54 ("all the agency"); Sheridan to Townsend, May 31, 1876, ibid., 55 ("fifty"); Poland to AAG, June 4, 1876, ibid., 59 ("the hostile"); R. William to AAG, June 8, 1876, ibid., 55; Bourke, *On the Border with Crook*, 296 ("all able-bodied").

51. Sheridan, letter, Nov. 25, 1874, LROIA, RCA, roll 718. As many as eight thousand Indians may have left Red Cloud Agency in the spring. See Thomas R. Buecker and R. Eli Paul, *The Crazy Horse Surrender Ledger* (Lincoln: Nebraska Historical Society, 1994), 6. The notion of Lakota warfare as a fundamentally individualistic endeavor sits deep among academics, too. See, in particular, McGinnis, *Counting Coup*, 213–15.

52. Stiles, *Custer's Trials*, 435–42; Robert M. Utley, *Cavalier in Buckskin: George Armstrong Custer and the Western Military Frontier* (Norman: University of Oklahoma Press, 1988), 169–77; Gray, *Centennial Campaign*, 309–20. For Arikara and Crow scouts, see Colin Calloway, "Army Allies of Tribal Survival? The 'Other Indians' in the 1876 Campaign," in *Legacy: New Perspectives on the Battle of the Little Bighorn*, ed. Charles E. Rankin (Helena: Montana Historical Society, 1996), 71–73.

53. Paul L. Hedren, *Great Sioux War Orders of Battle: How the United States Army Waged War on the Northern Plains, 1876–1877* (Norman: University of Oklahoma Press, 2011), 97; Donovan, *Terrible Glory*, 300–301; Stiles, *Custer's Trials*, 442; Gray, *Centennial Campaign*, 337–38; "The George W. Glenn Narrative Account," 193–94; Bradley, *March of the Montana Column*, 142–44; "William Jackson account," in *Battles and Skirmishes*, ed. Greene, 43.

54. The estimates of the village size vary wildly. Most modern estimates place the number of lodges around one thousand and the number of people between six and eight thousand. See Joseph M. Marshall III, *The Day the World Ended at Little Bighorn: A Lakota History* (New York: Penguin, 2007), 25; Donovan, *Terrible Glory*, 187; Gregory F. Michno, *Lakota Noon: The Indian Narrative of Custer's Defeat* (Missoula, MT: Mountain Press, 1997), 6–11; Gray, *Centennial Campaign*, 346–57; Bray, *Crazy Horse*, 212; and Utley, *Frontier Regulars*, 266. Crazy Horse and White Bull, however, believed that there were about eighteen hundred and twenty-three hundred lodges, respectively. See "The Crazy Horse Interview," IVCF, 35; and "White Bull Interview," box 105, folder 24, pp. 50–51, CC. What is critical is that Custer seems to have expected to face a much smaller village of roughly four hundred lodges. See Gray, *Centennial Campaign*, 337–38. For horses, see Jackson, *Black Elk*, 165.

55. "White Bull Interview," box 105, folder 24, pp. 49–52, CC; American Horse account, LC, 48–49; Michno, *Lakota Noon*, 25, 28, 30, 37–38, 41, 43; John Stands in Timber and Margot Liberty, *Cheyenne Memories* (1967; 2d ed. New Haven: Yale University Press, 1998), 194; Powell, *People of the Sacred Mountain*, 2: 1020; "The Story of Chief Runs-the-Enemy—Sioux Leader," in Joseph K. Dixon, *The Vanishing Race: The Last Indian Council* (Garden City, NY: Doubleday, Page, 1913), 170–71; "The John Stands in Timber Interview," CMCF, 168; Bray, *Crazy Horse*, 212–13. What became known as the Battle of the Little Bighorn is depicted here from Lakota and Cheyenne perspective. I have prioritized Native sources and focused on what the Indians saw and knew and what they did and tried to do. Many Native accounts were recorded decades after

the battle and through interpreters who were not always reliable. To dilute distortions, I have relied on several accounts on each phase and key event of the battle. Citing several accounts is necessary also because many of them open only a relatively narrow personal window into the battle.

56. Bradley, *March of the Montana Column*, 148 ("We are now").

57. "Interview with Respects Nothing," Tablet 29, 3–7, Ricker Collection, box 8, NSHS; Interview with One Bull, Mary Collins Family Papers, box 2, folder 35, SASDHS; Red Horse in W. H. Wood to AAG, Feb. 27, 1877, SF, roll 4; "Gray Whirlwind Interview," box 105, folder 14, pp. 11–15, CC ("Now my best," 13); "The Brave Wolf Interview," CMCF, 35; "The Brave Bear Narrative," "The Turning Hawk Interview," "The Little Soldier Interview," and "The Holy Face Bear Interview," IVCF, 83–84, 144–45, 174–76, 181; Oyawin Eder, "A Dakota View of the Great Sioux War," 69; "The Nicholas Ruleau Interview," "The He Dog Interview," "The Red Feather Interview," "The Moving Robe Woman Interview," "The Eagle Elk Interview," and "The Two Moons Interview," in *Lakota Recollections of the Custer Fight*, ed. Hardorff, 39–42, 74, 81–85, 92–94, 102–3, 134–36; "The Iron Thunder Interview," 61; Red Horse account, She Walks with Her Shawl account, American Horse account, and Soldier Wolf account, LC, 35, 37, 40, 42–45, 49, 51; "White Bull Interview," box 105, folder 24, pp. 53, 74, CC; "Interview with Thomas Disputed" and "Interview with One Feather," in *Custer & Company*, 121, 128–29; Joseph. M. Marshall III, *The Journey of Crazy Horse: A Lakota History* (New York: Penguin, 2004), 227; Michno, *Lakota Noon*, 23–89, 94–96; "The Story of Chief Runs-the-Enemy," in *Vanishing Race*, 172–73; "Black Elk Tells about the Custer Battle" and "Standing Bear Tells about the Custer Battle," SG, 181–83, 188; M. I. McCreight, *Firewater and Forked Tongues: A Sioux Chief Interprets U.S. History* (Pasadena, CA: Trail's End, 1947), 111–12; Vestal, *Warpath*, 192–94; Marquis, *Warrior Who Fought Custer*, 217–24; William A. Graham, *The Reno Court Inquiry: Proceedings of a Court of Inquiry in the Case of Major Marcus A. Reno Concerning His Conduct at the Battle of the Little Big Horn River, June 25–26, 1876* (Washington, DC: National Archives, 1951), 23–34, 40–44; "William Jackson Account," 48–50; Gray, *Centennial Campaign*, 174–76; Donovan, *Terrible Glory*, 227–30, 232–49. Major Reno was in charge of the initial attack on the Indian village. White Bull thought that Reno could have protected his position in the trees and had been "foolish to run across the river." See "White Bull Interview," box 105, folder 24, p. 73, CC. For the types and amount of firearms the Indians possessed, see Charles Windolph, *I Fought with Custer: The Story of Sergeant Windolph, Last Survivor of the Battle of the Little Big Horn* (1947; rprt. Lincoln: University of Nebraska Press, 1987), 92; Richard Allan Fox, Jr., *Archeology, History, and Custer's Last Battle: The Little Big Horn Reexamined* (Norman: University of Oklahoma Press, 1993), 77–79; and Michno, *Lakota Noon*, 225–31.

58. Utley, *Lance and the Shield*, 153–55; Marquis, *Warrior Who Fought Custer*, 224–25; Grinnell, *Fighting Cheyennes*, 343.

59. Michno, *Lakota Noon*, 93–155; "Story of Chief Runs-the-Enemy," 174–75 ("seemed," 174); "The Horned Horse Statement," "White Bull, Brave Wolf, and Hump Narrative," and "The Yellow Nose Interview," IVCF, 40–41, 46, 104–5; She Walks with Her Shawl

account, 45; "The White Shield Interview," "The John Two Moons Interview," and "Richard Throssel's Interview," *CMCF*, 50–53, 66, 126–27; Stands in Timber and Liberty, *Cheyenne Memories*, 197–98; "Interview with Respects Nothing," 7–8; Powell, *People of the Sacred Mountain*, 2: 1018–23; Marshall, *Journey of Crazy Horse*, 227–28; "The Eagle Elk Interview," 103–4; "The Two Moons Interview," 135–36; "The Two Eagles Interview" and "The Hollow Horn Bear Interview," in *Lakota Recollections of the Custer Fight*, ed. Hardorff, 143–46, 179–81; "White Bull Interview," box 105, folder 24, p. 56, CC; "Interview with Thomas Disputed," 122–23; Soldier Wolf account, 51–52; Red Horse account, Brave Wolf account, Tall Bull account, One Bull account, Little Hawk account, and Young Two Moon account, *LC*, 40, 46–47, 53–56, 62, 68–70, 72; Sitting Bull interview, *New York Herald*, Nov. 16, 1877, 4; Marquis, *Warrior Who Fought Custer*, 226–30; Vestal, *Warpath*, 195; Grinnell, *Fighting Cheyennes*, 337–39; Bray, *Crazy Horse*, 222–24; Donovan, *Terrible Glory*, 269–70; Thomas Powers, "How the Battle of Little Bighorn Was Won," *Smithsonian Magazine* (Nov. 2010), available at https://www.smithsonianmag.com/history/how-the-battle-of-little-bighorn-was-won-63880188/ (accessed Jan. 15, 2018). For Gall, see Michno, *Lakota Noon*, 148, 155, 167–68; and Larson, *Gall*, 126–29. Decades later Mrs. Spotted Horn, a Hunkpapa, provided one of the most astute analysis of the battle: Marcus Reno, leading the first attack against the village from the south, "had struck too early," allowing the allied Indians to concentrate overwhelming force against Custer. See Mrs. Spotted Horn, "A View from the Village," in *Our Hearts Fell to the Ground: Plains Indian Views of How the West Was Lost*, ed. Colin G. Calloway (Boston: Bedford, 1996), 147.

60. Michno, *Lakota Noon*, 155–93; She Walks with Her Shawl account, 45; Young Two Moon account, 70; "One Bull Interview," box 105, folder 24, pp. 55–56, CC; Marquis, *Warrior Who Fought Custer*, 230–31; "Story of Chief Runs-the-Enemy," 175–76; Powell, *People of the Sacred Mountain*, 2: 1023; "The Moving Robe Woman Interview," 95; Grinnell, *Fighting Cheyennes*, 339–40; Stands in Timber and Liberty, *Cheyenne Memories*, 199–20; Utley, *Lance and the Shield*, 155; Bray, *Crazy Horse*, 224–27; "The Flying Hawk Narrative," *IVCF*, 125; Peter Cozzens, *The Earth Is Weeping: The Epic Story of the Indian Wars of the American West* (New York: Alfred A. Knopf, 2016), 263–64; Donovan, *Terrible Glory*, 270–71; McCreight, *Firewater*, 112–13; Fox, Jr., *Archeology, History, and Custer's Last Battle*, 298–304; "One Bull Interview," box 105, folder 19, p. 44, CC.

61. "Joseph K. Dixon's Interview with Two Moons," *CMCF*, 130–32 ("swarming," 131); "The Two Moons Interview," 137–38 ("We circled," 137); "The He Dog Interview," 75; "The White Shield Interview," 53–54; Powell, *People of the Sacred Mountain*, 2: 1023–26; "Gall's Account of the Battle of the Little Bighorn," *St. Paul Pioneer Press*, June 18, 1886, available at https://www.nps.gov/parkhistory/online_books/hh/1b/hh10.htm (accessed Oct. 2, 2017); Larson, *Gall*, 131; "White Bull, Brave Wolf, and Hump Narrative," "The Little Knife Interview," "The Low Dog Interview," and "The Eagle Bear Interview," *IVCF*, 46–47, 54, 65, 84–85; "Interview with Respects Nothing," 18–19; Red Horse account, 37 ("became foolish," "did not"); 22; in "White Bull Interview," box 105, folder 24, pp. 57–58, CC; Flying By account, *LC*, 61; "The Nicholas Ruleau

Interview," 43–45; "The John Two Moons Interview," *CMCF*, 67; "The Moving Robe Woman Interview," 95; "The Red Feather Interview," "The Two Eagles Interview," "The Lone Bear Interview," "The Lights Interview," "The Hollow Horn Bear Interview," and "The Julia Face Interview," in *Lakota Recollections of the Custer Fight*, ed. Hardorff, 84–88, 147–49, 157–59, 166–71, 182–84, 189–92 ("they were driving," 189); "Story of Chief Runs-the-Enemy," 176–77; Michno, *Lakota Noon*, 203–86; Little Hawk account, 64; "Standing Bear Tells about the Custer Battle," 186–87; "Iron Hawk Tells about the Custer Battle," "Black Elk Tells about the Dead Soldiers and the Siege of Reno's Men," *SG*, 191–94 ("their arms," 193); "The Harness Gazette Interview with Two Moons," *CMCF*, 118; Vestal, *Warpath*, 198–200; One Bull account, 58; Grinnell, *Fighting Cheyennes*, 340–41; McCreight, *Firewater*, 113–14; Stands in Timber and Liberty, *Cheyenne Memories*, 199–203; Bray, *Crazy Horse*, 227–33; Donovan, *Terrible Glory*, 271–77; Fox, Jr., *Archeology, History, and Custer's Last Battle*, 142–221; "The Thunder Bear Narrative," *IVCF*, 88.

62. Oyawin Eder, "A Dakota View of the Great Sioux War," 70; "Black Elk Tells," 194 (I wasn't"); "Iron Hawk Tells," 191–92 ("They came," 191; "These," 192); "The Young Two Moons Interview," *CMCF*, 154; "The Flying Hawk Narrative," 126; "Story of Chief Runs-the-Enemy," 179; "J. M. Thrall's Interview with Two Moons," *CMCF*, 111; "Interview with Respects Nothing," 11–12. For Indian casualties, see Wood to AAG, Feb. 27, 1877, SF, roll 4; "White Bull, Brave Wolf, and Hump Narrative" and "The Little Soldier Interview," *IVCF*, 48, 177; and Herman J. Viola, "Red Horse and the Battle Drawings," *LBR*, 83.

63. "The White Bull Interview," *IVCF*, 164–65; Red Horse account, 37 ("As soon as"); "Standing Bear Tells about the Custer Battle," "Iron Hawk Tells about the Custer Battle," and "Black Elk Tells about the Dead Soldiers and the Siege of Reno's Men," 187, 189, 192–95; "White Bull Interview," box 105, folder 24, pp. 70, 89, CC; "Story of Chief Runs-the-Enemy," 177–78; White Bull account, *LC*, 65; Red Horse account, 37; "The Red Feather Interview," 88; "The Lone Bear Interview," 160; "The Hollow Horn Bear Interview," 185–86; "Two Eagles Interview," in *Lakota Recollections*, ed. Hardorff, 148; "The George W. Glenn Narrative Account," 195–97; Grinnell, *Fighting Cheyennes*, 341–42; Little Hawk account, 64 ("big guns"); "The Low Dog Interview," 66; *SG*, 195; Graham, *Reno Court Inquiry*, 162–63; Gray, *Centennial Campaign*, 180–82; Donovan, *Terrible Glory*, 279–99; Cozzens, *Earth Is Weeping*, 267–68; Waggoner, *Witness*, 131.

64. Bradley, *March of the Montana Column*, 152–58 ("communicate," 157; "in motion," "maneuvering," 159); Donovan, *Terrible Glory*, 303–9; Gray, *Centennial Campaign*, 188–90; Richard G. Hardorff, *The Custer Battle Casualties: Burials, Exhumations, and Reinternments* (El Segundo, CA: Upton and Sons, 1989), 20–21.

65. *SG*, 196–99 ("holy irons," 197; "A charger," 198); "The Brave Bear and Long Sioux Statement," 79–80; Stands in Timber and Liberty, *Cheyenne Memories*, 210–11; Bettelyoun and Waggoner, *With My Own Eyes*, 13; "White Bull Interview," box 105, folder 24, pp. 63, 69, CC; Joseph White Bull statement, 163–64; Gray *Centennial Campaign*, 338–41.

66. Marshall, *Journey of Crazy Horse*, 230–35; Bray, *Crazy Horse*, 240–42; Joseph Mills

Hanson, *The Conquest of the Missouri: Being the Story of the Life and Exploits of Captain Grant Marsh* (Chicago: A. C. McClurg, 1909), 325–27.

67. Jackson Lears, *Rebirth of a Nation: The Making of Modern America, 1877–1920* (New York: Harper, 2009), 43–45; Utley, *Lance and the Shield*, 174–76; Lewis H. Morgan to the Editor of *The Nation*, *Nation*, June 25, 1876 ("what are"); Lewis H. Morgan, *Ancient Society, or Researches in the Lines of Human Progress from Savagery through Barbarism to Civilization* (Chicago: Charles H. Kerr, 1877).

68. Edward Maguire, "Annual Report," July 10, 1876, *Annual Report of the Secretary of War, 1876–77*, 704 ("Sitting Bull"); J. D. Cameron to President, July 8, 1876, H. Ex. Doc. 184, 44th Cong., 1st Sess., 2–4 ("have for centuries," 2).

69. For similarities in American reactions to the Battle of the Little Bighorn and the Wounded Knee Massacre, see, for example, *New York Times*, July 7, 1876; *Louisiana Democrat*, July 12, 1876; *National Republican*, July 13 and 25, 1876; *New York Times*, Dec. 31, 1890; *Washington Post*, Dec. 31, 1890; and *Chicago Tribune*, Jan. 6, 1891. For an in-depth analysis of the press coverage of the 1890 Ghost Dance and the Wounded Knee Massacre, see Andersson, *Lakota Ghost Dance of 1890*, 192–250. For struggles over remembering and the meanings of Wounded Knee, see David W. Grua, "'In Memory of the Chief Big Foot Massacre': The Wounded Knee Survivors and the Politics of Memory," *Western Historical Quarterly* 46 (Spring 2015), 31–51.

70. Slotkin, *Fatal Environment*, 458, 466 ("a Golgotha," 466). For the number of military engagements, see Donald Fixico, "Federal and State Policies and American Indians," in *A Companion to American Indian History*, ed. Philip J. Deloria and Neal Salisbury (Malden, MA: Blackwell, 2002), 381.

71. Ostler, *Lakotas and the Black Hills*, 98–101 ("wish," 99); "Proceedings of Council Held at Standing Rock Agency, October 11, 1876, between the Indians at Said Agency and the Sioux Commission," Sen. Ex. Doc. 9, 44th Cong., 2d Sess., 55 ("I never"); Richardson, *West of Appomattox*, 165–66; Lazarus, *Black Hills/White Justice*, 91. For the centrality of landed property and its reallocation in the history of the American West, see Limerick, *Legacy of Conquest*.

72. YSF, 279; BTWC; R. H. Day to AAG, Feb. 5, 1877, Wood to AAG, Feb. 21 and 27, 1877, W. P. Clark to John G. Bourke, Mar. 3, 1877, and W. P. Clark to Adjutant General, Sept. 14, 1877, SF, roll 4 ("extremely" in Clark to Adjutant General), National Archives and Records Service; Anderson, *Ethnic Cleansing and the Indian*, 305–6; Olson, *Red Cloud and the Sioux Problem*, 222–46; Ostler, *Plains Sioux and U.S. Colonialism*, 64–105; Red Horse, Charger, Many Shields, and Tall Bull, "The Battle of Slim Buttes September 9, 1876," LC, 85–92; Paul L. Hedren, *After Custer: Loss and Transformation in Sioux Country* (Norman: University of Nebraska Press, 2011), 19–23, 55–57; Cozzens, *Earth Is Weeping*, 282–85; Jerome A. Greene, *Slim Buttes, 1876: An Episode of the Great Sioux War* (Norman: University of Oklahoma Press, 1982); Bray, *Crazy Horse*, 255–59, 297–390; Bennett A. Clements and Anson Mills, "The Starvation March and the Battle of Slim Buttes, September 9, 1876," in *Battles and Skirmishes*, ed. Greene, 96–115; Beth LaDow, *The Medicine Line: Life and Death on a American Borderland* (New York: Routledge, 2001), esp. xv, 40–42, 65–66; *New York Herald*, May 7, 1877; Marshall, *Journey of Crazy Horse*, 251–53.

73. BMWC, 39; RHO, 62; YSF, 282; Olson, *Red Cloud and the Sioux Problem*, 265–305; E. A. Hyatt, "Report," *ARCIA 1878*, esp. xxxii; DeMallie, "Teton," 812–18; Patricia Albers, "Sioux Women in Transition: A Study of Their Changing Status in Domestic and Capitalist Sectors of Production," in *Hidden Half: Studies of Plains Indian Women*, ed. Patricia Albers and Beatrice Medicine (Lanham, MD: University Press of America, 1983), 175–94; George E. Hyde, *A Sioux Chronicle* (Norman: University of Oklahoma Press, 1956), 26–66; Bettelyoun and Waggoner, *With My Own Eyes*, 110; Anderson, *Sitting Bull*, 136–61 ("I Wish," 140); Utley, *Lance and the Shield*, 234–47; Lears, *Rebirth of a Nation*, 39; Mark Ellis, "Reservation *Akicitas*: The Pine Ridge Indian Police, 1879–1885," *South Dakota History* 29 (1999), 185–210; Louis S. Warren, *God's Red Son: The Ghost Dance and the Making of Modern America* (New York: Basic, 2017), 240–42.

74. Ostler, *Plains Sioux and U.S. Colonialism*, 174–79, 291–92; YSF, 282 ("Col. McLaughlin"); RHO, 62; DWC, 24; Jeffrey Ostler, "'The Last Buffalo Hunt' and Beyond Plains Sioux Economic Strategies in the Early Reservation Period," *Great Plains Quarterly* 21 (Spring 2005), 117 ("right road"); Jeffrey D. Means, "'Indians Shall Do Things in Common': Oglala Lakota Identity and Cattle-Raising on the Pine Ridge Reservation," *Montana: The Magazine of Western History* 61 (Autumn 2011), 9–15; Richard White and Patricia Nelson Limerick, *The Frontier in American Culture*, ed. James R. Grossman (Berkeley: University of California Press, 1994); John Brennan, letter, Feb. 23, 1904, Doane Robinson Papers, box 3359A, folder 5: Correspondence, 1880–1946, SASDHS; Robert W. Larson, "A Victor in Defeat: Chief Gall's Life on the Standing Rock Reservation," *Prologue Magazine* 40 (Fall 2008), available at https://www.archives.gov/publications/prologue/2008/fall/gall.html (accessed Feb. 1, 2018); DeMallie, "Teton," 812–14; *New York Times*, Sept. 22, 1879; Sande Garner, "To Come to a Better Understanding: Complicating 'Two-Worlds' Trope," in *Beyond Two Worlds: Critical Conversations on Language and Power in Native North America*, ed. James Joseph Buss and C. Joseph Genetin-Pilawa (Albany: State University of New York Press, 2014), 282–85; Larson, *Red Cloud*, 217–48. For bison herds, see Isenberg, *Destruction of the Bison*, 153–62.

75. Frederick E. Hoxie, "From Prison to Homeland: The Cheyenne River Indian Reservation before World War I," in *The Plains Indians of the Twentieth Century*, ed. Peter Iverson (Norman: University of Oklahoma Press, 1985), 56–59; Ostler, *Plains Sioux and U.S. Colonialism*, 217–88; White, *Republic for Which It Stands*, 635–40; Prucha, *Great Father*, 633–86; Hyde, *Sioux Chronicle*, 184–228.

76. BMWC, 41; Robert M. Utley, *The Last Days of the Sioux Nation* (1963; 2d ed. New Haven: Yale University Press, 2004), 54–59; Andersson, *Lakota Ghost Dance of 1890*, 23–78; Warren, *God's Red Son*, 34–39, 55–58, 93–209, 106–7; Ostler, *Plains Sioux and U.S. Colonialism*, 243–73; Anderson, *Sitting Bull*, 173–79; White, *Republic for Which It Stands*, 641–42.

77. Ostler, *Plains Sioux and U.S. Colonialism*, 289–326, 365–66 ("Indians are dancing," 294); Anderson, *Sitting Bull*, 183–87; Heather Cox Richardson, *Wounded Knee: Party Politics and the Road to an American Massacre* (New York: Basic, 2010), 131–246; Warren, *God's Red Son*, 48–49, 271–83.

78. Ostler, *Plains Sioux and U.S. Colonialism*, 326–57; Utley, *Last Days of the Sioux Nation*, 200–219; Warren, *God's Red Son*, 286–89; William S. E. Coleman, *Voices of Wounded Knee* (Lincoln: University of Nebraska Press, 2000), 350–52.

79. John G. Neihardt, *Black Elk Speaks: The Complete Edition*, introduction by Philip J. Deloria, annotations by Raymond J. DeMallie (Lincoln: University of Nebraska Press, 2014), 55 ("A people's dream").

80. Frederick Jackson Turner, "The Significance of the Frontier in American History," *Proceedings of the Forty-First Annual Meeting of the State Historical Society of Wisconsin* (Madison: State Historical Society of Wisconsin, 1894), 79–112; Richardson, *West from Appomattox*, 275–77 ("as an illustration," 277).

EPILOGUE

1. YSF, 278–86 ("Big Foot," 286); BKWC, 364–65; BMWC, 37–41; RHO, 62; MBWC; MBWCV; CPWC; Prucha, *Great Father*, 659–71; Lears, *Rebirth of a Nation*, 35; Raymond J. DeMallie, "Pine Ridge Economy: Cultural and Historical Perspectives," in *American Indian Economic Development*, ed. Sam Stanley (The Hague: Mouton, 1979), 260–61; Ernest L. Schusky, "The Roots of Factionalism among the Lower Brule," in *North American Indian Anthropology: Essays on Society and Culture*, ed. Raymond J. DeMallie and Alfonso Ortiz (Norman: University of Oklahoma Press, 1994), 270; Limerick, *Legacy of Conquest*, 197–99; Hoxie, "From Prison to Homeland," 58–62; Akim D. Reinhardt, *Ruling Pine Ridge: Oglala Lakota Politics from IRA to Wounded Knee* (Lubbock: Texas Tech University Press, 2007), 19–20; Paul Robertson, *Power of the Land: Identity, Ethnicity, and Class among the Oglala Lakota* (New York: Routledge, 2002), 45–122; Warren K. Moorehead, *The American Indian in the United States, 1850–1914* (Andover, MA: Andover Press, 1914), 186 ("poor," "Think of it!").

2. Frederick E. Hoxie, *A Final Promise: The Campaign to Assimilate the Indians, 1880–1920* (Lincoln: University of Nebraska Press, 1984), 147–88; Thomas Biolsi, "The Birth of the Reservation: Making the Modern Individual among the Lakota," *American Ethnologist* 22 (Feb. 1995), 28–53.

3. Lears, *Rebirth of a Nation*, 31–40; Harvey Markowitz, "Converting the Rosebud: Sicangu Lakota Catholicism in the Late Nineteenth and Early Twentieth Centuries," *Great Plains Quarterly* 32 (Winter 2012), 3–23; Gibbon, *Sioux*, 136, 139; DeMallie, "Teton," 817; Kevin Bruyneel, *The Third Space of Sovereignty: The Postcolonial Politics of U.S.-Indigenous Relations* (Minneapolis: University of Minnesota Press, 2007), 97; Philip J. Deloria, "From Nation to Neighborhood: Land, Policy, Culture, Colonialism, and Empire in U.S.-Indian Relations, in *The Cultural Turn in U.S. History: Past, Present, and Future*, ed. James W. Cook, Lawrence B. Glickman, and Michael O'Malley (Chicago: University of Chicago Press, 2008), 364; Ostler, *Lakotas and the Black Hills*, 134–47.

4. Charles Wilkinson, *Blood Struggle: The Rise of the Modern Indian Nations* (New York: W. W. Norton, 2005), 10–11; Ostler, *Plains Sioux and U.S. Colonialism*, 361–65; Hoxie, "From Prison to Homeland," 58–60; Gibbon, *Sioux*, 142–44; DeMallie,

"Teton," 817–19; Thomas E. Mails, assisted by Dallas Chief Eagle, *Fools Crow* (1979; rprt. Lincoln: University of Nebraska Press, 1990), 43, 109–13; Benjamin Sewell, "Lakota Struggles for Cultural Survival: History, Health, and Reservation Life," *Nebraska Anthropologist* 19 (2006), 136–38.

5. Mails, *Fools Crow*, 145–49 ("as we," 145). For Collier and the Indian New Deal, see Wilkinson, *Blood Struggle*, 58–63. For the Indian Reorganization Act in the Lakota country, see Thomas Biolsi, *Organizing the Lakota: The Political Economy of the New Deal on the Pine Ridge and Rosebud Reservations* (Tucson: University of Arizona Press, 1992), 61–125 ("In every," 72); Reinhardt, *Ruling Pine Ridge*, 25–105; and Deloria, "Twentieth Century and Beyond," 407–18.

6. Michael L. Lawson, *Dammed Indians: The Pick-Sloan Plan and the Missouri River Sioux, 1944–1980* (Norman: University of Oklahoma Press, 1982); John E. Thorson, *River of Promise, River of Peril: The Politics of Managing the Missouri River* (Lawrence: University Press of Kansas, 1994), 82–83; Michael L. Lawson, "Federal Water Projects and Indian Lands: The Pick-Sloan Plan, A Case Study," *American Indian Culture and Research Journal* 7, no. 1 (1982), 23–40; Dennis M. Christafferson, "Sioux, 1930–2000," *HNAI* 13, Part 2: 821.

7. Vine Deloria, Jr., *Custer Died for Your Sins: An Indian Manifesto* (New York: Macmillan, 1969).

8. Paul Chaat Smith and Robert Allen Warrior, *Like a Hurricane: The Indian Movement from Alcatraz to Wounded Knee* (New York: New Press, 1996), 10–11, 18–35, 60–83, 107–11, 149–68; Sherry L. Smith, *Hippies, Indians, and the Fight for Red Power* (New York: Oxford University Press, 2012), 157–66; Ostler, *Lakotas and the Black Hills*, 168–69; Stew Magnusson, *The Death of Raymond Yellow Thunder and Other True Stories from the Nebraska–Pine Ridge Border Towns* (Lubbock: Texas Tech University Press, 2008), 11–24, 129–37, 139–56, 185–213.

9. Reinhardt, *Ruling Pine Ridge*, 117–38, 156–88; Robert Anderson, Joanna Brown, Jonny Lerner, and Barbara Lou Shafer, eds., *Voices from Wounded Knee, 1973: In the Words of the Participants* (Roseveltown, NY: Akwesasne Notes, 1974), 14–39; Smith and Warrior, *Like a Hurricane*, 190–97.

10. Smith and Warrior, *Like a Hurricane*, 200–222; Brown, Lerner, and Shafer, eds., *Voices from Wounded Knee*, 41–58, 111–32, 160–74; Smith, *Hippies, Indians, and the Fight for Red Power*, 170.

11. Smith and Warrior, *Like a Hurricane*, 222–65; Smith, *Hippies, Indians, and the Fight for Red Power*, 171–77; Anderson, Brown, Lerner, and Shafer, eds., *Voices from Wounded Knee*, 176–244; *New York Times*, May 9, 1973 ("leaped").

12. Troy Johnson, Joanne Nagel, and Duane Champagne, "American Indian Activism: Lessons from Alcatraz," in *American Indian Activism*, ed. Johnson, Nagel, and Champagne, 32–44; Anderson, Brown, Lerner, and Shafer, eds., *Voices from Wounded Knee*, 246 ("Our people").

13. Brown, Lerner, and Shafer, eds., *Voices from Wounded Knee*, 109 ("Real soon"); Smith, *Hippies, Indians, and the Fight for Red Power*, 211–12; George Pierre Castile, *To Show Heart: Native American Self-Determination and Federal Indian Policy, 1960–1975* (Tucson: University of Arizona Press, 1998), 43–174; Geoffrey D. Strommer and

Stephen D. Osborne, "The History, Status, and Future of Tribal Self-Governance under the Indian Self-Determination and Education Act," *American Indian Law Review* 39, no. 1 (2014), esp. 18–19, available at http://digitalcommons.law.ou.edu/ailr /vol39/iss1/1 (accessed Mar. 1, 2018).

14. Ostler, *Lakota and the Black Hills*, 134–63 ("a more ripe," 163); Sidney L. Harring, "Indian Law, Sovereignty, and State Law: Native People and the Law," in *A Companion to American Indian History*, ed. Philip J. Deloria and Neal Salisbury (Malden, MA: Blackwell, 2002), 452; Kristen Matoy Carlson, "Priceless Property," *Georgia State University Law Review* 29 (Spring 2013), 689; *Rapid City Journal*, June 30, 2011, available at https://rapidcityjournal.com/news/years-later-agreement-over-sioux-land -compensation-is-hard-to/article_8d9c71ba-a329-11e0-af75-001cc4c03286.html ("It's always") (accessed Feb. 22, 2018).

15. Albert White Hat, Sr., *Life's Journey—Zuya: Oral Teachings from Rosebud*, ed. John Cunningham (Salt Lake City: University of Utah Press, 2012), 7–13, 21, 111–21; George S. Esber, Jr., "Shortcomings of the Indian Self-Determination Policy," in *State and Reservation: New Perspectives on Federal Indian Policy*, ed. George Pierre Castile and Robert L. Bee (Tucson: University of Arizona Press, 1992), 215–19; George Pierre Castile, *Taking Charge: Native American Self-Determination and Federal Indian Policy, 1960–1975* (Tucson: University of Arizona Press, 2006), 49–109; Francis Paul Prucha, ed., *Documents of United States Indian Policy* (Lincoln: University of Nebraska Press, 2000), 335–36; *Washington Post*, Feb. 9, 2012; Ostler, *Lakota and the Black Hills*, 188–89 ("culture vultures," 189).

16. Magnuson, *Death of Raymond Yellow Thunder*, 6–7, 257–85, 291–92; David J. Wishart, *Great Plains Indians* (Lincoln: University of Nebraska Press, 2016), 119–22; Gibbon, *Sioux*, 193–201; *Los Angeles Times*, July 8, 1999; *New York Times*, July 9, 1999; *Nation*, July 16, 1999.

17. Nancy Bonvillain, *Native Nations: Cultures and Histories in Native North America* (Lanham, MD: Rowman and Littlefield, 2017), 47; *Bismarck Tribune*, June 13, 2017; *New York Times*, June 13, 2017; *Omaha World-Herald*, Sept. 30, 2017; *Guardian*, Sept. 29, 2017 ("liquid genocide"), available at https://www.theguardian.com/society/2017 /sep/29/pine-ridge-indian-reservation-south-dakota (accessed Dec. 27, 2017); Wishart, *Great Plains Indians*, 112–13. For persisting legacies of colonialism and conquest in the American West, see Limerick, *Legacy of Conquest*. The ongoing Lakota demand for sovereignty is a part of a larger movement for Indigenous sovereignty that has swept North America and much of the world in the early twenty-first century. The movement has been powered through art, writing, scholarship, and storytelling by Native elders, activists, politicians, lawyers, academics, artists, novelists and many others. For recent examples, see David E. Wilkins, *Hollow Justice: A History of Indigenous Claims in the United States* (New Haven: Yale University Press, 2013); Roxanne Dunbar-Ortiz, *An Indigenous Peoples' History of the United States* (Boston: Beacon, 2014); Aileen Moreton-Robinson, *The White Possessive: Property, Power, and Indigenous Sovereignty* (Minneapolis: University of Minnesota Press, 2015); Leanne Betasamosake Simpson, *As We Have Always Done: Indigenous Freedom through Radical*

Resistance (Minneapolis: University of Minnesota Press, 2017); Kent Blansett, *A Journey to Freedom: Richard Oakes, Alcatraz, and the Red Power Movement* (New Haven: Yale University Press, 2018); Lisa Brooks, *Our Beloved Kin: A New History of King Philip's War* (New Haven: Yale University Press, 2018); Nick Estes, *Our History Is the Future: Standing Rock Versus the Dakota Access Pipeline, and the Long Tradition of Indigenous Resistance* (New York: Verso, 2019); David Treuer, *The Heartbeat of Wounded Knee: Native America from 1890 to the Present* (New York: Riverhead, 2019); and Margaret Verble, *Cherokee America* (Boston: Mifflin Harcourt, 2019).

18. Alan Taylor, "Water Cannon and Tear Gas Used against Dakota Access Pipeline Protestors," *Atlantic*, Nov. 21, 2016, available at https://www.theatlantic.com/photo/2016/11/water-cannons-and-tear-gas-used-against-dakota-access-pipeline-protesters/508370/ (accessed Feb. 23, 2018); Louise Erdrich, "Holy Rage: Lessons from Standing Rock," *New Yorker*, Dec. 22, 2016, available at https://www.newyorker.com/news/news-desk/holy-rage-lessons-from-standing-rock (accessed Feb. 23, 2018); Bill McKibben, "Trump's Pipeline and America's Shame," *New Yorker*, Feb. 8, 2017, available at https://www.newyorker.com/tech/elements/trumps-pipeline-and-americas-shame (accessed Feb. 24, 2018); "Remarks by the President at Tribal Nations Conference," The White House, Office of the Press Secretary, Sept. 26, 2016, available at https://obamawhitehouse.archives.gov/the-press-office/2016/09/26/remarks-president-tribal-nations-conference ("sovereign to sovereign") (accessed Mar. 1, 2018); *Washington Post*, Dec. 5, 2016.

19. George Joseph, "30 Years of Oil and Gas Pipeline Accidents, Mapped," *Citylab*, Nov. 30, 2016, available at https://www.citylab.com/environment/2016/11/30-years-of-pipeline-accidents-mapped/509066/ (accessed Feb. 24, 2018); Colin Moynihan," A Murky Legal Mess at Standing Rock," *New Yorker*, Jan. 11, 2017, available at https://www.newyorker.com/news/news-desk/people-arrested-at-standing-rock-protests-fight-for-their-legal-rights (accessed Feb. 23, 2018); Carolyn Kormann, "For the Protestors at Standing Rock, It's Back to Pipeline Purgatory," *New Yorker*, Feb. 3, 2017, available at https://www.newyorker.com/tech/elements/for-the-protesters-at-standing-rock-its-back-to-pipeline-purgatory (accessed Feb. 28, 2017); *Guardian*, Nov. 3, 2016, available at https://www.theguardian.com/us-news/2016/nov/03/north-dakota-access-oil-pipeline-protests-explainer (accessed Mar. 1, 2018); *Washington Post*, Mar. 3, 2017; *Guardian*, May 10, 2017; *New York Times*, Jan. 24, Feb. 23, and Nov. 16, 2017.

GLOSSARY

akíčhita	marshal, soldier, camp police
blotáhuŋka	war chief
blotáhuŋka átaya	supreme war chief
Ȟaȟáwakpa	the Mississippi River, River of the Falls
huŋká	adopted relative
itȟáŋčhaŋ	chief, leader of a thióšpaye
iwáštegla	political philosophy that recognized that Lakotas would eventually have to coexist with the wašíčus
kȟolá	male friend
Matȟó Pahá	Bear Butte
Matȟó Thípila Pahá	Devil's Tower
Mde Wakan	Mille Lacs
Mníšoše	the Missouri River, muddy water
načá	chief, a member of the tribal council
Očhéthi Šakówiŋ	the alliance of the Seven Council Fires
oyáte	people, tribe, nation
Pahá Sápa	Black Hills
takúkičhiyapi	relatives, circle of kinship
thióšpaye	band, community
thóka	enemy, stranger
thuŋkášila	grandfather, Great Father, U.S. president
Wágluȟe	a Lakota band, often called Laramie Loafers, descendants of Ogala-white marriages
wakȟáŋ	sacred, holy, spiritual
Wakȟáŋ Tȟáŋka	Great Spirit
wakíčuŋzA	decider, an official responsible for guiding camp movements
wašíču	white person, person of European descent, Caucasian
wašíčuŋ	sacred power, spiritual power

wičháša wakȟáŋ	holy man, spiritual leader
wičháša yatáŋpikA	praiseworthy man, shirt wearer
wíŋkte	man who adopts womanly behavior and social roles
wíŋyaŋ wakȟáŋ	holy woman
wólakȟota	bonds of peace, friendship, peace treaty
wótakuye	ties of kinship, relatives

INDEX

Page numbers in **boldface** indicate illustrations.